Labour and Society in Britain and the USA

Volume 2

The Amalgamated Society of Engineers, formed in Great Britain, also established branches in the USA. The frontispiece, kindly supplied by John Smethurst, shows a membership certificate issued to a New Jersey machinist.

Labour and Society in Britain and the USA

Volume 2
Challenge and Accommodation, 1850–1939

NEVILLE KIRK

SCOLAR
PRESS

Published by   Ashgate Publishing Company
SCOLAR PRESS   Old Post Road
Gower House   Brookfield
Croft Road   Vermont 05036
Aldershot   USA
Hants GU11 3HR
England

British Library Cataloguing-in-Publication data.

Kirk, Neville
  Labour and Society in Britain and the
  USA. – Vol.2: Challenge and Accommodation,
  1850–1939
  I. Title
  331.1209

Library of Congress Cataloging-in-Publication Data

Kirk, Neville
  Labour and society in Britain and the USA / Neville Kirk.
    p.   cm.
  Includes bibliographical references and index.
  Contents: v. 1. Capitalism, custom, and protest, 1780–1850 – v.
2. Challenge and accommodation, 1850–1939.
    ISBN 1–85928–021–8 (v. 1) ISBN
1–85928–022–6 (v. 2)
    1. Labor movement–Great Britain–History. 2. Labor movement–
United States–History. 3. Working class–Great Britain–History.
4. Working class–United States–History. 5. Protest movements–
Great Britain–History. 6. Protest movements–United States–
History. 7. Capitalism–Great Britain–History. 8. Capitalism–
United States–History. 9. Great Britain–Social conditions.
10. United States–Social conditions. I. Title.
HD8388.K57   1994
305.5′62′094–dc20   93–47283
                    CIP

ISBN 1 85928 022 6

Phototypeset in 10 point Garamond by Intype, London, and printed in Great Britain at the University Press, Cambridge.

Contents

To David and Marty, Kate and Ella

List of Tables

Preface

This is the second volume of *Labour and Society in Britain and the USA*. The first volume offered the reader a survey of key features of capitalist development in Britain and the United States from the late eighteenth to the mid nineteenth centuries, and examined the nature, aims and fortunes of popular and working-class protest movements during this period. The aim of this volume is to pursue these themes between the middle years of the nineteenth century and the end of the 1930s.

Both volumes attempt to situate organised labour within its wider social context. The first chapter of Volume Two accordingly highlights key similarities and differences in the overall development of industrial capitalism in the two countries. Particular attention is devoted to the crisis of competitive capitalism during the latter part of the nineteenth century, moves towards the development of corporate or monopoly capitalism, and the attitudes and practices of employers and the state towards economic crisis, workers and organised labour. The second chapter examines workplace relations, trade unionism and other forms of workplace-based protest within the more general context established in Chapter 1. Chapter 3 extends our focus to politics, ideology and culture. Special attention is devoted in this chapter to the contrasting fortunes of independent labour politics in Britain and the United States. Chapters 1 to 3 concern themselves with the period from the mid nineteenth century to the early 1920s. Chapters 4 and 5 present an overview of key developments during the inter-war period. The reader's attention is drawn to the manifold contrasts both within and between the 1920s and 1930s, and the advances and retreats suffered by workers and organised labour in both countries. The conclusion offers some reflections upon the 'class and exceptionalism' debate which has informed both volumes, upon workers' achievements, and upon current and future directions in the study of labour and social history.

Neville Kirk
New Mills
September 1993

PART ONE

Capitalism, the Working Class and Labour Movements, 1860–1920s

CHAPTER ONE

Capitalist Development and the Transformation of Labour

OVERVIEW

The late nineteenth-century crisis of competitive capitalism constituted the material context in which labour's development between the onset of depression in 1873 and the early 1920s must be set. At various times between the early 1870s and mid–late 1890s falling prices, squeezed profit margins, increased competition, declining and erratic rates of growth and the growing strength of labour led employers and state institutions in both Britain and the United States to increase their resolve to subordinate labour to the will of capital.

Subordination was to be achieved in a number of ways. The formal, market-based dependency of labour upon capital, rooted in the wage earner's reliance upon the employer for work, was to be buttressed by more intensive and extensive capitalist penetration into and control of the process of production. Mechanisation, increased division of labour, simplification of tasks, the increased demand for semi-skilled workers within the burgeoning mass-production industries, 'Taylorism' and other managerial initiatives, were to be vital factors in the reduction of labour costs, increased productivity and output, and in the fight to wrest control over the labour process away from workers. In such ways 'transformed' (i.e. predominantly semi-skilled and dependent) labour was to be placed under greater formal and real capitalist control.

Simultaneously, increased concentrations of capital, characterised by oligopoly, integrated systems of production and distribution, close co-operation between finance and industry, sophisticated and bureaucratic managerial hierarchies, and high-powered marketing strategies would not only bring economies of scale but also stabilised and regulated markets. Such corporate features would become especially prominent in the United States. (In Britain competitive capitalism was far more resilient.) As Chandler has demonstrated, the visible, guiding hand of American big business increasingly predominated over the invisible hand of highly competitive markets tending towards equilibrium: competitive capitalism was superseded by corporate or 'monopoly' capitalism.[1]

The crisis of competitive capitalism, capital's intensified attempts to reduce labour costs and increase the surplus extracted from labour, and moves towards corporate business structures were both expressive and productive of heightened class conflict. As briefly noted at the end of the previous volume, large numbers of workers in the United States would adopt radical, and to a much lesser extent revolutionary, transformative strategies and ideologies in response to rapid and unsettling economic change. Support given to the Knights of Labor, socialism, Populism and other forms of agrarian radicalism, industrial militancy (both within and outside of the American Federation of Labor) and the syndicalism of the Industrial Workers of the World, and the increasingly mass-based character of labour 'unrest' provided adequate testimony to the depth and breadth of radicalism's appeal.

Similarly, in Britain the birth and growth of the Labour Party, 'new' unionism, the labour conflicts of 1889–91, 1910–14, 1915–16 and 1919–21, and the important if limited appeal of socialism, were reflective of heightened militancy, independence and general working-class consciousness. In both countries the development of a more homogeneous working class (as compared with the third quarter of the nineteenth century) constituted a profoundly radicalising influence, both within and beyond the workplace.

Heightened radicalism was both a major and incomplete part of labour's response. In the United States conservative, accommodative, sectional and racist initiatives and responses found an increasingly congenial home within the more influential sectors of the American Federation of Labor. And the development of more uniform work and extra work-based experiences did not signify the emergence of a unified working class. Severe racial and ethnic divisions and antagonisms, the latter directed particularly at the 'new' immigrants from southern and southeastern Europe and southern blacks migrating into the northern towns and cities, constituted a massive obstacle to working-class unity. Up to 1914, indeed beyond, the future direction of American labour lay in the balance. But by the early–mid 1920s the radical thrust had largely been defeated. Overall hegemony lay with the defensive and conservative American Federation of Labor.

In Britain radicalism displayed greater endurance and depth of appeal. But by 1922 British trade unions and workers were forced by depression into increasingly defensive actions, a position reinforced and accelerated by the defeat of the 1926 General Strike. Post-war gains registered by the Labour Party were significant if limited. Labour's rise was increasingly synonymous with the triumph of moderate labourism over socialism, and the Conservative Party was dominant throughout the mass unemployment of the 1930s. By the early–mid 1920s struggle and conflict had brought important, if limited, gains for workers in both countries, but within the confines of a seemingly stabilised and confident capitalist system.

The above represents no more than a highly schematised and, *ipso facto*, oversimplified account of key economic developments and worker responses during the years from the 1870s to the 1920s. As we will see in more detail during the course of this chapter, there existed differences both between and within the United States and Britain in relation to the nature of employer and state strategies, and the extent to which labour was transformed and subordinated.[2] British employers tended, for example, to respond to many of the economic problems common to their American counterparts (falling prices, 'sticky' labour costs and so on) more by intensifying traditional techniques of management (based upon increased work loads, speed up, and, more generally, low wage, labour-intensive policies), than by the (American) adoption of the new Taylorite and corporatist modes, complete with their emphases upon the transformation of the existing division of labour. Anti-trade-union strategies were also far more marked among American employers.

The picture presented so far is, furthermore, too narrowly economic and economic-reductionist in character. A more complete and balanced account demands that we pay full attention not only to the economic but also to the social, political, cultural and ideological determinations of labour action and consciousness.

Bearing in mind such guidelines, we can, nevertheless, take the notion of capitalist crisis as a useful starting point for our analysis. We will then proceed to an examination of employer responses to economic crisis and the effects of such responses upon labour. Of particular concern at this juncture will be the more rapid development of corporate capitalism and 'open shop' (i.e. anti-union) policies in the United States. We will suggest that the scale of violence and conflict between late nineteenth- and early twentieth-century employers and workers in the United States was generally higher than in Britain. This high level of raw industrial and (wider) class conflict was of crucial importance in the development of industrial and political radicalism, and makes a mockery of static and absolute notions of American 'exceptionalism'. Britain, whilst being less the 'peaceable kingdom' than sometimes supposed, did nevertheless possess employers and a state machinery generally more sympathetic to union recognition. And the system of 'modern' institutionalised collective bargaining which developed in this period in Britain was much weaker in the United States.

Our investigation of politics will likewise emphasise the complex and ambiguous structural determinations upon labour: the continued attempts of American's mainstream parties, especially the Democrats, to

assimilate workers' concerns and aspirations and to undercut independent third-party movements; the profound hostility of the courts and,
often, the machinery of the local state towards organised labour; and the
glaring contradiction between labour's traditional republican ideals and
the new and 'un-American' corporate reality.[3] In Britain, the employer
counter-attack against 'new' unionism, depression, the hostility of the
courts, the ambiguous role of the central state and the seeming indifference, indeed hostility, of the established parties towards organised labour
helped promote the cause of political independence, the growth of
socialism and the birth of the Labour Party. But the break from Liberalism on the part of organised labour was more uneven and slower than
sometimes believed.

This chapter will finally move to a consideration of the economic,
socio-cultural and ideological characteristics of the working classes
which developed at the turn of the century. We will argue that the trend
towards greater homogeneity was stronger in Britain and that internal
conflicts and divisions, revolving around ethno-cultural, political and
economic issues, were more pronounced in the United States. Such
conflicts and divisions were, furthermore, of crucial importance in
moulding the continued dual character of American labour: its tremendous capacity for militant industrial action combined, by and large, with
accommodation to the dominant political system. In contrast, by the
1920s British labour displayed greater political independence and a
stronger ability to create durable and increasingly mass-based trade
unions.

By the end of the chapter we will have identified some of the key
structural determinations shaping workers' ideologies and behaviour.
Chapters 2 and 3 will then consider the ways in which workers, as the
conscious and unconscious subjects of history, influenced the structured
world in which they were obliged to operate. Chapter 2 will focus upon
developments at the workplace from the era of the Civil War to the
1920s. The following chapter will concentrate upon political, cultural
and ideological currents during the same period of time.

ECONOMY AND SOCIETY: KEY FEATURES

The late nineteenth-century crisis of competitive capitalism can be properly evaluated only when placed within the wider context of the cardinal
features of economy and society in Britain and the United States. It is
accordingly to an examination of such characteristics that we must
initially turn.

Demography, Urbanisation and Social Structure

Between the 1870s and early 1920s the economies and societies of the two countries displayed both common and distinctive features. Population growth continued apace, doubling in Britain between 1851 and 1921 (from around 21 million to almost 43 million) and increasing more than fourfold in the United States (from 23.3 million to 106.5 million) between 1850 and 1920.[4] But in both countries declining fertility rates from around 1880 led to a deceleration in the rate of population increase.

Population growth was accompanied by accelerated urbanisation and the continued shift of the respective labour forces away from agriculture. Only 39 per cent of the British population was living in rural areas and a minority of 22 per cent of the labour force was engaged in agriculture, forestry and fishing at mid century: by 1911 these percentages had fallen, respectively, to 19 per cent and 8.3 per cent. As Hunt has observed, the towns, and especially industrial towns, 'had accommodated a fast increasing share of all people'. And this trend was to accelerate. In 1801, notes Hunt, one person in six lived in a town of 20,000 and upwards (the majority in London), yet by 1911 'considerably more than one-half' lived in towns of this size.[5] Moreover, many more people, particularly wage earners, increasingly lived in large urban areas. Thus Hobsbawm records that in 1911 there were thirty-six cities of over 100,000 inhabitants in Britain, compared to ten in 1851, and containing 44 per cent of the total population as compared to 25 per cent in 1851. And as early as 1881 the great conurbations of London, Manchester (including its surrounding towns), Birmingham and the 'Black Country', West Yorkshire (Leeds, Bradford, etc.), Merseyside (greater Liverpool) and Tyneside (centred on Newcastle) housed 40 per cent of Englishmen and Welshmen.[6] Finally, the latter part of the nineteenth century and the early decades of the present century witnessed the proliferation of 'boom' towns and areas – Govan and other parts of Glasgow, Burnley and Nelson, Barrow-in-Furness, Coventry, Swindon, Oxford, West Ham and many others – in which the demand for labour was both high and frequently met by migrant labour.

As predominantly urban dwellers, workers were increasingly concentrated in non-agricultural occupations. In 1851 Britain was already a heavily industrialised country, employing some 43 per cent of its labour force in manufacturing industry, mining and building: by 1911 46.4 per cent were likewise employed. However, the greatest shift away from agriculture in the post-1851 period was not towards manufacturing proper but to the tertiary sector of the economy (trade and transport, administration, and other services, especially 'white collar', occupations).

A deceleration in the rate of transfer of the labour force from agriculture to manufacturing in the second half of the nineteenth century should not obscure four important developments. First, between 1851 and 1911 the absolute increase in the size of non-agricultural labour force was particularly marked in relation to mining and transport. The number of railwaymen increased from less than 100,000 in 1871 to 400,000 in 1911, and the number of coalminers from 500,000 to 1.2 million in the same period. (The miners, in particular, were to provide a solid bedrock to the labour movement.) More generally, the relative decline of textiles and clothing was offset by the rapid development of metal working and food processing.[7]

Second, we should emphasise the predominantly *proletarian* (i.e. wage-earning) character of the post-1851 labour force. In 1901 about 85 per cent of the total labour force was in dependent employment, with some 75 per cent being manual workers. As McKibbin has observed, Britain was thus 'in the broadest sense... unquestionably a working-class nation' – a trend already well in evidence in 1851.[8]

Third, the working class was increasingly less 'artisanal' in character. 'In 1851', notes Hobsbawm, 'there were more shoemakers than coalminers, two and a half times as many tailors as railwaymen, and more silkworkers than commercial clerks.'[9] But the expansion of metals, mining and transport, combined with the continued importance of cotton, effected a profound shift towards a more industrial-proletarian base.

Finally, in comparison with the mid-Victorian period, the post-1870 decades witnessed the development of a more homogeneous working class. A combination of factors[10] converged to diminish those status-based and other divisions which had characterised the post-Chartist working class. Above all, widespread improvements in living standards and the expansion of demand for more regular, semi-skilled and better-paid jobs narrowed the hitherto massive gulf between the skilled élite and the rest. As such, strong foundations were laid for the growth of a truly mass labour movement in Britain between the 1870s and 1920. But, as we will show in due course, the working class did not become a totally unified and uniform mass. Homogeneity had its limits and solidarity and radicalism were uneven in terms of influence and character.

In many ways the United States experienced similar developments in relation to trends in urbanisation and the nature and distribution of the labour force. It might appear at first sight that urbanisation was less significant in the post-bellum United States than in Britain. The vast majority of citizens in 1865 lived in the countryside in small communities of under 2,500 inhabitants, and the westward settlement of the massive area between the Mississippi and the Pacific coast also swelled the number of rural dwellers. Indeed, not until 1920 would a majority of the American population live in urban areas.

Such a picture is, however, in many ways quite misleading. Between 1860 and 1890, notes Laurie, the proportion of Americans dwelling in municipalities with more than 2,500 residents almost doubled to 30 per cent. And as M. A. Jones has declared, from about 1870 onwards the city became, 'the controlling influence in national life.'[11]

Urbanisation did not spread evenly. Less than 10 per cent of Southerners lived in urban areas by 1890, and, despite westward expansion, the bulk of the total and urban populations continued to be concentrated north of the Ohio and east of the Mississippi. Nevertheless, urbanisation constituted an integral part of the settlement of the West, and even in the South the number of towns with more than 10,000 residents increased from about 100 in 1860 to in excess of 200 by 1890.[12] In sum, urbanisation fundamentally changed the nature and shape of American life.

As in Britain, the urban areas increasingly housed the American working class, especially manufacturing workers. In comparison with Britain, manufacturing, mining and construction workers in the United States constituted, at least in quantitative terms, a less significant proportion of the total labour force. Thus such workers comprised approximately 20 per cent of the American labour force in 1850–1 (as compared with 43 per cent in Britain), rising to 27 per cent in 1900 (46 per cent in Britain) and some 30 per cent (46.4 per cent in Britain) in 1911.[13] In addition, and despite a considerable decline in its share of the total labour force (from 64 per cent in 1850 to 38 per cent in 1900), agriculture continued to display greater strength in the United States than in Britain (employing 38 per cent of the labour force as opposed to Britain's 9 per cent as late as 1900–1).

Both countries had witnessed, nevertheless, very considerable shifts away from agriculture during the nineteenth century. Before, mid-century manufacturing had been the main beneficiary of such shifts. Thereafter, the tertiary sector (which grew extremely rapidly in the United States) was the main beneficiary. Even so, between the end of the Civil War and the outbreak of the First World War the manufacturing sector absorbed a proportional share of labour force growth. And, as in Britain, the absolute number of workers engaged in manufacturing, mining and transport showed substantial growth. For example, M. A. Jones has estimated that the total labour force in manufacturing, mining, construction and services in the United States increased from just over 4 million in 1860 to more than 18 million in 1900. And Lee and Passell calculate that the American manufacturing labour force rose from 2,470,000 in 1870 to 8,332,000 in 1910, whilst those employed in transport, and mining and construction combined increased from, respectively, 295,000 and 960,000 in 1870 to 2,005,000 and 3,017,000 in 1910. Significantly, as in Britain, miners, and building and transport workers would play prominent roles in the American labour movement of the late nineteenth and early twentieth centuries. Finally, David Montgomery has shown that the number of manual wage earners in American industry increased by 301 per cent between 1870 and 1910 (at a time when the population was rising by only 132 per cent).[14] And such wage earners were increasingly concentrated in New York, Pittsburgh, Chicago, Detroit and other urban centres throughout the country.

American and British workers shared other common traits. Rising living standards during the last quarter of the century, the central importance of a culture geared around mutuality, an easing of wage differentials and other differences and divisions between skilled and non-skilled, increased employment for women in factories, offices and shops, and a much greater demand for non-skilled labour in large units of production – such developments were conducive to greater working-class homogeneity in the United States as well as in Britain.

In important respects, however, the economies and societies of the two countries displayed marked differences. Of fundamental importance was size. Not only was the American population more than twice the size of the British population in 1900, but its labour force was also some 75 per cent larger and its natural resources (especially arable land) far more abundant.[15] The United States also possessed a much more extensive domestic market which, protected by tariffs and integrated in the post-bellum period by the completion of the railroad network (the first transcontinental line was completed in 1869; and by 1900 the United States had more railroad track than the whole of Europe), was particularly conducive to the mass production of relatively cheap and standardised goods and services. By way of contrast, industrial production in Britain was primarily geared up to meeting the needs of a variety of foreign and custom-based markets which did not so easily lend themselves to mass production.

Differences in size were accompanied by contrasts in social character and in the pace and direction of economic development. The most obvious difference in terms of social character lay in the largely immigrant nature of the American working class. As we observed in Volume One, by 1880 the vast majority of American workers were either foreign-born or the American-born sons and daughters of foreign-born parents. Moreover, between 1865 and 1914 immigration exceeded 26 million – a total, observes Maldwyn Jones, 'five times greater than in the previous fifty years'. The overwhelming mass of immigrants (a growing majority of whom hailed, by the turn of the century, from southern and eastern Europe) became urban-based wage earners. And, despite the quickened impetus towards economic homogeneity, stimulated by the mounting demand for semi-skilled labour, ethnic differences and conflicts often continued to confound attempts to unite workers.

Similar obstacles did not arise to anything like the same extent in Britain. The census of 1901 recorded only 165,000 foreign-born workers in England and Wales. And the largest post-1880 immigrant group, Jews from eastern Europe, never accounted for as much as 1 per cent of the British labour force. There was opposition to Jews and other 'new' immigrants in late Victorian and Edwardian Britain. And employers did often attempt to use immigrants as strikebreakers and as a source of cheap labour. But, as Lunn, Williams, Buckman and Holmes have noted, the traditional stereotype of non-union, strike-breaking and pliable immigrant labour is in need of serious qualification and refinement. Jews and others were frequently involved in strikes, trade unionism and political radicalism.[16] Finally, the absolutely smaller size of Britain's agricultural workforce, combined with the extremely high density of wage earners within that workforce, also made for greater homogeneity than in the United States.

Economic Growth, Retardation and 'Entrepreneurial Failure'

In terms of economic growth, the years from the 1870s to the 1920s saw the rise of the United States to a position of world supremacy and the relative, as opposed to the absolute, decline of Britain. If measured against previous performance, rather than against an external standard, then the British economy continued to perform reasonably well. There was a slowing down of the rate of growth of total output (2.7 per cent 1800–31; 2.5 per cent 1831–60; 1.9 per cent 1873–1907) and output per head (the parallel figures being 1.3 per cent, 1.3 per cent and 1.0 per cent). But this was partly to be expected in a mature economy and predated the 'Great Depression' of 1873.[17]

The vast weight of evidence discredits not only the notion of sudden retardation associated with the 'Great Depression', but also absolute notions of entrepreneurial 'failure' and the triumph of anti-industrial cultural conservatism. British employers continued to act 'rationally' (i.e. profit-maximise and cost-minimise, subject to prevailing constraints). And the tenacity of 'aristocratic' style within the British ruling élite should not obscure the close interpenetrations between different kinds of wealth, the powerful self-confidence of the bourgeoisie, and the overriding commitment of the economy to full-blown commodity production.[18] Nevertheless, Britain's early start to industrialisation and her unchallenged domination of the mid-Victorian period did in all probability induce, as suggested by Hobsbawn, a general sense of complacency and widespread reliance upon 'traditionalism', as reflected in methods, techniques, attitudes and employer behaviour.[19] But we must be acutely conscious of the dangers of viewing Britain's 'decline' from a position of hindsight. As Floud has astutely reminded us, not many Britons in the early twentieth century would have accepted a picture of gloom and despondency.[20]

Yet when British (and especially businessmen's) eyes were cast to the west rather than to the east there was a growing sense of unease. As the visits of British cotton trade unionists and engineering and cotton employers confirmed, Britain was increasingly falling behind the American industrial leviathan.[21]

Between the 1840s and the early 1890s American society underwent rapid industrialisation. Although capitalist industrialisation had been in clear evidence prior to the Civil War, it was in the post-war decades that the United States made the 'crucial transition to a modern industrial society'.[22] By the 1880s a society dominated by the northern bourgeoisie and rooted in full-blown commodity production had established national hegemony.

Thus the spread of the railway network brought with it not only an integrated national market but also the penetration of the wage labour–capital relationship into the furthest corners of the land. Whether in the South, the West or the North, in agriculture or in industry, clashes between the certainties and traditions of 'custom' and the uncertainties and dependent innovations of the capitalist 'octopus' would continue to spark fierce protests. But for the most part the post-bellum northern bourgeoisie successfully coped with popular insurgency and firmly established capitalist rule in the South.[23]

Once truly hegemonic, the northern bourgeoisie presided over a period of heady expansion. By the 1880s the percentage of non-agricultural workers was higher than agricultural workers, and the United States had outstripped Britain as the world's leading manufacturing nation. In terms of growth rates the United States was also forging ahead of Britain. Over the period 1873–1913 Britain experienced an annual average increase of 1.8 per cent in total output compared with 4.5 per cent for the United States. Comparisons in growth of output are to some extent misleading, output being produced by markedly different sized populations. The more reliable comparison, of growth rates of output per person employed, shows that although the difference between Britain and America was smaller than initially suggested, nevertheless the United States was clearly well ahead of Britain between 1873 and 1913 (a 1.8 per cent average annual increase being recorded as against 0.9 per cent).[24] Finally, Britain's growing reliance upon the United States for imports and financial assistance during the First World War was indicative of the changed balance of power. By 1918 the United States had become the leading capitalist nation.

THE CRISIS OF COMPETITIVE CAPITALISM

Common problems revolving around falling prices, worker strength and declining rates of growth in relation to profits, total output and output per head underlay the distinctive trajectories of the British and American economies during the last quarter of the nineteenth century. Such problems constituted the crisis of competitive capitalism.

In terms of Britain, we must be careful to distinguish the valid notion of crisis from the discredited term 'Great Depression' (1873–96). As Saul and others have convincingly demonstrated, the years from 1873 to 1896 did not form a uniform entity with respect to key economic indicators.[25] For example, there were sufficient variations in price, and levels of production and employment within the twenty years between the depressions of the mid 1870s and mid 1890s to invalidate the notion of unrelieved depression. In addition, as already noted, the economy as a whole continued to expand at a respectable rate. And increased levels of unemployment could not hide the massive improvement in living standards for the large number of workers who managed to stay in work and to benefit from the fall in prices, especially in relation to the price of foodstuffs. Indeed, there is some evidence to suggest that the last quarter of the century saw an increase in labour's share of the national income.

In sum, the term 'Great Depression' is an ideological construct, rooted in the growing problems of those late nineteenth-century contemporaries dependent upon profits, rent and interest as sources of income. It is significant that once prices, profits and (in all probability) capital's share of the national income rose between 1896 and 1914, at a time when real wages remained pretty stable, talk of depression largely disappeared from middle-class dinner tables.

If not synonymous with the 'Great Depression', capitalist crisis was nevertheless very real. It resided above all in the crisis of profitability attendant upon increased competition, falling prices, a marked decline in the rate of increase of productivity, a more pronounced deceleration of the growth of total output than in the pre-1873 years, and the ability of workers and their organisations (especially the trade unions) to prevent wages from falling as quickly as prices. Capitalists were thus caught not only in an economic crisis of accumulation, but also a *class-based* or social crisis in which a successful resolution to their problems demanded that labour be more fully subordinated to the will of capital. Nothing less than a marked shift in the balance of class forces was required.

As James Livingston has recently shown, a similar, and in all probability more pronounced, dual crisis situation existed in the United States between 1873 and 1896.[26] Domestic competition among employers was particularly fierce in the post-bellum decades in which general uncertainty, erratic growth and more frequent recessions characterised economic life. Intensified competition, combined with technological change, more integrated markets and improved methods of distribution and production resulted in a general (rather than uniform) fall in prices between 1873 and the mid 1890s. This decline in prices was not matched by a corresponding fall in wages. Indeed there occurred both a considerable advance in wages and a shift in the distribution of income from profits to wages. Furthermore, price deflation and the growth in real wages were not offset by a comparable increase in productivity. For alongside the deceleration of growth in industrial output (from an annual average of 6.5 per cent between the late 1830s to the mid 1870s, to 5.5 per cent between 1874 and 1899) and in gross national product (a progressive decline from 5.58 per cent per annum between 1869 and 1878 to 2.55 per cent between 1889 and 1898), output per worker declined 5 per cent from 1874–83 to 1884–93, as earnings per industrial worker increased about 4 per cent. More specifically, productivity in the non-farm sector, notes Livingston, 'barely improved' in the decade from 1884 to 1894 'while real wages continued to increase rapidly, at a rate five to six times faster than productivity'.[27]

Thus, capitalists in both countries were faced with a set of problems of accumulation which varied in degree both within and between the two nations but which, nevertheless, were fundamentally of the same kind. Rising wages set against falling prices, profit margins and decelerating rates of growth of output and productivity meant, in effect, that many employers faced a battle for continued economic health. That battle would not only align capital against labour, but also test to the limit capital's claim to be the true representative and moral guardian of the public good. There would emerge a profound legitimation crisis.

EMPLOYERS' RESPONSES AND GENERAL OUTCOMES: NATIONAL SIMILARITIES

Common problems produced, in part, similar responses. Employers on both sides of the Atlantic sought to secure markets, to stabilise prices and to reduce labour costs. The ultimate goal of employers was to achieve both formal and real control over labour.

Britain: Cotton, Railways, Coalmining and the Metal Trades

Specific examples of these general aims abound. In terms, for example, of the British cotton industry, the last quarter of the century saw intensified overseas competition, a slowdown in the rate of capital accumulation, falling prices, a marked trend towards labour-using and capital-saving investment, employment rising faster than net output, an increase in labour costs, and a subsequent squeeze upon profit margins, as reflected in labour's growing share of net output. As shown by Burgess, White and others,[28] cotton employers in Lancashire and elsewhere responded to their mounting problems by extending their range of products, by attempting to strengthen their traditional hold upon Third World markets and by making limited inroads into the West European market, and by pushing existing methods of labour management 'to the maximum limits of productivity'. Rather than transforming the prevailing division of labour by means of vertical integration, technological innovation and more direct managerial controls in relation to hiring policies (subcontracting spinners and weavers remained the norm), employers increased work-loads in spinning, weaving and the preparatory processes, speeded up mules and looms, utilised cheap and inferior raw cotton and yarn, and exerted greater pressure upon overlookers to 'drive' the operatives to increased output.

'Driving', especially the practice of posting the weavers' earnings by their looms, the intensified effort and lowered levels of production and actual earnings attendant upon the utilisation of inferior cotton (the latter led to an increase in the number of thread and yarn breakages and necessitated more effort in order to produce the same amount of output), and more widespread employer attempts to reduce wages – all resulted in embittered relations and frequent disputes in cotton during the last quarter of the century. For example, employers' demands for reductions in wage rates triggered off the weavers' Great Strike of 1878, the largest strike (involving 100,000 workers) that the cotton industry had experienced up to that time. Excessive mule speeds, bad materials and 'steaming' (excessive steam in weaving sheds), low wage rates, fines imposed on weavers for imperfections in cloth, and demands for equal pay for women weavers performing the same tasks as men, were some of the issues which underpinned the 'offensive strike wave of major proportions' in cotton during the 'new unionist' upsurges of the late 1880s and early 1890s. And yarn breakages and reduced earnings ('bad spinning') lay at the heart of the massive discontent of 1892. In that year employers in southeast Lancashire and northeast Cheshire spinning imposed two lock-outs in order to forestall demands for an end to bad spinning and a general wage advance. The second lock-out, to enforce a 5 per cent reduction in wages, stopped 16 million spindles and put some 45–50,000 operatives out of work.[29]

It is true that a picture of unrelieved conflict in cotton is inaccurate. Thus Burgess notes that the Oldham district, characterised by impersonal limited coarse spinning companies with heavy fixed charges and subjected to fierce international competition, was 'a cockpit of industrial strife', whilst the more cushioned fine spinning and family-dominated (and often paternalist) mills of Stockport and Bolton were less troubled.[30]

Emphasis upon quickened and widened conflict during this period of mounting competition must, however, be retained. Cotton may have constituted the showpiece for the system of institutionalised collective bargaining so admired by the Webbs. However, as McIvor has recently reminded us, trade union recognition and the development of collective bargaining in cotton had proceeded far less smoothly and evenly from the mid nineteenth century than Joyce and other advocates of 'institutionalised calm' would have us believe. Indeed, recognition, as demonstrated in the 1850s (in the wake of the 'Ten Per Cent' conflicts of 1853–4), in the early 1880s (following the violent conflict of 1878), and in the Brooklands agreement of 1893 (developing out of the 1892 lock-outs) was achieved, observes McIvor, only after 'the experience of extended and very damaging periods of industrial conflict when labour had illustrated its power to resist'. Indeed, turn-of-the-century employers in cotton continued to withhold full recognition to the relatively poorly organised cardroom operatives, female ring spinners, cloth-lookers and warehousemen. 'Clearly', concludes McIvor, 'employers' labour relations strategy was crucially affected by the bargaining power of particular groups of operatives'.[31]

The Scottish experience certainly bore witness to the willingness of some employers both to confront organised labour and to fully exploit less powerful groups of workers. For example, following the destruction of the seemingly powerful spinners' union in 1837, cotton employers in Glasgow and the surrounding areas pursued a consistent low-wage, anti-union and dictatorial policy throughout the mid and late Victorian decades. By the 1870s operative spinners in the Glasgow region had only weak trade-union defences and very limited power over the piecers. The manufacturers never fully accepted the spinners' union as a bargaining agent and exerted far more direct managerial control over the piecers (in terms of recruitment and pay) than their Lancashire counterparts. In addition the spinners never managed to establish a uniform list of prices, and from the 1880s onwards the minder-piecer system was replaced by a multi-pair system and young women took over all the spinning operations. Unlike Lancashire (but like the USA) institutionalised collective bargaining in the Scottish spinning sector did not take strong root. In Scottish cotton weaving, employer control was even more pronounced. There was no lasting trade-union organisation among the wholly female weaving workforce before 1907, weavers did not subcontract tenters, direct managerial controls and prerogatives were extremely powerful, and uniform price lists along the Lancashire pattern were never established. As Per Bolin-Hort has concluded in relation to the Scottish cotton industry:

> The general picture which emerges is one of employer domination, a very low degree of union authority, and an absence of collective agreements on price lists . . . The gradual acceptance of trade unions and the establishment of regional price lists and a formalized bargaining structure, which were distinct features of industrial relations in Lancashire, did not emerge in the Glasgow district.[32]

Not all Scottish employers relied upon the cheap labour policies and anti-unionism of the cotton textile masters. Joseph Melling has shown that carpet manufacturers such as James Templeton attracted women away from the cotton sheds by means of relatively high wages and decent working conditions. And the strong market position of the pre-First World War Clydeside shipbuilding industry (British mercantile tonnage constituted over a third of the world's total in the post-1870 decades, and domestic yards supplied most of this before 1914), combined with heavy managerial reliance upon the skills of the workforce, ensured that high, if fluctuating, wages and strong trade unionism endured.[33]

However, as Melling also notes, employer antagonism towards trade unionism was by no means confined to textiles. As in the country as a whole, railway employers in Scotland adopted a highly autocratic stance in relation to their employees. Especially in the more competitive post-1870 decades the employers made strenuous, if only partially successful, attempts to reduce the craft control of engineers and other skilled trades in the railway workshops. And railway directors were 'completely opposed' to the unionisation of their transportation and administrative grades. Given such opposition and growing worker confidence, it is not accidental that railways throughout Britain experienced acute industrial unrest in the pre-war years.

Finally, aggressive employer anti-unionism had played a key role in greatly weakening coalmining trade unionism in Scotland (and elsewhere in Britain) between the mid 1840s and the 1880s. From the latter decade onwards employers were generally more prepared to deal with 'responsible' trade unionism. And with the formation, in 1889, and growth of the Miners Federation of Great Britain coalmining trade unionism was to make remarkable advances. But economic fluctuations, declining productivity, the increasing concentration of production, and intransigent employers were also to bring great insecurity and instability to the system of industrial relations. The 1893 lock-out in mining was the largest dispute ever seen in Britain. And miners were to play a prominent role in the 'labour unrest' between 1910 and 1914.[34]

Melling concludes his general survey of employer policies and class relations in Scotland with two important observations. First, and despite important variations in employer behaviour and attitudes, generally deteriorating market environments from the 1870s onwards brought about a 'greater coherence' in employer strategies. This coherence was reflected in 'an impetus towards increased innovation and management'. In all the major sectors of the Scottish economy there occurred, albeit unevenly, 'tighter workplace controls, heavier workloads, fresh incentive systems, mechanisation and rationalisation'. Second, and notwithstanding the more widespread development of collective bargaining, intensified employer pressure upon Scottish labour stimulated quickened resistance on the part of established craft societies and greater confidence and militancy among previously unorganised workers. In addition, increasing numbers of workers looked to the state and radical and socialist politics as the means to fundamental economic and social reconstruction.[35]

Along with T. C. Smout, we might add another general observation. Given the plentiful supplies of cheap female, migrant (especially from the Highlands) and Irish immigrant labour in the west of Scotland, employers were consistently more adept at employing a cheap labour policy rather than an intensive and extensive capital investment strategy, in order to overcome their economic difficulties.[36] The full effects of this 'traditionalism' were reflected in both the deepseated and enduring suspicions and conflicts between workers and employers in Scotland and, increasingly, in the failure of post-First World War Scottish capitalism to restructure itself on the basis of Taylorism, mechanisation and a thoroughly transformed division of labour.

In addition to cotton, coal and transport, the metal trades constituted a key component of the late nineteenth- and early twentieth-century British economy. And, as in the cases so far discussed, the metal trades were feeling, to varying degrees, the effects of intensified competition, falling prices and reduced profits. In the engineering industry, so Zeitlin informs us,[37] such pressures drove employers 'to experiment not with new forms of capital-intensive investment, but rather with methods of cheapening and intensifying skilled labour within the existing division

of labour'. These methods embraced piecework and frequent rate cutting, the intensification of supervision in order to increase the pace of
work without a commensurate increase in labour costs, the subversion
of apprenticeship, the dilution of skills by means of mechanisation, and
the employment of rapidly growing numbers of semi-skilled machinists
upon the simpler machine tools. As in the United States, the overriding
aims of employers were to undermine craft regulation and control and
fully restore or implement managerial prerogatives.

Developments in engineering during the late nineteenth century
evoked strong memories of the battles of the 1850s. As a result of their
victory in the 1852 lock-out, engineering employers had won the formal
right to 'place labourers on machines, to employ non-union labour,
and to impose systematic overtime'. In many cases workers were also
compelled to sign the 'document', a renunciation of trade unionism and
all its workings. However, rapid export-led growth in the mid-Victorian
period had facilitated the re-emergence of strong craft regulations and
controls within the workshops. The resumption of the battle for control
climaxed in the 1897–8 lock-out when the employers won the fight
to employ non-unionists, to introduce piecework at rates agreed with
individual workers, to pay non-unionists at individual rates, to have full
control over the employment of apprentices, to enforce overtime, and
to place any worker on any machine at a mutually agreed rate. But craft
strength and the extraordinary fortitude and tenacity of work-group
loyalties (especially among the skilled) revealed themselves once again
in a further resurgence of craft militancy from 1909 onwards. And the
munitions crisis of 1915 and 1916 was to demonstrate the continued
centrality of skilled workers to engineering production.[38]

Despite such resistance, managerial innovations did take effect. Up to
the First World War and into the inter-war years engineering employers
continued to introduce automatic and semi-automatic machine tools,
and, according to Zeitlin, 'were able to undermine the long-term future
of craft regulation through the increasing employment of semi-skilled
and female labour; the multiplication of apprentices and the subversion
of the technical content of their training; and the rapid extension of
payment by results'. Effects were, however, by no means uniform
throughout the industry. In the older sectors, based on small and
unspecialised firms operating within diverse and varied markets, new
work practices and mechanisation were introduced 'within a workshop
organisation that remained structurally unchanged'. By 1914 such sectors
were not dominated by transformed and subordinate semi-skilled proletarians, mere instruments of production and appendages of machines.
Rather, skilled union members were often able to capture control of the

new machinery and still maintain a central position in the division of labour.

It was in the newer sectors of engineering – cycles, motor cars, electrical goods and in certain kinds of armaments – that managerial initiatives had a far more profound effect. In the face of rapidly rising mass demand for their largely standardised products, and confronted, in many cases, by fierce, direct competition from the United States and elsewhere, employers in the newer sectors of engineering did proceed with much greater purpose and speed in the transformation of the existing division of labour. For example, in the motor car industry there occurred extensive capital investment in new machinery, a veritable revolution in terms of methods of production and workshop layout, and an increasing concentration of power and control in the hands of management. Employers in the motor industry were, furthermore, largely successful in their opposition to mass trade unionism during the inter-war years.[39]

Three broad conclusions emerge from the foregoing discussion of the responses of selected British employers to the harsher economic and social climate of the late nineteenth century. First, as we have observed on numerous occasions, employers in a variety of industries acted quickly and often aggressively to offset falling profit margins and the power of organised labour. Such actions would strongly suggest that there was no absolute failure of entrepreneurship and no general triumph of an 'anti-industrial spirit' among employers. The will to make profits by means of industrial production was still alive and well.

Second, we have indicated above that employer actions frequently resulted in an escalation of industrial conflict. The full nature and extent of this conflict will be examined in Chapter 2. But at this point we can simply draw the reader's attention to the upsurges in militancy and conflict between the late 1880s and the early 1890s, the anti-union policies of employers in shipping and elsewhere in the 1890s, the series of anti-union judgements passed by the courts in the same decade (culminating in the Taff Vale case of 1901), and the widespread labour unrest of 1910 to 1914.

By no means all employers were anti-union. District and nationally based collective bargaining made rapid strides in the period up to the First World War. Furthermore, the state machinery generally favoured conciliation and union recognition rather than conflict and non-recognition. But the very existence of force and conflict in industrial relations, the increasingly large set-piece battles (as in cotton, coal and engineering in the 1890s), and the more widespread growth of radical class consciousness on the part of workers all suggested that mid-Victorian accommodation and stability were becoming very strained. The extent of worker dissatisfaction did not, as McKibbin has rightly observed, extend to mass support for the 'rejectionist' ideology of Marxism. But it was strong enough to cast serious doubt upon McKibbin's claim that fragmented and localised patterns of employment and the small scale of industrial organisation ensured the continuation of 'reasonably close and easy-going class relations'.[40]

Third, market situation crucially influenced employer responses. Thus where there existed (as in the case of motor cars) acute competition, especially from the United States, and where pressures upon accumulation were particularly marked, then employers did not hesitate to adopt radical, transformative managerial strategies. Similarly, Bill Lancaster has clearly shown that, under the pressure of American competition, the boot and shoe industry in Leicester was rapidly transformed in the late nineteenth century from an outworking industry to one based upon mechanised mass-production factories. In the process there occurred an intensified division of labour, a dilution of skills, and greater insecurity and unemployment. But, unlike the motor industry, workers in the boot and shoe industry remained strongly attached to trade unionism and many moved to embrace socialism and labourism in order to rectify their mounting grievances.[41] By way of contrast those employers (in cotton, shipbuilding and the older sectors of engineering) operating in less competitive and more secure markets (especially those of the British Empire) adopted, on the whole, more conciliatory labour strategies and less transformative industrial policies.

The United States: Iron and Steel, Cotton, the Metal Trades, Taylorism

Acute competition was a central feature of the late nineteenth-century American economy (at least before the massive merger movement of 1898–1903). For example, the iron and steel industries (especially the latter) were characterised by fierce employer rivalry and great instability (booms and slumps occurring with alarming frequency) within the overall deflationary character of the last quarter of the century. Employers made periodic attempts to stabilise prices and regulate market shares by means of trusts and pools. But in steel such combinations rarely outlasted depressions. The 1893 downturn, in particular, inaugurated a period of 'unmatched rivalry' in which Andrew Carnegie, with his enduring faith in cost cutting as the key to success, was to undersell many of his competitors and build up a large steel empire. As a result of his merger with the interests of Morgan and Moore, Carnegie created in 1901 the United States Steel Corporation, possessing a stock of over 1 billion dollars, and constituting the largest corporation in the world.

The Corporation controlled 60 per cent of the nation's steel business, regulated prices throughout steel, and owned, in addition to its furnaces and mills, vast ore and coking-coal lands, more than 1,100 miles of railroad and a fleet of lake steamers and barges. Run by a highly bureaucratic management, trained to set the greatest store by cost effectiveness, competition and incentives, United States Steel fully demonstrated the manifold advantages to be derived from the vertical integration of production stages from the iron or coal mine to the rolling mill.[42]

By the turn of the century, much to the amazement of visiting British steelmasters, the American steel industry had raced ahead of its once dominant British counterpart. In 1870 the American steel industry had been of 'minor consequence': by 1900 the Americans produced twice as much pig iron annually as the British. And American firms exported over a million tons of steel, some of it destined for British shores.

As David Brody had clearly shown, the 'impulse for economy' underlay the American achievement in steel.[43] During the 1880s, 1890s and 1900s mechanisation, extended seven-day working, irregular employment and greatly intensified labour instability and competition (with employers exploiting ethnic and other divisions among workers) brought a massive boost to productivity. Brody informs us that output per worker doubled in steel plants and tripled in blast furnaces between 1890 and 1910.

In addition, rapid and widespread mechanisation in steel eliminated jobs and diluted skills and conscious, collective workers' control over the process of production. Scooping machinery, larger barrows, and improved hoisting machinery greatly reduced the demand for the erstwhile large gangs of labourers in the ore yards, on the floors of blast furnaces and inside the mills.[44] In the rolling mills production became far less dependent upon the highly skilled, strongly mutualistic and formerly dominant rollers, roughers, catchers and heaters than upon the machine-tending abilities of the mass of semi-skilled 'transformed' workers who came to dominate the industry.

As Dawson and others have been quick to remind us, skill was not completely eliminated.[45] 'Men, not machines', notes Brody, 'continued to roll tin plate and puddle wrought iron'. But, generally speaking, manual operations in steel became extremely scarce. Once, 'the manipulators of raw materials and molten metal', steelworkers became, 'the tenders of machines'.[46] Furthermore, those whose skills remained at a premium were moved into ancillary and supervisory tasks, largely at the discretion of management, and production itself was dominated by the semi-skilled operatives. Thus, as Montgomery observes, the roller was transformed from, 'an inside contractor, and often a prominent member of a union that regulated the terms under which work was subcontracted from the employer by collective decisions of the workers involved' into 'a supervisory worker . . . a part of management'.[47]

Greatly enhanced managerial control and worker productivity were accompanied by the strict application of the principle of economy to wages. The aims of management were brutally simple: to deny a connexion between earnings and productivity; and to hold wages steady in a period of rapidly rising productivity.[48] A variety of means were employed to achieve these ends. Unilateral reductions in wages (in the interest of continued competitiveness), the massive employment of relatively cheap immigrant labour from southern and southeastern Europe, the adoption of the common-labour rate as the uniform standard for general wage calculation, and a systematic attempt at 'equalisation', to greatly weaken the position of high-priced workers and to narrow wage differentials, were all introduced to devastating effect. The wages of the ordinary labourer in steel were relatively stable before 1900, and there occurred an absolute decline in the earnings of those at the top after 1900. 'Labor savings were, in fact, the nub of the American accomplishment', concludes Brody, a view substantiated in the facts that between 1890 and 1910 the furnace worker's productivity tripled in exchange for an income increase of one-half, and the steelworker's output doubled in exchange for a wage increase of one-fifth.

A strong trade-union presence would, of course, have constituted a partial defence against the economising and authoritarian initiatives of Carnegie and his like. But as Brody, Montgomery and James Holt have demonstrated, this was not, on balance, to be the case in the steel industry.[49]

From its formation in 1876, the Amalgamated Association of Iron and Steel Workers did 'wage a formidable and persistent battle to oppose the employers' power with their own collective regulation of the industry' (Montgomery). But both iron and steel workers suffered major defeats and setbacks during the early–mid 1880s. It is true that the Association 'waxed', as noted by Montgomery, 'the strongest in its entire history' during the trade revival of 1888 to 1892. Indeed, Holt makes the important observation that, with a membership of some 24,000 in 1891, the Association had organised proportionately more iron and steel workers than its union counterparts in Britain (some 21,000 being organised in Britain). But from the early 1890s onwards, the fortunes of iron and steel trade unionism in the two countries sharply diverged to the detriment of American workers. Whereas total trade-union membership in British iron and steel had advanced to approximately 80,000 by 1913, the Amalgamated's membership had dwindled to a paltry 6,500 in 1914, largely concentrated among (a small percentage of) skilled men in the puddling and sheet and tin plate segments of the industry.[50]

This precipitous decline, from (in Gompers' opinion) 'probably the strongest organization in the American labour movement' to insignificance and impotence was caused in part by the excessive concentration of membership in iron (coverage of steel workers by the Amalgamated Association was never great), by the superior attitudes of the skilled towards the unskilled, which increasingly carried racial overtones (the mass of the unskilled being recent immigrants from southern and south-eastern Europe), and the grudging acceptance of the non-skilled into the union.[51]

Above all, it was the determined and ruthless hostility of the steel-masters towards trade unionism which constituted the key factor in the Amalgamated's demise. As Brody has declared, 'the maximization of labor savings required complete freedom from union interference'. Even cautious and moderate trade unionism was to be opposed. Trade unionism, by virtue of its very existence, challenged management's absolute rights to manage and control the plants.

The practical effects of such attitudes were truly devastating. In 1892 the Amalgamated Association was dealt a crushing defeat by Carnegie in the five months Homestead strike (which had been carefully set up by the management). Further anti-union onslaughts by Carnegie in the 1890s and by the United States Steel Corporation in 1901 spread the havoc beyond Pittsburgh. The last of the union steel mills fell in 1903, and the remaining tube mills followed in 1907 and 1908. In 1909, and despite the pleadings of moderate and increasingly obsequious union leaders, United States Steel formally initiated its open-shop policy. Thereafter, the company utilised a mixture of carrot (stock-subscription plans, low interest loans, opportunities for job advancement and so on) and stick (blacklisting of 'troublemakers', secret service tactics etc.) to exclude unions from its plants. But, despite such massive setbacks to trade unionism, worker discontent, as revealed most dramatically in the great strike of 1919 (which exploded the myth of immigrant docility) was by no means extinguished.[52]

At first sight cotton textiles in the United States would appear to have little in common with steel. The classic example of an early factory industry, cotton had, notes Montgomery, established its enduring patterns of mechanisation, gender division of labour, and methods of payment (rooted in piecework) by the end of the 1850s. And semi-skilled operatives were the norm in cotton, especially in weaving, long before mechanisation introduced them in large numbers into the steel industry.[53]

By the end of the century cotton and steel had, nevertheless, come to share many common features. Both industries were, for example, structured around high degrees of direct managerial control over labour. It is particularly significant in this respect that from the 1840s onwards American cotton employers departed from the English practice of sub-contracting. As Per Bolin-Hort has observed:

> When the self-acting mules were introduced in New England in the 1840s, the operative spinners were no longer allowed to hire any piecer assistants. The manufacturers demanded that they should perform all the piecing operations themselves, and that specific organization of work at the self-actors dominated for the rest of the century.[54]

There were exceptions to this general rule. In Fall River the minders were assisted by piecers and the mule spinners subcontracted the 'back-boys' who supplied the spinning machines with rovings. But Fall River's piecers were directly employed by management rather than being sub-contracted by the minders, and difficulties of labour supply as opposed to managerial concessions concerning control, determined the pattern of 'back-boy' recruitment.

Similarly, in Massachusetts weaving the weaver-tenter system, the characteristic form of organisation in Lancashire, was absent. Massachu-setts' weavers were restricted to the performance of the actual weaving operations. Ancillary tasks, such as cleaning the weft and cut carrying, were undertaken by special operatives under the direct control and employment of management. Likewise, the operations performed by piecers and creelers in Lancashire, under the supervision of the spinner, were carried out in Massachusetts by other workers under the authority of the overlooker.

The greater subdivision of tasks in American cotton and the more direct assertion of managerial control issued in part from extremely high patterns of labour turnover, and from the growing availability from mid century onwards of newly arrived, and in some cases relatively cheap, sources of immigrant labour (the Irish of the 1840s and 1850s being followed by the French Canadians and later the Portuguese, Greeks and Poles). But, as in the case of steel, the issue of control was of the essence. Thus American employers in cotton were determined to destroy competing sources of power and control within the workplace, and to undermine worker attempts to lay claim to certain types and areas of work. As Bolin-Hart observes, English operatives who emigrated to Massachusetts, 'often found the overlookers more authoritarian and overbearing than had been the case in Lancashire'.[55] And, by virtue of the power over other operatives which would be bestowed upon them by subcontracting, and their reputation for industrial militancy and allegiance to trade unionism, the spinners constituted a special object of employer attack.

In addition to their generally successful opposition to subcontracting, employers utilised a variety of means to achieve total control and increase profits. In the deflationary last quarter of the century there was intensified mechanisation in order to undermine skills and reduce costs. In spinning, new ring-spinning machinery, operated by unorganised women and juveniles, was introduced into the mule-spinning and textiles trade-union capital of Massachusetts, Fall River, in order to break the power of the men. Largely English immigrants, who had imported their customary attachments to subcontracting and trade unionism, Fall River's mule spinners had been involved in several disputes with the employers from the middle years of the century onwards. In 1886 they did manage to negotiate a sliding-scale list of prices with local and more distant employers which lasted until the First World War. But the list did not offer safeguards against speed-up. And whilst less dramatic and devastating in its immediate effects than immediately feared, the introduction of ring spinning did lead to the downfall of the union during the following three decades. By 1894, notes Montgomery, ten mills in Fall River had altogether dispensed with mules; and, 'Realizing that the days of their craft's existence were numbered', the union at Fall River, 'persuaded the National Mule Spinners' Association to recruit ring spinners and drop the word 'mule' from its name'.[56]

Beyond Fall River, exceptional in its trade union strength and chronic industrial unrest, employer successes were even more complete. In weaving, the automatic (Northrop) loom, complete with its low skill and low wage requirements and its facilitation of increased workloads, soon came to dominate the new mills in the South and establish a strong presence in the North. On the eve of the First World War 56 per cent of looms in the South and 29 per cent of those in New England were automatic, as compared with a corresponding figure of 2 per cent for Lancashire.[57] Ring spinning became truly hegemonic in both the North and South. The massive new woollen and silk mills of Passaic and Paterson, New Jersey, and Lawrence, Massachusetts, were run by relatively low-waged 'new' immigrants. And everywhere in textiles, employers intensified pressures upon speed-up, workloads and, most of all, upon the rate to be paid per piece of output. Finally, the corporate structures of power, the relatively high levels of employer co-operation (as compared with pre-1890s Lancashire), and the large financial resources which characterised American textiles, were of major importance in the widespread late nineteenth- and early twentieth-century employer offensive against trade unionism.[58]

Given the strength and determination of the employers, combined with the overall weakness of trade unionism, the degree and tenacity of worker resistance in cotton and other textiles were quite remarkable. As we will observe in some detail in the following two chapters, struggles to raise or prevent reductions in piece rates (especially among female weavers), to reduce the length of the working day, and generally to introduce standard rates and conditions into capitalist disorder were prominent features of late nineteenth- and early twentieth-century textile towns.

Unlike the examples of steel and cotton textiles, new machinery and more integrated processes and flows of production did not satisfactorily solve the problems of declining rates of productivity, increasing wages and squeezed profits in metal-working enterprises.[59] As Montgomery has shown, most late nineteenth-century metal-working firms, involved in the construction of railway locomotives, sewing machines, farm machinery, and in the electrical goods, machine-tool and, increasingly, auto industries, did not reap economies of scale from increased size. 'Quite small plants were the most efficient', writes Montgomery; and, furthermore, 'Large and small alike were hopelessly dependent on the skills of labor, in a multitude of different crafts: machinists, pattern makers, molders, blacksmiths, metal polishers, fitters, electricians, sheet-metal craftsmen, and others'. It is true that there occurred extensive mechanisation during the first two decades of the present century, but, notes Montgomery, 'the new lathes, boring mills, milling machines, and radical drills were no simpler to operate than the old'.[60]

Yet where mechanisation and increased size of firm failed to transform labour – to dilute skills, to increase the absolute numbers and proportions of the semi-skilled, and to transfer control of the labour process away from craft workers to management – so the introduction of scientific management and the open-shop policy adopted by many employers from 1903–4 onwards did strengthen the subordination of labour to capital, and did hasten the 'liberation' of, to use Haywood and Bohns' memorable phrase, the 'manager's brain' from 'under the workman's cap'.[61]

The open-shop movement followed hard on the heels of failed attempts by union officials and employers' representatives both within the metal trades and beyond (and largely under the auspices of the National Civic Federation), to sustain the development of a 'British' system of institutionalised collective bargaining (rooted in national agreements, the promotion of industrial peace and stability, and strict controls over the 'wildcat' actions of the rank and file).[62] In the metal trades, for example, the Murray Hill Agreement of 1900 granted the nine-hour day and no discrimination against union members (as opposed to the official recognition of the International Association of Machinists) in return for the termination of restriction on output and of strikes for the duration of the agreement. Many union officials and officers of the National Metal Trades' Association saw the agreement as a welcome release from the industrial conflict gripping the industry. But the failure of workers, especially in the militant stronghold of Chicago, to abide by the agreement led to its acrimonious breakdown. Both in the metal trades and elsewhere, workers continued to demand the closed shop, to restrict output, to engage in sympathy strikes and, as such, to defy the instructions of their national union officials and the American Federation of Labor.

Given this show of worker defiance, and the depression of 1903–4 (which transformed a labour scarcity into a surplus), employers generally jettisoned the National Civic Federation's plans for institutionalised collaboration between organised labour and organised capital in favour of an aggressive and organised Open Shop Drive. David Parry, of the National Association of Manufacturers, emerged as the leader of a crusade which sought the support of 'concerned citizens from all walks of life'. Montgomery has nicely captured the mood of this crusade:

> Starting with the Modern Order of the Bees in Dayton and Citizens' Alliances in numerous towns, local merchants, academics, professional men, supervisory personnel, fraternity boys from universities and anti-union workers were enrolled in local associations to combat 'union tyranny' . . . a national Citizens' Industrial Association was formed in 1903 to rally all 'those who believe in the maintenance of law and order and the perpetuation of our free institutions', first to defend the country's workingmen against 'the present programme of violence, boycotting, and tyranny now being carried out by the majority of labor unions', and second to resist 'legislation of a socialistic nature'.[63]

Within the metal trades employers did battle with the International Association of Machinists. The employers were aided by the National Metal Trades' Association which 'honeycombed the unions with spies', recruited and organised non-union strikebreakers, and 'provided struck employers with strategic advice, financial assistance, private detectives, legal assistance and a card file on every one of the 35 thousand workers employed by the Association's 325 firms'. In addition, employers' associations placed mounting and successful pressure upon the judiciary to issue anti-union injunctions and to outlaw boycotts and sympathy strikes; and pressed local police and magistrates to adopt aggressive anti-union and anti-strike tactics.

The results, both within the metal trades and within American industry as a whole, were farreaching. By the early 1920s, and in some cases much earlier, major sectors of the economy – steel, auto, meatpacking, electrical goods, rubber, chemicals and petroleum – were run mainly or wholly on non-union lines. Within the metal trades the open-shop movement 'effectively checked the growth of unionism' up to the eve of the First World War. Labour scarcity and massively increased demand for the products of machinists (especially munitions during the war), combined with worker militancy and self-confidence boosted the membership of the International Association of Machinists to 331,450 by 1919 (it had stood at 54,000 in 1910). But the depression of 1920–2, deregulation of the economy, the increasing hostility of the state towards organised labour, and a vigorously renewed Open-Shop Drive forced the weakened IAM very much on to the defensive in the harsh climate of the 1920s.[64]

The metal trades had also been at the forefront of experiments in scientific management.[65] Primarily associated with Frederick Winslow Taylor, the son of a wealthy middle-class family who had nevertheless trained as a machinist, scientific management was first and foremost concerned with 'the systematic organization of production' and the performance of work in 'the one best way', rather than with either technological change or corporate welfare reforms. Taylor's system, developed in the course of his experiences as gang boss in charge of the lathe department at Midvale Steel and as a supervisor at Bethlehem Steel, was concerned to transfer control over the labour process from workers to management. Taylorism sought to eliminate restriction of output ('soldiering'), to develop forms of payment and work to suit the character of individual workers, and to effect centralised planning and routing of the various processes of production, the precise and systematic analysis of these processes and greater supervision and closer instruction of workers in the performance of minutely divided tasks of work.

In both theory and practice, Taylorism amounted to a revolution in the sphere of management. Previously, most employers had negotiated a price for a particular job with the workers concerned and later sold the finished product. Actual control over the methods of work, the subdivision of tasks, and even the distribution of wages, had, as demonstrated by Montgomery for the iron industry, resided largely with the workers themselves. Taylorism thus presented a direct assault upon craft control, and, in seeking to individualise patterns of work and payment, was in fundamental disagreement with worker collectivism, especially trade unionism and its key principles of standard conditions, hours and rates of pay. Furthermore, as clearly demonstrated by Braverman, Taylorism represented not an objective 'science of work' but an ideology of management seeking 'an answer to the specific problem of how best to control alienated labor – that is to say, labor power that is bought and sold'.[66]

Taylorism was, in effect, part of the wider capitalist attempt to reduce labour costs, increase productivity and enlarge managerial control in response to the crisis of competitive capitalism. The impact of Taylorism was, however, limited, both by worker resistance and by widespread employer suspicion of a system which sought to swell the ranks of administrators and supervisors (armed with stop-watches, time cards, records of individual output and the like). Montgomery nevertheless notes that scientific management was part of 'a veritable mania for efficiency, organization and standardization' which 'swept through American business and literary circles' after 1900. And although not implemented in every detail, Taylorism found increasing favour among employers embroiled in 'control' conflicts with their workers. 'Employers in every major industry', records Montgomery:

> sought to develop an engineering staff, academically educated for its new role, which could plan and direct the flow of production on the basis of systematic research ... then assign each worker a very specific task ... based on time and motion studies, and finally, induce the worker to perform that task as assigned by a carefully structured system of incentive payments. By this innovation, the power of the craftsmen ... was undermined, and the traditional dualism of craftsmen operating the machinery while laborers fetched and carried was remodeled into a continuum of specialized machine tenders performing functions which required only minor variations in training and agility, and all of which were directly under the detailed supervision of a swarm of managerial officials.

Thus, concludes Montgomery, 'Although fewer than thirty factories had been thoroughly reorganized by Taylor and his colleagues before 1917, the essential elements of their proposals had found favor in almost every industry by the mid-1920s.'[67]

It was, above all, in the metal trades that Taylorism took early and explosive effect in relation to the subdivision and simplification of tasks, the shift from the all-around machinist to the specialised operative, intensive supervision and various forms of incentive payments. Skill was not eliminated. Indeed, Taylorism inadvertently created the new, and often militant, tool and die craftsmen who made the tools and fixtures operated increasingly by the specialised operatives. But skilled workers were transformed into tool makers or supervisors and, as such, became ancillary to the production processes dominated by the inexperienced machine tenders. Thus the number of machine operatives in the auto and farm equipment industries alone increased annually by almost 40 per cent between 1910 and 1920, an increase brought about not by mechanisation itself but rather by the simplification of tasks resulting from the use of prefabricated jigs and fixtures, and from the detailed instruction and supervision provided.[68]

Taylor always maintained that his system held great attractions for ambitious individuals seeking to maximise their income in return for increased productivity and managerial control. And there is little doubt that the large numbers of unskilled male labourers and women converted into machine tenders did experience significant improvements in earnings before 1920. But in general the spread of Taylorism was accompanied by widespread hostility. Opposition in the metal trades was concentrated mainly among those skilled workers experiencing a severe loss of control and independence. But they were joined during the years of the First World War by labourers and operatives (many of them recent immigrants) demanding increased wages to offset the rising cost of living. Premium pay systems, the dilution of skills, the stopwatch, the generally alienating and reificatory effects of Taylorism (as manifested especially in high rates of labour turnover, absenteeism and sabotage), and management refusals to establish standard rates and conditions, recognise shop committees and accept demands for the eight-hour day – all triggered major and bitter industrial conflicts. Taylorism, combined with the open-shop drive, transformed machinists from minor to major practitioners of strikes, and stimulated the development of socialist and syndicalist alternatives to 'pure and simple' trade unionism within the International Association of Machinists.[69]

Some other industries were less susceptible to Taylorism's 'embrace'. In coalmining in both the United States and Britain the hewer's 'place', deep underground at the coalface, hardly lent itself to close supervision by an army of white-shirts.[70] And, despite the growth of factory-produced standardised parts in the building industry, many construction workers in the United States successfully retained both their skills and local job control. Significantly, the largely non-transformed workers in construction and the coal mines made up half of America's trade-union members by the 1900s.[71] However, in both these industries and many others, employers attempted to reduce wage costs and worsen working conditions in order to increase profits.

RESPONSES AND OUTCOMES: NATIONAL DIFFERENCES

Our discussion of employer responses to the mounting problems of late nineteenth-century capitalism has so far emphasised similarities of response on both sides of the Atlantic. But it is now incumbent upon us to highlight three very different outcomes relating to the growth of concentration and corporate business structures; the extent and pace of the transformation of existing techniques of production and methods of management; and employer policies towards trade unionism.

In all three respects, the United States, as demonstrated in our preceding examples, adopted non-union corporate structures to a much greater extent than Britain.

Corporate Capitalism

The concentration of capital and the emergence of giant firms in late nineteenth-century and early twentieth-century America have been well documented by Chandler.[72] Up to the depression of 1873 American manufacturing firms were typically small (employing on average fewer than ten workers), owned by individuals or families, and expanded on the basis of traditional methods. But out of the depression emerged a new generation of business leaders who were to fundamentally transform their institutions. Hence, although only a minority of wage earners worked in factories by the 1880s, and despite the proliferation of small firms, nevertheless by the early 1900s the giant corporate enterprise had achieved a hegemonic position throughout industry.

Combination in industry developed in two phases. The first phase, the (mainly) horizontal concentration movement (1879–93), saw the combination of small manufacturers in the consumer-goods industries into larger units of production in order to counteract problems of overproduction and falling prices. 'By 1893', note Robertson and Walton, 'consolidation and centralization were well under way in those consumer-goods industries that manufactured staple household items that had long been in use'. The Standard Oil Company of New Jersey, headed by John D. Rockefeller, the Distillers' and Cattle Feeders' Trust, the American Sugar Refining Company, and the United States Rubber Company were the most prominent products of this first phase.[73]

The second phase (1898–1904) was characterised by the predominantly vertical combination of industries which lay mainly in the producer-goods sector. Sponsored by investment banks, employers in steel, copper, power machinery and so on extended their control over a wide range of operations from the mining of raw materials to the selling of finished goods. Some consumer-goods industries, responding to an integrated national and growing urban market, also effected vertical integration to achieve economies of scale. Thus Swift, Armour and Morris (in meatpacking) and Duke (in cigarettes) ranked alongside Carnegie, Moore and Morgan as prominent 'Robber Barons'. Altogether, some 328 major combinations were created between 1888 and 1905. Thereafter, the trend towards concentration slowed down, in part the result of successful prosecutions under the Sherman Act of 1890 (Standard Oil and the American Tobacco Company were spectacularly dissolved). But from the early 1920s onwards concentration once again made rapid advances, and the American economy as a whole was characterised by high degrees of monopoly and oligopoly.

Concentration was far less marked in Britain. There did emerge large units of production and distribution in food processing (for example, Cadbury's, Lipton's, the Co-op). And in both older and newer sectors of manufacturing there was, notes Cronin, 'a steady rise in the size of plant, the ratio of capital per worker, and in industrial concentration'.[74] Cotton, for example, saw the rise of limited liability companies and a general decline in the influence of the large, paternalist employer, whilst Britain's fastest growing coalfield, in South Wales, required levels of capital investment 'beyond the reach of most individuals and small partnerships'. By 1914 the Cambrian Combine, observes Benson, was responsible for two-thirds of the entire output of the Rhondda Valley; and the labour force at a typical South Wales mine stood at 376.[75] Similarly, relatively large units of production prevailed in the newer sections of engineering (in bicycles, armaments and cars). Late nineteenth-century shipyards 'were among the largest industrial enterprises in the country' (with, record Reid and McClelland, twenty employing over 2,000 men each),[76] and in Britain, as in America, the railway companies had pioneered large and bureaucratic methods of organisation and management.

But, in overall terms, large, corporate structures of the American type were rare in Britain. Elbaum and Lazonick have drawn attention to the continued centrality of the relatively small, specialised and 'traditional' family, or individually based firm:

> Britain's major nineteenth-century staple industries – textiles, iron and steel, coal mining, shipbuilding, and engineering – were composed of numerous firms with small market shares . . .
> Characteristically, firms were run by owner-proprietors or close family associates. Managerial staffs were small, and methods of cost accounting and production control were crude or non-existent . . . Most enterprises were single-plant firms that specialized in particular lines of manufacture of intermediate or final products.[77]

In those sectors where concentration did take place, it generally failed to match the scale of American experience. In cotton textiles, for example, the Lancashire weaving sector was generally dominated by small units of production (especially in the north and northeast of the county), and even in spinning the rise of the Limiteds was a phenomenon largely concentrated upon Oldham and district rather than upon the fine-spinning centre of Bolton. Lancashire's cotton employers tended, furthermore, to be more divided than their American counterparts. Despite the emergence of more broadly based and unified employers' organisations in British cotton from the 1890s onwards, employers at the local level often continued to be divided by economic competition. None of the Lancashire towns enjoyed the British equivalent of Fall River's Board of Trade, a corporate interlocking directorate which effectively regulated wages and concentrated ownership of between 30 and 40 of Fall River's firms in the hands of seven related families. Similar systems of corporate unity and concentrated power existed in cotton textiles in Lowell, Lawrence and other New England towns.[78]

Further examples abound. Thus Holt notes that the British iron and steel industry lagged behind its late nineteenth-century American counterpart not only in terms of the pace and extent of technological change, but also in terms of the scale of corporate organisation. 'By 1899', observes Holt, 'the Carnegie and Illinois Steel Companies had annual capacities of over one million tons of steel. As late as 1905 the ingot capacity of the largest British firm was somewhat less than half of this figure'.[79] Despite having large yards, the British shipbuilding industry did not experience a particularly strong movement towards the centralisation of capital. Reid and McClelland thus note that, 'with the exception of some significant mergers in the 1900s', ownership in shipbuilding 'remained widely scattered among over 100 predominantly family firms'. The large coal mines of South Wales and Durham, although typical of the industry as a whole, continued to exist alongside the small pits in Staffordshire, Lancashire and Cheshire. And in the engineering industry small firms continued to be the norm.[80]

Not only were British firms generally smaller and more fragmented than their American equivalents, but they also lacked commensurate long-term support and direct involvement in their affairs from the financial community. Whereas the late nineteenth-century merger movement in the United States was directly sponsored by the leading investment banks, eager to transform existing business structures and practices, no parallel development took place in Britain. In the latter country, long-term finance for businesses had customarily been raised by means of family fortunes, retained earnings and local banks. By the end of the nineteenth century national banks were providing credit to British businesses but, note Elbaum and Lazonick, only in the form of short-term working capital, largely in the form of overdraft facilities and bills of exchange. The increasingly strong attractions of overseas investment and the concentration of banking in the City of London meant that manufacturing industry and the financial institutions lacked the interdependence and common purpose characteristic of the American system. British banks did not provide industry with large amounts of long-term venture capital, and, in the absence of close and durable contact, possessed neither the inclination nor the power to fundamentally change industrial structures and practices.[81]

Managerial Innovations

The second major difference of response lay in the fact that, generally speaking, American employers were far more prepared than their British counterparts to introduce new techniques of production and management. Our selected examples have repeatedly demonstrated that bureaucratic managerial hierarchies, technological innovation, mass production techniques, and the new managerial practices of Taylor and his associates spread far more rapidly and widely in the United States than in Britain. One might add that technical and business education and personnel management also developed more profoundly in the United States. We have also seen that mechanisation, mass production and moves to organise production around semi-skilled workers were by no means absent in Britain, especially in those newer sectors of industry forced into open competition with America and Germany. But in the final analysis, as demonstrated in the cases of cotton, engineering and many other industries, British employers tended to push existing or 'traditional' methods of labour management to the full rather than, as in the American case, fundamentally transform existing plant layout and the division of labour by means of Taylorism and technological change.

In sum, as argued by Hobsbawn some twenty years ago, and recently elaborated by a number of scholars, British capitalism remained largely wedded to the competitive, small-scale and increasingly archaic structures and practices of the first Industrial Revolution whilst countries such as the United States rapidly moved to embrace corporate capitalism. Herein lay the roots of Britain's relative decline.[82]

Employers and Trade Unionism

The third difference lay in the adoption of markedly different policies by British and American employers towards trade unionism. Our focus upon selected industries has clearly revealed the existence in the United States of far more determined, aggressive and violent employer opposition to the very existence of trade unionism (however moderate) than generally existed in Britain (especially in England).

Carnegie's aims – to achieve the total submission of labour to the will of capital and 'complete freedom from union interference' – were widely shared by American employers. And the failure, in the face of rank-and-file unrest, of the National Civic Federation's attempt to achieve industrial harmony by means of institutionalised national collective bargaining, provided an important stimulus to the more extensive development of open-shop policies. American employers were, furthermore, determined to defeat trade unions by all possible means. On countless occasions spies and the full range of coercive forces available to the (especially local) state were enlisted in the cause of militantly anti-union capitalists. And the rhetoric of the latter, complete with references to union 'dictation', 'tyranny' and 'control', bore a striking resemblance to the language employed by British employers in the 1830s and 1840s when both competition and pressures of accumulation were more acute than during the balmier days of mid-Victorian world supremacy. Even so, it is difficult to call to mind an English equivalent of Jay Gould's threat to 'hire half the working class to shoot the other half'.[83]

American capital's drive for total domination resulted in much higher and more bitter levels of conflict than in England. But the American trade-union movement emerged from the tumultuous strike decade between 1912 and 1922 in a weaker state than its British counterpart. And determined, ruthless and unrelenting employer opposition was a key factor in America. Holt's comments concerning iron and steel could be widely applied to American industry:

> The determination to resist the growth of trade unions by employers who possessed vast financial resources, who controlled a rapidly changing technology, and who were uninhibited by political constraints, may not have been the only reason for the collapse of unionism in the American steel industry, but it is surely the most important one.[84]

In general terms British employers were far more prepared to accept trade unionism. To be sure, as noted, capitalism's late nineteenth-century crisis saw intensified pressures placed upon labour by capital, and an industrial and judicial attack upon 'new' unionism and some of trade unionism's basic functions. In some parts of Britain anti-union sentiments were especially pronounced. In the heavy industries of the West of Scotland, more undercapitalised, less productive and given more to acute cyclical fluctuations than their equivalents in England, employers fought long and hard against trade unionism. Melling and Foster have shown that trade unionism in and around Glasgow developed later than in England and was accompanied by much bitterness and deeply held suspicions towards the employers. In view of the fact that links between organised labour and Liberalism were less strong in Scotland than in England, and given the close ties between Scottish Conservatism and Orangeism, the Scottish labour movement turned more profoundly and quickly to independent labour and socialist politics than the movement in England. More generally, as seen in the cases of coal and cotton, large set-piece industrial battles between labour and capital became a prominent and regular feature of the late nineteenth- and early twentieth-century British industrial relations scene, whilst widespread conflict was a prominent feature of the immediate pre-First World War years.

Conflict was, however, accompanied by the development of a comparatively strong and increasingly mass-based trade-union movement, extremely high rates of union density in key occupations (over 90 per cent in cotton spinning and boilermaking, and 75 per cent in mining by 1900), and greatly accelerated moves towards employer recognition of unions and the development of collective bargaining procedures at both district and national levels. As we have seen, in contrast to their American counterparts, British employers in cotton, iron and steel, and engineering sought to eliminate 'excesses' of craft and union power rather than, generally speaking, trade unionism *per se*. Indeed, as Garside and Gospel have shown, the initiative behind the development of collective bargaining machinery in a number of industries between the 1890s and 1914 lay mainly with employers. And as Holt has declared, the goals of most British employers, even many of those involved in the 'counter-attack' of the 1890s, were 'limited' and their tactics 'generally timid when compared to those of many American employers at that time'. The British state was less hostile than its American equivalent. And many trade unionists would have endorsed the sentiments of John Hodge, a leading figure in British iron and steel trade unionism, that anti-union employers in the industry were in a minority and that the majority of employers were 'entitled to credit for always having played cricket' with the unions. Thus, whilst by no means a blessed 'Peaceable Kingdom', Britain was less afflicted than America by industrial conflict and anti-union employers between the 1870s and 1914.[85]

BRITISH 'TRADITIONALISM'

Britain's 'traditionalism', its much slower advance towards corporate capitalism, and its more tolerant attitude towards trade unionism have been explained in a number of ways. The range of explanations offered is, indeed, more extensive than wholly coherent. The 'institutional rigidities' of small-scale British capitalism,[86] its alleged addiction to 'short-termism' and the paucity of longer-term entrepreneurial vision; for some, such as Wiener, the increasing 'gentrification' and 'anti-industrialism' of Britain's employers;[87] the allegedly adverse effects of strong British trade unions upon technological and managerial innovation and dynamism;[88] the more diverse and custom-based nature of Britain's markets which were less conducive to standardisation and mass production than was

America's huge domestic market;[89] the abundance of skilled and comparatively cheap labour in Britain as a supposed disincentive to widespread mechanisation;[90] the different 'stages' of development reached by late nineteenth-century capitalism in Britain and America; and the more relaxed and 'corporatist' attitude adopted by the British state towards organised labour – these have constituted the key theses presented by historians and others.

Time and space do not permit a detailed assessment of the various explanations on offer. But we can observe that notions of 'gentrification', of overbearing and adverse trade-union power, and of *absolute* entrepreneurial 'failure' in Britain would appear to carry insubstantial empirical and theoretical weight. Similarly, the tendency to set up corporate America as the ideal to which Britain should have aspired (evident in the work of Elbaum and Lazonick) improperly erects an absolute standard of capitalist development, underestimates the extent of change within the British economy, and the importance of variety and national context, and unfairly assumes the availability to historical actors of degrees of foresight and choice which they rarely possess.

With reference to patterns of economic development, emphases upon the nature of markets and the chronology and pattern of industrialisation are more rewarding. America's large-scale domestic demand for relatively cheap and standardised commodities did undoubtedly provide a tremendous stimulus to the growth of mass-production industries. In turn, large size, vertical and horizontal integration, and hierarchical and bureaucratic management structures offered American business increased efficiency, economies of scale and the ability to meet mass demand. And the central involvement of the investment banks in the massive merger movement between 1898 and 1904 ensured that the impetus to economy, efficiency, combination and market control would not relent in America. Indeed, this impetus accelerated, and was increasingly reflected in the drive for overseas markets.

Britain's market structure and patterns of trade were very different. The British home market was, of course, much smaller than that of the United States, and its potential, in terms of mass demand for standardised commodities, was not adequately exploited until the inter-war period. By the end of the nineteenth century Britain's characteristic pattern of trade, based upon the export of manufactured goods and services and the import of raw materials, was firmly entrenched. Most significantly, foreign demand for British products was, with a few exceptions (such as that for cotton goods), highly varied in character. As in the case of shipbuilding, manufactured products for both the domestic and export markets were made to particular specifications to a much greater extent than in the United States. And, as argued by Elbaum and

Lazonick, the fragmented structure of much of British industry and the small scale of operations, in addition to the lack of close, long-term involvement with the banks, did not provide an institutional structure which could be rapidly transformed to meet changed market conditions and patterns of trade. Diverse markets and highly differentiated products were conducive more to small-batch production on the part of a multitude of relatively small firms than to bulk standardisation on the part of specialised giant corporations.

We have observed, nevertheless, that the crisis of competitive capitalism did compel British employers to reconsider their market strategies, and to make greater efforts to cut costs and increase profits. Significantly, we have seen that efforts to move British industry in a corporate direction were most pronounced in those sectors in which there existed either standardised mass demand or intensified and inescapable competition from abroad or both. Yet the overall fact remains that the development of corporate capitalism in Britain was far less profound and rapid than in the United States.

A key explanation of Britain's corporate retardation resides in the fact, as suggested by Hobsbawm, that, faced with mounting economic problems and competition, the majority of British employers (especially those in the staple export industries) concentrated most of their activities upon the vast, safe and protected markets of Empire. Given the profitability of such markets, there was no pressing reason for most engineering, cotton and other leading employers in the 'monopoly' export sectors to confront American and German competition head on. (In those industries, such as boots and shoes and automobiles, where competition could not be evaded, British capitalists carried out more profound restructuring.) In addition rising prices from the late 1890s onwards eased the pressure on profits; and Britain's continued domination of the world's shipping, insurance and banking reinforced a sense of complacent superiority. By the end of the nineteenth century Britain, as noted by Hobsbawm, was 'becoming a parasitic rather than a competitive economy, living off the remains of world monopoly, the underdeveloped world, her past accumulations of wealth and the advance of her rivals'.[91]

In such ways did Britain's patterns of trade cushion the effects of the crisis of competitive capitalism, inhibit widespread economic transformation and re-structuring of industry, and promote the values and practices of 'traditionalism'. In the relative absence of external cushions, and in response to the great inducements offered by the mass domestic market, determined American employers carried out a process of fundamental capitalist transformation.

Market structures were reflective of the overall nature and pace of

economic development. Without propounding a linear model of economic development, we should carefully note the later and more rapid
industrialisation of the United States. Part One in the first volume
suggested that full-blown commodity production and its associated
values of unrestrained individualism, competition and so forth were
more marked in Britain in the pre-1850 period. But between the 1840s
and the 1890s *laissez-faire* capitalism made giant strides in the United
States. During these decades industrialisation in America proceeded
more rapidly than during Britain's Industrial Revolution, was com-
pressed into a shorter period of time, was even more explosive (as seen
in the Civil War) and resulted in the more clear-cut domination of a
mature industrial society by an industrial bourgeoisie. Furthermore, as
in pre-1850 Britain, the pressures of capital accumulation, acute competition and sharp cyclical fluctuations, combined with the emergence of
determined and ruthless employer 'tyrants' and a permanent wage-
earning class, resulted in greatly intensified class conflict. The minority
standing of industrial wage earners within America's late nineteenth-
century population, the absolute triumph of a capitalist system red in
tooth and claw, the post-bellum hegemonic position of a fiercely anti-
collectivist northern bourgeoisie, the overall domination of political
structures and power by the propertied middle and lower-middle class,
and the continued centrality of the ideology of 'free labour' – all boded
ill for organised labour.

In late nineteenth-century Britain matters were, as we have seen,
quite different. There were continued instances of anti-unionism, but
these were not on a par with similar practices in the United States.
Many British employers did not *welcome* trade union recognition, an
attitude of mind which had been even more marked, more 'American'
during the mid-Victorian period. But, in the final analysis, dislike had
been effectively combined with greater accommodation. Thus, the gains,
in terms of recognition and financial strength, achieved by trade unionism during the third quarter, the official recognition of the movement
by the state, the cushions to anti-union employer practices provided by
Empire and safe markets, and the less severe anti-union ideological
climate, meant that trade unions had been and would continue to be
more readily accepted in Britain. In addition, by the turn of the century
many British employers had found it cheaper, more convenient and, in
all probability, more profitable to deal with 'responsible' trade unions
and their officials rather than fight to the death. As demonstrated by
Burgess for cotton, *détente* in the face of growing foreign competition,
combined with trade union 'moderation', proved a popular option for
many employers. Institutionalised collective bargaining structures and
procedures intended to offer greater stability and security against 'unof-

ficial' interruptions to production; diminished craft regulation and enhanced managerial prerogatives; demonstrably resilient and yet frequently moderate-led trade unions; and general consensus among union leaders and employers as to the 'rules of the game' – all became hallmarks of Britain's 'modern' system of industrial relations so admired by the Webbs.[92]

The State and Politics

Finally, the state had played a major part in the institutionalisation of industrial relations in Britain. Subjected to a variety of complex and, at times, contradictory forces – the facilitation of capitalist accumulation *and* due recognition of and concessions to contending social forces in the interests of stability and 'fairness' – the state in Britain had, as noted in Volume One, come to an early recognition of the legitimacy of the trade-union movement.[93] By the end of the 1860s the trade unions had become too strong to be simply wished away. The state and the employers could have destroyed the movement by force, but such a coercive policy would have run counter to the more accommodating stance adopted in the wake of the Chartist threat. Furthermore, in view of the growing moderation of organised labour and sustained economic expansion, accommodation made much greater sense than exclusion.[94]

By the end of the century, and despite the employer counter-attack, adverse legal decisions and growing tensions within Lib.-Labism, the trade-union movement still remained a recognised part of British society. Up to the First World War and beyond the state, as seen particularly in the actions of leading Liberal politicians, assumed a mediatory and conciliatory role between organised labour and organised capital. Ideology and public ceremonial, claims McKibbin, also acted as a powerful stimulus to consensus and stability. Thus, the workers' strong sense of class was, maintains McKibbin, 'highly conditioned by inherited ideologies which emphasized a common citizenship, the fairness of the rules of the game and the class-neutrality of the major institutions of the state'. The 'substantial exclusion of the market from politics', continues McKibbin, 'gave the British working class rights and immunities shared nowhere else; while it restrained the employing class from adopting the industrial techniques of its continental counterparts'. And the state's search for 'non-authoritarian social stability' was greatly aided by the seemingly neutral and consensual aims of the monarchy. The latter had 'apparently become the even-handed guarantor of the class-neutrality of Parliament, the institution which ensured that the rules of the game would be followed'.[95]

As we shall demonstrate in Chapters 2 and 3, this picture of a 'class-neutral' state, successfully excluding conflicts between labour and capital from the province of politics and promoting consensus and stability, is at many points in need of qualification and correction. The picture pays inadequate attention to conflict, the growth of independent labour and of a wider class consciousness, and the extent to which the British state employed coercion against those on Clydeside, Merseyside, South Wales and elsewhere who were not prepared to play solely by the rules of moderate, 'responsible' trade unionism and politics.[96] But, McKibbin's model does, nevertheless, usefully highlight the generally moderate policies of the British state towards trade unionism in contrast with the more authoritarian and 'free-market' strategies adopted in parts of continental Europe and in the United States.

In the latter country, the pre-First World War state did not, at least at the level of the federal government, interfere frequently and directly in the processes of 'private' negotiation between employers and workers. (The case of the railways, as having manifestly public concerns and engaged in inter-state commerce, constitutes the obvious exception to the general rule.) And as Howell Harris informs us, in the face of 'constitutionalism, separation and limitation of powers, federalism and local control' the United States' governmental system, 'remained extraordinarily weak and fragmented well into the twentieth century, in the face of structures of private interest and economic power already comparatively well-integrated at the national level'.[97]

By way of contrast, the political parties and the courts did wield large powers. Howell Harris' observations are again instructive:

> The United States' polity throughout most of the nineteenth century was one of 'courts and parties'. The parties controlled both the powerful legislative and the starveling, dependent executive-administrative branches of government, at state and federal levels. There they built, preserved, and balanced coalitions of voters and interest-groups by distributing public goods and devolving 'public' authority to 'private' interests. Courts created a legal framework to facilitate and stabilise a competitive, individualistic capitalism ... In the early twentieth century the United States began to build a centralised, regulatory administrative state. But that was a slow and uneven process. Through the 1920s, the judiciary still had a far greater part to play than the executive or legislative branches of state and federal government in defining public policies towards organised labour.

Enjoying a large measure of independence in terms of policy making, and staffed mainly by those extremely sympathetic to the cause of capital, the judiciary pursued a largely anti-union line between the 1880s and 1920s. As Howell Harris notes, 'even the most "conservative" spokesmen for organised labour in America came to an inescapable conclusion, the lesson of bitter experience, that the all-important judiciary played a role of contestant, rather than referee, in cases involving trade-union organisation and industrial conflict'.[98] In addition, the police, many politicians and editors, and others prominent in the local state machinery were, as demonstrated in the conflicts of 1877, at Homestead in 1892 and on countless other occasions, to be found arrayed against the interests of organised labour.

As noted in Volume One, the 'gift of the suffrage' meant that the mainstream parties were compelled to appeal to the interests of workers, including those involved in the labour movement. But, as will be shown in more detail in Chapter 3, there existed a number of important contrasts with the British experience. First, at least before the second decade of the twentieth century (when the American Federation of Labor moved close to the Democratic Party), there did not exist a national equivalent of Lib.-Labism to represent the specific interests of organised labour at the highest levels of government. Local alliances between organised labour and the mainstream parties (especially the Democrats) were often in evidence. As we have seen, the mainstream parties made strenuous efforts to undermine attempts at independent labour politics by means of the co-optation of labour's leaders and policies. In the process they were forced to take on board some of labour's class-based demands. But, in general terms, such demands were part of much wider programmes in which questions concerning religion, citizenship, ethnicity, race and so on often took precedence over the more particularist concerns of organised labour. Whilst by no means the sole determinant of politics in Britain, class-based issues did tend to occupy a more central place than in the United States. And, at least up to the turn of the century, the Liberal Party did prove to be a precise and largely successful institutional vehicle for the transmission of labour's demands to parliament.

Second, given the growing power of corporate capital over all aspects of public life and policy and its ideological hegemony, combined with the minority position of manual wage earners in American society and the numerically weak standing of organised labour, American politics, culture and society were increasingly pervaded by anti-trade union and labour movement sentiments to a much greater degree than in Britain. In effect, many saw organised labour as both unwelcome collectivist and, increasingly, 'alien' import. There is no way in which the late nineteenth-century and early twentieth-century labour movement could be remotely set alongside its British counterpart as an 'estate of the realm'.

A more sympathetic stance on the part of the federal government might have considerably changed matters. But, at least before the late 1890s when the federal government was forced to become interested in the 'labour problem', the dominant positions adopted were either non-intervention or intervention (in the form of federal troops) largely in the interests of capital. As Howell Harris and Tomlins have demonstrated,[99] it was within this general context of a hostile state machinery that the American Federation of Labor developed its philosophy of 'voluntarism'. In effect, the Federation sought autonomous space, free from the hostile attentions of judges and other agents of the state, in which labour and capital could conduct their negotiations.

Employers and the courts would not, however, permit the development of that space. By 1906–7, confronted with damaging injunctions and the sentencing of its president, Samuel Gompers, to prison for violating an injunction against a boycott, the AFL was compelled to seriously review its non-partisan political policy. Some members supported an independent political stance, largely along British lines;[100] others had their faith in allegiance to the Socialist Party re-affirmed; whilst the ruling Republican administration's attachment to the interests of anti-union big business was further reinforced in the minds of many of the Federation's leadership. In the opinion of Gompers and his supporters, more open attachment to the Democratic Party seemed to offer the best means of labour's survival and, hopefully, advancement, in a generally hostile climate. Thus, as Montgomery notes, 'With the formation of the federation's Labor Representation Committee in 1906 . . . the AFL began to move openly toward a national alliance with the Democratic Party.'[101] Competing political allegiances within the AFL delayed the effective consummation of that alliance up to the electoral triumphs of the Democratic Party in 1910–12. Thereafter, Woodrow Wilson's promises of mediation services actively supported by the federal government and legislated standards for working conditions 'proved irresistible to most union leaders'. It seemed at last that organised labour had won a true and effective friend in high places.

At a more general level the growth of a centralised, regulatory administrative state also suggested, for a time at least, that the picture of a state uniformly hostile to the interests of organised labour was misleading. In particular, as noted by Howell Harris, there developed during the early years of the present century a new conception of the 'public interest'. The federal government began to perform a mediatory role, to emphasise the importance, at least in its official rhetoric, of collective bargaining and 'industrial democracy' to the smooth, efficient and more harmonious operation of American society. As in Britain, recognition of moderate and 'responsible' labour, in the form of the AFL, would help to form a solid wedge against the 'extreme' demands of socialists and syndicalists and to promote greater stability and consensus within America.[102] The establishment by Congress of the Federal Mediation and Conciliation Service in 1914 and federal recognition, during the war emergency of 1916–19, of the 'right of workers to organise in trade unions and to bargain collectively through chosen representatives', were extremely important factors in identifying the AFL more closely with the ruling powers and as a staunch opponent of radicals within the labour movement.

The promise of harmony and integration was, however, shortlived. As we shall see in some detail in Chapters 2 and 3, the immediate post-war years witnessed the dismantling of war-time regulatory agencies such as the National War Labour Board, the sharp decline of effective governmental protection for unions, a militant crusade on the part of 'open-shop' employers, state repression against radicals, revolutionaries and strikers in general, the electoral triumphs, in 1918 and 1920, of a Republican Party committed to deregulation, deflation and to serving the interests of big business, and an AFL thrown on to the defensive. Throughout the 1920s the weakened labour movement was confronted by a state machinery, employers and an ideological climate generally unsympathetic to the cause of worker collectivism.[103]

On the basis of the foregoing discussion, we can therefore conclude that between the 1880s and the 1920s the various organs of the state adopted, on the whole, a hostile attitude to the claims of American trade unionism. The latter, lacking the absolute numbers, density and durability of the British trade-union movement, was afforded recognition and some protection in return for its commitments to the war-effort and the Democratic Party and its opposition to 'un-American' radicals, but overall state support was shortlived. In the face of consistently hostile employers, backed by the institutions of the state, late nineteenth- and early twentieth-century American workers displayed astonishing levels of militancy and support for collective forms of organisation and action.

We have seen, by way of contrast, that the British state generally adopted a more conciliatory policy towards the trade unions. This policy of accommodation was, in large measure, a reflection of the early strength and recognition, and of the durability of trade unionism in Britain. Having established a foothold within mid-Victorian England, and having secured official state recognition, the trade-union movement would have subsequently been dislodged only with the greatest difficulty and conflict. It is, nevertheless, extremely doubtful as to whether a movement possessing the strength of British trade unionism could have successfully withstood the concerted and persistent employer, and state-backed onslaught directed at American trade unionism.

EFFECTS: TRANSFORMED WORKERS?

To what extent did changes in the character of late nineteenth- and early twentieth-century capitalism lead to a 'transformed' working class, fitting Braverman's description of an increasingly de-skilled, routinised, alienated and degraded homogenous mass, subordinated to the hegemonic real and formal powers of a Taylorised capitalist class?

Braverman and his Critics

The question prompts a mixed response. As a number of critics have observed,[104] in its entirety Braverman's case is not convincing. Braverman offers an exaggerated and unduly uniform portrayal of developments within managerial practice and the labour process, largely infers worker consciousness from 'objective' economic structure, and underestimates worker resistance to the controlling desires of management. Simultaneously, however, Braverman's case cannot be dismissed out of hand. He has highlighted significant tendencies within late nineteenth- and early twentieth-century capitalism and has propounded a number of provocative and important arguments which have stimulated fruitful debate and research. In short, we can suggest that, despite the flawed deterministic (i.e. 'lawed') and unrefined nature of Braverman's case, particular elements of his thesis are valuable and merit extended scrutiny. To be more precise, we can usefully address ourselves to the issues of deskilling; the 'degradation' of and control over work, and worker resistance; and managerial strategies.

There is a general consensus among students of British and American economic and social history that skill was not undermined to anything like the extent claimed by Braverman in *Labor and Monopoly Capital* (1974). Andrew Dawson, for example, has suggested that while 'some small portion of the skilled stratum' in the United States was adversely affected by mechanisation and innovation, the development of corporate capitalism did not uniformly transform skilled 'labour aristocrats' into semi-skilled appendages of machines. Indeed, claims Dawson, the majority of the skilled benefited:

> The paradox is clear: in a period of rapid innovation and increasing monopolization of industry, when we might have expected a dilution of skills, the privileged stratum of the American working class not only maintained a marked degree of stability in terms of size, but also improved its economic position.[105]

Charles More's highly regarded *Skill and the English Working Class* (1980) has argued that the evidence against 'widespread deskilling' in nineteenth-century England is very strong. And a number of authors, including Montgomery and Zeitlin, have clearly demonstrated that skill was not eliminated, even in those sectors of engineering and the machinists' trades hit hardest by technological change and Taylorism. As noted earlier, the tool and die maker was an unexpected skilled creation of the transformation of the machinists' work by Taylorism. More generally, skilled workers were indispensable in terms of the repair of machinery, setting tools for the less skilled, and performing a variety of supervisory functions.[106]

Equally, however, an emphasis upon continuity, even improvement, must be set in the wider context of greatly increased threats to, and in some cases sharp deteriorations in, the position of skilled workers on both sides of the Atlantic during the period from the 1880s to the 1920s. It is their underestimation of the accelerated and generalised nature of such threats which seriously flaws the overall cases presented by Dawson and More. Simultaneously, it is Braverman's (albeit exaggerated) identification of such threats which merits retained interest in his argument.

As seen in the numerous examples presented earlier, and especially in the work of Montgomery, skilled workers themselves voiced a number of heightened fears at the turn of the century. Capitalist development and transformation were widely believed to involve an extensive dilution of skills, greater subdivision and simplification of tasks, increased managerial pressure on labour, diminished wage differentials, less opportunity to take pride in one's work, and markedly less control over the job. Especially in those sectors most affected by Taylorism and mechanisation, alienation and reification were rife (as reflected in extraordinarily high rates of labour turnover, worker resentment and sabotage, industrial conflict, and, increasingly, in the growth of personnel management and company welfarism).[107]

In addition, as seen earlier, skilled and other workers were confronted by more aggressive employers, judges and other representatives of the state machinery. In the United States, in particular, organised labour's very institutions were forced to fight for their lives. And, as emphasised by Montgomery, the increased marginality of the skilled within the process of production itself and the growing concentration of real control within the hands of management lay at the heart of the forward march of corporate capitalism.

'Skilled workers in large enterprises did not disappear', observes Montgomery, 'but most of them ceased to be production workers. Their tasks became ancillary – setup, troubleshooting, toolmaking, model making – while the actual production was increasingly carried out by specialized operatives.'[108] Spectacular growth in the numbers of the latter, especially in the mass-production industries, involved the movement of the poor and unskilled into better paid and more regular semi-skilled work. As claimed by Montgomery and Gordon, Reich and Edwards for the United States, and Hunt and Hobsbawm for Britain, there took place a greater homogenisation of work experiences (reflected primarily in the blending of the working worlds of previously separate labourers and operatives) rather than a complete unification of working people.[109]

As we have seen, the control issue lay at the heart of managerial responses to the crisis of competitive capitalism on both sides of the Atlantic. Craft regulation, 'soldiering' and general restriction of output were the 'evils' to be rooted out by Taylorite and non-Taylorite managers alike. Once again, Montgomery has penetrated to the heart of the matter. Writing of Carnegie's 'new managerial structure' which attached skilled workers on to the managerial hierarchy, Montgomery declares:

> This style of supervision, in one sense, did not represent a radical break with the past. It was built on both the technical knowledge of skilled workers, which remained indispensable, and the tradition of promotion within gangs. What had been eliminated was *collective, deliberate control from the workers' end*. In its place the company cultivated a hierarchy of fiercely competing individuals.[110] (emphasis added)

Management's efforts to roll back the frontiers of workers' control encountered strong and prolonged resistance across a range of industries in both countries. This process of class struggle at work has been underestimated by both advocates of 'degradation' (Braverman) and of stability and improvement (Dawson). It is, furthermore, extremely important to note that, despite worker resistance, the frontiers of control had been heavily redrawn in management's favour by the 1920s, not only to a greater extent in the United States than in Britain, *but also* in the most advanced and generally poorly unionised sectors of both countries' economies.

We are now in a position to summarise our arguments. It is certainly the case that the transformation of labour, as manifested especially in a deterioration of the position of skilled workers, did not operate uniformly across industrial and national boundaries. Transformation was most pronounced in the giant mass-production enterprises of corporate America and least marked in the relatively small-scale and more 'traditional' sectors of the British economy. Even in the most advanced sectors of the economies of the two countries it is at least arguable as to whether mechanisation and new managerial practices resulted in wholesale deterioration for the skilled. And for the traditionally large mass of the poor (women workers, casual workers, rural labourers, immigrants and blacks) the development of mass production did offer the tangible rewards of better pay and upgraded status at work. Taylorism did not hold unqualified blessings for employers, and was implemented, as a complete system of management, less quickly and extensively than argued by Braverman. Nevertheless, the position of the skilled at work generally deteriorated with sufficient force in both countries to induce intensified and extended industrial militancy and political moves to the left. The new-found material gains of the upgraded poor must be set within the wider context of continued insecurity and deprivation, and the high levels of speed up and close supervision, and general lack of respect and decency to which the new army of the semi-skilled were subjected by Ford and others. Increasing similarity of experience – in terms of experiences at work, the more extensive levels of individual and collective self-confidence and independence brought about by more regular work, and growing general concern with adequate common standards and protection in relation to wages, hours and conditions of work – all stimulated mass worker interest in organised labour on a scale unknown since the days of Chartism and the General Trades Unions of the 1830s.

The development of independent labour in the two countries was further stimulated by the hostile or seemingly indifferent attitudes and policies adopted by the state, employers and mainstream parties. Thus, albeit in ways described by Hobsbawm, Montgomery, and Gordon, Reich and Edwards, rather than by Braverman, the 'transformation' of labour and the rise of mass labour movements tended to go hand in hand in both Britain and the United States.

Homogeneous and Class Conscious Workers?

As observed above, a key part of the general notion of transformation resides, for all its proponents, in the increased 'homogenisation' of the working class. So far, the term homogenisation has been applied to experiences at work, especially the growth of the semi-skilled and the breaking down, or at least reduction, of nineteenth-century divisions between craftsmen, operatives and labourers. But the term has much wider application, to embrace life both outside and inside the workplace. It is to a discussion of homogenisation in this wider cultural sense that we must now turn.

Two questions present themselves. To what extent did the working classes of Britain and the United States become more homogeneous during this period? And was enhanced homogeneity synonymous with radical class consciousness and unity? We can respond to these questions by paying central attention to the views of Hobsbawm concerning

Britain, and Montgomery, and Gordon, Reich and Edwards in relation to the United States.

Attention has already been focused in this chapter upon the vastly increased demand for semi-skilled labour attendant upon the rise of mass-production industries and the great advances made by the transport, mining, construction, communications and service sectors of the British and (especially) American economies. Furthermore, as briefly noted in the early stages of the chapter, workers lived increasingly in large urban centres. Employment continued to be found in a variety of workplaces, but the factory came to exert dominance, in terms of numbers employed and patterns of organisation, across a wide range of industries. Paternalistic, family-owned businesses did not disappear, but the rapid growth of corporations in the United States and limited liability companies in Britain brought about more impersonal, standardised and, as suggested by Joyce, often more troubled relations between workers and employers.[111]

Developments in other areas of economic life were also conducive to a narrowing of differences among workers. In both countries the deflationary last quarter of the nineteenth century saw a massive increase in real wages of, approximately, 50 per cent in the United States and between 30 and 50 per cent in Britain.[112] The dramatic fall in the price of foodstuffs, combined with the overall growth of better-paid and more regular jobs throughout the two economies worked to the particular material benefit of the mass of non-skilled. Insecurity did, of course, remain an unwelcome fact of life for the majority of the working class. And, as we have seen, employers responded to narrowed profit margins by attempting to reduce unit costs of labour. But in many ways the resulting unemployment, insecurity and technological innovation acted more to the detriment of the established, regular and often skilled workforce than to the traditional poor who began to occupy the ranks of the semi-skilled.

Wage differentials did not disappear, and in some cases remained extremely wide (being, it should be noted, wider between the skilled and unskilled in the United States than in Britain).[113] However, as convincingly demonstrated by Gordon, Reich and Edwards, the United States' massive demand for semi-skilled labour between 1873 and 1896, 'narrowed wage differentials despite huge increases in the labor supply of unskilled workers'. (Between 1900 and 1920 the doubling of annual rates of gross immigration and changes in managerial wage strategies, 'appear to have reversed the earlier wage dynamic'.)[114]

In Britain, observes Hunt, differentials between craftsmen and labourers were both pronounced and enduring for most of the nineteenth century (many labourers receiving about half of the craftsman's rate).

But, 'This trend ceased well before the 1914–18 war and in some trades had begun to be reversed.' Increased demand for semi-skilled work, better educational standards which offered improved job opportunities, family limitation, the spread of mass trade unionism, a 'growing egalitarian sentiment' (as reflected in the Liberal Welfare Reforms of 1906–14), and wartime inflation – all worked, concludes Hunt, to reduce customarily high differentials.[115]

Beyond the workplace, life for working-class people became increasingly standardised and common. Hobsbawm has shown that from the 1880s onwards more commercialised patterns of life and leisure – organised around football, betting, the pub, the music hall, the popular press, the excursion to the seaside, and characterised by strong attachments to the home, neighbourhood, male-centredness and female support and sacrifice – took widespread root among British workers.[116] There occurred sharply increased residential segregation, as seen in 'the exodus of the middle and lower middle strata from formerly mixed areas' and 'the construction of new, and de facto single-class urban quarters and suburbs' – both developments stimulated by the expansion of the railway network, and the growth of the tram and the bicycle. The growing white-collar wedge between skilled manual workers and the middle class proper, the declining status attached to the achievement of manual skills and dexterity and the growing importance of formal schooling, deskilling, ostentatious display by the Edwardian rich and instances of ruling-class hostility towards organised labour – all these factors further enhanced working-class feelings of separation, indeed segregation and suspicion. As Hobsbawm astutely notes, 'The horizons of the skilled worker were thus increasingly bounded by the world of manual labour, and those of the less skilled even more so.' And, 'What all this amounts to is a growing sense of a single working class, bound together in a community of fate irrespective of its internal differences.'[117]

Similar processes were at work in the United States. The flaunting of their wealth and power by the 'robber barons' and the wealthy in general, and their seemingly weak sense of public responsibility, are well known. We have already referred to the hostile climate in which organised labour was compelled to struggle. We should further note middle-class fears of, condescension towards, and frequent recoil from workers, especially those born in southern and southeastern Europe; and, as in Britain, greatly accelerated residential segregation along the lines of class.[118] The urban workers' worlds revolved around family, the neighbourhood, the job, preservation of cultural traditions, and, with significant variations, around religion, temperance, dime novels, baseball, beer, betting, reading rooms, gymnasiums, debating clubs, fraternal orders and co-operative societies.[119]

As was the case in Britain, the burden of what Montgomery terms 'social condescension, deprivation, and toil', fell heavily upon the shoulders of American working-class women. From 1870 onwards women constituted in excess of 25 per cent of non-agricultural American wage earners. But some 80 per cent of these wage-earning women were single and lived at home. Married women were more than fully occupied in attending to countless and unending household chores. A widespread sense of partnership between husbands and wives was accompanied by a variety of gender-based inequalities.[120]

Historians are generally agreed that the norms and values of acquisitive middle-class individualism were of minor significance in most American working-class communities. Working-class Italians in Buffalo, Slovaks in McKeesport, Germans in Chicago and countless other ethnic working-class communities sought to achieve job security, decent living standards and general respect more by collective than by individual means. Above all, as documented by John Bodnar and others,[121] workers sought to attain their goals primarily as responsible members of families (one might add communities, even labour movements) than as self-seeking and isolated individuals. Social mobility and geographical mobility were of undoubted importance, especially (in terms of the former) to the native-born and 'old' immigrants, and (in respect to the latter) single unskilled men.[122] But we must not forget, as demonstrated in much recent research, that mobility existed within this wider and generally stronger context of collective priorities and mutualistic rights and obligations.

To what extent was working-class mutuality in both Britain and the United States translated into radical class consciousness? This is an extremely difficult and complex question which will be more fully addressed in Chapters 2 and 3. At this juncture we will simply outline some of the relevant substantive and methodological issues.

The responses of recent historians have generally been of four kinds. First, following the lead offered by Stedman Jones, there is a growing emphasis among British historians upon the defensive, conservative, fatalistic, apolitical and consolatory characteristics of late Victorian and Edwardian working-class culture, however mutualistic the latter may have been. This emphasis derives partly from an uncritical acceptance of the dismissive attitudes of some late nineteenth- and early twentieth-century socialists towards the allegedly passive and 'wrongheaded' commercial pursuits of the 'masses', in part from original research, and in part from organised labour's defeats under Thatcherism and the accompanying reassessment of the importance of class in modern British history.[123] Whilst a useful corrective to unduly uncritical and celebratory accounts of working-class culture, this first approach suffers from its excessively narrow focus and framework of analysis.

A second approach, associated closely with Bodnar and Emmons, views realistic pragmatism as the key characteristic of American workers' culture.[124] Steeped in mutualism, workers, according to this approach, had strictly limited objectives concerning steady work, decent pay and treatment, and secure family and community life. Bodnar does acknowledge that, in the course of pursuing these goals, workers could encounter obstacles which could push them in more radical directions. But both Bodnar and Emmons emphasise the predominantly modest, limited and non-transformative aims and results of American workers' culture.

The third approach, associated with Montgomery and Hobsbawm, would agree that the majority of British and American workers were pragmatists and that revolutionary socialist or syndicalist consciousness was the preserve of a minority. But equally, Montgomery and Hobsbawm situate class consciousness and behaviour, albeit of a largely limited and modest yet profoundly persistent and deepseated kind, at the very centre of their analyses of working-class culture. In the manner of E. P. Thompson, they do not see class consciousness as a given, but as something developed and created in the raw material of struggle and experience. In effect, Montgomery and Hobsbawm point to the complex and contradictory aspects of working-class culture (at times a defensive shell against a hostile world, at others the springboard for more radical, transformative strategies), the possible links between immediate and wider goals (family security and class advance), the necessity to situate working-class culture within the wider context of 'national' culture, and the centrality of class to working-class life.[125]

Finally, there is the longstanding and influential view that individualism, competition and all kinds of divisions (of skill, gender, income and so forth) have been more characteristic of workers' cultures than collectivism, class and mutuality. Thernstrom's emphasis upon individual mobility as the key to American culture, and Johnson's recent claim that competition and status-consciousness were the hallmarks of British working-class culture between 1870 and the inter-war period, constitute two notable examples of this fourth approach.[126]

Proper, detailed attention to the complexities and overall character of the historical evidence, context and conceptual rigour and consistency, constitute the criteria by which the different views must be evaluated. A full response must await the consideration of a range of cultural case studies in Chapters 2 and 3. But a preliminary judgement may be made in favour of Hobsbawm and Montgomery. Their approach is the more complete: alive to the complexities of the evidence; to the linkages between aims and unanticipated consequences; and to the fact that culture reveals its 'meanings' not in isolation, but only when adequately situated within the *ensemble* of social relations, structures and practices at particular moments in, and changes over, time. We will thus offer qualified initial support to Montgomery's emphases upon class and mutuality, and Hobsbawm's close identification between the growth of 'traditional' working-class culture, class consciousness, and 'The Rise of Labour'.[127] In comparison with the divided workers of the third quarter of the nineteenth century, late nineteenth- and early twentieth-century workers in Britain and America appear, as a mass body, to be both more homogeneous and class conscious.

We must, however, underline the fact that increased homogeneity did not equal complete or 'final' working-class unity. Contrary to the views of some of their critics, neither Montgomery nor Hobsbawm has suggested that working-class divisions suddenly ceased to exist. Classes are never undifferentiated, uniform or 'finished' wholes.[128] Rather, Hobsbawm, much like E. P. Thompson for an earlier period, has argued that internal differences and divisions were, for a time at least, over-shadowed by a sense of common working-class interests and expectations. The continued subordination of women and enduring general inequalities within the British working class could not mask the development of heightened solidarity.

The task of elevating class sentiments, ideologies and politics to a dominant position within the outlook and behaviour of American workers faced far more formidable obstacles than was the case in Britain. Greater similarities of experience at work and in leisure by no means signified total unity.[129] In the steel towns, for example, and despite Carnegie's policy of wage 'equalisation', differences between the (mainly native-born) skilled and (predominantly foreign-born) unskilled remained large. Susan Kleinberg has nicely illustrated such material differences in Pittsburgh:

> Photographs of affluent workers' homes in Pittsburgh show lace curtains, pianos, oak chairs, wallpaper, patterned carpets, and even the occasional parlor organ, the possession of which was a status symbol for nineteenth-century Americans.
> ... Mr. Smith could only obtain several days' work each week as a laborer in the steel mills ... His family's rooms contained few furbelows. The baby lay in a rope sling next to its parents' bed, not in a net-covered crib. In the absence of closets and wardrobes, clothes hung on pegs, over chairs, or on the bed frame. Instead of lace curtains, an odd scrap of cloth was nailed across the window ... Furniture, linen, and utensils were scarce and well worn among the very poor. Their barren homes contrasted sharply with the lavishly furnished and decorated dwellings of the skilled.[130]

Above all, the racial and ethnic heterogeneity of the American labour force frequently inhibited the growth of class unity. By 1880, as noted in Part Two Volume 1, the American working class was overwhelmingly composed of the foreign-born and their children. By 1920, records Montgomery, 13 per cent of the entire population were foreign-born, a statistic which rises sharply to almost 35 per cent once the children of the foreign-born are included. While not all of these people were working class, 'it is', observes Montgomery, 'safe to say that the immigrant milieu dominated urban working-class life at the time'. Of some 36,600,000 foreign-born and their children in 1920, Germans, Irish and Britons constituted the three largest ethnic blocs, accounting for approximately 40 per cent of the total. But, in terms solely of the foreign-born, the balance was moving strongly in favour of southern and southeastern Europeans. In 1860, notes Maldwyn Jones, natives of Ireland, Germany and Great Britain had constituted more than four-fifths of the foreign-born population: by 1910 the corresponding fraction was less than two-fifths. In 1860 southern and eastern Europeans had accounted for only 1.2 per cent of the foreign-born population: by 1910 they made up 37.5 per cent.[131] In sum, not only did the American working class continue to be dominated by the foreign-born and their children, but, as in the mid nineteenth century, was once again being reconstituted in terms of its social composition.

The changing social composition of the labour force, combined with upward occupational mobility for native white Americans and the children of the 'old' immigrants and persistently high rates of transiency for the less successful, posed, in themselves, important obstacles to the development and continuation of collectivism and class consciousness. In addition, the 'new' immigrants often met with suspicion and hostility on the part of the more settled working class, including large sections of organised labour. As we will later observe, this was not the total picture. The 'new' immigrants also partook in strikes, radicalism and other forms of working-class activity. But their overall reception by the host society was hardly favourable. The fact that many American workers and AFL leaders were opposed to unrestricted immigration more on economic rather than on overtly racial grounds, did little to still the fears of beleaguered immigrant communities.[132]

Class-based cultural allegiances and patterns of residence in the United States must, moreover, be set, in a number of contexts, against equally strong or stronger patterns of ethnically based, inter-class cultural and political attachments and residential developments. This is a matter to which we will return in some detail in Chapters 2 and 3. But we can briefly illustrate the point by reference to late nineteenth-century Pittsburgh and Detroit.

In Pittsburgh the developments of the omnibus, streetcar and commuter railroad enabled the middle and upper classes, mainly native-born whites, to abandon the city centre in favour of the pleasures of suburbia. The downtown area, as clearly shown by Kleinberg, became the preserve of workers, especially the Poles, Hungarians and other predominantly working-class 'new' immigrant groups.

This pattern of class-based residential segregation was a feature of many late nineteenth-century urban areas.[133] But the pattern was greatly complicated, and in some cases overshadowed, by the strong persistence, as in Detroit, of an ethnic inter-occupational and inter-class structure of residential development, and by powerful inter-class, ethnic cultural attachments (to religion, fraternal orders and so forth). As excellently demonstrated by Oestreicher, Knights of Labor radicals and socialists succeeded for a time in building a 'subculture of opposition' in Detroit, rooted in workers' common interests and problems irrespective of specific ethnic attachments. This class-based culture failed, however, to long withstand the pressures of opposition and repression from above, and internal ethnic tensions.[134] A further complication resided in the general fact that some ethnic communities, especially among the 'new' immigrants, were overwhelmingly proletarian, whilst others displayed much greater degrees of internal stratification and occupational differentiation.[135]

Finally, race and racism frequently constituted, in both the North and the South, massive oppositions rather than complications to class consciousness. As Nell Painter has suggested, racism, 'has affected the whole of American society, the whole of the American working class (including workers who were not its victims)'. And:

> White supremacy made it extremely difficult for workers who thought of themselves as white to combine with those they thought of as non-white. In the short term, lack of solidarity undermined numberless strike actions, making 'Negro' and 'scab' virtually synonymous terms early in the 20th century. As a consequence, white workers lost many a strike. Afro-Americans gained a toe-hold in industrial jobs in Chicago, East St. Louis, and Pittsburgh by crossing the picket lines of unions they were not entitled to join, but bigoted fellow workers did not permit them to strengthen workers' power overall.[136]

Further references to the oppositions between race and class, as well as instances of class-based inter-racial unity (which were few in number) will figure prominently in subsequent pages. But we should emphasise at this stage that racism was an extremely conservative and reactionary force, moulding the workers' mutualism to a defence of, rather than a rebellion against, the status quo, and allying white trade unions with white middle-class institutions.

Complexities and contradictions thus abounded to a much greater extent in the American than in the British case. Class undoubtedly constituted a factor in the making of the American working class, and on occasion class, ethnicity and race interrelated harmoniously. But in the period under review powerful racial and ethnic differences and divisions within the United States meant that class enjoyed a stronger presence among more unified British workers than among their American counterparts.

WORKER RESPONSES

The nature of worker responses and initiatives – in the face of capitalist economic change and the policies of employers, the state and political parties – will constitute the core of Chapters 2 and 3. Our purpose at this juncture is to offer some general guidelines to the detailed empirical material to follow.

Against 'Exceptionalism'

On the basis of information already presented in this chapter, it will be evident to the reader that worker responses were far less passive than suggested by Braverman, and more varied and complex than argued by advocates of American exceptionalism and the inexorable rise and triumph of business unionism. British 'new' unionism, intensified craft militancy, pre-war labour unrest, and immediate post-war industrial turbulence, allied to chronic industrial conflict in the United States, bore witness to workers' willingness to fight both in defence of established customs and in support of new demands. Similarly, the existence of a variety of workers' and 'producerist' movements in the United States – the Knights of Labor, socialist, anarchist, syndicalist, Greenbacker, and Populist, alongside the American Federation of Labor – the ideological battles within organised labour during the 1880s and 1890s, and the ensuing conflicts between 'pure and simple' AFLers, socialists and syndicalists for effective control of organised labour, hardly lend themselves to the Commons/Grob emphasis upon the 'natural' and relatively smooth hegemony achieved by the AFL leadership around Gompers and Strasser.[137]

Just as the 'triumph' of the AFL was not pre-ordained, so was American labour far less lacking in class consciousness, in relation to its British counterpart, than the 'old' labour history suggested. Indeed, it can justifiably be argued that *in some ways* late nineteenth- and early twentieth-century American workers were more militant, indeed more class conscious, than their British cousins. Such characteristics were displayed not only in industrial struggles, but also in the formation and growth (at least pre-1914) of a socialist rather than a labour party, and in the more spectacular successes of syndicalist organising drives in the United States rather than in Britain. We must, furthermore, remember that socialism was not welcomed by many trade unionists in pre-1914 Britain, that the Labour Party was electorally weak and hardly appeared as the natural successor to the Liberal Party in many parts of the country, and that, as forcibly argued by McKibbin, the 'rejectionist' ideology of Marxism had failed to find a mass base. Left-wing influences were to be found far more in the valleys of South Wales and on Clydeside than in the English industrial heartlands.

Britain and the Tenacity of Class

Necessary corrections and qualifications to the tenets of traditional labour historiography must not, however, obscure the extent to which the radical promise of early twentieth-century American labour was not fulfilled. By 1923 radical and socialist alternatives were in severe decline. By the mid 1920s a conservative AFL, intent on making its peace with, and becoming an accepted part of, corporate capitalism, had secured domination within the organised labour movement.

Furthermore, unlike the British case, mass trade unionism had (notwithstanding the unprecedented strike wave of 1916–22) failed to take strong root in the United States. In 1914 total trade-union membership in Britain and the United States stood, respectively, at 4,145,000 (23 per cent union density) and 2,566,000 (9.9 per cent density). By 1920 the corresponding figures were 8,348,000 (45.2 per cent) and 4,775,000 (16.7 per cent). During the 1920s union membership in both countries declined from the 1920 highpoint, but more markedly, in aggregate and percentage density terms, in the United States.[138]

Finally, the pre-1914 weakness of the Labour Party in Britain could not conceal both growing, if uneven, mass dissatisfaction with the established parties and, at least according to Hobsbawm and others, a widening and deepening of class consciousness. Certainly the period from 1918 onwards would witness the rise of *independent* British labour, especially in the form of the Labour Party, to a position of national prominence, a process unparalleled at the national level in inter-war America.[139]

Detailed explanations of independent labour's more pronounced rise and mass trade unionism's greater strength and durability in Britain will be offered in due course. But it is useful at this point to indicate our main areas of explanatory focus.

EXPLAINING NATIONAL DIFFERENCES

The first area revolves around the greater degrees of ideological and organisational fragmentation and competition within the American labour movement. The sense of 'moral universality' – of mutuality, producerism, of co-operation and independence within a democratic republic, and of opposition to 'un-American' 'wage-slavery', and concentrated, 'parasitical' and 'monopoly' power – which had sustained a variety of nineteenth-century popular movements in the United States, finally fractured from the 1890s onwards. Henceforward, 'conflicting groups of workers fought each other, rhetorically armed with different fragments of what had formerly been a coherent vision of redeeming the republic'. The transformative strategies of socialists and syndicalists now stood openly at odds with the pragmatic conservatism of the AFL. Thus Montgomery:

> The changing structure of American capitalism, the recomposition of the working class itself, and the new strategies of the bourgeoisie at the turn of the century did not destroy working-class militancy. They did disrupt the moral universality, which had given that militancy its nineteenth-century language.
>
> In its place emerged a trade union leadership explicitly committed not only to reforming American capitalism by strictly trade union means, but also to defending the state against foreign foes and domestic revolutionaries alike. Arrayed against that dominant group were two minority currents of great importance: the Socialist Party and the direct action movement, most clearly represented by the IWW.[140]

Differences and divisions existed within the British labour movement, as seen in conflicts between 'old' and 'new' unionists, among the various socialist factions and organisations, and in the divided political allegiances of the wider working class. But such sources of fragmentation were less pronounced than in the United States. Above all, Britain possessed a mass labour movement, embedded within an increasingly common way of working-class life, and enjoying relatively high degrees of internal cohesion and unity of purpose. For example, most socialists committed themselves to working within the mainstream of British labour in the interest of labour unity, despite the movement's predominantly labourist rather than socialist character. And the successful mass organisation of the non-skilled into general unions, operating alongside, as opposed to being largely in competition with, the established unions of the skilled, meant that problems of 'dual' unionism and jurisdictional disputes, which dogged organising drives in America, were not of comparable importance in Britain. Certainly by 1918 the strong British labour movement was largely united around the twin goals of trade-union development under the general umbrella of the Trades Union Congress and political advancement by means of the Labour Party. In the United States there existed only fragments of unity.

Further sources of organised labour's fragmentation and weakness in the United States in this period are to be found in the familiar areas of successful repression, internal working-class divisions, and, for some, the high benefits of material and social advancement. In addition, as emphasised by Oestreicher, the very size of the United States, the multiple tiers of the federal system (which made it difficult, in the absence of massive human and financial resources, to repeat local successes at higher levels of power, and to contest power at multiple levels), the entrenched two-party system and the vast resources commanded by the mainstream parties, and the relative openness and flexibility of the political system constituted formidable obstacles to the successful development of independent labour or socialist politics.[141]

Emphases upon American distinctiveness must, of course, be qualified. The contrast between a flexible and open American political system and an inflexible and closed British system can, for example, easily be exaggerated. After all, between the demise of Chartism and the late nineteenth-century growth of socialism and revival of independent-labour politics, the British labour movement and those workers possessing the vote were effectively contained within the two-party structure. Both the Conservatives and Liberals attempted to enlist working-class support and, especially from the 1860s onwards, to create popular partisan political institutions. Class issues were present within mainstream politics, but historians such as Joyce have argued that class was to a great extent transcended (much in the fashion claimed by Kazin for the United States) by the notions of 'the people' and 'the nation'.[142]

In the final analysis, however, the political example of the previous paragraph constitutes a qualification rather than a correction. The more limited extent of the franchise in nineteenth-century Britain imposed greater formal restrictions than in America upon the extent to which the established parties sought to enlist mass working-class support and active involvement in party matters. Questions concerning involvement and intra-party control were of great importance. Thus, while often presenting themselves as the paternalistic guardians of the welfare of the populace, the aristocrats who ran the Conservative Party would not countenance the control of substantive party matters by manual workers.[143] The idea of treating the latter as political or social equals was generally unthinkable. Similarly, despite its public face as the party of 'the People', the Gladstonian Liberal Party was loath to permit 'undue' worker influence within its ranks. By the end of the century the reluctance of the Liberals to endorse working-class Liberal candidates was creating serious tensions within Lib.-Labism.[144]

Such British examples stand in marked contrast to the much greater controls and powers exercised by manual workers in urban-based machine politics in the United States. Somewhat paradoxically, in view of the more limited franchise in Britain, the very strength of the British labour movement generally ensured that class-based concerns would be more forcefully and directly presented at the parliamentary level, especially by the Liberal Party, than was normally the case, at least at the federal level, in pre-1912 America. Moreover, as noted by Oestreicher, the flexible responses of Democratic Party machines to the concerns of labour, 'functioned more to identify class sentiments with existing partisan loyalties than ... toward a more explicitly class-based political consciousness'.[145] In addition, the established political parties in Britain did not offer the institutional opportunities for upward political and career mobility for labour leaders and workers to anything like the American extent. And 'machine' politics, complete with their powers of patronage and material rewards, did not exist on the same scale in Britain. Finally, while the Labour Party became a fact of national political life, neither reformist nor revolutionary workers' political parties in the United States ever 'seriously threatened the hegemony of the Republican and Democratic parties in the electoral system'. In such ways was American labour more firmly embedded within mainstream politics than its British counterpart.

The purpose of this chapter has been twofold: to identify the main structural constraints in which workers and their labour movements were compelled to think and act between the 1870s and the 1920s; and to briefly outline the main directions of worker response. It is now time to consider workers less as the carriers of structures than as the active creators of history who modify and change their structured conditions of existence. Chapter 2 will examine key developments in trade unionism and patterns of conflict and accommodation at work. The following chapter will move out of the field of industrial relations into the wider areas of politics, ideology and culture.

CHAPTER TWO

Conflict and Consolidation: Patterns of Workplace Organisation and Protest

KEY THEMES AND ISSUES

A number of key themes present themselves in terms of the development of work-based organisation and protest, trade unionism and industrial relations in Britain and the United States between the 1860s and the early 1920s.

Of foremost importance was the growth of a mass-based and strong organised labour, and especially trade-union, movement in Britain as compared with its less effective and more narrowly based organised counterpart in America. As James Hinton has observed:

> Between the 1870s and the First World War a mass labour move-ment was formed in Britain. Trade union membership grew from about half a million in the mid-1870s to over four million by 1914 ... Membership of the co-operative movement grew ... from about 600,000 in 1880 to over three million by 1914. Trades Councils ... spread rapidly over the whole country ... The forma-tion of the Labour Party in 1900 gave further expression to this sense of a working-class movement. By 1912 more than half of the total trade union membership was affiliated to the Labour Party.[1]

The movement was not without limitations and adversaries. Organised labour continued to occupy minority standing within the working class (being particularly weak among women and the poor); and, at least up to 1914, Liberal, as opposed to independent Labour, politics held mass appeal. The Taff Vale decision of 1901 and the Osborne judgement of 1909,[2] constituted serious setbacks to the legal freedoms and immunities won by the trade unions during the 1870s; and employers (particularly during the 1890s and 1910–14) and the state (especially during the 1920s) could still resist trade unionism, and especially trade unionism of a militant and radical kind.

However, as demonstrated in the previous chapter, the late nine-teenth-century British labour movement had secured a marked degree of official state and employer recognition to complement its growing numerical strength. And certainly by the post-First World War period, the labour movement was, by international standards, in an enviably strong position. In 1920 an astounding 45 per cent of potential union members had been organised. The Taff Vale and Osborne verdicts had long been reversed (in 1906 and 1913 respectively). Both trade-union leaders and Labour Party officials had assumed positions of unprecedented national importance during the First World War. And 1918 had seen a further step towards the creation of a mass electorate and the formal adoption of the aim of common ownership (the famous Clause IV) by the Labour Party. Liberalism was in decline and Labour seemingly not to be denied its continued rise to unprecedented power and influence.

In the United States developments were far less promising. Historians of American labour have traditionally emphasised the overall failure of (repeated) attempts to create a strong mass movement during this period. Both acute and chronic patterns of industrial conflict have been set against the extreme difficulties involved in the construction of *durable* trade unions (especially beyond the minority ranks of the craft and skilled) in the face of continued judicial and employer hostility (see Chapter 1) and working-class fragmentation. By the end of the First World War the cautious and conservative AFL ruled the roost, political radicalism was (certainly by 1920–1) in retreat, and the mass organisation of the semi-skilled and unskilled would have to await the 1930s. Both to John Commons and his associates and to those on the Left the American labour movement was demonstrating its 'exceptionalism' – its rejection of European-style radicalism and socialism and its adoption of American-style capitalist-minded business unionism.

There is little doubt that, as suggested by Hunt,[3] the British trade-union movement did, 'whether judged by numbers, efficiency, or strength', display remarkable growth from the mid nineteenth century onwards. Reliable statistics concerning trade-union membership and density are not available for much of the nineteenth century. We do, however, know that trade-union membership in Britain increased from approximately 250,000 in 1850 to about 500,000 in 1870 and thence to around the 1 million mark during the economic and trade-union boom of the early 1870s. The onset of the 'Great Depression' saw a reversion to the half-million mark. But the upswing in the trade cycle and the tightened labour market in the late 1880s and early 1890s were accompanied by the 'new unionist' explosion. Trade-union membership rose from 750,000 in 1888 to 1.5 million in 1892. By 1900 there were just over 2 million members (density of 12.6 per cent), a figure which increased to over 2.5 million (14.6 per cent density) by 1910. During the 'labour unrest' from 1910–14, which saw the second and more successful wave of 'new unionism', membership increased to 4 million (23 per cent density). By 1919 membership stood just below 8 million (43.1 per cent density), and reached its highpoint of 8,348,000 in 1920.[4]

In the United States trade-union membership was consistently smaller in both absolute and relative (i.e. trade-union density) terms. In 1850 there were approximately 200,000 trade unionists in the United States. Following the panic of 1857 and during the early Civil War years trade unionism was 'all but defunct'.[5] But Foner estimates that by 1864 about 200,000 workers belonged to trade unions. The later war and post-war years witnessed a massive upsurge in trade-union activity. Thus some 300,000 workers were enrolled in trade unions in the years immediately preceding the depression of 1873, a 'larger proportion of the industrial labor force ... than in any other period of the nineteenth century'.[6]

The depression from 1873–8 had an adverse effect upon trade union-ism (the national unions being reduced to about 50,000 members in 1878: total trade-union membership was higher). But in 1877 some 100,000 workers were on strike, a general railroad strike developing into 'a national conflagration that brought the country closer to a social revolution than at any other time in its century of existence except for the Civil War'.[7] The 1880s saw upsurges of trade unionism in relation to both the Knights of Labor (40,000 members in 1882, 100,000 in 1884 and approximately 750,000 in 1886)[8] and the American Federation of Labor (50,000 members in 1886 and 200,000 in 1890). In addition, the 'Great Upheaval' between 1884 and 1886 involved mounting industrial and class conflict, often among previously unorganised workers. The climax was reached in 1886 when a total of 690,000 workers struck for the eight-hour day and other demands.[9]

The severe depression of 1893–7, combined with fierce employer opposition, weakened the American trade-union movement. By 1897 there were approximately 447,000 trade-union members, a density of 3 per cent. By 1904 membership had risen to just over 2 million (11.3 per cent density). Between 1910 and 1914 membership increased from 2,102,000 to 2,566,000 (from 9 to 9.9 per cent density). As in Britain the war years saw a sharp rise in membership – to 3,285,000 American trade-union members (12.6 density) by 1918 – and a peak in 1920 (4,775,000 members, 16.7 per cent density). According to David Mont-gomery, trade union increases between 1912 and 1922 took place during 'a decade of strikes of unprecedented scale and continuity'. But from 1921–2 onwards both the number of strikes and trade-union member-ship showed a marked decline from the highpoint of 1920.[10]

Table 2.1   Aggregate Union Membership* and Density,** United
Kingdom and the USA, 1892–1925

	Union Membership (000s)		Union Density (%)	
	UK	USA	UK	USA
1892	1,576	400†	10.6	3.2†
1900	2,022	869	12.7	5.5
1910	2,565	2,102	14.6	9.0
1914	4,145	2,566	23.0	9.9
1918	6,533	3,285	35.7	12.6
1920	8,348	4,775	45.2	16.7
1922	5,625	3,821	31.6	13.0
1925	5,506	3,319	30.1	10.4

Source: G. S. Bain and R. Price, op. cit., pp. 8, 37, 79, 84, 88–9

 * Based, in the case of USA, upon the NBER series.
 ** That is, the percentage of the labour force unionised. Included in the labour
   force are the unemployed and those occupied in agriculture. Employers,
   the self-employed, members of the armed forces, and unpaid family workers
   are excluded.
  † The 1892 figures for the USA are based upon the calculations made by
   P. S. Bagwell and G. E. Mingay, op. cit., (p. 207) and, in contrast to all the
   other figures in Table 2.1, exclude agriculture.

The facts of a numerically stronger and increasingly mass-based trade-
union movement in late Victorian and Edwardian Britain are, therefore,
beyond dispute. But to see workplace relations, trade unionism and
industrial protest in Britain and the United States solely, or even mainly,
in terms of the adjectives weak and strong, or around the couplet
exceptional/normal, is to adopt a very limited, flat and misleading
approach to the issues involved. A more adequate, rounded approach
would be obliged to take full cognizance of the richness, complexity
and diversity of trends both within and between the two countries.

There are, for example, frequent references in texts and articles to
the slower development of mass unionism in the United States. But all
too often, and especially within traditional, institutional histories of
labour,[11] insufficient attention is devoted to a description and analysis
of the numerous and massive attempts made by late nineteenth-century
and early twentieth-century American workers, often non-skilled and
immigrant, to form unions. Rather, the weakness of *durable* mass unionism in 'exceptionalist' America (as contrasted with the success of 'new
unionism' in Britain) constitutes the conclusion of observation rather
than the starting point of analysis.

In common with the largely 'new' and certainly less heavily institutional histories of workers, we wish to pose a series of questions. Why, for example, did so many American workers risk life and limb (in the face of employer and state opposition and violence) to organise themselves? What do repeated attempts at unionisation tell us about the consciousness of American workers, and especially about the consciousness of those supposed trade-union laggards, non-skilled immigrants, especially of southern and eastern European origin? And why did high levels of industrial conflict between the 1870s and 1920s fail to secure more permanent and extensive trade-union gains in the United States?

Similarly, the 'old' labour history has, as previously noted, greatly exaggerated the inevitable 'triumph' of business unionism and the conservative nature and aims of the AFL. Along with Fink, Kazin, Montgomery and others among the 'new' labour historians, we must emphasise the diverse nature of the early AFL; the coexistence of radical, labourist and more accommodative-conservative perspectives within the Federation; the ability of craft, skilled and non-skilled workers to change their policies and consciousness (the equation, AFL equals aristocratic craft/skilled workers equals accommodation/conservatism, is far too simplistic and static); and the very solid presence of radical, reformist and non-business-unionist organisations within working-class communities. To provide the most obvious example, the Knights of Labor, far from being, as suggested by the 'old' labour history, on the periphery of the organised labour (especially trade-union) movement, was 'the first mass organisation of the American working class', exerting far more influence among a broad spectrum of workers than the AFL.[12]

Finally, many 'exceptionalist' accounts have also tended to gloss over the important links between urban and rural workers and petty producers in late nineteenth-century America. An excessively narrow equation of 'labour' with industrial and largely urban-based workers has often led to a great underestimation of the massive scale of post-bellum rural protest; the adoption, by discontented farmers, sharecroppers and labourers in the Alliance and Populist movements of the South and West, of the language of 'labor' and the 'industrial classes'; and the strong links forged between urban and rural workers via the institutions of the Alliance, Knights of Labor and Populism.[13]

We must thus move beyond teleology and institutional trade-union historiography in order to recapture the full range of experiences and patterns of consciousness which characterised American workplace protest during this period. In the process we can, along with many of the 'new' labour historians, reopen traditional questions concerning class and exceptionalism, and simultaneously widen our terms of reference.

In turn, such an exercise will compel us to re-examine key aspects

of British trade unionism and protest. Was Britain so profoundly different from the United States in terms of trade-union development, structure and practice? Were British workers really so much (if at all) more
class conscious than their American counterparts? In view of our criticisms of absolutist notions of exceptionalism in relation to the
1750–1860 period, would it not, at least on *prima facie* grounds, be
surprising to discover a massive divergence in terms of national patterns
of class during the late nineteenth and early twentieth centuries? And,
despite the growth of a mass labour movement in Britain, did not
sectionalism and all manner of other internal divisions (based on gender,
skill, income and so on) persist into the present century? Given the
considerable importance attached by the 'new' labour historians to class
in the lives of American workers between the 1860s and the 1920s and
the strong recent reaction on the part of some British labour historians
against class-based interpretations (of a predominantly Marxist kind) of
British trade unionism, politics and culture between the 1880s and 1920s,
the issues of class and exceptionalism assume acute importance and
urgency.[14]

Sensitive to context and complexity, we will proceed in the following
way. We will first present a chronological account of patterns of protest
and collective organisation in the two countries. Included in this first
section will be examinations of trade-union development, structure and
social appeal, and the nature and underpinnings of work-based protest
beyond the ranks of organised labour. The chapter will then move to a
consideration of the characteristics and causes of workplace organisation
and patterns of protest and the roots of success and failure. The policies and patterns of consciousness adopted by protesting workers will
form the next section. Included in the latter will be examinations of the
complex interplays between accommodating and more radical, challenging labour strategies, the shifting social and occupational roots of accommodation and challenge, and the multi-faceted relations between the
skilled and non-skilled. The chapter will finally return, on the basis of
the empirical material presented, to a discussion of the issues of class
and exceptionalism.

PATTERNS OF ORGANISATION AND PROTEST: 1860s–1880s

Britain: moderate trade unionism; ephemeral mass organisation

Reference has already been made (see Part Two, Volume One) to the
dominant position of the 'new model' unions within the British trade-

union movement during the third quarter of the nineteenth century. Epitomised above all by the Amalgamated Society of Engineers, the principles of 'new model' unionism spread rapidly during the 1850s and 1860s. Caution, moderation, conciliation, respectability, pragmatism, support for strikes only as a last resort, and the pursuance of the public (as opposed to 'class' or 'selfish'/sectional) interest – these were the watchwords of the leaders of the increasingly bureaucratised and central-ised craft and skilled unions.[15]

Cotton and Coal

A measure of the increased influence of more cautious and accommodat-ing trade unionism is seen in the mid-Victorian development of cotton trade unionism and in the divergent tendencies which emerged in relation to trade unionism among coalminers. Relations between employers and workers in cotton exhibited a variety of complex, and often contradictory, features during the third quarter of the century.[16] On the one hand, as demonstrated especially in the years 1853–4, 1861, 1867 and 1869, 'unrest', in the form of strikes and lock-outs, persisted throughout the 'golden years'. Many industrial conflicts arose during periods of bad trade and attempted wage reductions. But conflict was not confined to these periods. For example, in the relatively buoyant late 1840s employer attempts to circumvent the provisions of the Ten Hours Act of 1847 by means of the operation of shift working (or 'relays') among juveniles (which enabled them to work the legally unprotected adult males beyond the ten hours) set off protests in several cotton towns. Non-union policies had a similar effect. Indeed, whatever the immediate cause of conflict between operatives and employers in cotton, there is no doubt that the question of trade-union recognition continued to be the major long-term source of disagreement. Thus many cotton masters persisted in their opposition to trade unionism, irrespective of the latter's claim to moderation and good will towards capital. The fundamental issues at stake were power and control, the existence of trade unionism constituting a threat to the employer's 'right' to exercise total control in the factory. In the eyes of many masters, failure to abide by the rule that 'the master may do what he likes in his own factory' would automatically lead to 'subversion of the rights of property' and to communism.

It is further worth noting that the years of the Cotton Famine (1861–5), often seen as the highwater mark of class harmony and social cohesion in mid-Victorian Lancashire and Cheshire, witnessed class-based conflicts. It is true that contemporaries generally attributed the extremely high levels of unemployment experienced during the Cotton

Famine to the northern blockade of the southern ports of the United States, which cut off supplies of raw cotton to England. In addition the operatives did pay fulsome tribute to those employers who made strenuous efforts to run their mills throughout the Famine, to find alternative sources of raw cotton, and who displayed considerable generosity and care both at work and in the community (as seen in their contribution to local relief funds, distribution of free clothes and food, and the running of their mills at a loss).

As observed by Bridges, *The Times* correspondent in the north, 'deep and widespread irritation' did nevertheless underlie apparent calm and social harmony. Operatives were extremely critical of the low scales of relief provided by the Poor Law guardians, the physical separation of the sexes in the workhouse, and the continued performance of the 'humiliating' and 'degrading' tasks of the 'labour test' (stone breaking and oakum picking) by those in receipt of relief. In effect, operatives rendered unemployed by forces beyond their control were being treated with a lack of respect and decency, 'worse than felons in gaol'.

A further cause of 'irritation' lay in the miserly and uncaring attitudes of many of the wealthy (especially in southeast Lancashire) towards the plight of the unemployed operatives. In May 1862, for example, a local labour leader warned the masters of Ashton and Stalybridge that, 'starving people were no longer themselves', and that, 'it was dangerous to allow them to remain destitute in a country where there was enough for each and enough for all'. Finally, both the central executive committee in Manchester and many local relief committees were increasingly accused of 'partiality, arbitrary exercise of power, and of a marked tendency to imitate the parsimonious and "inhumane" activities of the Poor Law Guardians'.

These accumulated grievances came to a head in the early months of 1863 when rioting broke out in Stalybridge against the payment of recipients of relief in the form of tickets (the relief committee deciding in its collective wisdom that those relieved were incapable of spending their payments wisely: the tickets were to be cashed at authorised stores). Disturbances spread to Ashton, Dukinfield, Hyde and Preston, and there were protest meetings in other centres. Public works, introduced to ease the unemployment problem in 1864, prevented the outbreak of further incidents of worker protest during the Cotton Famine, but insults to the operatives' pride, self-respect and independence were not easily forgotten.

The mid-Victorian years were, therefore, neither so calm nor so harmonious in the cotton districts as is often supposed. But against continued sources of conflict we must equally set factors making for greater class toleration and accommodation, if not complete harmony.

For example, pragmatism did act as a partial counterweight to the ideological opposition of cotton employers to trade unions. Very few employers welcomed or liked trade unions. But the very tenacity and resiliency of the latter (their refusal to 'disappear'), the gains to be derived from union recognition in terms of uninterrupted production, greater stability in the workplace, the 'institutionalisation' of conflict, the regulation of competitive and unstable markets (by means of the adoption of uniform price lists and the negotiation of district rates of pay), the moderation of most cotton union leaders, and the disciplinary functions exercised by the latter over 'troublemakers' – these factors constituted powerful inducements to more widespread union recognition. The export-led boom in cotton products during the third quarter and the fact that many cotton employers had overcome earlier barriers to substantial capital accummulation (to acquire, by the mid-Victorian years, impressive fortunes)[17] added to the 'appeal' of trade-union recognition.

Employer recognition of the cotton unions was accordingly far more widespread than in the Chartist years. In the Blackburn area the adoption of the Standard List in 1853 (regulating prices and wages in an area of acute competition) and the recognition of weaving trade unionism (mainly in order to 'police' wage levels) constituted a watershed in the history of 'industrial relations'. In south Lancashire, however, weaving employers tended to operate in much less competitive markets than their Blackburn counterparts, and anti-unionism was much more persistent and widespread. Some of the large south Lancashire employers also used paternalism as an anti-union device. In overall terms, advances in union recognition in weaving were patchy. The East Lancashire Amalgamated Powerloom Weavers' Friendly Association, formed in 1858 (the First Amalgamation) did succeed during the 1860s in establishing a firm base in north Lancashire. But, despite a further wave of union organisation among weavers in the early 1870s, weaving trade unionism remained relatively weak in south Lancashire. It was not until 1884 that the second Amalgamation successfully signalled the arrival of durable mass unionism in weaving throughout Lancashire and Cheshire. And successful mass unionisation of the generally unskilled cardroom workers awaited the 1880s.[18]

Many of the operatives working in the weaving sheds and in the cardroom were unskilled or semi-skilled women. The unions of these workers tended to pre-figure the 'new' unions of the late nineteenth century. Thus mid-Victorian weaving trade unionism was 'open' (i.e. mass-based) as opposed to the 'closed' (i.e. exclusive) unions of the craft and skilled.[19] Weaving trade unionism sought to exert power in the workplace not by restricting the supply of labour (weavers did not possess scarce skills acquired through a long formal apprenticeship) but by enforcing a standard rate of pay for the job. The central significance of the Blackburn List of 1853 was that it created the precedent of a standard list which could be used as the point of reference in future negotiations, and that the adoption and *negotiation* of such a list implied union recognition. It is thus understandable that many of the weavers' disputes of the third quarter revolved either directly (as at Padiham in 1859) or indirectly (as in southeast Lancashire in 1861) around the issues of union recognition and the adoption of a standard list. Weaving unions charged, as a result of the very nature of their membership, low dues and were frequently obliged during long disputes to seek the aid of weavers in other areas and of workers outside cotton. Weaving trade unionism also tended to stimulate unionisation among other groups of cotton operatives.

Lacking the informal and unilateral controls over the labour process possessed by the highly skilled and indispensable autonomous craftsman, the semi-skilled weaver sought to achieve influence at work by means of mass organisation and the processes of formal recognition by employers and institutionalised collective bargaining. In the process the weaving trade unions acquired, somewhat ironically, the very same features of centralisation and bureaucratisation so characteristic of the 'new models'. Negotiation of the standard list and the complex adjustment of piece rates demanded that the union negotiator be possessed of mathematical and other technical skills. In 1858 the East Lancashire Amalgamated appointed an adroit negotiator, Mr Pinder, as full-time secretary of the union. Subsequent secretaries were to be appointed on the basis of their performance in competitive examinations. In addition the Amalgamated drew up an elaborate grievance procedure and consciously sought to concentrate decision-making powers (concerning the authorisation of strikes and other matters) in the hands of the district and executive committees. In such ways was a highly complex bureaucratic organisation created. But as a 'mass' trade union, often compelled to undertake mass (and sometimes militant) action in order to exert pressure on employers, and rooted in a semi-skilled membership, the Amalgamated faced more resistance from employers than the more exclusive craft and skilled unions.

Lacking a formal system of apprenticeship, and not qualifying as a 'craft' occupation, spinning and its associated unions nevertheless constituted 'closed' rather than 'open' areas. By the mid 1850s the spinners – both hand-mule and self-actor – had respectively recovered or gained much of the bargaining strength, privileged status, job security and high earning power characteristic of the hand-mule spinners in the period prior to their fierce and beleaguered 'control' struggles of the 1830s and early 1840s. The convenient, effective and proven system of labour management and speed-up offered by the spinner-piecer system, the spinners' control over the labour supply (spinners recruited the piecers and regulated their promotion into their own ranks by means of the principle of seniority), their partial job control (over the number of mules to be supervised per man and the ratio of piecers to mules), employer reluctance to restructure production relations radically during a period of economic boom, and the collective ability and determination of the spinners to improve their workplace bargaining position – all contributed to the growing power of the spinners within the structure of mid-Victorian cotton.

As Lazonick notes, during the 1850s and 1860s there developed 'a highly organised "craft" occupation of minders', well paid, and possessing strong and exclusive unions. The latter charged relatively high dues, did not normally concern themselves with the unionisation of other grades of cotton operatives, conducted separate negotiations with employers, emphasised the benefit features of trade unionism, and preached the virtues of caution and moderation. The strategically crucial place of spinners within the production process (yarn could not be woven until spun) and their labour management role meant that employer recognition of spinning trade unionism was far more marked than that of weaving trade unionism. Furthermore, the spinners more regularly won their demands without resorting to the mass actions characteristic of weavers.

Finally, bureaucratisation and centralisation developed more slowly in spinning trade unionism. Spinners' societies were, for the most part, local and independent in character, and jealous of their autonomy. However, from the late 1860s onwards moves in favour of federation bore fruit. In 1870 the Amalgamated Association of Operative Cotton Spinners, Self-Acting Minders, Twiners, and Rovers of Lancashire and the Adjoining Counties was established. The Amalgamated imposed a levy on affiliated societies, appointed a full-time secretary, and sought to concentrate decision making in the hands of the executive committee.[20]

Beneath the different patterns of development of trade unionism in weaving and spinning lay a crucial common feature: the sincere and dogged pursuit of moderation and accommodation by the leadership. Especially in the wake of the protracted, costly and largely unsuccessful 10 per cent wage struggles of 1853–4, weavers' leaders determined to advance their cause, if possible, more by the adoption of a moderate and respectable image and conciliatory policies towards employers than by costly mass action.

Insufficient funds had been a crucial factor in the defeat at Preston in 1854, and the leadership was determined not to repeat past mistakes.

Thus the weavers' leaders were reluctant to endorse the call for a strike throughout south Lancashire in 1861 on the grounds that sufficient funds were not in existence and that defeat would cripple the union. Similarly, the East Lancashire Amalgamated Powerloom Weavers Friendly Association made repeated overtures of friendship and moderation towards the employers (in the process sometimes alienating rank-and-file weavers), prided itself on its ability to restrain its more 'impulsive' members, and increasingly preached the virtues of conciliation and arbitration. Almost all officials were opposed to strikes and strenuously denied charges that they were 'intent on bringing down property, or encroaching on "managerial prerogatives" '. 'Unreasonable' and 'extreme' employers were, of course, to be opposed: in some instances strikes were unavoidable. But we should not underestimate union commitments during the third quarter to moderation and conciliation. The latter notions were, if at all possible, to be translated into concrete union policy. Union recognition and wage advances in weaving were to proceed more by quiet and determined moderation than by militant class conflict.

The 'aristocratic' spinners were even more anxious to avoid 'unnecessary hostilities' with their employers. As noted above, mutual dependency (upon the employer for a privileged work position and upon the spinner for labour management) increasingly bred toleration and compromise. By the 1860s the 'rules of the game' were widely in operation. Spinners, increasingly represented by their union leaders, sought wage advances during upswings in trade and tolerated reductions during downswings. Not all was permanent 'sweetness and light'. We have seen that union recognition by the spinning employers was by no means complete. And the onset of reduced profit margins and increased foreign competition during the final quarter of the century would lead employers to place the 'screw' upon the aristocrats of the industry. But typical of the mid-Victorian years were the attitudes of the Bolton and Ashton Spinners' Unions to strikes as, respectively, 'inimical and subversive to the rights of labour' and 'the scourges of civilisation'. By the 1860s the spinners' unions had cultivated 'friendly relations' with employers in a significant number of the cotton towns of Lancashire and Cheshire.

In terms of the trade-union leaders in both weaving and spinning, the desired end product was the creation of a 'modern' system of institutionalised collective bargaining in which 'strong', 'honest' and 'fair-minded' representatives of labour and capital would conduct negotiations with a view to the interests of both sides of industry and the public at large. This was the ideal of compromise, accommodation and 'fair play'. But given the continued opposition of some cotton employers (especially beyond spinning) to the 'baneful influence' of all matters union, it was to be the unions more than the employers who were to be the patient and long-suffering tutors in the realisation of this 'moderniser's' dream.

Mining trade unionism in the mid-Victorian period reflected the influences of both moderate accommodation and more militant radicalism. As John Benson and others have demonstrated,[21] fragmentation and the small scale of most early nineteenth-century production, divisions within the workforce (especially between the 'aristocratic' hewers and the oncost workers), considerable in- and out-migration in the coalfields (accompanied in Wigan and part of the Lanarkshire coalfield by marked ethnic and religious conflict), severe trade cycle fluctuations, the domination of the unions by the hewers and the neglect or exclusion of surface and some underground workers, and the widespread presence of powerful employers hostile to trade unionism and utilising all manner of devices (victimisation, the sack, free or low-rent colliery housing, free coal allowances, and even, in Northumberland and Durham, relief for injured miners) to prevent its growth – all combined to keep mining trade unionism weak and ephemeral before the middle years of the century. Thus the considerable trade-union activity of the early 1830s, which affected almost every coalfield, soon subsided. And the Miners' Association of Great Britain and Ireland, formed in 1842 and within twelve months having a membership of some 50,000 (approximately one-third of the country's miners), had effectively ceased to exist by the late 1840s.

Pressures against enduring mining trade unionism persisted well beyond 1850. Indeed, up to the last decade of the century (when the Miners Federation of Great Britain and mining trade unionism's overall membership showed massive advances), mining trade unionism, as noted by Hunt, was characterised by 'sudden upheavals and violent collapse'.

The mid-Victorian years witnessed two major organisational developments. In 1858 Alexander Macdonald's National Miners Association was formed. The Association concentrated upon political lobbying in order to improve the inspection and safety of the mines and adopted a very moderate and conciliatory attitude towards the coal owners. Macdonald's union received some support from Scottish colliers, but the bedrock of its support was in Northumberland and Durham. The northeastern hewers were the best paid in the country, had strong traditions of organisation, worked in the largest and most advanced of the coalfields, benefited from the boom in export markets, and combined class collaboration with a marked degree of sectionalism. Believing that their wages should be linked to prices (in order to maintain foreign markets) and themselves working fewer than eight hours, the miners of Northumberland and Durham would come into conflict with those miners (concentrated especially in those regions such as Lancashire and York-shire supplying the domestic market) advocating a minimum wage (as opposed to sliding-scale arrangements) and the eight-hour day. Further-more, Macdonald's policy of the avoidance of both militancy and co-ordinated industrial action across the coalfields of Britain was firmly in accord with the wishes of the well-organised Northumberland and Durham men to be left to manage their own affairs and to avoid the necessity of providing financial support to the miners in weaker and poorer districts.

The second development revolved around the growth of a radical alternative to Macdonaldism. In 1869 militant miners' leaders created the Amalgamated Association of Miners in an attempt to develop a centralised wages strategy and to promote collective industrial action across the various regions. Strongest in Lancashire and South Wales, the Association did for a time enjoy a fair measure of success. During the boom in the coal trade in 1871, wage victories were registered in both Lancashire and South Wales. James Hinton observes that, 'At its peak, in the spring of 1874, the Amalgamated Association had 100,000 members, almost as many as were claimed by MacDonald's Association.' However, as so often in the past, falling prices and wage reductions undermined militancy. In August 1874 the Amalgamated expired and many of its members returned to the National. By the late 1870s depression had destroyed many other rival organisations to the National. But this by no means signalled the death-knell of militancy. During the 1880s demands for a minimum wage and the eight-hour day revived – especially among miners in the coalfields supplying the home market – and became key policies of the Miners Federation of Great Britain created in 1889.

'New Unionism' in the 1870s

As Hunt notes, miners and cotton operatives, together with workers in engineering, shipbuilding and the building trades constituted in excess of two-thirds of all trade-union members in the years preceding the upsurge of 'new unionism' in the late 1880s. 'Traditional' craft and skilled workers in printing, glassmaking, coachmaking and other 'luxury' trades also enjoyed relatively strong trade-union defences.[22] Beyond cotton and mining the non-skilled mid-Victorian worker generally lacked durable trade unionism. The mass industrial upsurges of the Chartist years were not repeated, at least on anything like the same scale, during the 1850s and 1860s. The general economic boom and tight labour market of the early 1870s, combined with the impetus towards more general organisation provided by the relatively successful mid-Victorian unions, improved communications and literacy, and increasingly talented and determined trade-union leadership did, however, inspire a significant, if relatively shortlived, upsurge in 'new unionism' during the first half of the 1870s.

The 'new unionist' spirit manifested itself most spectacularly in agriculture. As seen in Volume One, the country's agricultural workers had been less deferential and apolitical during the first forty years of the nineteenth century than is often supposed. Agricultural protest had markedly declined from the mid 1840s to the end of the 1860s. But in Scotland opposition to the Highland clearances continued to manifest itself and reached its climax in the Crofters' Land War on Skye in the 1880s. And in England increased labour mobility (facilitated by the growth of the railways), the unusually tight labour market, and help from Nonconformists and trade unionists enabled Joseph Arch's National Agricultural Labourers Union of 1872 to gather rapid momentum. Between 1872 and 1874 between 100,000 and 150,000 labourers joined the union, support being especially strong in the labour-intensive corn growing areas of the south, the Midlands and East Anglia. In response the farmers organised Defence Associations, Anglican ministers condemned unionisation and the Eastern Counties lockout of 1874 successfully halted the 'Revolt of the Field'. Economic downturn from the mid 1870s militated against further successful organisation. Arch's union turned to the advocacy of emigration, land reform and the vote, but by the early 1880s agricultural trade unionism was 'largely extinct'.[23]

Elsewhere the early-mid 1870s had witnessed increased radicalism. As Hinton observes, the early 1870s strike wave had been triggered off by a five-month strike of engineering and shipbuilding workers in the northeast for the nine-hour day. But the significance of this strike lay in the fact that it was led not by the unions – 'whose national executives were sour about the whole business' – but by a Nine Hours League, 'representing ten times as many non-unionists, including labourers, as union members'.[24] London dockers, mostly Irish and Catholic and viewed as 'non-respectable' by the official labour movement, won wage increases in 1872 and formed a Labour Protection League which by 1873 had 30,000 members. There were signs of collective organisation among the dockers of Liverpool. And in addition to mining, trade unionism also made headway among railway workers: in 1871 the first all-grades union, the Amalgamated Society of Railway Servants, was formed.

The gains of the early 1870s were, for the most part, temporary. The period between 1875 and 1888 was not as barren as claimed by the Webbs and Cole. Indeed, one could point to the establishment of a stable organisation among London's stevedores, the first port-wide strike in Liverpool and Birkenhead in 1879 and the impetus given to renewed efforts at organisation, and the survival into the 1880s of 'new unionism' among railway workers, and boot and shoe operatives as examples of continuity. But the overall pictures was not rosy. Most of the advances of the early 1870s were lost in the depressed late 1870s. Economic revival between 1880 and 1882 did act as a spur to further trade-union activity. But the depressed years from 1883 to 1888 offset many of the earlier gains. Lovell endorses Clegg's view that, in so far as the major craft unions were concerned, the years between 1875 and 1888 were ones of 'steady expansion and continued effectiveness'. Conversely, overall trade-union membership had fallen by about 250,000 between 1874 and 1888. The narrow base of the movement was reflected in the fact that, despite their presence in weaving trade unionism and the formation in 1874 of Emma Paterson's Women's Protective and Provident League, women workers of the early 1880s were barely touched by trade unionism. Notions of female domesticity and a 'woman's place', and the continued employment and payment of non-skilled helpers by skilled men (Hobsbawm's notion of 'co-exploitation') were hardly conducive to the more widespread independent organisation of the non-skilled.[25]

Trades Councils, the TUC and Collective Bargaining

Final attention should be drawn to three important common characteristics of the generally narrow and sectional trade-union movement of the third quarter: the creation of trades councils; the establishment of the Trades Union Congress; and the more extensive, albeit chequered growth of collective bargaining.

Trades councils were the British equivalent of American city trades assemblies. Usually open to all organised workers within a particular locality, trades councils epitomised and stimulated a spirit of mutuality by means of the organisation of financial and other support for workers engaged in disputes, and by generally co-ordinating and speaking on behalf of local working-class activities and organisations. They increasingly represented workers' interests in local political forums and, especially when dominated by the 'new models' sought to encourage conciliation and arbitration. For example, the Manchester and Salford Trades Council, formed in 1866 and dominated by the 'aristocratic' bookbinders, printers, glassblowers and fine-spinners, had as its primary aim the eradication of the 'disastrous social evils' of strikes and lockouts. In 1868 members of the Council and the Manchester Chamber of Commerce established a Court of Conciliation and Arbitration to act as an adjudicator in disputes. The Trades Council itself was instrumental in bringing about amicable settlements in a number of local disputes and in generating 'a better feeling between employers and employed'. At the national level trades councils also set themselves the wider tasks of stimulating organisation among the unskilled and improving conditions in the sweated trades.[26]

Some trades councils had been formed in the Chartist years. But it was between the 1850s and the mid 1870s that they established themselves in most large towns. Their growing power, and especially their desires to create a legislative and general public climate more favourable to trade unionism also underlay the call (on behalf of the Manchester and Salford Trades Council) for a 'Congress of Trade Unions' in 1868. The result was the creation of the Trades Union Congress which, by the early 1870s, had established itself as the effective national voice of the trade-union movement.[27]

Collective bargaining, in the form of negotiations and written substantive agreements and disputes procedures between representatives of capital and labour, was (as in the United States) not well developed among the great mass of British workers throughout the whole of the nineteenth century. For much of the century those craft and skilled workers possessing strategic powers and/or skills within the realm of production relied heavily upon their economic indispensability *unilaterally* to impose all manner of rules (concerning wage and output levels, apprenticeship and so on) upon the employer. In the event of a refusal by the latter to agree to such rules, a strike or lockout would often ensue. Beyond the ranks of these 'autonomous' workmen, few workers possessed the scarcity value, collective organisation and skills necessary more or less automatically to compel the employer to heed their demands. And in the absence or weakness of trade unionism, few, if any, employers were willing to surrender any of their absolute powers at the workplace in order to meet worker demands for recognition. In such situations worker unrest often took the form of mass strikes or demonstrations, frequently community-based in character, and intended to place pressure upon the employer by means of marches upon the workplace to induce workers to 'turn out'.

What is nevertheless noticeable in Britain (especially England) from mid century onwards is that more formal, work-based and increasingly institutionalised means of negotiation become both more extensive and intensive. As we have seen, this was partly a result of the growth of trade-union strength and effectiveness, factors which employers could not permanently deny or ignore. Formalised negotiation was also part of a more general movement on the part of some workers and employers to practise greater mutual toleration and accommodation in the wake of the raw social conflicts of the second quarter. And, as astutely observed by Reid,[28] it was in large measure attributable to the decline, in the face of technological developments and changes in work organisation, of the numbers and influence of the fully autonomous all-round craftsmen. By the late nineteenth century these craftsmen constituted a minority within the labour force, and increasing numbers of 'craft' workers (in engineering, shipbuilding and elsewhere) now possessed more specialised and limited skills. The latter, in conjunction with the growing number of 'operatives' in iron and steel, coalmining and cotton, were increasingly dependent upon formal trade-union organisation and formal agreements with employers (rather than controls over apprenticeship and so on) in order to secure their bargaining strength. Finally, as demonstrated between 1888 and 1914, both the growing army of semi-skilled workers outside cotton and coal (increasingly concentrated in transport and communications) and the unskilled on the docks, in general labouring and elsewhere turned to formal trade-union organisation and employer recognition as the best means to improve their bargaining power. The second half of the nineteenth century and the early years of the twentieth century thus witnessed an enormous increase in the numbers and types of workers whose livelihoods were ultimately less dependent upon 'collective bargaining by riot' and other 'traditional' forms of protest than upon strong trade-union organisation and collective bargaining.

The latter developments were, however, far from linear. Complex and contrasting patterns could be found within the same industry and occupation at the end of the nineteenth century. Much depended upon local balances of power and the interactions of political, cultural and social as well as purely economic factors. But, in the midst of complexity, we can emphasise for the mid-Victorian years the growing importance of the negotiated standard list for cotton weavers, the negotiated agreement for coalminers and skilled workers in iron and steel, and (as seen most famously in Mundella's Nottingham Hosiery Board of 1860 but present also in parts of the shipbuilding, printing, silk and pottery industries) increasingly popular support for Boards of Conciliation whereby employers and workers or acceptable third parties investigated and settled disputes. From the employers' position, enhanced discussion and negotiation often brought tangible results: fewer interruptions to production and higher levels of output combined with 'a readiness to understand the employer's viewpoint' on the part of pragmatic and 'business-like' trade-union representatives. In such ways did increasing numbers of post-1860 workers come to be influenced by 'joint negotiating boards, conciliation and arbitration agreements, and other procedures designed to prevent disputes and to settle differences without resort to strike or lock-out.'[29]

The United States: union growth, defeats and conflict

The 1860s and early 1870s were also years of expanded trade-union numerical strength, influence, centralisation, bureaucratisation and moderation (or at least attempted moderation) in the United States. As David Montgomery and other historians have shown,[30] wartime hardship, followed in 1863 and 1864 by the quickened demand for labour and inflation, provided the context in which food riots in the South gave way to a revived labour movement in the North. The use of force and conspiracy laws to break strikes in 1864 and 1865, ostentatious displays of wealth by those who had made fortunes out of the war, the continued, if uneven, attacks upon craft standards and controls, and widespread determination to reap material rewards for the sacrifices made during the war (average real wages increasing, in fact, by 40 per cent between 1865 and 1873) combined with the preservation of the free-labour victories gained, all underlay the impressive attempts to create a national labour movement between 1865 and 1873.

The Skilled

Skilled and craft workers, organised into local and, in fewer cases, national and international unions, were at the centre of these attempts. In addition to the shoemakers, tailors, printers, carpenters and other artisans found in the ante-bellum labour movement, post-bellum trade unionism was to be greatly strengthened by the presence of miners, ironmoulders, rolling-mill hands, mule spinners, powerloom weavers, railway workers and other members of new or rapidly growing occupations. As in Britain, industrialisation was to highlight the importance of the metal, construction and transportation trades to the organised labour movement alongside coalminers and the traditional crafts. (As noted in the previous chapter, cotton operatives, outside mule-spinning Fall River, were to be less well organised in the United States than in Britain.)

In the post-bellum years there were accelerated moves to nationally based trade-union organisation, especially among the craft and skilled. Thus Montgomery notes that there existed approximately twenty-one national and international unions in the United States during the early 1870s with organisation being particularly marked among iron puddlers, iron moulders and coalminers. In all some thirty-four similarly structured organisations appeared between 1866 and 1875, but many enjoyed only short lives. Thus only three of the national unions created in the 1850s survived the depression of 1857 and the war years: the National Typographical Association; the Machinists and Blacksmiths International Union; and the Iron Molders International Union. These were joined between 1863 and 1865 by national organisations of miners, railway engine drivers, cigar makers, ship carpenters, plasterers, curriers, carpenters and joiners, bricklayers, painters, ironheaters, tailors, coachmakers and dry-goods clerks. In addition the Knights and Daughters of Saint Crispin enjoyed a large shoemaker membership (probably in the region of 20,000 to 30,000)[31] and, although based in Massachusetts, exerted considerable national influence upon organised labour.

Moves towards national organisation should not, however, blind us to the fact that most workers lacked nationally based organisational structures. The thousands of local unions, often embracing between twenty and thirty members and aloof from the national organisation of their trades, constituted, along with the city trades assemblies, the core of the trade-union movement. The city trades assemblies, comparable to British trades councils, were, according to Montgomery, 'the focal point of labor activity'. Made up of delegates from the trade unions of a single municipal area, the assemblies co-ordinated and initiated union activity in a variety of ways: raising subscriptions to aid strikers; providing arbitration; promoting boycotts of 'unfair' employers; sponsoring labour-reform journals (such as the hugely influential *Workingman's Advocate*); and exerting political pressure at the city, state and federal levels in the interests of organised labour. Thus most of the 300,000 or so workers who were involved in the labour movement during the early 1870s operated at the local rather than the regional or national level.

The revival of trade-union organisation during the 1860s did not, however, signify the widespread and longlasting development of formal collective bargaining. As noted by Montgomery, there were 'few written contracts before the 1880s and fewer salaried officers' (of trade unions). The fragmented and weak nature of much union activity, the strength of employer anti-unionism, and the heavy reliance of skilled and craft workers upon unilaterally imposed rather than negotiated work rules militated against widespread collective bargaining.

As in Britain, the 1860s and early 1870s in the United States did, nevertheless, witness accelerated moves towards formal negotiation. Especially among the national unions, there occurred increased centralisation (in relation to the power to call strikes and to accumulate and safeguard strike funds), bureaucratisation (the increased concentration of power away from the rank and file into the hands of elected officers) and arbitration (which embraced 'any form of organised negotiation of grievances between trade unions and employers', but which more often than not took the form of joint committees of worker and employer representatives rather than, as in the British case, the intervention of an independent third party). The aims of the trade-union leadership were to minimise conflict and violence, to avoid falling foul of the law, and to promote stability, moderation and toleration between labour and capital by means of the more efficient running of their organisations, by the greater adoption of 'responsible' policies, and by the exertion of tighter controls over the rank and file, especially over the more militant and 'unruly' elements.[32]

Like their British counterparts, American unions placed a high premium upon moderation and conciliation. While 'dishonourable' and 'unfair' employers were attacked, there was to be no generalised assault upon capitalists as a class. Rent and interest, as opposed to profit, were perceived as the gains of exploitation. The various eight-hour day campaigns of the late 1860s and early 1870s did bring the trade unions into repeated and extensive conflict with employers and a number of state legislatures (many of whom were, even if in principled agreement with labour, unprepared to *enforce* eight-hour provisions upon recalcitrant employers). But such conflict 'failed to make American labor reformers more class conscious' (at least in a revolutionary socialist sense).[33] As we will observe in more detail below, accommodation, conciliation and 'producerism' remained the dominant themes in labour's pre-1873 ideology.

Moderation and caution brought only limited results. Iron moulders, the Crispins, New York's cigar makers, iron puddlers, coal miners and train drivers did register important, if often limited and shortlived, gains in terms of union recognition by employers, and the adoption of standardised wage scales and price lists, written contracts, and in some cases arbitration procedures. But employer hostility to the very notion of trade unionism persisted in a multitude of industries and locations. Local union controls over wages, dues, apprenticeship and other substantive matters remained the general rule. Class and industrial conflict simply refused to disappear in the face of repeated union pleas for social harmony. And the depression of 1873–8 seriously damaged many of the institutional and material gains made by organised labour during preceding years. Lasting institutionalised collective bargaining was thus conspicuously rare.

Attempts to develop more effective unions and bargaining systems were accompanied by concerted efforts to centralise and co-ordinate labour-reform efforts on a national scale. Most important in this context was the career of the National Labor Union (1866–72).[34] In 1866 delegates from local and national unions, trades assemblies and reform associations (in this case eight-hour leagues) met in Baltimore to formulate common demands for organised labour. From the outset the NLU was, observes Montgomery, 'primarily a political organisation' rather than a congress of trade unionists along the lines of the English TUC. Trade unionists played a prominent role in the NLU, but jealously guarded the principle of individual trade-union autonomy and were not prepared to cede powers of the boycott, strike support and arbitration to the NLU. In effect the NLU constituted a vehicle for the formulation of labour's demands (the programme drawn up in 1866 supported the eight-hour day, homestead rights on public land, consumers' and producers' co-operatives, trade unionism and the organisation of Negro workers), and the realisation of such demands.

It is also important to note that the delegates at Baltimore narrowly adopted a resolution in favour of the creation of an independent National Labor Party. The purpose of the party would be to 'secure the enactment of a law making "eight hours" a legal day's work by the national congress and the several state legislatures, and the election of men pledged to sustain and represent the interests of the industrial classes'. The party did in fact come into being in 1872. It prospered in its initial stages, only, as in the case of so many previous experiments in independent labour activity, to fall foul of internal divisions and the machinations of professional middle-class politicians. However, the very fact that so many 'hard-headed' trade unionists within the NLU consistently supported the notion of independent labour politics serves as an important correction to the Commons-Grob view of necessary conflict between fuzzy-minded reformers and 'job- and wage-conscious' trade unionists. Immediate post-bellum labour activities, especially industrial and political actions, differed far less with respect to personnel and ideology (being largely complementary parts of a broad reforming movement) than to function. It is further significant that it was the Industrial Congress (formed in 1873), the industrial successor to the NLU, which quickly collapsed.

The Lesser Skilled, Immigrants, Women and Black Workers

So far the reader's attention has been drawn to the key role of craft and skilled workers in the post-bellum labour movement. But it is now incumbent upon us to point to the wider social base of organised labour and the extensive nature of post-bellum social protest. As Eric Foner has stated, 'drawing upon the traditional ideals of artisan independence and republican equality, the postwar labor movement mobilised the skilled and unskilled, the native and foreign-born'.[35] The profound commitment of workers to the Union cause, the great physical and material sacrifices made during wartime, and the unpopular impositions endured (inflation, taxes, a draft which discriminated against workers, and the 'encroaching power and centralisation of the federal government')[36] engendered a strong spirit of working-class unity.

The experience of Cincinnati illustrates the general point. Thus Ross:

> The battle for the Union ... assumed a new dimension after the surrender at Appomattox as the city's workingmen endeavoured to create new bonds of union among all wage earners. While workers of the 1840s and 1850s had occasionally joined together in common class protests, they nevertheless tended to remain divided by differing trade, ethnic, religious, and political loyalties. Yet, in the years after 1865, Cincinnati workingmen, bolstered by the belief that it was the nation's wage earners, not its capitalists, who had saved the Republic from dissolution, forged an unprecedented series of political and economic alliances which united all types of workers – skilled and unskilled, native and foreign-born, and even, on occasion, black and white – in a common struggle to obtain justice and preserve the free-labor victories of war.[37]

Those skilled workers facing 'the further erosion of their skills and the proletarianisation of their labor' – printers, shoemakers, iron molders, tailors and cigar makers – were in the vanguard of Cincinnati's post-bellum labour movement. But they were joined by Irish and black dock workers (who put aside memories of the anti-black dock riots of 1862 to march together in support of increased pay in 1866), Irish and German building workers (with a past reputation for mutual dislike), and unskilled labourers. Under the umbrella of a revitalised Trades and Labor Assembly, which called upon the skilled to 'abandon their traditional disdain for the plight of unskilled workers and help to encourage the "formation of unions among the unskilled laborers of this city" ', the broadly based Cincinnati labour movement united around the issues of the eight-hour day, improved wages and conditions, and a variety of other measures designed 'to restore ... greater ... equality between labor and capital'.

Similar patterns emerged elsewhere. In New York City, home of the most effective city central organisations in the country, the two largest unions were the Longshoremens' Union and the Laborers' Benevolent Society with a combined following of 9,000 workers (predominantly Irish). The Workingmen's Union of the city attracted delegates and leadership mainly from the skilled trades, as did the German-language trades assemblies. But the cause of the eight-hour day received support well beyond the ranks of the skilled, as reflected most dramatically in 1872 when some 100,000 of New York's workers 'left their jobs in unison'.[38]

Points to the east, north and south of New York City indicated the strong growth of organisation and protest. New York state, complete with 350 trade organisations, was 'the nation's foremost center of trade unionism'. Massachusetts, Connecticut, Missouri, Illinois, Pennsylvania, New Hampshire and California witnessed massive popular campaigns in favour of the reduction of the working day. (An eight-hour bill for government-employed workers became law in 1868, but most of the gains derived from the state legislatures were shortlived due to lack of enforcement provisions and clauses which permitted longer hours by the mutual agreement of employers and workers.) Trade unionism took root in the Mid-West and the far-West (especially in Chicago, Pittsburgh and San Francisco). In the West and parts of the South the expansion of the railroad and the unfettered capitalist market 'called forth a growing chorus of protest'. Directed against exorbitant freight rates, the high price of manufactured goods, the 'monopolistic' and 'un-Republican' character of the railway companies, the new-found insecurities, sufferings and dependencies of the 'liberated' market place, and the 'anti-social' (i.e. speculative, enclosing and monopolistic) practices of large landowners and financiers, western and southern popular protest was to pass through Grangerism (based on cash-only co-operative stores), strikes, anti-enclosure movements and even machine breaking to the Alliances of the 1880s and the People's Party of the 1890s.[39] Finally, as we will see below, the southern cotton belt was torn by class conflict (between emancipated blacks and white landowners) during the years of Reconstruction.

Of particular note were patterns of post-bellum organisation and protest among women and blacks. During the war some 300,000 women had entered the labour market, and from 1870 onwards approximately 25 per cent of non-agricultural workers were women.[40] In 1870 over 900,000 women worked in domestic service, the largest single occupational group in the entire economy. Clothing, laundry and cleaning, textiles and shoes also employed large numbers of (mainly non-skilled) women. A number of barriers – especially the male-dominated character of the trade-union movement, the widespread equation of womanly virtue with hearth and home, the temporary and isolated nature of much of the work performed by women, and employer hostility to collective organisation – continued to severely limit women's involvement in organised labour (as late as 1900 only 3.3 per cent of women engaged in industrial occupations were organised into trade unions).

A minority of women were nevertheless involved in the union upsurges of the 1860s and early 1870s. Thus Philip Foner lists women cigar makers, collar workers, tailoresses and seamstresses, umbrella sewers, cap makers, textile workers, printers, furnishers, laundresses and shoeworkers as organisers of unions. Despite the fact that most unions refused to admit women (advising the latter to form their own locals), both the Cigar Makers' International Union (in 1867) and the National Typographical Association (in 1872) began to directly admit women members and in shoemaking the Daughters of St Crispin catered for the needs of women. On other occasions male trade unionists lent their support to women's unionising efforts. In addition to trade-union organisation, women developed producer co-operatives (with limited success) and protective associations (which supplied women workers with legal protection against unscrupulous employers who unfairly withheld and reduced wages). Some also became involved in Susan B. Anthony's ill-fated Working Woman's Association (founded in 1868) which attempted to recruit working women to the suffrage cause by promoting 'the amelioration of working conditions and elevation of those who worked for a living'.[41]

Black workers, in both the South and the North, also faced formidable barriers to active participation in the labour movement.[42] Barred from the membership of almost all unions, and on the receiving end of persistent and pervasive racism, blacks were also used as strikebreakers on frequent occasions by northern and southern employers. The organised labour movement of the late 1860s displayed little understanding or sympathy with the desires of the freed people of the South for ownership of land, control over their own labour and for equal rights in the spheres of politics, culture and social life. Eric Foner's observations are instructive:

> The postwar National Labor Congresses either advocated the formation of segregated black locals, or concluded that the whole question of black labor involved 'so much mystery, and upon it so wide diversity of opinion among our members', as to defy resolution. These assemblies also ignored Reconstruction issues, aside from calling for the 'speedy restoration' of the South to the Union... Many labor leaders sympathised with Andrew Johnson... Others feared that to endorse blacks' political and economic aspirations meant associating with the Republican party, a step that would torpedo independent labor politics and offend workers loyal to the Democracy. Even those who advocated the organisation of black labor expressed little interest in blacks' own concerns... Thus, despite the parallels between blacks' quest for economic autonomy and its own hostility to 'wage slavery', the Northern labor movement failed to identify its aspirations and interests with those of the former slaves.[43]

In turn, as seen most dramatically in the Baltimore shipyards in 1865 (when white workers successfully struck against the continued employment of some 1,000 black workers), white working-class and trade-union opposition to the employment and membership of blacks frequently led the latter to seek the embrace and shelter of sympathetic employers. Isaac Myers, Baltimore ship caulker and future architect of the Colored National Labor Union (created in 1869), reacted to the events of 1865 by successfully seeking financial aid from a white merchant and leasing, along with a group of black businessmen, a shipyard. Myers and other leaders of the CNLU were to consistently advocate class conciliation and allegiance to the Republicans.

This conservative and accommodating strategy was to persist with great force within black communities of the South and North for the remainder of the century. We will observe black challenges to the tactics of caution and safety first. But the assertion of independence and the willingness to develop class ties with white workers in both the industrial and political fields invited the full and sickening wrath of racists and white demagogues (especially in the Democratic Party), charges of treason on the part of Republicans (especially in the South), opposition from the forces of capital, and resentments and worse on the part of those blacks who were not prepared to jettison the status quo. As Leon Fink has demonstrated,[44] the stakes of class and race insurgency were extremely high. Failure of independent class-based initiatives linking black and white could all too easily result in loss of employment, physical humiliation and, particularly in the South, death.

Such massive obstacles failed, however, to quell the creative agency and spirit of American blacks. After all, as we saw in Volume One, the 'Sambo' image bore precious little relation to reality under the conditions of slavery. During Reconstruction black people continued to draw heavily upon the resources of family, community, education and religion to sustain their drives towards freedom and equality.[45]

In the South the freedpeoples' overriding desires for cultural and economic autonomy (as manifested in the quest for landownership and deep opposition to becoming dependent 'wage slaves') and equal rights, combined with the equally powerful wishes of the planters to have a deferential and subservient black workforce (the idea of actually having to *negotiate* with blacks was anathema to the white owners) rendered class-based racial conflict inevitable. Such wishes and conflicts revealed themselves in several ways: in the widespread refusal of blacks to accept planters' labour contracts which 'prescribed not only labor in gangs from sunup to sundown as in antebellum days, but complete subservience to the planter's will'; in the restoration of land to its former owners (the work of President Johnson), and in the struggles mounted by black people (by means of refusals to move and, on occasion, armed resistance) against eviction by federal troops (Foner noting that the restoration of land 'required the displacement of thousands of freedmen throughout the South'); in the landowners' portrayals of the blacks as lazy, improvident and reckless beings who would work only under compulsion; and in the latter's characterisation of the former as unprincipled exploiters.

'Conflict was endemic on plantations throughout the South', observes Foner. It was, of course, in part economic. Hours of labour to be worked, methods of working (with intense black opposition to the revival of the labour gangs and close supervision of the days of slavery), and wages to be paid (in those instances in which owners and agents of the Freedmen's Bureau succeeded in creating a black rural proletariat) continued to agitate workers and employers well into the 1870s and beyond. But it was, above all, a cultural conflict, of class struggles concerning personal and social relationships and values, of patterns of authority, power and control. Foner has brilliantly penetrated to the heart of the matter:

> Clearly, the 'labor problem' involved more than questions of wages and hours. Planters' inability to establish their authority arose from the clash between their determination to preserve the old forms of domination and the freedmen's desire to carve out the greatest possible independence for themselves and their families ... Blacks, planters complained, insisted on setting their own hours of labor and demanded extra compensation for, or refused to do, work not directly related to the growing crop but necessary for the planta-tion's upkeep ... When a South Carolina planter ordered his employees to repair a fence, they asked, 'How it was they were doing this work for nothing?' Other blacks refused to weed cotton fields in the rain. Still others would not perform the essential but hated 'mud work' of a rice plantation ... forcing some rice planters 'to hire Irishmen to do the ditching'. House servants, too, had their own ideas of where their obligations began and ended. Butlers refused to cook or polish brass, domestics would not black the boots of plantation guests, chambermaids declared that it was not their duty to answer the front door, serving girls insisted on the right to entertain male visitors in their rooms.[46]

This most profound crisis of white supremacy and class rule was, as we know, increasingly resolved at the expense of the blacks. The state ultimately declared in favour of white landowners and against the redis-tribution of land to the blacks. The Freedmen's Bureau played an ambivalent role in simultaneously shielding the freedpeople against viol-ence from whites and offering some guarantees of judicial 'fair play' whilst also operating under the assumptions of 'free labourism' and seeing the blacks as 'natural' wage earners. The resort to coercion and intimidation by southern white Regulators, members of the Ku Klux Klan and landowners, and the control of local state machineries by racist whites, were also instrumental in preserving white class rule in the South.

The triumph of white domination must not, however, be seen as complete. Sharecropping, the characteristic relationship to eventually emerge between blacks and whites, represented a compromise rather than an imposition, 'a balance between the freedmen's desire for autonomy and the employer's interest in extracting work effort and having labor when it was needed'.[47] Sharecropping provided an escape from close supervision and gang labour, and croppers believed that they had a greater chance to secure a portion of the crop (the 'share wage') than they had to obtain the postharvest or 'standing' wage (all too often blacks were defrauded of all or a portion of the standing wage: the acute shortage of cash and credit in the post-bellum South meant that the freedpeople rarely had the option to receive a periodic cash wage in return for their labour).[48] Sharecropping offered, therefore, a certain amount of hope and security to the cropper and a stabilised workforce to the planter.

Conversely, the evolution of the crop lien system increasingly resulted in widespread and chronic insecurity, poverty and indebtedness for the croppers. In return for the acquisition of provisions, farm implements and other necessities with credit provided by local dealers and merchants (usually representing the sole sources of credit), croppers were compelled to pay the inflated prices and exorbitant rates of interest demanded by their creditors and also to offer them a first right, or lien, on the year's cotton crop. The growth of the crop lien system resulted in an excessive concentration upon cotton and its concomitants of overproduction and depressed prices. More and more croppers became hopelessly dependent upon middlemen, unable to raise even a meagre surplus above their inflated costs and charges, and firmly rooted in 'utter, unending poverty'. Ironically, if tragically, the blacks' regular adversaries, the white tenant farmers, also frequently became entrapped in the same cruel and unrelenting system, mortgaging their crops to the owner of land, for rent, and to the storekeeper, for supplies, and increasingly unable to maintain any semblance of comfort and economic independence.[49] It was out of such combustible materials that the southern Alliance and Populist movements were to explode in the 1880s and 1890s, complete with their attempts to link the grievances and aspirations of black and white tenants, sharecroppers and labourers.

Post-bellum black trade-union and industrial actions must be set within the wider context of black protest and activity outlined above. Sole concentration upon trade unionism presents an unduly narrow and understated account of black protest. However, even within the area of trade unionism and despite the many barriers erected against black participation, there is evidence of quickened activity during the 1860s and early 1870s.[50] For example, Jaynes has identified several black strikes and work slow-downs in southern agriculture and industry and supports Litwack's, Mandle's and Wiener's belief in the existence of 'an incipient labor movement among black workers during Reconstruction'. Black longshoremen in Charleston and Savannah, brickmakers, hod carriers and labourers in Philadelphia, and iron workers, labourers, waiters and factory hands in Richmond actively turned to unionism in this period. As demonstrated on the New Orleans docks in 1865 and among Philadelphia's brickmakers in 1868, black and whites could also on occasion engage in joint strike action. And, despite its lack of commitment to interracial trade unionism, the NLU convention of 1869 constituted, 'the first occasion in American history when a national gathering of white workingmen advocated the formation of labor unions by Negroes and authorized the admission of blacks to the annual sessions'.[51] Similarly, and despite its shortlived existence, the Colored National Labor Union, with its open advocacy of trade unionism, constituted a significant milestone in the history of black protest.

We have developed a picture of a labour movement and popular protest which had at their cores craftsmen and other skilled white males but which, nevertheless, extended their embrace to some of the non-skilled. Indeed, we would be well advised to heed Leon Fink's caution that it is the ephemeral nature rather than the absence of non-skilled collective organisations in the post-bellum years which merits special emphasis.

Notwithstanding its relatively wide, indeed class-based constituency, the American labour movement of the 1860s and early 1870s did possess severe limitations. For a start not only was organisation often shortlived, but it also fell prey to revived divisions and tensions. Black and white dockers who united in New Orleans in 1865 would clash as bitter foes in 1873. 'Immediately upon the war's end', notes Jaynes, 'race riots erupted in Memphis and New Orleans', and 'throughout the South, the thousands of atrocities and altercations between blacks and whites during the next ten years were replications of these situations'.[52] In Cincinnati and elsewhere in the North the promise of the immediate post-war years soon faded. By 1869 many women and other largely unskilled workers had once again become marginalised in terms of mainstream labour. And the cause of independent labour politics was struggling in the face of revived allegiances to the established parties. Finally, the onset of severe depression in 1873 provided a body blow to the continued existence of many trade unions and other institutions of organised labour. By the time of the massive strikes of 1877 American labour was once again in the position of having to revive its dispirited and in some cases collapsed constituent bodies. The perennial problems of employer and state hostility and ephemeral labour organisation were once more to the fore.

Ideology

In many ways the ideology of American labour in the 1860s and early 1870s displayed strong continuities with the revived 'producerism' of the 1840s and early 1850s (see Volume One). The central fact that the Civil War had been fought to preserve 'free labor' and 'equal rights' against the machinations of an 'aristocratic' slave power, the opening up of the West (beyond the Mississippi), the uneven process of capitalist transformation, continued opportunities (especially for the native born) to achieve non-proletarian economic and social independence, and the continued flexibility of the political system (especially the ability of the Democrats and Republicans to absorb working-class talent and labour leadership),[53] constituted factors of fundamental importance in preserving notions of artisan independence and republican equality and in erecting powerful barriers to the development of a more influential class-based ideology.

As we have seen, in mid-Victorian Britain the labour movement combined an acceptance of the permanent nature of a working class with strong desires to make its peace with capital and to find an acceptable place within the market-based social order. Karl Marx and the International Working Men's Association might have provided both intellectual and practical trade union stimulation for some of the leaders of the 'new models', but they most certainly did not induce the latter to abandon their central concerns with moderation and accommodation. In the United States the influence of revolutionary socialism upon the working class (outside of German workers in New York City) was equally negligible. As noted, moderation and class conciliation were also strong among American trade unionists. Strikes and the massive conflicts surrounding the eight-hour day campaigns placed strains upon the generally amicable relations between trade unionists and the Radical Republicans. And a minority of workers endorsed Ira Steward's belief that there existed necessary conflict between labour and capital (Steward was the influential leader of the Machinists and Blacksmiths International Union).[54] But American labour's ideology continued to be rooted in an anti-monopoly producerism uniting worthy employers and workers against a variety of 'parasitical', 'aristocratic' foes.

The central planks of labour's programme, as expressed in the NLU's formulations, thus revolved around the notions of equal rights, economic independence, and social and political harmony, especially among the 'producers'. The eight-hour day was demanded less for economic reasons (to increase employment and overall demand) than to remould 'American social realities to a shape consistent with American political ideals'. Excessive hours of labour undermined 'the virtue, the intelligence and the independence of the working classes', leading to 'wage slavery' which was, by its very existence, incompatible with the republican notion of active citizenship (a theme which would become central to the Knights of Labor).[55] In addition to reduced hours of labour, the keys to economic independence and proper citizenship were improved wages and the promotion of co-operative production. The latter, as in Britain, was seen as a means of both promoting economic citizenship and of restoring or promoting harmony and co-operation between the 'natural' allies of worker and employer. Indeed, co-operative production was, along with a suitable programme of education, preferable to a simple reduction of hours. The latter would ameliorate the position of the 'wage slave' while the former would abolish it. In time labour and capital would become virtually indistinguishable, untroubled by costly and uncivilised strikes and lockouts.

A citizenship of the land (widespread property ownership being guaranteed by effective homestead laws) combined with a government-owned banking system issuing paper money convertible into interest-bearing bonds (the Greenback scheme) would also ensure the triumph of the 'producers' over the 'parasitical monopolists'. Railroads, speculators and others would be prevented from amassing large tracts of land at the expense of genuine settlers. And Greenbackism would undermine the restrictive financial hold of the private banks and creditors over the 'productive' elements of society by 'transferring control of the currency from a parasitical "money power" to the democratic state'; by reducing rates of interest; by channelling investment into 'productive' sectors of the economy and so increasing investment, output, demand and employment; and by further promoting harmony between employers and workers.[56]

As emphasised in Volume One, notions such as 'class' and 'producerism' are not static and absolute categories. They are abstractions which embody human relationships and social structures. And, just as antebellum patterns of producerism' were subject to change, complexity, contestation and a variety of meanings, so the 'producerism' of the post-bellum years and beyond was far from one-dimensional in character. We have already observed – in relation to the comments made by Ross and to the eight-hour struggles – that class conflict operated alongside and within the overarching phenomenon of the 'producing classes'. And while Montgomery is undoubtedly correct to suggest that the language and ideology of 'producerism' held sway, there is a very real sense in which a non-revolutionary and non-socialist language of structured and experiential class antagonisms, interests and aims did begin to develop in the 1860s and gather increased momentum during the 1870s.

Ross's judgements in relation to Cincinnati are once again very instructive. Ross writes:

> Cincinnati workers of the 1860s did not initially view labor and capital as inherent enemies ... It was individual capitalists, rather than an intrinsically flawed economic system, that caused misery and distress among the working class ...
>
> However, when the postwar growth of industrial capitalism, monopolies, and corporations seemed to threaten this free-labor strain of ante-'bellum republican ideology, the cry of 'industrial slavery' emerged as a powerful metaphor ... The eight-hour day campaign, insisted TLA leaders, was less an attack upon what America was than what it was becoming: a nation of dependent, slave-like wage earners who could not fully exercise their rights as workers or citizens.

Cincinnati's workers did not wish to *abolish* the capitalist system but, like English Chartists and 1830s New York radicals, they did wish to regulate and civilise it, to make the market more responsive to the needs of workers, to balance moral/customary and market-induced imperatives, and to obtain 'due reward and protection' for the 'producers'. Increasingly, such desires and the widespread opposition of Cincinnati's employers to organised labour, did lead to conflicts, struggles and class-based modes of thought. 'Producerism' and 'class' began to coexist rather uneasily.[57]

This uneasy coexistence increased both locally and nationally during the 1870s. The growth of ever-larger units of production and a new generation of employers looking for the 'main chance', keen to maximise profits and minimise costs by driving competitors from the field, revolutionising the methods of production and unsentimentally cutting labour costs to the bone, depersonalised and embittered relations in the workplace. As in the 1830s, 'honourable' masters, abiding by the customs or the trade, were becoming rare. 'Dishonourable', grasping capitalist employers (increasingly donning new corporatist garb) were seen and felt to constitute an alien, 'un-republican' and fast growing system. Furthermore, as we saw in the last chapter, from the early 1870s to the late 1890s the American economy suffered from a severe crisis of competitive capitalism. Declining rates of profit, ruthless cost cutting and competition, rampant employer aggression and individualism, and the occurrence of economic depressions (in 1873–8, 1882–5 and 1893–7) over shortened intervals of time were hardly conducive to stability and social harmony.

1870s Depression and the 'Rising' of 1877

The depression from 1873–8 simultaneously weakened trade unionism and whipped up social tensions and class conflict. As noted by Eric Foner, 'The depression had a profound impact on the labor movement, shifting its focus from the issues of the 1860s – greenbackism, co-operation, and the eight-hour day – to demands for public relief, the desperate struggle to maintain pre-depression wage levels, and, for a few workers, socialism.'[58] There were widespread demonstrations in favour of public works during the winter of 1873–4 (which reached their climax in violent police action against demonstrators in New York's Tompkins Square in January 1874). The next two years witnessed acrimonious labour struggles on the railroads, in mining, and in textiles and the Molly Maguire trials which resulted (in 1877 and 1878) in the hanging of the twenty Irish mineworkers for the murder of colliery officials in Pennsylvania. In the West and Southwest falling prices and wages, and increased indebtedness, tenancy and waged labour induced farmers and others to join the Grange, attack the activities of speculators and the railroads (the latter symbolising the greed, corruption and unashamed drive for power of the new corporate business juggernaut), call for railroad regulation and fair prices, and to mount political insurgencies against 'monopolies'. Some craft and skilled unions attempted to weather the economic storm by running for cover and adopting a cautious, moderate stance. But such defensive and limited tactics gave little protection from the singleminded and hegemonic designs of corporate capital.

1877 was the climactic year. Wage cuts and changed working rules on the part of the major railroads sparked off strikes among railway and other workers across the entire country. The nature and atmosphere of the Great Strike have been well recaptured by Montgomery:

> In late July, 1877, train crews on the Baltimore and Ohio Railroad struck against a wage cut, triggering a chain of events which President Hayes was to condemn as an 'insurrection'. Popular anger over the dispatch of troops to reopen the line spread the strike to Baltimore, where huge crowds clashed with the militia. Simultaneously, work stoppages followed the rail lines across Pennsylvania ... Thousands of Pittsburgh iron workers and other residents defeated soldiers sent from Philadelphia in pitched battle, subsequently burning all property of the Pennsylvania Railroad. Across Ohio and Indiana, workers' committees simply took over their towns, halting all work until their demands were met by employers. A quickly organized strike in Chicago brought troops and artillery to the city ... In St. Louis, thousands of workers closed down the city's industry for several days ... In San Francisco, great crowds sacked railroad property and attacked Chinatown.[59]

Eventually defeated, the strikes merit comment on a number of levels. It is first of all important to acknowledge the sheer size and scale of the protests. Philip Foner[60] rightly describes the protests as a 'huge contagion', a general railroad strike which 'developed into a national conflagration'. Foner estimates that it involved some 80,000 railway workers and, quoting the *New York World* of July 1877, 'over five hundred thousand workers in other occupations'. We are thus dealing with a nationwide upheaval which embraced a wide cross-section of the working class.

Second, while not generally revolutionary or socialist in character and intention (only in St Louis did an explicitly revolutionary Marxist organisation, The Workingmen's Party of the United States, exert major influence over the course of events),[61] the strikes transcended narrow economic demands. Improved wages and conditions were of obvious importance to the railway and other workers involved. But opposition to a wage reduction symbolised much wider oppositions: to the 'monopolistic' and 'arrogant' powers of the railroads; to the latters' 'un-republican' behaviour; to the increasing exploitation and oppression of the worker by the railroads and other 'tyrannical' employers; to the domination of politics and society by special, 'sectional' and 'corrupt' interests; and to the unwanted intrusions of such 'monopolies' into the lives of local communities. As noted by Gutman, it is significant that actions of 'capitalists' frequently met with wide disapproval in small and tightly knit centres of population.[62]

In these various ways a multitude of community, producerist and class-based concerns interacted to produce a devastating indictment of the threatened capture of the Republic by alien, capitalist forces. Class still coexisted alongside and within producerism, but, notwithstanding the claims of Kazin, there was no doubting the heightened presence and influence of class. The defence of the Republic and of the interests of workers had become synonymous. Both were threatened by the depredations of aggressive capital. The language of class assumed the form of revolutionary republicanism rather than socialism. But corporate capitalists had, in effect, forfeited their right to be regarded as fellow producers. As would be made even more explicit by the Knights of Labor during the Great Upheaval of 1884–6, the language of anti-monopoly producerism thus contained within it the distinctly American version of non-socialist, class-based opposition to unregulated capitalism and capitalist control of the state machinery.

The depression of the 1870s and the events of 1877 had greatly intensified class divisions. Thus Eric Foner:

Rudely disrupting visions of social harmony, the depression of the

1870s marked a major turning point in the North's ideological development. As widespread tension between labor and capital emerged as the principal economic and political problem of the day, public discourse fractured along class lines ... in the nation's large cities, and at the upper echelons of both major parties, older notions of equal rights and the dignity of labor gave way before a sense of the irreducible barriers separating the classes and a preoccupation with the defense of property, 'political economy', and the economic status quo.[63]

Workers' refusals to meekly bow before the power of capital in the Gilded Age and their (to use Gutman's phrase) 'search for power' (involving the 'proper' recognition of labour's interests and reward for its contribution towards society's wellbeing) increasingly involved conflict with the forces of law and order. Thus, although some policemen, and even local militiamen, sided with the demands of the strikers in 1877, the state did not hesitate to use force to defeat the insurgency. 'For the first time since Andrew Jackson's administration', writes Philip Foner, 'federal troops were called in to suppress a strike'. All told, over 3,000 federal troops and several thousand more state militiamen were called out. There were upwards of 100 deaths, including the shooting of twenty civilians in Pittsburgh in July, and extensive destruction and damage to railroad property, engines and freight cars. Henceforth, state and federal troops, in addition to the police, and the private forces hired by employers, were to be employed with great frequency and intensity against the collective actions of workers. Laurie notes that, 'state troops were called out to calm labor unrest nearly 500 times between 1875 and 1910'.[64] And in the wake of the defeats of 1877 and 1886, and in opposition to the partiality of the law, the state and the established parties, workers turned to experiments in independent labour politics. Our fourth observation must be that workers in 1877 and beyond met with sustained state and employer hostility to their collective actions and demands.

How does the American situation compare with British experience? In terms of the scale of 'unrest', the number of fatalities and injuries, destruction to property, state coercion and employer repression, and the depth and extent of worker involvement, contemporary Britain offered nothing comparable to the American insurgencies of 1877. Britain did seem to be a relatively 'Peaceable Kingdom', possessing far more conciliatory workers and employers. More crucially, in terms of the 'class' and 'exceptionalism' issue, Britain was increasingly the laggard (a position which would become even more pronounced during the American strikes and mobilisations of 1884–6). The involvement of the non-skilled in the events of 1877 was far greater than any comparable involvement in Britain. Class conflict and class consciousness, American style, were hardly within the circumscribed world view of the 'respectable' British trade unionist. And American moves to independent politics during the late 1870s were not paralleled in Britain. In short, it is the more volatile and conflict-ridden nature of social relationships in 1870s America which merit special emphasis. Would such differences persist? Would Britain maintain its relative stability, its accommodation and growing 'institutionalisation' of class, and the domination of its labour movement by moderate and sectional trade unions?[65] In order to answer such questions we must proceed to an investigation of trade unionism and patterns of popular protest from the mid–late 1880s to 1918.

1880s–1918: CONFLICT, MASS UNIONISM AND THE POWER OF ACCOMMODATION

As compared with the much neglected middle decades of the nineteenth century, the period from the 1880s to the mass radical and socialist insurgencies of the immediate post-First World War years has been well served by historians of both British and American labour. This fact is understandable. The cautious 'new model' trade unionism of mid-Victorian Britain hardly captures the imagination in the same way and to anything like the extent of the explosions of 'new unionism' between 1888–91 and 1910–14, or the massive radicalisation of Labour between 1917–18 and 1920.

Similarly, alongside the ideological conflicts gripping American labour during the 1880s and 1890s or the mass strikes of the 1880s and 1912–22, moves in the 1860s towards bureaucratisation, centralisation and arbitration have a distinctly low-key appeal. But in many ways traditions and precedents were set in both countries during the middle years of the century – pragmatism, gradualism and reformism in Britain, the key importance of sound trade unionism and the dangers of mixing trade unionist with other concerns in America – which were to exert crucial influences upon subsequent labour movement developments. It is for these reasons, combined with the obvious requirement to provide the reader with a balanced and tolerably detailed account of overall developments, that the first part of the chapter has devoted a considerable amount of attention to the 1860s and 1870s.

On turning to an examination of the post-1880 period, we find that (as in the case of the exciting and 'heroic' 1830s and 1840s) coverage is far more detailed, and the narrative of events better known. Our intention is, accordingly, to provide a broad overview of key processes and themes rather than a detailed reconstruction of events. The British 'new unionism' of the 1880s will be our point of departure. We will then proceed to a consideration of the 'labour unrest' of 1910–14 and the effects of the First World War upon workers. Our focus will then move to trade unionism and popular protest in the United States with special reference to periods of mass activity and ideological conflict within the labour movement.

Britain: 'New' and 'Old' Unionism

As the British economy moved out of the severe depression and unemployment of the mid 1880s and as the labour market tightened, so the ephemeral attempts at 'new unionism' during the 1870s were renewed with increased vigour. Criticisms of the cautious and collaborationist stance of many of the older union leaders (the majority of whom were committed Liberals) were expressed by a new generation of young, confident, more militant and often socialist leaders. Opposition to the growth of more impersonal relations at work, to the adverse effects of change and capitalist transformation and to wage cuts and stagnant real wages stimulated both quantitative and qualitative leaps in the development of trade unionism.[66]

Between 1888 and 1892 trade-union membership doubled from approximately 750,000 to 1.5 million. As is well known, part of the upsurge took place in areas traditionally weak or non-existent in terms of trade unionism. As early as 1886 the National Labour Federation, composed of semi-skilled workers, began life in the northeast. The National Amalgamated Union of Sailors and Firemen, under the leadership of Havelock Wilson, was formed in 1887. By 1888–9 the Knights of Labor had some 10,000 members in Britain. In 1888 there occurred the famous strike by women and girls at the Bryant and May match factory. 'During 1889', notes Taplin, 'the momentum was increased with the appearance of unions for gasworkers, dockers, general labourers, carters, scavengers and tramwaymen among others'. Especially prominent were the successful organisation of the gasworkers and general labourers under the inspired leadership of Will Thorne of the Marxist Social Democratic Federation in 1889, and the justly celebrated London Dock Strike of August 1889 which not only won the dockers' 'tanner', but also stimulated union organisation elsewhere.

The 'new unionism' did have its limitations. Organisation among farm workers never remotely touched the heights of the early 1870s explosion. Among another traditionally ill-organised group, women, developments were more mixed.[67] Women, as we have seen, had been organised in weaving unions in cotton from mid century onwards. And the amalgamations in weaving and among card and blowing room hands in the 1880s greatly augmented the numbers of organised women in

cotton. It was, furthermore, in the cotton districts that the Women's
Co-operative Guild, formed in 1883 and providing a forum for the
discussion of a wide range of topics, proved to be immensely popular
among working-class women. But, despite their adoption of 'new' features, cotton unions were not creations of the 'new unionism' of the
late 1880s. Women boot and shoe workers, schoolteachers, woollen
workers, tailors, dressmakers and local government employees all joined
trade unions in increasingly greater numbers at the end of the nineteenth
century and the early years of the present century, a development resulting in part from the infectious general enthusiasm for unionisation
generated by 'new unionism'. And in 1891 the Women's Protective and
Provident League symbolically changed its name to become the
Women's Trade Union League.

In absolute terms significant gains had been made. Hunt notes that
there were 'fewer than 50,000 female trade unionists in 1888, more than
twice this number five years later, and around 432,000 by the end of
1913'. Relatively speaking, however, the picture was far from satisfactory. At the turn of the century women constituted over 30 per cent of
the labour force but only 7.5 per cent of the total number of trade
unionists. Isolated and personalised work situations (domestic service
still occupied 39 per cent of all employed women in 1911), seasonal and
part-time employment, hostile male attitudes and employer opposition
were enduring and potent influences upon women's low level of unionisation.

Notwithstanding such limitations, the 'new unionism' did, for a time
at least, construct impressively large organisations. As Richard Hyman
has observed, unions of the pre-1888 vintage were generally 'tiny and
fragmented' (the ASE, the largest union, had fewer than 52,000 members,
and at the beginning of 1888 'only a dozen claimed a membership of
over 10,000'). Between 1888 and 1891–2 matters changed dramatically.
Thus Hyman:

> Against this background, the mushroom growth of the 'general
> labour' unions necessarily created a profound impact. At the peak
> in 1890 the National Amalgamated Union of Sailors and Firemen
> officially reported 60,000 members and the Dock, Wharf, Riverside
> and General Labourers' Union 57,000. The other main waterside
> organization, the National Union of Dock Labourers, affiliated to
> the TUC on the basis of 40,000 members. For their part the
> (unregistered) National Union of Gasworkers and General Labour-
> ers claimed 60,000, as did the National Labour Federation, while
> the Tyneside and National Labour Union recorded 40,000. While
> such figures must be regarded with considerable scepticism, what
> was popularly defined as the New Unionism may have achieved a

maximum membership of some 300,000, or roughly a fifth of all trade unionists.[68]

The life-span of 1880s 'new unionism' was in most cases, however, very short. By the mid 1890s economic downturn and a fierce employer counter-attack (especially in the docks and ports) had halved 'new unionist' membership. And those organisations which managed to weather the storms of the 1890s were (as in the cases of gasworkers and dockers)[69] concentrated among workers occupying strategic positions within, or able to control, local job markets, and who were more regularly employed and less dispensable than the mass of unskilled. The Dockers' Union and similar organisations retreated from their wide ambitions of the late 1880s. Union recognition and advancement were to be secured more by the 'old' (i.e. 'new model') unionist methods of membership restriction, sectionalism, increased union dues, and caution and moderation than by militant and general (i.e. 'one man, one ticket') unionism. The fact that even from the outset the 'new' unions displayed no uniform pattern in terms of structure, policy and political orientation (socialist leadership and influence among the membership varying greatly from one 'new' union to another) has further strengthened the view of many historians that continuity rather than discontinuity (between the 'new model' and the 'new' unions) constituted the dominant theme in late nineteenth- and early twentieth-century British trade unionism.[70].

The position adopted here is that a traditionally exaggerated view of discontinuity does not, therefore, establish the validity of the case in favour of continuity. 'New' unionism did become more cautious and accommodating during the 1890s. As we have earlier noted, the 'new models' often did not conform to the picture of pacifism and capitalist-mindedness portrayed by the Webbs. And, as seen in cotton weaving, some mid-century unions did adopt 'open' policies and structures which anticipated the more concerted 'new unionist' practices of the 1880s. Equally, however, the 'new unionist' upsurge did, as argued by Hobsbawm and Hyman, mark a quantitative and qualitative leap in trade unionism in at least six main ways.

First there was the greatly increased (if ephemeral) penetration of trade unionism into previously unorganised or poorly organised areas (in this respect one can draw significant parallels with the American experiences of 1877 and 1884–6). Second, as noted above, 'new unionism' increased the average size of unions. Third, the upsurge signified a psychological break, a demonstration of the fact that large numbers of the non-skilled were breaking free from their seeming deference, fatalism and inhibitions of the mid-Victorian years to warmly embrace militant

trade unionism. This kind of mass-based self-confidence and assertiveness had arisen in the late 1820s and early 1830s, and again during
Chartism. But it had lain for the most part dormant during the post-
1850 years, at least as measured against the scale and intensity of organisation and protest of 1888–91. Fourth, while the mass of 'new' union
members were not socialists, at least in a formal, ideologically structured
(as opposed to a more fragmented, 'commonsensical') manner and while
the leaders were not uniformly left wing, advocates of continuity have
considerably underestimated the influence of socialists upon the formation and development of 'new' unions. Socialist organisations were small
in numbers, but, as demonstrated in the cases of Tom Mann, Eleanor
Marx, Will Thorne, Ben Tillett, Tom Maguire and countless others,
highly influential in terms of both national and local trade unionism.[71]

Fifth, many of the 'new' unions looked far more kindly upon
increased state intervention and independent Labour representation than
had been the case with the generally voluntaristic and Lib.-Lab. 'old'
unions. The relative weakness of their members' position in the market-
place, their general absence of strong allegiances to Liberalism, and the
obvious promise of a legal eight-hour day to improve material and
mental conditions, made many of the 'new' unions enthusiastic supporters of independent Labour politics.

Finally, as David Howell has suggested, the 'new organisations fused
together a series of elements which could provoke consternation in
respectable circles'. Mass assertiveness, mass strikes and militancy, the
shedding of 'natural' deference, and the influence of socialism led many
employers, politicians and others to complain of union 'dictation' and
'tyranny' on a scale and with an intensity far more reminiscent of the
1830s and 1840s than the 1860s and 1870s. The 'Peaceable Kingdom'
seemed to be losing some of its cohesion and stability, and it appeared
to many in authority that 'a fundamental change was occurring in British
trade unionism'. As Howell concludes, 'Such a prediction needs to be
set against the long-term factors diminishing the distinctions between
New Unions and their older, craft-based counterparts. The similarities
are perceivable with hindsight – the contrasts, real or imagined, were
apparent immediately'.[72]

Spectacular in its growth, the 'new unionism' did not, however,
embrace the majority of trade unionists. In the early 1890s the 'new'
unions accounted for about one-quarter of total trade-union membership (by 1896 for less than one-tenth). Indeed, during the late 1880s
and early 1890s growth was most pronounced among the more established unions. Cotton trade unionism extended its scope into the blow-
ing- and card-rooms, the ASE increased its membership by a third, the
United Society of Boilermakers and Iron and Steel Shipbuilders by a

half, and the United Operative Bricklayers' Trade Society increased threefold. Similarly, mining trade unionism was reconstructed and greatly revived under the auspices of the Miners' Federation of Great Britain, formed in 1889 and committed to the eight-hour day and the minimum wage. The railways, traditionally a weak site for trade unionism in the face of hostile employers (with their mix of welfarism and authoritarianism), also saw significant growth. In 1889 the General Railway Workers' Union was formed as a 'fighting union' to counteract the moderate Amalgamated Society of Railway Servants. Committed to the eight-hour day and mass organisation, the GRWU both displayed rapid recruitment (at least in the short term) and pushed the ASRS into a more militant, open and vigorous stance. In a parallel way the Workers' Union of 1898 would recruit heavily among semi-skilled engineering workers and force the leadership of the ASE at least to reconsider seriously its policy of excluding the non-skilled.

All told it was, therefore, the trade-union movement as a whole, rather than simply the 'new' unions, which benefited from the favourable economic conditions of the late 1880s and early 1890s. And the peak in strike levels between 1889 and 1891 was similarly due more to heightened conflicts in building, mining, metals and textiles than to the 'new' unionist explosion.[73]

The 1890s as a whole constituted a somewhat complex and contradictory decade. These were the years of adverse legal decisions, culminating in Taff Vale, of the employer counter-attack, especially against the 'new' unions, and, of accentuated employer attempts, in the face of increased international competition and reduced profit margins, to increase the 'squeeze' on labour and to assert management's undiluted right to manage in the face of 'obstructive' workers. As we saw in Chapter 1, the issue of craft control rather than the very existence of trade unionism was of central concern in the British context. And employers were generally successful in their attempts to (re)assert their 'right to manage'.

Thus, in a number of crucial battles – in cotton between the Stalybridge lockout of 1891, the general spinning lockout of 1892 and the Brooklands Agreement of 1893; in north Wales slate quarrying during 1896–7 and 1900–3; in the 1895 lockout in the boot and shoe industry; in most spectacular fashion in the engineering lockout of 1897–8; and (to a lesser extent) in the miners' lockout of 1893 – the employers won most of their demands.[74] Above all, they won the 'right' to impose unilateral changes in working conditions and practices, to defeat craft control, to stabilise and limit wage costs, and to reduce unwanted risks to production runs and profits.

In engineering the union had to abandon the eight-hour day and any negotiated influence over apprenticeship levels, the introduction of new machines and the rate to be paid to non-unionists. Employers also had total control over hiring and firing. In the boot and shoe industry defeat in 1895 meant that lasting machines would be introduced, would be controlled by the employers and that a semi-skilled mechanised factory industry would win the day over outwork and craft controls.

In cotton the Brooklands settlement placed a ceiling of 5 per cent on wage movements per annum, involved a wage reduction (albeit of half the magnitude originally proposed by the employers), and introduced a centralised disputes procedure which stated that unresolved local disputes had to be referred to a central joint committee before strike action could be considered. In effect, a growing accumulation of shop-floor grievances (and especially 'bad' spinning) were institutionalised and centralised, and their effective resolution postponed. Greater powers were concentrated in the hands of union officials, moderate, 'statesman-like' men who generally saw 'eye-to-eye' with the employers. Little wonder that Burgess can conclude that Brooklands represented 'collective bargaining on the employers' terms'.[75]

In the bitter mining dispute of 1893, which lasted for four months and involved the fatal shooting of two miners by troops at Featherstone, the outcome was less clear cut. The settlement maintained wages at existing levels and established a Conciliation Board. But, as Hinton notes, increased prices for coal offset the wage settlement, and 'in reality the miners had been forced to abandon their demand for a "living wage" '.[76]

Despite these serious setbacks, unions in mining, cotton, the boot and shoe industry, engineering and other industries were not destroyed, and in some cases workers would recapture some of their controls in the workplace. Indeed, as emphasised in Chapter 1, stalemate and compromise between unions and employers, as opposed to the elimination of the former by the latter, constituted the outstanding development of industrial relations between the early 1890s and 1908. Having gained formal mastery over the process of production, many employers operating within relatively cushioned markets were prepared to deal with officials of the 'old' unions. Moreover, although defeated in specific battles, such unions had amply demonstrated their staying power, their refusal to disappear or to submit to total employer domination of labour. And union officials were happy to 'do business' with pragmatic employers.

It was in this context that institutionalised collective bargaining made giant strides between the 1890s and the First World War. As Clegg and Lovell have shown, by the turn of the century unilateral regulation of working conditions had become greatly overshadowed by the development of collective bargaining. But whereas collective bargaining over substantive questions (conditions of employment) usually took place at a local or district level within each industry, the resolution of disputes was increasingly placed within a national framework. National, industry-wide procedure agreements arose in cotton weaving in 1881, in spinning at Brooklands, in boot and shoes in 1895, in engineering in 1898 and in building and shipbuilding in the first decade of the new century. Most significant was the fact that, as seen in the cases of cotton weaving (the industry-wide agreement of 1881 following the massive conflict of 1878) and spinning, boot and shoes, and engineering, the development of industry-wide disputes procedures and attempts to stabilise and harmonise industrial relations followed hard on the heels of acrimonious disputes.

The new-found position of *détente*, symbolised by the creation of conciliation machinery and institutionalised disputes procedures (before the 1914–18 war industry-wide *substantive* agreements were uncommon), amounted, of course, to formal union recognition on the part of the employers. And the unions eagerly took advantage of this situation to greatly increase their numbers and strength. Most spectacular in this context was the growth of the Miners Federation of Great Britain. Formed upon the initiative of miners from Yorkshire and Lancashire, the MFGB began life in an industry in which around one-fifth of miners were unionised. At its inception the MFGB also lacked support from Scotland and the key exporting coalfields of South Wales and Northumberland and Durham. The Federation did, however, crucially survive the 1893 dispute to become, by 1914, the largest bargaining unit in the country as a whole. In 1894 Scotland joined, to be followed by South Wales in 1897 and the miners of Northumberland and Durham in 1907–8. By the latter years the Federation had recruited some 600,000 members, a figure which represented 60 per cent of the country's miners and one-quarter of all trade unionists. The Federation's policies of industrial militancy combined with moderate political action (especially via parliamentary representation and lobbying) were increasingly successful. In 1908 the statutory eight-hour day was achieved for underground miners, and in 1912 the government accepted the principle of a statutory minimum wage for workers in the industry.[77] On a general level, improved economic conditions during the later years of the 1890s saw trade unionism rise to 2 million in 1900.

The collective bargaining machinery largely set in place during the 1890s helped to ensure that relations between employers and workers were relatively peaceful between the late 1890s and the end of 1907. Despite stagnant or falling real wages from 1900 onwards and the Taff Vale case, working days lost by stoppages continued to show a marked decline over the pre-1899 decade. This period of relative tranquillity was, however, rudely disrupted in 1908 when, in the midst of depressed conditions, attempted wage reductions on the part of employers in cotton, engineering and shipbuilding triggered off major disputes. Moreover, from 1908 onwards strike activity increased and, as noted by Lovell, 'the whole period down to 1926 – with the exception of some of the war years, when an industrial truce was in operation – was one of unprecedented industrial conflict'.[78]

Labour Militancy 1910–1914

The 'labour unrest' of 1910–14 constituted a key episode in this period of heightened industrial and class conflict. Our purpose is not to offer a detailed reconstruction of events,[79] but to sketch in the basic chronology, causes and significance of this pre-war explosion.

The conflicts of 1908 formed a prelude to the 'unrest'. In 1909 the economy came out of depression. The demand for labour quickened, and by 1910–11 the level of unemployment was very low. Wages increased but not sufficiently to keep pace with the sharply increased cost of living. Wage movements negotiated under the collective bargaining agreements of the 1890s proved (as in the case of the Brooklands Agreement) to be of insufficient magnitude to meet price increases. In addition, the centralised grievance machinery created during the 1890s had proven itself too unwieldy and slow to cope with accumulated grievances at the level of the workplace. In cotton and shipbuilding, for example, failure to satisfactorily resolve issues relating to, respectively, poor materials, speed up and various aspects of craft regulation, created pent-up grievances which were liable to break free from the bonds of institutionalised collective bargaining. The seeming indifference of some union officials to the grievances and demands of the membership, and the fact that established collective bargaining embraced only a minority of workers further worked to push 'unrest' beyond institutionalised channels. Finally, the growing sense of relative deprivation on the part of workers, the influence of syndicalists, and the unashamed flaunting of wealth in Edwardian Britain added fuel to the fire.

Mass insurgency began in earnest in 1910. 'There were', records Hunt, 'major disputes in the Clyde and Tyne shipyards, there was a strike of railwaymen in the north-east, and the cotton mills were stopped again'. And the issue of 'abnormal places' – adequate payment for coal hewers working difficult seams – was central to the Cambrian dispute in South Wales. This strike dragged on for almost a year, involving considerable violence (including the Tonypandy Riot in the wake of attempts to import strikebreakers), the use of police and troops, opposition to the conciliatory policies of the leadership, and efforts to commit the union to a revolutionary syndicalist perspective.

In 1911 the 'new' unionist thrust of the late 1880s was revived, strengthened and extended. In Bermondsey 15,000 sweated women workers walked off their jobs in search of increased pay. They were followed by London County Council's cleaners. In September there was a schoolchildren's strike. But the railways, ports and docks were at the very centre of the upsurge. The first ever national railway strike, in support of union recognition and better pay and conditions, saw concerted action on the part of the various unions. The railway companies displayed their traditional hostility to all matters union, and in the early stages of the strike were joined by a belligerent government. Troops were mobilised and martial law declared in some areas. The railway workers received support from dockers, miners and others. And in Liverpool a general transport strike took place. Eventually the government climbed down and persuaded the railway owners to accept conciliation. For the first time the companies conceded the right of full-time union officials to represent railway workers in the conciliation boards, but full recognition had not been achieved. However, in 1913 the various unions which had co-operated in 1911 merged to form the 'all grades' National Union of Railwaymen. Despite the loss of the engineers and firemen (in the Amalgamated Society of Locomotive Engineers and Firemen), the NUR became a genuinely industrial union. By 1914 it had recruited half the workers in the industry and, in effect, won recognition from the employers.[80]

The 1911 railway strike had been preceded by widespread and often united action on the part of seamen, dockers, carters, tramwaymen and other workers around the dock areas in support of demands for union recognition and improved pay and conditions. Once again mass action cut across occupational and other divisions within the working class (in Liverpool Catholic and Protestant dockers acted in concert), surprised union leaders by its scale and intensity, and compelled active state intervention. James Hinton has vividly portrayed the character of the transport strikes:

> This was no ordinary strike movement. The spontaneity and breadth of the strikes posed unprecedented problems both for union leaders ... and for the forces of the state. Union leaders ... rushed to formulate demands and to recruit unorganised bodies of strikers. George Askwith, the ubiquitous Board of Trade conciliator, toured the affected areas, grinding out settlements. In Manchester alone he spent five days ... co-ordinating the simultaneous negotiations of eighteen different unions, representing a bewildering variety of workers, all pledged not to go back until the other seventeen were

satisfied. And the longer settlements were delayed the more the strikers took on the character of a general social war.

... Troops were called out in several centres, and Salford was subjected to virtual military occupation. In Liverpool, with a gun boat standing by on the Mersey, two strikers were shot dead by the Army following three days of guerrilla warfare in the streets around the city centre.[81]

The generally successful strikes in transport were followed, in 1912, by a record number of days lost and, in mining, by 'the biggest stoppage the world had yet seen' (Lovell). Nearly 1 million miners quit work in support of a minimum wage. After five weeks the government resolved the dispute by rushing through minimum wage legislation. 1912 also saw renewed conflict in the London docks and a lockout in Lancashire weaving against weavers' demands for an industry-wide closed shop.[82]

In 1913 the number of recorded strikes reached a record level and union membership, especially among the unskilled, continued to soar. The unorganised metal trades of the Midlands were swept by a 'prairie fire' strike in which women played an important part. Dockers, railway-men and the miners formed the Triple Alliance to offer solidarity and mutual support. In London busmen and building workers were involved in industrial action. And in Dublin James Larkin led an eight-month transport strike. 'It seems probable', concludes Hinton, 'that, but for the outbreak of war, the strike wave would have continued into 1915'.[83]

The remarkable upsurge of agitation between 1910 and 1914 merits several comments. We must first observe the massive increase in trade-union membership, from some 2.5 million in 1910 to just over 4 million by 1914. Second, these years witnessed the second and far more durable phase of 'new unionism'. Thus, while the established unions in the crafts, in coal and in cotton did show gains between 1910 and 1914, by far the most significant and spectacular advances were registered by the 'new unions' among the unorganised and those in weakly unionised sectors. Transport and 'general labour' groups had, observes Hyman, come to organise well in excess of 1 million members by 1914 (a figure approaching 30 per cent of the total number of trade unionists). And by 1920 the 'new unions' would rival the strength of the combined forces of cotton, coal and the crafts.

The distribution of 'new unionist' forces in this pre-war phase showed significant differences from the 1888–91 period. Dockers and seamen were heavily involved in both periods of upsurge. But by 1912 railway workers stood at the very centre of 'labour unrest'. Furthermore, as conclusively demonstrated by Hyman, the 'new' unionism acquired a substantial base in manufacturing industries which had been barely touched by the earlier agitation. The Workers' Union, active in manufacturing, and especially among the semi-skilled in engineering, showed a dramatic rise in membership, from 4,500 in 1910 to 143,000 in 1914. By 1919 the Workers' Union constituted the largest single trade union in the country with 495,000 members. Women trade unionists were also drawn from manufacturing and the service sector to a much greater extent than previously. By 1914 some 9 per cent of women workers were trade unionists.[84]

A minority of participants in the 'labour unrest' were, as argued by Price, resisting attempts by employers and union officials to impose greater constraints upon craft-worker autonomy at the point of production. But the overriding goals of the vast majority of (non-skilled) participants were trade-union recognition combined with improved pay and conditions. Such demands cannot, however, be satisfactorily couched within a narrow 'industrial relations' framework of analysis. In pursuing their goals railway workers, labourers and the semi-skilled were obliged to confront intransigent and outraged employers, luke-warm trade-union officials anxious to institutionalise matters within established and accepted channels, and, often, suspicious and hostile government officials, policemen and even troops. In such a context, the established 'rules of the game' – piecemeal advancement by means of institutionalised collective bargaining on the part of representatives of workers and employers – were not of central relevance or importance. Government officials, such as Askwith, frantically attempted to impose institutionalised structures on movements which threatened to, and at times did, get 'out of hand'. But neither Askwith nor the trade-union officialdom was particularly successful in putting the lid on this mass insurgency. Our third comment relates, therefore, to the largely unofficial, spontaneous and insurgent nature of the 'labour' unrest.

To argue in this way is not, however, to suggest either that the 'unrest' was revolutionary or that Britain was on the verge of revolution in 1914. As suggested by Holton, syndicalists (complete with their support for revolutionary industrial unionism and workers' control) were active in South Wales, Liverpool and elsewhere, and the notion of militant, direct action did enjoy mass appeal. But practices which could, in part, be associated with syndicalism and syndicalist leadership, did not signify mass support for the ideology of syndicalism. Rather economic grievances both inside and outside the workplace, combined with the heightened self-confidence and collective awareness borne of a tight labour market and more regular and secure employment, and the occupational and class-based solidarities engendered by struggle and an increasingly similar way of life, constituted the deep sources of worker militancy.[85]

The Irish crisis, the women's suffrage agitation, and the budgetary crisis with the House of Lords all added to the conflicts and drama of Edwardian Britain. But events do not bear out Dangerfield's thesis that the outbreak of the war averted a revolutionary crisis. Large numbers of workers had turned to mass action in an effort to rectify their manifold grievances. But of central importance was the fact that mass insurgency had *worked*. By 1914 the primary goal of railway workers and hundreds of thousands of other 'new' unionists – union recognition – had largely been secured. The attainment of this goal did not mean that workers had suddenly become incorporated and pacified. The 1914–18 and immediate post-war periods would witness the continued dialectic of accelerated union recognition and institutionalised collective bargaining *combined with* fierce industrial and class conflicts and popular plans for social reconstruction. But the more successful advances made by mass unionism in Britain, as compared with the United States, increasingly served to strengthen the forces of 'labourism' (albeit often of a militant kind) rather than revolutionary socialism among the organised non-skilled.[86]

The application of a judicious mixture of coercion and conciliation by the state also worked against the development of a revolutionary crisis. As demonstrated in Chapter 1, the British state had long since sought to recognise 'responsible' trade unionism and to promote conciliation and arbitration. The state did not, however, generally look with favour upon mass strike action, especially when conducted by the non-skilled, influenced by revolutionary socialists and syndicalists, and liable to result in 'riot'. Troops had been used during the 1911 transport strikes and on various other occasions. The government had, however, backed down in the face of mass railway worker solidarity and determination, and had quickly sought to appease the miners in 1912. Askwith, the government's troubleshooter, redoubled his efforts at mediation, conciliation and the institutionalisation of conflict, and managed to convince many trade unionists of the 'fairness' of the government's intentions and actions.

Finally, there existed fears and differences of opinion rather than panic and irreconcilable splits within the ruling class. The latter was confronted by small and relatively weak revolutionary organisations. And trade-union strength was still limited. As Hyman has usefully reminded us, 'despite the extent of the prewar militancy and the remarkable advances in unionization ... the large majority of British workers did *not* revolt during these turbulent years, and ... by 1914 three-quarters of them remained outside the ranks of trade unionists'.[87]

The War Years 1914–1918

The First World War both stimulated trade-union development and national collective bargaining *and* created conditions in which militancy, radical and, to a lesser extent, revolutionary sentiments flourished, and in which state controls and coercion became more pronounced. The trade-union movement as a whole doubled between 1914 and 1920. The unprecedented demand for labour in the country's first experience of 'total' warfare, shortages of labour in key sectors (especially munitions), and the vastly expanded role of the state in the management of economic and social life (by 1917–18 government controls over prices, profits, imports and exports, areas of production and distribution, and manpower were extensive) all ensured that organised labour, institutionalised collective bargaining and 'planning' would assume major significance in the pursuit of the national interest. Above all, as noted by Schneer, 'the war emphasised labour's indispensability to society: quite simply, it could not be won if workers ceased to support it'.[88] Both Asquith's government and its Coalition successor afforded favourable treatment to labour leaders and their institutions. On a political level, leading figures in the Labour Party were incorporated into the machinery of high-level consultancy and government. On the economic front the most important piece of legislation affecting trade unionism was the Munitions of War Act (1915). This Act necessitated employer recognition of unions and increased union representation and direction in industry via local committees (the latter development was further strengthened as a result of the report of the Whitley Committee in 1917). The 1915 Act also introduced compulsory arbitration as a means of resolving war-time disputes. In turn, arbitration and increased government controls over parts of industry stimulated the growth of industry-wide pay settlements and organisation on the part of unions and employers. And, as a major employer the state directly encouraged the spread of trade unionism. White-collar unionism, for example, benefited greatly from government support for union recognition. And women employed in government work, munitions and elsewhere, made rapid advances, 24 per cent of women workers being organised in trade unions in 1920 in comparison with some 9 per cent in 1914. In overall terms there were 6,533,000 union members in the United Kingdom in 1918 as compared with 4,145,000 in 1914, representing an increase in density from 23 per cent to 35.7 per cent.

The carrot of union advancement and recognition was, however, accompanied by the stick of greater government and employer controls and submission of 'sectional' interests to the 'national good'. Under the Munitions Act strikes and lockouts were declared illegal for the duration of the war and provisions made concerning the introduction of dilution (these provisions, previously laid down in the 'Treasury Agreement' of March 1915, secured union support for dilution on the condition that craft privileges would be restored at the end of the war and that restrictions would be placed upon profits). In addition, the Act created a number of 'controlled establishments' in munitions in which manning levels, working practices and the selection of the workforce would henceforth come under the direct control of the state. Workers could, moreover, be assigned by the Ministry of Munitions to a particular place of work and not be allowed to seek employment elsewhere without the possession of a leaving certificate completed by the employer.

Such restrictions and controls were not lightly endured. In return for union recognition and compulsory arbitration, union leaders did their utmost to secure worker compliance with the provisions of the Munitions Act. However, given their strong position in the labour market, war-time inflation (in which wage rates, if not earnings, usually chased rising prices), and the heightened solidarity and confidence attendant upon full employment and the erosion of wage differentials within their ranks, workers were far from passive. In 1915 the South Wales miners struck successfully in support of a wage increase (and in opposition to the Munitions Act). And in Liverpool, London and elsewhere dockers reacted strongly to the longer hours, speed-up and increased regimentation involved in decasualised war-time production.

It was, however, Clydeside which rapidly became the industrial and political storm centre.[89] In 1915 and 1916 Glasgow and its surrounding areas experienced a series of important struggles and conflicts. There took place unofficial strikes on pay by engineering workers in munitions, strikes for union recognition and the closed shop among traditionally unorganised or weakly organised workers and impressive rent strikes in which women, and especially those women appointed as 'street captains', played a key role. There developed, furthermore, opposition on the part of shipyard workers to the dictatorial powers practised by some employers in relation to leaving certificates (workers being prosecuted, fined and imprisoned following complaints made by employers to Munitions Tribunals), and, most famously, the campaign of the socialists in the Clyde Workers' Committee to resist the government's dilution programme and 'formulate a radical policy of dilution which would secure workers' control' (the strike and the crisis of March 1916 leading to the deportation of CWC leaders).

Government concessions on wages, rents and the issue of leaving certificates did, at various points between 1915 and the end of 1916, induce relative phases of stability on Clydeside. And in the country as a whole the strong spirit of patriotism and the desire to 'pull together' in opposition to 'Kaiserism' undoubtedly placed a brake upon class conflict. But there is no doubt that 'discontent' became a widespread and major problem for Lloyd George and his allies in 1917 and 1918. Profiteering, low wage levels, continued inflation, food shortages, war weariness induced by the stalemate and appalling suffering on the Western front, the multiplication of shop-floor grievances in the face of official trade-union abdication of responsibility (dilution, speed-up, the regimentation of labour and so on), poor housing conditions, and 'industrial conscription' continued, notes Stevenson, 'to provoke unrest, so that strikes continued right up to the last days of the war'.

In 1917, for example, there was a national strike against the termination of the craftsmen's exemption from conscription and the extension of dilution to commercial work. In addition to Clydeside, Manchester and Sheffield became significant centres of the revolutionary Shop Stewards' Movement. The Russian Revolution gave a boost to revolutionary socialism. Anti-war sentiment grew. 'In Glasgow', declares Stevenson, 'there was talk of the creation of a Workers' and Soldiers' Soviet ... and one of the leading Marxist propagandists, John Maclean, was sentenced to five years' hard labour under the Defence of the Realm Act'.[90] Days lost to stoppages in 1917 totalled more than the combined numbers for 1915 and 1916: the total for 1918 was the highest recorded for the war years. The war ended amidst promises of social reform and reconstruction from Lloyd George, and threats of intensified demands from disgruntled workers and returning soldiers. As Cronin has observed:

> by the end of the First World War workers were demanding higher wages, greater control at the workplace, the nationalisation of coal and other industries, and a host of social reforms connected with housing, health and employment. The difficulty was compounded by their taste for 'direct action' in implementing these goals, and their distrust of the political process and independence from labour's formal leadership.[91]

Two major areas of controversy arise from workers' experiences between 1914 and 1918: the nature and extent of protest, militancy and radicalism, with particular reference to the supposedly 'Red' district of Clydeside; and an accurate and precise characterisation of the various responses of the state (largely oppositional and negative-coercive versus supportive and positive-conciliatory) towards official and unofficial labour actions and beliefs.

There is a general consensus among historians that, at least on a national level, 'unrest' was relatively muted during 1914–16 (with some obvious exceptions, such as South Wales mining and parts of engineering). Similarly, there is no doubt that 1917 and 1918 (indeed, the period up to 1921) witnessed mounting social conflict and dissatisfaction among a mass constituency. There is, furthermore, convincing evidence of growing consternation and fear in government and ruling-class circles between 1917 and 1920 (provoked in part by the Russian Revolution, and reflected in Cabinet plans to 'use the full powers of the state' against 'revolutionary activity').[92]

In relation to 'Red Clydeside' there exist sharp polarisations among historians. In opposition to the conventional wisdom of Hinton, McClean and Reid have recently argued against the notion that industrial struggles on the part of engineers and others (against dilution, managerial prerogatives and so forth) played a crucial part in the development of radical and revolutionary socialist politics on Clydeside between 1915 and the early 1920s. McClean and Reid have placed their key emphases upon craft sectionalism (especially in the shipyards) and divisions within the workforce; the rise of Labour, as opposed to revolutionary socialist politics; and the crucial influence of community-based issues and campaigns (especially the Independent Labour Party's campaigns concerning rents, housing and improved welfare and environmental provision via the municipality) rather than workplace-based conflicts upon 'the Rise of Labour' and the decline of Liberalism in Glasgow.

The importance attached by Reid and McLean to community-based issues and the construction of 'municipal socialism' is well taken.[93] Similarly, we must heed their injunction to pay careful attention to the specific and (at times) different chronologies of struggle in the shipyards, munitions factories and communities of Clydeside. But what is lacking from the accounts presented by both Reid and McClean is any real sense of *process* and the *interconnections* between seemingly disparate events. Their accounts are essentially too *compartmentalist* and too restricted in terms of chronological and geographical focus. As the authoritative recent articles by Melling and Foster have demonstrated, there were connections between shipyard workers, engineers, and women and other community-based activists. Their struggles were often linked in terms of leadership, constituency and socialist ideology (the role of the ILP being of central importance). As convincingly argued by Melling, opposition to mushrooming state and employer controls and 'tyrannies' over the lives of working people constituted an important unifying thread between the community and the workplace. The overall level of militancy, its geographical spread (beyond Glasgow's city boundaries) and its persistence (as seen especially in 1919) were, as shown by Foster, much greater than suggested in the revisionist case. And, again as demonstrated by Foster, the links between Labour and revolutionary socialist politics, and the influences of the latter upon the former, were much more pronounced on Clydeside than argued by

McClean. On balance, therefore, the notion of 'Red Clydeside' merits retention.

Debates concerning the nature and role of the war-time state have also been sharply drawn.[94] Hinton's usage of Belloc's notion of the 'Servile State' – to mean a bureaucratic state machinery geared to the interests of private capital, responsive to the wishes of class collaborationist trade-union and Labour leaders, and practising rigid controls and discipline over the mass of workers – has come under particularly strong fire. Reid has drawn attention to the positive gains and experiences of workers and organised labour during the war (in relation to trade-union strength, improved employment and earnings, especially for the non-skilled, and the importance of successful war-time collectivism to the future viability, confidence and mass appeal of Labour's socialism). He has also rightly pointed out that, in response to worker protest, the state was forced to offer concessions on pay, rents, leaving certificates and the overall regimentation of labour. Furthermore, Davidson has clearly shown that administrators were often reluctant to adopt statutory labour regulations (the practice being determined more by labour shortages than ideological preference), and that business interests had less direct and indirect influence upon government departments than claimed by Hinton. We might add that successful pursuit of the war effort constituted the overriding priority of war-time governments. Within such a context attention to the due and 'fair' balance of class and other forces and interests was of major importance: social instability represented a grave threat to the achievement of victory.

Equally, however, we must recognise the strengths of Hinton's case. Hinton is alive to the gains made by official labour during the war, both as a reward for participation in the war effort and the result of class struggle.[95] He is also aware of the complex and contradictory influences upon state policy. And there is no doubt that workers on Clydeside and elsewhere did see the state as a hostile force intent upon undermining their customary controls and defences in the interest of capitalist control in the workplace. The official union leadership was seen to be failing to defend members against the erosion of controls. As Melling has written in relation to Clydeside:

> Craftsmen found their initial bargaining strength removed and their skills jeopardised by a series of state policies in 1915–1916. The clear propensity of the state to underwrite the authority of management and impose conditions (and wages) on the workplace served to openly politicise issues of workplace bargaining... Union officials failed to protect their members against the aggression of the employers during the Munitions controversy and a crisis of confidence spread throughout the Clyde area.[96]

From: Jonathan Zeitlin <jzeitlin@wisc.edu>

The ASE merged with several smaller unions in 1920 to become the Amalgamated Engineering Union (AEU).   It has gone through a series of further mergers since 1967, and as the Amalgamated Engineering and Electrical Union (AEEU) recently joined with the white-collar/technical federation MSF to form Amicus, the UK's largest manufacturing union (with 1.2m members). Here's a brief history of the organization, taken from the Amicus website: The The Amalgamated Society of Engineers (ASE) was formed in 1852. By the beginning of the 20th century it had nearly 90,000 members. A head office was established in Peckham, South London and these premises remained the headquarters of the ASE until the merger with the EETPU in 1992.

In July 1920 the ASE and nine other unions merged to form the Amalgamated Engineering Union (AEU). The demand for armaments during the Second World War led to a rapid expansion of the engineering industry. This involved the widespread employment of women, who were finally admitted to the Union in 1943.

Foundry workers joined the AEU in 1967, followed by draughtsmen and construction engineers. In 1971 the federation became known as the Amalgamated Union of Engineering Workers. The AEEU was formed in 1992 from the merger of the EETPU and the AEU. The EETPU itself was the result of a merger of two unions the ETU (electricians) and the PTU (plumbers). The PTU was originally formed in 1865. This was followed soon after by the formation of the ETU in 1868, after the Amalgamated Society of Engineers refused membership to electricians. The inter-war years saw both unions making important industrial relations inroads, including the signing of the first national agreement on electrical contracting and the strengthening of ties with other building unions through the national wages and conditions council.

The merger of the ETU and the PTU was officially agreed in 1968. Important changes were made before this went ahead to prevent the kind of abuses and ballot rigging of which the ETU Communists were found guilty in 1961 and to ensure that the unions were truly democratic.

In 1971, the Electrical and Engineering Staff Association (EESA) was created as the white-collar section of the union. By 1989 a number of other professional associations had joined the union. They reorganised themselves under an umbrella organisation known as the Federation of Professional Associations. Hope this is helpful. Jonathan Zeitlin

At 11:28 PM 5/3/2004 +0000, you wrote:
<blockquote type=cite class=cite>From: Barbara Allen <allen1861@yahoo.com>

Does any currently existing British trade union consider itself to be
 the successor to or descendant of the Amalgamated Society of Engineers?

 Thanks,
 B. Allen

 =====
 Barbara C. Allen, Ph.D.
 Assistant Professor
 History Department
 La Salle University
 1900 West Olney Avenue
 Philadelphia, PA 1914
 Tel. (215)951-1179
 E-mail: allenb@lasalle.edu or allen1861@yahoo.com</blockquote> <x-sigsep><p></x-sigsep>
Jonathan Zeitlin
Professor of Sociology, Public Affairs, and History
 Director of the European Union Center
 Director-Elect of the Center for World Affairs and the Global Economy (WAGE)
 University of Wisconsin-Madison

 office/mailing address:
 3460 Social Science Building
 1180 Observatory Drive
 Madison WI 53706

 phone numbers:

(608) 262-1131 (3460 Social Science)
(608) 265-8040 (European Union Center)
(608) 255-4564 (home and voice mail)

john revitte

From: H-Net Labor History Discussion List [H-LABOR@H-NET.MSU.EDU] on behalf of
merithew@MAIL.H-NET.MSU.EDU

Sent: Tuesday, May 04, 2004 9:48 PM

From the point of view of the beleaguered minority of shop-floor activists the state appeared to be both servile and extremely hostile![97]

The United States

We shall return to the state and post-war radicalism in Britain in due course. At this juncture we must turn our attention to the major developments in popular protest movements in the United States in the wake of the upsurges of 1877.

Defeated in 1877, workers did not long remain quiescent. During the first half of the 1880s progress was slow. There was a downturn in the economy in 1882 which, although less severe than the depression of 1873–8, lasted until 1885. Given depressed economic conditions and bruised by defeats trade unions revived with great difficulty. But between 1884 and 1886 the United States was to witness another massive upsurge in strike activity and social conflict.

The 'Great Upheaval' 1884–1886

Known as the 'Great Upheaval', the mass insurgency of 1884–6 embraced well over 1 million workers.[98] Laurie notes that between 1880 and 1884 there were approximately 450 work stoppages per annum. They rose in turn from 645 in 1885 to a dramatic level of over 1,400 in 1886–7. And Montgomery informs us that in 1886 there occurred more than 900 strikes concerning wages and 286 in support of the eight-hour day, including city-wide movements in Chicago and Milwaukee. All told, over 690,000 workers were involved in the protests of 1886.[99] Significantly, labour organisations (especially the Knights of Labor formed in 1869, and the trade unions in the Federation of Organized Trades and Labor Unions of 1881) exercised much greater organisational influence and control over the actions of protesters (calling out over half of the strikers in 1886) than had been the case during the insurrectionary events of 1877. But the enhanced influence of trade unionism signalled neither accommodation to the existing order nor social harmony. Far from learning and accepting the 'rules of the (capitalist) game', workers were acquiring (to use Montgomery's phrase) 'the habit of solidarity', as expressed in allegiance to collective organisation, discipline, mutuality and determined opposition to the belligerence and 'unreason' of capital.

The socio-geographical bases of protest were impressive. In 1884–5 women carpet weavers in Philadelphia and New York sustained an industry-wide, eight-months strike against wage cuts. In the process the principle of trade-union membership came to the fore, the women strongly defending their right to belong to the Knights of Labor. Supported by women in shoemaking, the carpet weavers were largely successful in their endeavours. Meanwhile, the railroads were once again becoming both the central focus of industrial conflict and a trigger for more widespread action. 'Beginning in 1883', writes Fink,

> local skirmishes escalated into highly publicized confrontations with railroad financier Jay Gould, a national symbol of new corporate power. Strikes by Knights of Labor telegraphers and railroad shopmen touched off an unprecedented wave of strikes and boycotts that carried on into the renewed depression in 1884–85 and spread to thousands of previously unorganized semiskilled and unskilled laborers, both urban and rural.[100]

Throughout 1884 and 1885 workers, often as members of the rapidly growing Knights of Labor, successfully resisted wage reductions and dismissals on Gould's railway lines. And in 1885 the Knights achieved a highly symbolic victory when they forced Gould, the 'wizard of Wall Street', to honour a union contract. Victory was, however, shortlived. In 1886 Gould determined to crush trade unionism by precipitating a conflict across the Missouri and Texas Pacific lines. The deliberate and completely unjustified dismissal of a union spokesman in Texas provided the trigger for a strike which began in East Texas and rapidly spread across the West. The Great Southwest Strike saw unskilled railway labourers and skilled members of the railway brotherhoods, black and white, stand together for some two months against corporate might.

Ultimately, after a series of battles between strikers and deputies and militiamen, thousands of indictments, hundreds of imprisonments and several deaths, Gould won the day. Indecisive national leadership on the part of the Knights (especially on the part of Terence Powderly, Grand Master Workman, who disliked strikes), combined with ruthless determination on the part of the railroad management and strong state support for the latter, proved decisive. Thus Fink:

> Anxious from the beginning to resolve an unwanted conflict, the harried national leadership of the Knights proved no match for the skills of railroad management... By the beginning of April, state militia had placed Ft. Worth, Texas, and Parsons, Kansas, under martial law. On April 9, deputies fired into an East St. Louis crowd of strikers and killed nine people... Labor's final defeat... left hundreds of union men without jobs and dozens scattered in jails along the railroad route.[101]

In addition to conflicts on the railways in Texas, Kansas, Nebraska, Missouri and Arkansas, 1886 also saw a nationwide campaign to secure the eight-hour day. The campaign was launched by leading figures in the Federation of Organized Trades and Labor Unions. Despite the

cautious attitude displayed by some unions, and the hostility of Powderly to the idea, many workers eagerly formed Eight Hour Leagues in
a bid to attain, by means of direct action, the shortened working day.
The ineffectiveness of eight-hours legislation enacted (mainly) during
the 1860s, and successful strikes for reduced hours among building
workers in 1884, enhanced the mass appeal of direct action.

In total approximately 340,000 workers quit work in support of the
eight-hour day on 1 May 1886. 'Enthusiasm ran so high', comments
Laurie, 'that thousands of workers jumped the gun and in mid-April
petitioned employers for eight hours'.[102] Some 80,000 marched in the
May Day procession in Chicago, and there were further huge demonstrations of support in New York, San Francisco, Milwaukee and countless other industrial centres. Cincinnati experienced, 'the most dramatic
working-class protest of the nineteenth century'. In a mirror-image of
national trends, Cincinnati's May Day strikes were very large, effective,
embraced a wide cross-section of the working class, and centrally
included previously unorganised or weakly organised groups of
workers.[103]

This was a 'new unionist' explosion, American style. In Cincinnati
divisions of race, skill, gender and ethnicity were broken down. Irish,
German and black workers created a Central Labour Union. Single
factory-based or industrywide unions were brought into being. The first
weeks of May saw massive rallies and demonstrations in downtown
Cincinnati in support of the eight-hour day, union recognition and wage
increases. The language of popular republicanism was, observes Ross,
increasingly imbued with class-based meanings and demands. Workers
brought up and working in industrial contexts were demanding not a
return to a small producer past, but 'fairness' and 'republican justice'
within the framework of an advanced market economy in which
repeated 'tyrannies' on the part of capital were clearly perceived and
opposed. 'Under the impact of May', concludes Ross, 'a new sense of
class was forged within the working community'.

In Cincinnati and elsewhere the appeal of reduced hours of work
and increased pay proved immensely popular to workers who had suffered from a decade of almost unrelieved depression. As in the case of
Britain in the late 1880s, the lifting of the depression and the tightened
labour market provided important spurs to mass action in the United
States. But, as in the British case, trade-cycle analysis constitutes, in
itself, insufficient explanation. The increased scale of economic operations, especially the growing prominence of factory production, the
rise in demand for non-skilled factory workers, the latter's experiences
in the benefits of collective action (their acquisition of 'the habit of
solidarity'), the widespread opposition to the new corporate America,

the snowball effects of successful action, and, last but not least, the organisational and leadership vehicle provided by the Knights of Labor, were all important influences upon the mass explosion of 1884–6. Finally, success bred confidence, solidarity and imitation. Despite the disaster of Haymarket (when a bomb was thrown at a meeting in Chicago, with fatal consequences for policemen and anarchists), the campaigns and strikes of 1886 were generally successful. In Cincinnati most factory workers obtained shorter hours and increased wages. And in the country as a whole some 185,000 won a reduced working day.

The Knights of Labor

At the very centre of the 'Great Upheaval' stood the Noble and Holy Order of the Knights of Labor. Dismissed by many 'old' labour historians as peripheral to the innate 'job consciousness' of American workers, the Knights have been securely rescued from the condescension of posterity by Leon Fink, Susan Levine, Richard Oestreicher and other 'new' labour historians.[104]

We now know that the Knights constituted the most important labour organisation in nineteenth-century America. The 'first mass organisation of the American working class' (Fink), the Knights of Labor certainly touched and influenced the lives of more workers than would the AFL in its pre-1900 years. The beginnings were inauspicious. Founded as a secret society by Philadelphia garment workers in 1869, the Knights grew to only 6,000 members in 1877 (their strength being concentrated among coal miners in Pennsylvania). In 1878 the organisation became national in character with national officers assuming authority in relation to the trade and mixed local and district assemblies (despite the opposition of the Knights to craft sectionalism and élitism, most of the local assemblies were made up of members of one trade rather than of several trades and occupations). By 1880 there were just under 30,000 members, and in the early-mid 1880s skilled and craft workers were heavily attracted to the Knights. Dual membership of the Knights and the forerunner of the AFL, the Federation of Organized Trades and Labor Unions, was, as seen in the case of Samuel Gompers and others, common. It was during the explosions of 1884 to 1886 that the Order mushroomed. By the middle of 1886 membership had reached the astounding figure of 750,000, an increase of some 600,000 in a year. This meteoric rise was, however, to be followed by a precipitous fall. 'By the early 1890s', notes Laurie, 'membership cards were collectors' items and lodge halls gathered dust'. However, between 2 and 3 million people had come within the embrace of the Order between the 1870s and

1890s, and 'no other movement had such an impact on the American working class'.[105]

The Knights merit investigation from a number of perspectives. But we must limit ourselves in this chapter to a consideration of the constituency, ideology and rise and decline of the Order (the Knights and politics will be considered in Chapter 3).

The Knights set out to organise the 'producing masses' in pursuit of a wide-ranging reform of American society by means of education (personal, moral and political), co-operative production and land settlement. Somewhat ironically in terms of the events of 1884–6, important leaders of the Knights, especially in the person of Grand Master Workman Terence Powderly, were hostile towards strikes (much preferring arbitration as a means of settling disputes) and lukewarm towards trade unionism, especially of a craft and skilled type. Powderly associated the latter with sectionalism, divisiveness and élitism within the working class, and saw trade unionism as a purely defensive and ameliorative force. The Knights were interested in social transformation rather than defensive craft sectionalism. But the leadership of the Order did sanction strikes in cases of worker victimisation or employer refusals of arbitration. And, as Montgomery, wryly notes, these two categories 'allowed hundreds of strikes to be waged under the Order's auspices'. In practice, the Knights were also very actively involved in trade unionism in order to counteract the 'unreasonable' actions of 'dishonourable' employers.

The Knights were catholic in their appeal. Limits and boundaries were drawn primarily in 'moral-experiential' rather than in structured and abstract economic terms. No *necessary* conflict was perceived between labour and capital, and, as with radicals in the NLU, 'fair' profit was perceived as the perfectly legitimate reward for industry and guidance. 'Honest producers', as the backbone of the nation, could include manufacturers as well as workers, merchants as well as small shopkeepers. As Fink has written:

> For the Knights the concept of the producing classes indicated an ultimate social division that they perceived in the world around them. Only those associated with idleness (bankers, speculators), corruption (lawyers, liquor dealers, gamblers) or social parasitism (all of the above) were categorically excluded from membership in the Order. Other social strata such as local merchants and manufacturers were judged by their individual acts, not by any inherent structural antagonism to the workers' movement. Those who showed respect for the dignity of labor (i.e., who sold union-made goods or employed union workers at union conditions) were welcomed into the Order. Those who denigrated the laborer or his product laid themselves open to the righteous wrath of the boycott or strike.[106]

As the reader will appreciate, in their emphases upon lived experience and customary morality as setting the boundaries of the social and ideological dimensions of their movement, the Knights had much in common with the Chartists.

In actual fact membership of the Knights (as in the Chartist case) was predominantly working class. The 'middling sort' of shopkeepers, 'honourable' small employers and independent-minded, autonomous craft and skilled artisans were extremely active, especially at the leadership level. Skilled workers experiencing the adverse effects of capitalist transformation (especially shoemakers) were prominent, as were coalminers and many other trade unionists who would eventually find a home within the AFL. But the real basis of the Knights successes in 1884–6 was their institutional and ideological appeal to the mass of factory and other non-skilled workers generally lacking strong trade-union traditions. In their eschewal of craft sectionalism and élitism, and in their provision of a broad ideological umbrella which covered a variety of tendencies, groups and individuals the Knights (again very much like the Chartists) constituted a congenial home for virtually all manner of workers. There were limits. Chinese workers were the target of Knights' racial abuse and physical assault. But black workers and women were welcomed. As Susan Levine has demonstrated, the Knights viewed women's labour, both inside and outside the home, as productive. The Order supported women's suffrage, and women in the Order, whilst not challenging the idea of a domestic women's sphere, did insist upon 'full equality with men, including equal pay, equal rights within the organization, and equal respect for their productive work whether in the home or in the factory'.[107] Levine also shows that the Knights' 'labor feminism' attracted large numbers of women from a variety of occupations across the country. In 1887 there were some 65,000 female members of the Order, about 10 per cent of the total membership. Textile workers, followed by shoeworkers, were the most heavily represented occupations. But tobacco workers, domestic servants, housekeepers, farm hands, waitresses and schoolteachers were also members. Most women were organised in separate 'ladies' locals' of the Knights. There were, however, some mixed assemblies of women and men, and in the South white and black male and female Knights occasionally belonged to the same assembly.

The importance attached by the Order to both the workplace and the community, and its emphases upon active citizenship, rights and duties, temperance, self-respect and improvement and 'wholesome' family- and community-based life (the American workers' equivalent of Chartist 'respectability'), further enhanced the importance attached to female members. As important guardians of 'hearth and home', as bearers and instructors of children, and as an assumed 'civilising', 'caring' and 'moderating' influence upon the 'rougher' inclinations of men (especially in relation to drink, brawling and gambling), women thus stood at the very forefront of the Knights' moral crusade against personal and corporate greed, corruption, acquisitive individualism, and lack of conscience and responsibility. But 'labour's true woman' was not confined to the domestic sphere. As Levine concludes:

> Rather than providing an isolated refuge from the world of work, labor's true woman engaged in productive toil and participated in a class movement. The notion of equal rights modified Victorian ideals of domesticity and allowed working-class women an expanded area of action.[108]

In practice male Knights of Labor sometimes found great difficulty in accepting women as equals both inside and outside the workplace. But the expanded vision of the Knights in relation to gender-based issues stands in marked contrast to the narrow and constricting notions of female domesticity and 'separate spheres' so prevalent in mid-Victorian labour movement circles on both sides of the Atlantic.

Concentrated mainly in unskilled jobs, black workers in both the North and South were also welcomed into the Order.[109] 'Powderly genuinely believed in racial brotherhood', notes Laurie, 'and unlike the chieftains of the NLU who had headed a loose federation of trades, he could get compliance with his orders'. The cause of trade unionism prospered for the first time among large numbers of blacks during the 1880s, especially during the 'Great Upheaval', and the Knights of Labor was by and large the institutional beneficiary. The New Orleans docks were 'a stronghold of bi-racial unionism' (Montgomery), and black tobacco workers and iron workers (Richmond) and construction workers (in many parts of the South) were active in union matters. There was also an upsurge of activity among blacks in the North. Black coalminers in both North and South would be welcomed into the young United Mine Workers (by 1900 there would be 20,000 blacks in the UMW).[110] The Knights' emphasis upon land reform, their evangelism and 'associationalist idealism' (Fink), rooted in self-help and respectability, also nicely meshed with elements of black popular culture. The results were truly spectacular and unprecedented. Although black and white Knights tended to form separate assemblies, they joined together in a common movement. By the summer of 1886 some 60,000 blacks had joined the Knights, almost 10 per cent of the total membership. 'No labour movement had ever claimed such a prominent black presence', declares Laurie, 'and none would until the coming of the Congress of Industrial Organizations (CIO) in the 1930s'.

In sum, committed to the organisation of the producing classes, the Knights nevertheless constituted the largest *working class* and 'new unionist' movement in nineteenth-century American history. Borderline occupations were present. But the middle class proper (especially in urban areas) recoiled from the 'revolting masses' and accordingly were barely involved in the Order.

A number of experiential grievances underpinned the growth of the Knights. The adverse effects of capitalist industrialisation upon autonomous craftsmen, the desires of the non-skilled for improved conditions and union recognition, the widespread unease concerning the rise of 'unrepublican' corporate America, the hardening of European-style class divisions, the partiality of the law and the growing influence of corporate power and corruption upon a supposedly neutral state, were all factors of central importance. As Fink has observed, 'The permanency of wage labor, the physical and mental exhaustion inflicted by the factory system, and the arrogant exercise of power by the owners of capital threatened the rational and progressive march of history'. Declaring 'an inevitable and irresistible conflict between the wage-system of labor and republican system of government', the Knights sought to arrest and reverse, 'the recent alarming development and aggression of aggregated wealth' and the consequent 'pauperization and hopeless degradation of the toiling masses'.[111]

Alarming developments necessitated root and branch remedial and transformative action. Trade unions were in practice supported as necessary defences against the monstrous acts of capital and as schools of collective solidarity. But the attainment of true republican independence, balance and harmony demanded far more. Education would reawaken Americans as to their just rights and obligations, co-operatives would restore independence, end 'wage-slavery' and promote harmony between labour and capital, land settlement would strengthen democracy, the nationalisation of the railways and telegraphs would strike at the heart of corporate power, and customary morality would promote greater mutuality, understanding, co-operation and civic mindedness. As in the cases of many nineteenth-century popular movements (one thinks immediately of Chartism), the appeal to customary 'moral' norms and values served both to legitimise and 'root' the actions of the Knights and to provide a sharp indictment of prevailing practices and relationships. Contrary to the wisdom of the 'old' labour history, the Knights did not seek to turn the clock back to a mythical pre-industrial golden age. Rather, they accepted industrialisation and technological change, but were opposed the forms and practices which were increasingly coming to characterise corporate America. As in the Chartist case, 'custom' provided, in a period of rapid change, a very radical tool and an important ingredient in the development of class consciousness.

The termination of 'wage slavery' and the restoration of 'true' republican practices were not, however, synonymous with revolutionary class consciousness of a socialist kind. All historians of the movement agree that the majority of Knights were opposed to the *excesses* of capital rather than capitalism itself. 'Fair' profits, as noted earlier, were welcomed and a certain amount of competition was deemed to be healthy. Furthermore, the Knights, as excellently demonstrated by Fink, did not welcome a more activist role for the state. Centralised and bureaucratic government was associated with despotic power. Nationalisation of basic industries (apart from 'natural' monopolies) was not welcomed. State socialism was frequently associated with denial of individual initiative and freedom. Much like the Chartists, the Knights wished government to ensure 'equal rights', 'balance' and 'due reward' for all deserving citizens, but not to go beyond this minimalist role. Ultimate salvation was to be achieved by individuals and groups operating freely in the sphere of civil society, by the means of a pervasive spirit of 'associationalist idealism' rather than under the auspices and control of 'big brother'.[112]

Whilst not revolutionary socialists, the Knights did nevertheless offer a 'producerist' critique of American society in which class played an important part. In attacking capitalist society as it actually presented itself, the Knights did, of course, enter into fierce conflicts with real capitalists. And in the course of such conflicts, and particularly during the struggles between 1884 and 1886, many Knights came to see corporate capitalism as constituting a new and hostile force, rooted in conscious agency and patterned structure (maximisation of profits, unbridled individualism and competition, ruthless opposition to trade unionism, and unashamed exploitation of workers). As we observed in relation to Chartism, the 'dishonourable' employers were perceived to be achieving an obnoxious dominance within economic and political life, and had certainly forfeited the right to be counted among the morally upright 'producers'.

In pursuing a more regulated, harmonious, civilised, democratic, equitable and co-operative/collective version of a market-based society, both the Chartists and the Knights acquired the habits and consciousness of class. The latter was manifested in widespread articulated hostility to the thoughts and actions of employers, and in the creation of independent and wide, class-based constituencies and practices which went far beyond the limits of craft sectionalism. The language of class exploitation and conflict continued to be expressed within a largely 'producerist' shell. But, as Palmer has recently noted,[113] the languages of both class *and socialism* acquired great force during the 1880s. In Detroit and elsewhere, many socialists were in fact active members of the Knights. In general terms there existed a fluidity and an overlap of personnel and ideologies within the various strands of 'Labour' and an overarching sense of class separation and conflict.[114] In many respectable circles Labour had become the great problem and fear of the day, and middle-class America resorted to a mixture of coercion and concession in order to effectively banish the Knights and the 'Great Upheaval' to an unwanted past.

At the height of their popularity in 1886, the Knights nevertheless experienced severe problems in sustaining their mass appeal. There were important experiments in independent labour politics between 1886 and 1888; and in the late 1880s and early 1890s alliances with agrarian radicals in the Alliances and Populism and with the American Railway Union bolstered membership levels. But by the mid 1890s the Order could not compete with the ascendant AFL. Employers counterattacked strongly in the wake of the defeated Southwest strike. Powderly's half-hearted attitude towards the issue of the eight-hour day, his betrayal of the Southwest strikers, and his hostile attitudes to the anarchists arrested and hanged after the Haymarket incident (much of the labour movement supporting Parsons and his comrades on the grounds of false arrest and conviction) fuelled disillusionment and divisions. And recurrent conflicts between the Knights and the national unions were detrimental to the continued health of the Order.[115]

The diminished appeal of the Knights constituted a severe blow to broad reforming and radical impulses within American society. As noted in Chapter 1, labour's moral universe was fragmented and its cohesion undermined by the emergence of fiercely competing philosophies and groups. Most prominent would be the AFL, increasingly suspicious, under Gomper's directing hand, of both militant conflict of the 1884–6 variety and of radical, transformative socio-political strategies. Reacting strongly to the Knights' attempts to oppose the principle of trade-union autonomy and to mix trade unionism and independent labour or socialist politics, Gompers and his allies increasingly settled for what Leon Fink has termed a 'self-protecting incrementalism', more defensive, more cautious and limited, more exclusive and far more accommodating than the broad democratic vision of the Knights.[116]

Rural Radicalism

We must not, however, run ahead of our story. Radicalism suffered setbacks in the late 1880s, but it was far from dead. Rather its geographical focus shifted from the urban North to the rural South and West. In episodes all too often neglected by labour historians, millions of farmers, croppers, labourers and tenants were to mount, in the Alliances and Populism, a further challenge to the rise of corporate America.[117]

As demonstrated earlier in this chapter, the post-bellum decades witnessed mounting agrarian protests in the South and West around a variety of issues. Much as some economic historians might doubt the extent of American farmers' absolute and relative financial impoverishment between the 1870s and the mid 1890s,[118] there is absolutely no question as to the depth and scale of rural 'unrest', the reality and validity of the grievances articulated, and the wide-ranging nature of the solutions proposed. An influential approach within economic history continues to see farmers as simple-minded victims of fluctuations in world markets (especially for wheat), largely unaware of the 'true' causes of their plight and given to largely unfounded conspiracy theories against speculators, railroads, creditors, banks and middlemen in general. But this approach erects a crude positivist model of 'false consciousness' around the notions of objective ('true') economic structure and the subjective ('flawed') consciousness of historical actors.[119] It unjustly belittles the intellects and 'true' perceptions and actions of the 'plain people'.

Interest rates, freight charges and general railroad rates, selling prices for agricultural produce, the price of manufactured goods, fluctuations in supply and demand (especially during the generally deflationary 1870s to 1890s), and wage levels were, as emphasised by Douglas North and other economic historians, of crucial daily concern to rural producers. However, an unduly quantitative-economic approach to the issue of rural protest obscures the human relationships and values which lie behind economic categories and measures of 'the quality of life'. Furthermore, such human relationships cannot, as we have repeatedly observed, be properly defined and understood in purely economic terms. Questions of power, customs, needs and expectations are also centrally involved. Post-bellum rural protest revolved around living standards and much more. We have already seen that the consolidation of the crop lien system, chronic indebtedness, the new-found insecurities and dependencies of the extended and (especially in the cases of cotton and wheat) narrowed market, enclosure and more keenly observed property rights, and growing tenancy and waged labour constituted some of the most potent sources of protest.

The scholarship of Hahn, Goodwyn and Woodward has extended our focus into the 1880s and 1890s and sharpened our awareness of continued, indeed heightened, clashes between customary and fully fledged market values, between notions of 'fairness' and unrestrained self-interest. As seen in reference to some members of the family of Tom

Watson, the charismatic Alliance member and Populist from Georgia, *downward* social mobility and poverty was the lot of many southern farmers. (Watson's father moved from 'bepillared mansion' befitting a solid member of the southern squirearchy, to 'miserable shanty', and William, his younger brother, was forced to pursue 'a wretched existence' as a share cropper.) There was, furthermore, profound opposition on the part of 'the plain people' to the monopolisation, commercialisation and alleged corruption of America by financiers and corporate interests. Country people longed for a more democratic, secure and prosperous future. And the impressive 'movement culture' of radical newspapers, lectures, picnics, rallies, wagon trains and summer encampments which developed among members of the National Farmers Alliance stimulated solidarity, self-respect and collective confidence.

It was out of such grievances, practices and aspirations that protest developed its mass character and impressive socio-geographic spread. Goodwyn records that:

> The agrarian revolt first stirred on the Southern frontier, then swept eastward across Texas and the other states of the Old Confederacy and thence to the Western Plains. The gathering of democratic momentum required almost fifteen years – seven within a tier of counties along the Texas farming frontier, three more to cover the rest of the state, and another five to envelop the South and West.[120]

During the years from the late 1870s to the late 1880s Texas (in particular), Alabama, piedmont Georgia and Kansas became strongholds of agrarian radicalism as expressed in the formation of rural dwellers' co-operative organisations or Alliances. In terms of the South, Alliance members were less numerous in South Carolina, Mississippi and the Black Belt in general. But, as Woodward observes, the Alliance movement had attracted a membership of 3 million in the South alone by 1890. And radicalism had developed a wildfire momentum. Thus Woodward:

> In March, 1887, two organizers from Texas entered the virgin territory of Georgia, touched a match to the tinder of discontent, and almost immediately the state was aflame. Hundreds of 'lodges' sprang into existence, each with its 'lecturer'; organizers rode all over the state; dozens of papers and journals were founded, or changed their tone and adopted the new slogans; great quantities of reform literature were distributed. In less than three years 134 out of 137 counties in the state sent delegates to the state convention; well over 2,000 lodges were established with a membership of more than 100,000.

Georgia's experience constituted a single instance of what was rapidly becoming 'one of the most amazing feats of organization in American history'.[121]

'In general', notes Woodward, 'the Southern Populists were mainly the agrarian masses, including tenant, small landowner, and a surprising number of large landowners, together with the industrial proletariat'. Southern Alliance members and Populists variously described themselves as, 'the peasantry of America', 'the yearning, upward tendency of the middle and lower classes', the 'producing classes' and even the 'working class'.[122] Poor white landowning dirt farmers often constituted the core of southern membership. But of great significance was the embrace held out to croppers and labourers, and especially black workers of these descriptions. Alliance members and Populists called for a united front between black and white against the divisive influences of racism and the Democratic and Republican political machines of the South, and in opposition to the works of 'financial despotism' and capitalist oppression in general. Blacks faced, of course, formidable obstacles to successful and open public organisation. But the crop lien system sorely afflicted black tenants, and in 1888 the Colored Farmers' National Alliance and Cooperative Union came into being. Despite the opposition of white Bourbons and black Republicans (fearing the far-reaching consequences of black and white industrial and political alliance), the Colored Alliance had recruited approximately 250,000 members by 1890.[123]

Beyond the South the agrarian revolt had, by 1890, demonstrated promising growth in Missouri, Kansas, Colorado and the Dakotas. Kansas in particular would become a great source of strength, leading the Alliance to the People's Party in 1892 (see Chapter 3). In Nebraska, Iowa and Minnesota a 'shadow movement' of Populism emerged, but 'without organic roots in the Alliance network and its political culture'.[124] Populism embodied the third-party hopes of millions of rural dwellers *and* urban workers. In Illinois, Ohio, Massachusetts and under the auspices of the Knights of Labor and the American Railway Union, Labor Populism enjoyed significant support. And throughout the South the white supremacist Democratic Party fought for its very life against Populist insurgency.

Collective economic and cultural self-help and democratic practice underlay the mass appeals of the Alliance movement and its Populist successor. During the 1880s farmers and others created an extensive network of co-ops or Alliance stores which, observes Gavin Wright, 'offered members discounts and reasonably priced credit on supplies, and the advantages of cooperative marketing of the cotton crop'.[125] The massive and, for a time at least, highly successful Texas Alliance Exchange in Dallas illustrated the benefits to be derived from bulk purchasing and selling, and promoted the cause well beyond Texas. But it was Macune's sub-treasury plan, outlined at the St Louis convention of 1889, which offered a revolutionary *national* plan to strike at the very heart of the high-interest, crop-mortgage system and to enable farmers to exert a greater measure of control over the timing of the sale and the price of the crop.

Under the sub-treasury scheme federal warehouses, erected in the nation's main agricultural counties, would constitute 'sub-treasuries' for the deposit and store of crops. Farmers would be allowed to sell their crops at the most advantageous moment, borrow up to 80 per cent of the local market price upon storage, and to pay interest to the government at 2 per cent per year, plus small charges for storage, insurance and grading. At a stroke the plan would obliterate the existing system of credit (especially in the South) and dependency upon the middleman or furnishing merchant, establish a governmental source of the money needed to advance against crops at low rates of interest, and promote greater price stability and overall security and control for the farmer. In addition to planks in support of Greenbackism (the abolition of the national banks and the substitution of legal tender treasury notes for national bank notes), government ownership of the means of communication and transportation, the free coinage of silver, abolition of 'alien land ownership', equitable taxation, and government economy, the sub-treasury plan constituted the basis of the programmes of the 1890 Alliance movement and Populism.[126]

The promise of these movements was not, however, to be fulfilled. By 1890 lack of access to low-cost credit and the vigorous opposition of banks, merchants and capital in general had reduced many of the co-operative exchanges to financial ruin. Populism maintained radical hopes between 1892 and 1894. But subsequent serious disagreements concerning the relative merits of continued third-party action on the basis of the broad Omaha Platform of 1892 (itself largely a re-statement of the 1889 St Louis programme) versus 'fusion' with the Democrats on a narrow 'free-silver' platform, and the Populists' eventual support for the Democrat, William Jennings Bryan, in the 1896 presidential election signalled the end of the mass agrarian revolt. Tom Watson waged a hopeless presidential campaign in 1908 on behalf of the diehard independent Populists. But Watson's anger at 'fusionist betrayals' and Democratic intimidation and coercion of southern Populists was subsequently translated into the vicious scapegoating of blacks, Catholics and Jews for national popular ills. Others did, however, move in very different directions. 'If the agrarian revolt was over in 1896', writes Montgomery, 'the march of these workingclass voters through Populism into the

Social Democracy of America and later the Socialist Party had only begun'.[127] (See Chapter 3 for the political aspects of agrarian protest).

Mass agrarian radicalism had thus fallen victim to internal divisions, the manoeuvrings of the mainstream parties (especially the Democrats), and the concentrated opposition of the forces of capital. In addition, internal contradictions between blacks and whites and landowning and non-landowning Alliance members had proved difficult to contain. Landless labourers and many sharecroppers had no first legal title to the crop grown and consequently enjoyed no substantial interest in the sub-treasury plan. The demands of wage labourers were, furthermore, sometimes in conflict with the interests of their Alliance employers. Thus, when in 1891 the Colored Farmers' Alliance announced its intention to call a general strike of black cotton pickers in support of a wage increase opposition was immediately forthcoming from the *Progressive Farmer*, the paper of the president of the white National Alliance. According to the paper, the pickers were attempting, 'to better their condition at the expense of their white brethren. Reforms should not be in the interest of one portion of our farmers at the expense of the other'.[128] More generally racist demagoguery and the caution of black Republicans increasingly undermined the viability of independent and inter-racial third-party politics in the South. In the aftermath of agrarian revolt southern blacks, and indeed many poor whites, were disfranchised and 'Jim Crow' legislation (enforcing segregation in education, leisure, marriage and many other areas of life) became the norm. A racist and class-based backlash returned power firmly into the hands of the white minority of the plantation districts.[129]

Economic factors also played their part in radicalism's demise. Attention has already been drawn to the problems faced by co-operatives in the pre-1896 years in securing cheap credit, aid from banks and merchants, and in coping with falling prices. In the post-1898 period increased world demand and rising prices, combined with an easing of the credit situation and slowed rates of tenancy, brought greater levels of stability, security and even prosperity for white farmers.[130] By 1896 Populism was, of course, a largely spent force: economic recovery was very much the successor to, rather than the central cause of, agrarian radicalism's decline.

One final issue remains. Often regarded as the embodiments of rural 'producerism', did the Alliance and Populist movements offer a class-based position within and alongside their familiar 'anti-monopoly' stance? At first sight the question might appear to be perverse. We have observed that these movements appealed to a wide range of country people rather than to rural proletarians alone (or as the core group in an alliance with other social forces), that there existed certain divisions and contradictions within radicalism's constituency, and that ultimately 'fusionist' sentiments triumphed over third-party politics. We should also carefully heed Woodward's comment on the Southern Populists that (p. 217), 'Individualist and middle-class in tradition and aspiration, they accepted the basic capitalistic system.'

This was, however, by no means the complete story. As Woodward himself demonstrates, the *experiences* of poverty, dependency and the opposition of the forces of capital to their plight, moved many Alliance and Populist members in distinctly collective, class-based ways. 'Obviously the Populist attack did not strike at the whole system of capitalist exploitation, as did socialism', observes Woodward (p. 219), 'but in its time and section the Populist party formed the vanguard against the advancing capitalist plutocracy'. As in the case of the Knights, the enemy was not, therefore, capitalism in the abstract, but actually existing corporate capitalism. In fighting for their rights, in the process of *struggle*, farmers and others came to embrace in their 'movement culture' the practices of mutualism, mass collective self-help, and direct democracy which were antithetical to bourgeois acquisitive individualism. They did not wish for the most part to transform society in a socialist direction (Norman Pollack had tended to overstate the socialist inclinations of Populism), but, like the Knights, they did wish to create a more regulated, civilised, co-operative, equitable and harmonious market order.

It is also important to note that many agrarian radicals identified themselves as (to quote Montgomery) 'labor' and 'their movement as one of the "industrial classes" ' rather than as one of businessmen. The language of producerist populism *and* of class and perceived class interests and conflict abounded. Thus Watson in 1891:

> 'We are the people. We have created the corporations. They are our legal off-spring. Shall it be said that the servant is above the master, or the child above the father?' . . . 'Will you Knights of Labor help the farmers and laborers in the field of their fight on the common enemy?' What of this cry of 'class legislation'? 'What has this country ever had but class legislation? The second law Congress ever passed was aimed to build up commerce and manufactures at the expense of agriculture. Our statute books are filled with legislation in behalf of capital, at the expense of labor . . . If we must have class legislation . . . what class is more entitled to it than the largest class – the working class?'[131]

Similar sentiments abounded in both the South and West. Class was being employed in an elastic yet undeniable manner. This fact may not meet the test of admission set by post-structuralists and others scanning historical texts for examples of 'true' articulations of class. But the problem lies far less with the class-based expressions of real historical subjects than with the unduly formalistic, narrow and de-contextualised procedures of post-structuralist methodology. Agrarian radicals were presenting a sharp critique of existing social relationships and values, and class was an integral part of that critique.

The constituency of the Alliances and Populism also reflected the influence of class. It is highly significant that bonds of solidarity were offered not only to blacks and non-property-owning elements within the countryside, but also to urban-based workers and their labour organisations. Thus verbal and material support was provided to those involved in the Southwest strike of 1886, to the Knights of Labor, to the Homestead strikers of 1892, to miners and to countless others involved in disputes with 'despotic capital'. (Of equal significance was the fact that Gompers and some of the more 'hard-headed' trade unionists rejected the Populists as constituting a *petit bourgeois* diversion from the trade-union struggle).[132] And structural divisions within the 'producing masses' of the countryside should be set against *common* experiences and articulations of oppression. Woodward's comments in relation to the southern Populists are, once again, highly instructive:

> They were united by their resentment of the crushing oppression of capitalist finance and industrialism. Watson himself recognized the complexity of his ranks. 'There is a gradation in servitude', he said. The laborer was the first to feel the lash, the cropper next, the tenant next, and the landlord next – in Watson's hierarchy of serfdom. 'But', he added, 'the livery of the serf is there all the same'. This livery, he believed, would become the uniform of the army that he led against its oppressors.[133]

And it *was* the common sense of oppression which led multitudes of farm owners and tenants, croppers and labourers, and sections of the urban working class to place their faith in independent third-party politics.

Ideological Conflicts and the Rise of the American Federation of Labor

In many ways the mid 1890s constituted a watershed in the history of popular protest in the United States. By 1897 the transformative visions of the Knights and agrarian radicals had given way to the defensive and limited strategy of Gomper's AFL. In addition, the massive depression from 1893–7, combined with the hostile endeavours of employers, the state and the judiciary, had hit trade unionism hard.

In 1892 black and white workers in New Orleans successfully campaigned for the ten-hour day in a bi-racial general strike. But this outstanding example of labour solidarity was immediately damaged by the conviction of New Orleans unions for violation of the Sherman

Antitrust Act of 1890 (which was directed more at labour unions than big business).[134] During the same year workers suffered a massive and highly significant defeat at Carnegie's Homestead steel works. The twenty-week lockout at Homestead where Carnegie sought to impose a wage reduction and the 'open shop', involved the fortification of the mills by superintendent Henry Clay Frick (who had made his reputation as the anti-union 'Coke King'), the attempted importation of three hundred Pinkerton detectives, the river battle between Pinkertons and workers (in which nine workers and seven guards were killed and a total of sixty wounded), and the surrender of the Pinkertons (who were then forced to run the gauntlet of the line of irate Homesteaders). The July battle of 'Fort Frick' did not, however, bring success to the workers. The subsequent ninety-five days of military occupation of Homestead by 8,000 Pennsylvania National Guardsmen and the arrest and trial of workers on charges of murder, riot and conspiracy for their parts in the July battle (none were convicted) allowed Frick to import strikebreakers and gradually re-open the works. By the end of November non-unionism ruled at Homestead.[135]

The Homestead dispute was of the utmost significance in a number of ways. It demonstrated the capacity of large numbers of workers to do battle with one of the leading employers of the day. It further illustrated the capacity, indeed increased necessity, for co-operation between skilled and non-skilled, native-born and immigrant, and men and women in the face of determined corporate hostility to the very existence of trade unionism. Women played a prominent role in the dispute, being heavily involved in the confrontation with the Pinkertons and in supplying domestic and community-based support to the locked-out men. The Amalgamated Association of Iron and Steel Workers had around 800 members in Homestead, and generally regarded the non-skilled with 'aristocratic' disdain. But some 2,500 non-skilled and non-unionised workers voted to quit work in solidarity with the skilled men. Most crucially, 600 eastern Europeans (generally regarded as 'submissive' and 'docile') actively opposed the company and played their full part in the dispute. The non-skilled viewed the élitist and sectional Amalgamated Association as providing a necessary shield against attempts by management to worsen the *general* conditions of work. Once the lines of the skilled had been breached then all were likely to fall. Herein lay important (and inadequately heeded) lessons for future union structures and strategies in the fight against corporate capital: 'craft' unionism was of limited value in the new corporate world of mass production, de-skilling and Taylorism.

Above all, Homestead demonstrated the formidable powers of corporate capital operating in alliance with the courts and the military. It was the intervention of the National Guardsmen which proved decisive at Homestead. And the military commander, General George Snowden, and Chief Justice Edward Paxson of the Pennsylvania Supreme Court both demonstrated fundamental ideological opposition to the claims of workers and their collective organisations. Snowden declared in his official report, 'Philadelphians can hardly appreciate the actual communism of these people [in Homestead]. They believe the works are their's [sic] quite as much as Carnegie's.' On his visit to Pittsburgh in September 1892 Chief Justice Paxson charged that the members of the union's advisory committee did, 'unlawfully, falsely, maliciously and traitorously compass, imagine and intend to raise and levy war, insurrection and rebellion against the Commonwealth of Pennsylvania'. Their actions had, furthermore, constituted, 'a deliberate attempt by men without authority to control others in the enjoyment of their rights'. As David Montgomery has tersely stated, Paxson's judgement amounted to a 'crisp and firm declaration that workers' control was illegal'.[136]

As we suggested in Chapter 1, the high level, persistence and concerted nature of employer and establishment opposition to trade unionism in the United States are of fundamental importance in explaining the comparative weakness of American trade unionism and formal collective bargaining procedures. If Homestead constituted a stark example of this naked and powerful opposition, then the Pullman Boycott of 1894 amounted to conclusive proof.

In the spring of 1894 wage cuts imposed upon workers at George Pullman's 'palace car' railway carriage workshops outside Chicago precipitated a walk out. Workers had long complained of 'tyrannical' and 'abusive' acts on the part of Pullman's managers and foremen, and the wage cut constituted the final straw. The strikers appealed for a national boycott of Pullman cars which was successfully observed by some 250,000 railway workers. The courts and the federal government then moved to terminate the boycott on the grounds of the disruption of interstate commerce. An injunction ordered the strikers back to work and 12,000 federal troops were despatched to Chicago, the hub of the dispute. Attacks on railroad property and battles between strikers and federal troops and state militia left scores dead and hundreds wounded or injured in Chicago and elsewhere. Eventually, Eugene Debs and other union leaders were arrested and subsequently imprisoned. Debs' appeal for a sympathy strike met with a negative response from Gompers and his allies who issued a call for an immediate and unconditional return to work. The boycott ended in failure.

Many workers were sacked, and the American Railway Union, which had recruited 150,000 members to its industrial unionist cause in less than a year (at a time when the entire AFL peaked at around 275,000 members) was greatly weakened. As in 1877, the cause of industrial unionism had dramatically soared among railway workers, only to show a precipitous decline. Thereafter the federal government courted the conciliatory and highly sectional railway brotherhoods. The mass of railway workers were left without unions. Debs himself left Woodstock jail largely converted to the cause of socialist political action (although industrial unionism retained its attractions into the early years of the Socialist Party).[137]

Homestead and Pullman had thus both ended in defeat for unionised workers. Similarly, there were bitter and unsuccessful miners' strikes in 1894 which almost destroyed the United Mine Workers of America. The very severity and success of American employer anti-unionism thus casts the British counter-attack of the 1890s in a relatively modest role. British 'new unionism' had been checked and constraints placed upon trade unionism in general, but, unlike its American counterpart, the British union movement had become an established part of national life.

There was a final, political, dimension to the mid-1890s watershed. As Stromquist has shown,[138] during the early 1890s 'political agitation for an increasingly collectivist program erupted within the organized trade union movement'. It was especially among groups of workers and unions with industrial or general unionist tendencies – miners, many railway workers, brewery workers, shoemakers, some machinists and furniture and woodworkers, and hotel and restaurant workers – that the causes of independent labour politics and trade unionism went hand in hand. Such groups operated both within and outside the AFL. Following the 1893 AFL convention affiliated unions were requested to consider the political programme which had been put forward at the convention and which included in its collectivist agenda the famous plank 10 calling for 'the collective ownership by the people of all means of production and distribution'. The programme was in fact approved by a majority of members in AFL unions. But at the 1894 Denver convention Gompers' opposition and effective wire-pulling, general opposition to the sectarian and seemingly anti-union Socialist Labour Party, and a strong collective desire to avoid irreparable splits within the AFL, led to the defeat of the programme. Gompers was defeated in his bid for president. But he successfully ran in 1895. Thereafter Gompers effectively imprinted his philosophy of non-partisan politics upon the Federation. The cause of independent labour politics had, along with the general thrust against the narrowness of craft unionism, been effectively checked. Such causes would re-awaken, but, at least in the AFL, without the mass appeal and force of the early 1890s.

In somewhat parallel ways to the British situation of the late 1840s and early 1850s, the defeats suffered by American industrial and political radicalism, and the hostility of the state and employers, led in the 1890s to greater fragmentation within the labour movement and contributed to the development of a more divided working class. American labour responded to the defeat of transformative strategies and movements by adopting a variety of competing strategies, tactics and general goals. The AFL became more cautious, conservative and exclusive. The socialists and supporters of independent labour politics splintered in 1895 (mainly around the issues of sectarianism and working inside or outside the AFL), only for many to come together in the Socialist Party in 1901 in an attempt to capture state power and transform American society in more democratic and collectivist ways. And a militant minority turned their backs on both the AFL and political road of the socialists to proclaim, in the Industrial Workers of the World and elsewhere, the virtues of One Big Union and revolutionary industrial action. The AFL may have become the dominant voice by the early 1920s (some would suggest much earlier), but a range of forces vied for supremacy, and increasingly militant mass strike action between 1912 and 1922 threatened the official leaderships of both the AFL and the Socialist Party.

A more fragmented labour movement operated, at least during the second half of the 1890s and early 1900s, within the context of sharpened divisions within the working class.[139] Thus, against the increased demand for semi-skilled workers and the more pronounced role of class in patterns of residence (see Chapter 1), we must set the following: opposition to unrestricted 'new' immigration and continued anti-Chinese feeling; heightened anti-black sentiments, segregation, and exclusion (from trade unions and other working-class organisations) throughout the South and the North; the conscious exclusion of most women from the labour movement; and a skilled white working class which was experiencing, at least in the East and parts of the Midwest, the contradictory forces of opportunities to climb on to the lower rungs of management combined with Taylorism, de-skilling, loss of control and threats to their security from the 'masses' below.

This highly volatile combination of factors increased the seeming chaos and insecurity of industrial life. At least for many white workers, the cautions and exclusive 'craft' unionism of the AFL offered some hope of security, improvement and protection against threats from both above and below. The wide and generous embraces of the Knights of Labor and the Alliances gave way to exclusion, narrow sectionalism and scapegoating. Class was in retreat.

This picture was, of course, not static and one dimensional. Attention has been drawn above to a variety of factors making for greater homogeneity among late nineteenth- and early twentieth-century British and

American workers. But the countervailing factors of racism and ethnic conflict were far more pronounced in the United States. The British working class was not immune from internal conflicts. But at that crucial period of time, from the late 1880s to 1914, when all manner of British workers were in the process of creating a mass (rather than totally unified) labour movement, American workers were splintering into competing strands.

The American Federation of Labor became the most important of these strands. Officially formed in December 1886, the AFL had nevertheless grown out of the Federation of Organized Trades and Labor Unions established by the national unions in 1881.[140] A confederation of local, national and international unions and state labour councils, the AFL demonstrated great staying power. Under the presidency of Samuel Gompers, poor immigrant from London, cigar maker, and tough pragmatist, the Federation successfully fended off unwanted Knights of Labor interference in the affairs of the national unions, the 1890s campaign for independent politics, the attentions of Daniel De Leon's Socialist Labor Party, and 'dual unionist' opposition (i.e. attempts to set up rival unions to those of the AFL).

Most significantly, the AFL survived the severe depression of 1893–7 and employer hostility to a degree unmatched by trade unionism in previous downturns. During the subsequent boom, from 1898 to 1903, the Federation greatly increased its affiliated membership from under 500,000 to 2 million. By 1903, observes Montgomery, the AFL 'for the first time secured its place as the "House of Labor" '. And:

> Although many unions large and small continued to function independent of the AFL after 1900, and the Industrial Workers of the World openly challenged its right to speak for America's workers, the federation not only dwarfed the independent organizations in size but also came to represent in the minds of most union activists the arbiter of what was or was not 'bona fide' trade unionism.[141]

Further economic downswings and fierce employer attacks upon trade unionism were experienced in 1903–4, the latter part of 1907, and 1911. But by 1914 the AFL had some 2.5 million members, a figure which had increased to over 3 million by 1918.

The AFL leadership attributed their success to sound, pragmatic, 'common sense' and the avoidance of ambitious schemes for social transformation. Much like the mid-Victorian 'new models', the majority of AFL unions saw capitalism as a strong and seemingly permanent structure in which 'wage slavery' constituted a hard, if unwelcome, fact of life. The overriding aim was to achieve strength and recognition within capitalist society and in the process to 'civilise' anti-union employers and state agencies. The AFL leaders continued to employ a republican vision, but of a much narrowed variety. Central concern lay less with the economic independence conferred by co-operative production and democratic structures of power and ownership than with the more limited achievements, as unionised wage earners, of home ownership, a steady job, decent wages and, increasingly, of the consumerist pleasures of modern corporate America. In many ways the AFL of Gompers was a recognition of, and accommodation to, the triumph of corporate power. In a world fundamentally hostile to the claims of organised labour, there appeared to be little practical sense in waging an all out assault against the social system. Truly substantial and lasting gains were to be made by painstaking attention to organisational detail and limited and gradual advancement. Much like the 'wild and visionary' Owenites and Chartists, the Knights of Labor were perceived to have paid the price of failure for their 'unrealistic', grandiose plans.

For Gompers and his allies fundamental and undivided concentration upon 'pure and simple' trade unionism constituted the key to survival and growth. According to Gompers, past failures to achieve durable trade unionism were to be partly explained by excessive ambition, especially the mixing of trade unionism with politics and various 'isms'. Such schemes had proved to be highly divisive. The AFL accordingly sought to build upon what was *common* to workers, namely the economic necessity to labour for wages, to confront profit-seeking bosses, and the 'natural' tendency to organise collectively within the workplace in order to safeguard their interests. This hard-headed economic realism, which was partly a reaction to Gompers' earlier involvement with Marxian socialism, did nevertheless have severe limitations. Although we must be careful not to confuse the 'craft' unionism of the AFL with a purely craft memebership ('craft' unions were not confined to craftsmen, and the AFL embraced miners, semi-skilled operatives and women garment workers as well as craft and skilled workers), many of the Federation's unions were increasingly highly sectional. Women, black workers and the unskilled, and large masses of the semi-skilled working in corporate enterprises were, with honourable exceptions (such as the United Mine Workers and the International Ladies Garment Workers Union) largely excluded by the national unions.[142] The Amalgamated Association of Iron and Steel Workers, for example, was extremely reluctant to organise beyond the ranks of skilled white males, and, as we have seen, paid a high price for its antiquated stubbornness.

There were those in the AFL and beyond who clearly identified the deficiencies of craft unionism within a corporate capitalist structure, especially in view of the latter's heavy demand for semi-skilled work and its proven ability to revolutionise methods of work. Gompers, for example, was keen to develop the principles of union amalgamation and

co-ordination of effort.[143] But in practice the wide jurisdictional powers
enjoyed by the predominantly craft-based AFL unions (sometimes, as
in the case of steel, over entire industries), their fear of competition, their
general reluctance to unionise the mass of workers, and the Federation's
adherence to the principle of trade-union autonomy meant that Gomper's principles were of very limited practical effect. Rather, initiatives
in favour of a wider union base and more inclusive union structures
generally arose in opposition to AFL union leaders and were frequently
led by syndicalists and socialists (the latter being critical of their party's
excessive concentration upon politics). The attachment of many AFL
unions to the 'new model' features of relatively high dues and the
attempted control over the supply of labour also militated against
the creation of a mass, 'new unionist' membership.

In addition to 'pure and simple' trade unionism, the AFL leaders set
great store by the notions of non-partisan politics and voluntarism. Keen
to separate politics and trade unionism , the AFL was not, however, as
is often claimed, apolitical or anti-political. 'Politics was a central concern for the AFL from its earliest days', notes Julia Greene. It was not
politics as such, but the *kind* of politics to be pursued which agitated
the minds of AFL leaders.[144] In Gompers' view, attachment to a particular party circumscribed the unions' political choices and constituted a
source of conflict among union members with diverse political
allegiances. As demonstrated in the past, claimed Gompers, politics also
offered illusory hopes of salvation from economic and social ills. The
solution lay, therefore, in the bond of trade unionism and in the adoption of a labour programme which would be submitted to representatives of the various parties.[145]

In practice, however, non-partisanship increasingly amounted to support for the Democratic Party. The Republicans were seen as the party
of big business, while by the mid 1890s Gompers and his friends had
little sympathy towards socialist and independent labour politics. The
very effective entrance of the anti-union National Association of Manufacturers into political activity in 1903, the 'open-shop' drive, and the
increased use of injunctions and the provisions of the Sherman Anti-
Trust Act did force the AFL to expand, intensify and even broaden its
political activities between 1906 and 1909 (and even included, in the
event of Democratic and Republican lack of support for organised
labour's demands, the nomination of independent labour candidates).
But by the end of the decade the mainstream AFL had effectively
narrowed its allegiance to support for the Democrats.[146]

Voluntarism, the principle of effective improvement and change by
means of trade unionism rather than by means of the efforts of the state,
complemented non-partisan politics. The state, as a proven opponent of

labour, and, in bloated 'European' form, the enemy of individual freedom, was to be kept at arm's length. The courts, in particular, possessed
very strong powers within a system in which centralised state power
was weak and were, generally speaking, supporters of individualism
rather than the collectivism of the unions. With their powers of judicial
review the courts could strike down (as unconstitutional) pro-labour
legislation and, at least in the opinion of Forbath, thus acted to strength-
en the AFL's commitments to voluntarism and to lobbying within the
powerful mainstream parties rather than to emancipation by means of
independent politics (the latter being seen as a futile venture). The
Democrats would be expected to wring legislative concessions to organised labour from this grudging state apparatus. But more crucially,
friendly Democrats would provide a shield against state aggression and
in so doing help the AFL to proceed with its true goal of working-class
'emancipation' by means of market-based collective bargaining.[147]

Conscious of the successes enjoyed during the second half of the
nineteenth century by the Amalgamated Society of Engineers and other
conciliatory British 'new models', Gompers preached the virtues of
patience, responsibility, respectability and, where possible, the cultivation of amicable relationships with employers and their representatives. Bruce Laurie has usefully offered the description of 'prudential
unionism' to encompass such practices. The AFL leadership recoiled in
horror from the militant mass conflicts of Homestead and Pullman.
Usage of the union label, binding trade agreements, friendly relations
with members of the National Civic Federation and other means of
'civilised' behaviour were to replace raw and, for the most part, unsuccessful class conflict.

'Prudential unionism' did not empower the AFL either to vigorously
challenge capital in its corporate power centres or to unionise the mass
of non-skilled workers. By the time of the declaration of war in 1917,
the AFL's power bases lay, apart from mining, in building, printing and
other sectors outside the corporate heartlands of steel, auto, meatpacking
and electrical goods. But, within a far more restricted sense, 'prudential
unionism' had brought tangible results in terms of increased trade-union
membership, material improvements for members, and concessions, recognition and support from both the Democratic Party and the state.
The important Clayton Act of 1914 offered the reduced use of federal
injunctions in labour disputes, and Wilson's administration was keen to
consult with Gompers, to provide mediation and conciliation services
in industrial conflicts, to encourage employers to negotiate with the
responsible AFL, and 'to shun the IWW and other groups deemed
"outlaw" by the AFL'. Active AFL support for the war effort in 1917
and 1918 would, as in Britain, involve organised labour's patriotic leader-

ship in the promotion of state policy at the highest levels (as seen especially in AFL involvement in the National War Labor Board). In turn, the state conferred its official stamp of approval upon the AFL's campaign for union recognition and union standards. Anti-war radicals and socialists were not so fortunate, becoming the target of espionage and sedition laws, state committees of public safety and all manner of patriotic and increasingly anti-'Red' citizens' associations.[148]

Making due allowance for self-congratulation and general hyperbole, it is useful to draw attention to Gompers' article in the *American Federationist* of 1919 as an index of the perceived achievements of the AFL's non-partisan politics and its voluntarism. 'It is not true', began Gompers,

> that the American Federation of Labor is a nonpolitical organiz-
> ation. As a matter of fact, the workers of the United States and the
> organized labor movement act voluntarily in the exercise of their
> political right and power. We have changed the control of our
> government from the old-time interests of corporate power and
> judicial usurpation. We have secured from the government of the
> United States the labor provision of the Clayton Anti-Trust Law,
> the declaration in the law that the labor of a human being is not a
> commodity or article of commerce ... We have secured the eight-
> hour workday not only as a basic principle but as a fact ...
>
> There are other laws in the interest of labor which we have
> secured, more than I can mention off-hand, but far above all these
> are the improvements brought into the lives and work of the toilers
> by their own actions as organized workers. We have established
> unity of spirit; we have brought about the extension of organization
> among the formerly unorganized, and our organized free existence
> to function and to express ourselves is now practically
> unquestioned ...
>
> Suppose in 1912 we had had a labor party in existence ... would
> the American Federation of Labor have been permitted to exercise
> that independent political and economic course ... How long would
> we have had to wait for the passage of a law by Congress
> declaring ... that the labor of a human being is not a commodity
> or an article of commerce – the most far-reaching declaration ever
> made by any government in the history of the world.[149]

While increasingly dominant, conservatism and accomodation did not hold undisputed sway within the AFL. The reader's attention has already been drawn to the existence of competing ideological currents within the early Federation and the important thrusts towards more inclusive union structures and independent politics. It is also important to note that Gompers and his close lieutenant, Adolph Strasser of the Cigar Makers' International Union, had both been involved in Marxian-inspired socialist activity in New York City, that Gompers had been a member of the Knights of Labor, and that the formation of the AFL had (contrary to the wisdom of the 'old' labour history)[150] revolved far more around the issue of trade-union autonomy than any fundamental disagreement with the Knights' broad, reforming vision. Indeed, as Kaufman and Tomlins have noted, Gompers continued, up to the early 1890s, to combine support for limited, immediate gains with the Federation's ultimate goals of 'abolition of the wages system' and the achievement, by means of aggressive trade unionism, of workers' 'rights to the product of their labor'.[151] During these early years Gompers strongly opposed racism and demanded equal pay for equal work on behalf of men and women.

Despite radicalism's defeats in the mid 1890s, the post-1900 AFL did not constitute a uniformly conservative bloc. 'True Womanhood' might continue to be associated in the minds of many AFL members with the domestic sphere, but economic necessity and, especially among the young, the search for independence pushed masses of (particularly unmarried) women into the labour market. Some of them undoubtedly saw their jobs as temporary or as a means of asserting their wills against attempted parental controls. In such cases, as suggested by Kessler-Harris, Tentler and others, trade unionism was probably given low priority. But, as demonstrated by the 1909–10 strike of women in New York's garment industry and their extensive involvement in the 1912 Lawrence textile strike and the mass strikes between 1912 and 1922, women did, given the right circumstances, act in militant ways. And, despite its somewhat uneasy relationship with the AFL leadership, the Women's Trade Union League, formed in 1903 by middle-class sympathisers and female trade unionists, took 'a giant step toward organising wage-earning women'. Significantly, the aim of the WTUL was to recruit women into the ranks of the AFL.[152]

Socialists continued to enjoy solid support within a number of AFL unions (the political fortunes of the Socialist Party will be discussed in Chapter 3). Thus, as Montgomery clearly shows, the International Association of Machinists, the United Mine Workers, the International Ladies Garment Workers Union, the Western Federation of Miners (which joined the AFL in 1911) and the unions of brewery workers and tailors were important centres of socialist agitation. In 1911 and 1912 socialist-led movements successfully defeated seemingly secure conservative leaders within the ranks of the machinists, hatters, pattern makers, journeymen tailors, sheet-metal tradesmen and carpenters. And in 1912, at the height of both their political and industrial powers, the socialists won almost a third of the votes cast for the presidency of the AFL and secured important municipal offices throughout the country. Generally supportive of amalgamation and firm industrial action in the face of corporate power and aggression, the Socialist Party had, nevertheless, little effective response to either Taylorism or the erosion of skills and collective control at the workplace. The party asked workers to place their faith in the efficacy of political action: in practice the 'craft' structures and practices of the AFL were not widely challenged. Between 1914 and 1917 both the Socialist Party and the AFL leaderships were increasingly outflanked by groups of dissident socialists and revolutionary syndicalists who preached the virtues of industrial unionism and mass militancy. The Socialist Party did show a recovery in 1916 and 1917. But by 1920 repression, faction-fighting on the Left, and the attractions of the Democrats had greatly reduced the party's influence within the AFL.[153]

Independent labour politics also received backing from a number of important AFL affiliates. As excellently shown by Michael Kazin, the powerful Building Trades Council in San Francisco combined 'the Gompers brand of "business unionism" and a kind of syndicalism like that being advocated at the time by radical craftsmen in Western Europe' with support for independent labour politics and an expanded welfarist role for the local state machinery.[154] In 1905 Patrick McCarthy, president of the BTC and mayoral candidate of the Union Labor Party, was swept into office. Local political involvement and militant trade unionism were seen as complementary activities, the former providing a legislative shield for the gains of the latter. 'BTC spokesmen', notes Kazin, 'often chided Gompers and his associates for not confronting businessmen and the state'. And in their support for the establishment of an eight-hour day on all public works in California, the setting up of public works to absorb the seasonally unemployed, and public health insurance, the leaders of the BTC were championing 'a spate of measures that, if enacted, would have made California the most advanced welfare state in the nation'. Much like many Labourites in Britain, San Francisco's building trades craftsmen thus sought to create a social order responsive to the wishes and power of organised labour, a 'commoner's paradise'.

Gary Fink and others have demonstrated that San Francisco's experience was far from unique. Especially in St Louis, Chicago and other urban centres in the Midwest, German-born workers and their allies sought municipal representation in order to secure governmental reform, workmen's compensation, health insurance, protective legislation (such as minimum wages for women) and municipal ownership of key local services.[155] Widespread at both the local and state levels, such endeavours had far more in common with the 'municipal socialism' and 'progressivism' of British workers (see Chapter 3) than with the voluntarist philosophy of the national AFL leadership.

'Prudential unionism' similarly experienced more chequered fortunes both within and outside the AFL than the conventional wisdom would suggest. For example, the western mining areas witnessed extensive and bloody conflicts during the late nineteenth and early twentieth centuries. Western workers had been hit particularly hard by the depression of 1893–7. For so long operating in relatively favourable market conditions, many western workers found by the 1890s that labour markets had become saturated and that burgeoning corporate enterprises were intent upon non-unionism and the slashing of unit costs of labour. As Shelton Stromquist observes, 'sharply declining wage rates, high levels of unemployment and only modest capital investment precipitated serious conflict'.[156]

Conflict surfaced most acutely in the Colorado 'mining wars' of 1903 and 1904. Cripple Creek, a stronghold of the Western Federation of Miners, was at the centre of the storm. In the Cripple Creek district, notes Elizabeth Jameson, 'thirty-six unions organised everyone from waitresses and laundry workers to bartenders and newsboys', and, 'through successful organization, workers achieved a large measure of control over job conditions and over the social, political, and economic life of the towns'.[157] Relations between the gold miners and the operators had been fairly peaceful for much of the 1890s. But in 1903 the Mine Owners' Association, in conjunction with Governor Peabody and the local Citizens' Alliance (an anti-union body) resolved to break a sympathy strike and 'do up this damned anarchistic federation'. Troops were sent in, martial law declared, and members of the Western Federation of Miners driven out of the district. 'The mine owners' campaign destroyed the Western Federation of Miners throughout virtually all of the metalliferous mining areas of Colorado', concludes Taft.

Of equal significance was the successful opposition of the Colorado Fuel and Iron Company to the United Mine Workers' attempts to organise the Colorado coal fields. Matters came to an appalling climax in 1914 when soldiers fired upon the miners' tent colony at Ludlow. Eleven children and two women died in the Ludlow Massacre. In addition three strike leaders were murdered, and forty-six people (mainly company guards) died in further battles.

Given the levels of anti-unionism displayed by employers and the state in the West, in conjunction with the sheer scale of violent conflict, it is hardly surprising that western workers retained their allegiances to general organisation and radical independent labour politics to a much greater extent than many of their skilled eastern counterparts. Whereas the 1898–1903 boom brought tangible, if hardly unqualified, benefits to many eastern workers (and increased the appeal of cautious, sectional unionism), relative and absolute declines in material conditions in the West aided the mass appeal of general radical organisations such as the Western Labor Union (1898–1902), the American Labor Union (1902–5) and the IWW (1905–).

To be sure, there were variations of experience within the West. David Emmons, for example, notes that the Butte copper union, although affiliated to the Western Federation of Miners, shared none of the parent organisation's revolutionary ardour.[158] In Butte the existence of extremely high wages, a closed shop, a core of settled and stable mining families, a pro-union and community-minded dominant employer (Marcus Daly), and Irish domination of the union, the town and the supply of labour, ensured that relations between labour and capital were far more harmonious than in the more unstable, transient and ethnically heterogeneous gold and silver settlements. Between 1879 and 1915 the Butte Miners' Union did not call a strike, a sure sign, according to Emmons, of worker conservatism.

As Emmons himself informs us, this is, however, only part of the story. From 1906 onwards Rockefeller's Amalgamated Copper Company assumed increased importance within Butte. Keen to reduce union power, the corporate giant enlarged and widened its supply of labour (to embrace the 'new' immigrants), cut its costs and introduced new-found insecurities and dependencies into the lives of Butte's workers. In 1912 the company discharged hundreds of socialist Finnish miners. Speed-up, increased accidents and arbitrary managerial decisions became facts of industrial life. Against a moribund BMU young Irishmen, Finns and Slavs established a militant Metal Mine Workers' Union in 1918. The mining companies responded by importing strike-breakers and succeeded in destroying the union.

Similar corporate triumphs and union defeats were evident in San Francisco. Between 1916 and 1921 a formerly fragmented local élite was superseded by a self-confident and unified anti-union social bloc. McCarthy's once powerful empire was challenged and defeated. By the 1920s the open shop prevailed in much of the Bay Area's industry. McCarthy's retreat into AFL-style accommodation and alliance with the city's Progressives had failed to deter militantly anti-union businessmen. A radical challenge within the BTC came too late to salvage trade unionism.[159]

1910–1918: Years of Conflict

The 'prudential unionism' of 'civilised' binding trade agreements and the avoidance of mass strikes was, by the end of the first decade of the twentieth century, being challenged in the Midwest and East as well as in the West. Montgomery has chartered the growth in militancy:

The economic boom of early 1907 saw more workers out on strike than in any other year between 1904 and 1910 ... Militant dockers' strikes in Brooklyn and New Orleans gave a preview of the 1910–13 'revolt of the laborers' ... Then, in the fall of the year, the economy collapsed, leading to sweeping layoffs ... The open-shop drive was dramatically joined by U.S. Steel ... As the crisis gave way to renewed prosperity in the summer of 1909, aggressive strikes in McKees Rocks and Newcastle, Pennsylvania, the West Virginia coal fields, and New York's garment markets, all ably conducted under Socialist or IWW leadership, contributed immensely to the prestige of the Left. The general strike of 146,000 workers in Philadelphia in 1910 and the briefly effective fusion of the AFL and Socialist Party efforts in Job Harriman's campaign for the office of mayor in open-shop Los Angeles the next year bore eloquent testimony to the class solidarity the Socialists preached.[160]

Matters were to develop even more dramatically in the years between 1912 and 1922 a decade of chronic and extremely large-scale 'unrest'.[161] Economic upturn in 1912 was preceded by the famous IWW-led strike against wage reductions in the woollen mills of Lawrence, Massachusetts. In the same year the UMWA began a major organising drive in West Virginia, demanding wage increases, the eight-hour day, the check-off system and no discrimination against union members. The mining companies refused these demands. There ensued violent conflicts between miners and private guards and National Guardsmen, culminating in attacks on the miners' tent colony at Holly Grove in February 1913.[162] By April 1913 the country was reportedly suffering from an 'epidemic of strikes'. Textile workers in New England and New Jersey, unskilled workers in rubber, and building trades workers were at the forefront of demands for improved pay and conditions.

In anticipation of future 'control' strikes, shopmen on the Illinois Central Railroad and Harriman lines formed systems federations in 1911 on behalf of the various occupations involved to demand the abolition of premium pay schemes, time study, personnel records and the dilution of skill. When the railroads refused to deal with the workers' federations (recognising only the national unions of the various crafts), the federations called a strike involving over 16,000 workers. In the face of railroad opposition, the importation of strikebreakers, violence and the imprisonment of more than 500 strikers, the strike was called off in 1916, four years after its inception.[163]

The outbreak of war in Europe vastly increased the demand for American goods and capital. Given booming demand and ever-tightening labour markets masses of workers sharply raised their material expectations and demands. In the summer of 1915 the munitions strikes 'swept out of New England across the whole northeastern part of the country'. Bridgeport (Connecticut) and the Westinghouse plants in the East Pittsburgh district were the centres of titanic struggles involving skilled and craft workers and semi- and unskilled labourers and operatives, many of the non-skilled being 'new' immigrants.[164] In 1915 and 1916 (the latter year setting a record for the number of workers on strike) 'munitions' strikers were joined by machinists, textile workers and clothing operatives. And in order to head off the unprecedented call for a national railway strike (in support of the eight-hour day), Congress enacted an eight-hours bill.

The years between 1916 and 1922 were to see between 1.5 and 4 million workers strike work each year in 'the most continuous strike wave in the history of the United States' (the ratio of strikers to non-agrictural workers being more than double those in the periods 1886–7 and 1933–4).[165] As in Britain, miners, railway workers, dockers and maritime workers, and engineers were prominent in this period of mass insurgency. But of equal importance was, as in the case of the British 'labour unrest' of 1911–14, the large-scale involvement of 'new' unionists. Thus Montgomery:

> The abundance of employment between early 1916 and the summer of 1920 gave millions of workers the confidence to quit jobs and search for better ones and to go on strike on a scale that dwarfed all previously recorded turnover and strike activity. Union membership almost doubled, rising from 2,607,000 in 1915 to 5,110,000 in 1920, leaving a larger proportion of American workers unionized than is the case in the 1980s. More important than the overall size of the union movement was the influx of workers who had previously been on the margins of union organization, at best: recent immigrants in textiles, steel, longshore, maritime, railroad construction and other activities; workers in the open-shop strongholds of metal fabrication; and 396,000 women, whose prominence among the clothing and textile workers, railway clerks, and electrical workers swelled union ranks and brought their proportion of total union membership up to 7.8 per cent, roughly what it had been in 1886–7.[166]

The increased demand for labour, combined with claims for wages sufficient to meet the rising cost of living, brought many of these semi- and unskilled workers into the labour movement. But more than short-term economic factors were involved. By the time of the First World War many more immigrants were coming to see themselves as permanent American citizens rather than as temporary residents intent upon accumulating the means to acquire property 'back home'. Immigrants warmly embraced the nationalist aspirations of their mother countries *and* notions of 'American' standards and 'equal rights'. Moreover, some, such as Finns and Jews, imported their radicalism, internationalism and socialism into the United States. And, as exemplified in the case of

Slavic strikers in Pennsylvania, many 'new' immigrant communities were bound together by strong ties of mutuality and religion. Once engaged in industrial action, whole communities of immigrants proved themselves to be united and determined fighters. In sum, immigrant consciousness cannot adequately be described in terms of a cautious and conservative accommodation to the status quo.[167]

Furthermore, as in Britain the 'new' unionists wished to secure union recognition and union standards in order to introduce greater stability and security into their working lives. And herein, as noted by Montgomery, lay an important reason for the relatively slight role played by the IWW in the 'New Unionism'. IWW leaders could provide inspired, charismatic leadership and invocations to smash capitalism, but they were far less attentive to the daily needs of workers for stability, recognition and material improvement by means of durable trade unionism.

The search for order amid the growing chaos of 'flexible' patterns of working and individualised systems of payment and reward within America's increasingly Taylorised and mechanised corporate order was, of course, not confined to the non-skilled. The craft and skilled workers involved in the 'munitions' struggles at Westinghouse, the Remington Arms Company and elsewhere were desperately attempting to establish 'collective control over their conditions of work' and to achieve a secure place for their unions within the new corporate world. Demands for common standards and ground rules (for the eight-hour day, for union rates of pay and conditions of work, for the abolition of 'stretch-out' and premium payment schemes designed to set worker against worker, an end to the victimisation of union members, and recognition of shop committees) in conjunction with a fair and proper system of 'scientific management', under the joint control of workers and engineers, underlay the struggles of craft and skilled workers throughout the decade of mass strikes.[168]

Mass struggle thus united the 'control' issues of the skilled worker with the predominantly 'wages and hours' perspectives of the non-skilled. Harmony was by no means total. Skilled opposition to dilution could take the form of opposition to dilutees, and especially female dilutees. As in the British engineering industry, craft sectionalism and exclusiveness (especially directed against the masses of 'foreign' and black competitors) were by no means defunct in America. But of the utmost significance in terms of the 1912–22 period is the massive and repeated extent to which skilled and non-skilled, men and women, and 'old' and 'new' immigrants and native-born did act in concert in mass strikes. This was the case not only in specific industries but also in specific geographical areas. Thus wide cross-sections of the working class were involved in the city-wide general strikes which occurred in

Springfield, Kansas City, Waco and (twice) in Billings, Montana, between the autumn of 1917 and the late spring of 1918. And this pattern of mass and most un-AFL-like strikes would continue after the War.

In the course of these mass struggles workers developed forms of organisation which were at odds with the narrow craft unionism and sectionalism typical of the AFL. The impetus towards the formation of all-grades unionism, industrial unionism and various forms of combined action or federation on the part of different occupations was present in engineering, in men's clothing, in the garment industry, in steel, in meat packing, on the railways (stretching back to 1877) and elsewhere. Co-operation offered, for many, a much more realistic chance of collective success than the divisive structures of the AFL. Differential standards, conditions and rates of pay did, of course, exist within the various industrial-unionist experiments. But unity did equal strength. The non-skilled in particular were more prepared to accept differentials on the grounds that the unionised skilled acted as pacesetters in the establishment of better conditions for all.

Both in the pre-war and post-war periods industrial unionism ran foul not only of the national officers of many of the AFL's unions, but also of antagonistic employers. Furthermore, and somewhat ironically, neither the IWW nor the One Big Union assumed, notes Montgomery, the 'leading role in any of the big strikes of the epoch'. Individual IWW members and members of the Socialist Party were active. But the mainstream socialists were consumed by political action and the IWW increasingly concentrated its attentions upon the organisation of timber and agricultural workers in the South and West. Striking skilled and craft workers, even if motivated by more inclusive industrial unionist goals, frequently met with little sympathy from the IWW. In addition to being, more often than not, members of the AFL machinists and others were far too 'aristocratic' for the IWW's liking. And, as noted earlier, the non-skilled workers' desire for secure, stable trade unionism did not meet with the IWW's requirement for continuous class struggle.[169]

America's direct entry and participation in the war effort in 1917 and 1918 failed to end mass strikes.[170] As in Britain, workers combined strong patriotic sentiments with determined efforts to take advantage of the tight labour market and to keep pace with inflation. In 1917 strikes reached, in fact, a record level, and workdays lost surpassed the record years of 1912–13 and 1915–16. In descending order of prominence, the metal trades, shipbuilding, coal mining, copper mining, textiles and lumber led the workdays-lost league, and the IWW was particularly influential among timber, agricultural and mining workers in the West.[171] For a time, notes Montgomery, it seemed that the strike wave of the summer of 1917 might effectively mesh with the anti-war movement (the anti-war socialists performed well in the local elections of November). But the government's generous wage increases to the lower paid, its courtship of the 'responsible' AFL and its creation of the National War Labor Board in 1918 (in an attempt to resolve industrial disputes), combined with anti-radical propaganda and repression, effectively stilled dissent.

'By early 1918', writes Montgomery, 'factories were saturated with agents of military and naval intelligence, and War Industry Committees, made up of workers and foremen, staged patriotic rallies and combatted "slackers" on the job'.[172] But while patriotism proved extremely damaging to the cause of the Socialist Party, it signally failed to eliminate mass industrial protest. As we will observe below, the immediate post-war years were to witness, as in Britain, both continued high levels of industrial militancy and concerted attempts to reconstruct American society along the lines of nationalisation and 'workers' control'.

Conclusions

The foregoing survey of the main developments within American labour and workplace protest between the 1880s and 1918 would lend itself to three central conclusions. First, the AFL was, especially up to 1913, far from being the uniformly conservative and pragmatically 'hard-headed' force portrayed by many historians. Second, the labour movement as a whole, and large sections of the working class, were subjected to, and influenced by, a variety of competing institutional and ideological forces ranging from mainstream AFL craft unionism to revolutionary industrial syndicalism. Third, in comparison with Britain, one is immediately struck by the greater scale, intensity, violence and sustained character of industrial conflicts in the United States during these years. Even allowing for differences in geographical size between the two countries and phenomena such as 'Red Clydeside' and the 'labour unrest', one is still left gasping by the naked and massive industrial *and class* conflicts of corporate America.[173]

An absolutist notion of American exceptionalism stands, once again, in need of severe correction. Yet ultimately there did emerge crucial national differences in this period. In Britain mass 'unrest' successfully produced a mass trade-union movement largely recognised by employers and the state. In the United States the sad fact remains that the vast majority of the mass strikes between 1912 and 1918 *failed*. By the end of the war, and despite the upsurges in trade-union strength, a secure and *recognised* mass union movement had not materialised. Key corporate sectors of the economy were still without unions, and would remain so until the 1930s. And the fact that massive class struggles had failed to produce mass trade-union recognition, and that Gompers' brand of unionism was dominant, largely resulted from the effective opposition of corporate capital and its allies to the collective (and especially radical and mass-based) organisations of workers. We can thus reaffirm the conclusion advanced in Chapter 1 that the weaker state of trade union-ism in the United States in this period was attributable less to an 'exceptionalist' working class than to the power and hostility of corpor-ate capital and key sectors of the state.

THE POST-WAR YEARS, 1918–22

In the immediate post-war period three common themes inform work-place protest and trade unionism in Britain and America: mass insur-gency; plans for social reconstruction; and the containment, and in many cases defeat, of workers' ambitions by the actions of sections of the official labour movement, employers and the state. Given the existence of these common threads, this final part of our chronological narrative will directly compare experiences in the two countries.

Mass Insurgency

Mass strikes (especially in the United States), combined with a wider mass insurgency against the status quo, informed important parts of the British and American labour movements during these years. Thus Montgomery informs us that, 'In the four years following the armistice, control strikes persisted at high levels, while the phrase "workers' con-trol", seldom heard before that time, became a popular catchword throughout the labor movement'.[174] The Seattle General Strike, called in support of striking metal trades workers, took place in 1919. The national steel strike of the same year involved 367,000 workers. Embra-cing large numbers of recent immigrants, the strike unsuccessfully attempted to unionise steel and saw the deaths of 28 people.[175] The miners' and railway switchmen's strikes of 1920, running disputes in construction, textiles and clothing, the attempts to unionise meatpacking on a mass, interethnic and interracial basis, and the extraordinarily large, if unsuccessful, fights against the open-shop 'American Plan' in 1922 (involving 400,000 railroad shopmen, 600,000 coal miners, 60,000 textile operatives and 45,000 in meatpacking)[176] were also illustrative of the magnitude and persistence of industrial conflict.

In Britain, as in America, union membership reached an all-time high in 1920. In the same year Councils of Action were formed to protest against government plans for intervention in Russia.[177] The previous year had witnessed Clydeside's protests climax in the forty-hours strike of January–February. During this strike some 40,000 striking shipyard and engineering workers were supported by 36,000 miners, 10,000 iron moulders, and many other trades in Glasgow and the surrounding areas. May Day in Glasgow saw 100,000 pass resolutions in support of 'the Russian Revolution, demands for British withdrawal from Russia and for a socialist revolution in Britain'.[178] The year 1919 had also seen serious conflicts in engineering, the mines and on the railways. The government granted wage increases to the railwaymen and created the Shaw Inquiry for the dockers in an effort to detach them from the miners. The latter were temporarily appeased by the appointment of the Sankey Commission.

In such ways was a generalised strike on behalf of the members of the Triple Alliance avoided. But the situation remained grave. As John Stevenson notes, 'Cabinet minutes have revealed genuine fears of revolutionary activity and plans to use the full powers of the state against it.' All sections of the labour movement were growing in unprecedented ways and its constituency was deepened and extended (to embrace women and others concerned with housing, welfare and neighbourhood issues). And days lost to stoppages surged from almost 35 million in 1919 to 85 million in 1921.

Similar grievances and demands underlay mass insurgency in both countries. Continued inflation, determination to protect the gains (such as union recognition and union standards) achieved during the war and to avoid a return to pre-war inequalities and deprivations, and desires for better housing, welfare provision and a more civilised and just society were to the fore. Total participation in the war effort (especially in Britain) thus engendered the feeling that people deserved the reward of a qualitatively and quantitatively better life in a reconstructed world.[179] And for many of the workers involved in mining, clothing, textiles, the dock and port industries, and on the railways demands for nationalisation and democratic control constituted essential features of this anticipated social reconstruction. War-time experience had taught the valuable lessons that planning and common standards were economically viable and had the potential to be more socially just than the unfettered market mechanism. The massive improvement in the post-war fortunes of the British Labour Party and the various experiments in Farmer-Labor and progressive politics in early 1920s America constituted direct political manifestations of this mushrooming radical consciousness.

Defeats and Retreats

By the end of 1922 radical hopes were either shattered or tempered by a 'new realism'. Especially in the United States the forces of the Left, indeed of the labour movement as a whole, were in hasty retreat. The progressive bloc of leaders within the UMWA and other AFL unions did not manage to win a majority voice within the Federation. Gompers survived radical and other challenges to his leadership to defend the status quo, to preach allegiance to all things 'American', and to lead the fight against 'bolshevism, IWWism and red flagism in general'.[180]

Acute divisions surfaced both within the American working class and the labour movement. The split between the newly formed Communist Party and the Socialist Party in 1919 fragmented the forces of the Left. Massive immigrant participation in strikes failed to eliminate the hostility of the skilled native born and the leaders of many of the national unions. And the migration of some half million southern blacks to the North during the war years brought in its wake a racist backlash. Very limited numbers of black workers were accepted into the labour movement. Thirty thousand blacks were used as strikebreakers during the Great Steel Strike. And in East St Louis in 1917 and Chicago and several other cities in 1919 there took place sickening race riots.[181]

Post-war workers also faced a hostile state and aggressive employers. The vigilante activities, deportations, trials and 'patriotic' outburts used to devastating effect against the IWW during the war were extended in the period between 1918 and 1922. A witch-hunt, directed particularly at 'Red' Eastern European immigrants, accompanied the steel strike. As Brody notes:

> an assiduous search began for the radical conspirators behind the strike. At its start, the *New York Times* reported that in the Chicago district Federal agents 'stepped in with the avowed purpose of suppressing radical agitators, lest the strike be used as a means of advancing Bolshevism'. The Department of Justice, already scouring the country for radicals, now concentrated on the strike centers. Hundreds of steelworkers were detained, most of them aliens who could be deported as undesirables ...
>
> General Leonard Wood, commander of the Central Military District at Chicago, enthusiastically shared the spirit of the Red scare. The country, he confided to U.S. Steel's George W. Perkins, had to 'make a much more serious and thorough effort to Americanize the immigrant who comes to us' and 'of promptly getting rid of the alien or naturalized Red, either by deportation or proper legal procedure'.[182]

Such advice was liberally taken and interpreted. The years 1919 and 1920 saw Attorney General Palmer's witch-hunt against 'alien radicals'.

In 1922, a year of massive and protracted strikes, 'soldiers', records Montgomery, 'swarmed over American industrial towns . . . , patrolling the streets, and escorting strikebreakers through angry crowds'.[183] Republican victories in the congressional and presidential elections of respectively 1918 and 1920 had provided the green light to militantly anti-radical forces within the state machinery. Patriotism became synonymous with anti-radicalism. Many, including the middle-class leaders of immigrant communities, furiously waved the flag and adopted the 'American Creed'.[184] Those suspected of harbouring 'impure' thoughts and deeds were routinely deported throughout the 1920s.

The Republican shield added strength to the general business clamour for an end to war-time regulations, controls and federal restrictions upon market 'freedoms'. Deflation, deregulation, cost cutting and anti-unionism proceeded apace from 1920 onwards. During the era of mass unrest many large employers used a mixture of the carrot of welfarism (profit-sharing schemes, pension plans, company sporting clubs and so on) and the stick of non-unionism (described as opposition to 'outside interference'). As unemployment began to bite hard from 1920 onwards (remaining at persistently high levels throughout the 'roaring 1920s'), and as militant mass strikes receded so employers played down 'welfarism' in favour of the anti-union 'American Plan' and the 'natural' controls of the market.[185]

By the mid 1920s union membership had fallen from its 1920 high-point of 4.75 million to some 3.3 million. There were still more union members than in the pre-1914 years, but the climate of optimism and progress had been replaced by one of grim 'realism'. Autocratic voices within the higher echelons of the AFL demanded opposition to radicalism and acceptance of capital's will in the hope of preserving union recognition. Even the progressives in the AFL counselled worker participation in all manner of Taylorite deals in an attempt to minimise unionism's losses. Anti-union capital, aided and abetted by the Republicans, much of the judiciary and influential sections of the media, was seemingly in total control. By 1925 patriotism had become synonymous for many not only with anti-radicalism but also with anti-unionism.

Montgomery has provided the lament for 'The Fall of the House of Labor':

> Because so many of their activists refused to abandon the dreams that had inspired them in the heady postwar days, international officers . . . resorted to autocratic control of their own organizations. Beleaguered unions clinging to minority sectors of their industries, surrounded by a hostile open-shop environment and governed by ruthless suppression of dissent within their own ranks – that was the legacy of 1922. Most men and women who punched in daily to

tightly supervised jobs where no union steward was to be found at all felt lucky to have the income. Business's successful mobilization for the 'world contest of peace succeeding that of war' had persuaded them that to desire more was folly.[186]

While less dire than those of their American brothers and sisters, the fortunes of British workers had also declined in the early 1920s. In the immediate post-war context of heightened militancy and economic boom Lloyd George and his coalition partners had been careful to tread softly. Rent and other controls were maintained, the unemployed benefits scheme extended and broadened, and a formal commitment made to extensive social reconstruction. The government played for time in its dealings with the miners, and used wage concessions, a public inquiry and promises of future improvement to fragment the Triple Alliance of miners, railwaymen and dockers. By the end of 1921 the government's line had hardened. The growth of mass unemployment was placing formerly insurgent unions on the defensive. And, as Cronin observes, the defeats of the miners in 1921 and the engineers and textile workers in the following year 'began the process of lowering expectations and deflating hopes'.[187] By 1922 deregulation and decontrol were well advanced, the 'land fit for heroes' had largely vanished, and a resurgent Conservative Party was beginning to relish the prospect of 'putting the unions in their place' and demonstrating the futility of mass industrial action.

These parallels with the United States were extended in three other directions. Racism, so long a feature of British attitudes towards many subjects of the Empire, dramatically demonstrated its ugly domestic face in attacks upon West Indian workers in London, Newport, Cardiff, Tyneside, Glasgow and Liverpool in 1919.[188] Second, trade-union membership declined significantly, from 8,348,000 in 1920 to 5,506,000 in 1925. And third, the trade union leadership attempted, with considerable encouragement from the authorities, to assert their control over the massively rebellious rank-and-file membership.

But we must end this section by emphasising an important difference. In Britain both the state and the majority of employers wished to discipline and contain organised labour, to restore authority to a 'responsible' leadership which 'knew its place', rather than to crush trade unionism. This was to be the mainstream strategy employed in the months preceding and during the General Strike of 1926. In the United States even the conservative AFL unions were barely tolerated for much of the 1920s. And the key corporate sectors of the economy remained, of course, largely immune from trade-union 'interference'.

WORKPLACE ORGANISATION AND PROTEST: OBSERVATIONS AND ASSESSMENTS

We are now in a position to draw together the various strands of our chronological narrative in order to highlight key characteristics of workplace protest and organisation, assess the causes of success and failure, and evaluate radical and more conservative influences upon the developments of the period.

Characteristics

We can begin, at the most general level, by indicating the enlarged constituency and scale of trade unionism and other forms of work-based agitation between the 1860s and the early 1920s. Despite the central importance of craft and skilled trade unionism to the British labour movement during the third quarter of the nineteenth century and its continued, if lessened significance thereafter, the outstanding features of the period as a whole were the development of mass trade unionism and a strong, recognised labour movement in Britain. As we have seen, from a solid base in mid-Victorian cotton and coal, non-skilled trade unionism rapidly expanded during the late nineteenth and early twentieth centuries into transport and manufacturing. Some groups, especially agricultural labourers and women, remained on the margins of the male-dominated trade-union world. But the enlarged constituency of that world is undeniable.

One might reasonably expect that in a world increasingly dominated by factories and enlarged units of production trade unionism would 'naturally' shed much of its former 'artisanal' and 'aristocratic' character. The experiences of both countries, but especially the United States, suggest that the nature of the relationship between trade-union structure and policy and economic structure was more complicated.

In terms of the United States we have witnessed repeated moves away from narrow craft unionism towards more open and inclusive forms of industrial organisation and, especially in the immediate post-Civil War years, in 1877, 1886, the early–mid 1890s, and between 1912 and 1922, explosions of mass activity and organisation. The trade-union and labour movements were increasingly forced to take cognizance of the growing importance of semi-skilled workers and the predominantly immigrant character of the American working class. Often considered by the native-born and 'old' immigrant trade-union leaders to be docile and malleable to the wishes of capital, the 'new' immigrant workers in particular demonstrated their ability to undertake impressive collective strike action during the mass struggles between 1912 and 1922.

And moves towards amalgamation, industrial unionism and all-grades movements in American trade unionism were reflective of both the shifting social composition of the workforce and the changing requirements and structure of the workplace. The rapid growth of the modern corporation hardly augured well for the continued viability of old-style craft unionism dominated by a native-born or 'old' immigrant élite.

Countervailing forces were, however, extremely resilient. Not only did American employers and the state mount repeated assaults upon mass strikes and mass trade unionism but also many AFL unions refused to shed their antipathy towards the 'masses', especially if the latter were black, female or 'foreign'. Given their wide jurisdictional claims and powers, such 'craft' unions continued to provide a serious institutional and ideological obstacle to strong mass organisation.

Sectional craft unionism did not, of course, expire in Britain. Indeed, it has retained significant force and influence up to the present day. But, given its more limited sphere of influence and jurisdictional claims as compared with its American counterpart (to occupations and groups of workers rather than to whole industries), it left more effective space for the mass (i.e. general) unions of the non-skilled to develop.[189] Despite the greater scale, intensity and more violent nature of industrial disputes in America during this period, the trade-union movement of the early 1920s lacked the solid mass foundations of its British counterpart.

The enlarged constituency of workplace protest in the later nineteenth and early twentieth centuries was accompanied by the increasingly central influence of trade unionism. During the third quarter of the nineteenth century both countries had experienced a transition, however gradual and uneven, from more informal, community-based protests of the Chartist type to greater emphasis upon the more formal, structured and trade-union orientated types of organisation and agitation. This transition often involved a narrowing of aims from wide-ranging community grievances to concentration upon wages and hours and a diminished role for women in workplace protest.

As the second half of the century progressed trade unions, as observed by Montgomery[190], became a major importance in conducting strikes and in putting forward wages and conditions demands on behalf of workers. Strikes were still called without union approval and, as we have noted, many mass strikes were conducted against the wishes of the union leadership. Furthermore, we have seen that institutionalised collective bargaining developed more strongly in Britain than in America and that mass agrarian protests of the Alliance and Populist variety were not generally rooted in trade unionism. But the general points remain. By the last quarter of the nineteenth century workers were far more inclined to operate through the mechanism of trade unionism (which could, and often did, provide both a shield and a bargaining base for both unionised and non-unionised workers in the same workplace) than by means of more informal community-based workplace protest, sanctions and networks. Workers, as we noted earlier, were learning the habits of collective solidarity and collective organisation.

'Learning the rules of the game' did not, however, lead to the smooth and unquestioning assimilation of bourgeois values. We have thus emphasised the mutualism of American workers which stood in opposition to the dominant acquisitive individualism of the times. Similarly, even while the 'new model' trade unionists in Britain were adapting customary values to take greater account of the power of supply and demand in affecting wages, they offered far from unqualified support for the tenets of orthodox political economy. Many believed that an 'objective' social science masked the class interests of the employers. According to William MacDonald, president of the Operative House Painters in Manchester, teachers of political economy were, 'mere partisans of the strongest side, on a level with paid agitators, or special pleaders'. 'False opinions in the garb of science', were propounded to, 'maintain class interests, and not the welface of society'. More generally, British trade unionists adopted a pragmatic approach to political economy, endorsing those beliefs which suited their needs and rejecting those which were inimical to trade unionism and which denied the effectiveness of collective organisation in the determination of wage levels.[191]

Furthermore, contrary to the claims of 'modernisation' theory, the maturation of industrial capitalism did not, at least in the period under review, witness a decline in the intensity of worker protest and workers' more widespread support for the free-market order. We have observed in this chapter that relations at the workplace did not develop in straight, linear ways. Thus trade unions in mid-Victorian Britain could combine 'sweet talk' with a determination to correct 'unjust' and 'unreasonable' behaviour. Despite its relative stability, the third quarter of the century witnessed some extremely bitter disputes, both in the 'aristocratic' sectors and beyond. A similar process was observable in post-bellum America, the idea of the use of strikes as a last resort being combined with massive disputes in favour of the 'republican' demand for the eight-hour day. The late nineteenth and early twentieth centuries saw mass conflicts in the United States which dwarfed earlier disputes and record days lost to stoppages.[192] During the same period Britain experienced *both* the growth of a relatively sophisticated system of institutionalised collective bargaining and the largest set-piece industrial battles (especially in mining) in her history. There was, in addition, pre-war, 'labour unrest', wartime militancy and post-war insurgency.

There is no doubt that this period witnessed a greater differentiation of the functions performed by the various parts of the labour movement (trade unions, for example, being involved in politics but generally leaving the articulation of political demands to political organisations). And accommodation to the structures of industrial capitalism constituted an important response on the part of sectors of the trade-union world in both countries. To this extent the 'modernisation' thesis does have some validity. But, as we have been at pains to demonstrate, the total picture was far more complex. 'Pure and simple' trade unionism of the AFL variety constituted a single instance of a wide variety of trade-union responses and initiatives. And trade unionism was not unchanging in its tactics and strategies.

Causes

In turning to the causes of workplace organisation and protest we must also emphasise complexity and a wide-ranging number of influences. In itself, for example, an explantion based upon the business cycle is insufficient. There was a *tendency* for strikes and trade unionism to grow during upswings in the business cycle, and the chances of *successful* organisation and development were certainly improved by tight labour market conditions. In Britain, as noted by Hobsbawm and others, the upswings of the early 1870s and the late 1880s did see trade-union 'explosions', as did the post-First World War boom. And 1910–14 'labour unrest' was closely related to the accelerated demand for labour (albeit in conditions in which money wages were lagging behind prices).[193] Similarly, as the work of Montgomery and others makes clear, American trade unions were far more likely to benefit from booms rather than slumps. But a connection is not synonymous with a hard-and-fast rule. Neither trade-union organisation nor strikes were limited to periods of 'improvement'. Thus the Great Depression in Britain saw attempts to organise in 'bad' years. In the United States the correlation between 'explosions' or quantitative and qualitative leaps in work-based protest and economic upswings is not strong. The strikes of 1877, the early years of the 1880s 'Great Upheaval', some (such as the Pullman boycott and mining disputes) of the major conflicts of the 1890s, and a limited number of the mass actions between 1912 and 1922 took place in conditions of mild or extreme depression. And agrarian protest was most definitely not confined to 'good' years.

In truth, such 'explosions' were, as observed by Hobsbawm and Montgomery, associated with the extension of trade unionism and other vehicles of protest into new or previously weakly organised regions and/or groups of workers and petty producers. And the grievances and

demands of the protesters often both included and extended beyond the
narrowly economic and instrumental concerns suggested by cyclical
analysis. Anti-union employers and courts, grasping creditors, gender-
based exclusion and exploitation, and popular notions of 'fairness' and
'just reward' were simply not confined to years of 'bad' trade.[194] In
concrete historical situations narrowly calculative 'economic man'
expanded his personality greatly and was joined by similarly multi-
faceted woman. Movements in the business cycle thus provide too
limited, mechanistic and reductionist an account of workplace protest
to qualify as a sufficient explanation.

Attempts to explain developments in trade unionism, protest and
industrial relations through an institutional focus also bring useful yet
limited results.[195] As Hugh Clegg and his associates and, more recently,
Jonathan Zeitlin have reminded us, any complete account of trends in
workplace relations must pay careful attention to the character, tactics,
strategies, institutional and market-based contexts, and power bases and
goals of the organisations of employers and workers. As we have
observed throughout this book, employer practices towards organised
labour were of crucial importance in moulding the character and fortunes of trade unionism in both countries. Futhermore, Hobsbawm,
Montgomery and many others have shown that the quality of leadership,
of active agency, was significant in determining the outcomes of disputes,
and in modifying and changing seemingly permanent structures.

As associated with Clegg and the 'Oxford' school of industrial
relations (and embracing the work of Lovell and Zeitlin), the institutional focus is nevertheless unduly narrow, exclusive and in many
ways too conservative to provide more than a partial explanation of the
events and phenomena covered in this chapter. Both employers and
workers are influenced, whether consciously or unwittingly, by factors
beyond the immediate workplace environment to a much greater degree
than we are led to believe. And, as demonstrated by Gutman, Thompson
and several other historians of America and Britain, concerns rooted in
ethnicity, race, gender and other aspects of culture and ideology are
carried into the workplace with important effects. The problems of an
institutionally based focus have been clearly perceived by Richard Price:

> Such a focus ... would contain no room for the history of gender,
> for community studies, for popular culture or for workgroups that
> stood outside the official institutional channels. This model is avow-
> edly conservative. The history of institutions is the history of win-
> ners, of local and national establishments whose procedures and
> ideologies tend to be treated as inherently rational and natural. If
> labour history were to be written around this model, it would
> implicitly exclude the poor handloom weaver or the deluded fol-
> lower of Joanna Southcott, and it would tend to discourage the

> notion that the way things actually turned out ... was the product
> of an historical process of change in which alternative strategies of
> equally rational action and organisation competed for dominance
> and control.[196]

Institutional and business-cycle factors thus constitute, in themselves, inadequate areas of explanation. They are, however, necessary parts of a wider and deeper explanatory framework.

This must take as its point of departure the further development of industrial capitalism and market-based relationships in the period after the 1860s. These developments were, for example, absolutely central to the agrarian radicalism of the South and West of the United States. As we have seen, in the post-bellum period capitalist relationships and the capitalist market-place spread rapidly throughout the United States. And capitalist expansion brought in its wake the heightened insecurities, dependencies and clashes between 'custom' and unbridled, free-market capitalism which moved millions of rural petty producers and workers to chronic protest. It is important to remember that farmers and others were the victims not only of expanded markets and crop specialisation and the accompanying booms and slumps in production, but also of *perceived* changes in relationships and patterns of power. As demonstrated in relation to the Alliance and Populist movements, it was the new-found power exercised by 'middlemen' of all descriptions, of the greatly increased stranglehold of industrial and finance capital over the lives of the 'plain folks' which caused such widespread anger. Conflicts also undoubtedly revolved around the issues of South versus North, and urban versus rural. But at root it was the changed economy, society and polity – as symbolised in the burgeoning of 'monopoly' and 'un-republican' power – which was of fundamental concern.

We have also traced the massively disruptive and unwelcome effects of industrial capitalist triumph upon black people in the post-bellum South. Seeking the independence conferred by landownership and control over their labour, the freedpeople were confronted by hostile, racist whites and a Freedmen's Bureau which, in reflection of the aims of the northern bourgeoisie, aimed both to protect the political, social and legal freedoms of blacks and to confirm, indeed enforce, their status as propertyless wage earners. Given this context, conflict was inevitable. With the consolidation of sharecropping and other forms of subordinate status among southern blacks from the late 1860s onwards, the chronic ills of indebtedness, poverty and crop lien dependency formed a unifying link for 'producerist' blacks and whites. This link surfaced most strongly in the Knights of Labor, in the Alliances and in Populism. But all too frequently and depressingly the race card was produced and successfully played to tear apart blacks and whites.

The effects of capitalist expansion, at least up to the early 1870s, were arguably far less disruptive of the lives of many skilled and predomin-antly urban workers in the northern states of America and in Britain. Mid-Victorian economic expansion brought unprecedented material rewards to the 'labour aristocracy'. We have observed that tensions and conflicts did exist. But the necessary adjustments made to the workings of the market and the 'accommodation' reached with the state and employers were far less painful and profound than the conflicts of the first half of the century. Skilled workers in the United States had to contend with anti-union employers and waged largely unsuccessful struggles for the 'republican' eight-hour day. In addition, the sacrifices made during the Civil War heightened popular expectations and demands in the post-war years. But commitments to defend their Republic and to the values of 'producerism', combined with the con-tinued realities (at least for the native born) of upward social and political mobility, subdued the power of class conflict.

During the last quarter of the nineteenth century and onwards to the early 1920s this scenario, especially in relation to the United States, changed dramatically. The crisis of competitive capitalism, the growth of monopoly structures, complete with ruthlessly cost-conscious and anti-union employers, triggered off repeated large-scale industrial con-flicts. In Britain the transition from competitive to monopoly capitalism proceeded far more slowly and attacks upon trade unionism were far less intense and widespread. But Britain's late nineteenth-century relative economic decline did see intensified efforts to increase labour pro-ductivity, to challenge craft control and to reduce labour costs, and the counter-attack against 'new' unionism and resurgent 'old' unionism. The upshot was heightened industrial conflict.

If industrial capitalism posed problems for the continued autonomy, status and privileged material standing of many craft and skilled workers during the late nineteenth and early twentieth centuries, it also offered greatly improved prospects for those sections of the poor upgraded into more regular, better-paid and semi-skilled jobs. We have noted that in both countries the growth of a semi-skilled workforce reduced the 'traditional' divisions between the poor and the skilled, and gave large numbers of workers the heightened confidence and expectations borne of regular work and increased cultural cohesion. Living standards for the mass of workers had likewise improved dramatically over the period as a whole (the rise being more persistent in early twentieth-century America).

Expectations and demands grew in other ways. In Britain, mass education, extensions to the franchise (by 1918 there existed a mass electorate), improved communications and literacy, and the common sufferings induced by the First World War were largely conducive to expanded notions of 'citizenship' and 'natural rights'. Civilised conditions and hours of work, protected by trade unions, had become an integral part of workers' social vision.[197] Demands for the eight-hour day – the veritable touchstone of a civilised existence – had been common to labour's agenda on both sides of the Atlantic. And American workers' strong desires to preserve and extend their political rights and their place within a 'republican' society had figured prominently in the campaigns of the National Labor Union, the Knights of Labor, the AFL and striking immigrant steel workers in 1919. Thus, both capitalism's denial of expected rights, needs and customs, and its generation of rising popular expectations and demands contributed to the 'leaps' in protest and organisation studied in this chapter.

As implied above, needs, customs and expectations transcended purely economic matters. For example, and especially during periods of war, growing numbers of workers looked to the state to improve their lives and to recognise trade unions. The crucial role played by leadership also extended beyond economic immediacy. Particularly during periods of mass insurgency, successful leaders related not only to the material aims of their constituents but also to their widest dreams and hopes. As in our discussion of pre-1860s protest, we must therefore continue to be attentive to the cultural and ideological dimensions of 'unrest', as reflected in workers' continued demands for 'due reward, protection and balance' and in the responses, demands and expectations of other classes and the state.

Workers' successes and failures must also be situated within this wide explanatory framework. Upswings and downswings in the economy and changed patterns of labour supply were important factors in the determination of the fortunes of protest movements. But ideas and ideologies, structures of power and authority, and the overall balance of class forces were frequently of great significance. On balance, trade unionism's early attainment of a 'place' within the British system offered relative security and strength. The far more hostile balance of forces in the United States convinced many that hard-headed 'pure and simple' trade unionism offered the best hope of survival.

Policies

The wide and changing variety and balance of policies adopted by workers and their organisations in this period should also be placed within this wide context. Broadly speaking, we have identified two dominant and contrasting policy positions on the part of protesters: *accommodation* to the general structures of capitalism (rather than wholesale *incorporation*): and more challenging radical responses and initiatives (which often took socialist or syndicalist forms). It is initially tempting to identify the first position with sectional craft and skilled trade unions and the second with more 'open' general or industrial unions. But, as we have demonstrated in this chapter, closer attention to the evidence makes it extremely difficult to simply 'read off' policy from trade-union structure.

We have encountered several 'new model' unions which, whilst not unqualified practitioners of capitalist values and norms, did nevertheless preach and practice accommodation to the existing order, and which largely turned their backs upon the inclusion or organisation of the non-skilled. Railway engine drivers and firemen (in ASLEF), many shopfloor engineers (in the ASE) and some sectors of the shipyard workforce (especially in the Boilermakers' Society) were to continue their élitist, exclusive policies beyond the First World War. Similarly, as illustrated in cigar making, and the building, and iron and steel industries, many AFL unions were sectional and 'aristocratic', particularly in their dealings with blacks, women and 'new immigrants'.[198]

Policies of accommodation and exclusion were not, however, confined to the craft and skilled. In the early–mid 1890s context of mounting unemployment and employer hostility, some of the 'new' unions retreated from their broad radicalism of the late 1880s to practise a narrow pragmatism. The Dockers' Union, for example, attempted to create local job monopolies, to restrict the occupational base of the eligible membership, and to exclude potential competitors from waterside employment.[199] Accommodation (as reflected in sliding scale agreements and the leadership's conciliatory stance towards employers) had constituted a strong element in the policies of the relatively 'open' unions of coal miners and cotton weavers from mid century onwards. And, as in America, the overriding desires of the non-skilled for union recognition and security during the period of 'labour unrest' severely limited syndicalist influence. In the United States, as seen in the cases of Bakers' and Confectioners' International Union and the Boot and Shoe Workers' Union, socialist idealism and inclusive policies often gave way, in the interests of survival and advancement, to 'pure and simple' methods.[200] And conservatism could exist within radical or even revolutionary enclaves. Thus, as Emmons informs us, the Butte Miners' Union, conservative and class collaborationist in character, formed local no. 1 of the Western Federation of Miners. The latter was of course, an industrial union, committed to socialism, a founder member of the IWW, and a sworn enemy of AFL conservatism.[201]

Unions of craft and skilled workers should, furthermore, not be viewed as uniformly unchanging and conservative blocs. Within a number of industries and unions employer hostility, union weakness and the changing structure of work and workplace relations led to sharp disagreements as to the appropriate structures and strategies to be pursued. Thus Stromquist informs us that in America railway expansion, labour scarcity and high wages were conducive to the sectionalism, élitism and moderation preached by the Brotherhood of Locomotive Engineers. But economic adversity, the growth of a labour surplus, the mixture of anti-union authoritarianism and welfarism practised by many railroads, the tightening up of work rules, the decline in promotion prospects for the skilled, and reduced wages led many, both within the brotherhoods and beyond, to question the viability of the craft model of organisation and class collaboration. During the great upsurges of railway protest – in 1877, 1886, 1894, 1914–16 and 1922 – radical factions within the brotherhoods, shopcraft workers, and less skilled workers thus sought, especially by means of federation, to develop broader organisations which would unify workers across trades. The most famous example of this development was the American Railway Union formed by Debs in 1893. Significantly, Debs himself had moved from the conciliatory stance of the Brotherhood of Locomotive Firemen to the belief that the only permanent solution for railway workers' ills lay in militant industrial unionism and (in the wake of the Pullman boycott) socialism.[202] Similar, if less turbulent developments had, of course, taken place on Britain's railways. The General Railway Workers' Union saw itself as a 'fighting union', intent upon organising those neglected by the Amalgamated Society of Railway Servants. In 1913 three unions merged to form the industrially based National Union of Railwaymen (although the footplatemen maintained their separate organisation).

Brief reference may also be made to the conflicts between socialists and conservatives within the ranks of the International Association of Machinists, between socialist 'progressive' and straight 'craft' factions within the AFL as a whole at various points of crisis (the early–mid 1890s, 1912–13 and in the post-war period of insurgency), and to Gompers' support, at least in principle, for the notion of amalgamation. In Britain, many of the socialists involved in the engineering disputes of Clydeside, Sheffield and elsewhere and socialist leaders of the ASE were keen to open up the union to the ranks of the non-skilled. And in the iron and steel industry John Hodge's British Steel Smelters' Amalgamated Association demonstrated an active willingness to broaden the base of organisation, a policy which stood in marked contrast to the complacency and conservatism of the Associated Iron and Steel-workers' Union. The Iron and Steel Trade Confederation of 1917, covering all the important unions except the Blastfurnacemen, represented the climax of the movements for amalgamation, federation and more inclusive unionism.[203]

Both within the workplace and within trade unionism the interests of the skilled and non-skilled were by no means *necessarily* antagonistic. Skilled union members could act as pacesetters for general improvements in pay and conditions in particular workplaces and industries. Pat Duffy's study of the mid-Victorian Manchester building trades, for example, finds strong support among both unionised and non-unionised labourers and others for craftsmen in dispute. Such support extended to financial aid in the expectation of the achievement of generalised benefits.[204] The general decline during the second half of the nineteenth century of the employment, payment and exploitation of helpers by skilled men also reduced structural antagonisms. And, as variously seen among machinists, engineers, boot and shoe workers, and shipyard workers, the practices of 'taking the rate to the job' and of preserving occupationally and custom-based distinctions and divisions on new jobs, could unify rather than divide all manner of grades and occupations.[205] The establishment of a standard rate for the job, as opposed to control of the supply of labour, was, of course, well established in the weaving sector of the late nineteenth-century British cotton industry.

Our analysis of trade-union policy must also incorporate the dimension of change. Under the pressure of employer hostility, state repression, adverse technological change, the experiences of wartime 'collectivism' and so on, relatively strong and hitherto accommodating workers could move sharply to the Left. Montgomery has thus identified a strong leftwards movement in America's 'control' struggles and mass strikes. Similarly, by the end of the First World War many of the previously conservative engineers, firemen, trainmen and conductors in the Brotherhoods were coming to seriously consider nationalisation of the railroads and a 'progressive' alliance with miners and machinists within the AFL. Hobsbawn has drawn our attention to a shift to the Left at the end of the nineteenth century and beginning of the twentieth century on the part of once conciliatory British 'old' unionists. And the specific studies of Hinton (engineers), Lancaster (boot and shoemakers) and Haydu (skilled metalworkers in Coventry, England, and Bridgeport, USA)[206] have added detailed strength to Hobsbawm's general case.

As Alastair Reid has been anxious to remind us, there was, however, no uniform movement to the Left. Craft and skilled workers could and did (as in the cases of some American iron and steel workers, building trades workers in San Francisco and elsewhere, the dominant voices in the AFL, and some skilled workers in engineering and other industries in Britain) respond to adversity by advocating caution, moderation, sectionalism and 'realism'.

We must insist, therefore, upon the complexity of change and, once again, upon very different responses among workers within the same occupation and union. In San Francisco some building trades workers followed the lead of their president, McCarthy, by responding to the emergence of powerful anti-union employers in cautious ways: a minority adopted more radical tactics and goals. The same responses could be observed in copper mining in Butte and among engineers (to the dilution issue) in Britain.[207]

The spotlight accordingly falls upon those factors which moved workers in different directions. This is an exceedingly complex area. But we may suggest that trade unionists and other workers were motivated by three crucial influences: the overall balance and character of competing social and political forces; the attractiveness and plausibility of 'realistic' tactics and strategies; and the guiding hand of past experiences and traditions.

Of central importance was the question of realism, of the relative costs and benefits of conservatism and radicalism. Some AFL unions, such as those of the bakers and confectioners and of the shoemakers, found that 'pure and simple' unionism brought the material and institutional advances which prior allegiance to low dues and 'open' socialist principles had failed to deliver. Given the oppressive machinery of the state and employers and the past failures of mass insurgency, transformative strategies and independent politics, Gompers and his allies plumped for accommodating, 'safety-first' tactics. Ethnic and racial divisions within the working class, combined with the fluidity and relative receptivity of the American political and party systems (especially as epitomised by the Democrats) to workers' demands reinforced Gomper's choice. There were moments of circumspection and doubt (particularly during the period of adverse legal decisions against trade unionism between 1906 and 1908), but this limited and conservative position generally held firm. By 1918 it had acquired a distinctly anti-radical character.

Contradictory voices were raised. In the eyes of American socialists the 'monopoly' concentration of power was a logical step on the road to 'true' political and social democracy. Monopoly capitalism thus presented opportunities for inclusive trade unionism and radical, transforming change. The revolutionary unionism advocated by the IWW was likewise seen as the 'natural' corollary of mass-production methods. The political complexion of the trade-union leadership, employer policies, workplace traditions, the character of the labour force, and economic and political trends also constituted important factors in the determination of radical versus accommodating policies and outcomes.

The latter cluster of forces were especially operative in Britain. The

greater strength, unity and recognition of the British trade-union movement softened revolt against the industrial system. But, despite the
largely separate organisational structures of skilled and non-skilled trade
unionism and problems of sectionalism, the adverse pressures upon
trade unionism and workers were strong enough, the labour movement
sufficiently united, and the allegiances to Liberalism shaky enough, to
push British labour in more independent and, by 1918, leftward directions. In America relentless hostility from 'above' frequently resulted
in short-term radical responses. But the longer-term outcomes were in
many cases demoralisation, despair, fatalism combined with cynicism,
and a narrowing of aims and aspirations. In the United States the risks
of revolt – in terms of personal, family, and community welfare and
security – were extremely high. In Britain workers were pounded less
frequently and severely, and there was accordingly greater space for
socialists and advocates of independent labour action to implant their
messages within key sectors of the labour movement.

In the midst of myriad complexities we can nevertheless discern some
general patterns of behaviour. We suggest that strong craft and skilled
unions, operating within the wider context of vibrant economies, did
undoubtedly provide powerful, if incomplete, forces for accommodation. This was certainly the case in mid-Victorian Britain. Once
competitive capitalism entered a period of uncertainty and crisis from
the early–mid 1870s onwards and new pressures were exerted upon
labour, so the latter's position became far less secure. Both insecurity
and mounting mass opposition to monopoly capitalism fragmented the
labour movement in America to a much greater extent than in less
transformed Britain. By the end of the century ideological conflicts,
ranging broadly around strategies of accommodation and challenge,
raged with far more intensity in labour movements on both sides of the
Atlantic than in the 1860s and early 1870s. And the outcomes of such
conflicts were determined by a wide mixture of forces rather than by
economic factors alone.

The Issue of Class

A final question remains. Where, if anywhere, in the wide-ranging and
complex picture of events presented in this chapter do we find class?
One is immediately moved to reply everywhere, or almost everywhere.
The ability of large numbers of workers to join together in independent
organisations, sometimes in alliance with petty producers, to fundamentally shape their ways of life, values and norms and to demonstrate
ideas and actions antagonistic to the actual forces of capital (rather than
to some abstract or 'essential' embodiment of the latter) has been amply

shown in the course of our survey. In the great upsurges of 1877, the 1880s, 1892–6, 1898–1903 and 1912–22 millions of male and female labouring Americans, representing different occupations, levels of skill, religions, ethnic groups, geographical areas and even different races, joined together to protest against the injustices of the new corporate system. As Stromquist has observed in relation to the years between 1873 and 1896:

> Ethno-cultural differences, always a factor within the heterogeneous American working class, were increasingly subsumed by class differences. Many English, Irish and German immigrants brought with them an already sharply honed consciousness of class: for others a process of Americanization 'from below' produced a creative synthesis of ethnic and class identities. No period in American history before the 1930s saw a more direct attack on the formidable barriers of racial and sexual segregation within the working class. Within the Knights of Labor and the Farmers' Alliance, black and white, male and female producers groped toward common bonds of class that subordinated differences of race and gender.[208]

The immediate post-bellum years had also witnessed a 'direct attack' on the various sources of fragmentation, and the 'craft' based AFL was far from being the purely sectional and élitist body suggested in much of the 'old' labour history.

In the course of the upsurges outlined above more and more workers and small producers turned away from the dominant institutions of American society to create their own oppositional organisations. Trade unions, assemblies of the Knights of Labor, Alliance exchanges and stores, AFL locals, city labour councils, branches of the IWW and the Socialist Party were all reflective of a burgeoning independence of spirit among the labouring people. And, as emphasised by Montgomery, these institutions were infused by an ethos of mutualism and struggle which caused widespread consternation in the ranks of middle-class America.

Labouring people in America struggled against a variety of injustices ranging from poor living standards to 'monopoly' power. And, as we have seen in this chapter, notions of 'producerism' and 'the people' remained key themes in the consciousness of the people during this period. Simultaneously, however, we have shown that the languages of class feeling and class conflict constituted integral parts of producerist and populist mentalities. During the 1870s and 1880s workers, farmers and others increasingly set themselves up in opposition to the workings of the unfettered market and 'monopolistic' capitalists. By the 1890s, and through to the 1920s, explicitly and directly class-based ideas and languages, rooted in socialism, independent labour politics and syndicalism, competed for the loyalties of workers against the narrower, more exclusive views of Gompers and his associates. But even Gompers, especially in the early years of the AFL, assumed that a wage-earning class and a certain degree of class conflict had become integral features of American capitalism.

We have seen that in Britain too class, as reflected in an increasingly common proletarian life-style, in narrowed wage differentials, in a more homogeneous occupational structure, and in the development of a mass labour movement, exerted itself with great force upon everyday life. By 1920 the British working class enjoyed a degree of internal cohesion which stood in marked contrast to its highly sectional and fragmented form in the mid-Victorian period. The influences of revolutionary socialism and syndicalism were extremely limited. But class consciousness, expressed in the notion of 'Us' and 'Them', in the growth of a mass labour movement, in the renaissance of independent labour politics, and by the 1920s in the Labour Party's gradualist socialism, and involving an acute sense of opposition to capitalist injustice and desires for greater equality and social justice, had greatly gained in strength in Britain since the accommodation and moderation of the 1850–70 years.[209]

To establish the presence of class in working-class life is not, however, to demonstrate the measure of its importance. And, as the recent 'revisionist' historiography of Gareth Stedman Jones, Alastair Reid, Jonathan Zeitlin, Duncan Tanner and David Emmons informs us, there were sufficient divisions, ambiguities and contradictions, and conservative and fatalistic elements in working-class life in both Britain and the United States to undermine notions of a completely 'made' and radical working class. Many of the methodological assumptions and procedures of the revisionists are, however, flawed. Having attributed to 'Marxism' a unified, largely undifferentiated and economic view of class, they then proceed with the easy work of demolition.[210] But, as we observed at the end of Chapter 1, the views of 'Marxists' such as Hobsbawm, Montgomery and Thompson (indeed Marx himself) do not conform to this reductionist and undifferentiated model. These historians also emphasise complexity, the influence of non-economic forces upon class, the contradictory features of fragmentation and solidarity within working-class life, and the enduring and changing battles for supremacy between conservative, radical and revolutionary forces.

Having attended to complexity and contradiction, Hobsbawm and Montgomery do nevertheless emphasise the great power of class in the period under study. And the evidence presented in this chapter would largely support their case. Class did face tremendous obstacles in the form of craft and skilled sectionalism, conciliatory attitudes to employers, and all manner of gender-based, racial and ethnic divisions. James Barrett and David Brody, for example, have clearly detailed the various ethnic and racial barriers which confronted attempts to unionise steel and meatpacking. But both authors emphasise that class and ethnicity were neither static identities and relationships nor automatic foes. Indeed, Slavic and other 'new' immigrant groups in steel and meatpacking often lent their powerful ethnic and neighbourhood ties to the cause of trade unionism. Unions provided a point of common focus and unity for all manner of disparate individuals and groups in Chicago and Pittsburgh. As Barrett demonstrates, the experiences of mass-production work and neighbourhood also contributed to the process of class bonding:

> On Chicago's South Side, the varied work experiences of skilled Irish butchers, recent Slavic immigrants, and black migrants were reinforced by the physical and social barriers separating these groups.
> Yet this study also suggests that such divisions can easily be overdrawn. In opposition to the clear tendencies toward fragmentation in this era, there were countervailing pressures inherent in the changing character of manufacturing and neighborhood life. Huge plants with finely integrated production systems linked the fates of very large, socially diverse groups of workers who might otherwise have had little in common with one another. In packing, a significant intensification of work, the downward pressure on wages caused by casual hiring methods, and the army of the unemployed at the yard's gate provided a rationale for more skilled, Americanized workers to reach out to the unskilled black and Slavic newcomers . . .
> As in the workplace, there were also points of contact among immigrant workers and between them and native-born whites in the community. Some institutions of big-city life – the saloon and the settlement house, for example – provided a common ground and facilitated the acculturation of newcomers.[211]

Similarly, the 'conservatism' of Emmons' Butte miners must be set within the wider and more balanced context of western working-class radicalism and the mining wars of the late nineteenth and early twentieth centuries.[212] Within the Butte Miners' Union and within Butte itself the growing failure of corporate capital to meet miners' needs for security, stability and decent wages led to increased radicalism. The demand for a settled, secure way of life was thus by no means necessarily synonymous with 'conservatism'. Much depended upon the political and socioeconomic contexts in which demands and needs were articulated, and the extent to which they were met. Furthermore, as in the case of the San Francisco building trades, relative stability and decent living standards were often achieved by means of strong collective organisation and struggle.[213] The militant unionism and independent political stance adopted by many members of San Francisco's building trades derived just as much from desires for steady, well-paid work as did the aspirations of Butte's workers. But San Francisco's building workers lacked the narrow ethnic character of Butte's copper miners (the vast majority of the latter being Irish), their very close attachment to the dominant employer (Marcus Daley conscientiously providing work and welfare for his compatriots in the mines), and their tight allegiance to Catholicism and the Democratic Party. Wider context could thus influence both the meanings and the outcomes of needs and demands.

Stedman Jones's picture of a defensive, fatalistic, consolatory and largely apolitical working class in parts of late nineteenth- and early twentieth-century London must also be put in its proper 'place'.[214] There is evidence that workers in West Ham and parts of London's East End behaved in far less conservative, resigned and pessimistic ways than described by Stedman Jones. And, as noted by Winter and others, working-class culture cannot be interpreted in a straightforward, one-dimensional manner ('conservative' versus 'radical'). Rather culture carries within it the possibility of a variety of meanings and outcomes. Much depends, once again, upon the *ensemble* of social forces, practices and values. And Winter is surely right to insist that during the first two decades of the twentieth century (and especially during and immediately following the 1914–18 war) ever growing numbers of workers attached themselves to radical politics (including socialism) and unions in an attempt to substantially increase the presence and the power of organised labour in Britain. This was hardly the behaviour of defensive consolation.[215]

Alastair Reid's identification of divisions within the workplace has, along with Paul Johnson's emphasis upon competition and individualism within working-class life, alerted us to the dangers of exaggerating the unified and co-operative characteristics of the British working class. But, as revealed throughout this chapter, we must insist that the period from the 1870s to the 1920s did see the development of extremely powerful countervailing forces to fragmentation and competition. Hobsbawm's notion of the 'making' (or, more accurately, 're-making') of the working class between 1870 and 1914 would appear to carry overall conviction.[216]

The similar class-based experiences of British and American workers should not, however, obscure important national differences. There were, for example, contrasts in both the chronologies and influence of class. Class, in conjunction with producerism, was probably stronger among American workers than their British counterparts between 1873 and the early–mid 1890s. Thereafter, and despite repeated industrial conflicts both the American labour movement and the working class were more divided, especially along ethnic and racial lines, than was the case in Britain. For example, building craftsmen in San Francisco combined an acute sense of class with a profound aversion to the employment of Chinese workers. And Chicago's race riot of 1919 effectively ended the drive to organise the packinghouses.[217] As we will observe in Chapter 3, strong labour movements were far more likely to develop in relatively homogeneous and culturally cohesive communities than in places where ethnic and racial conflicts were pronounced.[218] The less settled and durable character of class among American workers also derived from the highly repressive and effective actions of the establishment. Finally, class arguably expressed itself in more long-lasting and powerful forms in British rather than American politics. But this is a hypothesis which requires detailed investigation and substantiation. It is to a consideration of popular politics, ideology and culture that we will proceed in Chapter 3.

CHAPTER THREE

Citizenship and Emancipation: Politics, Ideology and Culture

PARTY LOYALTIES AND INDEPENDENT INSURGENCIES

In moving to an examination of the central features and developments in the political cultures and allegiances of workers from the mid nineteenth century to the early 1920s, we are immediately faced with a number of intriguing and difficult issues and seeming contradictions. Why, above all, were the high and persistent levels of industrial conflict and violence in America which we described in Chapter 2 not accompanied by more successful attempts to break the grip of the Republicans and Democrats upon the political loyalties of workers? How, to quote Eric Foner, do we explain, 'the coexistence in American history of workplace militancy and a politics organized around non-ideological parties appealing to broad coalitions, rather than the interests of a particular class'?[1] Is the answer to be sought in the 'exceptionalism' of American workers' political consciousness? Did, as Paul Kleppner and likeminded 'new' political historians have claimed, that consciousness revolve far more around the 'ethnocultural' issues of family, religion, tradition and the cultural aspects of daily life than around the predominantly economic tie of class?[2] Is is possible to compartmentalise workers' lives and outlooks in such clinical ways, and to underestimate the cultural dimensions of class? Would it not be more plausible to argue, along the lines suggested by Richard Oestreicher, that both class-based and ethnocultural concerns interacted in powerful ways upon the lives of American workers but that the daily sentiments and practices of class did not automatically and necessarily translate themselves into radical political consciousness and action? The creation of strong, durable and successful radical political movements required plentiful effort and resources and inspired and tireless leadership and organisational skills. Agency and institutions were the necessary translators of the daily 'commonsense' of class into structured and powerful political ideologies and causes.[3]

As we will observe in due course, there were numerous occasions between the mid nineteenth century and the 1920s when American workers and their 'producerist' allies sought to assert their radical political presence both against and within the established parties. There was a proliferation of labour parties and labour 'tickets' during the post-bellum decades of the century. There were also attempts to take over and radicalise mainstream political organisations in the 1880s and beyond, a strong farmer-labour presence throughout much of the entire period, local and state involvement in Progressivism on the part of AFL activists (in opposition to the stated 'voluntarism' of the national AFL), trade unionists running as Republican or Democratic nominees and 'friends of labour' from within the political mainstream. We should finally note the importance of the Socialist Party in the pre-First World War years (the *socialist* presence in the United States being much stronger than in Britain). In sum, such factors testified to the enduring radical political presence, pressure and indeed independence of sections of the labour movement and the working class.

Most significantly, this spirit of radical, even socialist, political inde-pendence flatly contradicts an absolute view of American 'exceptional-ism', of laggardly political consciousness as compared with allegedly more class-conscious British workers. Possession of the vote and allegiance to the first modern political democracy did induce a strong spirit of *citizenship*, of the possession of a stake in the political system, on the part of white adult males. And, as a result of northern victory in the Civil War, political citizenship was extended to many black adult males. But this notion of integrated citizenship did not guarantee *unconditional* and *permanent* attachment to the political system. Con-trary to the claim of Alan Dawley, the ballot box was *not* 'the coffin of class consciousness'.[4] Black disfranchisement and generalised oppression at the hands of whites would take place with a vengeance towards the end of the century. And the growth of 'un-republican' corporate strength complete with its grasping designs upon the levers of economic, social, ideological and political power, would radicalise workers politi-cally as well as industrially.

Ultimately, however, radical political class consciousness lacked the strength to successfully challenge the hegemony of the Republicans and Democrats. We will see that there were many instances of solid, indeed spectacular short-term success (one thinks immediately of the Populists and of some of the municipal gains made by the Socialist Party), but all too often, as in the 1830s, independent labour (and socialist) political experiments were shortlived and frequently unable to translate local victories into wider gains. By the early 1920s, and despite the blood and thunder of post-war political and industrial conflict, the labour movement and American workers were predominantly accommodated within the two-party system. Indeed, the latter has demonstrated formi-dable long-term strength. As Gary Marks has noted:

No country has seen a greater number of parties contest elections than the United States, yet nowhere over the last century have third parties been so weak. Since the Civil War the number of parties that have contested local, state, and national elections have to be counted in the hundreds, yet only eleven times over the last hundred years have third parties gained more than 5 per cent of the total vote in a presidential election, and no party has managed to accomplish this feat more than once.[5]

Thus, as recorded by Oestreicher, since the 1850s, 'no new political aspirant in American politics – no party, no politician, no social movement – has gained significant national power except through the Democratic or the Republican party'.[6] It is thus both the frequency and shortlived character of American third-party movements, rising and falling within the context of an extremely stable political system, which demand explanation.

In comparison, British workers turned far less frequently but, by the early 1920s, ultimately more successfully to independent labour politics. As briefly noted in Part Two of Volume One, there developed upon the decline of Chartism close links between the labour movement and Liberalism. In parts of the country, especially in Lancashire, the Conservative Party also developed strong working-class support. One might have expected that extensions to the parliamentary franchise under the Second and Third Reform Acts of respectively 1867 and 1884 (the latter including the counties in the household suffrage provision established in the boroughs in 1867) would provide a considerable fillip to the momentum of independent labour representation. But this was not to be the case, at least in the short term. General working-class accommodation to Liberal domination during the third quarter of the nineteenth century and to Conservative rule from the mid 1880s to the early years of the new century may in part have been related to the facts that all women and approximately 40 per cent of adult males still lacked the vote.[7] But it was far more likely that mellowed Liberalism and Conservatism in the post-Chartist decades successfully tapped the cultural, social, political and economic sentiments of large numbers of working men and women. In any event, and unlike the situation in the United States, working-class moves to establish an independent political presence from the 1850s to the 1880s were largely conspicuous by their absence. As noted by Edward and Eleanor Marx-Aveling and Engels, during the 1880s American workers turned far more readily to independent labour politics than their counterparts in Britain.[8] More generally, 'cultural politics' exerted considerable influence not only in the United States but also in Britain during the mid- and later-Victorian periods.

Between the 1880s and the 1920s the crisis of competitive capitalism underpinned the enhanced importance of class-based issues in the politics of both countries but especially in Britain. As in the United States, more hostile courts, employers and agencies of the state, combined with important developments within working-class life (growing cultural uniformity and separation, the militancy and organisation of the non-skilled and so on), placed independent labour politics and (to a much lesser extent) socialism on the late nineteenth- and early twentieth-century Britain political agenda. The creation of the Labour Representation Committee in 1900 and its subsequent development into the Labour Party testified to the revival of class. As noted earlier, socialism continued, at least numerically, to carry more weight in the United States than in Britain. And an important recent strand in the historiography of labour politics in Britain has highlighted the ideological affinities and continuities between Labour and Liberalism, and the slow and uneven nature of the Labour Party's advance in the pre-1914 period.[9] Nevertheless, as convincingly demonstrated by David Howell[10], significant continuities should not obscure the fundamentally important fact that the issue of *independent* labour politics had by 1900 assumed a degree of importance lacking since the days of Chartism. Moreover, by the early 1920s the Labour Party had achieved a position of strength, durability and national significance unparalleled by radical political movements in the United States. Throughout the 1920s the question of American 'exceptionalism', as manifested in the decline of socialism and independent labour politics, and in Republican hegemony, came to the fore.

Questions concerning the varied fortunes of independent labour and socialist politics thus lie at the heart of this chapter (and Chapters 4 and 5). We are simultaneously concerned with the character and resources of power and hegemony, and with the generation and nature of popular political consciousness. What were the economic, political and cultural determinations of politics? How do we unravel and evaluate the class, ethnocultural and gender-based factors involved? Why were revolutionary socialist politics of marginal importance in both countries? And what kind of political consciousness did the Labour Party express in the early 1920s? Did this consciousness revolve around class? And did it signify a qualitative 'break' with developments in the United States?

We will proceed in the following manner. The first part of the chapter will identify and explain the main features of popular politics from the mid nineteenth century up to the mid 1880s. Trends outlined in Volume One – the transition from Chartism to popular Liberalism and Toryism, the consolidation of partisan political loyalties in the United States, and tensions within these inter-class structures of politics – will be amplified. We will then investigate the various challenges mounted by American workers to the political hegemony of the Republicans and Democrats, and draw some contrasts with the pre-1880s British experience. The second part of the chapter will centrally address itself to the rise and 'triumph' of the Labour Party in Britain and the continued inability of independent labour and socialist politics to put down firm roots across the Atlantic.

POLITICAL STRUCTURES AND POPULAR POLITICS: FROM MID CENTURY TO THE 1880s

Britain

As we demonstrated in Part Two of Volume One, a key feature of national Chartism was its mistrust of mainstream Toryism and Whiggery and its emphasis upon the importance of political *independence*. And that political independence was a reflection of the acute class consciousness of Chartism and its supporters. From the late 1840s important counter-currents and departures were discernible. The defeats endured by Chartism persuaded many leaders and supporters that continued emphasis upon the primacy of independent political means of emancipation offered little hope of success in the forseeable future. Chartism continued into the 1850s, but became progressively weaker. By 1860 the vast majority of Chartists had moved into Liberalism and had come to accept the Liberal emphasis upon the inseparability of free trade and economic and social improvement. We saw in Volume One that from the mid 1840s onwards growing numbers of the more regularly employed workers adopted trade unions, friendly societies, mutual improvement societies and co-ops as the best means of advancement. 'No politics' rules within trade unionism were extended and hardened.[11] And the tangible, if uneven, successes achieved by non-political working-class institutions during the 1850s and 1860s, combined with the overall stabilisation and expansion of the economy, promoted 'reformism' (by predominantly economic and social means) within the working class.

In addition, mellowed Liberalism (especially) and Conservatism from the mid–late 1840s onwards provided increasingly popular political attractions for workers, particularly working men (the mid-Victorian world of formal party politics being dominated by men). The profound shock provided by Chartism to the security of 'respectable' property owners, the growing 'respectability' and 'responsibility' of sections of the mid-Victorian working class, and the passage of many large Conservative and Liberal employers from the miserly and grasping practices of the 1830s and 1840s (imposed, in part, by the pressures of capital accumulation and declining rates of profit) to the more generous and socially responsible actions of the 1850s and 1860s, provided the determining context of the 'liberalisation' of the main parties. As we will see, 'liberalisation' was by no means a smooth and even process, free from tensions and class conflicts. But we cannot doubt the greatly accelerated extent to which leaders of Conservatism and Liberalism sought to create mass followings, to 'reach' workers, and to better accommodate their interests and claims. The aim was not only to generate strong partisan support but also to create an effective wedge against the re-emergence of radical popular movements of the Chartist type.

Popular Liberalism

Between the mid 1840s and the late 1860s Liberalism achieved ascendancy in British politics and Liberal radicalism permeated the British labour movement. Throughout Scotland, Wales and England the vast majority of former Chartists and new labour leaders adopted the Liberal creed. In terms of the labour movement, Conservatism attracted minority support, although its wider working-class base was much stronger.

Liberalism's appeal to workers was multi-layered.[12] Commitments to progress, reason, the extension of civil, political and religious liberties, social and political reform, civic-mindedness, and a culture rooted in self-help, moral earnestness, temperance and the 'improvement' ethic were of central importance. Liberals contrasted their Enlightenment ideals with the 'baser instincts' of a Toryism rooted in 'ignorance, reaction, intolerance . . . rowdyism, bellicosity . . . and the privileges of Wellington boots and the humble and reverent submission of clogs'.

Mid-Victorian Liberals strenuously attempted to cast aside images of Whig dogmatism and 'Gradgrindery'. By the mid 1840s Liberals in Bolton and elsewhere were far more prepared to countenance factory reform than during the acute industrial conflicts of the late 1830s and early 1840s. Among Bolton's employers and middle-class reformers there was a heightened concern with social stability and reciprocity between employer and worker. On a national basis Liberals were enthusiastic supporters of friendly and co-operative societies as being conducive to self-help, independence (a key word in the Liberal dictionary), and the cultivation of 'capitalist' values. Trade unions continued, however, to receive a mixed reception throughout the third quarter of the century. John Bright and other Liberal luminaries saw unions as dangerously 'wrongheaded' in many of their activities (their collectivism, their 'unnatural' interference with the 'laws' of the market, and their resort to strike action). But in overall terms Liberal hostility towards trade unionism was far less pronounced than during the Chartist period. Trade unions' emphasis upon their benefit features, their assiduous cultivation of a moderate and respectable public face, their reduced condemnations of capitalist 'tyranny', and their greater acceptance of the workings of the market all helped to allay Liberal fears of trade-union subversion and irresponsibility. It is thus significant that by 1870 all except two of the members of the Manchester and Salford Trades Council were Liberals – a pattern reflective of trade unionists' political loyalties throughout the country.

The softened economic and social visage of Liberalism can be illustrated with reference to developments in Ashton-under-Lyne and Stalybridge. Both towns had been strongholds of Chartism and were, in addition, dominated by Liberal and predominantly Nonconformist employers. As P.F. Clarke has observed, 'Ashton and Stalybridge... probably came as near as anywhere to exhibiting that conflict between bourgeois Liberalism and working-class Conservatism which was the staple myth of Tory Democracy'.[13] Much of the Chartist anger in Ashton and Stalybridge had indeed been directed against the 'purse-proud', 'haughty' and 'hypocritical' Liberal cotton masters who preached 'freedom' and 'liberty' and simultaneously practised opposition to trade unionism, factory reform and other manifestations of collective independence on the part of the cotton operatives. Charles Hindley, a local Liberal millowner, had contested elections at Ashton during the 1830s and 1840s on very progressive platforms (support for a ten-hours bill, universal male suffrage and total repeal of the New Poor Law). But, as Sykes remarks, Hindley had to contend with the popular Tory-radicalism of Joseph Rayner Stephens and the 'particularly naked' class divisions of Ashton. As a result, Hindley 'occupied an uneasy position between the radical wing of Liberalism and the popular political tradition', and a Chartist-Liberal alliance was not properly consummated.[14]

Between the late 1840s and the 1860s the labour movement in the Ashton-Stalybridge area did forge an alliance with the Liberals. Hindley's continued support for factory reform, the vote and other progressive causes secured him the support and friendship of leading local labour activists. And his attempt to present Liberalism as a broad reforming and crusading movement, concerned as much with fairness and the public good as with the workings of political economy and efficiency (looking forward to the day when workers, 'would cease to be regarded as looms or spindles, or cast metal, and be treated as creatures possessed of souls as well as bodies')[15] did much to broaden the base of the movement. This attempt to give Liberalism a 'human face' was strengthened in 1855 when the newly created *Ashton Reporter* announced its support for factory legislation, political reform, the creation of a national elementary system of secular education and, at least in principle (if not always in practice), trade unionism. The rabid 'No Popery' of local Toryism also strengthened the libertarian resolve of many Liberal labour activists.

However, of major importance in advancing the fortunes of Liberalism in the Ashton-Stalybridge area were the softened work- and extra-work-based practices and general 'change of heart' on the part of many of the wealthiest and most prominent local Liberal employers.[16] Illustrated in the extensive spread of paternalism (see Part Two, Volume One) and, for many, a *volte face* on the question of factory legislation, this 'change of heart' was most dramatically seen in the case of Hugh Mason, mayor, leading Liberal, and wealthy employer at Ashton. Opposed to Chartism, trade unionism and factory reform in the 1840s and spouting self-help, 'restraint' Nonconformity and abidance by the tenets of orthodox political economy, Mason was reputedly one of the most unpopular men in 1840s Ashton. However, the class conflicts of the Chartist years, combined with Mason's growing fortune from cotton spinning, induced a 'remarkable transformation':

> In 1859 he admitted that the Ten Hours campaign, 'had been nobly fought, and fairly won ... By the 1860s his harsh political economy of the 1840s had been softened by humanitarian concerns: 'He was not indifferent to the teachings of political economy, but he should be very sorry if the rigid and abstract rules of political economy alone prevailed in his workshops. It would be impossible for him to buy the labour of his workpeople ... the same as an ordinary commodity over the counter of a shopkeeper. He felt a deep interest in the welfare of his workpeople ... The bond which united them was not the cold bond of buyer and seller.[17]

Mason held his position as an employer to be 'far more sacred than that of a mere capitalist'. 'Brothers and Sisters' at the Oxford colony (the site of Mason's works and company-owned housing), they were, according to Mason, 'marching together for one common end – the mutual welfare of the workpeople and the employer'. The new-found 'responsibilities' of Mason were demonstrated in numerous ways: trips and 'treats' for his workers; the provision of a library and reading rooms at his mills; opposition to the parsimonious attitudes of many local millowners during the Cotton Famine; the distribution of free food and clothing during the Famine and vociferous support for public works and increased scales of relief for the unemployed operatives; and post-Famine advocacy of the Saturday half holiday, better inspection of the mines and the eight-hour day for miners. From 1840s 'haughty tyrant', Mason had, by the mid 1860s, become, in the opinion of the *Ashton*

Reporter, 'the most energetic, public spirited, and capable man the town has ever raised'.

Mason's transformation at mid century is significant in a number of ways. First, it dramatically illustrates both the mellowing of employer attitudes and the more civilised and caring character of Liberalism. Second, it demonstrates the changed nature of Liberalism in what had been one of the strongholds of Chartism and of class conflict. Even though the mid-Victorian Conservatives in Ashton and Stalybridge continually opposed the 'Manchester School' views of the Liberal Nonconformist millowners, Conservative propaganda met with only limited support. Indeed, throughout the 1850s and early 1860s local Liberals maintained that a Conservative workingman was 'the strangest creature imaginable'. Conservatism had largely failed to address itself to the changes within Liberalism. And in some centres beyond Ashton and Stalybridge, in, for example, Edinburgh and Kentish London, where social conflicts between workers and employers were generally far less marked and where Liberalism was not the dominant preserve of a highly visible and tightly knit Liberal Nonconformist mill-owning élite, a mass base for Liberalism had often developed both earlier and more harmoniously.[18]

Liberalism's attempt to consciously tone down the 'heartless' tenets of orthodox political economy did, third, have limits which were often productive of continued tensions, even class conflicts. Mason and many of the Liberal employers in the Ashton area long retained their suspicion of trade unionism. And some of the most prominent Liberal (and Tory) employers used paternalism as a conscious strategy to counteract the 'baneful' and 'disruptive' influence of trade unionism. Robert Platt, cotton manufacturer and a leading voice in Stalybridge Liberalism, offered trips and 'treats' in order to 'beat all trade unions out of court'. Dan Lynne, long-serving employee and 'trusted servant', and the key speaker at many of Platt's carefully orchestrated paternalist functions, preached deference and non-unionism: 'They wanted no third party to interfere between them and their employer; they acknowledged no paid secretary or committee in a back room, drinking brandy and water, and smoking cigars at the expense of the public'.[19]

Platt's aims and methods were shared by many other Liberal employers. Significantly, as emphasised in Volume One, instances of employer 'tyranny' and opposition to trade-union and legislative 'interference' in their concerns continued to generate bitter and protracted industrial disputes during the mid-Victorian period. And Conservatives in south Lancashire and elsewhere were quick to exploit instances of 'Manchester School' 'despotism'.

The patronising 'social control' aspect of Liberal and Tory paternalism also often aroused the indignation of those self-respecting, proud and *independent-minded* workingmen who were likely to be trade unionists, members of co-ops and, not infrequently, supporters of Liberalism's stated commitments to the principles of independence and liberty. Continued contradictions between structures of dependence and independence, of attempted middle-class control versus working-class desire for self-management, were to be found not only in mid-Victorian workplaces but also in the increasing number of 'cultural' endeavours (the opening of libraries and public parks, educational provision, soirées and co-operative and friendly society functions) which bound together Liberal (and Tory) 'respectables' from both the middle and working classes.[20] That Liberalism did soften its economic and social message is clear. But the process was less smooth and even than is sometimes supposed.

The consolidation of Liberal hegemony over the labour movement cannot be sufficiently explained with reference to economic and social factors alone. As Joyce has emphasised, the political and cultural (especially symbolic) appeals projected by the likes of Bright and Gladstone (the 'John the Baptist' and 'the Christ of popular liberal democracy')[21] were of fundamental importance. Above all, mid-Victorian Liberalism embraced the notions of citizenship, democracy, progress and embodied a crusading moral zeal.

Gladstone and Bright appealed to 'the people'. Significantly, 'the people' were not primarily identified in narrow 'factional' and 'selfish', class-based economic ways but in terms of moral attributes. The temperate, self-improving, respectable, decent, socially responsible, and liberty-loving producers from all classes were asked to join together in a crusade of common citizenship against reactionary and unthinking defenders of the status quo. The enemy included those besotted by drink, betting and all manner of brutal sports, 'unproductive' and 'parasitical' landlords, exacting and unrepresentative Churchmen (especially in Ireland), and those lacking in virtue, 'restraint' (especially of a sexual character) and firm commitment to the values of 'hearth and home'.[22] In effect, in comparison with the Chartist period, the notion of 'the people' had been expanded. The 'self-helping, self-educating working man with his co-operative society, savings bank, and chapel' was being invited to discard outmoded and exclusive class-based allegiances in favour of the brand new, progressive and inclusive embraces of citizenship and community. In Gladstone's opinion, 'respectable' workingmen had become, 'our fellow-subjects, our fellow-Christians, our own flesh and blood'.[23] All would henceforth march together under the banner of progress.

For the mid-Victorian Liberal progress was synonymous with com-

mitment to a number of causes: the extension of the parliamentary
franchise; (for some) the abolition of property qualifications for town
councillors; civic improvement and urban reform (the building of public
libraries, hospitals and town halls, the opening of public parks, better
educational facilities and environmental, especially public health,
improvement); the preservation and extension of civil and religious liberties (particularly opposition to compulsory Church rates and to the
dominance of the Established Church in Ireland); patriotism at home
and liberal nationalism abroad; and (for many) Nonconformity and
temperance.

The crusading zeal of the 'masses' against the 'classes' was clearly
shown in the great demonstrations preceding the Second and Third
Reform Acts. Smout has vividly recaptured the scenes in Scotland:

> These processions were pure street theatre, encapsulating more than
> anything else in the nineteenth century the character of proletarian
> Liberalism, and emphasizing its civic and craft pride, its class feel-
> ings against landlords, its sense of belonging to a coherent tradition
> of reforming zeal that stretched back at least a century, and its
> loyalty to the Liberal leaders felt to be its modern standard bearers.
> The Glasgow demonstration of 1884, intended to put pressure on
> an obstructive Tory House of Lords involved... 64,000 in the
> procession and another 200,000 gathering to greet them on Glasgow
> Green. They carried countless pictures of Gladstone and many of
> Bright, a flag from as far as back as 1774, banners from 1832 and
> from Chartist days, and models and mottoes old and new... The
> basic message was clear – the 'class' obstructed reform, the 'masses'
> were here to demand it.[24]

In such ways and by such means did Liberals establish a strong national
presence and a radical and earnest political culture around mid century.
Two further aspects of this culture should be highlighted. First, as
astutely noted by Joyce, the 'appropriation of the past to the cause of
Progress' was important not only in terms of Liberalism's radical self-
image but also the continued support offered by workers to Bright and
Gladstone. Thus Joyce wrote 'Political Liberalism set out with much
success to annex the radical past: there is no more telling a symbolic
expression of this than the construction of the Free Trade Hall on the
site of the Peterloo massacre.'[25] Emphasis upon a broad, consensual
radical tradition was not confined to events in Manchester. In the late
nineteenth century the Liberal press looked with (appropriately distant)
fondness upon the Chartist movement. W. H. Chadwick, for example,
who moved from Manchester Chartism to Liberalism, maintained in the
1890s that Chartism and Liberalism had naturally united around
common commitments to political and social reform and individual
freedom.[26]

Second, Joyce has also emphasised the central role of the Liberal (and Conservative) employer in creating and cementing political cultures at the local level.[27] Thus in Blackburn, Bolton, Bury and other Lancashire mill towns employers (and especially the wealthy paternalist employers) played, claims Joyce, a key part in setting the 'tone' and the culture of the neighbourhoods surrounding their mills. Employer influence, we are informed, was reflected not only at work and in patterns of leisure but also in voting preferences: those workers living in proximity to a particular mill generally adopted the political 'colours' of the millowner. And such employer hegemony was allegedly rooted far less in coercion and working-class instrumentalism (especially the desires to retain one's job and house) than in genuine worker internalisation of the views of the employer.

As was the case with its economic and social programme, mid–late Victorian Liberalism's political and cultural platforms were not lacking in internal tensions and contradictions which were often related to the question of class. For example the Liberal attempt to generate a tradition of broad, consensual radicalism was highly selective, propagandistic, contained within itself a number of silences and ambiguities, and glossed over important class conflicts (whether at Peterloo or between Chartists and middle-class reformers) within the history of radicalism. Victorian Liberalism's 'invention of tradition' must thus be approached critically. Too many of those historians currently bedazzled by 'the Word' (particularly in its absolute, non-referential form) have accepted Liberalism's claims to a broad, consensual, and longlasting intellectual and political tradition in far too uncritical and literal ways. We cannot simply accept words and their meanings at face value. In order to fully comprehend the shared and contested, continuous and changed meanings of words we must situate spoken, written, physical and symbolic forms of language in specific and changing historical contexts. By such means we will integrate ideas, actions, and the intended and unintended consequences of thought and action.

These methodological concerns have a bearing upon the nature and appeal of Victorian Liberalism. We can illustrate this point with reference to a key word in nineteenth-century political vocabularies, *independence*. As James Vernon has shown, mid-Victorian Liberals and Tories shared a strong attachment to the notion of independence, yet interpreted the word in largely different ways. Within the political culture of Liberalism independence signified, above all, self-improvement and proud, upstanding, and 'respectable' individuals. To many Conservatives the 'vision' of independence revolved around, 'the protestant nation proudly preserving the liberty and prosperity of the independent Freeborn Englishman in his cottage against the tyranny of Europe's Catholic states and Lancashire's satanic mill-owners'.[28] We have seen in Volume One that the notion of independence also lay at the heart of Chartism, being associated with personal and collective independence, class pride, and the ability and strong desire of workers to determine their own destinies free from cloying middle- and upper-class condescension and patronage. During the mid-Victorian years independence retained some of its associations with class pride in labour-movement circles. But simultaneously, the language of economically and socially 'successful' co-operators, trade-union leaders and others became more individualistic, status-conscious and privatised in character. There developed closer, if far from untroubled, links between the language of independent and 'respectable' ex-Chartists and middle-class Liberals. Politically conscious workers still resented the superior and condescending postures adopted by some Liberal 'friends of the working classes'. But the language of improvement, rooted in independence of character and determination, constituted a basis for cultural *rapprochement*. The 'poor', seemingly scorning self-help, had become a source of embarrassment and anger to the successfully independent workingman. Class conflict had, at least for many Co-operative leaders, become a relic of an 'uncivilised' past. In such ways did independence become synonymous more with inter-class harmony and co-operation rather than conflict. And economic changes, especially the material improvements in the position of the mid-Victorian Co-operative movement, did undoubtedly exert a powerful, if partial, influence upon the changed significance of independence.[29]

The changes were not, however, complete. Independence in the workplace continued to invite opposition to the absolute will of the boss. In political terms, a 'substantial minority' of Lancashire mill workers continued, in days before the introduction of the secret ballot, to vote against the wishes of the local employer.[30] The politics of civic improvement, whether predominantly Tory or Liberal in character, did sometimes provoke class-based conflicts. Who was to benefit most from the provision of parks, libraries and hospitals? Who was to exercise control over matters of general public concern? Who was to meet the cost of improved public provision? Was increased public provision compatible with adherence to free-market economics? As Koditschek has shown, such questions, debates and conflicts placed important constraints upon the extent to which Bradford's ruling Liberals translated fine words into the concrete practice of urban improvement in the mid nineteenth century. Public health, and especially sanitary conditions, remained a disgrace in Bradford and countless other northern towns in the 'Golden Age' of mid-Victorian capitalism.[31] Similarly, John Cole's recent work on Rochdale strongly suggests that John Bright and his mainstream Liberal allies were far less committed to popular, democratic and progressive movements than the conventional wisdom has led us to believe. Up to the early 1860s Rochdale's reputation for 'advanced' measures and causes (the possession of 'the most democratic local franchise in the country', and successful opposition to the establishment of a 'union' workhouse) owed far more to the endeavours of Thomas Livesey and his group of radical ex-Chartists on the town council than to the wealthy millowners who stood at the apex of local Liberalism.[32]

Rochdale also epitomised the continued mistrust between radical ex-Chartists and mainstream Liberals. During the Chartist period industrial conflict, and the issues of the New Poor Law, Sturge's Complete Suffrage Union and the repeal of the Corn Laws had created profound divisions between reformers of the Bright stamp and the Chartists. From the mid–late 1840s onwards, Livesey held out the hand of friendship to the reforming sections of the middle class on the basis of a possible compromise with the Chartists around the desired extent to which the parliamentary franchise should be extended. But throughout the 1850s there were important divisions between Bright's proposal for household suffrage and the radicals' continued call for universal manhood suffrage. Cole informs us that there remained a strong and independent local radical movement which resisted incorporation into mainstream Liberalism. Thus:

> local middle-class attempts at proselytisation met with very little success throughout our period. The working classes retained a remarkable independence of spirit, selecting those planks of reformism which suited their purpose and rejecting those which they considered to be irrelevant or actively detrimental to their interests.[33]

This spirit of independence was further fortified and sustained by the reputation of many of the Bright family for 'tyranny' in their mills. Opposition to trade unionism and the attempted enforcement of total control over the workplace on the part of the Brights constituted, according to many local people, acts of downright hypocrisy – formal commitments to 'freedom' and 'independence' being combined with haughty, dictatorial practices. As Ernest Jones declared in 1852, many of the 'Manchester Reformers' were 'hypocrites and traitors, who make of political liberalism a cloak under which to carry on social tyrannies unquestioned.'[34] Significantly, in late nineteenth-century Rochdale the memory of John Bright the 'tyrannical millowner' was probably more pronounced than that of 'standard-bearer of the people'.[35] The language of Bright, and especially his attempts to portray himself in a publicly favourable light, must thus be set into engagement with Bright's utterances and actions in the workplace (and in other contexts) in order that a balanced character portrayal may be offered. To offer portrayals of Bright and Liberal politics based solely or mainly upon language is to invite charges of partiality and a failure to transcend ideology.

Tensions and contradictions within post-Chartist Liberalism, largely overlooked by advocates of continuity and consensus, arose in many other urban areas. Two further examples will suffice to reinforce our argument.

First, in Halifax Chartist, and later radical-Liberal, politics demonstrated great tenacity during the 1850s and 1860s, albeit with diminished levels of popular support as compared with the 1840s. As late as 1868 a 'working man's candidate' was adopted to contest the parliamentary election against two opponents situated more firmly in mainstream Liberalism. In the aftermath of the election there were attempts to mend fences within Liberalism. But it was not until the mid 1870s that effective unity between the radicals and the more middle-of-the-road Liberals was achieved. In 1872 the newly created Halifax Liberal Association accepted a largely radical programme (based upon 'perfect religious equality'; the adoption of a national system of education, publicly funded and divorced from 'distinctive creeds'; the ballot and so on). But as Kate Tiller, the historian of late Chartism in Halifax, has declared:

> The partnership was an uneasy one. At the grand inaugural [of the Liberal Association] Edward Akroyd [local Whig] and the guest of honour, Gladstone's nephew Lord Frederick Cavendish, were heckled and there were interventions from the floor on republicanism and the bastardy laws. Only a new 'democracy', the first School Board elections of January 1874, finally brought anything like harmony to the sections of Halifax Liberalism with an unsectarian 'working man', John Snowden, heading the poll.

The general election of 1874 'cemented this united "popular" Liberalism' which finally 'overtook any overt, independent working-class political activity in the Chartist tradition'.[36]

Tiller's conclusion, that the 'political passage of Chartism into popular Liberalism was never an easy, passive, untroubled or complete process in Halifax', would appear to require some qualification in relation to our second case study, Bolton. As Taylor has observed, ' "reformist" radical-Liberalism achieved a mass base of support (in Bolton) before the consolidation of the grass-roots popular Liberalism of the 1850s and 1860s'.[37] The issues of 'Old Corruption', taxation, the conflict between 'productive' and 'unproductive' wealth, corn law repeal, and the agitation to repeal the tax on raw cotton, had provided much of the basis upon which a broad and 'gradualist' reform movement developed. At the 1852 parliamentary election campaign non-electors praised the principles and effects of free trade, condemned aristocratic 'privilege' and 'monopoly', and strongly supported Liberal proposals to extend the franchise.[38] But not all remained sweetness and light. Thus Taylor:

> But the consolidation of a grass-roots popular Liberalism proved not to be an untroubled merger of consenting ideas and values. In particular some sections of the Liberal big bourgeoisie believed that their aims could be achieved with only limited parliamentary reform and were slower to embrace democracy than the more 'advanced' middle-class reformers ... and working-class reformers.

During the 1859 parliamentary election in Bolton there was considerable opposition, especially on the part of workingmen, to the limited nature of Bright's household suffrage proposal. A Manhood Suffrage Association was set up to press for radical reform against the moderate intentions of the local 'Whig clique', and to support the candidature of Joseph Crook MP, 'the people's advocate'. Crook himself had supported the Ten Hours Bill for bleaching works, was opposed to the Whigs, thought Bright's proposal to be insufficiently radical, and expressed 'his adhesion to the principles of the Charter'. Crook received substantial popular support. The other Liberal candidate, Barnes, was 'the object of suspicion and detraction by the more democratic of the Liberal party'. Several of the gentlemen on Barnes' committee expressed 'strong repugnance to favouring in one way the return of Mr. Crook, with whose extreme democratic views they did not agree'. Given the split within Liberal ranks, and his lack of strong popular support, Barnes withdrew in order to permit Crook to carry the Liberal standard. During the 1860s Bolton Liberalism represented a relatively broad and united front although, as in the country at large, working-class Republicanism and charges of Liberal 'dictatorship' and 'hypocrisy' (as seen in the employment of the 'screw' during elections and Liberal employer 'tyranny' in the workplace) did at times create tensions.[39]

Popular Conservatism

We have seen both that Liberalism came to dominate the political complexion of the mid-Victorian labour movement and that Liberalism was not totally immune from internal conflicts. From time to time dreaded memories of 'physical-force' Chartism, of torchlight parades, drillings, and open class conflict, arose to threaten the image of political consensus and harmony. Furthermore, Liberalism did not have a monopoly upon the political allegiances of mid-Victorian workers. Conservatism, with its various emphases upon social radicalism and Tory Democracy, its links with Orangeism and 'No Popery', employer paternalism, and a relaxed and expansive political style rooted in the culture of 'beer, bonhomie, and Britannia' had, by the late 1860s, established important bases in many working-class communities.[40] It is to a consideration of popular Toryism that we will now move.

We have noted in Volume One that during the Chartist period the Operative Conservative Associations generally failed to develop strong working-class support and that, outside of the West Riding of Yorkshire, Tory radicalism was weak. There is precious little evidence that mass Conservative organisations developed before the mid–late 1860s (Liverpool and Wigan, their politics based upon religion and ethnicity, constituted obvious exceptions to the general rule)[41]. Tory radicalism continued to be extremely limited in terms of both extent and influence (the vast majority of national and regional Conservative leaders being far more concerned to defend traditional hierarchies, inequalities and, above all, the interests of property than to promote the causes of social reform, trade unionism and the more general interests of workers)[42], and links with the labour movement were weak. Furthermore, Liberalism's mellowed nature limited the extent to which Tory radicalism could score direct hits upon its main rival.

There were, nevertheless, certain parts of the country, and especially the cotton districts of Lancashire and Cheshire, where mid-Victorian Conservatives sought to advance their cause by attacking the 'inhuman doctrines' of the 'Manchester School' Liberal employers and their allies. As Patrick Joyce has perceptively remarked:

> If the Tory politician was tarred with the brush of reaction, the Liberal was tarred with that of social and economic *laissez faire*. No matter how much the rigours of political economy had been moderated, something of the charge stuck, and the Tories did their best to see that it stuck.[43]

In Manchester leading Conservative, W. R. Callendar, 'worked closely with the Tory leaders of the Manchester and Salford Trades Council, W. H. Wood and S. C. Nicholson, in order to promote the public acceptance of trade unionism'. The *Stockport Advertiser* and the *Oldham Standard* regularly attacked Liberal opposition to factory legislation and social reform. And in the 1868 parliamentary elections Conservative candidates in the cotton districts frequently referred to John Bright's opposition to the Ten Hours Act.[44]

In the Ashton-Stalybridge area Tory-radicalism developed a strong presence from the mid 1840s onwards. We have already seen that the majority of millowners in this area were Liberals. And, despite the 'change of heart' displayed by Hugh Mason and others, local Conservatives mounted fierce and unrelenting attacks upon Liberal 'dictatorship' and 'intolerance' (those in Mason's Oxford Works succumbing to the temptations of beer, tobacco and general 'frivolity' were allegedly in great danger of losing their jobs and rented homes), and the 'coldness' and 'indifference' of the Liberal 'Manchester School' élite. Joseph Rayner Stephens continued to occupy an important political place, advocating a union between the 'Altar, The Throne and The Cottage', and 'The Aristocracy and The People' in order to recreate pre-industrial social bonds and community ties in the face of the disruptive, anti-social, selfish and immoral forces unleashed by capitalist industrialisation. Opposed to political democracy (and in favour of an organic union between rich and poor), Stephens supported factory legislation and trade unionism as means of strengthening individual and collective defences against the ravages of unrestrained individualism and class oppression. In 1860 Reverends Verity and Stephens were to be found in the Ashton area exhorting workers to join the weavers' union. Verity supported combination in order to, 'vindicate humanity from its mighty tyrants'. Stephens in turn attacked 'wage-slavery':

> All that independence as citizens, as yeomen, as independent free-men had disappeared; they now lived on wages ... and if work be suspended they were thrown into the streets, helpless and powerless, and as a consequence, compelled in thousands ... to accomplish by union what they could not accomplish in their individual capacity.

During the 1860s and early 1870s Stephens supported the Conservatives while simultaneously opposing the anti-Irish feeling which swept across the northwest. Stephens led opposition to the miserly practices of (especially Liberal Nonconformist) millowners during the early part of the Cotton Famine, espoused the National Church as 'the church of all degrees and kinds', and actively defended the 'Englishmen's right' to 'the mug that cheers' against the temperance sentiments and endeavours of Hugh Mason and his Nonconformist Liberal allies.[45]

Even in Ashton and Stalybridge Stephens was regarded as something of a maverick by those who controlled local Toryism. And in many of the other cotton towns the strong presence of Conservative employers greatly weakened the extent to which Stephens' brand of populist social radicalism could develop. But in Stockport and elsewhere some of the (mainly older-established) wealthy Tory millowners did support factory legislation. In the West Riding of Yorkshire, especially in Huddersfield (the heart of Oastler's campaign for factory reform), Bradford and Keighley, the Tory Radical cause remained strong. This resulted in part, notes Joyce, from 'the antagonism between early-established Anglican-Tory business, with its landed links, and *nouveau riche* radical Noncon-formity.[46]

A variety of social radicalism associated with the Orange Order and other militant Protestant organisations also worked to the benefit of popular Conservatism. The massive increase in post-Famine Irish (predominantly Catholic) immigration into mainland Britain, combined with the Pope's restoration of the Catholic hierarchy in England and Wales in 1850, touched off a loud and aggressive backlash against Roman Catholicism in general and Irish Catholics in particular. In the early 1850s this backlash was predominantly middle class in character. But anti-Catholicism, touching upon deepseated fears of 'alien domination' and Papal 'mumbo-jumbo' and 'despotism', and defence of the 'liberties of Freeborn Englishmen', did generate an increasingly mass following, especially in Lancashire where Anglicanism and Irish Catholic immigration were particularly strong. And Orangemen and other militant Protestants frequently combined 'virulent attacks on Roman Catholicism with support for the economic and social grievances of English workers'.[47]

At Salford, for example, Reverend Hugh Stowell, ultra-Protestant, anti-Chartist and anti-socialist, supported the Ten Hours Bill, trade unionism and the principle of 'a fair day's wage for a fair day's work'. In 1850 Stowell warned that the Catholic church intended, 'to get England under her power ... to persecute and prosecute every Protestant ... to set up the inquisition in our land ... and to make Queen Victoria a Papist'. An extremely well-known and influential figure in Manchester and Salford Protestantism, Stowell had established by the 1860s a Sunday school system strong enough to render the Crescent district of Salford 'a Tory stronghold for years to come'.[48] At Ashton-under-Lyne Booth Mason, Deputy Grand Master of the Orange Order, prided himself upon his long and friendly contacts with local workers and in 1857 and 1865 contested Ashton upon the remarkable platform of manhood suffrage, 'No Popery', and support for factory legislation. Unlike many Conservatives and Orangemen, Mason welcomed the effects of political reform:

> He had been brought up with the working classes ... and was not afraid of them. He called them brethren, and he called them so because the great mass of those present were Orangemen. If they enfranchised the working classes, they would have Church and Queen, and down with dissent.

Throughout 1868 – the climactic year when 'No Popery' riots occurred in several English urban areas – extreme Protestants reiterated their identification with the oppressed (Protestant) masses. Reverend Heffill of Audenshaw (near Manchester) cultivated a 'proletarian' image by sporting clogs, defending 'ignorant' workingmen Tories who wore clogs themselves, and branded Liberal manufacturers as 'haughty, hypocritical, and effeminate snobs'.[49] And William Murphy, member of the Protestant

Electoral Union, and anti-Catholic firebrand whose itinerant lectures triggered off the appalling riots against Irish Catholics in Ashton, Stalybridge and elsewhere in 1868, consciously sought to exploit the anti-Catholic and economic and social grievances of Protestant and native-born non-Catholic workers. Sensationalist 'exposes' and violent denunciations of Roman Catholicism (the latter being equated with 'mumbo-jumbo, political despotism and Fenianism, and the alleged gargantuan sexual appetites of the priests') mingled in Murphy's speeches with 'attacks upon the immigrant Irish Catholics as puppets of the Pope, sympathisers with Fenianism, and as a profitable source of cheap labour for Liberal employers'. Thus:

> In December 1867 he claimed that employers were, 'anxious to put their lectures down', because Orangemen, 'showed up the system of Romanists working for such low wages'. The following month Murphy eulogised the colliers on strike in the Stalybridge area, and promised to raise a subscription to aid their cause. During his election campaign at Manchester he styled himself the 'working-man's candidate' and pledged, if elected, to introduce a bill into parliament to increase the wages of the working class and to outlaw female factory employment. 'Now, Milner Gibson will not do that', cried Murphy, 'Milner Gibson will keep you in the mill . . . and so will John Bright and Gladstone too'.[50]

Significantly, Milner Gibson, the Liberal candidate, was defeated in the parliamentary election at Ashton in 1868. A tide of anti-Catholic feeling swept the Conservatives to power in much of Lancashire and northeast Cheshire. Mid-Victorian Liberal ascendancy in the cotton districts was overturned. As in Liverpool, Wigan and other parts of west Lancashire, and parts of the Lanarkshire coalfield, Orangeism thus assumed an identification in the eyes of some workers with economic and social radicalism.

Even more significant were the mass base achieved by mid–late 1860s Orangeism and the channelling of that mass base into effective support for Conservative Party candidates at the 1868 elections. In Liverpool and areas of west Scotland the links between nineteenth-century Orangeism and Conservatives are well known. In Liverpool, for example, a mixture of Protestant and Catholic immigrants from Ireland, Anglicanism and Nonconformity effectively meant that politics would revolve around ethnicity, religion and class. Conflicts between ultra-Protestantism and Catholicism also constituted much of the staple fare of popular politics at Widnes, Wigan and Birkenhead. And, as Philip Waller has clearly shown, the formation (in 1868) and subsequent strength of the Liverpool Working Men's Conservative Association ensured that the 'defence' of Protestantism, combined with support for the trade unions and socio-economic interests of Protestant workers, would continue to dominate Liverpool's politics up to 1914 and beyond.[51]

Less well known is the strength achieved by Orangeism and other organs of extreme Protestantism in the cotton towns. Generally speaking, such organisations progressed from being small, predominantly middle-class bodies during the 1850s to large and mainly working-class institutions by the late 1860s. In 1868 Gladstone's plan to disestablish the Irish Church, combined with the riotous effects of Murphy's lectures, led to an upsurge in support. Throughout 1868 members of the Order addressed extremely large and noisy audiences. For example, at Stalybridge, where the principles of Orangeism had spread with 'astonishing rapidity' from the early 1860s, 800 people attended an Orange meeting in October. Between 1868 and 1870 the influence of Protestant groups remained very strong in south Lancashire with many, including former Chartists, adopting the slogan, 'The Queen, Garibaldi and Murphy'.

Ties between extreme Protestantism and Conservatism were close in the cotton districts. As I have noted elsewhere:

> In south-east Lancashire the Order was almost a branch of the Tory party; the men who ran the Order were very often the same men who ran the clubs and local Conservative Party Associations. In 1868 many Conservative candidates were either self-proclaimed Orangemen ... or ... close sympathisers with Orangeism. Many of the leading Conservatives of the area were to be found at Orange functions between 1868 and 1870.

By no means all Conservatives were anti-Catholic in their outlook (and there was a strong tradition of indigenous and wealthy Roman Catholicism in Lancashire). Similarly, many leading Conservatives and Liberals were quick to condemn the demagoguery and 'excesses' of Murphy and his riotous followers. Nevertheless we cannot escape the fact that many Conservatives, especially in south Lancashire, did endorse (albeit in more 'respectable' fashion) Murphy's sentiments. The Conservative Party's campaign at the 1868 elections was one of 'aggressive Protestantism'. Terrified by Gladstone's proposed disestablishment of the Irish Church, the Conservative Party readily adopted 'No Popery' as its election battle cry. Fears of Papal despotism in Britain, the Irish Catholics as the Pope's agents, and the termination of 'English liberties' and Queen Victoria's reign, dominated Conservative propaganda. And the Murphyite crowds who pillaged Catholic chapels and neighbourhoods in 1868 provided the shock troops of the Tory candidates. At Ashton, for example, Murphyites 'continually disrupted Liberal meetings and groaned or hooted outside the homes of prominent Liberals'. While Sidebottom and Mellor, the Conservative candidates, were portrayed as 'true Protestant heroes', Liberals were accused of being, 'crypto-Papists who wished to 'scatter the Established Church of England to the four winds of heaven" '. In truth, as argued by the *Manchester Guardian*, in 1868 Gladstone had been 'kicked out of Lancashire for not being a Protestant'. And working-class identification of social radicalism with Orangeism and Conservatism and popular anti-Catholicism had constituted important elements in Conservative successes.

Anti-Manchester School social radicalism and anti-Catholicism thus formed important popular points of entry into mid-Victorian Conservatism. But they were not exclusive. In many places, as noted earlier, Conservative employers were dominant and in others anti-Irish Catholic riots and 'Murphyite' influences were far less significant than in the turbulent 'frontier' towns of Ashton and Stalybridge. We may suggest that urban popular Toryism, especially in Lancashire, arose out of two other key influences: employer paternalism and 'influence'; and the ability of Conservatism to firmly root itself in the more robust and outgoing varieties of working-class culture. Disraeli's authorship of the Second Reform Act of 1867 (a 'leap in the dark' occasioned far more by 'one-upmanship' with Gladstone on the reform issue than by any commitment to Tory Democracy) also helped to reverse the Conservatives' (well-grounded) reputation for opposition to political reform.[52] But it was in the experiences and structures of daily life and 'common-sense' that Victorian Conservatism developed a more longlasting hegemony.

During the 1850s and 1860s the 'new' paternalism was a feature of Conservative as well as Liberal employers. And, as demonstrated by Joyce in relation to Blackburn, Bury, Bolton and elsewhere, the political and cultural influences of Tory employers matched those of their Liberal counterparts. But of great interest to contemporaries and historians were the different political styles, images and cultures projected by Liberal and Tory employers and respective party leaders. It is to a discussion of the distinctive style and political culture of Toryism that we can now usefully turn.

Whether in Blackburn, Stalybridge or Wolverhampton the Tories prided themselves upon their broad, relaxed, informal, tolerant, robust and patriotic appeal to 'the people'. Shared customs, habits and values, as opposed to strict adherence to political programme, party line or ideological purity would constitute the basis for Conservatism's mass appeal. Much like the Liberals, the Tories consciously attempted to create a political culture rooted in the notion of 'community'. But whereas the Liberals sought 'community' in the earnest, temperate, self-improvers of all social strata, the Tories were far more tolerant of the 'weaknesses' of the people. The 'respectable' workingman – who nevertheless liked sports, including 'manly' blood sports, betting, drinking (an integral part of the 'liberties of the Freeborn Englishmen'), and was sociable and easy going, who was a 'natural' defender of Church and State, who was far more 'practical' and determined than 'intellectual' and faint-hearted, who identified a close affinity between himself and his family and the propertied rulers of society, who disliked the self-righteous, morally intense and priggish among Liberal working-men, and who had a strong sense of 'place' as embodied in local and national pride – constituted the target of Tory propaganda. Conservatism thus situated itself within the culture of 'conviviality and bonhomie', of 'beer, 'bacca, billiards, and Britannia' rather than within the strait-jacketed Liberal domain of 'moral exhortation' and the 'improving tract'.[53]

This is not to suggest that earnest and improving Conservatives were totally absent, and that Liberalism, drink, and 'non-respectable' practices and habits were invariably at odds. But, as Joyce, has argued, Toryism was generally less inflexible and narrowly based than Liberalism. Thus:

> There were many 'improvement'-conscious Tory employers and 'improving' Tory workingmen, but Toryism is general, rather more than Liberalism, was adaptable, and capable of appealing to all social and cultural levels, the godly and the godless, the 'abstinent' and the indulgent. The Tory voice often spoke of things the chapel knew not, in the accents of indiscipline and unrespectability. It spoke of the poor man's right to his glass of beer and his idle pastime. It spoke to the Blackburn of 1867: '. . . it is a thoroughgoing Tory community. Strong drink is the secret of its own and Britain's greatness; after that its heart has been given for long years to the Church and cockfighting'.[54]

Toryism, at least in intention, thus cast its social net wide and deep. The identification, often made by Liberals, of Toryism with the riotous 'rags and tatters' of society was, in essence, wide of the mark. It was the robust sociability of the amiable and respectable John Bull rather than the 'roughness' and 'depravity' of the 'residuum' which met with Conservative approval. And it was the 'dictatorial intolerance' of the likes of Hugh Mason which was roundly condemned.

Something of the tone, character and appeal of Conservatism in an urban context can be gained from a study of the north Lancashire weaving town of Blackburn. The latter, as richly portrayed by Walsh, Joyce and Trodd,[55] constituted along with Stalybridge, a veritable strong-hold of working-class or 'clog' Toryism during the second half of the nineteenth century. Blackburn was dominated by Conservative employers, and especially the Hornbys in cotton who epitomised Tory paternalism and the town's Conservatism.

During the Chartist period the Hornby family had encountered considerable popular opposition. William Henry Hornby, an employer of over 1,400 operatives at mid century, had been thrown into the town's river by the radical 'mob', forced to barricade his house, and shot at during the strikes of 1842. From the mid 1840s the Hornby family and local Conservatism changed course. At the 1847 parliamentary election in Blackburn local Conservatives were reputedly seeking the votes of Chartists, and William Henry Hornby had become, by the late 1840s, a fervent supporter and defender of the Ten Hours Act. In 1852 the Liberals defeated Hornby. But thereafter, until Labour's Philip Snowdon captured one of the town's two parliamentary seats in 1906, Tory hegemony prevailed in Blackburn. And that hegemony revolved around social radicalism, paternalism and that mixture of 'traditional',[56] 'John-Bull'-like qualities depicted above.

In 1853, for example, William Hornby treated members of the Operative Conservative Association to a trip to Blackpool and a ball and banquet on their return. In his speech at the banquet Hornby, 'congratulated them on their continued existence and on the recent success of the town's working class... in gaining an increase of 10 per cent'. He further 'defended the legitimacy of trades unionism, and denounced the "tyrannical masters" like Montague Fielden' (the latter being a Liberal and newly elected MP for Blackburn). This was the beginning of some fifty or so years of 'flamboyant Hornbyism'. As Trodd observes, Tory successes were more dependent upon social and cultural endeavours and broad appeal within the community than upon political programme. For example, imperialism, 'often reduced to a rather mystical adulation of monarchy and empire and an anti-foreigner chauvinism', was used as a vote catcher during many elections, but the natural 'commonsense' of Conservatism was grounded in the routines of daily life. Thus Trodd:

> Of greater significance for the long tradition of working-class Toryism... was a wider network of loyalties inspired through the operation of paternalism and underlying those issues that surfaced at elections. The success of the Tories lay in a permissive attitude to popular activity, an astute identification with the central institutions of working-class culture, coupled with the sponsoring and patronage of essentially middle-class institutions designed to win working-class acquiescence.[57]

In order to achieve cultural hegemony, Blackburn's Tories permeated the institutions of the community – the pubs, friendly societies, co-operative societies, local burial societies, workingmen's clubs, football teams and sections of the trade-union movement – with their partisan presence. The Hornbys themselves placed a premium upon their intensely local and personal connections and their service to the community. The informal, populist approach was carefully cultivated:

the Tory party owed a great deal to the 'common touch', a benevolent tolerance with 'a larger share of original and mundane humanity'
than the Liberals with their concern for 'getting on'. W. H. Hornby
had once been a steeplechaser and Harry Hornby's brother, the
cricketer A. N. Hornby, was known as 'a bit of a card' and 'The
Boss', rode to hounds, had been a member of Blackburn Rovers
for a time and taken on boxers in fairground booths. John Ruther-
ford, 'owd Jack', kept a prizewinning racehorse and liked to end
his speeches by drawing a union jack from his pocket like a conjuror
and waving it at the audience.[58]

Harry Hornby trusted to 'common sense and instinct' rather than to
political theories. As Trodd observes, 'Much of the Hornbys' appeal, in
fact came from this apparent apoliticism, an appeal more easily understood when one remembers the general cult of amateurism in English
political life and the working-class distrust of politics and officialdom.'
An approachable gentleman, Hornby gave generously to football clubs,
church schools and boys' clubs, being regarded as 'almost their patron
saint' by many members.

In such ways did Blackburn's Tories set themselves up as the party
of the community, the 'workingman' and the 'nation'. By way of contrast the Liberals were regarded as sectional and puritanical 'killjoys',
many of them allegedly 'namby-pamby foreigners', unused and unsympathetic to 'local ways'. As we will observe later, the Labour Party's
challenge to the Conservatives in Blackburn involved struggles to gain
hegemony over the institutions and mores of the local working class,
to combat the traditional hierarchical social arrangements of the mill,
the Church, the Orange lodge, the pub and its related leisure-based
activities, and to create a new political 'commonsense' based upon co-
operation, 'true' democracy and greater equality.

Elsewhere in urban and rural England, the mixture of paternalism and
expected deference, 'traditionalism', and links to a robust, predominantly
'masculine' culture were evident in the growth of popular Toryism. Far
from being in some way 'unnatural' or 'deviant', post-1860s Conservatism would increasingly pose a formidable challenge to the electoral
popularity of Gladstonian Liberalism.[59]

Arguments

Before proceeding to an examination of the main political developments
between the Second Reform Act and the mid 1880s, we should pause
to take stock of the arguments so far offered. We have suggested, above
all, that the political and cultural independence which so marked the
Chartist movement was greatly diluted during the mid-Victorian years.
In so far as they were politically involved, most workers increasingly

came within the orbits of Conservatism and Liberalism. Furthermore, politics extended beyond formal institutions and elections deep into the cultures of local communities. Tensions continued to exist within Liberalism. And Toryism was distrusted by large sections of the labour movement on account of its associations with defence of the status quo and its 'sham radicalism'. But the outstanding facts of the mid-Victorian period of popular politics were the marked decline of class-based independent labour politics and popular accommodation to Tory and Liberal rule.

We should add that this process of accommodation was spread unevenly across Britain. Tony Taylor's current work shows, for example, that Chartism and other manifestations of popular radical political independence enjoyed longer and more robust life in mid-Victorian London than in Manchester.[60] The more 'open' nature of politics in London, the capital's less highly developed political organisations, the more restricted extent of the parliamentary suffrage, the continuing problems of London's trades and the maintenance of stronger links between economic and political means of salvation, and the much weaker presence of antagonistic Liberal Nonconformists and Anglican Tories and Orangemen, all meant that the solutions offered by independent politics and manhood suffrage maintained a sizeable appeal in London well into the 1850s and beyond. In contrast, by the early–mid 1850s the highly organised Liberals (benefiting from the organisational, leadership and propagandistic techniques successfully developed by the Anti-Corn-Law League) and the social-radical and anti-Catholic Tories were effectively closing down the political space in Manchester. Room for Chartist manoeuvre was further restricted by its loss of the battle of ideas to the Liberals, to Chartism's increasing failure to offer an effective antidote to the spread of anti-Catholic popular feeling, and to the general movement away from political solutions into economic and social means of improvement in the Manchester area.

Taylor's interesting work highlights the value of detailed comparative investigation, exposes massive areas of unexplored and potentially fruitful terrain for the mid-Victorian labour historian, and rightly details the complexities of change and continuity at mid century. The equally impressive researches of Peter Taylor, Tiller, Gray and Crossick outlined earlier also emphasise variations in the pace, timing and extent of political and social changes around 1850. But within this complex mosaic we can detect the dominant pattern of the demise of political independence and the sharp changes in consciousness and policy frequently involved in the decline of Chartism and the rise of popular Liberalism and Conservatism.

Party Attachments and the Onset of 'Mass' Politics

From 1867 onwards the two main political organisations were obliged to compete within the context of 'mass' politics. The Act of 1867 enfranchised borough householders. The Third Reform Act of 1884 extended household suffrage from the boroughs to the counties, in the process enlarging the electorate by a further 76 per cent. As Belchem observes, 'this was still far from universal suffrage'. Women continued to be denied the parliamentary franchise (although the Municipal Franchise Act of 1869 did enable many women to take an active part in local politics). And up to 1918 some 40 per cent of adult males failed to qualify for the vote.

In ushering in the age of male political democracy, the Second Reform Act was, nevertheless, of profound significance. In the cotton town constituencies of Lancashire, for example, the electorate was increased five- or sixfold. Moreover, although the Liberals under Gladstone were the national beneficiaries of the extended franchise in the elections of 1868, the Reform Act also demonstrated, to the surprise of many contemporaries, the depth of popular Conservatism. As already seen, this was particularly the case in Lancashire. As Walton notes, in the 1865 general election Lancashire's twenty-eight seats had been evenly divided, but in 1868 the Conservatives won twenty-four seats to the Liberals twelve. Numerous mid-Victorian cotton strongholds of Liberalism passed to the Tories, a fact in part explicable in terms of boundary changes but which also undoubtedly owed much to the Conservatism of the new working-class voters. Furthermore, despite fluctuations in the national fortunes of the political parties (power alternating between Liberals and Tories between 1868 and the mid 1880s), the Tories continued to 'rise' in Lancashire. Thus Walton:

> In the cotton seats overall, a 12–6 Liberal lead was reversed, and in 1868 the Conservatives prevailed by 13–7, as well as winning all 8 of the county seats. This was a remarkable reversal of fortunes, and it was recognised as such at the time. Moreover, it was no mere flash in the pan. The Conservatives held on to most of their gains in 1874, and the Liberals recovery of lost ground in 1880 was only temporary. Under the wider county franchise of 1884, and the ensuing redistribution which increased the number of Lancashire seats to 58, the Conservatives won 38 seats in 1885 ... and they continued to dominate the country's electoral map until the Liberal landslide of 1906.[61]

Between 1885 and 1905 the Conservatives dominated the national scene, losing power only between 1892 and 1895 over the entire period. This was a remarkable achievement, partly arising from the substantial movement of the propertied middle classes into Conservatism, but also attributable to that significant minority of the working class (constituting about one-third by the inter-war period) who were attracted to the Conservative cause.[62]

The Clubs

Mass support for the Tories and Liberals in the post-1867 period issued from a variety of factors. Both parties attempted to come to terms with and capitalise upon the advent of 'mass' politics by by putting down stronger organisational roots within the working class. Thus working-class Liberal and Conservative clubs and associations emerged in many places after the Second Reform Act. Initially Disraeli was lukewarm about the creation of Conservative clubs, believing class-based institutions to be incompatible with the 'one nation' appeal of Conservatism. But he relented once the clubs were firmly placed under the control of the propertied elements within the constituency organisations. Both Liberal and Conservative clubs offered 'political education', in the form of lectures and debates, and some had libraries and reading rooms. But increasingly the social side of club life became of more importance. Cards, draughts, billiards, 'smoking concerts', picnics, dances, bowls and (especially among Tory workingmen) alcohol assumed by the 1880s greater attractions than party political work. As Joyce has remarked, by the 1880s 'complaints about gambling, and the primacy of "bacca, billiards and beer", were legion in respectable circles'. But, Joyce continues, popular wishes prevailed:

> The clubs developed under the pressure of what the members wanted rather than what their betters thought they should have. Instead of lectures and reading rooms, what mattered was the round of comedy evenings, bazaars, tea parties and outings. Billiards, bowls, and above all the bar, rapidly dominated club life, especially in the elaborate clubs of the 1870s and 80s, the solid, square presence of which is still a considerable feature of northern recreational life.[63]

Above all, and especially in the north, the clubs were popular. Joyce's observations once again merit attention:

> In 1871 there were twenty-two party clubs in Bolton, in 1889 forty-three in Oldham, and in Rochdale seventeen out of twenty-nine clubs in the town in 1885 were political. In 1867 the first flush of renewed activity produced membership figures for the Conservative clubs as follows: 500 in Ashton, 700 in Stalybridge, 1,000 in Rochdale and a reputed 5,000 in Manchester. After the second wave of club development in the late 1870s and 80s there were nearly 3,200 members in thirty-one Bolton Conservative clubs.[64]

Give such figures, there appears to be little doubt that the bulk of rank-and-file club members in urban Lancashire were working class (clerks and others from the lower middle class tended to be prominent at the committee level).[65] Prepared to lend a hand with leafleting, registration and canvassing, most club members nevertheless saw the clubs as a welcome change from work. Finally, the growth of party-based friendly, burial and co-operative societies added to that peculiar cultural milieu of the English workingman in which political partisanship mixed with the increasingly mass-based pursuit of apolitical social and leisure activities. In any event the club movement of later Victorian Britain put down much firmer popular political roots than comparable Liberal and Tory endeavours of the 1830s and 1840s.

The Parties and Women

Of particular interest were the greatly accelerated attempts of the post-1867 parties to attract women to their respective causes. As Linda Walker has informed us,[66] women were drawn into the 'hitherto sacrosanct world of male party politics' for 'pragmatic rather than feminist reasons'. Women had, as we have seen in Volume One of this study, been involved in Chartism and other forms of popular community-based protests. But the decline of Chartism, the growth of more formal work-based forms of action, and the increasing popularity of the notions of the 'family wage' and 'separate spheres' had relegated women to a position of marginality in the mid-Victorian labour movement. The general permeation of the two main parties (with the exception of some pro-feminist Liberals) by patriarchal ideas had also greatly limited the extent to which women were to be afforded an official public presence.[67] Indeed, until the achievement of the vote for women over thirty, in 1918, women were excluded from the two main party organisations. However, the extension of the franchise in 1884 and the Corrupt Practices Act of the previous year, which outlawed the payment of canvassers, compelled party leaders and organisers to give added thought to the development of organisational structures which could more widely and effectively enlist the voluntary efforts of supporters, including women. The latter, it was envisaged, could help with a variety of unpaid practical tasks from the work of registration to canvassing. Indeed, party leaders soon came to attach special importance to the role of the female canvasser. Women, it was argued, were far more likely to present a 'caring touch' and 'winning appeal' on the doorstep than their male colleagues, and were far less susceptible to physical assaults from hostile householders.

In later Victorian times women were accordingly brought more into the structure of party politics, albeit in subsidiary associations. Walker informs us that Women's Liberal Associations 'first appeared from about 1880'. The Women's Liberal Federation was formed in 1887 (its splinter group, the Women's National Liberal Association, being born in 1892), and the Women's Liberal Unionist Association began life in 1888. These sex-segregated women's Liberal organisations found a partial echo in Conservative organisation. The Primrose League, formed initially (in 1883) as 'a semi-secret society of Conservative gentlemen' (to further the cause of Churchill and his clique), was soon transformed into a mass organisation committed to the defence of the Church and Crown and traditional hierarchies and seeking to enlist the support of those Tory worthies beyond the existing network of clubs and associations.[68] Following pressure from society hostesses, women were admitted to the League in 1884 and a sex-segregated Ladies Grand Council was established in 1885.

Gender- and class-based divisions frequently coexisted within the Primrose League. Thus the Ladies Grand Council was subservient to the overall control and policy direction of the exclusively male and aristocratic Grand Council. Furthermore, the financial subscriptions made by male and female members (known as Knights and Dames) to the local branches or Habitations were usually beyond the means of labouring people. The latter were accordingly enrolled as lowly Associate members, paying lower subscriptions but, if deemed worthy by their courtly betters, capable of being raised to the ranks of honorary Knights and Dames. Absurdly preoccupied with issues of rank and status, the League ironically effected degrees of sex integration in the local Habitations (most were mixed) unknown to the self-styled progressive and segregation-minded Liberals. Thus, while the Ladies Grand Council deferred to the wishes of male aristocrats and excluded women who were not 'ladies', nevertheless the local Habitations were (financial standing and membership status excepted) open to men and women on an equal basis. This was in marked contrast to the Liberals. Furthermore, Pugh suggests that, 'In the typical mixed habitations ... women were not merely passive footsoldiers marshalled under male leadership' (approximately 25 per cent of leading office holders sampled by Pugh being women).[69]

Both the Primrose League and the various Liberal organisations for women developed strong bases. The former, in particular, attracted very considerable working-class support. According to official estimates (which undoubtedly contained a degree of upward bias), total membership of the League increased from 957 in 1884, to over 200,000 by 1886, to 1,001, 292 in 1891 and a very impressive 2,053,019 by 1910. No other popular political organisation could compete with such growth or overall membership. Furthermore, as Pugh observes, 'uniquely for a Victorian political institution' hundreds of thousands of women belonged to the League. Almost half the total membership was female. And there is evidence to suggest that in some areas both levels of membership and women's involvement were extremely high. Thus the League's Habitation at Bolton, comprising some 6,000 members in 1900, was equal to the total national membership of the leading socialist organisation of the time, the Independent Labour Party. And Lynn Cooper's current research suggests that Bolton's Habitation was not only one of the largest in the country but was also dominated by women, constituting the *de facto* women's wing of the local Conservative Party.[70]

By the turn of the century the Women's Liberal Federation had increased its initial membership by over sixfold (from 10,000 in 1886 to 66,000 in 1904). And by 1910 the Federation claimed to have 104,759 members. Other women were members of the Women's National Liberal Association which found the Federation's brand of feminism (including active campaigning for women's suffrage) too strong for their more moderate taste. Women's single sex and predominantly middle-class Liberal organisations thus flourished, albeit less spectacularly and with less success among working-class women than the Primrose League.[71]

Walker has drawn a sharp distinction between the roles of women in Conservative and Liberal organisations. Thus:

> A striking difference between Primrose League and Liberal women was the latter's deliberate cultivation of female political power – not simply as canvassers but as voters, candidates and makers of policy. Their practical objectives were fourfold: to improve women's political education, to make sure that women voters used their prerogative in local elections, to encourage women candidates for Poor Law Boards, School Boards, town and county councils and, ultimately, to enhance their claim to the Parliamentary suffrage.

And, 'by virtue of being women-only', Women's Liberal Associations offered 'more of their sex an education in political management'. Walker does concede that an important part of the Primrose League's work lay in the political education of its male and female members, and that women attained positions of authority and skills in public speaking. But, we are told, such activities were set within 'clearly defined limits': the acceptance of a low profile and the fact that 'women were only extending their domestic managerial role'; the exertion of indirect and supportive influence, 'to be the complement and never the rival of men in politics'; and the recognition that women's *forte* lay in social activities and practical political work rather than in framing policy and ideology. Women were thus central to the tea and garden parties, concerts and lantern shows of the League and to the mundane, if essential, tasks which surrounded elections.[72]

There is doubtless much truth in Walker's portrayal of middle-class Liberal women as being more assertive, independent-minded, and committed to the feminist cause than most women in the League. Whereas, for example, the Women's Liberal Federation actively campaigned for women's suffrage, the League was 'always careful to dissociate itself from... militant feminism', delighted in comparing its ' "masculine" women with the more womanly Dame', and declared the subject of women's suffrage to be beyond its official remit.[73]

Equally we must, however, delve beneath official pronouncements issuing from head office. And Cooper's important and controversial local findings – that Bolton's predominantly middle-class Liberal women did not display a confident and independent feminist presence, that they did not adopt a corporate stand on the issue of women's suffrage (and generally put the interests of the Liberal Party above those of women), and that they were an exclusive group, preaching self-help and 'improvement' to workers and largely insensitive to the structural underpinnings of poor housing, unemployment and so on – should certainly be set against the established national picture. In addition, the question of votes for women was often sympathetically treated in Bolton's League meetings. And the Tories' reputation for sociability and informality, discussed earlier in this chapter, may well have extended to women. Thus Vernon has observed, in relation to the early–mid Victorian years, that, 'In the cultural politics of gender... the Oldham Tories were light years ahead of the town's radicals.' While the latter staged 'respectable' family entertainments and social events under male supervision, the 'Female Operative Conservatives met under their own auspices to drink, dance, and talk in local pubs and clubs.' By the end of the century the Primrose League in Bolton provided a congenial home for those working-class women seeking sociability, a warm welcome and genuine acceptance, fun and entertainment, respect borne of their contribution to political work, and an escape from middle-class homilies on the need to practise self-denial and hard work.[74]

Despite their differences of appeal, both Tory and Liberal endeavours to secure women's support had the common effect of challenging the mid-Victorian notion of hard and fast 'separate spheres'. Given their increased participation in the public business of politics, women could no longer be so easily confined to the private sphere of the home. Male politicians frequently attempted to downplay or counteract the increased political presence of women by re-emphasising women's 'primary' duties to home and children and the notions of the 'male breadwinner' and the 'family wage'. Women in turn frequently defended their enhanced public position on the grounds that, as wives and mothers, they would inject a more caring 'mother-spirit' into the 'rough-and-tumble' of political life. Such a defence could convey conservative and radical meanings. In terms of the former, many men and women in both Britain and the United States continued to lay great stress upon the supportive role provided by caring and public-spirited women to men. But for a minority of female feminists and socialists, especially in the United States, the special caring and sisterly attributes of women assumed much more radical, indeed revolutionary, meanings. Such attributes would provide the basis for the purification and transformation of both personal and social relationships and the moral inspiration for the creation of a truly co-operative and egalitarian society. According to this latter scenario, women stood, therefore, in the vanguard of change.[75]

Ideologies, Limitations and Tensions

Organisational endeavours to meet the needs of 'mass' politics were accompanied by a mixture of old and new ideological emphases. In terms of the Conservative Party, commitments to the legislative defence of 'responsible' trade unionism, to limited degrees of social reform (in the spirit of 'One Nation' Toryism) and to the defence of 'the family' and the 'Englishman's castle' (against the 'unwarranted intrusions of an increasingly interventionist state' and against the alleged 'free-loving' and 'nationalising' desires of 'atheistic socialists' upon personal relationships and child care) were combined by the early twentieth century with support for tariff reform (as the guarantor of steady employment and the funds with which to finance social reforms). These commitments were added to the attachments to Church, Monarchy, Empire, social radicalism and the distinctive cultural appeal of the party described earlier.[76] Gladstonian Liberalism, complete with its crusades for Home Rule and against aristocratic 'privilege' represented something of a radical departure from the security and stability epitomised by Palmerstonian 'moderation'. Furthermore, Liberalism's general identification with 'progressive' causes, its close ties with organised labour (from the late 1860s onwards the trade-union movement offered institutionalised support to Liberal candidates), and towards the end of the century the rise of 'New Liberalism' (with its support for 'collectivism', social reform financed by means of graduated taxation and death duties, and its partial accommodation of some of the class-based issues of Labour) propelled increasingly large numbers of the propertied classes into the arms of the Conservatives.[77] Liberalism's late nineteenth- and early twentieth-century claim to represent 'the People' was in fact increasingly endangered not only by propertied Conservatism but also by growing demands for independent labour representation and 'class' justice.

This last point obliges us to turn our attention to the limitations of popular Liberalism and Toryism between the late 1860s and the mid 1880s. As in the mid-Victorian period the two parties generally accommodated workers' interests, but working-class integration was not total or untroubled. For example, there were largely class-based organisational and ideological boundaries beyond which neither party wished to venture. As Joyce and Garrard have shown, the political clubs created in the wake of the Second Reform Act appealed to a mass constituency while remaining under the strict control of the propertied elements within both Liberalism and Toryism. 'Excluded from political power', observes Joyce, 'the working class was nevertheless included in the political process by means of the manipulation of the fiction of consultative democracy'. In the clubs, political caucuses, and on the town councils representatives of industry and wealth continued to operate the levers of power while simultaneously streamlining 'the machinery of a make-believe democracy'.[78] And the 'social control' element remained strong. Although largely given over to social activities, the clubs, Habitations and associations did encourage workers to develop 'correct', 'responsible' and 'respectable' modes of thought and behaviour in accordance with middle-class views and experiences of the world.[79] Similarly, working-class women enjoyed enhanced space and independence within the Primrose League and Liberal political organisations. But the overall direction and ideological content of such organisations lay ultimately in the hands of middle-class and aristocratic men and women. And, although not often voiced in this period, demands for an increase in the numbers of working-class Liberal members of parliament during the early 1870s had no major impact upon the Liberal Party. Thus before 1886 only two workingmen, Burt and Macdonald of the miners, were selected and elected to parliament as Liberals, and both were returned without Liberal opposition 'on orthodox programmes unexceptionable to middle-class radicals'.[80]

Ideological constraints and contradictions were also in evidence. The notion of Tory Democracy, for example, was more rhetorical than real. Despite the trade-union and social reforms of his 1874–80 ministry (which, in any case, were limited and piecemeal and in part inherited from Gladstone's 1868–74 government), Disraeli was committed far more to the defence of property and inequality than the radical advancement of working-class influence and power. As Belchem has noted, 'under Disraeli's leadership, the Conservatives remained overwhelmingly rural and aristocratic in ethos, attitudes and electoral calculation'.[81] Much of the party leadership was 'disdainful of the new middle-class conservatism' into the 1870s, and Salisbury, having resigned in alarm over the 1867 Reform Act, remained extremely fearful of the working class. Salisbury believed the masses to be inherently radical, and that Tory Democracy would 'lead ineluctably to the dispossession of the wealthy'. Under Salisbury's late nineteenth-century leadership the Conservatives thus adopted a quietist or inactive policy towards the 'masses'. As E.H.H. Green has argued:

> In Salisbury's mind there was no possibility of converting the democracy to Conservatism, all that could be done was to discipline the masses on their inexorable path to political ascendancy.
> ... Salisburyian Conservatives were opposed to any systematic appeal to the masses on the basis of a 'constructive' programme ... The futility of a 'constructive' appeal was that it would concede the necessity of systematic reform and allow radicals and Socialists to take up the stakes, thereby drawing the Conservatives into a game of bid and counter-bid which they could never hope to win. The counter-productive aspect of attempting to appeal to the working class vote on constructive lines was that it posed the risk of alienating propertied support.[82]

It was precisely the task of defending the interests of landed, commercial, and industrial wealth and property which Salisbury placed at the top of the Tory agenda. Plans for social reform via the Liberal model of increased taxation were to be avoided at all costs. The inherently radical and untrustworthy 'masses' were, in so far as it was possible, to be kept off the electoral register, trust placed in the new 'villa Toryism' of the suburban middle and lower-middle classes alongside the 'traditional' instincts of the solidly wealthy, and tariff reform used as a counterweight to the socially disruptive schemes of the Liberals in order to deliver employment and social reform. There was precious little radicalism or democratic spirit evident in this electoral shopping list. Joyce's shrewd judgement upon northern Toryism can be extended to the national scene:

> Tory Democracy ... had more to do with the Toryism of the democracy than any democracy in Toryism. Despite the genuine sympathy of some individuals, the history of Toryism and social reform makes this plain. The national leaders, and the vast majority of the regional ones, were set fair on the course of bourgeois business Conservatism that led from Palmerston, *via* Disraeli, to the modern party. It was with this kind of party that the labour interest had to deal.[83]

Tensions were also present within popular Liberalism. It was Gladstone's 1868–74 ministry which introduced both legal recognition for trade unions *and* the Criminal Law Amendment Act which made pickets liable to prosecution for intimidation, molestation and obstruction.

Many trade-union leaders reacted angrily to this measure, and some called for independent labour representation. But nothing substantive emerged from this call, at least in the short term. Disraeli subsequently introduced more adequate legislative protection for the unions. And on a general level the unions maintained their allegiance to Lib.-Labism.[84] But by the mid–late 1880s economic and social tensions – which had frequently been a thorn in the side of projected alliances between Chartists and middle-class Liberals – were once again posing considerable dangers to inter-class social and political harmony. As we will observe in due course, 'Old Liberalism' was frequently unable to come to terms with militant 'new unionism', industrial conflict, and demands for the eight-hour day and the right to work. And, despite its collectivist garb, 'New Liberalism' generally failed to assimilate the growth of 'class' politics, especially at the municipal level. Similarly, growing demands for independent labour representation and the selection of more working-class men as candidates placed serious strains upon the continued prosperity of Lib.-Labism.

In short, during the 1880s we can sense that increasing numbers of workers were growing tired of being the footsoldiers of the two established parties. Much like Chartists (and Chartist memories were still strong in some parts of the country, such as the West Riding of Yorkshire), late nineteenth-century sections of the working class were beginning to demand much greater *control* over their destinies. This spirit of independence was reflected culturally, socially and politically, and was fuelled by the crisis of competitive capitalism, and employers' and politicians' attempts to resolve the crisis at workers' expense. The Conservative Party, for example, relegated much of its cultural politics to a position of secondary importance in favour of hard-nosed *laissez-faire* attacks on trade unionism and socialism. As a number of historians have observed, community-based politics were giving ground to those of class and class conflict. But before we begin our examination of these late nineteenth-century developments in Britain, we must first of all identify the key features of popular politics in the United States from mid century to the late 1880s and draw comparisons and contrasts with the British experience.

The United States

Civil War, Reconstruction and the Politics of Nationhood

We can usefully remind ourselves of the structure and character of American workers' politics on the eve of the Civil War. As Bridges shows, by the 1850s most workers were part of the Democratic and

Republican structures of partisan politics (the Republicans having arisen in 1854 out of a merger of Free-Soil, Whig and nativist elements). Issues of class were present in both local and national politics, but in the overall scheme of things were overshadowed by ethnocultural issues.

The Civil War and the Reconstruction years did regenerate the politics of class and independent labour. But this process of regeneration was a sub-theme in the wider story of American politics. In truth the broader issues raised or strengthened during the Civil War decade – slavery, black emancipation, the defence of the Union and democracy, and the relative merits of government 'greenbacks' versus money issued by private banks – dominated politics down to the end of Reconstruction (in 1877) and beyond. Class constituted a part of many of these issues, but it was not generally the whole or dominant part. Above all, it was the outstanding fact of the Civil War, and its attendant loss of some 600,000 American lives, which dwarfed all other public and private concerns, and which constituted a major contrast with the class-ridden yet generally peaceable kingdom of Britain.

In effect the growth of cultural politics in mid-Victorian Britain was paralleled by the dominance of the politics of nationhood in 1860s America. As Martin Shefter has written:

> the war strengthened the attachment of the working class to the American regime. It united wage workers and employers in defense of a nation that was the world's only democracy and in opposition to a society based upon the principle of slave labor. Although American labor conflicts were more violent than those of any other industrialized nation, the number of workers killed by the Confederate Army exceeded by a factor of more than one hundred the number killed in conflicts with their employers. The loyalties to the regime forged during this titanic conflict were strong and enduring.[85]

Alan Dawley has stated the case even more forcibly, arguing that the Civil War and its related issues effectively 'sidetracked' workers from class-based concerns. Thus:

> At a time when scores of industrial communities like Lynn were seething with resistance to industrialism, national politics were preoccupied with the issues of war and reconstruction. Economic and social issues arose, such as factory reform, the hours of labor, the distribution of wealth, and cheap money, but they were crowded off the center stage of debate by issues of military strategy, presidential impeachment, racial adjustment, and reconstituting the Union...
>
> Thus a special configuration of events having to do with the inter-class character of the American Revolution, the radical, anti-monopoly critique of capitalism, and the nationalist impact of the Civil War established among nineteenth-century workers an orien-

tation away from class consciousness and toward a view of labor
as one interest group in a pluralist society.[86]

Whether class was so narrowly confined to the economic and social
issues highlighted by Dawley and so absent from the political, cultural
and ideological issues of the Civil War period is a matter of considerable
doubt. We will return to this matter. At this juncture it is sufficient to
emphasise the centrality of the question of political identity to 1860s
Americans.

The Republicans

The Republicans, as the party of Lincoln, the defenders of the Union,
the staunch opponents of the Slave Power, and the emancipators of the
slaves, emerged with massive support from the war. Part of the Republican appeal to artisans, small farmers and industrial workers from New
England to the far West derived from pre-war loyalties to the principles
of Free-Soilism, Whiggery and nativism. Continuities rooted in pietistic
Protestantism, 'strident Yankee moralism', temperance, self-help and
'improvement', centralising nationalism, moral regulation, equal rights,
free labour, the 'producerism' of farmers, masters and artisans (often
living in close-knit and small communities), the high tariff, and suspicion
of, if not downright opposition to, non-pietistic Protestant immigrants
and, more especially, Catholic immigrant 'dupes' of the 'despotic' and
'aggrandising' Papacy, fed into 1860s Republicanism. As Goodwyn has
remarked:

> By 1868 the white farmers of the North who had filled the ranks
> of the Grand Army of the Republic found a settled home in the
> army's political auxiliary, the Grand Old Party ... Throughout
> the North the politics of army pensions, orchestrated by loyal
> Republican leagues, contributed additional political adhesive. From
> New England to Minnesota, hundreds of small towns, as well as
> broad swaths of rural America, became virtual rotten boroughs
> of Republicanism. The original prewar coalition of free soilers,
> abolitionists, and Whigs which had carried Lincoln to the White
> House thus found in postwar sectionalism a common ground that
> proved far more serviceable than the controversial issue of Negro
> rights.[87]

Broadly equivalent to the British Liberals (with the marked exception
of the latter's more tolerant attitude to Irish Catholic immigration and
their general defence of religious liberties), the Republicans thus built
upon their earlier appeal to earnest and 'respectable' elements within
the labouring and farming populations of the North. Suspicious of
great wealth, corporations and other forms of 'monopoly', native-born

puddlers in Pittsburgh and farmers in Pennsylvania, Kansas and Iowa rushed to join Union Leagues and Wide Awake companies – in defence of equal rights and in opposition to 'parasitical aristocracy'. By way of contrast, in Civil War New York City Republicanism was widely identified (by the predominantly immigrant working class) with 'a repressive government apparatus and an unyielding defense of the interests and outlook of "aristocratic" reformers'.[88]

Much in the manner of Liberalism, Republicanism embraced a relatively broad spectrum of opinions. Of particular significance to workers and small producers in both the North and the South were the Radical Republicans, the American counterparts of John Bright and his 'Manchester School' colleagues in Britain.[89] Strong defenders of the Union, democracy and the ideologies of free labour and producerism, the Radical Republicans constituted a powerful voice in the post-bellum Congress in favour of black suffrage ('the logical consequence of negro emancipation'), the general extension of the virtues and responsibilities of citizenship to blacks, and the thoroughgoing reconstruction of the South 'in the image of the small-scale competitive capitalism of the North'. More the expression of the broadly based notion of free labour than of the interests of a narrow group of northern businessmen, Radical Republicanism sought to utilise the expanded machinery of the national state to provide the institutional and cultural conditions in the South in which the freedpeople could prosper 'on the basis of character and merit'. The key, notes Foner, was to give all citizens 'a perfectly fair chance' by means of 'equal standing in the polity and equal opportunity in a free labor economy'. Most Radical Republicans believed that legal equality and formal equality in the market-place would eventually give rise to a black yeomanry. But few were prepared to tackle the economic (i.e. property-based) determinations of inequality in the South which existed alongside political and legal forms of oppression. The widespread confiscation of planters' land and its redistribution to the freedpeople was far too radical a proposal to meet with substantial approval from northern bourgeois radicals. As Foner has written:

> It is hardly surprising that many Radicals proved reluctant to support a program that so contravened the *sanctity of property* as confiscation; what is striking is how few suggested an alternative, other than holding out the prospect of individual advancement in accordance with the free labor ideology. (emphasis added)

Most agreed with Edward Atkinson, a 'business radical', that confiscation would 'ruin the freedmen' by inducing the belief that they could obtain land without '*working* for it and purchasing'.[90] This insult to the long years of back-breaking work performed by successive generations of black slaves was illustrative of the growing gulf between the aspirations of the freedpeople and even the more radical sections of the white population in the post-bellum years. Given the limits of Radical Republicanism's ideology, its declining influence within the Republican Party as a whole, and the general white retreat from the promises of Reconstruction into the organisational, spoils-based politics of the Gilded Age, it is not surprising that black optimism gave way to mistrust and a more cautious and in some ways defensive political stance. Blacks in the South would generally retain their allegiance to the Republicans, as the party of emancipation, but the resuscitation of more ambitious dreams would all too often call forth the wrath of both the Republicans and the white-supremacist Democrats.

Labour and the Radical Republicans

The emergence of a revived and strengthened labour movement and of the 'politics of class feeling' in the post-bellum North also, observes Foner, 'raised fundamental questions for the free labor ideology'.[91] In many ways, as demonstrated by Montgomery, labour activists and the Radical Republicans had much in common. Both groups had supported the war effort with courage and passion, could justifiably 'wave the bloody shirt' in the face of the 'traitorous Peace Democracy', and could look forward to the advancement of democracy, reason and progress in the post-bellum years. Many Radical Republicans and labour movement stalwarts also demonstrated shared commitments to self-help and independence, the free upward mobility of individuals on the basis of merit, temperance and 'respectability', to the 'producing classes' as against 'unproductive' financiers and 'aristocratic monopolists', and to an expanded greenback currency (in the interests of reduced interest rates, increased levels of employment and overall economic activity, and more democratic control of the economy). With the obvious exception of the greenback issue, the parallels between labour and the Radical Republicans in America and labour and the Liberals in Britain, are manifest. In Britain there was, of course, strong Liberal and labour movement support for the cause of the North during the Civil War in opposition to the 'aristocratic' South.[92]

However, as already demonstrated in relation to labour and mid-Victorian Liberalism, there similarly emerged a number of tensions between the labour movement and the Radical Republicans. To return to Foner, the labour movement set obstacles for the ideology of free labour by 'questioning the equity of Northern labor relations'. And:

> Like freedmen seeking land and Western farmers advocating regu-

lation of the railroads, labor reformers called upon the Republican
party to move beyond its commitment to equality before the law
to consider the realities of unequal economic power and widespread
economic dependence, and the state's responsibility for combating
them.[93]

Thus the perceived reality of the growth of a permanent wage-earning
class in supposedly un-European and equal rights America presented a
major problem for the ideology of free labour. According to the latter,
only those lacking in character and determination would fail to rise in
the social scale. But the contradictory evidence offered by life histories
of innumerable 'upright' and 'honest' Yankee workingmen suggested
that all was not well in the land of the free. Furthermore, in opposition
to the teachings of political economy, the rule of the market was visibly
failing to generate that expected 'natural' harmony between 'productive'
workers and employers. Rather, under the pressures of wartime inflation
and expected rewards for their participation in the war effort, workers
were increasingly turning to the 'sectional' and 'selfish' devices of trade
unionism and collective action in general in order to realise their goals.
And trade unionism, especially of a militant kind, and class conflict, as
manifested in escalating strikes and demands for the legal eight-hour
day (see Chapter 2), had no place within the Radical Republicans'
scheme of things. While some of the Radical Republicans were prepared
to concede the compatibility of the principle of citizenship and the
performance of eight hours' daily labour, they were not generally prepared to countenance the legal imposition of eight-hour rules upon
formally free and consenting employers and workers. As in the case of
confiscation, the legal enforcement of the eight-hour day represented an
unwarranted intrusion upon the rights of property and 'freedom'.

As Marx and Engels suggested, the contradiction between the formal
market-based freedoms of bourgeois liberalism and the actual indignities
and oppressions endured by the dependent proletarian created objective
conditions for the development of class consciousness and socialism.
But, as the post-bellum development of the American labour movement
suggests, the notion of 'objective condition' or 'interest' does not automatically lead to the adoption of a particular point of view and course
of action. Between position in the production-based market-place and
articulated consciousness lie relatively autonomous cultural, political
and ideological forces which greatly influence both consciousness and
behaviour. As Montgomery has shown, the experience of class conflict
in the late 1860s and early 1870s failed to push American workers in
the direction of revolutionary socialist consciousness. Class consciousness did, as we saw in Chapter 2, become more pronounced. And class
conflict did *partly* explain the demise of Radical Republicanism

(although, to quote Foner, the latter foundered more on 'the all too visible politics of race and Reconstruction'). Furthermore, as we will see below, economic class conflicts and political disillusionment with the existing parties did push groups of workers in the direction of independent labour politics. But the socialist content of such politics, at least down to the depression of 1873, was, at best, marginal. Rather, notes Montgomery, the workers' movement turned to the 'traditional producerist' analyses and solutions offered by Greenbackism (of producers versus non-producers rather than classes versus classes) to effect labour's salvation.[94]

The Democrats

The Democrats did not take kindly to either 'soft' money or high tariff panaceas. Rather, they argued in favour of the anti-inflationary effects of a 'sound' monetary policy and a low tariff which would not impose a heavy tax burden upon the imported goods consumed by workers. As the 'true home of the working classes', the Democrats emphasised their party's devotion to Jeffersonian principles and personal liberty'.[95] As we observed in Volume One, ante-bellum Democrats had portrayed themselves, much in the manner of British Conservatives, as the defenders of personal liberty and choice, cultural diversity, toleration, and the bonhomie of robust popular culture against the centralising, regulatory, intolerant and self-righteous 'pietistic cultural police' of Whiggery, nativism and Republicanism. Democrats thus championed the rights of male workers to drink, to engage in the 'rough-and-tumble' of street life, to practise 'muscular' and 'manly' forms of leisure, to be proud of their protective and patriarchal attitudes towards 'their' womenfolk, and generally to pursue life-styles which went beyond the boundaries of 'respectability' defined by the narrowly self-helping and 'improving' Republicans.[96]

American Democrats held out the strong hand of friendship to immigrants. Unlike British Conservatives, the Democrats offered a protective home to Roman Catholic immigrants, the majority of whom arrived on American shores from Ireland in the wake of the Famine. (Non-pietistic Protestant immigrants to America, such as German Lutherans, who shared the Irish Catholics' attachment to a sociable, drink-based culture and their dislike of state regulation of personal behaviour, were generally part of the Democratic fold. These Protestants would have been accepted by British Conservatives.) Thus the Irish Catholics who were at the centre of New York's anti-draft riots in 1863, loudly voicing their opposition to federal conscription, exemption for those able to afford the commutation fee, rising taxation, increased federal powers, black competition in the labour market, and black emancipation, were loyal Democrats.

The advantages offered to such immigrants by the Democrats have been outlined by Lawrence Goodwyn:

> Uneasily adrift in a sea of Yankee Protestant Republicanism, the largely immigrant and overwhelmingly Catholic urban workers clustered defensively in makeshift political lifeboats fashioned after the Tammany model. Generally run by Irish bosses, these scattered municipal vessels essentially conveyed patronage and protection. Though nominally Democratic, little in their design reflected Jeffersonian patterns; their chief function, aside from affording their captains a measure of income and status, was to provide the immigrant masses with local security in an alien world.[97]

It was upon their provision of jobs and all manner of local services, combined with their opposition to the 'haughty' and 'aristocratic' moral regulators who ran the city's Republican machine, that New York City's Democratic leaders, Fernando Wood during the 1850s, and 'Boss' William Tweed between 1864 and the early 1870s, claimed to be the 'true representatives' of the 'working classes'. The corrupt Tweed 'ring' did have connections with some of the trade unions, especially in the building trades and in and around the docks. But, as Bernstein has clearly shown, Tweed's appeal to his predominantly Catholic and working-class constituency was rooted primarily in ethnocultural concerns and populist rhetoric against 'aristocratic' Republicans rather than in a radical, class-based programme. Independent labour and anti-capitalist politics were to be opposed. As in the case of Conservatism in the Lancashire cotton districts, social radicalism was set, for both Wood and Tweed, within defences of the existing social order and private property. Indeed, as with the Radical Republicans, it was to be the eight-hours movement and intensified industrial conflict of the late 1860s and early 1870s which exposed the deficiencies in Tweed's claim to be the champion of the workers.[98]

In both the pre- and post-war periods the Democratic Party was heavily influenced by racist, white supremacist sentiments. We have seen in volume one that during the 1840s and 1850s Mike Walsh and his 'shirtless Democrats' had combined anti-capitalism with defence of 'southern rights', the latter amounting to de facto support for states' rights and slavery. Anti-abolitionist views flourished among Democrats in the 1850s. And violent opposition to blacks, and especially black competition in the labour market, was widespread among Democratic (and to some extent Whig and Republican) workers in both the North and the South during the ante-bellum period. There were, of course, those within the Democratic Party who opposed the war, advocated immediate peace, and were opposed to black emancipation. In New York City, the Peace Democracy, active in the 1863 riots, was, notes Bernstein, 'branded the provocateur of an insurrectionary working class and traitor to the Northern cause'. And New York's Catholic leaders set a tone which was hardly conducive to racial harmony. Thus Bernstein:

> New York's Catholic leaders . . . attacked Protestant abolitionists as both revolutionary sowers of chaos . . . and as infidels . . . Slavery, Archbishop Hughes insisted, was best left alone. The *Irish American* hailed New York's Catholic clergy for declining 'to preach the nigger from their pulpits'. The shift in Northern war aims to include emancipation enraged local Catholic opinion. The Republican government, in the words of the vitriolic John Mullaly, had now made Irish army volunteers 'subservient to the emancipation of the negro'. The anti-Republicanism and racism of the Catholic press began to crescendo through winter and spring 1863 and reached fortissimo by early July.

It was, of course, in July that the riots took place. And many of the Catholic clergy added legitimacy to the widely expressed view of the rioters that Republican employers planned to flood the labour market with low-paid black labour. Brazenly racist views also characterised the views of New York's influential merchants and others grouped together in the Young America organisation.[99]

Its popularity threatened by war-time charges of traitorous and insurrectionary behaviour, the Democracy nevertheless succeeded in maintaining its mass support in the post-bellum period. The careful cultivation of a patriotic and responsible, conservative image was crucial to the Democrats' continued prosperity. In New York City, for example, the steadfast support provided to the war effort by William Tweed and Tammany Hall from the first days of fighting meant that an important section of the Democracy could not be charged with the disloyalty levelled at Fernando Wood and his Peace Democrats. Furthermore, the Tammany Democrats accepted the fact of black emancipation, if somewhat grudgingly (denouncing, 'any attempt to bolster black economic and political status at the expense of the white Southern élite'), later opposed, 'the use of federal power to enforce black suffrage', and 'only reluctantly' came to support black citizenship. In addition, and despite their dislike of blacks and their commitment to the Democratic Party, the vast majority of Irish Catholic immigrants were 'deeply loyal to the Union' and were 'by and large enthusiastic supporters of the war effort'. And the patriotic sentiments displayed on the battlefield by the Irish redounded to the cause of Tweed and Tammany. Vigorously waving the flag of loyal nationalism, associating Tammany patriotism 'with a defense of the social order', carrying the support of the Irish Catholic immigrants, and blending the causes of Irish nationalism and democratic American nationhood, the Tweed circle ruled New York into the 1870s. As Bernstein concludes, Tammany thus became a 'bastion of immigrant loyalty to the Union cause and . . . patriotic defender of private property and the social order'.[100] In the process the Irish in New York City acquired new-found status and respect as 'true' American patriots and left behind the 'taint of proletarian treason' associated with their involvement in the Draft Riots.

At the national level the 'unholy alliance' between former slaveholders and most southern whites and Catholic and some Protestant immigrants in the North continued to serve the Democracy well up to the Alliance, Populist and labour movement explosions of the 1880s and 1890s. In such ways did the Democrats and Republicans forge strong popular bases in the era of the Civil War and Reconstruction.

Organisational Politics in the Gilded Age

The decline of the fierce ideological conflicts of the Civil War years and the early period of Reconstruction and the rise of the politics of organisation and compromise in the Gilded Age added to the seeming stability of the party-political system and its hold upon the mass of workers. As Goodwyn has written:

> the passing of radical abolitionism proved rapid. The bankers, manufacturers, shippers, and merchants who had provided much of the direction for the G.O.P. from its inception soon wearied of their attempt to build a postwar party in the South based on black suffrage. As election victories in the 1860's and 1870's proved that the G.O.P. could rule with a basically Northern constituency, Negroes, their morale declining and white radical abolitionists, their numbers thinning, lost the intra-party debate over Southern policy.[101]

By the late 1860s the Freedmen's Bureau had been 'allowed to lapse'. Thereafter the Republican Party 'gradually abandoned both the cause of the freedman and the commitment to a "reconstructed" South that it implied'. Increasingly the politics of strict electoral calculation prevailed over principle. The Republicans, secure of the black vote in the South (in opposition to the racist Democrats), and cognisant of the wide extent of anti-black feeling among their own supporters in the North, consciously chose to 'wave the bloody shirt' rather than to parade its former abolitionist and emancipatory credentials. Similarly, faced with economic contraction and an increasingly restless working class, former Radical Republican advocates of 'soft' money preached the virtues of 'restraint' and financial 'responsibility' during the depression of 1873–8.

'Realism' and 'pragmatic commonsense' were indeed coming to prevail in Republican circles.

In turn the Democrats generally came to accept the main features of Reconstruction. Increasingly winning control of state governments in the 1870s, the 'New Departure' Democrats, notes Shefter, 'permitted blacks to vote, hold public offices, serve on juries, and patronize many of the same public accommodations as whites'. However, as Shefter further observes, the ugly features of white supremacy and violence towards the blacks also continued to characterise the South.[102] Nationally, the post-bellum Democrats placed more emphasis upon their long and established political pedigree (the 'party of the fathers') than upon their appeal to a particular class of the population (the 'true home of the working classes').

Neither party achieved the political hegemony in the post-bellum decades which the Republicans would come to enjoy from 1896 down to the 1930s. Depression was the main factor in the spectacular Republican defeat of 1874. Between 1874 and 1896 stalemate characterised the political scene and effectively placed a brake upon new national policy initiatives. The increasing dominance of both parties by the interests of business in the North and the South and party professionals seeking compromises on the formerly divisive issues of the Civil War and early Reconstruction periods, induced the 'issueless', organisational mode of politics which dominated the 1870s and 1880s. Patronage, power, sound and streamlined party organisation and the rewards of office, rather than reform, became the guiding concerns of politics.[103]

As Shefter and Foner have observed,[104] the rise of the 'professionally managed politics' of the Gilded Age was partly class-based in origin. The intense ideological conflicts of the Civil War period and the growth of class feeling and conflict during the 1870s depression prompted competing social and political élites to reach a settlement as to the restabilised rules of the political game. The main features of this compact were fiscal and monetary conservatism (the United States returned to the gold standard in 1879), defence of property rights, growing mistrust of the 'masses' and the practices of popular political democracy (with an accompanying emphasis upon the importance of professional expertise and efficiency), and a renewed determination to 'educate', 'improve' and firmly incorporate the masses within the élite-dominated structure of politics. The extent to which such incorporationist aims succeeded is the subject to which we will now turn.

Political Assimilation and Revolt: from the 1860s to the 1880s

As noted in this chapter and as earlier demonstrated (see Volume One) in reference to the 1840s and 1850s, there is no doubt that the nine-teenth-century political system in America was extremely adept at meeting the needs of the mass of the population. The reader's attention has already been drawn to the importance of possession of the vote and the flexibility of the political parties. In addition, the extremely fragmented and decentralised structure of politics, and the ability of local political machines to exercise degrees and ranges of power (over jobs, all manner of 'favours', services, public agencies and elected officials such as police chiefs, mayors and magistrates) unmatched in more hierarchical and undemocratic Britain, meant that American politics were relatively open, often directly relevant to local material and other needs, and generally subjected to popular influences to a much greater extent than across the Atlantic. We have seen in relation to post-1850s Britain that, despite the 'rootedness' of politics in popular culture, workers were primarily *supporters* of Conservatives and Liberals rather than active framers of policy. In the United States active (and at times central) popular partici-pation in the processes of politics was far more pronounced. The truly popular nature of nineteenth-century American politics was reflected (in contrast to the late twentieth-century pattern) in general turnout rates of 85 per cent or more of the eligible electorate on polling day.[105]

With specific reference to the 1860s–1880s period, the mass sectional loyalties generated by the Civil War continued to dominate politics. In addition, observes Shefter, the two main parties offered concessions to organised labour in the form of the establishment of bureaux of labour statistics, limitations upon the use of convict labour, and in 1885 prohibi-tion of the importation of immigrant contract labour. And several trade unionists and members of the Knights of Labor achieved state and local political offices as nominees of either the Democrats or the Republicans. As David Montgomery has declared:

> In the early 1870s and throughout the 1880s, Republicans and Democrats alike eagerly snatched up prominent workers to be can-didates in their own neighborhoods. Here was an important avenue of social advancement for ambitious workers, which played a major role in inhibiting the development of a national labor party.[106]

The forces of integration and consensus were manifestly very powerful. But total harmony did not prevail. As in Britain, workers continued to push their interests within the two-party structure and in so doing invite charges of 'selfishness' and 'sectionalism'. Montgomery thus notes 'evidence of workers' caucuses emerging inside the Republican fold during Reconstruction' and 'a profound working-class orientation among the Irish and German leaders of the Democrats who usually came to ascendancy locally in late 1860s or the 1870s'.[107] We must, of course, be careful to define the precise nature of working-class influence. By no means every intervention in the mainstream political process revolved around class. But the significance of the latter was reflected in the fact that the notion of independent political action, often crucially concerned with class, retained its appeal in the period between the 1860s and 1880s to a much greater extent in America than in Britain.

Within this general period there were three key phases – the late 1860s and early 1870s, the late 1870s and, most markedly, the years from 1886 to 1888 – when predominantly class-based independent politics developed. We can highlight the importance of the following factors in the growth of independent labour politics: unresolved grievances arising out of the Civil War and its immediate aftermath; growing trade-union strength (according to Montgomery, 'workers' independent political influence rose and fell together with their local power on the job'); the inadequacy of the policies and concessions offered to organised labour by the main parties; the latter's identification with 'monopolistic', élitist and anti-labour employers and officials; the hostility of the courts to trade unionism and strike action; defeats suffered in the industrial arena; and perceived inequalities and injustices in terms of political, social and economic arrangements and practices.

Economic and social causes were paramount in the political agitation of the late 1860s and early 1870s. In Chapter 2 we saw that the Civil War gave rise to a strengthened labour movement, which expected 'due reward' for the many sacrifices endured by workers during the war and which advocated the creation of an independent labour party in order to facilitate the achievement of labour's demands. And in both Chapters 2 and 3 we have argued that questions concerning the *enforcement* of eight-hour statutes, revived trade unionism and strikes in favour of the legal eight-hour day placed severe strains upon labour's relations with the Democrats and Radical Republicans.

The specific examples of Cincinnati, New York City and Massachusetts highlight the general developments outlined above. Unsuccessful in their attempts to gain the eight-hour day by means of political lobbying, leaders of Cincinnati's Trades and Labor Assembly called on workers in 1867 to, 'emancipate themselves from their degrading party influences' and to support a 'straight-out workingmen's candidate'.[108] A Workingmen's Party was created and ran former Civil War general, Samuel Cary, in the 1867 special congressional election on the platform of 'an eight-hour work day, more stringent laws to prevent "soulless corporations" from gaining control of public lands, and the restoration of a truly neutral republican government'. The leaders of the party consciously appealed to German and Irish voters, emphasising the united interests of all workers and support for Irish land and nationalist struggles. In the event local Democrats threw their support behind Cary who went on to win the election. Emboldened by this success, the Workingmen decided to contest the municipal elections of the following spring. But an all too familiar process of co-optation then took place. Thus Ross:

> Mainstream parties, as they had done before and would continue to do, quickly moved to co-opt the workingmen's most popular candidates by endorsing them on their own tickets. While several of these 'coalition candidates' went on to win their campaigns, not a single one of the lesser known men who ran solely on the Workingmen's ticket was elected to office. Working-class efforts at further independent political action soon ground to a halt when the TLA's most influential leaders ... accepted important positions in the Democratic and Republican organizations.

Ross accepts Montgomery's thesis that the 'lure of office' for labour leaders within the main parties and the latter's wider ability to 'absorb talent from the working classes' constituted mighty obstacles to the development of revolutionary consciousness. Socialists and radical trade unionists did continue to run independent candidates in Cincinnati from the early 1870s to the mid 1880s, but they 'rarely succeeded in attracting more than a few hundred votes'. In addition, much 'waving of the bloody shirt' by Cincinnati's Republicans and white-supremacist rhetoric by local Democrats, combined with appeals to patriotism (above the 'sectional' claim of the eight-hour day), and the more mundane yet extremely effective abilities of the main parties to deliver jobs and patronage, helped to still the appeal of class. By the end of 1868 Cincinnati's Germans and Irish had returned to their respective Republican and Democratic 'homes'.

In Massachusetts independent labour politics experienced similar fortunes, spectacular initial success giving way to rapid decline.[109] In the post-war years the state witnessed an upsurge in both trade unionism and independent politics. There were several Radical Republican state legislators in Massachusetts who were generally favourable to the causes of voluntary eight-hours agreements, the prohibition of child labour, and more stringent safety legislation; and abolitionism had brought together labour leaders and middle-class radicals in the ante-bellum period. However, the state legislature would not enact a compulsory measure in favour of eight-hours work, and in 1869 refused to grant a charter to the Knights of Saint Crispin to enable the union to set up co-operative ventures. Thereafter members of the Crispins played a leading role in the creation of a Labor Reform Party. Advocating reduced hours of labour, co-operative production and other radical measures, the party received 10 per cent of the vote and elected twenty-three members to the state legislature in the 1869 election. In the following year Wendell Phillips, the Labor Reformers' candidate for governor, collected 15 per cent of the statewide vote. Promising beginnings were not, however, to be maintained. By 1872 internal wrangles and the successful opportunism of local Radical Republican, Ben Butler, spelt the end for the Labor Reform Party in Massachusetts.

In New York City the bricklayers' strike in 1868 in support of the eight-hour day, the stonecutters' procession of 1871, and the massive eight-hour strikes in the spring of 1872 were crucial illustrations of the rise of an impressive labour movement and the decline of Tweed's hold upon workers. In the wake of the 1868 strike Tweed's acceptance of the state legislature's eight-hour law was emphasised (union bricklayers employed on Tweed's County Court House having previously been faced with the sack on account of their refusal to work a ten-hour day). But cracks soon began to appear in the Democratic edifice. In 1869 and 1870 a growing number of workers, especially in the German community, supported independent labour candidates and expressed their support, in opposition to Tammany, for the Fifteenth Amendment. Adolph Douai, editor of *Die Arbeiter Union*, had long supported abolition and the rights of black citizenship, including the suffrage, and 'regarded the demise of black slavery as an auspicious omen for the emancipation of the white working class from the wages system'.[110] The German Association of United Workingmen's belief that 'both of the existing parties are corrupt, serving capital instead of labor', became the battle cry of the new labour reform movement. As Bernstein notes, these developments in 1869 'represented a new and dramatic conjuncture in the history of the New York City working class'. Under the leadership of English-speaking and German trade unionists, 'the two great projects of the middle decades – the establishment of an independent working-class politics and the regulation of the trades – now merged'.

In 1869 growing working-class unity and links between industrial and political struggles failed to present a serious challenge to Tweed's domination at the polls. But by 1872 Tweed's demise had resulted not only from public outrage at revelations of fraud but also from 'the emerging power of the organized working class'. Thus in September 1871 some 8,000 workers marched in procession to 'express sympathy with the stonecutters' eight-hour strike, demand general enforcement of the state eight-hour law, and denounce Tammany rule'. Of special note among the marchers was the presence of a committee of black trade unionists and members of the International Workingmen's Association.

The latter had grown in influence, especially among German workers, and labour's new-found interracial unity presented a direct challenge to the Tweed Ring's white supremacist views. As Bernstein observes:

> The stonecutters procession ... was also a symbolic racial repudi-
> ation of the draft riots by workers in many of the same trades that
> eight years before had taken to the streets ... the themes of Septem-
> ber 13 were the interracial cooperation of labor, the power of
> organization, and, for many working people, independent politics.

And, 'the loyal white working class that brought the Tweed regime to power ultimately presided over its demise'. Finally, the eight-hour day strikes of 1872, involving some 100,000 workers in New York City, constituted an awesome reminder of the growing power, influence (the eight-hour day being temporarily achieved), and, above all, the economic and political independence of New York's labour movement.

Independence was, alas, transient. At both the national and local levels independent labour politics, in the form of the National Labor Reform Party, fell victim to internal divisions and middle-class inter-vention and control. And the onset of depression in 1873, combined with the vigorous pursuit of anti-unionism by the new crop of thrusting entrepreneurs, dealt hammer blows to the trade-union movement.

Between 1873 and 1878 there were instances of workers turning to independent tickets or exerting concerted pressure upon incumbent poli-ticians and local officials to meet the 'labour interest'. Quickened interest in politics was most apparent during or immediately following industrial disputes, especially in order to punish politicians who had 'sided with employers or broken promises to organized workers'.[111] It was, there-fore, not surprising that the most pronounced turn to politics occurred in the wake of the defeated 1877 'uprising'. Louisville, Kentucky, set the pace. The Marxist Workingmen's Party of the United States elected five out of seven candidates for the state legislature in Louisville in August 1877 and prompted fears of the establishment of a 'Kentucky Commune'. The local *Courier-Journal*, bitterly critical of the 'mob movement', clearly perceived the connection between the 1877 insur-gencies and radicalised political allegiance:

> Its victory followed on the heels of the late strike, of which it is
> the representative and is a reflection of the bitterness of the defeated
> strikers. It will surely, unfortunately, have a profound effect wher-
> ever the strike made itself felt.[112]

As Philip Foner shows, the *Courier-Journal*'s prediction proved to be accurate. Workingmen's Party tickets were 'nominated in city after city', and in several places socialists and greenbackers joined forces. Indeed, it was the Greenback-Labor Party (founded in 1876 but established nationally in 1878), rather than the WPUS (which became the Socialist Labor Party in late 1877), which gained the greatest popular support. The Greenback-Labor Party thus elected a number of mayors (including Terence Powderly at Scranton, Pennsylvania) in industrial and mining communities in Pennsylvania and New York state, and the party's candidate for governor of Ohio, Stephen Johnson, polled well in Toledo and other industrial towns in the state which had played prominent roles in the industrial struggles. Representing the interests of workers, farmers and other small producers, the burgeoning political movement added currency reform and opposition to financial 'monopoly' to demands for the eight-hour day, the abolition of child and contract convict labour, compulsory education, abolition of conspiracy laws against labour organisations, arbitration in industrial disputes, and distribution of the public lands to settlers only.[113]

This revived political momentum at the end of the 1870s both merits further attention from historians and questions the views that ties between urban-industrial workers and rural producers were tenuous and worker commitment to greenbackism generally weak.[114] Two years after its national foundation the Greenback-Labor Party received 2 million votes in its electoral fight for 'the people's money'. Its demise arrived in 1884. But many former supporters henceforward channelled their energies into the Alliances and Populism. Once again, however, the fortunes of third-party politics had, by the early 1880s, nosedived. The successes of 1878 and 1880 were not to be repeated by Greenback-Laborites. By the early 1880s the 'no politics' rule in many trade unions meant, in effect, that the day-to-day business of running and organising politics fell to those middle-class reformers who, to quote Shefter, 'alone could afford to devote their time to party business between annual conventions'. And while the unions of the Federation of Organized Trades and Labor Unions were more concerned to perfect their organisational structures and build up their industrial strength rather than to contest political contests, the official leadership of the Knights of Labor saw education and co-operation, as opposed to the 'dirty' business of politics, as the keys to labour's emancipation. Finally, the increasingly fragmented (and to some extent competing) elements of the labour movement were once again prey to the co-optive schemes of Republicans and Democrats.

By the mid 1880s this scenario had, however, changed dramatically. The 'Great Upheaval' (see Chapter 2) was both accompanied and followed by an unprecedented movement in favour of political independence. The very depth and extent of the 'Upheaval', the strong degrees of working-class unity engendered, the hostility of employers and key sectors of the state, and the violent defeats suffered by striking workers led, notes Leon Fink, 'many Knights of Labor to reconsider the political option'.[115] The achievement of political power could serve as a useful complement to, and safeguard of, workers' power within the workplace – providing limits to the power and influence enjoyed by élites; safeguarding equal rights and an inherently neutral and accessible state; curtailing 'abuses' of state power, and, as in the 1870s, punishing labour's and democracy's enemies; and facilitating the effective introduction of 'class specific' pieces of legislation such as the eight-hour day.

According to Fink, labour's defeat in 1886 at the hands of the state and (in the words of labour editor, John Swinton) an 'anti-democratic Money Power', triggered 'what may still stand as the American worker's single greatest push for political power'. Adopting 'Workingmen's', 'United Labor', 'Union Labor', 'People's Party' and 'Independent' labelled tickets, or locally capturing one of the established parties, the Knights entered electoral contests in '189 towns and cities in thirty-four (out of thirty-eight) states and four territories'. The range and depth of the Knights' political activities have been well captured by Fink:

> Areas affected ranged from Eureka, California, to Gardiner, Maine, from Red Wing, Minnesota, to Fort Worth, Texas. The activity encompassed tiny rural as well as major metropolitan areas, frontier settlements as well as old New England towns, marketing centers as well as manufacturing and mining communities. The movement linked old immigrant farmers with new immigrant industrial workers, skilled white artisans with unskilled black laborers.

There ensued, for a time at least, important advances and heady successes. In Richmond, Virginia, and other parts of the South, the Knights temporarily brought together the political and industrial interests of black and white workers. The seeming stranglehold of the Republicans over the black South and the Democrats over the white South was briefly threatened and in some cases broken – developments which anticipated the climactic challenge to established power in the South mounted by Populism in the early 1890s.[116]

In 1886 the greatest political excitement was centred upon New York City. In New York representatives from various wings of the reform and labour movements – Gompers and others from the AFL, members of the Knights, socialists, greenbackers and the Single Tax followers of Henry George – united under the banner of the United Labor Party. 'This unaccustomed unity', observes Dawley,

> was imposed ... by the strike wave, the major parties' subservience to plutocracy, the judicial lynching of the Haymarket anarchists, the assassination of strikers by Gould's mercenary army – all of which momentarily fused the inchoate class consciousness of American workers into a unified movement.[117]

George himself narrowly lost his battle for New York's mayoralty. In Chicago the United Labor Party elected seven assemblymen and five judges. Nationally labour tickets were successful in municipal elections in 'dozens of communities'. And in November 1886 the Knights 'claimed to have elected a dozen Congressmen'. 'For a brief period', records Fink, 'labor reform leaders held high hopes of building a national independent political movement'.

Steps were accordingly taken towards this end. In 1887 a Cincinnati meeting of Knights, greenbackers, socialists, Alliance members, single-taxers and anti-monopolists set up the National Union Labor Party. But by the end of 1887 this grand project lay in ruins. In turn by 1888 the Democrats and Republicans 'emerged . . . with a stronger grip than ever on the working class'. 'Ironically, concludes Fink, 'a movement that began by defying the contemporary party system may in the end have left workers even more firmly within its confines'. Why had such a remarkable reversal taken place in such a short period of time?

The answer lies in a familiar roll call of factors. Fatal internal divisions were very much to the fore. In Cincinnati's United Labor Party, for example, conflicts between moderates, conservatives and radicals under-mined the early promise displayed at the spring 1887 elections when candidates had received the largest vote ever cast for a third party in the city. By the end of 1888 Cincinnati's ULP had virtually ceased to function. Conservatives wished to jettison the radical, class-based image of the party, and there was growing opposition to George's Single Tax (a uniform tax on land designed to transfer the 'unearned' profits of rent and land speculation from the individual to the community). And integral to the Cincinnati Party's change of name to the Union Labor Party (in line with the decision made earlier by the national convention) was renewed emphasis upon respectability and patriotism: links to Hay-market and to 'Socialism and other 'isms antagonistic to American institutions' were to be avoided at all costs. German socialists and radical Georgites reacted in kind to the conservatives.[118]

Elsewhere a similarly dismal picture of splits and recriminations pre-vailed. In New York City there occurred ruinous battles between social-ists and single taxers. And both Georgites and socialists 'refused to work under the banner of the western-oriented Union Labor people'. Nationally, the decline of the Knights, Powderly's opposition to political involvement (only in the early 1890s did the Knights make solid contact with agrarian radicals), and the rise of a strong non-partisan group within the AFL, further contributed to the demise of independent politics.

Second, the varied structures and arrangements of local politics, and especially the extent to which the 'labour interest' had been accommo-

dated by the mainstream parties, constituted a key ingredient in the
mixed fortunes and overall failure of independent politics. Fink, for
example, notes that while labour tickets were successful in many small
and medium-sized towns, they were generally unsuccessful in the 'major
urban-industrial centers'. In terms of the latter, only Chicago, Cincinnati
and Milwaukee witnessed successful independent campaigns. The explanation, continues Fink, lay less in the size of the community than in
politics. Thus, in those communities, such as Pittsburgh, Boston and
San Francisco where the major parties had already attempted to meet
the interests of labour and to promote labour leaders within their organisations, there existed a pluralistically inclined basis to politics and the
appeal of independent labour politics was very limited. Conversely, in
those communities, such as Chicago (especially), Cincinnati, Kansas City
and Milwaukee where local politicians had been 'irreversibly tainted by
[the] complicity of party officials with the state repression of industrial
protest' and where politicians were, for a time at least, perceived to be
the close allies of anti-labour movement social forces, then the appeal
of independent action was correspondingly high. In addition, it was in
those communities, such as Rochester, Rutland and Richmond, where
paternalism, employer hegemony and racial factors had inhibited independent labour's influence up to 1886, that industrial conflict and class
polarisation suddenly created space for the development of labour radicalism.[119]

Varied patterns of independent labour politics worked, however,
against mainstream political structures which rapidly reasserted their
power and control throughout the country. Industrial defeats did
undoubtedly move large numbers of people in the direction of political
radicalism. But the defeats suffered by and the splits within the latter
produced cynicism and a more fatalistic acceptance of Republican and
Democratic hegemony. And, as in Cincinnati and Rochester, the two
main parties soon busied themselves in tempting radical labour leaders
with the 'lure of office'. But a consolatory dialectic of change and
contradiction was simultaneously at work. In order for the 'lure' to be
successful and for independent labour politics to lose their wider appeal,
the two main parties were also frequently obliged to make policy concessions to the radicals. In New Hampshire, for example, state Republicans reacted to labour's insurgency by passing a ten-hour law and
prohibiting child labour in mills and factories. We can thus endorse
Fink's conclusion that the 'demise of the Knights of Labor and their
political tickets ... did not end workingmen's influence in local and
state affairs'.[120]

Third, we must also support Fink's suggestive notion that the failure
of independent politics in the 1880s should in part be related to radical-

ism's intellectual heritage and orientation.[121] Of particular importance were the attitudes of the Knights to politics, the role of the state, and to the place of political action in the movement's overall strategy. We have already noted that the leadership of the Knights did not afford primary importance to independent politics. The producers' liberation was to be ultimately achieved within the sphere of civil society by means of the 'associationalist idealism' embodied in education, moral persuasion and example, and co-operation. The political experiments of 1886–8 constituted an important phase in the Knights' history but, at least for Powderly and his associates, a largely involuntary one, thrust upon the movement by the 'capture' of the state by the 'Money Power' and the enthusiasm of the rank and file. As Fink perceptively informs us, 'To the extent that the state had become an appendage of the money power, the Knights believed that it had to be liberated before rational self-government, as organized by the people in civil society, might flourish'.

This necessary intervention on the part of the Knights to 'purify' society and politics, and to return an essentially pluralistic state to its rightful constituency, 'the people', did not, however, signify a new-found conversion to the primacy of politics. Powderly was all too soon to be found advising his fellow Knights to 'let political parties alone'. As Fink suggests, efforts to develop a labour strategy based first and foremost upon the creation of a national third party and a more inter-ventionist and transforming state 'surfaced in only the most tentative form until the rise of the People's party in the 1890s'. At root the Knights' leadership viewed party politics as a 'dirty business' (illustrated in 'boss' rule and the machinations of unscrupulous 'fixers', such as lawyers) and did not welcome any increase in the 'baneful' power of the central state. But, as the heirs of a long tradition of active republican citizenship, they were obliged to act to safeguard the interests of 'their' state. The move to independent politics was thus designed more to correct political 'abuses' on a short-term, limited basis rather than to initiate long-term change by means of the primary agencies of the state and party politics.

It is useful at this point to make some brief comparisons with British labour in the 1880s. As noted earlier, emphases upon economic and social means of worker advancement, upon voluntarism, and upon mutuality within the sphere of civil society took a firm grip upon the British labour movement, especially in the post-Chartist period of 'new model' unionist domination. In the earlier part of the nineteenth century many British workers had viewed the state as an agent of propertied oppression and exclusion rather than as a neutral force responding sympathetically to a plurality of interests. But from mid century onwards labour's institutional advancement had been accompanied by both an accentuated voluntarism and a growing belief in the class-neutrality of the state. In all these ways there thus existed transatlantic similarities.

During the latter part of the nineteenth century and early years of the twentieth century there did, however, take place important shifts in Britain. The growth of 'new' unionism with its demand for the legal eight-hour day and with a more sympathetic eye to the benefits of state intervention than the 'old' unionists, the employer counter-attack, the mounting hostility of the courts and adverse legal decisions culminating in Taff Vale, and the seeming unwillingness or inability of both Conservatives and orthodox Liberals to adopt labour's cause, meant that voluntaristic mutualism (the special preserve of the skilled workman) no longer seemed adequate to the task of defending labour's interests. The very facts that organised labour was being challenged at the national level and that reversal of the Taff Vale decision would necessitate parliamentary legislation, compelled British labour to turn its attentions to parliament, the state and the question of independent political representation.[122] And the voices of numerically small yet highly influential socialist groups were added to the growing chorus for political independence and 'collectivism'.

Similarities must thus be set against new departures. But before we rush to instant judgements of American difference, even 'exceptionalism', we must consider the case further. For late nineteenth- and early twentieth-century developments in British politics were paralleled, albeit to varying degrees of influence, within America. In the latter country the period between the 1890s and the early 1920s also saw serious and sustained campaigns on behalf of independent labour and socialist politics and the more active utilisation of the state in order to achieve 'true' democracy and equality. It is to a study of the fortunes of these radical independent political forces on both sides of the Atlantic that we will now turn.

INDEPENDENT LABOUR AND SOCIALIST POLITICS, 1880s–1920s

Exceptionalism, Class and Politics

The notion of American 'exceptionalism' has traditionally been employed with great force to the period between the 1880s and the early 1920s. Whereas most European societies witnessed the rise of mass labour and socialist parties in these years and the emergence of Marxism as a major political philosophy, the United States experienced the failure of socialist and independent labour experiments, the general rejection of Marxism as an 'alien doctrine', and in overall terms the continued dominance of the two-party system. Indeed, during a period of political radicalisation in Europe, the United States saw the Republicans, the party of big business, enjoy political hegemony between the election of 1896 and the depression of the 1930s. In 1906 Werner Sombart posed his famous question, 'Why is there no socialism in the United States?', and ever since historians, sociologists and others have eagerly suggested and debated answers.[123]

Sombart's contemporaries, Engels and Lenin, recognised that Britain, and especially England, was not in the same socialist league as the Germany of the SPD and Marxist revolutionaries. In the late 1870s and early 1880s, for example, Engels was to be found bemoaning the fact that, 'no real labour movement in the continental sense exists here' (while Marx himself was dismissing the English working class as 'nothing more than the tail of the Great Liberal Party, i.e., of its *oppressors*, the capitalists'). And despite the rise of 'new' unionism and the revival of socialism, Engels could still, in 1894, be,

> driven to despair by these English workers with their sense of imaginary national superiority, with their essentially bourgeois ideas and viewpoints, with their 'practical' narrow-mindedness, with the parliamentary corruption which has seriously infected the leaders.[124]

Lenin's *Left-Wing Communism: An Infantile Disorder*, written in 1920, welcomed the militancy of British workers, yet simultaneously condemned the 'old, trade unionist, opportunist and social-chauvinist Labour Party' and characterised MacDonald and other party leaders as 'hopelessly reactionary'.[125]

Deficient from the standpoint of revolutionary socialism, the British labour movement was, however, increasingly regarded by those on the Left as more 'advanced' than its American counterpart. Thus, despite his 'despair', Engels also noted, in 1894, that, 'the *masses* are moving forward – slowly, it is true ... but unmistakably'; and in the following year that, 'the socialist instinct is getting stronger and stronger'.[126] And as a mass party, however 'reformist' and 'opportunistic', the Labour Party constituted, in Lenin's opinion, a more solid base for revolutionary socialist activity than the less substantial independent political movements in the United States. Furthermore, and despite the current historiographical reactions against the importance of class and discontinuity, the conventional wisdom has generally equated the birth and development of the British Labour Party with a revived class consciousness, however modest and reformist that consciousness may have been. The American 'failure' to establish a durable labour or socialist party has thus been set against not only European socialism but also British labour's non-revolutionary yet independent Labour Party.[127]

As noted at several points in this study, hypotheses in favour of American 'exceptionalism' have all too frequently been formulated in static and timeless ways, without due attention to chronology, historical specificity, contradiction and change. We observed at the beginning of this chapter that key questions revolve far less around the absence of labour and socialist politics in the United States than upon their shortlived character, and upon the contrast between high levels of work-place militancy and conflict and assimilation into mainstream political structures.

These general observations bear heavily upon late nineteenth- and early twentieth-century political developments. For a start, as empha-sised by Eric Foner, Werner Sombart failed to observe that there *was* socialism in America in 1906. And,

> In the first fifteen years of this century, the American Socialist party appeared to rival those in Europe, except the German, in mass support and prospects for future growth. Around 1910, the Ameri-can Socialist party had elected more officials than its English counterpart; certainly, Sombart's question might as readily have been asked about Britain as the United States before World War I.[128]

James Weinstein and others have clearly demonstrated American socialism's strength up to 1912 and beyond.[129] Up to the formation of the Socialist Party in 1901, socialism in the United States had been of marginal importance. The Socialist Labour Party, created in 1877, had suffered from splits between Lassalleans (with their dismissal of the effectiveness of trade unionism and emphasis upon political action) and Marxists (who sought to combine trade-union and political activities). Similarly, Daniel De Leon's denigration of AFL labour 'fakirs' and his creation of the dual unionist Socialist Trades and Labor Alliance in 1895 had created further divisions in socialism's ranks. But those socialists who rejected De Leonism to form the new party registered important successes. Between 1901 and 1912, the 'Golden Era', the Socialist Party enjoyed strong support at the polls, a vibrant and popular press, wide-spread geographical and social appeal, a significant base within trade unionism, and an influential effect upon American politics in general.

It was above all the Party's opposition to corporate greed and power, its powerful defence of democracy, its equation of republican virtues with socialism, and its support for organised labour and producers in general against parasitical capitalists and 'monopolists' which elicited a favourable mass response. Support for women's suffrage, civic improvement and municipal socialism, for improved education, and the 'truly scientific organization of society' by means of democratic, collective ownership, added to the Party's appeal. But it was the appeal of socialism as the 'true' heir of American revolutionary and democratic ideals which mattered most in the new 'unrepublican' climate of monopoly capitalism. Thus Buhle:

> They brought under their banner native-born small-town workers, miners, lumberjacks, tenant farmers, railroad men, and petty merchants who saw capitalism destroying the old American ideals and who accepted the Socialists as proper successors to Tom Paine and Abe Lincoln.[130]

In part a customary movement, and the voice of capitalism's dispossessed and exploited, socialism nevertheless looked forward to the construction of a co-operative, egalitarian and rational society. Significantly the Party prospered during a period of material prosperity. As a reflection of its close ties with organised labour, its electoral fortunes rose and fell in line with fluctuations in union strength.[131] At its peak in 1912 the Party had 118,000 members (which declined to 79,000 in 1915, rose to 109,000 in 1919, and plummeted to 36,000 during the following year in the wake of the split between socialists and communists). In 1912 Eugene Debs, the Party's presidential candidate, received 6 per cent of the vote. And, comparatively speaking, the Party performed reasonably well at the polls. As Marks observes:

> Electoral support for the Socialist party of America was not much weaker than that for the British Labour party before the First World War. The peak for the Socialist party was 6.0 per cent for Debs ... while the prewar peak for the Labour party was 7.6 per cent in January 1910. Moreover, the American Socialist party was one of the most radical left-wing parties to be found in any Western society; the Labour party was one of the most moderate.[132]

It should also be noted that the British Labour Party lost four seats in the fourteen by-elections fought between 1910 and 1914, and, in terms of Westminster politics, remained subservient to the Liberals on the eve of the First World War. Few in Britain in 1913–14 would have predicted Labour's rise to national power and unprecedented strength in the post-war years. By way of contrast in 1912 the American Socialist Party was riding high: over 1,000 of its members held office in 340 cities, including 79 mayors in twenty-four states. In 1916 Meyer London was elected to Congress and socialists made gains in municipal contests in several large cities. As late as 1918 the Party had over thirty members of state legislatures. The *Appeal to Reason*, a Party organ operating out of Girard, Kansas, was 'for a time, the best-selling political weekly of any kind in the world', and achieved a weekly circulation figure of half a million. And in 1912 the Party claimed over 300 English and foreign-language publications with a total circulation probably in excess of 2 million.[133]

The Party's socio-geographical appeal was also impressive. In addition to the native-born males struggling to safeguard their skills, independence and political voice in the new corporate world, the Party received support from workers and small employers in the former Knights of Labor mining and industrial strongholds of the rural Southwest and Midwest, and from miners, lumber workers, tenant farmers and labourers in midwestern and western areas of former Populist strength. Many midwestern and western women, who had been involved in the Women's Christian Temperance Union and various strands of the nineteenth-century women's movement, took their reforming and Christian-Socialist principles into the Socialist Party. Indeed, some of these admirable and highly principled women saw themselves as being in the vanguard of the socialist crusade, and attached distinctly revolutionary meanings to the conventionally conservative ideologies of domesticity and separate spheres. As Mari Jo Buhle has written:

> from her position as head of the household, woman could reach out to purify all aspects of the human condition . . . Ada K. Schell of Ponca, Nebraska, admitted that the Socialist party might not directly 'touch on the domestic and private relation of the people', but if Socialism meant anything at all, it meant the 'freedom of woman will be the ennoblement of man'. The husband, purged of his masculine vices, would be able to share with his wife the consecration of the abode of human happiness and, once purified, would also be capable of moral political and economic acts . . . According to this interpretation, the dialectic of history was certain: the purified home as the necessary setting for Socialism, the imperative of womanhood the determining factor.[134]

Organised in mainly small-town autonomous women's clubs, such tough-minded and independent women were joined in the Socialist Party by urban immigrant women (especially German and East European Jewish incomers) who tended to place party before gender. The integration of women into the mainstream Party and the decline of separate organisations were increasingly accompanied by the primacy of socialist and class-based issues over those of gender and feminism.

Immigrant men, especially Germans, Jews, Finns, Slavs and Italians were also attracted to the Party in significant numbers. These ethnic groups provided socialism with much of its strength in New York City, Chicago, Milwaukee and other northern urban areas. A new wave of immigrants, largely from eastern and southeastern Europe, flocked into the Socialist Party during the First World War years, especially in the wake of the Russian Revolution, and accounted for the dramatic increase in the Party's foreign-born membership – from 20 per cent in the pre-war period to 53 per cent in 1918.[135] Government repression, intense pressures to become 'American', and internal faction fighting soon led to the precipitous decline in the Party's membership and general fortunes.

By the early–mid 1920s socialist optimism and strength were in tatters. The causes of this decline will be examined in due course. At this juncture we should simply note an obvious and crucial manifestation of socialist weakness: the failure of the Party to secure majority support within the AFL. We saw in the last chapter that the Socialist Party did build important bases in the United Mine Workers of America, the International Association of Machinists, the International Ladies' Garment Workers and other unions. Furthermore, an important minority within the Party were actively promoting, against the official line, revolutionary industrial unionism and were prominent in the massive strike waves between 1912 and 1922.[136] However, the majority of Socialist Party trade-union members and leaders generally accepted the 'craft' structures and practices of the AFL unions. And from 1912 onwards much of the trade-union support for the Socialist Party was transferred to Woodrow Wilson's ruling Democrats. Socialist influence within the AFL did not suddenly perish in 1912, but it did henceforth diminish. Laslett offers an appropriate comparative dimension to the picture:

> The S.P. of A. never secured the support of more than a minority of the A.F. of L.'s trade unions, which meant that it was unable to acquire the kind of mass labour base that enabled most Western European socialist parties to become a force to be reckoned with. This was probably the most important reason for the S.P. of A.'s long-range lack of success.[137]

By 1914 even the majority of British trade unions, many of them officially anti-socialist and a fair number still articulating the principles of liberal-radicalism, had pledged their support to the Labour Party. This was a telling contrast with American labour.

Independent labour and third-party politics in the United States were not, of course, solely to be equated with the Socialist Party of America. Populism (especially) and Labor-Populism were of major significance during the first half of the 1890s. And in 1893 and 1894 Thomas Morgan's Political Programme, urging the AFL to commit itself to independent political action (along the lines of the Independent Labour Party in Britain), to the famous 'Plank 10' (calling for the 'collective ownership by the people of all means of production and distribution'), and to the legal eight-hour day, municipal ownership of streetcars, gas and electricity, and nationalisation of telegraphs, telephones, railways and mines, received strong support in many affiliated unions. However, the AFL's 1894 convention defeated Morgan's Programme. This action was in part a reaction to the revolutionary implications of collective ownership, in part revulsion against the verbal onslaughts launched upon AFL policies by Daniel de Leon and the SLP (a revulsion shared by many advocates of independent labour politics), and partly a strong desire to preserve the unity of the Federation. Members were all too aware of the tender age of the AFL, the parlous general state of trade unionism during the depression, and the ways in which politics had frequently proved detrimental to trade unionism and divisive to partisan workers in the past. Gompers, well known for his opposition to independent politics, was unseated in 1894 by John McBride of the United Mine Workers (whose sympathies lay with independent labour politics), but successfully contested the presidency in 1895. Thereafter, Gompers (for the remainder of his life), 'pure and simple' trade unionism, voluntarism and non-partisan politics were to be the dominant forces within the Federation.[138]

The events of 1893–4, combined with the decline of Populism, and the Pullman boycott and other industrial defeats, constituted something of a watershed in the history of American workers and the AFL. As we suggested in Chapters 1 and 2, the AFL leadership increasingly lowered its sights and sought accommodation within the 'system'. The formulation by the AFL of demands to be placed before politicians in a non-partisan manner remained the official 'political' line, despite the increasingly close practical connections between the Federation and the Democratic Party (especially from 1908 onwards). The cause of independent labour did not, however, die in the mid 1890s. Faced with hostile courts, open-shop employers and generally unsympathetic Republican congressmen many within the AFL seriously considered the possibility of turning to independent labour politics between 1906 and 1908.

In the event such a 'turn', at least for the majority of AFL unions, did not take place. Advocates of labour politics did continue to make their voices heard at AFL conventions. There was support for a labour party on the part of John Fitzpatrick and some of his colleagues in the Chicago Federation of Labor. And, as seen earlier, the building trades of San Francisco provided strong backing for the city's Union Labor Party. As demonstrated most dramatically and successfully in the case of the Minnesota Farmer-Labor Party, radical third-party popular politics (the Minnesota party was committed to public ownership and production for use) did continue to operate into the inter-war years. However, as in the case of American socialism, the cause of independent labour politics failed to progressively increase its support within the AFL. The post-1908 situation has been accurately described by Marks:

> Over the next decade the demand for independent labor represen-
> tation came up directly or indirectly at several AFL conventions.
> Without ever marshalling a majority of AFL delegates behind the
> idea, supporters of a labor party were entrenched in some of
> the largest unions ... and regularly polled up to one-third of the
> votes at AFL conventions.
>
> However, support for a new independent political role for unions
> did not increase over the years as it did in Britain in the years
> around the turn of the twentieth century.[139]

In time-honoured American tradition, many post-1880s American workers addressed independent labour and, at times, class-based, interests within and to the mainstream political organisations. Although still committed to final goals which transcended class-based concerns, both the Republicans and Democrats continued, as in the pre-1880s decades, to attempt to accommodate workers' manifold concerns. We will return to this matter later in the chapter. But we should make reference at this point to four ways in which workers adopted independent stances in order to exert pressure upon, to change, and in some cases to protest against, the dominant political structures.

First, the AFL's non-partisanship amounted, at least up to its growing involvement with the Democratic Party, to a form of independent pressure-group politics. This form of politics was, of course, by no means concerned solely or often even mainly with class. The AFL was primarily concerned to represent the 'labour interest' rather than the 'class' interest. And the 'labour interest' usually amounted to the representation and defence of predominantly white and relatively skilled and privileged males, mainly of native-born or 'old'-immigrant stock. We have seen on numerous occasions that blacks, women and 'new' immigrants did not get a fair deal from the AFL. At albeit unrepresentative moments (the early-mid 1890s, 1906–8 and, to some extent, during mass organising drives and strikes) the official AFL did, however, embrace the interests and aspirations of much wider groups of workers. We have also seen that there was opposition within the AFL to narrow and exclusive 'craft'-based policies. And the official support given to the eight-hour day, extended municipal provision and selective nationalisation meant that to some extent the AFL was adopting class-based political demands which went beyond 'labour aristocratic' confines.

Second, as demonstrated by Gary Fink and others, at the local and state levels many AFL members and their unions busied themselves in independent pressure-group and protest politics in order to improve their lives both inside and outside the workplace. Not only did such activity contravene the official orthodoxy of voluntarism, but, especially in its widespread Progressive form, posed an independent challenge to the conservatives of the two main parties. (The Progressives embraced dissatisfied Republicans, Democrats, ex-socialists and others.) In its attempts to simultaneously civilise, harmonise and render more efficient American economy and society, Progressivism both addressed and transcended the politics of class. The point to note in the immediate context is that workers often viewed Progressivism as an effective and independent form of protest against the unresponsive 'old-style' political parties. In its attempts to minimise insecurity (via more extensive insurance provision), to improve public services and the extra-work environment (by means of municipalisation, reform and efficiency), and conditions at work (through restrictions on child labour, the promotion of health and safety measures and so on), the Progressive movement expressed both the class-based concerns of workers and the improvement- and humanitarian-minded concerns of workers and larger communities of American citizens.[140]

Our third and fourth examples of independent political expression – the Nonpartisan League and the Conference for Progressive Political Action – were explicitly radical and contained within them powerful class-based sentiments.[141] As Montgomery informs us, many supporters of the pre-war Socialist Party increasingly left the Party to aim for greater success in 'purely electoral movements which emphasized the immediate needs of working people and proclaimed their loyalty to the government during the war'. The most significant and successful of these was the Nonpartisan League. The League began life in North Dakota in 1915. There the state legislature's rejection of the farmers' request for a state-owned grain terminal elevator sparked off a phenomenal mass movement. Arthur Townley, former rural organiser for the Socialist Party, took the initiative by forming an independent organisation of farmers and workers. Strong in its condemnation of the greed and exploitation of the banks, grain dealers and railways, the fledgling North Dakota League supported state-owned banks and grain elevators among its planks. Convinced of the futility of the third-party road, Townley set out to build an independent organisation sufficiently powerful to 'force its demands on the politicians of the major parties'.

In North Dakota the chosen strategy was to capture the dominant Republican Party. The results were immediate and highly encouraging. In 1916 the League took both the Republican primary and the fall election, and successfully put forward a candidate for the post of governor. Further, 'almost miraculous' successes were registered in North Dakota between 1917 and 1919. Thus Montgomery:

> In 1917 seventy-two of the ninety-seven Republican legislators, and fifteen of the sixteen Democrats were in the NPL caucus ... The 1919 session, where the NPL controlled both houses as well as Governor Lynn Frazier, was the only one in the state's history to

finish its business within the constitutionally mandated sixty days, and it created a state bank, grain elevators, hail insurance, workmen's compensation, income and inheritance taxes, home buyers' assistance, restrictions on injunctions in strikes, and the country's best mine safety law. No more dramatic demonstration of democracy has occurred in American history.

The NPL, flushed by its triumphs in North Dakota, soon extended its activities into neighbouring states and Canada. Depending upon specific political contexts, Leaguers either worked within or set out to realign the existing two-party system in order to achieve their goals. In any event, in addition to North Dakota, impressive victories were achieved in Wisconsin, Idaho, Colorado, Montana and South Dakota. By 1920 the League had also built a strong organisational and membership base in Minnesota. Following a series of electoral defeats in Minnesota, the League jettisoned non-partisanship in favour of a third-party strategy. Farmers were joined by trade unionists advocating public ownership of industry. Together, they entered the Farmer-Labor Party in the 1922 elections.

The year 1922 also saw the formation of the Conference for Progressive Political Action. Hit hard by the 1920–2 depression, anti-union employers and Republicans, and the mounting anti-radicalism of Gompers and his allies, leaders of the machinists, railroad brotherhoods, coalminers and needle-trades (the progressive bloc within the AFL) formed the CPPA to campaign for 'nationalization of rails and mines, restoration of civil liberties, and an end to U.S. military intervention in the Caribbean and Central America'.[142] Calculating, much in the manner of the NPL, that an independent, non-partisan approach was more likely to bring greater rewards than third-partyism, the CPPA supported candidates from across the political spectrum who were sympathetic to its goals. Important Congressional electoral victories were registered in 1922. Many Republicans who had supported the government's adoption of harsh measures against strikers in coal and on the railways, were defeated by labour-endorsed candidates. Indeed, advocates of American exceptionalism would be well advised to note David Montgomery's salutary comments on the 1922 elections. 'Never before', writes Montgomery, 'had the American working class asserted itself so decisively at the polls. The conservative tide that had grown ever stronger in local and congressional elections since 1914 had been reversed.' Success at the polls convinced some both within the CPPA and the wider labour and farmers' movement that the time was ripe for the birth of a labour party. But the majority within the CPPA disagreed. Without in any way watering down their radical, indeed class-based demands, they argued that a party identified with 'sectionalism' and 'class warfare' would not win elections in the United States. Accordingly, the CPPA threw its support behind the independent candidature of Robert La Follette of Wisconsin in the 1924 presidential contest.

Class and 'Exceptionalism' in America: Conclusions

We are now in a position to summarise our findings concerning American politics, class and 'exceptionalism'. We have seen that a simple equation of socialist and labour party failure with the absence or negligible influence of class is wide of the mark. Such an equation fails to do justice to the complexities of American workers' political allegiances, especially the various attempts to form labour parties, the initial successes of the Socialist Party, and the various expressions of political independence outside third-party structures. Such attempts were shortlived, and we cannot doubt the overall and continued domination of American politics by the main parties. Nevertheless, class-based concerns did inform politics in a variety of ways and contexts, ranging from pressure upon and within established parties to full-blown third-partyism. All too often protagonists of 'exceptionalism' have far too narrowly identified class with socialist and labour parties, and failedt to sufficiently explore other avenues of class expression. Along with Eric Foner, we argue that questions concerning 'exceptionalism' be 'historicised' and reformulated. The puzzles to be solved are not why socialist and independent labour politics have been absent in the Untied States, but why they 'once rose and fell', and the *disjuncture* of industrial relations and political practice'.

Britain: The Nature and Appeal of Socialist and Labour Politics

Equally, an insistence upon the automatic or inevitable 'Rise of Labour' in Britain is inadequate. The growth of an increasingly common way of life and shared attitudes and values, combined with similar economic pressures upon large numbers of workers and the emerging importance of the semi-skilled (see Chapters 1 and 2), did not find expression in socialism or independent labour politics.

As we have argued at a number of points in this study, politics must be afforded its own importance and internal dynamics, its own relatively autonomous space. Whilst important connections exist between politics and other forms of social action and thought, politics cannot be treated as the necessary outcome of economic, cultural and social processes. Furthermore, between everyday political, economic, and cultural acts and thoughts and *structured* political outcomes (in the form of political parties complete with programmes and formal ideologies), exist insti-

tutions and individuals engaging in power struggles to elevate daily
'commonsense' into the dominant national political 'sense'. Such political actors thus play a crucial role in translating daily experience into
structured political behaviour (or 'interest' into 'action'). Once again,
political outcomes are crucially influenced by conscious human subjects,
by 'agency' as well as 'structure'.

More concretely, there *were* connections between, on the one hand,
the revival of British socialism in the 1880s and the birth of Labour
and, on the other, the crisis of competitive capitalism and the growth
of a more homogeneous working class. But political determinations
also crucially affected the fortunes of radical politics. For example, the
replacement of 'community' by 'class' politics worked to independent
labour's advantage. Conversely, the élitist 'cultural politics' of some
socialists, as manifested in their hostility to 'popular' culture, limited
socialism's mass influence.[143] Furthermore, up to the First World War
and its aftermath, labour and (particularly) socialist politics had a strictly
limited appeal to British workers. The most influential socialist group,
the Independent Labour Party (formed at Bradford in 1893) had a dues-
paying membership of 4,504 in 1893–4, rising to 10,720 a year later, but
standing only at 9,556 in 1905–6. The leadership of the ILP, observes
David Howell, was heavily drawn from white-collar occupations,
although the rank and file were mainly from the organised working
class. But the ILP generally failed to reach the 'lower depths'. Thus
Howell:

> It seems reasonably clear that the poverty of many members was
> that of the later Victorian tradesman, miner and railwayman . . . The
> party struck few chords amongst very poor, unskilled, unorganised
> workers. The ILP counted for little in the teeming slums of great
> cities, where trade unionism and Victorian institutions of self-help
> had little foothold.[144]

Contrary to standard political practice, women were admitted as full
members of the ILP, enjoying formal equality with men. And, as June
Hannam remarks, 'Women were not just to be found behind the scenes
in the ILP. They also took a more prominent political role as speakers,
journalists, trade union organizers and elected members of public
bodies.' Party women were often not of the 'submissive, doormat
material', and actively supported women's suffrage, social reform and
trade unionism. There were, however, limits. The ILP as a whole was,
note Liddington and Norris, 'ambivalent on the question of women's
suffrage' (some being unreservedly in favour, others favouring 'adult suffrage', and others agreeing in principle but prioritising other issues).
And deep attachment to the principles of the family wage and female
domesticity meant, according to Hannam, that the ILP 'failed in the

end to challenge in any fundamental way women's unequal position in
the workplace and in the home'. It was the Women's Co-operative
Guild with its solid constituency of wives and mothers (membership
reaching 32,000 in 1919 and rising to over 50,000 during the inter-war
years), and its commitments to women's self-government and 'married
women's right to economic independence', which did more to boost the
self-confidence and material fortunes of women. In some cases the ILP's
formal rhetoric of equality was at odds with the reality of women as
makers of tea and organisers of bazaars.[145]

The two other main socialist organisations, the Social Democratic
Federation (1884) and the Fabian Society (1884) also admitted women
on formally equal terms with men. But the Fabian Society, notes Pugh,
'though interested in the conditions of life of women, displayed little
sympathy for their political-legal status'.[146] And Karen Hunt has shown
us that the SDF viewed women primarily as a *problem*: as a 'nagging'
hindrance to the full political participation of their husbands; as a potential source of cheap and 'scab' labour; and as a generally conservative
force. As a 'problem', women had, therefore, to be 'educated' to 'proper'
political awareness. A few SDF women achieved positions as public
speakers, but the vast majority of female members and wives of members
were essentially viewed as auxiliaries to politically active male comrades
and, once 'correctly trained', as 'the means to the children'. Education
and social activity – these were the key spheres of influence for SDF
women. Much like many German socialists in the United States, the
SDF saw women, above all else, as mothers. It was accordingly
the caring, educative, longsuffering, provisory and supportive 'virtues'
of motherhood which were 'venerated as women's contribution to
socialism'.[147]

Neither the SDF nor the Fabians achieved mass standing. The SDF,
despite the official contempt of its national leadership, and especially
the aristocratic Hyndman, for trade unionism, did achieve a presence
among some of the 'new' unions and the London unemployed. Much
like the ILP, the SDF attained a degree of influence in the labour
movement out of proportion to its numerical strength (the SDF probably had 'no more than 3,000 members at any one time', and in 1911
joined with disaffected ILPers and others to form the British Socialist
Party). Robert Roberts, a native of Salford, could claim that Hyndman
Hall, the home of the local SDF branch, 'remained for us mysteriously
aloof and through the years had, in fact, about as much political impact
on the neighbourhood as the near-by gasworks'. But as Hobsbawm has
suggested, the SDF's 'greatest achievement' was 'to provide an introduction to the labour movement and a training-school for a succession of
the most gifted working-class militants: for John Burns, Tom Mann and

Will Thorne, for George Lansbury and even for Ernest Bevin'. It was in its political aims – the creation of a strong Marxist Party and the revolutionary transformation of British society – that the SDF failed.[148]

The influence upon organised labour of the ILP was far more pronounced than the SDF. Not only did the ILP supply leaders of the calibre and national importance of Keir Hardie, Philip Snowden and Ramsay MacDonald, but also invaluable apprenticeships for trade-union officials and future Labour backbenchers and councillors.[149] Most crucially in terms of comparisons with the activities of American socialists, the ILP consciously subordinated its socialism to the overriding task of building a mass base within the mainstream trade-union movement for the cause of independent labour representation. The fruits of the ILP's endeavours lay in the creation of the Labour Representation Committee in 1900. By way of contrast, the 'dual unionist' tactics of Daniel De Leon's Socialist Trades and Labor Alliance had resulted in splendid isolation from the mass ranks of the AFL. This is a matter to which we will return.

Despite its claims to the contrary, the Fabian Society exerted little influence upon organised labour.[150] Mainly middle class in character, generally adopting a superior cultural pose to the 'masses', having virtually no influence upon trade-union development, and preferring permeation of the Liberal Party to the creation of an independent party of Labour, the Fabians remained 'drawing-room' socialist intellectuals and planners. Indeed the main contribution of the Fabians lay in 'paper-work' – as 'drafters of propagandist material for the labour movement and of various concrete propositions of reform'; and in exercising their administrative and intellectual influences upon politicians, administrators and other government officials. But, unlike the ethical socialists of the ILP and William Morris's Socialist League, Fabian efficiency and élitist expertise 'opened no windows on the soul' (R. H. Tawney).[151]

The various socialist groups were thus small in numbers, and, despite the influence of the ILP and the SDF on the labour movement, did not enjoy the organisational and membership strength and wide appeal of the American Socialist Party in its 1902–12 heyday. Independent labour politics met with a more receptive audience in Britain than in the United States. But progress was by no means smooth and even. The Scottish Labour Party had been established in 1888 in the wake of Keir Hardie's defeat in the Mid Lanark by-election, and from 1892 onwards there was significant, if limited, trades council and trade-union support for the Scottish party.[152] South of the border prospects for independent labour appeared to be less propitious. For much of the 1890s the TUC was most heavily influenced by the Liberal persuasions of its 'old guard' leadership. Adverse legal decisions, economic threats to skills, wage levels and workplace control and independence, hostile employers, indifferent or increasingly adversarial establishment politicians, and growing pressure from socialists (especially the ILP) and 'new' unionists did, however, force change. In 1899 the TUC set up a meeting of the unions, co-operative societies and socialist organisations to plan for labour representation in parliament. A year later the Labour Representation Committee held its inaugural meeting, and in 1906 gave birth to the Labour Party.

The fortunes of the infant Labour Party were mixed. Mainly in response to the Taff Vale decision of 1901 (which rendered unions, as corporate bodies, liable for the payment of damages), union-affiliated membership of the LRC rose from 375,000 in early 1901 to 861,000 in 1903. In the latter year agreement was reached as to the necessity to establish a fund for the payment of Labour MPs. The important Miners Federation of Great Britain formally affiliated to the Party in 1908 (thus ending official ties with the Liberals), but 45 per cent of miners voted against affiliation, and in 1913 some 40 per cent of miners would vote against the creation of a political levy to support the Labour Party. Up to the First World War and beyond several unions were opposed to the 'socialism' of Labour. And pre-war allegiances to Liberalism were far from confined to workers in the coalfields of Yorkshire and Nottinghamshire. In his celebrated thesis of 1971 P. F. Clarke argued that the 'New Liberalism' of progressive reform and enhanced collectivism, as manifested in the actions of Lloyd George and Churchill and the 1906–14 welfare reforms (old age pensions, unemployment insurance and so on) accommodated, in Lancashire and elsewhere, the rise of class-based politics. Clarke's views have subsequently suffered some damaging blows.[153] But there is no doubt that liberal-radicalism did continue to exercise an important influence upon sections of the working class. Indeed, a number of recent contributors to the debate have emphasised ideological affinity, rather than conflict, between the policies of 'New Liberalism' and the Labour Party.[154]

It is certainly true that, in terms of national politics, the Progressive Alliance between Labour and the Liberals generally maintained itself up to 1914. And, as noted earlier, at Westminster Labour remained very much the junior partner in the electoral pact negotiated between Herbert Gladstone and Ramsay MacDonald in 1903. The pact did facilitate the election of thirty Labour MPs in the 1906 general election. But, despite growing support at the municipal level and much improved organisational structures, the national party was, at best, only holding its own in electoral terms between 1910 and 1914. As Hunt observes, 'there were rather less Labour MPs in 1914 than the combined strength of miners and Labour MPs in 1906. This record . . . fuelled the mood of disillusionment and frustration.' The stark fact that the Labour Party 'held only thirty seats in a House of Commons of 670 members', underlay MP Phillip Snowden's gloomy observation in 1913 that, 'The present labour representation in parliament is there mainly by the good-will of the Liberals, and it will disappear when that goodwill is turned into active resentment.'[155]

Between the war years and the early–mid 1920s the Labour Party's fortunes were, however, to undergo a dramatic improvement. As Tanner notes, 'During the war the Progressive Alliance fell apart.' The split between Asquith and Lloyd-George in 1915–16 and painful contradictions between the individualist beliefs of many Liberals and the collectivist requirements of total warfare gravely weakened the Liberal Party. By way of contrast, Labour's collectivist case was strengthened. Tanner's observations are once again instructive:

> Local Labour parties increasingly came under the influence of expanding trade unions with an enhanced interest in the Labour party. They encouraged wholehearted support for the war ... and reinforced Labour's *social* roots. The *economic* impact of war also helped Labour's competitive position. War collectivism made state involvement in ... the coal and railway industries seem a viable means of altering wages and conditions. The affected workers became more confident in the method ... , less confident in the parties currently governing its practical application. Labour ... became an attractive force. Its commitment to protecting the gains made by the unskilled workers who often dominated Tory areas also gained some credibility from the experience of war collectivism. To many, Labour seemed the party most likely to protect these gains.[156]

Combined with the appearance of a truly mass electorate in 1918, and heightened and widened demands for post-war reconstruction and 'fairness', the collectivist experiences of warfare thus considerably advanced Labour's cause. And, especially in the west of Scotland, and parts of England and South Wales, socialist advancement went hand in hand with the rise of Labour. By 1924 a minority Labour government was in office and Phillip Snowden had become Chancellor of the Exchequer.

General Observations

We must pause at this point in our story to make three general observations. First, however halting and chequered, independent labour and socialist advances in pre-war Britain and the United States arose from similar causes. As seen in Chapter 1, the serious strains experienced by competitive capitalism in both countries and the intensified pressures placed upon workers to increase production at relatively lowered costs, combined (especially in the United States) with capital's accelerated drive for mastery over the workplace, provided the broad material context in which political developments must be situated. Albeit to varying degrees, workers in both countries once again began to feel that economic problems and crises were being tackled primarily at their expense. Dissatisfaction with the courts, employers and existing parties, and the serious depression and unemployment common to both countries during the mid 1890s, stimulated workers' feelings of being under siege, of even being outside of and rejected by the 'system'. As we know from our discussion of Chartism, attachment of 'outsider' status to proud and independent craftsmen and others could have profoundly radical effects. There were a number of countervailing influences at work (the flexibility of the political system in the United States, the strong constitutionalist and gradualist traditions of British labour and so forth) which greatly limited the mass appeal of what Ross McKibbin has termed the 'rejectionist' ideology of revolutionary Marxism. But especially in Britain, the very fact that the solid, if unspectacular advances achieved by the 'reformist' post-Chartist labour movement were being challenged and in real danger of being reversed, pushed even 'old guard' Lib.-Lab. trade unionists to the Left. And in both countries the increasingly *mass* character of organised labour's social base and of industrial conflicts meant that workers would not passively submit to hostile treatment.

Second, implicit in the first observation is the total rejection of a crude, unqualified notion of 'exceptionalism'. Especially during the late 1880s and 1890s independent labour politics in both countries enjoyed growing support. There was less of a 'permanent structural determinism' at work to inhibit the growth of a third-party voice for American labour, than 'a dynamic and indeed somewhat fortuitous convergence of events'.[157] The United States did not trail Britain in the socialist stakes right up to the First World War.

Third, during the war and the post-war years important differences did emerge between the two countries. Despite the massive American strike wave between 1916 and 1922, industrial militancy did not lead to successful independent labour or socialist politics. The AFL's effective attachment to the Democrats was the dominant feature of organised labour's politics, and was to continue as such throughout the inter-war period. In Britain, and despite the inter-war hegemony of the Conservative Party (complete with significant working-class support), Labour did come to replace the Liberals as the 'alternative' party of government. Such differences demand explanation.

Explaining National Differences

Institutional Factors

Answers are, in part, to be found in institutional factors. Notwithstanding its internal complexities, the AFL constituted a generally permanent and certainly formidable obstacle to the adoption of independent labour and socialist politics. As we have clearly seen in the present and previous chapters, Gompers and his allies' official attachment to non-partisanship, and increasingly unofficial allegiance to the Democrats, stemmed from a number of causes. Past experiences of the divisive and bruising effects of partisan politics and clashes with socialists and Populists were of key importance. The costs of attempting to transform a hostile state, including a very strong judiciary,[158] and an established and successful political system were set against the tangible benefits of 'incremental gradualism'. And in the post-1912 years support for Woodrow Wilson, and the AFL leadership's growing patriotism, conservatism, racism, nativism and unmitigated opposition to all radical 'isms' – all strongly worked against the durable success of both socialism and independent labour politics. We must not forget that the AFL was the *dominant* force in American labour. Realistic chances of radical success were in effect dependent upon either the transformation of the AFL or its replacement by a more radical and influential body. Neither alternative, either in the form of 'dual unionism' (De Leon, the IWW) or 'boring from within' (the Socialist Party's line) was ultimately successful. In contrast, and despite the continued imprints of liberal-radicalism and anti-socialism, the TUC did, nevertheless, throw its support behind independent labour representation. And from modest beginnings, and despite its setbacks and disappointments, independent labour representation did develop a strong momentum. This momentum was stimulated by growing class consciousness at the grass-roots level (a matter to which we will return), and a series of events (particularly between 1914 and 1918) which boosted the Labour Party's confidence to achieve national prominence, indeed to govern the country.

Second, as emphasised by Gary Marks, the strong impetus provided by 'new' unionism to independent labour politics in Britain was, at least in a formal, organised sense, lacking in the United States. We have thus seen that while semi- and unskilled workers in America did engage in industrial action, they were markedly less successful than their British counterparts in building durable mass unions which posed an increasingly effective challenge to the voluntarist and Lib.-Lab. or non-partisan loyalties of the more established unions.

Third, instructive, if ambiguous, lessons can be drawn from the roles played by socialists in the two countries.[159] Historians such as Philip Foner have roundly condemned those American socialists, especially De Leon and his Socialist Trades and Labor Alliance, who placed doctrinal purity above practical effectiveness in forsaking the potentially fertile recruitment base of the AFL. Weinstein has, of course, argued that the socialist cause was fatally wounded less by external factors (such as high wages and opportunities for upward social mobility) than by internal conflicts between socialists and Communists. In addition, Laslett and others have pointed to the debilitating effect of the Socialist Party's anti-war stance. And Montgomery has convincingly shown that the mainstream Socialist Party lacked an effective response to Taylorism and mounting shop-floor grievances and conflict: workers were generally advised to abide by the structures of the AFL and to place their faith in the vote. Possibly far-reaching ties between industrial struggle, militant mass unionism, and socialist politics were thus rarely consolidated.

We have noted that the various socialist groups in Britain were small, that doctrinal purity was present (especially in the case of the national leadership of the SDF), and that the ILP played down its socialism in the broader interests of labour unity and the advancement of independent labour representation. Cultural élitism also distanced some socialists from their potential working-class allies. But general socialist influence, as seen in the formation and consolidation of 'new' unionism, in the pre-war 'labour unrest', in many wartime and post-war industrial struggles, in the politics of housing and municipalisation (see below) and post-war demands for 'socialist' reconstruction, and in terms of the propagation of new and radical ideas, values and ways of living (along ethical and co-operative lines), frequently compensated for small numbers. It is also worth recalling that, formally at least, the post-1918 Party was committed to Clause IV; and that MacDonald and many other national leaders did regard themselves as the inheritors of a liberal-radicalism which, in its higher stages, would evolve into socialism. Above all, in contrast to the United States, socialism in Britain remained an integral, if often subordinate part of the mainstream labour movement.

Social Factors

Even if the American socialist movement had been able to resolve its internal conflicts and to achieve a more effective role in the AFL, it would still have encountered a formidable array of enemies and obstacles in the wider society. Arguably, such hostile forces were more powerful and damaging than in Britain. Many of the largest American corporations were, of course, not only anti-union but (often violently) anti-socialist, and were prepared to spend large sums of money, time and effort in order to smash the 'Bolshevik menace'. Likewise, the American state, as seen in wartime and post-war repression, was more intensively and extensively anti-socialist than its British counterpart. As Laslett has argued:

> opposition to the war placed the S.P. of A. entirely beyond the pale of respectability, as far as much of the middle-class was concerned; and this was one of the acts that helped to precipitate the 1919 Red Scare which had far more serious consequences for the American Left than did the anti-Bolshevik movement in Britain in the immediate post-war period'.[160]

Furthermore, the Catholic church, complete with its massive working-class flock in the United States, frequently adopted an aggressively hostile stance towards 'statist' socialism with its allegedly detrimental effects upon personal independence, family life and motherhood. As Elizabeth and Kenneth Fones-Wolf have demonstrated, religious enthusiasm and trade unionism could march hand in hand and prove attractive to Catholic as well as Protestant workers.[161] But, notes Montgomery, despite internal qualifications and contradictory practices, the Catholic church organised 'a deliberate, coordinated antisocialist bloc in the leadership of the unions', and 'attacked the Socialists with arguments bound to be convincing to large numbers of workers'.[162]

In mainland Britain, especially in the west of Scotland and in Liverpool, there were attacks from the pulpit upon 'atheistic', 'free-loving' and 'statist' socialists. These attacks issued from Tory-Anglican-Methodist as well as Catholic sources. But in overall terms they were neither so pronounced nor so effective as in the United States. Furthermore, there did develop in Glasgow, Liverpool and elsewhere important ties between Catholicism and the Labour Party and, to a lesser extent, Catholicism and socialism.[163]

Political Factors

The relationship between Catholicism and socialism leads us into the wider, and crucial, explanatory framework of political systems, political parties and political processes. We have earlier argued that there was no necessary underlying structural dynamic which greatly limited the fortunes of independent labour and socialist politics in the United States. Contrary to the views of Dawley and Laurie, we have suggested that the gift of the vote and the tradition of republican citizenship did not necessarily induce allegiance to the political system throughout the nineteenth and early twentieth centuries. Indeed, at several points in this study we have described instances of political revolt, independence and third-partyism. Class was generated within politics as well as within the workplace. Equally, however, we have repeatedly observed that the mainstream parties and the established political system consistently proved to be remarkably adept at nipping political insurgencies in the bud. Co-optation, accommodation and realignment proved to be key *leitmotives*, rather than necessary structural imperatives, in the history of American workers' political allegiances.

These general remarks can usefully be applied to the period from the late 1880s to the early 1920s.[164] Populism, Labor-Populism and radical political movements within the AFL did offer serious challenges to the cosy, bland and 'non-ideological' organisational politics of the Gilded Age. The politics of 'fusion' did water down the far-reaching demands of the Alliance and Populists such as Tom Watson, but they also pushed the Democratic Party, temporarily at least, to the Left and re-opened 'ideological' issues at the national level. Thus in the crucial 1896 presidential election Bryan stood as the professed candidate of the 'toiling masses' against 'parasites' and 'monopolists'. In the event the Republican McKinley won in 1896 to usher in the long period of Republican hegemony. Political conflicts, splits and insurgencies, as witnessed especially in the rise of socialist and progressive strength, and the formation in 1912 of Theodore Roosevelt's Progressive Party ('the strongest third party the nation had known since the emergence of the Republicans'), did continue to characterise politics. But conflicts occurred within the overall strength of the existing political system and, most significantly in terms of the labour historian, the continued allegiance of the great mass of workers to the established parties.

There is no doubt that the Republicans, despite their identification with the interests of big business, did tap significant popular sentiments in 1896 and into the twentieth century. Support for the tariff continued to attract workers to the Republican cause, especially in the urban and industrial Northeast and Midwest (the heartlands of Republican strength). Identification of the severe 1893–7 depression with the Democrats and the Republicans with economic boom, general prosperity and improved wages and farm prices was a factor of extreme importance. The Republicans thus advertised themselves as the party of industrialisation and the 'full dinner pail'. The Democrats were, in part, identified with reactionary rural interests, and Bryan's commitment to 'free silver' with a devalued dollar and diminished working-class purchasing power. Furthermore, argued the Republicans, it was Democrat Grover Cleveland who had deliberately employed federal troops against the Pullman boycotters and acted in generally aggressive ways towards organised labour. From the turn of the century onwards the Republicans did suffer, in the eyes of organised labour, as a result of their connections with anti-union employers, and especially the National Association of Manufacturers. But, as Julia Greene has recently shown, the Republicans attempted in the 1908 elections to play down any overt connections with NAM and its specific attacks on Gompers, believing that, 'a connection with the open shop drive would cost them labor's support'.[165] Finally, and despite its appeal to Catholic and German Lutheran voters in the somewhat unique circumstances of 1896 (when Bryan assumed the traditional Republican mantle of evangelical crusader), the twentieth-century Republican Party soon re-established its reputation as the defender of pietistic Protestantism. And the Democratic Party reverted, in turn, to its traditional allegiances. As Sundquist concludes:

> By the second and third decades of the twentieth century, the Republican party had clearly established itself as more sympathetic to prohibition and to such nativist causes as immigration restriction, and as the preferred party of northern Protestants of pietist denominations. The Democratic party was as firmly identified, throughout the North, as the party of the Catholics, the 'wets', and the immigrants.

In such ways did 'the religious and ethnic character of the party division throughout the North' become 'even more pronounced than previously'. In addition there developed the close alliance between the AFL and the Democrats, an alliance which gained in strength with the accession of the progressive Woodrow Wilson to power in 1912. Indeed, as Laslett notes, Wilson's famous pro-labour measures (especially the Clayton Act, recognising the legality of trade unionism and many of its 'respectable' practices, and the appointment of the first Secretary of Labor) brought support to the Democrats not only from within the mainstream AFL, but also from many of the Federation's unions which had previously supported the Socialist Party.[166] Finally, both the major parties continued to vigorously and largely successfully recruit workers and particularly local labour leaders to their respective partisan causes.

Between 1900 and 1917 the progressive movement, made up of reform-minded Republicans, Democrats, ex-socialists and others, also developed strong working-class support.[167] Having a national appeal, and strongest in urban areas, Progressivism embraced a wide range of goals including government regulation of the economy, the 'purification' of politics and public life and the curtailment of inefficient and costly 'boss' politics, women's suffrage, Prohibition, municipal reform, the conservation of natural resources, and the improvement of working conditions. Such goals were to be achieved by the exertion of effective pressure upon the more conservative-minded sections of both major parties rather than by the creation of an independent party (Roosevelt's shortlived party of 1912 was the exception rather than the norm).

Much like 'New Liberalism' in Britain, Progressivism represented a particular reform-minded moment in the history of politics in western capitalism. Tired of the inefficiencies, waste, class conflict, and gross inequalities and divisions of unregulated *laissez-faire* capitalism, sections of the bourgeoisie in both Britain and America sought to achieve greater harmony and efficiency by the promotion of a more regulated or 'collectivist' form of political economy. It is important to note that the Progressives and the 'new' Liberals were not socialists. They did not believe in full-blown collectivism, but rather in a 'social service' state in which government intervention would help to both streamline and advance business and government practices and provide a safety-net for those who had lost most in the competitive stakes of the market-place. The strengthening, as opposed to the transformation, of capitalism was the overriding common goal of both groups. Maldwyn Jones has clearly outlined the class-based élitism and anti-socialist nature of Progressivism:

> Progressivism was free from the taint of radicalism that had so damaged Populism. Progressivism leaders were preponderantly middle-class city dwellers, generally comfortably off and well-educated. In exposing the seamier side of American society Progressives were not demanding a thoroughgoing transformation of the existing political and economic system. While concerned for the victims of the new industrial order – slum-dwellers and exploited factory workers – they abhorred class conflict and did not envisage any radical redistribution of wealth and power.

Samuel Hays and other historians have, furthermore, emphasised the anti-working-class and anti-democratic character of much of the Progressive programme. In many ways, for example, Progressivism formed part of a long line of élite and middle-class 'reform' movements aiming to fashion the American polity and society more in their own image: to improve the 'habits and customs' of the (especially Catholic immigrant) 'masses'; to substitute middle-class efficiency and expertise for 'rough-and-tumble' local democracy and 'boss' rule; and, to quote Leon Fink, to 'sanitise' local affairs by means of city manager and commission forms of government and 'divesting economic decision-making from locally elected officials to appointed bodies'.[168]

Progressivism did, nevertheless, attract considerable working-class involvement, especially at the local level. The appeal was multi-layered. On the level of political idealism and the active duties of citizenship, middle-class Progressives in San Francisco and elsewhere wished to include workers in a broad-based alliance against all forms of corruption and 'un-republican' behaviour. Workers were thus being offered the friendly hand of political inclusion in a harmonious, liberal-minded community, as opposed to the class-based hand of rejection. Michael Kazin has neatly captured this sentiment:

> out of the crisis of the 1890s sprang a new breed of reformers who turned their wrath against men from *all* social classes whom they accused of using money and power for selfish purposes. The progressives wanted to humble or eliminate utility monopolists, merchants of sex and alcohol, corrupt urban bosses, and extortionist union officials, and they were willing to work with anyone who would further those ends. Workers were no longer seen as a rebellious, alien force. Instead, they belonged to a sizable interest group whose mistrust of employers could, progressives hoped, be broadened into an attack on all varieties of immoral privilege.[169]

Progressivism also offered material and environmental improvements in the form of municipalisation and improved public services which did not fleece the consumer, workmen's compensation and health insurance, the abolition of child labour, minimum wages for women, and improved health and safety provision at work.

There were, however, pitfalls. According to the Progressive scheme of things, organised labour's autonomy and sectional interests would have to play second fiddle to the wider and 'higher' interests of the entire liberal community. Furthermore, as Kazin has aptly demonstrated for San Francisco, in allying themselves with middle- and upper-class reformers labour leaders were often compelled to dilute parts of their own programme. In the event of Progressivism's decline, organised labour (as in San Francisco) frequently found itself more exposed and isolated than ever to the anti-union designs of hostile businessmen. 'Having jettisoned the class combativeness of old', concludes Kazin, 'they could not convincingly revive it'. By the early 1920s San Francisco had joined Los Angeles as a predominantly 'open shop' city.

The legislative achievements of Progressivism also generally fell short of its ambitious aims. Despite the very real achievements of La Follette in Wisconsin (relating to the regulation of banks and railroads, the introduction of primary elections, the provision of income tax and death duties, and improved working conditions for women and children) and Roosevelt and Wilson at the national level, the United States generally lagged behind Britain in terms of social welfare provision (old age pensions, unemployment insurance, workmen's compensation and so forth). However, weaknesses at the national level should not be allowed to obscure important progressive achievements at the local level. Finally, we can endorse Stromquist's view that Progressivism did much to attach workers to a liberal-reforming strain of inter-class politics and to provide an attractive alternative to the Socialist Party.

Beyond the confines of political parties and pressure groups, there were also embedded within the structures of the American political system key factors which worked against the ultimate success of socialist and independent labour politics. To briefly return to the early concerns of this chapter, the very nature of the federal system, complete with its different levels of power and authority, made it difficult to translate immediate and local into longer-term and wider achievements. Geographical size also presented formidable obstacles of organisation, communication and finance. And, as Oestreicher has convincingly argued, the translation of class interests into nationally based class actions required resources and financial reserves which were far more the preserves of big business than organised labour. Given also the flexibility and adaptability of strong coalition-based parties, complete with established social bases of support and powerful financial backers, it is hardly surprising that, *in toto*, independent labour and socialist politics did not make greater headway. When all these political factors are brought together (and added to divisions within the working class, state repression and labour defeats), the 'minimalist' non-partisan approach of Gompers becomes more readily understandable. In sum, class sentiments undoubtedly existed alongside and in conjunction with ethnocultural concerns, but political factors, as argued by Lipset and Laslett, played a major role in limiting the influence and success of left-wing, class-based politics.

In Britain the parties and the character of the political system provided less effective bulwarks against the successful development of independent labour. We have earlier remarked that the late nineteenth and early twentieth centuries saw the more widespread development of class – as opposed to status- or community-based 'cultural' politics in Britain. Generally speaking, the two main parties, and especially the Conservatives, were far less able or willing to meet and incorporate the politics of labour and class into their wider ideological terms of reference than were American parties. Flexibility, splits, insurgencies and shifting positions were (as variously seen in the divisions arising from the Home Rule issue, in Lib.-Labism., the tariff reform question, and in the changing social composition of Conservatism) far from absent in British politics. But in relation to questions of labour's *independence* and growing class assertiveness, British politicians were markedly more 'traditional' and inflexible than their American counterparts.

As demonstrated earlier in this chapter, Conservatives in Lancashire and elsewhere had successfully played the game of cultural politics from the mid-nineteenth century onwards. They encountered far more

difficulties in coping with the 'new' politics of class. To be sure, appeals
to Monarchy, Church and Empire, to 'Englishness', to paternalism and
deference, to the growing 'selfishness' of trade unions, to the 'evil'
designs of socialism upon women's virtue, domestic bliss and personal
independence, and, for some, to tariff reform as the provider of work
and the financial means towards non-radical social reforms, continued
to provide the Conservatives with a strong base in the working class.
As Pelling has suggested, 'traditional' personal or family allegiances (to
Conservative Clubs, Orangeism, or the Anglican church), inter-class
family connections, and instrumental factors (hopes of material advancement, the Tory defence of certain occupations against foreign competition, and other forms of 'connection' and protection) would be among
the major factors persuading some 30 per cent of the twentieth-century
British working class to vote Conservative. (In all likelihood 'deference'
has been far less important, although it may have operated with more
force among 'the poor' than the more regularly employed and better
paid working-class strata.)[170]

The Tories proved incapable, however, of preventing the growth of
independent labour politics. There were a number of influences at work
in this context. The extensive movement of sections of the propertied
classes from later Victorian Liberalism into Conservatism was extremely
important. Many of the propertied prescribed large doses of economic
liberalism and tough anti-trade unionism as the only effective remedies
for Britain's growing economic ills. In ideological terms the Conservative
Party as a whole became far more hard-headed, offering support for
employer attempts to increase the screw upon labour in order to increase
productivity, achieve true 'mastery' of the workplace, defeat the 'tyrannical machinations' of trade unionists, and arrest declining profit rates
and reduced shares of world markets. In effect, in its new 'ideological'
form, late-Victorian and Edwardian Conservatism forfeited much of its
former identification with a wide community of interests, and became
more narrowly identified with the sectional interests of those propertied
people who had little regard for organised labour. Furthermore, set
within the context of the growth of larger units of production, more
impersonal relations at work, district and even national 'systems' of
collective bargaining, and increased industrial conflict, old-style Conservative paternalism, informality, and bonhomie lost much of their
earlier influence. Workers turned away from political structures dominated and controlled by their 'betters' to effect – by political, as well as
economic and cultural means – their own autonomous advancement.
Enraged by such displays of 'ingratitude' and 'insubordination', Tory
grandees and others vented their wrath against Labour candidates and
trade unionists. In the process they unwittingly drove workers even

further away from establishment control, and aided the growth of worker self-confidence and class awareness.

Developments in our nineteenth-century Tory stronghold of Blackburn illustrate the general trends outlined above.[171] In late nineteenth- and early twentieth-century Blackburn, notes Trodd, the longstanding Tory hegemony associated with the Hornby family finally came to grief upon the issues of economic change, political response and the re-emergence of class (in the widest sense of the word). In the face of cotton's declining international competitiveness and reduced profit margins, and despite the system of institutionalised collective bargaining which existed in the Blackburn district, many local employers took to 'driving' their workers and putting up stiff resistance to trade-union demands. The predominantly pro-employer local and trade press became increasingly vituperative in its attitudes towards the unions. In the early 1890s, for example, the *Textile Mercury* maintained that, 'Trade unionism was thoroughly demoralising our working classes and making them into ... tyrants'. And the *Lancashire Evening News* argued that, 'the prime necessity ... is to curb the revolt of labour and re-establish authority in the workshops on oldfashioned lines'. The climax arrived in 1901 when, as a result of the local version of Taff Vale, involving a strike against a Liberal employer (there were several such local 'Taff Vales' throughout the country), the Blackburn weavers' union lost over £6,000. Significantly, within two years the weavers had affiliated to the Labour Representation Committee.

The presence of both Tories and Liberals in anti-union activity, the weavers' union's dissatisfaction with the deficiences of the legislation gained on 'steaming', and employer failure to abolish fining at work and opposition to midday Saturday closing of their mills, all advanced the cause of independent labour in Blackburn. The Tories and Liberals also voiced considerable opposition to increased Labour representation on the town council; and the Hornbys were outraged by the nomination of an 'outsider', Phillip Snowden, as Labour's candidate at the 1906 general election. In the event Snowden was elected along with the 'natural' representative, W.H. Hornby. This was the first time in the period of national and local Tory hegemony from the mid 1880s onwards that Blackburn's Tories had lost a seat in the two-member constituency. In 1906 local employer and Tory stalwart, W. Coddington, retired, to be followed in 1910 by W. H. himself. Indeed, Tory fortunes in Blackburn reached an unprecedented low in 1910 when they lost both seats to Snowden and the Liberals. Snowden, in fact, became the leading member for the constituency.

Labour did not emerge in Blackburn for political reasons alone. Attention has already been drawn to the importance of economic issues and the increasingly close associations between economic prescriptions and political allegiances. It was also the case that a class-based independence was increasingly present in cultural and leisure-based matters. Significantly, the Labour Party, the trade unions and to a lesser extent the socialists, all began to relate to, and to build up a 'natural' constituency within those leisure-based activities and institutions – the pub, football, cricket, friendly and burial societies, and other clubs and pastimes – which had sustained the paternalistic Toryism of Hornby. In Blackburn the rise of Labour was, therefore, related more to the politics, economics and cultures of class than to the narrowly institutional matter of labour representation. Beneath Tory and Liberal opposition to Labour representation and independence lay all manner of conflicts and differences of outlook which centrally revolved around class.

We must, however, add a final cautionary note. Labours' 'rise', in Blackburn and elsewhere, was to prove uneven and limited. Thus, in the elections of 1918, 1922, 1923 and 1924 Labour was defeated in Blackburn by Tories and Liberals. Only in 1929 did Labour prove victorious, capturing both seats (this was a familiar national pattern). But throughout the 1930s Blackburn returned only Tory members. The case of Blackburn also counsels us against the adoption of a cultural determinist model of politics. The late nineteenth- and early twentieth-century working class in Britain may have adopted a more uniform or 'traditional' style of life and general culture, but increased cultural homogeneity did not constitute a sufficient guarantee of the adoption of labour and socialist politics. In truth, between culture and political allegiances and actions lay a complex *ensemble* of personal, institutional, economic, political and ideological determinations.[172]

If the subject of popular Toryism has been somewhat neglected (often, given the strength and resiliency of working-class Toryism, quite unjustly), then the same cannot be said about popular Liberalism. P. F. Clarke's thesis that the 'New Liberalism' successfully accommodated the growth of class-based politics, as reflected in the general viability of the Progressive Alliance between the Liberals and Labour up to 1914, has stimulated voluminous and often impressive research and continuing argument and counter-argument.[173] Our present purpose is not to investigate every nook and cranny of debate but to offer some general observations and evaluations of the highly complex relationship between Labour and Liberalism.

There is, first of all, no doubt that 'New Liberalism' and the Progressive Alliance did enjoy some notable successes. Clarke has detailed such achievements in Lancashire. Chris Wrigley, John Davis, Susan Pennybacker and, most recently, Pat Thane have also clearly shown that parts of London were strongly influenced by Progressivism.[174] Given the more recent nature of much of the work on London (which nevertheless rests upon the strong foundations built by Paul Thompson's *Socialists, Liberals and Labour* (1967), and Gareth Stedman-Jones' *Outcast London* (1971)), we can usefully delineate the main features of Progressivism in the metropolis.

Official or orthodox Liberalism (rooted in retrenchment and *laissez-faire*) was relatively weak in mid–late nineteenth-century London. Attention has earlier been drawn to the continued vitality of radical traditions, especially among artisans, in the post-Chartist metropolis. And the formation of the London County Council in 1889 provided the opportunity for the various radical groupings, and especially radical Liberals or 'Progressives', to fight elections on the basis of commitments to municipal reform and opposition to privilege and monopoly. The Progressives demanded municipal control of water, electric lighting and tramways, the municipal provision of parks, libraries and baths, 'fair' (i.e. union) wages and conditions for those employed on council contracts, the employment of unionised 'direct labour' by councils, 'work creation' by public means (to counteract unemployment), better sanitation and housing (the latter being of crucial national importance), an end to sweated labour, and reductions in the length of the working day. As Pat Thane has observed, Progressive demands centrally revolved around the assumption of a more activist role by a largely democratic, accountable and progressive local state. There existed obvious parallels with Progressivism in the United States. Above all, both movements represented movements away from *laissez-faire* towards increased state intervention in economic and social affairs.

In London the Progressives controlled the County Council up to the Tory victory of 1907 (a reaction against 'profligate' Progressivism by economy-minded ratepayers and anti-collectivists). And in some parts of the capital, especially Battersea, West Ham, Woolwich, Bow and Bromley (particularly Poplar), there developed close links between trade unionists, socialists, Labour Party members, and 'New Liberals'. The very facts that London Labour's successes at the polls in the post-First World War years were most pronounced in those parts of the city in which pre-war Progressivism had flourished and that the Labour Party inherited much of the ideological bag and baggage of Progressivism, have led Thane and others to play down the ideological differences between radical Liberalism and Labour. Similarly, on a more general note, Reid and Biagini have highlighted the radical-liberal (and inter-class) rather than socialist or even 'labourist' (and more class-based) characteristics of the rising Labour Party. According to these two authors, ideological continuity and broad reforming traditions were far more important to Labour's growth than ideological ruptures and burgeoning class conscious.[175]

Whether in its unreconstructed (as in Wales), reconstructed (as in parts of the northeast), or hybrid form (parts of Yorkshire and Lancashire), Liberalism, as recently demonstrated by Duncan Tanner, undoubtedly retained the allegiances of workers beyond the boundaries of London and Lancashire.[176] Ultimately, however, it was the overall failure of Liberalism to prevent the rise of Labour which mattered most. A number of key factors arise at this juncture. First, as manifested most dramatically in the case of Poplar (where mainstream Liberals united with the Tories in opposing Progressive and Labour commitments to the 'right to work' and 'fair' levels of relief for the unemployed) the Liberal cause was sometimes damaged by conflicts between 'new' and 'old' party members. Such conflicts usually centred upon cost, 'economy', and the nature and extent of collectivism. Second, as a number of historians have demonstrated, the influence of 'New Liberalism' upon the Party as a whole was less profound than argued by Clarke. As Belchem notes in relation to the famous Liberal general election victory of 1906, it was the free-trade 'Liberal crusade against tariff reform . . . old-style revivalism, not any progressive revisionism, which brought the Liberal party back into power'. And, having achieved power by revivalism rather than by any widespread commitment to social reform, 'the Liberals looked to progressivism to add an attractive gloss to their remarkable victory, to consolidate support particularly among the working class'.[177] Third, 'New Liberalism' possessed its own limitations and deficiencies. In London, for example, the city's trades council, representing some 60,000 trade-union members, became increasingly disillusioned with the 'fainthearted' commitment of the Progressives to municipalisation, improved housing and to the LCCs inadequate attention to the grievances of its own workforce. In the crucial elections of 1907, notes Pennybacker, the London Trades Council endorsed 'only certain Progressives', and called for 'direct labour . . . the creation of a labour exchange and work for the unemployed, and for metropolitan-wide wage standards in municipal employment'. Increasingly, trade unionists in the capital moved away from Progressivism to the Labour Party.[178]

Finally, and most crucially, both 'new' and 'old' Liberalism frequently foundered upon the rocks of largely class-based economic and social conflicts. From Scotland to South Wales there arose, albeit unevenly, areas of disagreement which, while not generally manifest in the political deals of Westminster and in national voting patterns, nevertheless were of major importance in modifying and transforming local political cultures, allegiances and, increasingly, voting preferences. The 'right to work', to relief 'without pauperisation' for the unemployed, to the eight-hour day, to (especially for women) a minimum wage, to trade-union wages and conditions, to decent housing at fair rents, to efficient, expanded and accountable public services, and opposition to local 'Taff Vales', to the antagonistic policies of employers, and to collusion between the latter and local political establishments – these were the key issues which, time and time again, variously moved workers to champion independent labour representation in preference to Liberalism.[179]

Reference to local case studies reinforces the general point. In the West Riding of Yorkshire autocratic and 'old-style' Liberal employers, chafing against workers' demands for collective organisation and legally reduced hours of labour, and strongly attached to voluntarism, unwittingly advanced the cause of independent labour. In Glasgow, industrial conflict, 'control' issues at work, housing and the influential role of the ILP were crucial catalysts in Labour's growth. In Leicester unemployment, rapid mechanisation, the rise of young, militant and influential socialists, and the opposition of local Liberals to the right of the unemployed to decent and rewarding work at fair rates of pay were significant factors in the decline of long-established Lib.-Labism. In Burnley in the immediate pre-war years the weavers' union's demand for a closed shop taxed the Liberals commitment to 'collectivism' to breaking point. In Blackburn and Manchester 'New Liberalism' offered 'too little, too late'. In the mining valleys of South Wales escalating industrial conflict, irregular earnings, fluctuating market conditions, hostile employers organised in large, impersonal companies, the birth of the South Wales Miners' Federation (in 1898), growing socialist and syndicalist influence, the largely homogeneous and tightly knit character of many mining villages, and the rise of the miners' lodge to a hegemonic position within the community, underlay the post-1914 transition from Liberalism to Labour. Even in the Nottinghamshire coalfield, complete with its class-conciliatory traditions and its paternalistic employers, economic and social changes were loosening the grip of Liberal politics.[180]

In sum, notwithstanding the complexities of the relationship between Liberalism and Labour, and despite the chequered character of the latter's development, the dominant national picture – of Labour's growth – cannot be denied. Our second general observation must therefore be that American mainstream parties and Progressivism proved to be far more adept at halting the rise of independent labour politics than did British Liberalism. In its overarching reluctance to *strongly* intervene in the mechanisms of the market-place and consistently to place collective, class-based needs and demands above those of 'individual freedom', 'independence', and the virtues of 'restraint' and 'proper self help' (especially in relation to the needs of the unemployed), British Liberalism frequently exposed the limitations and contradictions of its new 'collectivist' face. In opposition to the claims of Kenneth Brown, Alastair Reid and Eugenio Biagini, we thus argue that the pre-war development of the Labour Party cannot be viewed mainly or purely within a context of the 'continuity of radicalism' and in relation to Liberal resistance to the selection of working-class Liberal candidates. Organisational factors and ideological continuities were inextricably bound up with predominantly class-based economic, political, ideological and (as we will observe) cultural changes.

Beyond the ideologies and practices of the political parties there were features of the British political system which did not inhibit the development of independent labour politics to the same extent as in the United States. The smaller size of Britain and the absence of a federal system meant that Labour had fewer hurdles to cross before translating local into national gains. Furthermore, despite the development of 'boss' politics in parts of the country (such as Liverpool), machine and patronage-based politics, complete with their attention to the material (especially job-based) needs of their constituents and their strong pull upon working-class loyalties, were far less pronounced in Britain than in America. And, notwithstanding the facts that significant numbers of those men lacking the parliamentary franchise in the pre-1918 period were younger and single males, lodgers, and the highly mobile of all social strata rather than simply working-class in occupation, and that the political preferences of indeterminate numbers of the unenfranchised (both male and female) lay with the Conservatives and Liberals, there is little doubt, as demonstrated by McKibbin, Matthew and Kay, that (in conjunction with class-based changes in political culture) the achievement of the mass franchise in 1918 did give a considerable boost to the electoral fortunes of the Labour Party.[181]

Cultural Factors

Finally, we can now turn away from politics to usefully explore possible links between developments in working-class culture and politics. We can take as a starting point the hypothesis, suggested by a number of historians, that independent labour and socialist politics were more likely to take firm root and flourish in relatively homogeneous cultural contexts in which elements of solidarity and mutuality greatly outweighed those of fragmentation, competition and individualism.[182] We can also add two important qualifications to the hypothesis: that, as noted at several points in this study, the meanings of culture are not fixed and one-dimensional; and that there exists no necessarily direct and unmediated line between a particular kind of culture and type of politics. Individuals, institutions and various political, economic, and ideological forces both contest cultural meanings and attempt to harness culture to desired political ends.

How, in view of such considerations, did matters stand in Britain and the United States? Attention was drawn in Chapter 1 to the growth of more standardised and common cultural and leisure patterns among workers in the late nineteenth century. Just as football, pub life, the music hall, betting, the cloth cap, and close attachments to family and neighbourhood became the 'traditional' characteristics of British workers, so large numbers of American workers congregated in saloons, belonged to fraternal lodges, supported baseball, gambled, flocked to the amusement parks, dancing halls and other symbols of the new commercialised world of leisure (dancing and amusement parks being particularly attractive to young men and women), and were similarly strongly anchored in the immediate experiences of home and neighbourhood.[183] By no means *all* workers adopted the same life-styles and pastimes, and, as we will see, there continued to exist intra-class cultural conflicts and divisions. But especially in Britain, the period from the 1880s to the 1920s saw the rise of a more distinctive, segregated and *experienced* (i.e. felt and articulated) form of class-based culture among workers.

The enhanced sense of class as a way of life was both reflected and informed in other ways. British and American workers, from San Francisco to New York, from London to Glasgow, provided highly effective resistance to élite and middle-class attempts to refashion their norms, values and patterns of behaviour in more individualistic and 'improvement'-minded ways. As Roy Rosenzweig has written in relation to pub life in Worcester, Massachusetts:

> In the saloon, Worcester's immigrants created a distinctive social institution that symbolized not only a rejection of some of the cornerstones of the dominant culture (e.g., mobility) but also an endorsement of alternative public modes of mutuality, conviviality, and collectivity.[184]

In truth, 'making ends meet' by a means of a variety of predominantly mutualist strategies (and centrally via the family) rather than the single-minded pursuit of individual escape from the world of manual labour, remained the overriding preoccupation of the great majority of British and American workers.

As recorded in Chapters 1 and 2, numerous economic and sociological trends – the vastly increased demand for semi-skilled labour, the narrowing of differentials, more marked residential segregation along class lines, hostile, anti-union employers and state officials, and (in some instances) growing material inequalities between classes in urban areas[185] – were also conducive to greater cultural homogeneity and solidarity. Indeed, we have seen that in Chicago, Pittsburgh and other centres of fierce industrial conflicts unifying economic, sociological, cultural and political developments (and especially attitudes of employers, politicians and judges) could overshadow divisions of race and ethnicity.

Notwithstanding such common trends towards enhanced cultural homogeneity, there did, however, develop significant differences between the two countries in relation to the issues of cultural unity and fragmentation, and the ties between culture and labour politics. It would be fatuous to present a picture of an undifferentiated British working class totally united in its mutualist and oppositional values and way of life. As noted by a long line of commentators – from Engels to Robert Roberts – divisions rooted in skill, income, religion (e.g., Catholic Glasgow Celtic fans versus Protestant Glasgow Rangers supporters), politics and, we might add, gender, did not disappear among culturally 'traditional' British workers. Similarly, we have earlier observed (in Chapter 1) that some historians have highlighted the competitive and status-seeking or defensive and conservative aspects of workers' lives. Evidence produced in Chapters 1, 2 and 3 of this study has, however, hopefully demonstrated that class-based solidarity, mutuality, confidence and the rising popular groundswell in favour of radical, forward-looking change by independent and largely autonomous working-class means increasingly took precedence over intra-class divisions and consolatory fatalism.

In the United States, and despite numerous instances of culturally informed desires for class-based space and autonomy, working-class culture was generally more fragmented than in Britain. As Couvares, Rosenzweig and others have demonstrated, 'class and cultural conflict, though they interacted, often proceeded along different lines'.[186] Thus issues such as nativism, Prohibition, religious beliefs, Sunday baseball and the general right to partake of commercial entertainments frequently allied evangelical Protestant workers with similarly minded employers against capitalist 'purveyors of pleasure' and their working-class allies. In Worcester, concludes Rosenzweig, saloon-based working-class culture was, '*alternative* – separate and distinct from the dominant society – but not *oppositional* – not a direct challenge to that society'. And, 'the "alternative culture" ... did not provide ... the basis for class-wide solidarity or consciousness. In Worcester, at least, this culture remained rooted in distinctive, insular, and often antagonistic ethnic communities.' Ethnic conflicts were, of course, frequently paralleled by debilitating racial antagonisms.[187]

These antagonisms must in turn be set within the wider social context of significant opportunities for upward social mobility (especially on the part of the native-born and the 'old' immigrants), improved living standards from 1898 onwards, and, perhaps most crucially, the triumph of Taylorism and monopoly capitalism. For long periods skilled and non-skilled workers had fought against the 'un-republican' development of corporate capitalism, for their independence and autonomy, and for recognition of their collective institutions. By the early 1920s corporate capitalism had seemingly become a permanent fixture and radical labour had lost many of its battles. Workers now had to find means (as in late-1840s Britain) to come to terms with the 'system', to survive and, hopefully, to advance within it. The defeats of socialism and mass industrial struggle, combined with the sheer strengths of big business and the state dictated that less ambitious, and in many cases more privatised, courses of action be followed.

Political Implications

The political implications of divided and united cultures were far-reaching. Populist, labour and socialist parties had indeed put down strong roots among relatively tightly knit and unified working-class, ethnic (e.g., Jews in New York City and Germans in Chicago) and 'producerist' urban and rural communities. But the defeats outlined in the previous paragraph, allied to the culturally fragmented nature of many American working-class communities, allowed the mainstream parties to cultivate 'ethnocultural' and other popular allegiances to a much greater extent than in Britain. In the latter country, the continued appeals of Toryism and, to a lesser extent, Liberalism to 'traditional' working-class voters meant that there was no automatic link between relative cultural homogeneity and Labour politics. But, as Hobsbawm has suggested, there was an increasingly close connection between Labour and the image of the cloth cap. Strongly reflecting its cultural roots, Labour's programme was constitutionalist and (at least during the 1930s) reformist, and in some instances modest and limited. But it did contain within it very powerful collectivist ties and thrusts, and frequently suggested a grass-roots consciousness of 'Us and Them'.[188]

By the early 1920s the Labour Party in Britain had become an established fact of national political life. Ties with the unions remained strong. But increasingly important in a number of localities was the attempt of the party to extend its appeal and constituency, to, for example, women around neighbourhood-based and social-welfare issues (see Chapter 4).[189] In the United States class consciousness, whilst not defunct, existed in far more dilute form in the established parties. Furthermore, the rapid expansion of commercialised leisure, mass culture and largely conformist notions of 'Americanisation' and 'Americanism' brought workers more fully into the cultural mainstream, reduced the level of culturally based class conflicts, and promoted the virtues of mass consumerism. Workers were being enticed to partake of the benefits of monopoly capitalism rather than to question its fairness. But such trends did not signal the advent of absolute incorporation and consensus. By the 1930s conflicts were once again manifest in America in the areas of both production and consumption.[190] And the CIO would be the instrument of mass-production union organisation. Indeed, it is to an overview of the major economic, social, political and ideological developments of the inter-war years that we must proceed in Chapters 4 and 5.

PART TWO

Advances and Retreats:
The Inter-war Years

INTRODUCTION

Contrasts and Similarities, Changes and Continuities

The history of workers and organised labour in inter-war Britain and the United States abounds in similarities, contrasts, contradictions, advances and reversals. The purpose of Chapters 4 and 5 is to unravel and give meaning to the myriad influences and cross-currents which affected labour's development in the two countries.

Transatlantic similarities clearly revealed themselves in relation to trade unionism, economic and social trends, politics, culture, and ideology. As observed in Chapter 2, both countries had experienced upsurges in post-war industrial militancy and conflict. However, between 1921 and 1933 trade-union membership and the overall strength and the incidence of strikes and militancy declined on both sides of the Atlantic. It is, of course, the case that the General Strike occurred in Britain in 1926. Furthermore, trade-union membership in both countries remained above 1914 levels throughout the 1920s and early 1930s; and American workers were not totally passive during the 'lean years'. But such qualifications should not obscure the dominant picture of defensive and (especially in the United States) retreating trade-union movements in both countries.

Matters improved from 1933 onwards. Economic upturn and 'recovery' in Britain were accompanied by a significant revival in the fortunes of trade unionism. Between 1933 and 1939 membership increased by 42.7 per cent; and by the latter date there were almost as many trade-union members in Britain as there had been in 1918 (6,298,000 as opposed to 6,533,000). In America there was truly dramatic change. The 'turbulent years' from 1933 to 1939 were less strike-prone than the 1916–22 years had been; sudden and profound experiences of depression and suffering may well have induced more fear, division and 'realism' among workers than portrayed in the more heroic accounts of the 1930s; and welfare capitalism continued to exert more influence among selected groups of workers than customarily portrayed. But we surely cannot doubt the depth and extent of changes in popular consciousness exerted by the Great Depression and the feeling that established sources of security, stability and general wellbeing (employers, churches, ethnically based institutions and élites, and so on) had failed to sustain their responsibilities towards 'the People'. Unemployed protests in the early 1930s were succeeded by the massive strikes of 1933 and 1934. Thereafter 'new' unions were organised under the auspices of the Congress of Industrial Organizations (formed in 1935 as the Committee for Industrial Organization) and with the vital legal protection of New Deal legislation. Despite the continued hostility of major, open-shop employers and setbacks in 1937–8, the CIO and the AFL (which also prospered during the second half of the 1930s) achieved combined (if separate) memberships of just over 7 million in 1940 – as compared with 2.8 million trade-union members in 1933. On the eve of the Second World War total trade-union membership in the United States was higher than in Britain, and far exceeded (by some 1.55 million) the membership highpoint attained in 1920.

Similar trends in the fortunes of trade unionism occurred within a broader context of shared features and processes. In terms of economic life, business amalgamations, industrial concentration, welfare capitalism, mass production, and new methods of organising production, such as the Bedaux system, proceeded apace (albeit unevenly) on both sides of the Atlantic. Similarly, depressed 'old' industries, such as coalmining, shipbuilding, textiles and agriculture co-existed with 'new' sectors of advanced production in motor cars, electrical goods and elsewhere. Socially and culturally, British and American workers were increasingly affected by the spread of commercialised forms of leisure, by the growing influence of business beyond the workplace, and the rise of the service sector. Insecurity also continued to be a common feature of working-class life. And the Wall St Crash of 1929 and the ensuing Depression brought the harsh facts of unemployment and poverty into the lives of millions of Britons and Americans. Indeed, between 1929 and the early 1930s the very existence and continued viability of industrial capitalism seemed to many contemporaries to be in doubt. Significantly, however, capitalism in Britain and America survived its crisis. In the United States Roosevelt's regulatory and interventionist New Deal largely succeeded (with important help from the economic stimulus provided by the outbreak of war) in restoring corporate liberal capitalism to health. In Britain no 'New Deal' departures were required. Recovery in 1930s Britain was mainly 'market-led' and involved remarkably little political and social instability and conflict. From 1931 onwards the Conservative-dominated National Government ruled the country. The national fortunes of the Labour Party never fully recovered from the debacle of 1931. The Left made precious little headway. And despite the image of the 'Red Decade', the 1930s in Britain were largely notable for Conservative hegemony and overall stability.

Similarities must, however, be set against significant, and in some ways more important, contrasts. Within this context a multitude of examples spring to mind: the generally more depressed state of the British economy during the 1920s, complete with its higher levels of unemployment (between 1921 and 1940 there were never less than 1 million people out of work – about one-tenth of the insured population), its predominantly more 'traditional' employers, its less defensive and weak trade unions (at least up to the defeat of the General Strike), and its established system of institutionalised collective bargaining. Similarly, employer 'welfarism' and anti-unionism, combined with deep corporate influence over all aspects of life (ranging from politics to the 'Americanisation' of cultural and social life) were of far more profound influence in 'roaring twenties' America. Whereas the American working class seemed to be relatively helpless in the face of corporate might, unable to transcend its overwhelming internal divisions rooted in race, ethnicity, income, skill, and gender, and politically fatalistic or committed to one of the two business-dominated parties, the 1920s British working class appeared to be recovering from post-war setbacks to begin its 'historic forward march'. Above all, the Labour Party, rooted in the tenacious loyalties of 'traditional' working-class culture, was the rising political star, briefly achieving office in 1924 and confidently assuming power in 1929. The world was about to be transformed: the promise of working-class power to be demonstrated; and laggardly American workers left to observe the transformative wonders of 'socialism'.

The historical deficiencies of the notion of Labour's 'forward march' were, however, soon to be revealed. The failure of the General Strike had already constituted something of a watershed in trade-union history. The more extensive and intensive attitudes of caution, moderation and 'responsibility' induced among trade unionists (and especially the leadership) by the events of 1926 and its legislative aftermath were to prevail throughout the 1930s. The trade-union movement, dominated by the highly bureaucratised, anti-Left, and militantly pragmatic general unions, lacked overall vision and flair during the 1930s (despite its post-1933 membership recovery); and effectively controlled and imprisoned the Labour Party within a hegemonic ideological structure of parochialism, empiricism and closure. Rooted in the smothering fog of immediate 'experience' (as perceived mainly by centrist male trade unionists), Labour's prevailing ideology was ill-equipped to successfully confront the greatest economic crisis in the history of capitalism and the rise of Fascism abroad. There were some countervailing successes, as seen in the revival of trade unionism, Labour's municipal successes during 1933 and 1934, and the Party's capture of 37.8 per cent of the vote at the 1935 general election. But the National Government reigned supreme while mainstream Labour Party and trade-union members and Communists, ILPers and others on the Left remained in conflict.

By way of contrast, the American Labour movement of the 1930s achieved spectacular growth both within and beyond the narrow confines of the AFL. Of great significance was the ability of the CIO to 'reach out' to previously unorganised and/or marginalised workers and to root its 'culture of unity' within families and communities as well as in the workplace. Whereas in 1930s Britain, working-class experience was in many ways becoming more differentiated (in terms of living standards, employment, status, consumption, leisure 'preferences', geographical and economic location, and so on), there developed a strong contrary impetus in the United States towards a more common way of working-class life (as reflected in the sudden onset of mass suffering, and in the largely successful attempts of the CIO to break down intra-class, ethnic, racial and other divisions).

There emerged, nevertheless, ironies and partly unintended consequences within the world of the 1930s American worker. Despite the efforts of the CIO, cultural divisions were rarely entirely overcome and, indeed, received continued support from the revived AFL. Likewise, the notion of 'Americanism', rooted in a more standardised way of life, could simultaneously undermine all manner of parochialisms and ethnic and other barriers to extended class consciousness, and relentlessly and profoundly convey the benefits of the 'normal', classless American citizen (usually the middle class in disguise) to a mass audience. There was, furthermore, considerable irony in the fact that the mass movements and protests of the 1930s, often led by left-wingers and inspired by radical class solidarities, were largely contained within traditional trade-union demands for recognition and collective bargaining. It was the scale and success, as opposed to the very fact, of industrial unionism which conveyed novelty. Some of the workers involved in mass agitation were undoubtedly extremely critical of actually existing 1930s American-style capitalism, and some of them wished to create an independent party of labour. But a 'tamed', 'civilised' and 'moral' social order more regulated, guided and directed to meet workers' longstanding demands for due protection, equity and recompense was the dominant aim of organised labour. This aim was far more in accord with the civilising vision of the Knights of Labor and the long tradition of radical republicanism (albeit in a new setting) than with the revolutionary designs of communists and many socialists. In several localities there were close parallels between the roles of the Labour Party in Britain and the Democrats in the United States, both organisations advancing and protecting the material interests of workers against their foes. But at the national level the Democrats represented a broad coalition of (arguably competing) interests (ranging from industrial workers to industrialists, to southern planters) to a far greater extent than did the British Labour Party. Finally, out of the mass struggles of 1930s America there arose a highly formalised, bureaucratised and centralised system of collective bargaining over which rank-and-file workers exerted diminishing influ-

ence, and which involved a high degree of state intervention and regulation. The hallowed voluntarism of the AFL and the 'associationalist
idealism' of the Knights of Labor had fallen prey to the ambitions of
the liberal capitalist state, and mass revolt had resulted in organised
labour's accommodation to and recognition by 'official' society.

As the reader will have gathered from previous paragraphs, contrasts,
discontinuities and contradictions existed within as well as between
Britain and America. The changing fortunes of the Labour Party
between the 1920s and the 1930s and the growing divide between the
improved living standards of those employed in 'new' industries and
the unemployment and poverty of many of those in the 'old' sectors,
constitute obvious examples of contrast. Generally speaking, however,
contrasts and breaks were more pronounced in the United States. In
this context one immediately calls to mind images of the 'booming' and
quiescent 1920s as set against the depressed and radical 1930s, and of
New Deal interventionism as opposed to *laissez-faire* post-1921 orthodoxy. In addition there existed (at least from a position of hindsight)
glaring contradictions between apparent economic wellbeing and dis-
equilibrium, between advancing wealth and growing inequality, and
between the capacity to produce and the means with which to consume
in 1920s America. Such contrasts and contradictions will in the course
of Chapters 4 and 5 be refined and qualified. But of their existence
there can be little doubt. And while it will be argued that America's
economic and social contradictions of the 1920s issued in large measure
from the common problems afflicting agriculture and 'old' industries
across the western capitalist world, it will be suggested that America's
inter-war contrasts outlined above merit a more specific, nationally
based explanation.

Above all, it was the sudden and preciptious fall in America from
overall prosperity to the massive and profound suffering of the Great
Depression, combined with the mass disintegration of faith in the ability
of the existing 'system' to rectify matters, which produced a general
crisis of legitimation. This crisis in turn induced mass radicalism and
radical state intervention of an unprecedented type and scale. In contrast,
the British economy was subjected to less intensive and sharp discontinuities. Without wishing to devalue the awful effects of capitalist crisis
in Britain, it should be remembered that Britain was not booming during
the 1920s, that unemployment was already extremely high, that the
1929–32 collapse had less adversely monumental consequences than in
America, that the post-1933 'recovery' was more marked and sustained
than in the United States, and that the slump gave rise to a 'safety-first'
and largely non-interventionist National Government rather than an
interventionist New Deal administration. Less profound shocks to, and

sudden ruptures within, the British economic system occasioned more moderate political and social continuities than in the United States.

The material presented above constitutes a summary of the main subject areas, to be covered in Part Two. The summary is pitched at an oversimplified and abstract level and will be rendered more complex and concrete in the course of our discussion. Part Two is organised in the following manner. In Chapter 4, identification of the main features of economy and society in 1920s Britain and America is followed by due attention to key developments among workers and in labour movements. Chapter 5 adopts a similar procedure in relation to the 1930s, paying special attention to the forces of militancy and reformism.

CHAPTER FOUR

Economy, Society, Culture and Politics in the 1920s

ECONOMY AND SOCIETY: THE 1920s

The United States

'Despite the blemishes in some sectors of the economy', writes Jim Potter, 'the years 1922–9 constitute one of the longest periods of sustained prosperity in American history. Profits, wages and employment all increased ... Economists, business-men and journalists spoke of a new era and believed the millenium to be at hand.'[1] The period of post-war recession and readjustment between 1920 and 1921 was followed by some seven years of heady growth. Between 1922 and 1929, notes Potter, America's GNP (in constant dollars) rose by 38 per cent in real terms. The *per capita* growth rate, while lower, was 'still spectacular: 3¾ per cent in the seven years 1923–9 and about 5 per cent in the four years 1923–6'. The population of the United States increased from 106.5 million in 1920 to 123.2 million by 1930 (a declining rate of growth resulting from severe restrictions upon immigration in 1921 and 1924, and falling birth and death rates), and the total labour force from 42.2 to 48.7 million during the decade. Between 1923 and 1929 the index of manufacturing production rose by almost 30 per cent despite the constant size of the manufacturing workforce. The key to this rise lay in dramatically improved productivity. Average output per manufacturing worker increased by over 60 per cent between 1920 and 1929. Rapid technological change and the continued capitalist transformation of the organisation and methods of work underlay the impressive gains in productivity registered throughout the economy. Wages and salaries rose by about 45 per cent during the 1920s, and prices, reflecting reduced unit costs of production, were steady or falling. Profits rocketed in key industries and the market value of shares listed on the New York Stock Exchange boomed (rising from 4 billion dollars in 1923 to 67 billion dollars in 1929). Finally, by the 1920s the United States was confirmed as the leading financial as well as manufacturing power in the world economy.[2]

The nub of the American 'miracle' lay in the successful application of science, technology and general know-how to production, to a single-minded desire to succeed, to a commitment to change and to the exploitation of mass markets for relatively cheap, standardised products. As Tom Kemp has observed:

> The new techniques of the twentieth century, based upon applied physics, chemistry and mechanics, were generally first applied on a large scale in the United States . . . The financial resources of the big corporations, the huge size of the internal market and the innovative flair of its entrepreneurs made the American economy the trailbreaker, not only in new technology, but also in organizing the large-scale manufacture and marketing of the product.[3]

Growth was evident in older sectors of the economy such as (especially) construction and parts of agriculture. Workers in the former industry resisted the forward march of scientific management and were tenacious in their defence of craft privileges and job control on the building sites. But increasingly during the 1920s worker resistance ended in failure; union recognition in construction being preserved only on the condition that the modernising drives of employers for control over the labour process and the standardisation and mechanisation of parts (window frames, doors and so on) be allowed to flourish. Parts of agriculture, especially in the South, retained their largely 'traditional' character during the 1920s, but 'agri-business' – revolving around mechanisation, high levels of capital investment and utilisation, wherever possible, of the techniques of mass production – had made steady progress in cereal cultivation (on the Northwest prairies), ranching (in parts of the West), and fruit growing (in California and Florida). Indeed managerial and technological developments in construction and agriculture point to the dangers of an oversimplified division between backward 'old' and progressive 'new' industries.

It was, nevertheless, in the heavily capitalised 'new' or newer industries that growth in the 1920s was most spectacular. For example, automobiles, electricity and electrical goods, food processing, mass distribution and retailing, chemicals and machine making, variously reliant upon economies of scale, scientific advances, mass markets, the most up-to-date managerial and productive and distributive methods, and the production of long runs of standardised products at decreasing unit costs, symbolised the wonders of American entrepreneurship and ingenuity. Automobiles and electricity stood in the van of economic progress. Kemp has outlined the phenomenal growth and massive economic effects of motor-car production:

> The most striking feature of the 1920s was that for the first time in history, and some thirty years ahead of Europe, a nation took

to four wheels. The automobile industry had already grown to adolescence before the First World War; now it became a leading sector, drawing other industries behind it through its manifold backward and forward linkages. Most obvious was the new market it offered for such industries as steel, aluminium, rubber and petroleum. By 1929 total sales of cars reached over 4,455,000 vehicles, with another 881,000 trucks and buses. In that year there were over 26 million vehicles on the road, one for every 4.5 inhabitants of the United States ... Service stations, garages and wayside eating places sprouted like mushrooms. US production of cars in 1929 was nine times that of Britain and France combined.[4]

The socio-cultural effects were equally profound: journeys took less time and distances appeared less daunting; people's lives and sense of time were speeded up; mobility and freedom enhanced; the divorce between home and work, as reflected in rapid suburbanisation, often increased; rural isolation broke down; more privatised forms of leisure (based on the 'family car' rather than the neighbourhood) made possible; and the dangers of pollution and reification and 'macho' individualism accelerated.

The assembly line and continuous flow systems greatly benefited from the spread of electric power. Equally, the corporate generators of electricity quickly appreciated the advantages of the mass domestic market and turned to the manufacture of all manner of electrical goods. Of central importance, of course, were the cookers, vacuum cleaners, washing machines, refrigerators, electric irons and other household appliances which revolutionised housework and (albeit to a limited extent) liberated women from hours of household drudgery and 'service' to the family. On a more general level, it should be noted that the cinema and the radio, central features of the inter-war 'revolution in leisure', were dependent upon electricity.

In conjunction with improved living standards, hire purchase, mass advertising, and developments in transportation, cars, electricity and electrical goods thus effected very powerful changes in the lives of Americans. For many, the 'American way of life' became identified with mass consumerism and more standardised and commercialised patterns of leisure. 'Americanism' was thus extended from the workplace of Henry Ford into people's living rooms, kitchens and leisure pursuits. And the 'Americanisation' of politics constituted the final ingredient in the conscious corporate attempt to standardise, control and 'purify' the entire culture.[5]

Despite the advances and prosperity of the 1920s, by no means all sections of American industry and society flourished. Agriculture, for example, was of declining importance within the economy. In 1920 about 15 per cent of GNP arose from agriculture, as did some 40 per

cent of the total value of exports. Furthermore, 29 per cent of the
occupied population and over 31 million Americans still respectively
worked and lived on farms. Nevertheless, by 1921 the urban population
exceeded the rural for the first time in the nation's history, and throughout the inter-war years the farm population declined both absolutely
and relatively.[6] During the 1920s well over 19 million people left farms
for urban areas. Many returned, but the total farm population decreased
by about 1 million people. Poor wages, unemployment, under- and
seasonal employment, the pull of urban jobs, expanded opportunities
and freedoms (such considerations being of particular importance to the
2 million or so blacks who had migrated from the South to the North
between 1915 and 1930), declining prices and downward mobility underlay the mass exodus to the towns and cities. And just as these rural
migrants increasingly occupied the unskilled and poorly paid ranks of
the mass-production workforce, so exploited Mexican and Chicano
migrant workers were recruited by wealthy capitalists in California and
elsewhere to pick fruit and vegetables.[7]

Peter Fearon has observed that farm income fell to a very low level
in 1920–1, rose sharply to 1925 to reach pre-war levels, and stabilised
up to 1930. Fearon concludes that agricultural income 'grew at a satisfactory rate during the 1920s and many farmers could improve their living
standards considerably'. But much depended upon the size of the farm,
geographical location (many tenants in the South and elsewhere living
from hand-to-mouth), and location within the agriculture sector. Certainly, as Fearon emphasises, a growing common problem for small
farmers was indebtedness. Between 1919 and 1922 many farmers had
gone into debt to buy land which had rapidly increased in value. During
the 1920s, however, the value of farm property declined. But farmers
were still compelled to repay long-term mortgages at extremely high
levels. As a result of inability to pay, there occurred widespread fore-
closures and evictions. Many farmers were forced down into the ranks
of tenants and wage labourers. Between 1930 and 1934 almost 1 million
farms were repossessed, arousing great anger in rural communities.
Ominously, agricultural prices collapsed in 1929. The industry was about
to enter its awful agonies of the Great Depression.[8]

Other traditional stalwarts of the economy also suffered. Coalmining
experienced acute competition among the operators, declining prices,
rapidly mounting unemployment (the number of coalminers falling from
704,000 in 1923 to 439,000 in 1940), widespread mechanisation of load-
ing and cutting, and fierce attacks on the United Mine Workers by
determinedly anti-union employers. The cotton industry also underwent
bitter conflicts. Competition from synthetic fibres and the low-wage
mills of the South persuaded northern employers to 'drive down labour

costs, intensify production, and obtain a free hand to weed out employees they considered inefficient or undesirable'. Some northern textile and clothing firms also moved away from centres of trade unionism. But none of these measures could still the decline of northern textiles. In the South aggressively anti-union employers utilised cheap labour and the protection offered by local state machines to successfully undercut their northern competitors: but during the late 1920s and early–mid 1930s there was an explosion of protest among southern textile workers.[9] Shipbuilding, as in Britain, lost the increase in demand stimulated by the war and 'suffered from over-capacity in a period of sluggish foreign trade'. Finally, the railways, frequently unable to meet competition from road transport, went into what was to be a long period of decline.[10]

As we will see in more detail below, both the 'old' and the 'new' sectors of the economy constituted increasingly unfavourable sites for trade unionism during the 1920s. In Chapter 2 we examined the ways in which the employers generally emerged victorious from the industrial conflicts between 1916 and 1922. From the latter date onwards employers in the 'new' sectors consolidated their non-unionism; and in the declining older sections unions were generally faced with increased employer hostility and the stark alternative of patchy recognition in return for more or less total employer control over the organisation of work. In addition, workers were confronted with depressions in 1924 and 1927 and the nagging worry of economic insecurity. As we will see below, while there was an unmistakable and significant upward general trend in real wages during the 1920s, by no means all workers enjoyed 'American' standards. Unemployment and underemployment, combined with speed-up, lack of federal social-welfare provision, and loss of independence at the point of production constituted the flipside of the American dream. Indeed, a recent article by Frank Stricker has concluded that 35 to 40 per cent of all US non-farm families in 1929 were poor.[11]

Britain

In comparison with the robust health of the United States, Britain in the 1920s was generally ailing. Indeed, it has become a commonplace in British economic history to refer to depression during the 1920s and recovery from 1933 onwards. However, as recognised in some of the literature, the 1920s were not depressed in an absolute or blanket sense.[12] There were distinctive and varied phases within the economic history of Britain between 1918 and 1929.

At the end of the war there took place a frantic and spectacular re-stocking boom, 'fuelled', notes Stevenson, 'by rising prices, the release of wartime profits in the form of bonus shares, and the widespread belief that pre-war conditions would return and with them the demand for British goods'. This highly unstable speculative boom was characterised by increases in capacity, production and a rash of transactions in cotton and elsewhere at hugely inflated prices in anticipation of a return to pre-war market conditions and prices. In fact, the return to 'normalcy' did not materialise for the staple export industries, the basis of Britain's nineteenth-century economic supremacy. The year 1920 saw an increase in government borrowing rates, a fall in prices and rising unemployment. The following two years witnessed further reductions in exports and production and a sharp rise in unemployment, especially in the staple industries. Short post-war boom had given way, observes Von Tunzelmann, to 'a deep and sustained slump as Britain was finally compelled to come to terms with the losses and dislocation arising out of the war'. Indeed, the appearance of new substitute goods and materials, intensified foreign competition and the erection of tariff barriers, overcapacity and 'overcommitment' (in terms of the excessively heavy reliance of the economy upon the staple industries), the falling purchasing power of the primary producers for manufactured goods, the return to gold at an inflated rate of exchange in 1925, insufficiently forward-looking and comprehensive managerial strategies, and serious industrial conflict were to ensure the continued suffering of cotton, coal, iron and steel, and shipbuilding throughout most of the inter-war period.

The total economic picture was not, however, uniformly gloomy. There was a slow, if weak and unsteady, upturn between 1923 and 1929. By 1924 the 1913 level of production had been reached; and between 1924 and 1929 net national product grew at an average rate of 2.5 per cent per annum, as compared with 0.5 per cent between 1899 and 1924. Indeed, despite the 1929–32 Slump and mass unemployment, the economy as a whole performed reasonably well between the mid 1920s and mid 1930s. Thus Hobsbawm:

> The output of *all* British manufacturing industry (including, that is, the declining ones) grew considerably faster between 1924 and 1935 than between 1907 and 1924 ... Total industrial output per head may have just about doubled between 1850 and 1913, or a little more. It hardly changed between 1913 and 1924. But from then until 1937 it rose by about one third, considerably faster than in the heyday of the Victorians.[13]

In addition, retail prices tumbled during the 1920s while wage rates either remained fairly stable (1927–30) or fell at a slower rate than prices (1920–6). Herein lay the trend which was to dominate the inter-war years: improved real wages for those in regular employment in the midst of falling living standards for the unemployed (see Table 4.1, p. 295).

On balance, the 1920s constituted a period of disruption, uncertainty and the beginnings of reorientation for the British economy. Contrary to the dominant views of politicians, bankers, industrialists and economists, there was to be no return to the free trade, economic individualism, and British domination of the prosperous and less contested international markets of the pre-war era. Traditional deflationary strategies to restore competitiveness – cutting wages and other costs, increasing hours and workloads, and 'sound money' – were also to reveal their limitations and social costs during the 1920s. The former 'workshop of the world' was, in effect, in the process of making painful adjustments to its diminished importance in the post-war economic order.

There were optimistic signs. Alongside improved macro-economic performance in the post-1922 years, there was the development of 'new' industries in motor cars, electrical goods, chemicals, pharmaceuticals, rayon and in the burgeoning service sector (distribution, transport and administration). Against the serious employment losses of the staple industries (half a million in coal between 1911 and 1938, a reduction from 621,500 to 393,000 in cotton between 1912 and 1938, and a quarter of the workforce lost in shipbuilding between 1924 and 1937), we must set increases of 318,000 and 107,000 in, respectively, construction and the electricity supply industry between 1920 and 1938. 'The biggest absolute gains in employment', records Stevenson, occurred, however, in wholesale and retail distribution: an increase from 1,773,200 in 1920 to 2,438,200 in 1938.[14] Significantly, British trade unionism was to be weak in these new growth sectors while simultaneously on the defensive in the declining areas of the economy. But this is to run ahead of our story. The important point to note at this juncture is that whereas the 'new' industries peaked in the United States during the 1920s they would only fully prosper in Britain during the 1930s. By the late 1920s the slack left by the decline of the traditional industries had not been adequately taken up by the sectors of growth, and Britain was about to be hit by the Slump.

BUSINESS STRUCTURES AND EMPLOYER STRATEGIES TOWARDS LABOUR

Workers' experiences and trade unionism were affected not only by the conditions of health of the sectors of the economy but also by levels of economic concentration and power, the extent to which employers controlled and transformed the organisation of work and social relations of production, and by more general employer attitudes and policies towards the collective organisations of workers. We will now turn to an examination of these issues during the 1920s.

In Chapter 1 we described the ways in which American employers, responding to market conditions, the workers' bid for power, and, above all, the late nineteenth-century crisis of competitive capitalism, transformed their organisations along corporate, Taylorite and non-union lines to a much greater extent than was the case among more 'traditionalist' British employers. This picture persisted, despite important qualifications, throughout the inter-war period.

At several points in this study we have observed that the mass-production centres of the American economy had, by the early 1920s, resisted the impetus to unionisation. Non-unionism was to remain the norm in steel, meatpacking, automobiles, electrical goods and parts of machine-making for the remainder of the decade. These and other economic sectors were for the most part dominated by corporate giants, jealous in defence of their freedom of action and autonomy at the point of production, increasingly mechanised, 'Taylorised', and resorting to 'rational' bureaucratic procedures and structures (as epitomised by the development of personnel methods of labour recruitment at the expense of the more arbitrary practices of foremanship; in the recruitment of college-educated business graduates; and in an increasing interest in the 'human' problems of production – to be resolved with the aid of psychology and sociology).[15]

The successful pursuit of the 'open shop' was viewed as an indispensable factor in gaining management the 'right to manage', and the means to reorganise working practices, relations and the very nature of the job itself without 'outside' union interference. And this pursuit was carried on as relentlessly in the cotton mills of the South as in the steel mills of the North.[16] There were exceptions to this general rule. In the highly competitive needle trades, dominated by sharp fluctuations in output and employment, and declining prices and chaotic wage structures, recognition of the Amalgamated Clothing Workers and the International Ladies Garment Workers helped to stabilise, regulate and improve matters. Interestingly, these unions pressed employers to accept scientific management, operated in conjunction with workers and union officials, in order to more successfully compete and safeguard jobs and wages.[17] The United Mine Workers of America similarly attempted to standardise conditions and wages in a highly competitive industry. But the general point of emphasis remains; by and large anti-union American employers continued to mechanise and transform production relations in the interests of power and profit maximisation within domestic and foreign markets.

If non-unionism constituted the stick, then 'welfarism' was the carrot in the employers' drive for control. We observed in Chapter 1 that in response to high labour turnover and worker militancy between 1916 and 1922, many of the large employers adopted more conciliatory policies towards sections of their workers in order to diminish the appeal of unions, induce company loyalty, reduce turnover and instability, and promote security, reliability and efficiency. Employee representation schemes (in effect company unions which often took their inspiration from the shop committees promoted by the National War Labor Board, but lacking the union dimension), savings and home-ownership plans, stock-purchase, a multitude of sports and social clubs, insurance protection against accident, illness and death, provision for old age, allotments, holidays and evening classes came to typify the labour policies of employers at General Electric, Westinghouse, United States Steel and elsewhere. By no means all the wealthy corporations followed identical policies – some were more paternalistic, and some more liberal (i.e. tolerant of workers' views) than others. But the very existence and spread of the phenomenon should not be doubted.[18]

The benefits of welfarism were not unlimited. By 1930 employee representation covered some 1.5 million workers. But welfarism affected the lives of a distinct minority of workers (the more skilled and valued 'labour aristocrats'), did little to prevent unemployment and reduce hours, and had lost some of its former impetus during the post-1922 years of persistent unemployment, reduced labour turnover, and severely battered workers and trade unions. Welfarism was not a novel development, having being present at Lowell and elsewhere during the nineteenth century, and some of its elements would survive the Great Depression.

Such considerations have led some historians to doubt the centrality of welfarism to the growth of employer hegemony and worker quietude during the 1920s.[19] The massive psychological and sociological effects of welfarism should not, however, be undervalued. As David Brody has argued,

> The flawed performance of welfare capitalism was not a true measure of its significance. Welfare capitalism exceeded the sum of its parts. It was also an idea: that management accepted an obligation for the well-being of its employees.[20]

Welfarism thus raised worker expectations of 'economic well-being and security' (Brody) which had not previously existed to anything like the same depth and extent. And although some of these expectations were lowered in the post-1922 economic climate, welfarism (and especially the benefits linked to seniority) persisted with considerable force down to the Great Depression. It was, of course, the dynamism of the 1920s economy which made welfarism a viable proposition. 'All in all', observes David Montgomery, 'American management in the 1920s enjoyed an international reputation for organizing efficient production by faithful employees comparable to that of their Japanese counterparts in the 1980s'.[21] And the deepened perception of employer *responsibility* for the welfare of the worker played an important part in creating that reputation. The onset of the Great Depression undermined the material foundations of welfarism, and, as argued by Brody, 'generated a profound sense of betrayal among industrial workers against their corporate employers'. More contentious is Brody's further conclusion that, 'had not the Depression shattered the prevailing assumptions of welfare capitalism, the open shop might well have remained a permanent feature of American industrialism'.[22]

Welfarism, transformation of the labour process, corporate structures committed to more-or-less permanent technological innovation and advanced managerial practice, and anti-unionism were far less widespread in 1920s and (to a lesser extent) 1930s Britain. This is not to suggest that the 1920s British economy remained totally static or sluggish. 'A wave of mergers and combinations', notes Cronin, 'began in 1919 and continued through the 1920s'. Indeed, Hobsbawm has suggested that whereas in 1914 Britain 'was perhaps the least concentrated of the great industrial economies', by 1939 it had become 'one of the most'.[23]

Concentration was evident in a number of sectors.[24] In cotton and elsewhere there was an acceleration of the decline of family-owned and largely self-financing firms and of the growth of large combines (English Sewing Cotton, Tootal Broadhurst Lee Company, Fine Cotton Spinners' and Doublers' Association and others) looking to the stockmarket or the banks for finance.[25] It was, however, in the newer and new growth sectors that concentration and mergers were most pronounced. As John Stevenson has observed:

> Out of the mergers of the twenties and thirties emerged industrial giants like ICI, EMI, Unilever, Courtauld's and Royal Dutch Shell. Several of these large firms were involved in trading in different countries, but in many cases the impetus to rationalization came from the rise of mass consumer markets, new forms of distribution through motor transport and the economic advantages given by size and concentration. Significantly a large number of the giant concerns were involved in the new industries, such as Nestlé's in food processing and Dunlop in tyre-making. Factories too tended to be larger ... Ford, for example, employed seven thousand people at its Dagenham factory by 1932.[26]

By the mid–late 1930s 'chain stores' such as Marks and Spencer, Liptons,

Sainsburys and Woolworths 'had become household names in almost every medium-sized town' (Stevenson), and in chemicals, engineering and vehicles, and iron and steel 40 per cent or more of the workforce were, according to Hobsbawm, employed by the top three firms. As in America, albeit on a reduced scale, the 'discovery' of a mass domestic market for relatively cheap, standardised products constituted the key impetus to increased and more oligopolistic production.

High rates of capital investment, an emphasis upon high wages and increased productivity, upon 'welfare' or personnel management, and more generally upon advanced methods of production also increasingly characterised the growing industries, and did something to offset the British reputation for labour-intensive methods of production utilising (for the most part) cheap labour. Mass-production techniques were, of course, most pronounced in the car industry of the South and Midlands. But the Bedaux system, a form of Taylorism seeking to increase productivity by means of time and motion study, was quite widely introduced. Richard Price informs us that by 1929 about 250 firms had adopted Bedaux and possibly as many again influenced by its techniques. Food processing, hosiery, textiles, tobacco, engineering and chemicals experienced speed-up as a result of the adoption of Bedaux and, in some cases, industrial conflict.[27]

A minority of 'progressive' employers sought to improve methods of production by means of trade-union recognition and joint employer and union consultation. Most prominent in this respect was Alfred Mond of Imperial Chemicals who in 1928 (in the wake of the defeat and bitterness of the General Strike) set up a series of meetings between TUC leaders and 'advanced' industrialists (the latter including a significant element from the newer, expanding sectors). The Mond-Turner Talks (Ben Turner being a leading textile trade unionist and president of the TUC) recommended trade-union recognition and the reinstatement of those unfairly dismissed as a result of their activities during the General Strike. Mond-Turner also supported the creation of a National Industrial Council (composed of equal numbers of trade-union and employers associations' representatives) to discuss general industrial relations issues and to provide, upon request, conciliation machinery to resolve disputes; the rationalisation of industry, including mergers, reorganisation and the easing or abandonment of restrictive practices in order to maximise efficiency and wage levels; and the idea that the government be urged to consider the deleterious effects upon industry of the high exchange rate of the pound.

The 'corporatist' aims of Mond-Turner were rejected by the majority of employers who resented interference in their own concerns and the imposition of standards and conditions which they could not meet.

Significantly, Mond's proposals met with a good deal of support among leaders of the more modern and prosperous industries, but were opposed by the National Conference of Employers' Organizations, dominated by the engineering and shipping employers. Autonomy and 'traditionalism' were the guiding principles of the latter group. The TUC offered support in the face of protests of 'class collaboration' from union militants. Ultimately the Mond-Turner Talks came to very little.[28]

A minority of (especially wealthy 'new' or newer) employers also practised the welfarism of their American counterparts. Stephen Jones has shown that paternalism was 'recast, if not transformed' by the wealthy cotton combines into 'organized industrial welfare':

> In the immediate post-war years the more progressive firms introduced and extended specialist welfare departments to oversee the welfare of their workforce. The minute books of the Fine Cotton Spinners, the English Sewing Company and Tootal Broadhurst Lee reveal the range of welfare programmes in operation from pension and profit-sharing schemes to schools and dental clinics . . .
>
> Mill recreation was an integral element in the industrial welfare movement, and recreational facilities were provided by most of the larger companies. The Fine Cotton Spinners' and Doublers' Association had football, hockey, bowling, and swimming clubs, whilst Tootals had excellent amenities for both indoor and outdoor entertainment, including an array of sports clubs and even an operatic society.

Jones concludes that by the 1920s paternalism in cotton was 'no longer based on Victorian ideals of "individual employer benevolence and workers' duties" ', but had become more firmly geared to the notion of rational economic efficiency. As in America, the overriding aims were more efficient and healthy workers, greater company loyalty and better relations between workers and employers.[29]

The industrial welfare movement of the 1920s extended well beyond the confines of cotton. GEC and Courtaulds had sporting clubs, ballrooms, ran works outings, operated works canteens, offered some forms of medical and sickness provision, and a range of incidental benefits. The 'traditional' paternalism of firms such as Cadburys and Rowntrees (as seen in company housing and the provision of 'trips' and 'treats') assumed more routinised and systematic welfarist form. ICI achieved renown for its profit-sharing endeavours, and company-based pension schemes became far more widespread than in the past. Increasingly, 'welfarist' initiatives were undertaken by 'labour' or 'employment' managers who then developed into 'personnel' managers.[30]

As in America, welfarism and non-unionism often went hand in hand in the growth sectors. This was certainly the case in much of the car industry for most of the inter-war period. 'The motor firms were a

Trade Union desert', notes Stephen Tolliday of inter-war Coventry. Much the same could be said in relation to Luton, Oxford and Dagenham, other key centres of automobile production. Skilled men might preserve their union attachments, but autocratic managers paid high wages, bullied and 'drove' the raw semi-skilled and unskilled car workers, and offered welfarism as a substitute for mass trade unionism.[31] Some of the 'new' employers, such as Alfred Mond and Samuel Courtauld, prided themselves upon their 'enlightened' views towards trade unionism and the necessity of worker-employer consultation. But general practice was by no means necessarily consistent with well-meaning individual intentions. The unions failed to penetrate chemicals to any significant extent. Samuel Courtauld did negotiate with the Workers' Union for his Essex factories. But elsewhere the picture was very uneven. In Coventry, for example, Courtaulds did not officially recognise the Transport and General Workers' Union until 1937. GEC also tended to be anti-union. And some companies in the growth sectors deliberately paid above the union rate in order to preserve a free hand to manage. In cotton there did, of course, exist an established tradition of collective bargaining, although during the 1920s the cotton unions were very much on the defensive. Finally, most employers in the service and distributive sectors successfully set their faces against trade unionism.[32]

'Progressive' corporate and welfarist developments in the growth sectors did not match either the speed or profundity of such developments in 1920s America, and were characterised by marked limitations. During the 1920s, notes Cronin, increased concentration of ownership 'was not translated immediately into major technical rationalization'. Much depended upon the specific economic sector, but concentration and mergers could signify the age-old capitalist concern to 'corner the market' rather than to promote rapid technological change and scientific management. And at the aggregate level, including 'old' as well as 'new' sectors, technological modernisation, increases in firm size and industrial concentration proceeded, concludes Cronin, 'only gradually from 1919 to 1939'.[33] Furthermore, welfarism touched far fewer workers and employers, both absolutely and relative to labour force and employer group size, than in the United States. Howard Gospel's pithy observation is most apposite: 'the majority of British employers, though they might talk about the "human touch", did little to develop such schemes'.[34] The speed and extent to which personnel management, systematic recruitment, and job analysis and grading were introduced should not be exaggerated. In 1939, notes Gospel, there were only about 1,800 welfare workers and labour managers in Britain. And British companies were far less prepared than their American counterparts to recruit managers direct from the ranks of business graduates. 'Natural' seniority, experience, including apprenticeship, pragmatism, a blinkered if not blind empiricism (which bit hard into the national culture), and a suspicion of 'booklearning' were important features and values of even the most advanced businesses.[35] Finally, even when introduced in the more 'progressive' sectors, scientific management often degenerated into 'merely another technique to expand output on the cheap', rather than to fundamentally transform class relations at the point of production.[36]

What we are witnessing during the 1920s is the continued general 'failure' of British employers to fundamentally change the existing division of labour (by means of new working practices, the organisation of work and technological change) and to subordinate labour to capital to anything like the American extent. And when we move to the older sectors of the British economy, this 'failure' and, above all, reliance upon the traditional methods of increasing profits by cutting wages and increasing hours and workloads rather than by capital investment and high productivity, become far more marked.

In cotton, for example, the majority of employers (beyond the untypical combines) responded to adverse market conditions by attempting to reduce wages (especially in weaving) and by raising workloads (particularly by increasing the number of looms per worker). In contrast to cotton employers in the American South, British cotton masters did not extensively employ (and at times did not utilise at all) new labour-saving machinery, job reorganisation and other de-skilling techniques, non-unionism, new supervisory practices (such as time and motion study) and personnel (the employment of young, college-trained supervisors), and breakneck driving and speed-up. To argue as such is not to suggest that American managerial practices constituted the absolute yardstick against which all 1920s capitalist practice should stand or fall. But it is to strongly claim that most British cotton employers were less 'entrepreneurial', ruthless and single-minded than their counterparts in the American South. Many cotton employers in the northern states of America also found themselves unable to compete with southern textiles. But this inability owed far less to 'traditionalism' of the British kind (northern employers did mechanise and reorganise production methods to a much greater extent than their British counterparts) than to the more successful cheap labour and non-union policies of employers in the South. The latter were also strongly supported by powerful and repressive local states.

Despite government intervention designed to reduce excess capacity and stimulate rationalisation (in 1936 and 1939), most pre-Second World War British cotton employers relied upon 'tried and trusted', highly individualistic, fragmented, and competitive labour and production strategies to counter their growing problems. Fine spinners in Bolton, for example, were little interested in the acute problems of coarse-spinning Oldham. The industry as a whole markedly failed to develop a concerted policy in relation to the pressing issues of marketing, outmoded plant and equipment, and excess capacity. The growth of the large, advanced combines could not hide the fact that most of inter-war British cotton was far too small-scale, fragmented and outmoded to successfully compete in international markets.[37]

Conservatism was rife in other established industries. Employers in 1920s shipbuilding responded to deteriorating market conditions far less by increasing capital investment and the reorganisation of the division of labour than by cutting wages, 'driving' workers and by containing craft practices within narrowed limits. In engineering the employers' victory in the 1922 dispute did seriously damage trade unionism and strongly advance the cause of managerial prerogatives. But islands of craft autonomy and strength remained (in all sectors of engineering), and would reassert themselves during the economic upturn and rearmament of the late 1930s. Finally, in coalmining employer attempts to improve the inefficient structure and outmoded attitudes and practices of the industry were, at least during the 1920s, largely conspicuous by their absence. As clearly revealed in the troubled industrial relations of coalmining, and above all in the 1926 General Strike, entrenched and conservative employers expected the miners to shoulder the burdens of the industry in the form of reduced wages and worsened conditions of work.[38]

Heavily banking upon the 'cure-all' policy of a return to free trade and deflationary pre-war 'normalcy', employers in the established sectors of the economy thus did little to improve existing technologies and work organisation. Managerial prerogatives were more forcibly reasserted in the staple industries during the 1920s, but largely within the context of relatively unchanging divisions of labour and established systems of institutionalised collective bargaining.

We can thus conclude that, although less small-scale, competitive and, in some ways, archaic than in the pre-1914 period, British capitalism in the 1920s was still far more reliant upon low wage, labour intensive and low productivity policies than its American counterpart. British 'traditionalism' also revealed itself in other important ways: in the narrow perspectives and 'short-termism' of many employers in the older sectors; in the fragmentation of decision making; and in the premium placed upon practical experience as opposed to practice informed by structured and formal knowledge. British and American employers did, however, share a common distaste for 'undue outside interference' in the affairs of their businesses. Trade unions were more widely tolerated

in Britain, albeit within the confines of strictly defined managerial prerogatives. But, apart from exceptional circumstances (such as during
wartime), the majority of employers were opposed to government 'med-
dling' in business matters. As revealed in the breakdown of the Mond-
Turner talks, most British employers did not welcome 'corporatist'
attempts to resolve their economic problems. This *laissez-faire* attitude
would persist with great force throughout the inter-war period. More
corporate and oligopolistic in character, most American businesses also
wished to be left alone by the federal government. Their wish was
hugely fulfilled during the Republican 1920s. But during the interventionist 1930s American capitalists were largely prevented from
mounting co-ordinated *national* opposition to the New Deal by their
very insistence upon business 'autonomy' and the fragmented structure
of their organisations (which were largely industry-wide in character).
As David Montgomery has remarked, 'The autonomy of the enterprise
was the *sanctum sanctorum* of interwar management.'[39] This is a matter
to which we will return.

THE SOCIAL STRUCTURE OF THE WORKING CLASS

The occupational and social characteristics of the working classes in
1920s Britain and America were intimately linked to the economic
changes described above. Of foremost importance was the continuing
and greatly accelerated shift from manual (and especially manufacturing)
work to white-collar occupations.[40] In both countries the 'traditional'
working class, rooted in manufacturing industry, was at its strongest
during the period of the First World War. As Alan Dawley has observed
in relation to the United States:

> the years immediately after World War I marked the climax of
> what Lewis Mumford dubbed 'carboniferous capitalism'; that is, the
> nexus of coal, rails and factories laid down by the Industrial Revolu-
> tion. Measurements vary, but it is clear that in this moment indus-
> trial capitalism peaked – mining and manufacturing accounted for
> about one-third of GNP, and 'industrial' employment (including
> mining, manufacturing, transportation, and construction) reached
> 44 per cent of the gainfully employed, most of whom were wage
> earners. The 'old working class' of blue-collar manual workers, then,
> amounted to something more than two-fifths of the workforce. It
> is worth emphasizing that these proportions were the peak for the
> entire twentieth century. Deindustrialization (at least of the labour
> force) did not begin in the 1970s but the late 1920s.[41]

In Britain manual workers comprised 80 per cent of the paid work
force in 1911. Twenty years later this figure had fallen to 77 per cent:

by 1951 it stood at 70 per cent. During the 1920s in Britain the largely stationary demand for workers in manufacturing production was offset, notes Cronin, by a 'steady upswing' in the service sector. White-collar groups in teaching, nursing, the civil service, clerical work in general, sales and distribution increased by some 27 per cent between 1920 and 1938. Recruitment to these occupations came largely from the middle and lower-middle classes, but increasingly that minority of working-class children who had received a year or two of grammar-school education moved into the ranks of the lower-middle class.

Clerks, teachers, and other clerical and lower professional groups were generally keen to distance themselves from the manual working class. In some cases the financial gap between manual and white-collar strata was not wide. But questions of status, life-style, and family background and connections served to forge powerful divisions. Whilst by no means an undifferentiated, homogeneous mass, and whilst some (such as technicians, local government workers and clerical workers on the railways and in the civil service) were attracted to trade unionism, most white-collar workers thus stood outside, and often in opposition to, the inter-war labour movement.[42]

A similar, if more pronounced, picture emerged in the United States. During the inter-war period the proportion of the paid labour force engaged in primary and secondary activities (agriculture, mining, construction and manufacturing) declined from 61.8 per cent in 1920, to 54 per cent in 1930, to 51 per cent in 1940. Total tertiary employment increased from 38.2 per cent, to 46 per cent, to 48.9 per cent. While employment in the American primary and secondary sectors increased by something under 1.5 million during the 1920s and 1930s, employment in services and the rest of the tertiary sector grew by almost 10 million, a truly staggering rise. Indeed, by 1940 almost half of America's paid workers were employed in the tertiary sector. Thus, not only was the rate of increase of white-collar employment far more rapid in inter-war America than in Britain, but the absolute imprint of white-collar workers upon American society was also more profound. And in the United States white-collar status, consumerism and an increasing aversion to the collective organisations of labour were particularly marked. It would, after all, be in the mass-production industries, rather than in services and so on, that trade unionism would make its greatest leap forward during the New Deal era.

The ethnic, racial and sex-based characteristics of the respective American and British labour forces merit comment. Of major importance in 1920s America was legislation, enacted in 1921 and 1924, to restrict immigration and close the long-established 'open-door' policy. As Montgomery has noted, 'the closing of immigration by the quota and national origins laws had a greater impact on working-class life than any other government measure since the emancipation of the slaves'.[43] Under the terms of the 1924 legislation an annual ceiling of 150,000 was set upon European immigration. 'New' immigration from southern and eastern Europe, which had provided much of the labour force for the expanding corporate giants of the late nineteenth and early twentieth centuries, was virtually ended. Immigration from Asia was now banned. Slack in the labour market was to be taken up by migrants from the American countryside, new immigrants from Europe, increased numbers of women workers, and Mexicans and Canadians. It should also be remembered that as late as 1920 over half of America's workers (some 57 per cent, according to Montgomery) were the children of parents who had emigrated from northern Europe.

Reference has already been made to the large numbers of largely non-skilled southern blacks and Mexicans who moved into northern and western agriculture and industry during the 1920s. Women also constituted an important, if generally undervalued, part of the American labour force, especially in the burgeoning tertiary sector. During the First World War years women had moved into 'men's jobs' in manufacturing. But such gains were mainly temporary. 'With few exceptions', notes Kessler-Harris, 'jobs returned to male control when the conflict ended'. The story was, however, very different in the expanding sectors of the wartime economy such as telephone and telegraph, advertising, sales, and the financial and government sectors. 'What women as a group failed to gain in manufacturing', concludes Kessler-Harris, 'they more than made up for in white-collar areas that encompassed office staff at all but the highest levels'. By 1920 more women worked in clerical or sales occupations (25.6 per cent) than in manufacturing (23.8 per cent), in domestic service (18.2 per cent), or in agriculture (12.9 per cent).[44]

These trends accelerated during the inter-war period. Between 1920 and 1930 paid female employment increased from 8.3 million to 10.6 million, a 27 per cent rise. By 1930 women made up 24.3 per cent of the total labour force (rising to 25.1 per cent in 1940); and, despite considerable male opposition and the operation of formal and informal 'marriage bars' (in teaching, government work and elsewhere), both the absolute and relative numbers of married women in the paid workforce showed an impressive rise (from 28.8 per cent of all wage-earning women in 1930 to 35 per cent by 1940). As with women in general, married women tended to be concentrated in those sectors (clerical work and light industry, and to a lesser extent domestic service) which both suffered less than centres of heavy industry during the Great Depression, and which also recovered more quickly after 1933.[45]

Extended employment opportunities for women were part and parcel of expanded female horizons and self-confidence. As in Britain, involvement in the war effort had brought a new-found independence into the lives of many American working-class women. The attainment of the vote on a nationwide basis in 1920, the declining size of families and the amount of time spent upon household chores, the inter-war women's movement's fight for sexual independence and the more widespread questioning of sexual taboos and male domination, the freedoms associated with the 'flapper', and the pleasures provided by the affordable and accessible world of commercialised leisure – all pointed to the greatly enlarged element of *choice* (rather than unremitting grind, struggle and necessity) in women's lives.

An unqualified picture of 1920s 'liberation' is, however, misleading. For some, and especially black women, the ending of the war resulted in a narrowing of choice in the labour market: a return to domestic service and other menial jobs as contrasted with the greater variety of employment opportunities created during wartime. For many American working-class women outside the growth areas, the post-war years involved a retreat into the home and the return of 'men's jobs' to the 'natural breadwinner'. Throughout the inter-war period, as noted by Kessler-Harris, the great majority of married women remained in the domestic sphere and most of those in paid work 'were still poor and black'. The 'flapper' image – of a 'flighty, apolitical, and irresponsible stance', of 'limited economic and sexual freedom' combined with 'an extension of women's supportive functions in the male world without the threat of competition' (Kessler-Harris) – held out some attractions to young working-class women; but its central appeal was to middle-class women entering the business and professional worlds. Working-class women continued to be highly concentrated in low-paying and low-status occupations, in which routinised, Taylorised, divided and alienating tasks were the norm. Women, as shown by Susan Porter-Benson, did develop their own 'bonds of solidarity', their own cultures at the workplace. But such bonds only rarely found expression in male-dominated, hierarchical and largely unsympathetic trade unions. Women's priorities rested by and large less with the world of work (in which opportunities for fulfillment and promotion were minimal) than with family, neighbourhood and personal relationships. As we will see below, most trade unions failed to relate to the needs and perspectives of women.[46]

In 1920s Britain the labour force continued to be far more homogeneous than its American counterpart. The late nineteenth and early twentieth centuries had seen increased immigration from southern and eastern Europe into Britain (Jewish immigrants being particularly important in terms of the clothing trades of Leeds, Manchester and the East End of London); and black workers found employment as seamen and in related activities in Liverpool, Cardiff and other ports. Significantly, the motor car and other growth industries of the Midlands and the southeast were to be operated by large numbers of predominantly 'raw' and young migrant workers from Wales, Scotland, the northeast and other depressed areas. But large-scale immigration, and especially black immigration from the West Indies, would await the boom of the post-Second World War years.

As in the United States, women did, however, constitute a significant section of the labour force. Indeed, in terms of their share of the total labour force (35 per cent in 1911, 33.7 per cent in 1921 and 34.2 per cent in 1931) women in Britain were more conspicuous than their counterparts in the United States (24.3 per cent by 1930).[47] The First World War had greatly expanded jobs for British women, but, in line with the US experience, the immediate post-war years saw a 'shake-out' of women in heavy industry. Women in inter-war Britain did move into the service sector, electrical goods and artificial fibres. But in contrast to the great advances made by American females, the progress achieved by British women was less impressive. As James Cronin has remarked, 'Job opportunities for women were extremely limited and improved only gradually.' For example, while the number of women in paid employment in Britain rose by 500,000 between 1921 and 1931 (from a total base of 5,701,000 paid women in 1921) the corresponding increase in the United States was 2.3 million (from a total of 8.3 million in 1921). Not until 1951 would the level of women's labour force participation in Britain be restored to the 1914 mark.

A number of factors contributed to the slower rate of growth of job opportunities for British women. In the first place, expansion of the service sector in Britain was far less spectacular than in the United States (in Britain electrical engineering and vehicle production generated employment at a faster rate than services).[48] Second, the steady decline of traditionally heavy areas of womens' employment, particularly textiles and clothing, were not sufficiently offset by gains in services, engineering and parts of the 'new' industries (such as electrical goods and artificial fibres)[49] to generate rapid overall growth. As Cronin has noted, 'There was no noticeable increase in women employed in chemicals, food, drink and tobacco, public utilities or transport from 1923 to 1935, and only a modest 10–15 per cent increase from 1935 to 1939.'

Third, a variety of largely non-quantifiable forces also exerted varying degrees of influence. For example, advocates of the notion of 'patriarchy first', and most notably in the British context Sylvia Walby, have emphasised the historical importance of male-dominated trade unions in excluding women from employment, and especially from the more secure, well-paid and high-status jobs. But, as argued by Mike Savage, the 'patriarchy first' argument has extremely limited explanatory value in relation to women's employment during the inter-war period. It is true that, apart from textiles and clothing, defensive and beleaguered unions in the largely depressed traditional sectors of both the British and American economies did intensify their efforts to restrict and even close their male-dominated ranks against female and other competitors during the 1920s. But trade unionism was very weak in those 'new' sectors in which British and American women either made occupational advances (services and so on), or in which (for example, cars) males dominated employment. On balance, as argued by Milkman (for the United States) and Savage (for Britain), male and female employment patterns were determined less by the existence and power of trade unionism than by (at least from the employers' point of view) economic and financial considerations. Thus in labour-intensive settings (such as parts of electrical engineering) where labour costs were of paramount importance, employers could 'secure large gains by substituting women's labour for men's wherever possible'. (Interestingly, continues Savage, unions in parts of British electrical engineering did oppose employer utilisation of cheap female labour.) However, in the more capital-intensive automobile industries of Britain and America, where profits derived from high productivity under a system of high, if fluctuating, wages, then 'employers were relatively uninterested in cheap labour'. Rather they preferred to employ what they saw as a more 'reliable' male workforce.[50]

To argue in the above manner is not, however, to suggest that gender-based constructions and representations were insignificant. Employer and trade-union notions of 'cheap' and 'reliable' labour were saturated in gender-based expectations and stereotypes. As noted by Savage, the question of age was also an important consideration for many employers in the growth sectors. Large numbers of both male and female workers in the 'new' British and American sectors of the economy were young or youngish, and were, by imputation, 'highly productive' and largely untutored in the ways of trade unionism. The combined effects of sex, gender, age and economic influence upon women's employment patterns merit further investigation.

Further cultural and ideological influences should also be examined. Did, for example, the 'marriage bar' operate more profoundly in Britain than in the United States? Did the grossly unfair and excessive attention visited upon women workers by the British social-welfare authorities during the 1920s (under the 'not genuinely seeking work' regulation of 1922) and under the Anomalies Act of 1931 (which meant that married

women's right to means-tested transitional payments 'virtually
disappeared') act as deterrents to the search for employment?[51] To what
extent did the 1920s feminist movements in Britain and America concern
themselves with and influence employment opportunities for working-
class women? A provisional answer would seem to be that feminism on
both sides of the Atlantic was relatively more interested in social-welfare
issues (such as birth control, maternity provision and family allowances),
and increased employment opportunities for middle-class women, rather
than in either trade unionism or working-class women's employment
prospects.[52]

Finally, despite the attainment of the vote, and greater freedoms and
self-confidence during the immediate post-war years (as reflected in
dress, appearance and bearing), did not 1920s British women suffer more
than their American sisters from revived, indeed strengthened, notions
of a 'woman's place'? In the depressed climate of 1920s Britain, 'traditionalism' may well have exerted a more profound influence than in
booming, self-confident, outgoing and increasingly consumerist
America, complete with its stronger traditions of citizens' rights, opposition to deference and individual assertiveness.

Many of the questions posed and 'answers' provided in the previous
two paragraphs are highly speculative in character. As with so many
aspects of inter-war British and American social and labour history, it
is far easier to set questions concerning patterns of women's employment
than to provide well-documented replies. Further research is required.

LIVING STANDARDS

Doubtless owing much to their seemingly 'hard' (i.e. quantitative and
economic) character, questions concerning living standards have been
far more thoroughly investigated by historians and social scientists.
Scattered references to workers' living standards in the 1920s have
already been made in this chapter. It is now time to pull these threads
together.

Four main conclusions emerge. First, there is no doubt that in aggregate terms both depressed 1920s Britain and prosperous 1920s America
experienced improvements in average annual real wage earnings. As
demonstrated in Table 4.1, between 1920 and 1926 weekly wage rates
and retail prices in Britain both declined, but the latter fell more than
the former. Between 1927 and 1930 wage rates remained fairly stable
while prices continued to fall. In overall terms real earnings rose by
roughly 8 points during the 1920s. Crucially, this improvement in living

Table 4.1 Wages, Prices and Real Earnings in Britain, 1920–30

Year	Weekly wage rates (1930 = 100)	Retail prices	Average annual real wage earnings
1920	143.7	157.6	92.2
1921	134.6	143.0	94.1
1922	107.9	115.8	93.2
1923	100.0	110.1	90.8
1924	101.5	110.8	91.6
1925	102.2	111.4	91.7
1926	99.3	108.9	91.2
1927	101.5	106.0	95.8
1928	100.1	105.1	95.2
1929	100.4	103.8	96.7
1930	100.0	100.0	100.0

Source: J. Stevenson, *British Society 1914–45*, p. 117

standards would continue and accelerate in Britain during the worst years of the 1930s depression.

The achievement of the 48-hour working week by many trade union-ists during the period of post-war militancy, improved health, edu-cational and unemployment provision (between 1913 and 1938 the proportion of the national income spent centrally and locally upon social services rose from 5.5 per cent to 13 per cent), increased family expenditure upon non-essential items and a greater variety of foodstuffs (especially fruit and fresh vegetables), the growing popularity of the annual holiday (until the end of the 1930s the vast majority of workers did not receive holiday pay) and commercialised forms of leisure, and the inter-war shift in resources in favour of wage-earners – all reflected improved living standards. Some of these manifestations of improvement would fully reveal themselves only during the 1930s, but undoubted signs of prosperity were evident during the 1920s. Finally, and perhaps most significantly, the continuing decline in family size made possible, according to Cronin, 'an improvement in the standard of living of nearly 70 per cent' for workers between 1914 and 1937–8.[53]

Second, advances in working-class living standards in America not only accompanied but also outstripped gains in 1920s Britain. The earlier growth of the 'new' industries in America and general economic dyna-mism made possible truly significant advances in general living standards and consumerism. According to Robert Zieger real wages 'leapt by 38 per cent between the beginning of World War I and 1929', while hours of work in manufacturing 'slid downward, from over 59 in 1900 to just

over 50 in 1926'. Allowing for unemployment, Lebergott estimates that
'the average annual real earnings for all employees rose from 639 dollars
in 1922 to 793 in 1929'. Similarly, Brody has observed that, 'after slowing
under wartime inflationary pressures' and plummeting during the acute
recession of 1920–1, real earnings 'now resumed their long-term upward
march'. Thus, while prices stabilised around the level of 1922, real
weekly earnings rose by almost 15 per cent between 1922 and 1929.[54]

In comparison with increases in productivity and national income,
workers' wage gains during the 1920s were far from spectacular. But
what was truly revolutionary was the massively changed, far less arduous
and (at least as measured in consumerist terms) greatly improved way
of life which extra pay could now command. Thus Brody:

> What was extraordinary was the qualitative leap in living standards
> accompanying the rising real income of the 1920s. A revolution had
> taken place in household technology. The age of electricity, central
> heating, and indoor sanitation had arrived. From American industry,
> too, there now began to flow the consumer durables of modern life
> – home appliances, the radio and phonograph, and the automobile.
> All these wonders had come first to the well-to-do, then to the
> middle class. In the 1920s they became accessible to the working-
> man. The life that his family thereby achieved truly separated him
> from the workingman of 1900.[55]

It is, of course, difficult to calculate 'average' living standards. As
Fearon has insisted, the search for the American 'average' in terms of
1920s real earnings and a satisfactory base year upon which to construct
decadal trends is highly problematical. There existed all manner of
variations in wage rates and earnings in the 1920s (based upon geog-
raphy, economic sector, skill level, sex, race and so on), and wages were
unusually depressed in the 'natural' base year of either 1920 or 1921.
To raise such qualifications and complications is not to argue against
the possibility of adequate generalisations; but it is to suggest that
aggregate 'optimistic' data must engage 'pessimistic' aggregates, and
that both sets of aggregates must be broken down to take account of
complexities and contradictions. Balanced conclusions can then be
reached concerning living standards. It is to this task that we now turn.

In both 1920s Britain and America (and especially the former) chronic
and, in some cases, high levels of unemployment, offset a picture of
unqualified improvement. As seen in Table 4.2, official levels of unemployment were roughly two times higher in 1920s Britain than in the
United States. The serious problems encountered by the staple export
industries, the attempted return to 'normalcy', the overvaluation of the
pound, the continued allegiance to orthodox (i.e. deflationary) economics, and the changed post-war international trading and political

situation all ensured that Britain would live, in an unprecedented way, with persistent mass unemployment of 1 million plus (at best about 10 per cent of the insured labour force, at worst 22 per cent) for most of the inter-war period. Unemployment and sickness benefits, increasingly provided by the state rather than trade unions and friendly societies, did mitigate the worst effects of being out of work and ill. But such benefits were limited. National health insurance covered insured indi-viduals (largely men) rather than families. And, as Paul Johnson has observed, 'unemployment benefit was never generous ... was increas-ingly restrictive, particularly towards married women, and was paid only for a limited period, whereafter means-tested unemployment assist-ance was available'.[56] In addition, while long-term unemployment was the lot of a minority of workers, 'very few manual workers could be confident that they would avoid some interruption of employment'. Short-time working and general underemployment were present in a variety of economic contexts. In the depressed weaving towns of north and northeast Lancashire, notes John Walton:

> the vast majority spent some time out of employment; in Blackburn, Burnley and Darwen ... 77 or 78 per cent of the insured population claimed benefit at some point during 1930, with the figure for women reaching 92 per cent in Darwen.

In the most depressed areas – of Scotland, South Wales and the northeast – unemployment and underemployment entrapped whole communities. And even in early 1930s London and the southeast 'very few manual workers', records Johnson, 'could be confident that they would avoid some interruption of employment'. 'In fact,' concludes Johnson, 'even for those in fast-growing sectors, such as motor manufacture, employ-ment incomes were far from regular, as employers would typically lay off part of their workforce and put others on short-time during the slack summer months'.[57]

The traditional sectors of the US economy also experienced very high levels of unemployment during the 1920s, and there occurred severe fluctuations in employment for the mass of non-skilled workers in the expanding sectors. In addition, American workers did not benefit from a national system of unemployment insurance. In the absence of a systematic attempt on the part of the federal government to ascertain national unemployment levels, it is exceedingly difficult to present accu-rate figures. 'Official' estimates would suggest a 5 per cent unemploy-ment rate for the 1920s, roughly half the British level. But there appears to be agreement among economic historians that the 5 per cent figure should be realistically doubled to take full account of unemployment,

Table 4.2   Unemployment in Britain and the USA, 1921–30

	*Unemployment in millions		Percentage of labour force	
	Britain	USA	**Britain	USA
1920		1.7		4.0
1921	1.8 (2.2)	5.0	17.0 (12.2)	11.9
1922	1.5 (1.9)	3.2	14.3 (10.8)	7.6
1923	1.3 (1.5)	1.4	11.7 (8.9)	3.2
1924	1.1 (1.4)	2.4	10.3 (7.9)	5.5
1925	1.2 (1.5)	1.8	11.3 (8.6)	4.0
1926	1.4 (1.7)	0.9	12.5 (9.6)	1.9
1927	1.1 (1.3)	1.9	9.7 (7.4)	4.1
1928	1.2 (1.5)	2.1	10.8 (8.2)	4.4
1929	1.2 (1.5)	1.6	10.4 (8.0)	3.2
1930	1.9 (2.3)	4.3	16.1 (12.3)	8.9

Sources: J. Potter, *The American Economy Between the World Wars*, p. 69;
T. Kemp, *The Climax of Capitalism*, p. 72; W. R. Garside, *British
Unemployment 1919–1939: A Study in Public Policy* (1990), pp. 3–5.

  * The British figures refer to insured persons and (in brackets) to total
    workers; the American to the total labour force.
 ** i.e. the insured unemployed as a proportion of insured employees.
    Feinstein's calculations (in brackets) are based on the 1931 census and
    attempt to measure the total unemployed as a proportion of total
    employees. They suggest a consistent downward revision of the insured
    figures. For the strengths and weaknesses of the two sets of calculations
    see W. R. Garside, op. cit.; C. H. Feinstein, *Statistical Tables of National
    Income, Expenditure and Output of the U.K. 1855–1965* (1972).

short-time working and chronic underemployment (especially in
agriculture).[58]

Material improvements by-passed not only the unemployed, but also
several of the lower paid in full-time work. In 1920s Britain cotton
weavers suffered from considerable reductions in money wages
(Lancashire's reputation as a high-wage county waned during the inter-
war years); and agricultural employees, women workers, some coalminers and many juvenile workers were poorly paid. In the United
States large numbers of black, agricultural and 'new' immigrant workers
received wages below the 'American standard'. And the range of consumer durables and home comforts available to a fair number of 1920s
American workers would come within the means of a majority of British
workers only during the 1950s and 1960s. In parts of inter-war Salford
the possession of a wireless set was 'a sign of relative affluence in the

working-class home'. 'You were *somebody* if you had a wireless', was the declaration of one local.[59]

If economic insecurity remained at the very core of working-class life on both sides of the Atlantic, then poverty and ill health continued to afflict a substantial minority of working-class Britons and Americans.[60] The most recent work on inter-war working-class culture has reinforced the view that poverty, both primary – and secondary or 'insufficiency' – based, 'was an intractable feature of urban life'. Indeed, Andrew Davies both acknowledges the findings of Rowntree and other contemporaries – which suggested that almost one-third of the working-class populations of York, Bristol and Merseyside were living in or on the boundaries of poverty in the 1930s – and also conclusively shows that in parts of Manchester the incidence of poverty was much higher. In all these areas unemployment, low pay, irregular work, old age and sickness remained the principal causes of poverty. In Salford, observes Davies, 'many of the families of men who spent heavily on drink or gambling were already living below or close to the poverty line': expenditure on leisure thus 'tended to exacerbate, rather than "cause" poverty'.

Illness and poverty were frequently close companions. The loss of the (generally male) breadwinner through sickness or accident (many workers being 'worn out' and debilitated by excessive labour, speed-up, and 'working in all weathers'; and 'there was still a casual attitude to injuries and even deaths in many parts of British industry')[61] frequently had a seriously adverse effect upon the material wellbeing of their families. Death could prove devastating in more ways than one. Significantly, Davies has found that families headed by widows 'were among the poorest' in Salford: much the same pattern existed elsewhere in the country. In terms of the overall position of health, Charles Webster has persuasively argued that, despite undoubted average improvements in morbidity and mortality (and especially infant-mortality) rates, there persisted strong and largely unvarying sex, class, occupationally and regionally based inequalities throughout the period. 'For those substantial sections of the population in a position of disadvantage', concludes Webster, 'it is difficult to maintain that the interwar period was marked by any meaningful improvement in health'.[62]

In the United States economic insecurity 'driving' at work (sometimes under appallingly tyrannical conditions), ill-health and poverty continued to impair the lives of many workers. This was especially the case in relation to black and migrant workers, women workers, and large numbers of second-generation 'new' immigrant workers who suffered much hardship and hostile treatment during the 1920s (being regarded as unwelcome aliens by large sections of the 'host' society) and who would express their grievances in the momentous upsurges of the

1930s.[63] Economic insecurity remained a central feature of working-class life. And there is a strong, if incomplete, element of truth in Stricker's claim that, 'the struggle for economic security, not the struggle to keep up with the Joneses dominated working-class life in the prosperity decade'. Utilising a poverty-line figure of 1,550 dollars for a non-farm family of four, Stricker concludes that '35 to 40 per cent of the non-farm families in 1929 were poor'.[64]

As will be evident from previous pages, material deprivation did not fall equally upon working-class shoulders. As a number of historians have recently observed, poverty, unemployment, and general hardship were centrally structured by sex. Women, and especially married women, were generally expected, whether in British, or black, immigrant or native-born American families, to 'make ends meet', to manage the household budget, to feed and clothe the rest of the family, and to 'go without' or 'clem' (a phrase frequently heard in my own childhood in a supposedly 'aristocratic' carpenter's family) in the event of scarcity. In sum, women were taught to see their needs as secondary to those of their families. In Salford and elsewhere women socialised far less than men, were far more tied to the home and immediate neighbourhood, and for the most part saw *self-sacrifice* as 'natural', as an integral part of being a 'good mother'.[65]

We are now in a position to present our third and fourth conclusions concerning workers' living standards during the 1920s. General advances in material standards must be balanced against continuing unemployment, underemployment, poverty and uncivilised conditions of existence for significant minorities on workers on both sides of the Atlantic. And gender-based constructions of inequality, power and 'appropriate' spheres and roles for men and women ensured that deprivation (and much of the attendant turmoil and violence within families)[66] would fall most heavily upon women, and particularly married women.

WAYS OF LIFE, VALUES AND NORMS

Women contributed, of course, to the development of those 'traditional' norms, values and practices which, as observed in earlier chapters, dominated working-class communities from the late nineteenth century onwards. During the 1920s and 1930s ways of life revolving around the pub/saloon, football/baseball, cheap and commercialised amusements (fairs, dancing halls and so on), various forms of gambling, the annual holiday, and the family and local community were more deeply and extensively subjected to commercialisation.[67] Commercialisation, consumerism and mass advertising were more pronounced in the United

States than in Britain. But in both countries the very epitome of commercialised leisure, the cinema, was most popular among workers.

Simultaneously, communal and informal street-based leisure activities, (gathering to talk with friends, to play games and to 'click', or pair off, with members of the opposite sex during 'monkey parades' down the streets), still accounted, at least in Manchester and Salford, 'for most of the leisure time of young workers'.[68] The regular pursuit of commercialised leisure activities necessitated levels of expenditure often beyond the means of young people, especially in less prosperous Britain. Married women were also far less centrally involved in commercialised leisure pursuits than were their husbands. As noted earlier, women's worlds centred for the most part less around the place of paid work, the pub or saloon, and the baseball/football park than around the home, family and immediate neighbourhood. Women did occasionally visit the cinema or pub, often in the company of other women, and were sometimes 'treated' by their menfolk. And female independence may well have manifested itself more strongly in 'consumerist' inter-war America. But cash-based exchanges and relationships belonged more to the world of males than females. At the same time, however, many working-class women were less strictly confined to the private space of the home than an unqualified view of 'separate spheres' would suggest. As Melanie Tebbutt has recently observed,

> While the respectable working class might retreat into domestic privacy as a means of hiding poverty under an appearance of coping, the poorest could ill-afford to maintain such illusions. Lack of privacy was endemic in the poorest working class areas, where street life inevitably became an extension of the domestic. These public characteristics are a reminder that the definitions of public and private space ... had a more rigid application in the lives of middle class than working class women, the very openness of this presence in street life testifying, despite its ambivalent aspects, to a desire for companionship, participation and public affirmation otherwise denied by their impoverished surroundings.[69]

As noted in Chapters 1 and 3, the meanings assumed by working-class culture are complex, often ambiguous, rest upon the specific convergence of a mixture of wide-ranging influences, and can and do change over time. In terms of the 1920s we find that a number of competing descriptions – competitive versus co-operative, individualistic and community/class based, status conscious and privatised versus class conscious and mutualistic, and conservative and integrated into the mainstream versus radical and challenging – have been applied to 'popular' culture.[70] The very existence of so many definitions reflects the complexity and indeed diversity of workers' worlds. But, at the risk of oversimplification, we will offer the following observations upon working-class life.

First, despite Gerstle's important emphasis upon the radical potential of the 'Americanism' of inter-war American workers, it would appear to be the case that workers' cultures in 1920s (as opposed to 1930s) America were more privatised, fragmented, conflicting and integrated into the mass mainstream than was the case in Britain.

The industrial defeats of the early 1920s, combined with improved living standards, and the mounting conformist pressures of mass consumerism and patriotic, anti-radical 'Americanisation' drives persuaded many workers to concentrate more upon the narrowed goals of personal and family improvement than upon wider mutualist and class-based notions of justice and fairness. For example, in their famous study of Middletown, published in 1929, Robert and Helen Lynd emphasised the decline of a strongly collectivist 'traditional' way of working-class life and the growth of privatisation and, to some extent, *embourgeoisement* among Middletown's workers.[71] It is, of course, difficult to evaluate the typicality of Middletown's workers. James Green, for example, cites examples of 1920s working-class communities in which ties to neighbourhood life, mutuality and so on were still very strong.[72] And in the light of post-Second World War English debates concerning affluence and worker *embourgeoisement*, we must be extremely careful not to paint idealised pictures of 'traditional' homogeneous and class-conscious working-class communities, and then to counterpose such idealised pictures against 'modern' fragmented, instrumental, privatised and largely non-class-conscious workers. The historical record is usually more complex and messy than such a simple 'traditional'–'modern' dichotomy would suggest.[73] Nevertheless, there was a more pronounced trend towards privatisation and narrowly based consumerism in 1920s America. This trend fell short, however, of 1950s consummated consumerism when, to quote John Bukowczyk, 'Americanism, mass consumption, and mass culture' would become the 'new Father, Son, and Holy Ghost' to which Catholic Poles and other immigrants would turn.[74]

As a number of recent works have usefully reminded us, growing involvement in mass culture did not lead to the disintegration of ethnic and racial allegiances. Lizabeth Cohen has well expressed the persistence of dual identities,

> When black workers patronized chain stores or bought packaged goods, they were asserting independence from the surrounding white society, not enslavement to cultural norms. No doubt their consumption of mass cultural products ... gave them interests in common with mainstream American society and subjected them to

the vagaries of the capitalist market. But with mass culture as raw
material, blacks fashioned their own culture during the 1920s that
made them feel no less black . . .
      And although attracted to mass culture, ethnic youth and urban
blacks constructed their own versions of it, which differed from the
mainstream.[75]

There thus existed continued diversity and the potential for cultural
conflict. Largely denied the opportunities by racism to assimilate into
the mainstream, black music (and especially jazz) and black employment
became, notes Cohen, 'a vehicle for making a claim on mainstream
society that racism had otherwise denied'; and mass culture, 'which
offered ethnics a conservative retreat, became in the hands of blacks a
way of turning blacks' vulnerability and dependence on mainstream
society into a demand for respect'.[76]

Many middle-class professional and business people within the 'new'
immigrant communities found themselves in an ambivalent position. On
the one hand they had cultivated ties (by means of wartime patriotic
and Americanisation campaigns) with the host society, and were keen
to demonstrate their responsibility, respectability and patriotism. Furthermore, during the 1920s they began to occupy important positions
within the business-dominated Republican and Democratic Parties; and
they gave their ethnic constituents links to corporate employment, local
governments and the political parties. Simultaneously, however, they
wished to maintain the vitality and integrity of their ethnic communities
– by means of 'language maintenance, cultural preservation, political
and ecclesiastical representation, resistance to nativism, and upward
social and economic mobility' – in the face of consumerist and other
trends towards cultural uniformity. In essence, such middle-class ethnics
were attempting to have the best of both worlds – acceptance by and
assimilation into the mainstream of the American business world, combined with domination within their distinctive, if tamed, ethnic
communities.[77]

In practice, such middle-class control was often achieved; and revived
ethnic nationalism during the 1920s cut across the potential for working-
class unity. As John Higham and James Green have argued,[78] the pressures of Americanisation, the 'red scare' of 1919–20, immigration restriction and '100 per-cent Americanism', and the massive growth of the Ku
Klux Klan (which by 1920 had millions of members, supported the
open-shop drive and denounced 'all immigrants as "un-American" and
"agents of Lenin" ') generated strong, resistant forms of nationalism
among many beleaguered 'new' immigrant groups and blacks. The
growth of Zionism, Marcus Garvey's Universal Negro Improvement
Association, and the popularity of Al Capone (as 'benefactor' and

defiant opposer of Prohibition) and Mussolini (as reviver of Italian nationalism) among Chicago's Italian-Americans, were powerful manifestations of the ethnic nationalisms abroad.

Occasionally, such nationalisms assumed radical form. This was most plainly the case in the mass movement which arose to defend Sacco and Vanzetti, the anarchist shoemaker and fisherman executed in 1927 for robbery and murder on the basis of extremely flimsy evidence. As Green notes, 'the ordeal of Sacco and Vanzetti . . . seemed to symbolize the fate of those who resisted Americanization and rejected the authority of the state'. But in the vast majority of instances ethnic nationalism was synonymous with what Higham termed 'compensatory chauvinism(s)'. Green's observations are most appropriate:

> Ethnic assertiveness developed at the expense of integrationism, socialism, anarchism, and other pre-war ideologies which stressed internationalism and working-class unity . . .
>   The popularity of Italian nationalism and Fascism rose as radicalism declined. Business values gained new respect as the anti-capitalist elements lost ground.

The cause of working-class unity was not aided by those AFL unions which 'capitulated almost entirely to racism in the "tribal twenties"' (Green). A. Philip Randolph's Brotherhood of Sleeping Car Porters was admitted to the AFL only on a segregated basis and was not afforded the status of 'a full-fledged "international" organization'.

In overall terms American working-class cultures of the 1920s were thus characterised more by divisions and accommodating aims than by widespread solidarity and radicalism. Only during the late 1920s and 1930s would the traumatic experiences of the Depression induce strong bonds of unity and a weakening of ethnic and racial fragmentation. Significantly, both the 1920s and 1930s American labour movements would take much of their colouration from the contrasting decadal cultural pictures of the inter-war period.

In Britain there also existed divisions and differences in working-class communities. Local, regional and national points of identification and perception remained strong, as reflected in speech, mannerisms and in sporting rivalries (especially in the world of football). During the 1920s differences between the employed and unemployed, between the more prosperous Midlands and south and the more depressed north, Scotland and Wales, and between the more privatised world of workers in 'new' industries and the long-established neighbourhood ties of workers in the staple industries, were attracting comment. Similarly, shared attachment to a 'traditional' way of life was sufficient guarantee of neither 'collectivism' (versus 'individualism') nor of political support for the Labour Party or left-wing politics. Adequate understanding of the full range and interaction of influences upon inter-war popular politics, and the complex relations between culture and politics, must await (and urgently merits) further historical attention, especially across a range of localities. But we do know that Conservative as well as Labour politics did flourish in 'traditional' working-class communities (Bolton is a good example), and that for some families status, competition and individualism were stronger motivating forces than mutuality, neighbourliness and collectivism.[79]

It was, however, more during the 1930s that the *differential*, and to some extent competing, experiences and strategies of workers assumed a dominant position. During the 1920s differences and divisions tended to be overshadowed by common or similar experiences and attachments. Such bonds of unity were forged and demonstrated in numerous ways: in post-war industrial conflict; in the outstanding solidarity, very real sacrifices, and awesome generosity of spirit displayed by workers during the General Strike; in the widespread and tenacious loyalties to family, home, neighbourhood and 'our kind'; in the profound and shared experiences of depression and the battles for survival and security; and in the continued tendency for the labour aristocracy and the casual poor of the nineteenth century to dissolve, thus leaving, at least according to Hinton, 'an altogether more homogeneous bloc at the base of the social pyramid'.

In addition, mass consumerism and 'mass' culture, complete with a blurring of social divisions, outlooks and values made very little progress in 1920s Britain (certainly in comparison with the USA), and did not erode the bedrocks of class and attitudes of 'Us and Them'. There continued to exist profound differences and divisions between working- and middle-class Britons, as reflected in speech, life-style and attitudes. Indeed, as respectively emphasised by Hinton and McKibbin, large sections of the middle and lower-middle classes in Britain responded to the country's economic problems and the rise of a more *politicised* labour movement and working class in the post-war years far more by distancing themselves from (indeed, 'patriotically' opposing) than identifying with manual workers. The political effects of this social and psychological aversion were seen in the massive support delivered to the Conservative Party in suburbia.[80]

Workers were in turn far less given to privatised patterns of behaviour than their more affluent American cousins. In any event, as suggested by Cronin, 'for most working people home and community were not alternative foci, but part of a single world of daily life'.[81] And distinctive local, regional, and even national loyalties and customs were articulated within the context of a broadly shared national and class-based culture. As noted in Chapter 3, there were race riots in a number of British ports in 1919 and racist rumblings into the 1920s. But racial and ethnic conflicts were of minor significance as compared with the United States. As Neil Evans has recently written.

> The black populations were very small in Britain... Blacklegging was hardly an issue, whereas in America it was vital... The marginality of blacks in casual occupations like shipping also limited their visibility... Britain's black population lacked the relatively strong middle class that characterised America and this brought it much closer to the white working class. It was usually unionised and ethnic politics hardly developed at all... The great diversity of Britain's black population also brought it closer to the white working class in many respects.[82]

In truth, the British working class was far more homogeneous than its American counterpart during the 1920s.

Finally, the absence of an unbroken link between 'traditional' working-class culture and support for the Labour Party should not mask the development of a close connection. As I have written elsewhere:

> Labour often did take strongest root in those communities in which the co-op, trade union, friendly society, the pub, football, betting and all manner of collective norms, habits and values were strong, and in which women were expected to play the part of willing yet subordinate partners.

Such was certainly the case in the west of Scotland, in South Wales, and many of the urban heartlands of England.[83] Even in many erstwhile areas of political apathy and fatalism, indeed popular Toryism, the Rise of Labour was a marked feature of the 1920s. Robert Roberts' observations on post-war Salford are instructive:

> In factory, mine and workshop... a new and graver spirit moved. Men were changing their minds. From 1918 to 1920 the ILP had increased its membership by half. We noted change, too, in the little streets above the shop. Poor families, dyed-in-the-wool Tories, who had voted Conservative since getting the franchise, were now talking not 'Liberal' but 'Labour'.

'Old deference died', continued Roberts, 'no longer did the lower orders believe *en masse* that "class" came as natural "as knots in the wood"'. Marxism continued to exert little appeal in Salford, but the return of Roberts' constituency's first Labour MP in 1924 had far from defensive, consolatory or conservative effects on the local population. 'Simple socialists like my mother', records a somewhat patronising Roberts, 'wept for joy and we, the young, felt ourselves heralds of a new age'.[84] It was in this setting of increased cultural and political cohesion, optimism and confidence that early 1920s Labour Party politics developed.

LABOUR MOVEMENTS

Overview

We have so far traced the economic, social and cultural contexts in which 1920s labour movements must be placed. Our attention will now turn to a discussion of the main industrial and political features of organised labour.

Of absolutely crucial general importance was, as we have already implied, the predominantly defensive contexts and characteristics of labour movements on both sides of the Atlantic. Defensive struggles on the part of unions desperately fighting for survival were especially pronounced in the United States. We have observed that a mixture of positive and negative forces underpinned worker quiescence in 1920s America. Thus, changes in occupational structure, quantitative and mass-ive qualitative improvements in living standards, increased access to commodities, welfare capitalism, persistent and successful open-shop policies, divisions within the working class, conformist cultural and political pressures, rapid technological and managerial changes, and the mainly depressed state of organised labour's traditional areas of recruit-ment, were all instrumental in rendering the 1920s the 'lean years' (Bernstein) in the United States. In addition, as we will see below, the vast majority of workers remained rooted within the two-party political structure (although increasing estrangement from the system of formal politics, especially among 'new' immigrants and migrants, became a feature of the 1920s). In any event alternative, and more class-based, politics went into decline after 1924. Attempts to set up third parties did not entirely disappear, but they were predominantly unsuccessful and shortlived. Socialism lost much of its former appeal, the Communist Party was very small, and big business seemingly exerted a powerful grip upon the Democrats and the hegemonic, *laissez-faire* Republicans.

In Britain a more complex and, in significant ways, less bleak picture prevailed. The generally depressed state of the economy did place trade unionism on the defensive. And the defeat of the General Strike consti-tuted a watershed in the history of the unions. Nevertheless, British trade unionism continued to operate from a comparatively strong base (in relation to both the United States and many European countries), and was extremely *resilient* during the inter-war period. British employers and the state were, despite the General Strike and its legisla-tive aftermath, more conciliatory towards 1920s trade unionism than their American counterparts; and in Britain institutionalised collective bargaining was well established. Despite the growth of the poorly union-ised service sector, and growing differences between workers in the

Table 4.3 Trade-union Membership and Density in Britain and the
USA, 1920–30

	Union Membership (000s)		Density (%)	
	GB	USA (NBER)	GB	USA
1920	8,348	4,775	45.2	16.7
1921	6,633	4,553	35.8	15.5
1922	5,625	3,821	31.6	13.0
1923	5,429	3,418	30.2	11.3
1924	5,544	3,334	30.6	10.7
1925	5,506	3,319	30.1	10.4
1926	5,219	3,299	28.3	10.2
1927	4,919	3,343	26.4	10.1
1928	4,806	3,269	25.6	9.6
1929	4,858	3,213	25.7	9.3
1930	4,842	3,162	25.4	8.9

Source: G. S. Bain and R. Price, op. cit., pp. 37, 88–9

growth and depressed areas, the working class in Britain was less fragmented than in America, and British class divisions persisted with great
force. Above all, the years between 1918 and 1929 saw a massive
improvement in the electoral fortunes of the Labour Party. Politically
at least, the 1920s truly witnessed the Rise of Labour.

Trade Unionism and Industrial Relations

We will return to workers' politics in due course. First we must survey
the main developments in trade unionism and industrial relations. Table
4.3 clearly reveals the setbacks suffered by trade unionism on both sides
of the Atlantic during the 1920s.

From its highpoint in 1920, trade-union membership in 1920s Britain
thus showed, apart from modest increases in 1923–4 and 1928–9, a
consistent decline. A very similar picture was evident in the United
States, the only increase occurring between 1926 and 1927. Trade unionism in both countries did remain above the 1914 levels of 4,145,000 in
Britain and 2,566,000 in America. But this was little consolation to those
millions of workers who had extended the boundaries of unionism to
unprecedented degrees between 1914 and 1920.

As will be observed from Table 4.3, during the 1920s trade unionism
(in terms of both absolute numbers and density) remained much
stronger in Britain. We have previously seen that by the end of 1922
corporate might, government repression and mounting unemployment

had successfully repulsed the massive movement of post-war industrial militancy in the United States. Thereafter, militancy quickly subsided and trade unionism was thrown into heavy retreat. As Montgomery has declared, the legacy of labour's lost battles in meatpacking, mining, on the railroads and elsewhere in 1922 was, 'beleaguered unions clinging to minority sectors of their industries, surrounded by a hostile open-shop environment, and governed by ruthless suppression of dissent within their own ranks'.[85]

There were continuing struggles in the post-1922 years. Coalmining, for example, experienced bitter conflicts in 1923 and 1927–8 between workers fighting against non-unionism, unemployment, mechanisation and declining wages, and employers intent upon cutting costs to the bone. By 1930 the employers were triumphant. The UMWA, long established as the largest union in the AFL, 'found itself virtually without members'. The economic decline of bituminous coal, rising competition from other fuels, fierce conflicts within the UMWA (especially between John L. Lewis and the official leadership on the one hand and communists and radicals on the other), and militant anti-union employers and their allies were at the root of the union's decline. 'I have just returned from a visit to 'Hell-in-Pennsylvania', wrote Lowell Limpus, a reporter with the *New York Daily News*, of the mining war in 1924–5,

> I went into the coal camps ... and saw for myself. ... Many times it seemed impossible to think that we were in modern, civilized America.
>
> We saw thousands of women and children, literally starving to death. We found hundreds of destitute families living in crudely constructed bare-board shacks. They had been evicted from their homes by the coal companies. We unearthed a system of despotic tyranny reminiscent of Czar-ridden Siberia at its worst. We found police brutality and industrial slavery. We discovered the weirdest flock of injunctions that ever emanated from American temples of justice.
>
> We unearthed evidence of terrorism and counterterrorism; of mob beatings and near lynchings; of dishonesty, graft, and heartlessness.

What Irving Bernstein has termed, 'the combination of armed power and starvation', smashed the UMWA in Pennsylvania. By 1930 Lewis was the authoritarian head of a fallen union.[86]

The UMWA's sad decline held a mirror to wider brutalisation and defeats. In southern textiles, for example, night work, stretch-out and widespread employer 'Czardom' were rife. In 1927 worker patience and stoicism snapped. Hall, Leloudis and Korstad take up the story:

> In 1927 resistance to management tactics by individuals and small

groups gave way to labor conflict on an unprecedented scale. The battle opened in Henderson, North Carolina, where workers struck for restoration of a bonus withdrawn three years before. Then on March 12, 1929, young women in a German-owned rayon plant in Elizabethton, Tennessee, touched off a strike wave that spread quickly into the Carolinas. The involvement of the communist-led National Textile Workers' Union and the shooting deaths... brought Gastonia, North Carolina, a special notoriety. But the carnage was even worse in nearby Marion, where deputies opened fire on demonstrators, wounding twenty-five and killing six. In 1930, revolt hit the massive Dan River Mill in Virginia – a model of welfare capitalism.

Revolt would continue into the 1930s among these white operatives. Most of them had either spent their whole lives in or moved as children from the countryside to the mill villages. Employer control over housing, official religion, education and, in effect, the machinery of the local state could not prevent the development of worker mutuality and self-help, and the fashioning of 'a language of resistance from established cultural forms' (country music being of particular importance as a means of stimulating collective pride and bonding). In the face of growing hard times, and employers 'united in their refusal to tolerate even the mildest form of unionism', victories were rare. But these southern workers would return to the fore in the national textile strike of 1934.[87]

Textile and clothing centres in the North experienced fierce competition and industrial conflict during the early 1920s. Both the International Ladies Garment Workers' Union and the Amalgamated Clothing Workers' Union sought to regulate competition by means of union recognition and standardised lists and prices. Employers who recognised unions received union support for the introduction of scientific management. And, unusually for American industry as a whole, the needle trades were important sites for the development of arbitration systems. Despite internal faction-fighting between socialists and communists, the ACW found support for its goals of stability, advance planning, security and regulation from a small élite of large modern concerns within the clothing industry, and largely managed to weather the storms of the 1920s. The ILGWU was, however, not so fortunate. As Bernstein observes, 'torn asunder by competition from nonunion shops and a bitter conflict between right-wing and Communist forces in the mid-twenties', the union disastrously declined from 105,400 members in 1920 to 32,300 in 1929.[88]

Other prominent unions, such as the Mine, Mill and Smelter Workers, the Brewery Workers, the Seamen's Union, and the Hotel and Restaurant Employees also fell upon very hard times. Strikes did not disappear. In fact, as Montgomery reminds us, they lasted longer on average during the 1920s than the 1930s. And, despite their largely unproductive factional battles, socialist and communist militants (the latter especially in W. Z. Foster's Trade Union Educational League, formed in 1920) battled hard in a number of unions in support of union amalgamations, greater rank-and-file control, improved pay and conditions, and opposition to 'class collaborationist' leaders. Such battles were, at least in the short term, mainly lost. And the Communist Party's credibility and effectiveness at the workplace were hardly aided by the inauguration in 1928 of its Moscow-dictated 'class and class' policy. Between the late 1920s and the mid 1930s the Party abandoned 'boring from within' in favour of the attempted creation of revolutionary dual unions under the auspices of the Trade Union Unity League. In the longer term, the proven ability of communists and socialists to withstand employer victimisation and great hardships in the cause of radical labour would inspire the unorganised to unionise under the leadership of those with whom they often voiced sharp political disagreements. But such developments appeared in 1929 and 1930 to be so much 'pie in the sky'. By the latter year strikes had fallen to an all-time recorded low, and unionism was in dire straits. The appropriate lament is provided by Bernstein:

> By 1930 union membership constituted a bare 10.2 per cent of the more than 30 million nonagricultural employees counted in the census, a marked drop from 19.4 per cent in 1920.
> ... Great segments of American industry were either totally devoid of unionization or showed only a trace. This was the case with most of manufacturing, including such important industries as steel, automobiles, electrical equipment, rubber, cement, textiles, chemicals, and food. In the extractive industries effective unions existed in neither nonferrous metals nor petroleum. Motor transportation revealed only a smattering of membership. Utilities, banking, insurance, retail and wholesale trade, the professions, and domestic and personal service were predominantly unorganized.[89]

Battered and bruised, the AFL nevertheless refused to expire. Rather the Federation retreated into a much narrower basis of 'craft' strength than in the post-war years, and desperately preached 'responsibility', in the form of acceptance of Taylorism, improved productivity on the part of workers, general union-management co-operation, largely autocratic leadership with highly centralised powers, and militant anti-radicalism, as the keys to survival and future viability.

Significantly, areas of production lying beyond the white-collar and mass-production sectors (especially in construction, printing and some craft parts of the railroads), were key areas of AFL strength. The construction industry, for example characterised by local product markets, small units of production, and the possibility of control over the supply of (particularly skilled) labour, prospered during the 1920s and was the site of strong unionism. The fortunes of the United Brotherhood of Carpenters, in particular, markedly improved under the autocratic control of Republican William Hutcheson.[90] Maintaining that 'anything made of wood was carpenters' work', and successfully fighting a series of jurisdictional battles to enforce this claim, Hutcheson established the Carpenters as the strongest union in the AFL. By 1929 the union had a membership of 322,000, and was the leading light in the building trades, the group, notes Bernstein, 'that made up the largest and most important element within the AFL'. And 'boss' Hutcheson had eliminated all opposition, to concentrate formidable power in his own hands.

The needle and printing trades also tended to be geared up to local markets, and in the latter there was scope to control the labour supply. Significantly, while membership in building trades' unionism increased from 789,500 in 1923 to 919,000 in 1929, unions in printing also rose, if modestly, from 150,900 to 162,500. Elsewhere, as observed by Howell Harris, 'unions were confined to sick industries, like coal, railroads, and textiles . . . and to employees of some public utilities and branches of government service'. On the railroads the operating crafts were 'entrenched in a major industry under federal supervision', which offered great scope for political lobbying and some legal protection, but which simultaneously could embrace company unionism and temporary prohibitions against strikes.[91]

With the significant exception of the building trades, most AFL unions were very much on the defensive during the 1920s. And moves towards the acceptance of Taylorism and general union-management co-operation were far more signs of union weakness than strength. In effect, the unions were prostrating themselves before the employers in the hope that the latter would appreciate the value of union recognition to increased production, stability at the workplace, and the rooting out of 'troublemakers'. Significantly, however, experiments in union-management co-operation were both scarce and shortlived; and in the improved politico-legal climate of the mid–late 1930s AFL unions would jettison much of this abject submissiveness to the dictates of 'tyrannical capital'.

Three further effects of the defensive 1920s upon American trade unionism and industrial relations should be noted. First, whether from a position of union weakness (as increasingly in the case of John L. Lewis) or strength (as with Hutcheson), union leaders successfully placed premiums upon intra-union loyalty and unity in order to both increase their bargaining strength with employers and to consolidate their own powers. As will be evident from our brief survey, a central feature of 1920s unionism thus resided in the more pronounced growth of the union 'boss', brooking no opposition (especially from 'un-American' communists) and exercising increasingly unlimited powers. Internal union democracy was a casualty of the process. Equally, centralised unions effectively surrendered claims to control over the nature and organisation of work to oligopolistic and bureaucratic corporations in return for recognition. There were, of course exceptions to this general pattern (in building and printing, for example), but it is highly significant that the *control* issue, and especially the *moral* or *'legitimate'* exercise of power and authority, would be at the very heart of workers' industrial protests during the 1930s. The 'bullying', 'driving', 'tyrannical' and 'Czar-like' boss, foreman, or 'man with the stopwatch', stood in direct opposition to the republican ideals of 'the brave and the free'.

Second, the more restricted base of the union movement meant that the counsels of craft conservatism and sectionalism came to dominate the AFL. We have seen that neither conservatism nor sectionalism were strangers to the Federation. But during the first two decades of the twentieth century industrial unionist and other radical sentiments had contested more conservative patterns of thought. David Brody rightly informs us that the AFL was not rigidly and uniformly bound by 'craft' structures, and that there was, for example, some support from Gompers and his successor William Green, for more 'open' union structures and amalgamation. But during the 1920s most unions jealously protected and sought to extend their jurisdictional 'patches'. Not only did narrow, 'craft' jurisdictionalism stand in the way of a more co-ordinated and unified trade-union response to the adversities of the 1920s, but it would also fatally obstruct the *mass* organisations of the mass-production industries by AFL unions during the 1930s.

The dominance of conservative and narrowly exclusive white male views within the 1920s AFL was clearly manifested in the failure to recruit large numbers of black workers and women.

Reference has already been made to the racism rampant within the AFL during the 1920s. We need only add that the Federation's leadership frequently adopted a more liberal line than many of the affiliated unions. Officially, the AFL continued to bar racial discrimination in union membership. But many unions discriminated either directly or indirectly against potential black members; while employers frequently practised segregation in employment structures and opportunities, recreation and education. Faced with such a massive wall of white racism, many blacks saw little hope of improvement via the unions. But hope was not completely extinguished. As Rosalyn Terborg-Penn has shown, black women, 'drawing upon traditional African mutual aid and collective survival strategies', constructed organisations of collective resistance 'even in the most "unorganizable" of occupations'. The northern garment and laundry industries, along with parts of the South, were areas of such prominent, if generally shortlived, resistance during the late 1920s.[92]

Between 1910 and 1920, observes Alice Kessler-Harris, the total number of women in trade unions had quintupled. By 1920 almost 400,000 women were trade-union members (6.6 per cent of all non-agricultural wage-earning women, and 18 per cent of women in industry). This expansion had been part of the great, if temporary, extension of trade unionism to previously marginal and non-unionised groups. However, the defensive 1920s saw a retreat into union exclusivity and attempted closure. Women workers were, once again, widely regarded as a threat to male job security, wages and conditions of work. And a number of convenient stereotypes and rationalisations – women as lacking the requisite 'reliability', 'stability' or 'fighting spirit' for industrial struggle – were widely utilised, even by unions such as the ILGWU, to exclude or marginalise women. There is, of course, much substance to the thesis offered by many historians that women's priorities lay more with the home, community and social life than with the worlds of 'work' and trade unionism. But we must be careful, in taking on board the thesis, not to mistake the victims for the culprits. We have repeatedly observed in this book that, given favourable conditions, women did form and support trade unions. We must, accordingly, be attentive to Susan Porter-Benson's suggestion that in 1920s America some young women were 'far from frivolously indifferent to unions', and 'may have seen them as potential guarantors of their right to have a good time'. In fact, unions generally failed to relate to women's entitlement to 'the right to consume' (Benson) or to their general material needs, and accordingly paid a heavy price. By 1930, records James Greene, 'only 250,000 of the 4 million women wage earners belonged to unions, half of them to the Garment and Clothing workers' organizations', and 'one of every nine male workers enjoyed union protection, as compared to every sixteen female workers'.[93]

Third, in view of the adverse conditions facing trade unionism, it is hardly surprising that institutionalised collective bargaining was not achieved by the mass of American workers during the 1920s. Outside of (and sometimes within) the unionised sectors of American industry, workers lacked effective grievance machinery. And the continued hostility of the courts (as seen especially in the granting of injunctions against strikers, the outlawing of secondary boycotts, and restrictions upon peaceful picketing), other agencies of the state, and the Republican administrations of the 1920s towards organised labour ensured that open-shop practices characterised most of 1920s American industry.[94]

The recession of 1921–2, chronically high unemployment levels, the serious difficulties facing the staple industries, post-1920 government de-regulation of the economy and the obsessive concerns with 'sound money' and 'orthodoxy', and mounting employer determination to resolve economic problems at the expense of workers and organised labour – all ensured that British trade unionism would face an extremely testing time from 1921 onwards.[95] By 1921, for example, unemployment had soared (to afflict over 20 per cent of trade unionists by the summer), post-war militancy was less visible, and Lloyd George's coalition government felt more confident of its ability to de-control and de-regulate the economy without provoking mass protest. As James Cronin has observed:

> Before the summer of 1920, the workers had emerged victorious from key industrial confrontations; neither the government nor private employers felt confident of the outcome of a showdown. From late 1920 on, however, labour was forced onto the defensive. Lloyd George sensed the shift almost immediately, telling Bonar Law in 1920 that the era of compromise was finished. 'It would have been a mistake', he explained, 'if the fight had come sooner – the nation had not settled down' and a dangerous 'restlessness' was about.

In 1921 the process of taming labour began in earnest. The government's withdrawal from intervention in agriculture resulted in the scrapping of the minimum wage established in 1917, massive reductions in wages, and in 1923 the outbreak of a strike involving between 6,000 and 10,000 workers in Norfolk. In coalmining government de-control in March 1921 was the signal for the employers to demand savage wage reductions. The miners appealed in vain for support from their allies in the Triple Alliance, the railwaymen and the transport workers. This unsuccessful appeal, on 'Black Friday', effectively killed off the Triple Alliance. The ensuing three-month miners' strike resulted in great bitterness, a government subsidy to the industry, and a settlement made on a district rather than a national basis. As Chris Wrigley comments, the miners 'had exhausted their union funds, their personal savings, and their credit with the Cooperatives and other shopkeepers. As a result they were in a much weakened state when they faced the employers and the government in 1926.'

Cotton and engineering workers also suffered serious setbacks.[96] Viewing wage cuts as the key to restored competitiveness, employers launched major offensives in support of their aims in both weaving and spinning in 1921. Despite their mass memberships and, especially in the case of the spinners, substantial financial resources, the cotton unions met with defeat in 1921, accepted a wage cut in 1922, and generally remained quiescent up to the launching of a further employer offensive in 1928. Its funds reduced by mounting claims for unemployment benefit, the Amalgamated Engineering Union was dealt a severe blow by the employers in 1922. Choosing to fight on the specific issue of their unilateral right to introduce overtime and the wider question of managerial prerogatives, the engineering employers won a national lockout. Engineering trade unionism subsequently suffered from severe membership losses. Only during mid–late 1930s economic recovery, and especially under the impetus of rearmament, would engineering workers rediscover much of their former militancy and strength. Early 1920s recession also allowed engineering employers to sack many activists and leading figures in the shop stewards' movement.

The negative experiences of agricultural workers, coalminers, cotton operatives and engineering workers were symptomatic of a general reversal of trade unionism's fortunes since the heady days of post-war militancy. By the middle of 1921, observes Wrigley, industrial production was 'down by over 18 per cent, exports by 30 per cent, and some 2.4 million workers were unemployed'. Wages had sharply declined from their high levels of 1918–20, with particularly heavy falls in engineering, shipbuilding and agriculture. And the 35 per cent overall decline in trade-union membership between 1920 and 1923 had severe specific manifestations in agriculture, horticulture and forestry (68.9 per cent), bricks and building materials (54 per cent), pottery (49.4 per cent), clothing (47.3 per cent) and metals and engineering (47.1 per cent).

There were attempts, especially at the grass-roots level, to revive the fortunes of trade unionism. The call for '100 per cent trade unionism' was made by trades councils and, most notably, members of the Communist Party's National Minority Movement.[97] Formed in 1924, the NMM sought 'to convert the revolutionary minority within each industry into a revolutionary majority', to develop an alternative leadership to the established trade-union officialdom, and to wage a vigorous struggle against capital. The NMM achieved considerable influence between 1924 and 1926 in mining, engineering, the railways, the docks, the building industry and in some trades councils. Demands for a minimum wage, a 44-hour week, the abolition of overtime and workers' control of industry undoubtedly struck a responsive note in those areas in which war and post-war militancy had flourished. Indeed, as James Hinton notes, on the eve of the General Strike, the 883 delegates at a Minority Movement 'Conference of Action' 'could claim (with a good deal of double counting) to represent nearly a quarter of the total membership of the trade unions'. Simultaneously the National Unemployed Workers' Movement, founded in 1921 and dominated by Communists, mounted 'hunger marches' and other forms of protest against unemployment, low scales of relief for the unemployed, and evictions.

In the event neither the NMM nor the NUWM achieved much

success during the 1920s as a whole. The latter organisation would achieve a position of significance among unemployed workers during the early 1930s. The former relied heavily upon the belief that left-wing trade-union officials would produce an alternative polity to that of the TUC's General Council during the General Strike. Such an alternative was, however, not really forthcoming. And, as Hinton has claimed, the NMM overestimated the capacity of workers to launch a militant offensive against capitalism and the existing trade-union leadership at a time of mass unemployment and general union defensiveness. The NMM's strategy might have succeeded at the height of worker militancy in 1919: by 1926 it was doomed to failure.

Indeed, notwithstanding the courage of the miners and the widespread support for their cause from workers in general, the General Strike itself stood little chance of success.[98] In 1925 the government had intervened in the coal industry to prevent a strike against employer proposals for wage cuts and the termination of national agreements. A nine-months subsidy was granted to the industry in order to maintain wage levels. In return, the miners were to co-operate with the Royal Commission, headed by the Liberal Sir Herbert Samuel and given the task of examining the economic state of the coal industry. The Samuel Commission reported in March 1926 in favour of the long-term reorganisation of the industry under private ownership. The Commission was opposed to employer proposals for increased hours and district agreements, but it did recommend heavy wage cuts.

Industrial harmony did not ensue. The miners were totally opposed to wage cuts, as were the owners in relation to reorganisation. Moreover, the nine-month waiting or 'cooling-off' period had enabled the government to perfect its plans for the maintenance of supplies in the event of a strike. Indeed, despite Rodney Lowe's claim to the contrary, there is much evidence to suggest that Baldwin's government, and especially the 'hawks' gathered around Churchill, welcomed a confrontation in order to excoriate the memories of post-war insurgency and to firmly teach organised labour its proper place within the post-war settlement. Given the indifference or hostility of the government, the intransigence of the coal owners, and the widespread feeling within the ranks of workers that the miners were being made a scapegoat for the employer- and government-induced problems of the British economy (the return to an overvalued pound in 1952 being of acute and debilitating importance to coal and other export sectors), conflict became inevitable.

Called by the General Council of the TUC, the General Strike began at midnight on 3 May. The government, questioning the very constitutionality and moral legitimacy of the strike ('selfish' and, in some cases 'sinister' class forces 'holding the nation to ransom'), put into place the provisions established under the Emergency Powers Act. In the event the strike elicited massive working-class support, but lasted only nine days. The leaders of the General Council took fright at the prospects of protracted and 'uncontrolled' direct action and direct democracy. On the basis of having reached a 'gentleman's agreement' with Samuel (concerning reorganisation, the renewal of the subsidy, and the issue of wage reductions), the leaders of the General Council called off the strike. This was, in effect, total surrender, the 'Samuel Memorandum' having no binding effect upon the parties involved in the dispute. Most workers immediately returned to work. The miners struggled on for a further nine months, but were eventually forced back to work by starvation, suffering, the threat of company unionism and repression. Longer hours, wage cuts and a return to district agreements constituted the price of defeat. Many militants, and especially Communist Party activists, were 'blacklisted' in coal.

It is difficult to envisage ways in which the General Strike could have resulted in victory for the miners. The government was determined and well prepared. The ruling and propertied classes were largely united in their opposition to 'politically motivated' trade unions and workers. The leaders of the General Council and many of the trade unions were moderate, cautious, opposed to 'unconstitutional' direct action, and ready to make peace at the first opportunity and on the basis of flimsy evidence. And the vast majority of trade unionists, while loyal to the miners' cause, were also obedient to the wishes and commands of their union and General Council leaders. Communist and other left-wing activists did play very important, and often heroic roles during the strike. The loyalty, determination and capacity for sacrifice and suffering on the part of miners and mining families were frequently beyond belief. But in the final analysis, the changed political economy of British capitalism from 1918–20 on the one hand, to 1926 on the other made it extremely unlikely that a general strike, and even a largely *defensive* general strike (against wage cuts and increased hours rather in support of revolutionary socialism), would carry much hope of success.

The legislative aftermath of the General Strike and the failure of the Mond-Turner talks to move British capitalism in a more 'progressive', class-collaborationist direction further contributed to the defensive and increasingly cautious mentality of British trade unionism. The provisions of the Trade Disputes and Trade Union Act of 1927 did not seek to obliterate trade unionism in a manner familiar to 1920s Americans. Rather, organised labour was to be firmly reminded of the due place, and proper respect, obedience and deference befitting a minor, if recognised, estate of the realm. As Lowe reminds us, the legislation of 1927 accordingly did not attack trade-union funds, substitute criminal law for civil law in industrial relations, extend the Conspiracy Act of 1875, or introduce compulsory strike ballots and arbitration – all course of action variously advocated by a number of politicians, employers and prominent figures in British judicial circles during the years from 1919 to 1926.

To the extent outlined above, the vindictive character of the Trade Disputes Act should not be exaggerated. Simultaneously, however, we are dealing with a serious legislative and judicial attack upon 'politicised' and militant trade unionism, upon some of the established functions of trade unionism, and upon the links between the unions and the Labour Party. The Act banned general strikes and laid down a maximum prison sentence of two years for those so defying the law. Sympathetic strikes were outlawed, civil service and local government workers forbidden to join unions which could affiliate to the TUC, the closed shop outlawed in public sector employment, and the right to strike restricted. In a move designed to reduce union members' financial support for the Labour Party and so slow down or halt the 'Rise of Labour', contracting in to the political levy was substituted for contracting out. Finally, the legislation of 1927 must be viewed alongside the Board of Guardians (Default) Act of 1926 which increased central control of the purse strings of poor-law relief in an attempt to halt the 'profligacy' of Labour Guardians in Poplar and elsewhere at the local level. There also developed much outraged Conservative feeling at the thought of 'undeserving' striking miners receiving poor relief. In sum, although designed not to destroy unionism, the legislation of 1926 and 1927 was most certainly designed to punish organised labour for its 'extremism' and 'un-British' turn to 'unconstitutional' direct action.[99]

To some extent this legislative backlash had unintended consequences. The highly partisan nature of the attack on labour drew the unions and the Labour Party closer together. The return of a Labour government now became an urgent priority of the unions. Similarly, as we will see below, British labour retained much of its stoicism and resiliency in the face of adversity. But caution and moderation were reinforced. Militants, and especially Communist militants, were thrown very much into retreat. As Hinton has written, 'the widespread demoralisation which followed the General Strike was accompanied by the rapid dissolution of the amorphous left-wing of 1925–6, leaving the CP isolated and exposed to disciplinary action from the right'. Communists now began to be widely expelled from the Labour Party, and the Communist Party was about to enter its unproductive 'class and class period'. On a more general level, there was a continued decline, as opposed to catastrophic post-General Strike collapse, in trade-union membership (from 5,219,000 in 1926 to 4,919,000 in 1927 to 4,806,000 in 1928). But the coal miners'

unions were hit very hard, union density in coalmining falling from
61.9 per cent in 1926 (albeit from 76.7 per cent in 1921) to 51.8 per
cent in 1928. In addition, employers in cotton were beginning to mount
another offensive against wages and workloads in 1928. By the end of
1929 and into the 1930s the devastating effects of capitalist breakdown
upon jobs and expectations were awfully visible to British trade
unionists.

As one would logically expect, the defences, defeats and retreats of
British trade unionism during the 1920s had an adverse effect upon
established centres of trade unionism. Predictably, and while less
adversely affected than many other unions in the early 1920s, coalmining
trade unionism suffered heavily during the entire decade, losing,
observes Wrigley, 'more members (48.6 per cent) then the trade unions
as a whole (42.4 per cent)' between 1920 and 1928. Whereas aggregate
trade-union membership in Britain declined by 12.5 per cent between
1925 and 1928, the miners' unions lost 32.9 per cent during the same
period. Much like the American situation, union losses in coal took
place against a backcloth of mounting unemployment in the industry.
Unions in the other staple industries also suffered. And trade unionism
in the expanding sectors of building, distribution and transport was
generally weak. The car industry was largely non-union; and, despite
the organisation of teachers and other professional workers, white-collar
trade unionism 'as a major force in its own right and within the
broader trade-union movement was to be a post-1945 phenomenon'
(Hinton). Following the war the majority of women returned to the
home or into traditional areas of paid employment such as domestic
service. Hinton notes that, 'the expanding female workforce in distribution, clerical work and the new industries remained low paid and
poorly organised'. Wrigley adds that, 'with the recessions of 1921–2
and 1929–30 male trade unionists gave explicit or tacit support to women
being pushed out of jobs first when industry contracted'. Little wonder
that between 1920 and 1923 female trade-union membership fell more
markedly than the corresponding figure for males (by 38.5 per cent as
opposed to 34.1 per cent). Union density among women was much
lower (roughly 13.8 per cent to male union density of 33.8 per cent).
And between 1923 and 1938 the number of women trade unionists
increased by only 100,000 (to a total of 926,000). The 'marriage bar'
became common in a number of occupations, including those in that
traditionally high employer of women, cotton.[100]

As in the United States, the more restrictive attitudes adopted by
British trade unionists towards women's employment were symptomatic
of the development of more widespread exclusivity, caution and
narrowed vision within an increasingly defensive trade-union movement.

But we must emphasise two key differences. British trade unionism in the 1920s was more deeply and broadly based and generally more resilient than its American counterpart.

Of fundamental importance in Britain was the accelerated development and prominence of non-skilled trade unionism. Amalgamations (which extended beyond the non-skilled sectors) created, in 1922 and 1924, the two respective general-union giants of the Transport and General Workers' Union and the National Union of General and Municipal Workers. The TGWU initially brought together dockers and road transport workers, and, as a result of its merger with the Workers' Union, was strengthened in 1929 by the addition to its ranks of semi-skilled workers in engineering, building and elsewhere. The more diverse membership of the NUGMW was scattered across a number of industries including local authority employment, gas, electricity supply, engineering and building. Increasingly in the post-General Strike years these two highly bureaucratised, centralised and cautious unions were to set both the tone of trade-union policy and the dominant ideology of the labour movement as a whole. In conjunction with the continued, if somewhat diminished, importance of trade unionism in coal, cotton, shipbuilding and other traditional sectors and in its limited spread into the services, new mass-production industries and the professions, the British trade-union movement thus offered a far more solid presence than was the case in 1920s America.

The comparative strength and resiliency of British trade unionism were demonstrated in numerous other ways. David Montgomery makes the telling observation that British unions 'lost more members between 1920 and 1926 than American unions ... enrolled'. And James Cronin notes that, 'though the General Strike did discredit direct action, its failure did not signify a mass reversion to non-unionism and so did not license the sort of wholesale attack upon unions demanded by some employers'. Despite the undoubted severity of the early 1930s depression in terms of employment and trade unionism, trade-union membership consistently remained above its 1914 level and money wages held up well in comparison with the savage cuts introduced in 1921–2. There is undoubtedly much truth in James Hinton's claim that, notwithstanding its failure, the General Strike 'taught employers that there were limits beyond which it was dangerous to push their workers'. In marked contrast to the United States, institutionalised collective bargaining, increasingly concentrated (with the most notable exceptions of post-1926 coalmining and the woollen industry) at the national level, was further developed in inter-war Britain. The 'frontier of control' moved in general favour of the employer, but trade-union bargaining rights were preserved in the staples and many other industries. And despite the 'corporatist bias' evident in the immediate post-war discussions and attempted institutional 'arrangements' between unions, employers and the government, and the resort to consultations and informal under-standings during the 1920s and 1930s, formal attempts to institutionalise corporatism generally failed (as seen in the cases of Mond-Turner, the National Industrial Conference and the Economic Advisory Council). Most employers and unions remained jealous of their cherished auton-omy and voluntarism. And governments did not generally wish to impose policies upon resentful employers and unions. As Lowe has concluded:

> Government policy in fact remained resolutely the decentralisation, not the centralisation, of responsibility. Each industry was to be responsible for its own affairs whilst government itself stood above the fray, free to defend its perception of the 'national' interest. Corporatism or 'corporate bias' had to await the Second World War when economically the two sides of industry were more equally matched and, politically, the purpose of such a deal was uncon-tentious.[101]

Alongside continuities within British trade unionism there did, how-ever, develop important changes. The generally more defensive context has already been noted. Furthermore, as in the United States, trade-union officials played upon threats from unemployment, employers and governments to emphasise the need for worker loyalty to the union and strong union leadership. National collective bargaining stimulated union centralisation and bureaucratisation. And the failure of the 'direct-action' methods of the General Strike presented moderate union leaders with heaven-sent opportunities to augment their own powers and to root out 'malcontents' and 'extremists'. Thus Chris Wrigley:

> After the General Strike trade union officials appear more powerful within their organisations both in settling wage negotiations on their own authority and in dealing with militants within their unions. Thus the TGWU and the ETU both expelled London com-mittee members in the mid-1930s, and earlier, in 1927, the General and Municipal Workers Union banned communists outright from being elected to union posts. Under Bevin and Citrine the TUC also took an anti-communist and more 'statesman-like' line generally.[102]

Indeed, the failure of the General Strike constituted a watershed in British trade-union history far less on account of its effects upon union membership levels than upon attitudes, behaviour and expectations – upon the tremendous fillip given to moderation, caution, constitutional-ism, intra-union loyalty and unity, and upon intra- and inter-union commitments to seek the election of a Labour government. Post-war militancy and the experience of 1926 were increasingly to be cast, by trade-union leaders and Labour Party officials, as 'aberrant', as not properly belonging to the gradualist and constitutionalist traditions of British Labour.

Furthermore, within organised labour's increasingly dominant paradigm of 'commonsense', gradualism and constitutionalism, issues of power and patronage – of how to extend the influence and 'connections' of the movement, both locally and at the highest national level – became of paramount importance. Attempts, especially by left-wingers, to raise questions concerning alternative aims and means were, at best, regarded as unnecessary irritants, and, at worst, as treachery and sabotage to the quests for unity of purpose and the singleminded pursuit of office. As David Howell's current work clearly demonstrates, the pursuit of power rather than the formulation of refined ideas and ideologies mattered most to organised labour's national leaders during the second half of the 1920s.[103] Parallels with organised labour in the 1980s, especially in the post-Bennite and post-Scargillite periods, are striking.

Workers and Politics

To return to our comparative perspective. We have seen that by the end of the 1920s defensive trade-union movements in Britain and the United States differed in terms of their respective strengths, powers of resilience, and their relations with employers and governments. In the field of labour politics, the differences become more pronounced, Britain experiencing the 'Rise of Labour' and the United States continued Republican hegemony and the general decline of worker experiments in third-party politics. We can now usefully elaborate upon these developments.

As James Sundquist observes, 1920s American prosperity was accompanied by the ebbing of reform-minded movements within the political mainstream, the 'normalcy' or orthodoxy of the ruling Republicans under Harding, Coolidge and Hoover, and the domination of both the Republican and Democratic Parties by 'big business and high finance'.[104] In this era of political complacency, popular challenges of the magnitude of Populism, socialism and Progressivism to established political structures and the conventional wisdom were conspicuous by their absence. Simultaneously, however, there did arise independent, radical political movements and radical challenges inside the Democratic Party which belied a picture of complete harmony and which, in some instances, anticipated the radicalisation of the Democratic Party during the 1930s.

We have, for example, already made reference (in Chapter 3) to the emergence of a progressive political bloc within the AFL during the post-war years, the formation of the Conference for Progressive Political Action, and its successes, in the 1922 elections, of supporting 'friends of labor' from across the entire political spectrum. The rewards of this non-partisan approach, while self-evident to leaders of the AFL and a majority of the leaders of the CPPA, were seen by the highly successful Minnesota Farmer-Labour Party, John Fitzpatrick and other leaders of the Chicago Federation of Labor and the Workers' (Communist) Party as a signal that the time was ripe for the creation of a labour party. In 1923 the Chicago farmer-laborites bolted the CPPA and put out a call for a convention to form a labour party along British lines. Strong counter-pressure from the non-partisan AFL and CPPA leaders meant that the convention attracted few progressives from the mainstream labour movement and was dominated by the communists. Thereupon, the leaders of the Chicago Federation of Labor voiced their mistrust of the communists' motives and left the third-party movement. The call for the creation of a national third party was subsequently taken up by the Farmer-Labor Party. But the continued opposition of the AFL to the notion of a labour party, and disputes between the communists and the Farmer-Laborites at the 1924 St Paul convention ensured that third-partyism would, once again, quickly perish. Meanwhile, the CPPA and the AFL, the latter temporarily abandoning its non-partisan line, threw their support behind Senator Robert La Follette in the 1924 presidential race. La Follette, denouncing the 'class' politics of third-partyism, ran as an independent candidate and received a very creditable 4.8 million votes 'from farmers, workers, intellectuals, and others who were disgusted with the two-party system'.[105]

However, as James Green notes, La Follette's campaign, 'proved to be an end rather than a beginning of independent labor politics'. La Follette, whilst obtaining 16.6 per cent of the total vote cast, mounted a serious threat to the main parties 'only in places where the building blocks of a radical political party were already in place – in other words, in the Northwest' (Sundquist). Farmers and agricultural workers, continuing to feel the economic squeeze for much of the 1920s, did rally to La Follette's cause in large numbers. And economic difficulties, as manifested in unemployment and underemployment and high mortgage repayments, the opportunity and political space to be effective at the state level, and the presence of seasoned and talented radical and socialist political activists, ensured that the Farmer-Labor Party of Minnesota would continue to exert a major influence upon the state's affairs throughout the inter-war years. (In 1930 Floyd Olson, a farmer-laborite, won the governorship of Minnesota, and was re-elected in 1932 and 1934.)[106]

The Northwest was the exception to the general rule. 'In the East', observes Sundquist, 'organized labor made a similar showing for La Follette in only a few areas'. In the post-1924 years the communists turned more and more to trade-union work, and the AFL reverted to its policy of non-partisanship. David Montgomery usefully reminds us that the League for Independent Political Action, founded in 1928, did continue to fight for the creation of a labour party. But the immediate effects of this fight were negligible. In the 1928 presidential election contest, Governor Alfred ('Al') Smith of New York, 'a Catholic, a friend of labor, a friend of the slum dweller, an enemy of Prohibition, and a leader who had made his mark in the enactment of factory laws and other pioneering social legislation', received very impressive support from the urban working class (especially from 'new' immigrants, Jews and Catholics) and significant backing from western farmers. The economic grievances of farmers notwithstanding, the 1928 contest was dominated by the 'status' issues of religion and Prohibition, and the defeated Smith 'went to great pains *not* to be the voice of protest' (Sundquist). In effect, Smith *did* address the grievances of the dispossessed 'status, ethnic and religious minorities yearning for equality'. But AFL support for Smith was not forthcoming, and more explicitly class-based forms of political protest would await the 1930s. Finally, left-wing parties performed very poorly in 1928. William Foster, a leading communist, received 48,000 votes, while Normas Thomas obtained 268,000 votes on the socialist ticket. On the eve of the Great Depression political preferences were a fair reflection of the generally fragmented state of the American working class.[107]

From the point of view of the radical labour activist, political matters appeared to be far more satisfactory in late 1920s Britain. Indeed, from the end of the war up to 1929 support for the Labour Party showed an 'unmistakeable upward secular trend'. As John Stevenson has written:

> Labour's share of the vote rose from under 8 per cent in the two elections of 1910 to 22 per cent in 1918. In 1924 Labor formed its first, minority, Government on the basis of a 30 per cent share of the vote and 191 seats, overtaking the Liberals in votes and seats. The General Election of 1924, although reducing Labour representation to 151 seats, witnessed an increase in the share of the vote to 33 per cent... The theme of the 'three-party' situation in the 1920s was the gradual decline of the Liberals as an effective national political force and the establishment of the Labour Party as the principal opposition. In 1929 the coming to power of the second Labour Government with 288 seats and almost 40 per cent of the total vote, with the Liberals reduced to a mere 59 seats in spite of an attractive and revamped programme, seemed to confirm a major realignment of political forces.[108]

Labour's seemingly inexorable rise owed something to the sudden increase of the electorate, from some 7 million to 20 million voters, in 1918, to the consolidation of 'traditional' working-class culture, and to its increasingly powerful ties with the trade-union movement. As in the case of the cotton unions, there was a widespread feeling among trade unionists in the 1920s that the election of a Labour government would do a great deal to reverse the declining fortunes of the movement and its members, and attempt to improve the economic situation at the expense of the employers and financiers rather than on the backs of workers, both the employed and unemployed.[109]

The Labour Party did not, of course, enjoy undisputed power and influence within the working class. Despite its overall decline, the Liberal Party, complete with its established tradition of Nonconformity, still exerted considerable popular appeal in Wales, parts of the northeast of England, and in some rural areas. And, as we will observe in more detail in relation to the 1930s, traditions of popular Conservatism remained very strong, especially in Lancashire and the West Midlands. McKibbin in fact suggests that throughout the 1920s 'the Tories (probably) had a majority of the working-class preferred vote and in the 1930s (almost certainly) a majority of the actual vote – a reasonable estimate is 55 per cent in 1931 and 50 per cent in 1935'.[110] On its left flank the mainstream Labour Party had to contend with an increasingly restless and frustrated ILP and a revolutionary Communist Party. Still, when all qualifications have been made, the rise of the Labour Party during the 1920s was a fact of primary importance. As Stevenson notes, in establishing itself as a party of government, the Labour Party critically provided an alternative means to industrial militancy 'for organized Labour to press its claims in the polity as a whole'.

In addition to the political, cultural and economic factors already outlined, Labour's successful development owed much, especially up to and including the 1929 election, to the Party's ability to portray itself as a vehicle of progress, improvement, idealism and a more civilised and harmonious life. Living in an age in which the leaders of the Labour Party have assiduously cultivated an image of business-suited efficiency, pragmatism and (bland) consensus, it is hard to appreciate the extent to which 1920s Labour offered the breaking of a new dawn in which the co-operative socialist commonwealth of independent and community-minded citizens would 'naturally' replace an outmoded, conflict-ridden and anti-social form of capitalism. Ramsay MacDonald and many other leaders did, after all, define themselves as labour socialists rather than mere 'reformists' or patchers-up of the system: dull reformism properly belonged to the 1930s rather than to the constitutionalist and evolutionary labour socialism of the 1920s.

For example in his *Socialism: Critical and Constructive* in 1921, Mac-

Donald provided a thoroughgoing critique of the capitalist system. The latter was characterised by 'individualistic disorganisation', 'a servitude to things', divisive social classes and competing nations, and materialism as a substitute for 'human qualities', 'personal excellence of mind and character' and 'social gain and happiness'. MacDonald's socialism posited an altogether higher order of civilisation. By means of the vote and the attainment of parliamentary office, moral persuasion and reasoned discourse, the mutualist activities of the trade unions, co-operative societies and other voluntary and collectivist institutions of 'the movement', and by the encouragement of greater co-operation in industry and elsewhere, Labour would build its new order. 'The Socialist', wrote MacDonald,

> seeks to educate into community and co-operative frames of minds, so that people will think of their partners in different fields of service, rather than of their subordinates, or their employees ... Such a change in thought will lead to a revolution in social organization right from beginning to end – from class relationships to workshop control. It has begun. It may be hampered, it cannot be dammed back. The Socialist State is already appearing within the capitalist State. Its creative force is an intelligence which can conceive of organized communal service, not as a purposeful exercise of sacrifice and moral strenuousness like the discipline of a religious fellowship, but as an ordinary grouping of human effort for production, for distribution and for culture.[111]

Ideas were, of course, insufficient to build a mass base. Effective leaders and institutions at all levels, large constituencies of support and initiative, and policies which carried an appeal beyond the Labour Party's 'natural' trade-union base, were also requirements of national political success. During the 1920s such requirements were largely met.

As demonstrated by Michael Savage and others, the Labour Party extended, albeit unevenly, its key bases of support from the trade unions into neighbourhoods and from males to women. The rise of ward organisations during the 1920s permitted the individual payment of Party subscriptions weekly to a visiting collector. In addition, ward and women's representation at constituency level increased. Other neighbourhood-based organisations – clothing clubs, co-ops and the like – provided further institutional bases for political mobilisation. Of central importance were the Women's Sections of the Party. Between 1906 and 1918 Labour women had enjoyed separate organisation within the Women's Labour League. But under the terms of the new constitution adopted in 1918 women were absorbed into the mainstream Party, and, notes Sam Davies, 'the formation of Women's Sections at a local level became a priority'.

There took place a remarkable growth in the numbers of formal

Labour women in the 1920s, from the 5,500 members of the Women's Labour League in 1918 to the 200,000 women members of the Party at the national level in 1925. And, while women's achievements within the national Party generally fell way short of their actual ambitions (due mainly to the continued power of patriarchal values and practices within Labour), they did, for a time at least, significantly influence the shape of policies and, especially in 1930s London, manage to get elected to municipal positions of power within the Party (Thane). As suggested by Savage:

> women campaigned over a number of issues: women in paid employment, unemployment among women, social services, education for 'working women', Trade Boards, the need for equality in employment, minimum wages, the end of marriage bars and family allowances paid for out of a wealth tax.

Finally, as seen in the movement of Liverpool's nationalist Irish Catholic community into Labour, the Party also acquired distinctive ethnic and/ or religious constituencies.[112]

The enlarged constituencies of post-war Labour stimulated the Party to move beyond its 'traditional' commitments to the largely 'economistic' policies of the trade unions and the 'mutualist' concerns of the friendly societies and co-ops. As Savage has convincingly argued, the 'tapping of female and neighbourhood bases of support . . . led to consumer-oriented statist politics'. During the 1920s local Labour parties throughout Britain thus pursued a number of, especially social-welfare, policies which issued from the direct needs of their constituents and which were closely embedded within local cultures and patterns of political 'commonsense'. Municipal undertakings were pursued in the fields of housing, electricity supply, the provision of nursery schools for children of 'working' mothers, school meals, school clinics and improved maternity facilities. Labour sought adequate levels of relief for the unemployed, union rates of wages and civilised hours of labour for those employed by the municipality, the creation of direct labour departments, slum clearance and the provision of council houses at low rents. Finally, demands to raise the school-leaving age, for family allowances and birth control (issues which excited the negative passions of, respectively, male trade-unionist 'breadwinners' and Roman Catholics), and for more 'direct' (i.e. community-based) control and democracy also lay at the heart of the 1920s popular labour-socialist project.[113]

By no means all these policies and demands were successful. The Party conference declined to adopt the causes of birth control and family allowances. And from the mid 1920s onwards tightened central government financial and administrative controls erected barriers to progressive local initiatives. But in localities from Glasgow to London Labour did sufficient to significantly enlarge its basis of support.

Four further observations on Labour's 'statist turn' should be noted. First, Labour was particularly successful in those communities in which the abstractions of labour socialism (concerning common ownership, community spirit and so on) were shown to be directly relevant to people's lives, and in which a Labour élite did not set itself above and deride popular culture. Second, as will be evident from our discussions in Chapter 3, many of Labour's social-welfarist policies of the 1920s were anticipated, and in some cases practised, by pre-1918 socialists and labourites. During the 1920s such policies assumed more widespread importance and improved chance of realisation. Third, along with Pat Thane, we should emphasise the importance to 1920s labour socialists of notions of local democracy and accountability. Many of Labour's policies were to be achieved by means of community- and gender-based empowerment and under the auspices of democratic local states. Both personal and collective independence on the one hand and rational local state planning on the other were central to Labour's thoughts. The notions of heavy, centralised, bureaucratic and impersonal central state control and, arguably, diminished independence and autonomy both for individuals and voluntary organisations, would properly belong to post-1945 rather than 1920s British socialism.

Fourth, notwithstanding its great electoral triumph of 1929, there is evidence to suggest that the Labour Party was beginning to change its course in the post-General Strike context, to narrow its focus somewhat, and to lose some of its large-hearted vision of the earlier 1920s. As is well known, at the national level the rhetoric of labour socialism was no substitute for concrete measures to arrest the awful rise of unemployment. Labour's victory in 1929 had been largely based on the promise to immediately tackle the problem of unemployment. But in the event little of substance was achieved. As observed by McKibbin, the minority Labour government was extremely unfortunate to be in office at a time of capitalism's most profound crisis to date. The Slump wrecked the electoral fortunes of incumbent governments throughout the western world. In 1930 Labour did increase and widen access to benefits, but in McKibbin's considered opinion the worsening economic situation, the weight of orthodox economic opinion and practice in Britain and elsewhere, and the severe budgetary and exchange-rate crises of 1931 rendered a commitment to deflation more or less inevitable. But this was surely not the total picture. Increases in benefits must be set against the penalties meted out to married women in the Anomalies Act of 1931. And, as Cronin suggests, Labour suffered from an embarrassing and disastrous lack of clarity, precision and rigour in terms of macro-economic policy. 'Keynesian' tinkering with demand was to be eschewed, and the leadership maintained that in the absence of socialist planning (the only 'true cure' for unemployment and capitalist instability) mere palliatives could be offered to the unemployed. Simultaneously, however, Snowden, as Chancellor of the Exchequer, was committed to deflationary orthodoxy.[114]

In sum, Labour's economics was a chaotic mess. Unable to agree upon a 10 per cent cut in unemployment benefit, the government resigned in August 1931. MacDonald stayed on as head of a National Government, and he and Snowden, his ally, passed down into labour movement folklore as the 'great betrayers'. In October 1931 the National Government fought a general election, 'at which it won the most sweeping victory in modern British history, obtaining 554 seats (of which the Conservatives won 470) to Labour's 46'.[115] The great expectations and high hopes of 1929 thus ended in disaster. Conservative hegemony, in the form of the National Government, would prevail throughout the 1930s.

If the years between 1929 and 1931 brought Labour's policy deficiencies and disagreements into full public glare, then there had increasingly been signs of a narrowing of focus, a closing down of 'unsafe' and 'irresponsible' alternatives from 1926 onwards. Above all, the failure of the General Strike induced greater caution, not only in the industrial but also in the political wing of the labour movement. There were also growing tensions between (largely socialist) 'intellectual dreamers' and 'down-to-earth' realists (especially trade unionists), and between those seeking 'higher' and 'nobler' forms of 'socialist culture' and the (largely working-class) pursuers of the 'delights' of commercialised popular leisure. Moderate trade-union leaders, such as Ernest Bevin of the TGWU, increasingly imposed their fundamentally 'labourist' or 'incremental collectivist', as opposed to transformative socialist, views upon the Labour Party. Contacts with 'unsound' elements, such as 'extreme' feminists and revolutionary Communists in the National Unemployed Workers' Movement, were discouraged. The expulsions of these elements proceeded apace.

Similarly, by the early 1930s women in Preston, Liverpool and elsewhere were being pushed to the margins. Growing unemployment rendered male Labour Party members far less tolerant of women's continued presence in the labour market. 'Women's issues' increasingly took a back seat to the more pressing issue of (mainly male) unemployment. Women's sections became more marginal, tending to 'fight shy of political campaigns and . . . to become a support organisation for the party, organising such things as fêtes and baking competitions' (Savage).

Finally, by 1931 the radical alternatives offered by the ILP (with its underconsumptionist and robustly socialist emphases) and the expansionist and protectionist Oswald Mosley had been rejected by the mainstream Labour Party.[116] Caution, 'responsibility', the paramount important of the 'national interest', the growing influence of trade-union control over Party affairs, and avoidance of contacts with 'revolutionaries' were thus the most important legacies of organised labour's defeats in 1926 and 1931. As we will see below, the experience of mass unemployment reinforced centrist and 'realistic' Labour politics.

CHAPTER FIVE

Militancy and Reformism in the 1930s

DEPRESSION AND MASS UNEMPLOYMENT

The appalling effects of the British 'Slump' and the American 'Great Depression' upon employment levels from the end of the 1920s to the late 1930s are revealed in Table 5.1.

A number of key trends emerge. Of foremost importance was the sudden, massive and unprecedented rise in the early 1930s in the number of people thrown out of work in the United States. Thus, between 1929 and 1933, the trough of the depression, unemployment rose from 1.6

Table 5.1 Unemployment in Britain and the USA, 1930–8

	*Unemployment in millions		Percentage of labour force	
	Britain	USA	**Britain	USA
1929	1.2 (1.5)	1.6	10.4 (8.0)	3.2
1930	1.9 (2.3)	4.3	16.1 (12.3)	8.9
1931	2.7 (3.2)	8.0	21.3 (16.4)	16.3
1932	2.8 (3.4)	12.0	22.1 (17.0)	24.1
1933	2.5 (3.0)	12.8	19.9 (15.4)	25.2
1934	2.1 (2.6)	11.3	16.7 (12.9)	22.0
1935	2.0 (2.4)	10.6	15.5 (12.0)	20.3
1936	1.7 (2.1)	9.0	13.1 (10.2)	17.0
1937	1.4 (1.7)	7.7	10.8 (8.5)	14.3
1938	1.8 (2.1)	10.4	12.9 (10.1)	19.1

Sources: J. Potter, op cit., p. 69; T. Kemp, op. cit., p. 72; W. R. Garside, op. cit., p. 5

  * The British figures refer, respectively, to insured persons and (in brackets) to total workers. The American figures refer to the total labour force.
** The British figures refer to the insured unemployed as a proportion of insured employees and (in brackets) to the total unemployed as a percentage of total employees.

million to 12.8 million. It eased off to 7.7 million by 1937, but Roose-velt's deflationary-induced recession of 1937–8 saw unemployment rise to almost 10.5 million in 1938. In 1929 only 3.2 per cent of the American labour force was unemployed. By 1933 fully one-quarter of the labour force was out of work. As late as 1939 9.4 million Americans, or over 17 per cent of the workforce, lacked jobs. The Great Depression represented, therefore, a profound crisis for the richest country in the world. In addition unemployment spread from agriculture and the depressed staples into the most dynamic sectors of the economy. Car workers, electrical workers, and native-born white-collar workers suf-fered alongside blacks, sharecroppers, labourers, and the sons and daughters of 'new' immigrants. Wages plummeted throughout the econ-omy, the banking system fell apart, millions of small businessmen and farmers were ruined, and 1920s welfare capitalism was no longer a viable proposition. Moreover, the standard economic views that depression would (via the unfettered market mechanism) more or less automatically lead to recovery, and that generalised capitalist collapse was (via the operation of Say's law) an impossibility, were shown to be patently false.

The sorrowful details are provided by Tom Kemp:

> National income, which had been growing at the rate of 5% per annum in the period 1922–9 went down at the rate of 14.4% between 1929 and 1933; output of manufactures fell by half, and in 1933 private domestic investment was only one-eighth of what it had been in 1929. The general price level fell by 25%, while the prices of farm products were less than half what they had been in 1929 . . . The fall in prices cut incomes severely and thus contributed to a further decline in demand for manufactured goods . . .
>
> One result of the general fall in prices and a lower cost of living was that consumption fell less than income and output. Indeed, some people might have been better off than before; but they were a minority. The general fall in income meant a disproportionate fall in the demand for house space . . . and for durables.[1]

As we will see in due course, the suddenness, scale and persistence of the Great Depression, combined with fears of increased social conflict and political radicalism, gave rise to radical departures in state and government policies during the New Deal era. And workers reacted to the crisis by turning to radical protests in order to lay claim to their full material, social and political rights of American citizenship.

In Britain the Slump was less precipitous, less severe and less sus-tained than in the United States. As we have already seen, large sectors of the British economy had been in depression throughout the 1920s and mass unemployment was an established feature of the British political, economic and social landscape. Unemployment did, however, bite very hard between 1929 and 1932, rising from 10.4 per cent to 22.1 per cent of insured employees. And single industry towns in South Wales, northeast England and parts of Scotland were devastated. In Jarrow 68 per cent of the insured workforce were unemployed in 1934. In the same year – and this at a time when recovery had begun – 37 per cent of Glamorgan's labour force and 36 per cent of Monmouth's were out of work. Poverty continued to blight the lives of large numbers of working-class families during the 1930s. And there is little evidence to support Benjamin and Kochins' view that the availability of state benefits in Britain raised the level of unemployment. The vast majority of the unemployed preferred the activity and self-respect of paid work to the enforced inactivity of the 'dole' and the indignities of the means test. Then, as now, 'voluntary' unemployment was far more a case of special right-wing pleading than of concrete working-class reality and choice.[2]

Unemployment rates in Britain from 1932 onwards were, however consistently and significantly lower than those prevalent in 1930s America. In addition, as noted in Chapter 4, British growth rates rose impressively between 1924 and the end of the 1930s. From 1933 onwards the number of unemployed fell, and a mixture of factors – cheap money, the building boom, protection and the slack taken up by the continued growth of the service sector and the flowering of the 'new' industries such as motor cars, electrical goods and aircraft construction – stimulated economic recovery. The technical fruits of 1920s amalgamation began to take effect, productivity and organisational gains were made in some of the older sectors (such as mining and parts of cotton), and rearmament gave an important boost to engineering and the metal trades in general.[3] Finally, as demonstrated in Table 5.2, retail prices

Table 5.2 Wages, Prices and Real Earnings in Britain, 1930–8

Year	Weekly wage rates (1930 = 100)	Retail prices	Average annual real wage earnings
1930	100.0	100.0	100.0
1931	98.2	93.4	105.1
1932	96.3	91.1	105.7
1933	95.3	88.6	107.6
1934	96.4	89.2	108.1
1935	98.0	90.5	108.3
1936	100.2	93.0	107.7
1937	102.8	97.5	105.4
1938	106.3	98.7	107.7

Source: J. Stevenson, *British Society 1914–45*, p. 117

continued to fall faster than wage rates up to 1933, and thereafter did not generally keep pace with rising wage rates. As a result, for those in work, the 1930s saw 'a substantial improvement in living standards compared with the 1920s'.[4]

The overall effects of the distinctive 1930s British experience were far-reaching. The less sudden and convulsive effects of the Slump upon the British system, combined with improved living standards for the employed, general middle-class affluence and more widespread consumerism (see below, pp. 360–61), and more pronounced economic recovery than in the United States, largely accounted for the greater stability and political, economic and social continuities evident on this side of the Atlantic. In Britain the increasingly *differential* experiences of workers, based upon geographical and economic location (between 1918 and 1939 almost one-fifth of British workers were rehoused, many of them on 'green field' estates: J. Cronin, p. 82), patterns of employment, living standards and leisure preferences, stood in marked contrast to the *common* economic disasters befalling all manner of workers in the United States. In the latter country the heterogeneous and frequently conflict-ridden working class of the 1920s became more homogeneous during the Great Depression. In Britain the relative working-class homogeneity of the 1920s gave way to greater fragmentation. Finally, and despite the limited advances registered by both the trade unions and the Labour Party from 1933 onwards, the British labour movement became even more defensive and cautious, desperately seeking out the 'responsible' and 'respectable' middle-ground of politics, eager to please and to demonstrate its electability. In the United States, in stark contrast to the 1920s, large numbers of workers turned to radical forms of protest, and the 1930s would see the successful development of 'new unionism' in the United States. Indeed, we can now usefully turn to a consideration of the nature, aims and general characteristics of popular protest movements in the two countries.

1930s POPULAR PROTEST: THE UNITED STATES

The story of the quickened and extended radicalism of American workers during Bernstein's 'turbulent years', and particularly the rise of the CIO, has been told many times. The purpose here is not to rehearse the full story, but to provide a summary of key events and developments and then to offer some evaluations. A similar procedure will be adopted in relation to Britain. We will then be in a stronger position to make further transnational comparisons, especially in relation to our dominant theme of class and exceptionalism.

The pre-CIO Years

The hunger marches and unemployed struggles of the late 1920s and early 1930s were indicative of the growing unrest among America's workers.[5] In Chicago, Harlem, the Bronx, Detroit, Washington, San Francisco and elsewhere thousands protested against unemployment, cuts in relief and evictions. At the forefront of such struggles were the Unemployed Councils, organised by the Communist Party, and gaining substantial support, especially in black communities. As Green notes, 'In Chicago alone, party members and other radicals mobilized over 2,000 demonstrations demanding relief and blocking evictions, especially in the South Side "black belt." ' Party demands for immediate federal assistance to the unemployed, a moratorium on mortgages, and national unemployment insurance also won considerable backing. Civil-rights work in the South, as seen most dramatically in the defence of the 'Scottsboro boys' (unfairly tried and convicted of rape), in the brutally repressed Sharecroppers' Union in Alabama, and close involvement in the union struggles of Kentucky miners and southern textile workers, further gained respect and admiration for Party comrades from predominantly non-Communist workers. Other radicals in the Socialist Party and the American Workers' Party were also prominent in unemployed struggles.

Green observes that the struggles of the unemployed 'met with brutal opposition from authorities'. A sit-in by First World War veterans in Washington was 'routed by tanks and army troops' in 1932. In the same year marchers in Detroit, protesting against unemployment and conditions in the Ford factories of the area, saw four of their number killed by police fire and over fifty wounded. Repression failed, however, to silence growing popular radicalism. As Robert Zieger remarks:

> The wide range of protest – the demonstrations, anti-eviction actions, relief riots, and street marches – never coalesced into a mass movement or achieved the kind of political consciousness Communists and Socialists sought. Yet these protests made it abundantly clear that working people would fight for their homes, and that those in power could not count on permanent quiescence, and that if traditional leadership did not respond to the crisis, working people could turn to corps of energetic, articulate radicals for support.

By 1935 the combined unemployment movement had organised some 450,000 workers. But in the wake of Franklin D. Roosevelt's victory over Herbert Hoover in 1932, his assumption of presidential office and the creation of the National Recovery Administration in 1933, the focus of popular struggle increasingly moved to the workplace. By no means unambiguously supportive of the labour movement, the early NRA did nevertheless seek to rescue American capitalism from the edge of the abyss by resurrecting consumer demand and effecting a more economically productive balance between labour and capital. In return for exemption from anti-trust legislation, capitalists were compelled 'to adopt presidentially sanctioned codes that established minimum wages and maximum hours, eliminated child labor, and recognized the right of workers to organize unions and bargain collectively'.[6] Section 7a of the National Industrial Recovery Act, while providing state support for workers' rights to organise and choose their own unions, nevertheless lacked the crucial power of legislative enforcement. In practice many employers used their considerable powers to simply defeat unionising drives and to create company unions.

There was, however, to be no return to the 1920s. Many saw Section 7a as symbolic of 'official' support for unions, as marking a complete break with the state's support for non-unionism during the 1920s. Unions had been badly hit by the Depression, membership in 1933 standing at 2,805,000, approximately one-tenth of the non-agricultural labour force and 0.5 million and 1 million fewer members than in, respectively, 1929 and 1923. But, as Milton observes, 'workers throughout the country responded to ... Section 7a ... with the greatest strike wave since 1921'.[7] Car workers, textile operatives, miners, steelworkers and others struck in support of union recognition, improved conditions and general opposition to employer 'despotism'. Hall, Korstad and Leloudis provide a vivid account of developments in the textile South:

> Across the Piedmont, mill hands listened eagerly to Roosevelt's fireside chats and signed on as 'members of the NRA'. Recovery legislation seemed to place the federal government's imprimateur on ideals of equity, independence, and cooperation. Everyone, from the lowliest sweeper to the most skilled loom fixer, could join in a fervent campaign to put the industry, and the nation, back on its feet ... But the NIRA also promised something altogether new: the intervention of a powerful third party as leverage against local élites and a guarantor of workers' rights. Within less than a month, union locals had sprung to life in 75 per cent of South Carolina's mills. UTW membership jumped from an estimated forty thousand members in September 1933 to two hundred seventy thousand by August 1934. To the shock of government officials and businessmen alike, southern workers organized.[8]

Mass militancy, mass participation and seemingly spontaneous enthusiasm for collective organisation on the part of many considered 'unorganisable' by many AFL bureaucrats, mushroomed in 1934. Approximately 1.5 million workers went on strike in support of issues such as union organisation and recognition, wage increases, common ground rules concerning layoffs and promotion (the issue of 'recall by seniority' becoming 'a central feature of the emerging industrial unionism'),[9] greater worker controls over labour supply (by means of the closed shop and union hiring halls), and opposition to speed-up and intolerable working conditions. There were four major city-wide strikes and social upheavals (in some ways reminiscent of those in 1877, 1886 and at various points between 1912 and 1922): in Toledo (centring upon auto-parts workers); in San Francisco (led by the longshoremen, and involving a longshoremen's shutdown of most of the Pacific Coast ports and a four-days' general strike in San Francisco); the truckers' strike in Minneapolis; and the national strike in textiles lasting 22 days and involving some 400,000 workers. The demands of workers in Toledo, San Francisco and Minneapolis were largely successful, but the textile strike was lost. 'Picket lines', note Dowd Hall, Korstad and Leloudis, 'faltered before machine guns and fixed bayonets'. Federal mediation proved unhelpful (Roosevelt himself refused to intervene), and employers sat out the conflict and then purged activists from their cotton mills. The South returned to non-union 'normalcy' and defeated workers once more reined in their ambitions:

> Mill hands learned from their history, and in 1934 the lesson for many was a deep distrust of government and trade unions alike. Above all, the General Strike drove home the cost of challenging the established order. Better the familiar securities of job and home than 'air and promises', followed by exile, suffering and defeat.[10]

Elsewhere there were unmistakeable, if limited, signs of advance. 1934 saw workers organise themselves in auto, rubber and the electrical industry. The AFL enrolled some of these predominantly semi-skilled and second-generation 'new' immigrants in large federal unions. But the growing militancy of sections of the mass-production workforce and the unwillingness of AFL unions to change their organisational structures and modify their jurisdictional claims would place great strains upon the Federation's ability to control labour developments in steel, auto and elsewhere. As realised by Lewis and Hillman, the mass organisation of these industries necessitated the creation of mass, industrial unions. The refusal of the AFL to take the necessary steps would create the space for the emergence of the rival CIO in 1935.

Comments

Before considering developments during the second half of the decade it is, however, important to pause in order to comment upon the upsurges of 1933 and 1934. The first, and most obvious, point to make is that these two years witnessed a revival of widespread workplace militancy which had lain largely dormant since the early 1920s. Second, the capacities for mass independent rank-and-file activity and organisation were extremely marked. As David Brody has argued, 'the brief upsurge of the early NRA period was probably the high point for mass participation during the entire period. Thereafter, rank-and-file activism was confined to relatively small numbers, although present in all the mass-production industries'.[11] Third, the CIO was in many ways grafted on to this prior movement of mass insurgency. Mike Davis has well recaptured this relationship:

> the original Committee for Industrial Organization was an alliance of dissident trade-union bureaucrats, with important financial resources and friends in high places, created for the purpose of capturing an already existent mass movement of industrial shop committees and rebel locals – a movement with dangerous embryonic proclivities toward an anti-Gompersian model of class struggle unionism.[12]

Fourth, the constituency of protest was extensive, embracing skilled and non-skilled workers from varied ethnic backgrounds, and groups such as longshoremen and auto-parts workers who were radical members of the AFL, presenting a challenge to the caution and conservatism of the Federation, and greatly extending the boundaries of 'craft' unionism (Harry Bridges, for example, wished to organise the whole of San Francisco's waterfront).

Fifth, as a portent of developments within the CIO, two groups played key leadership roles in 1933 and 1934: left-wing revolutionaries (such as the Communist Party members active in San Francisco and the Trotskyites in Minneapolis); and, as Ronald Schatz has shown in relation to the electrical industry, skilled and often 'old-stock' 'autonomous workmen', generally indispensable within production yet being subjected during the Depression years to downgrading pressures and nagging and infuriating insults and humiliations (on the part of foremen and managers) to their strong pride and independence. These 'autonomous workmen' also frequently hailed from radical socialist or communist backgrounds.[13] As in Britain during the late 1880s and early 1890s, the American insurgencies of 1933 and 1934 were thus not solely confined to 'new' unionists. Threatened 'labour aristocrats' were also key players in the unfolding American drama.

Finally, it is highly significant that many of the disputes revolved, at least directly, less around hours and conditions than the issue of union organisation. The primary aim was to counteract employer 'despotism' by means of collective organisation. Notions of pride, self-respect, democracy within the workplace, and control were at the very centre of 1930s American workers' struggles. Indeed, David Brody calculates that, 'no less than half the strikes of the mid-1930s were fought over basic rights of organization rather than over wages, hours and conditions'.[14] The sons and daughters of 'new' immigrants, who had been subjected to the full effects of employer 'tyranny', poor wages and often appalling working conditions during the open-shop 1920s, duly stood at the forefront of the 1930s mass struggle for citizenship rights at the workplace.

The CIO Years

The second and third phases of 1930s workers' industrial struggles, from 1935 to 1937 and from 1937 to the outbreak of the Second World War, have been extensively documented and accordingly demand less description than the first phase.[15] The year 1935 saw the birth of the CIO and the Wagner Act. The latter's crucial importance lay in the fact that it buttressed the abstract right to union organisation of the NIRA with powers of *legal enforcement*. The Act, as noted by Brody, made it 'unfair labor practice for an employer to "interfere with, restrain, or coerce employees in the exercise" of "the right of self-organization" '. Employers were henceforth 'prohibited . . . from dominating or supporting a labor union', and 'having proved its majority in an "appropriate" unit, a union became the certified bargaining agent for all employees in the unit'. A National Labor Relations Board, 'clothed with powers of investigation and enforcement', would oversee the whole process.[16] This was a truly remarkable development. The American state, long noted for its support for *laissez-faire* policies, had intervened to legally safeguard the existence of trade unions duly receiving majority support from workers in the appropriate workplace unit of representation. No longer, as so often in the past, would employers be able to employ naked power and force to defeat popularly supported unions. Company unionism was, in effect, outlawed and workers sacked on account of their union activities would be reinstated with back pay.

As Brody declares, 'assured of their safety, workers flocked into the unions'. Between 1936 and 1937 some 4 million workers were active in the CIO, and approximately half a million were involved in the famous sit-down strikes at Flint and elsewhere. The bedrock of the CIO's support lay with second-generation 'new' immigrant workers in the mass-production industries of steel, auto, rubber and electrical manufacturing. And, frequently under the class-conscious leadership of local communists and socialists, determined efforts were made to recruit black workers, to break down ethnic and other divisions among workers, and to 'root' the CIO in the lives of people both inside and outside the place of work. Of special significance were the constructive efforts of unions such as the United Electrical Workers to help unemployed members in obtaining relief payments, in overcoming bureaucratic hurdles, and in maintaining their active involvement in union affairs.[17] (All too often AFL and British unions effectively failed to meet the needs of unemployed members during the inter-war period.) The CIO's commitment to a 'culture of unity' also extended to leisure. Lizabeth Cohen's comments in relation to Chicago are instructive:

> CIO unions put great efforts into developing social and recreation programs where workers who had little contact inside or outside the plant could develop stronger ties to each other through sharing leisure time. The pages of CIO newspapers were filled with reports of dances, picnics, summer camps, softball teams ... and bowling leagues ... Recreation could provide a glue to bind workers of different races, ethnicities, and ages together.[18]

The CIO also made significant, yet limited, efforts to recruit women. In meatpacking the union's demand for 'equal pay for equal work' elicited strong women's support, and Kessler-Harris notes that the relatively small but growing numbers of low-paid women in automobile, rubber, the metal trades, glassware and leather 'eagerly joined CIO unions in the mass drives of 1936–9'. Similarly, there were important attempts to extend the benefits of unionism to the large numbers of women in clerical work, and to some women workers in the South. There were, however, limitations. The CIO's central commitment to a 'family-oriented union culture' included a belief in the virtues of 'traditional womanhood'. Women were accordingly mainly viewed 'as temporary workers and potential wives and mothers, not as equals in their unions' (Sharon Hartman Strom). In Chicago and elsewhere women played a predominantly supportive role in the labour movement, founding women's auxiliaries which raised money, operating soup kitchens, and generally encouraging women to support their striking menfolk. And Hartman Strom concludes that office-worker unions continued 'to be institutions which mirrored the sexual division of labor at work. Male unionists shaped policy in such a way as to win benefits mainly for themselves and to prevent women from climbing out of the lower levels of clerical work.' This conclusion could usefully be applied to vast segments of the American economy.[19]

On balance the CIO did, nevertheless, make determined, and in many cases highly successful efforts, to break out of the narrow membership and constituency straitjackets of the AFL. As in so many other periods of mass insurgency – in the 1830s and 1840s and 1910–14 in Britain, the 1880s and 1916–22 in the United States – there developed an

expanded radical constituency and an emphasis upon the community-
as well as the work-based aspects of working-class life. There also
undoubtedly existed many radical spirits within the ranks of the CIO,
and a greatly enhanced feeling of 'Us and Them'. Class was at the heart
of the CIO experience. The question, What kind of class consciousness?
is, however, a query which we will return to at the end of our story.

By the autumn of 1937 the CIO appeared to be all conquering.
Impressive solidarity, tactical daring and innovation (as seen most dramatically in the 477 sitdowns conducted in the spring of 1937), determination and inspired leadership had, records Mike Davis, 'breached for
the first time the main bastions of capital'. Victories at US Steel, General
Electric, Chrysler and General Motors, however dramatic, did not mean
that the war was over. Labour's titanic struggles could not conceal the
fact that the era of *mass* involvement belonged more to the first phase
of protest rather than the second. As demonstrated by David Brody,
Peter Friedlander, Steve Jefferys and others, militancy was more patchy
than often thought and in many cases victories were achieved on the
basis of the activities of a 'militant minority' within the workforce.
Furthermore, its constitutional standing unclear, the Wagner Act was
'virtually ignored by antiunion employers' between 1935 and 1937. The
depression of 1937–8 saw unemployment soar and union membership
gains threatened. Indeed, between the end of 1937 and 1939 the unions'
massive advance (in 1937) considerably slowed down. It would take the
soaring demand of the war, worker militancy and government support
for 'responsible' bureaucratic trade unionism to spectacularly advance
the gains made by 1938.[20]

Comments

The industrial protests of the 1930s invite a number of comments. We
should first of all acknowledge the important union breakthrough
achieved by the CIO (the AFL also showed vigorous evidence of recovery during the second half of the 1930s). As demonstrated in Table 5.3,
from 1934 onwards the trade-union decline of the early 1930s was
reversed. Indeed, by 1939 the United States had more union members
than Great Britain, 6,339,000 as opposed to 6,298,000, (although union
density remained far higher in the latter country, 31.6 per cent to 14.9
per cent), and had easily surpassed the union highpoint of 4,775,000 in
1920. The war would greatly accelerate such favourable trends. 'By
1944' notes David Montgomery, 'the average production worker in basic
industry was a union member for the first time in American history'.[21]

Trade-union growth resulted from the convergence of specific influences and longer-term structural factors, most of which we have already

Table 5.3 Trade-union Membership and Density in the USA, 1931–9

	Union membership (000s) NBER	Density (%)
1931	3,142	8.6
1932	2,968	7.9
1933	2,805	7.3
1934	3,448	8.9
1935	3,609	9.1
1936	3,932	9.8
1937	5,563	13.6
1938	5,850	14.0
1939	6,339	14.9

Source: G. S. Bain and R. Price, op. cit., pp. 88–9

touched upon if not brought together. It was above all the collapse of the 1920s 'system', its inability to 'deliver the goods', its raising (by means of welfare capitalism and consumerism) and then deflating of popular expectations and 'needs', and its widespread inducement of a sense of betrayal against employers and establishment institutions (such as banks) which provided the broad context in which reawakened popular protest and the rise of the CIO must be situated. The evils and excesses of the 'drive system' at work, the adverse effects of technological change upon the nature and performance of jobs (for both the skilled and non-skilled) and workplace relations,[22] the 'despotism' of the bosses, the changed consciousness and greater unity and cultural toleration within the working class, talented and dedicated local leadership and the powerful national presence of John L. Lewis, Sidney Hillman and others,[23] and the essential protective shield provided by the Wagner Act, were all interrelated factors of major importance. The negative effects of the Agricultural Adjustment Act upon share croppers and tenant farmers (with subsidised richer farmers who severely cut back on production and letting arrangements) and its promotion of waged labour may also have advanced the appeal of the CIO, especially in the South.[24]

As argued by historians such as Schatz, Dubofsky, Davis, Brody and Dawley,[25] we must be careful not to romanticise 1930s trade-union developments. Thus Davis:

> The CIO was not, as it has often been popularly depicted, the product of a single, heroic upsurge of working-class ardor. On the contrary, the new industrial unions were formed by highly

uneven, discontinuous movements of mass organization which mobilized different strata of the proletariat.

Similarly, fear, passivity and militancy often existed among different
workers within the same workplace. In parts of the electrical goods
industry welfare capitalism, employer paternalism and non-union company loyalty survived the 1930s. And, as Dawley usefully reminds us,
'the level of strikes in the 1930s never approached that of 1919–1920'.[26]

The outstanding facts of unprecedented union breakthrough in mass
production and of greatly extended official recognition and institutionalised collective bargaining cannot, however, be denied. It is also beyond
doubt that radicals and left-wingers continued, in the years from 1935
onwards, to play important roles in providing union leadership, organisation and policy. Furthermore, as highlighted by Montgomery, there did
occur significant, if uneven, changes in popular consciousness which
have been often overlooked by those New-Left historians seeing the
CIO as the agent of working-class incorporation into 'corporate liberalism'. Thus Montgomery:

> Contemporaries sometimes discerned profound changes in workers'
> consciousness and in local politics associated with the coming of
> the CIO – changes that historians have only recently started to
> appreciate. Louis Adamic wrote in *My America* of Slavic communi-
> ties tingling with a realization that they could humble mighty bosses
> and politicians, and live no longer 'under America'. Peter Fried-
> lander has indicated how this process unfolded day by day...
> George Powers revealed that a toppling of long entrenched political
> machines all along the Monongahela Valley was the immediate
> consequence of the unionization of U.S. Steel. Similarly the simul-
> taneous emergence of union, political and race consciousness which
> Horace Cayton and St. Clair Drake sensed among Chicago's black
> packinghouse workers, has recently been discovered by Horace
> Huntley in Alabama's iron mines and by Meier and Rudwick in
> Detroit.[27]

Radicalism, socialism and communism were nevertheless subordinated,
as pinpointed by Brody, to that 'wholly conventional trade-union objective – a collective-bargaining contract'. The vast mass of workers
involved in 1930s protest and 'orthodox' trade unionism were converted
neither to revolutionary socialism nor to independent labour politics.
The local studies of auto workers by Friedlander and Jefferys make
specifically clear an important general fact: communist and socialist
activists were welcomed by the mass of workers far less on account of
their 'private' politics than of their unstinting efforts on behalf of trade
unionism. In conjunction with the spirited revival of the 'old' AFL, the
'new' unionism of the CIO thus occurred, concludes Brody, 'within
the framework of traditional trade unionism'. Part of the story resides

therefore not in a simple dichotomy between *either* 'spontaneous rank-and-file militancy' or 'bureaucratic trade unionism's sell-out', but in the complex and ongoing interplays between radical and conventional goals and tensions within 1930s popular movements.[28]

We can develop the story further. Although 'traditional', the demand for union recognition was by no means necessarily moderate or assured of success. As we have seen in the cases of Chartism, the Knights of Labor, the Populists and strikers in both countries in the immediate post-war years, goals which appear to their holders to be eminently reasonable, just and moderate may not appear to be so to employers and those in the commanding heights of the state. In such contexts seemingly moderate goals can trigger off sustained and radicalising conflicts. It is thus the overall context in which ideas and goals are expressed which renders them 'moderate', 'reformist' or 'revolutionary' rather than in the very nature of the words themselves. Yet the outstanding irony of 1930s American trade unionism was the fact that what began, to quote Schatz, as 'a locally based, rank-and-file effort', resulted in 'bureaucratic international unions and a system of labor relations regulated by federal law and codified in national contracts'.[29] Not only had the AFL's prized and long-established 'voluntarism' bitten the dust, but so also had the far from 'incorporationist' aims of many 'new' union pioneers. By the late 1940s the CIO had, at least at the national level, become a very powerful incorporationist and conservative force. Communists and other radicals had been largely purged from its ranks, and the Congress was resolutely pursuing the Cold War. As Montgomery has observed, 'assimilation through opposition' had become the dominant feature of American labour from the mid 1930s to the mid–late 1940s.

Wherein lay the roots of the CIO's accommodation to Roosevelt's New Deal? The answer lies in part in the traditional and predominantly economistic goals of many trade-union leaders and sections of the rank and file. But, more crucially, the responses to organised labour's demands and to wider working-class protest by the New Deal administration, key figures in the state machinery, and by the Democratic Party mattered most. It is to this issue of responses that we will now turn.

We have already established that massive sections of American industry did not welcome trade unionism. Only declining profits, the competitive disadvantages of non-recognition of unions, sustained worker pressure and effective legislation brought about significant changes in the policies of the major employers. But even on the eve of the war the battle for recognition had been far from completely won.[30] The wartime experience was, as in so many other areas, to prove of crucial importance in the field of workplace relations.

Far less hostile than the employers, the Roosevelt administration, especially in the pre-1936 years, was nevertheless somewhat cool towards the claims of trade unionism.[31] As Paul Edwards has declared, the aim of the NRA 'was to restore American capitalism to profitability'. This was to be achieved by curbing 'excessive' corporate power, and by regulating and stabilising competition and prices via 'the promulgation within each industry of codes of fair competition which would establish minimum labour standards and permit the fixing of minimum prices, so that a process based on industrial self-government could be initiated'. The state was to become more interventionist in an attempt to revive the fortunes of, rather than supplant, private capital. The fact that there was widespread opposition by employers to intervention in their affairs was far more a reflection of American capitalists' prized attachment to autonomy than sufficient evidence in favour of the wholly autonomous role of the state in public affairs. The state, as self-proclaimed guardian of the 'national interest' and the (especially perceived) overall legitimacy of the system, as well as a key player in the continued reproduction of labour power and the generation of surplus value under conditions of private ownership, was keen to be seen to act on behalf of 'the People' as a whole rather than of sectional interests. In pursuance of these holistic goals, and especially during this period of massive economic crisis, the state was prepared to come into conflict with and overcome the sectional interests of labour and capital.

The New Deal experience does indeed invalidate a simple, instrumentalist or reductionist view of the state – as the direct agent of the self-expressed views of individual and collective units of capital. But, contrary to the view expressed in much recent writing, a reductionist notion of the state is not synonymous with a historical-materialist approach. We can largely accept Marx's view of the state – as a complex means of class rule, simultaneously responding to and shaping the outcomes of contradictory pressures (from employers, workers and others) in specific contexts over time, in the overall interest of the dominant mode of capitalist production and its attendant social relations.[32]

These general considerations had immediate bearing upon the actions of Roosevelt and the NRA. As 'national saviour', healer of social divisions, and restorer of capitalist efficiency, Roosevelt was not primarily concerned with the demands of organised labour. And his attitudes and policies towards the union movement have been variously described as problematic, cool and inadvertent (Brody and Edwards). As Brody informs us, the 'notion that labor should have the right to organize and engage in collective bargaining had long preceded the coming of the New Deal', and was embodied in the Norris-LaGuardia Act of 1932. Section 7a of the NIRA was, according to Howell Harris 'so largely the unintended result of an incredibly confused legislative process that it is still difficult ... to explain quite how or why it happened'. 'But', continues Harris,

> it is clear that the initiative for including what became 7(a) came from the AFL, not from any section of organised business or the administration; and that the subsequent beefing-up of 7(a) in committee similarly owed nothing to administration support, which was conspicuously absent, and occurred over the desperate opposition of the National Association of Manufacturers (NAM) and other weak and disunited business groups.

Beyond 1933 Roosevelt 'persisted in seeing the industrial problem as getting the workers to work and not of giving them the right of self-organization' (Edwards). According to Howell Harris, Senator Wagner, 'almost singlehandedly, and against the odds, sustained the campaign for federal labor law reform in 1934 and 1935'. The Roosevelt administration had 'torpedoed' Wagner's initiatives in 1934, and 'withheld support from the second version until the Senate was about to pass it' (Brody). And, notes Brody, the other public-spirited men 'who carried labor's fight, occupied state houses, mayors' offices, and congressional seats' worked 'independently of the New Deal administration'. 'Only during World War II', concludes Brody,

> can it be said that the Roosevelt administration pursued labor policies that deliberately promoted union growth, but even conservatives understood that this had nothing to do with reform, and everything to do with carrying on an efficient war effort.

Roosevelt's conservatism did not, however, constitute the total picture. Of major significance were popular perceptions and expectations of the New Deal. As we demonstrated earlier in relation to southern textile workers, large numbers of workers believed that Section 7a symbolised official presidential support for unionisation. And shrewd union organisers capitalised upon such legitimising beliefs. Most famously, Lewis, in 1933, and the CIO, in 1936, employed the slogan, 'The President Wants You to Organize', to great effect. Furthermore, in large measure a response to the widespread popular protests of 1934 (involving not only strikes but Huey Long's 'Share the Wealth' movement, Upton Sinclair's popular 'End Poverty in California' gubernatorial campaign, and the important campaign organised by the Southern Tenant Farmers' Union) and the mounting unpopularity of big business (especially its perceived 'selfishness' and economic ineffectiveness), the New Deal of 1935 took a progressive turn away from its prior pro-business stance.[33] In addition to his endorsement of the Wagner Act, Roosevelt threw his support behind progressive taxation and social security legislation. And during 1936 and 1937 Roosevelt's implied support for the CIO, as manifested in his advocacy of mediation rather than state repression of industrial disputes, allowed him 'to appear as the savior of industrial unionism' (Davis). In the Flint sit-down strike of 1937, for example, Roosevelt and Murphy, Michigan's New Deal governor, refused to evict the strikers by force. 'Had either man ordered troops', declares James Green,

> political history might have taken a different turn. Labor party sentiment, already on the rise in the UAW, might have been hard to resist. Instead, UAW leaders ... joined other CIO officials in developing a working relationship with professional politicians in the Democratic party.

Similar developments took place in many other parts of the country, Democratic officials providing an important political shield against forces hostile to mass unionism. Indeed, Howell Harris claims that the Democratic Party was recast 'into a close approximation to a labour party in numerous industrial districts'.[34]

Albeit in the somewhat unintentional and chequered manner described above, the New Deal administration, important sectors of the state machinery, and the Democratic Party thus did play important roles in the development of mass-production unionism. By 1937, in marked contrast to most of the period considered in this book, organised labour in America had found effective defenders at the highest levels of the state.

We should finally note that the CIO's support for the Democratic Party, effectively in place by 1937, was neither preordained nor unproblematically achieved. Alternatives to the left of the Democratic Party, and especially the creation of a national labour party, were an important part of organised labour's political agenda during the 1930s. In the 1932 presidential election the Communists and Socialists achieved a combined total of almost 1 million votes (880,000 of them being Socialist). But, given the depth of the Depression and the seeming accuracy of left-wing propaganda that capitalism was on the point of collapse, this total was not encouraging.[35] The following four years did, however, bring more promising political signs. The Farmer-Labor Party in Minnesota, for example, strengthened its hold on the levers of power. Floyd Olson was re-elected governor in 1932 and 1934. In the latter year the FLP's convention demanded 'immediate steps ... to abolish capitalism in a peaceful and lawful manner'. And in 1936 the Party's candidate for governor, Elmer Benson, 'won a record 58 per cent of the votes ... five of the nine congressmen were FLP, and the party had 50,000 dues-paying members and 100,000 subscribers to its paper'.[36] The employment of force by Democratic governors to defeat the textile workers' strike in 1934, Communist agitation in favour of a new party and the brief agreement of the Communists and Socialists on this issue, and Roosevelt's refusal to support Wagner's bill all kept alive the idea of independent labour politics. Indeed, despite the Wagner Act, CIO militancy in 1936–7 meant, according to Brody, that 'for a brief moment . . . a labor party seemed a genuine possibility'.[37] Finally, the economic crisis of 1937–8, the renewed determination of anti-union employers to fight their corner, the conservative political revival of 1938, and state repression of strikes and relief riots in 1939 once more raised the possibility of the emergence of a national labor party.[38]

As so often in the past, possibility was not, however, translated into reality. In 1936 labour's Non-Partisan League, officially the independent political creation of the CIO, mainly acted in support of Roosevelt, and did not form the basis for a new party as hoped for on the Left. In reality, Roosevelt's impressive re-election victory in 1936 and his increasingly progressive stance cut away the ground on which a new party could be based. In Minnesota, effective anti-'Red' propaganda by New-Deal style Republicans and others, divisions within the ranks of farmers created by Roosevelt's favours to richer farmers, conflicts between Communists and Trotskyists, and the besieged Farmer-Labor Party's desperate attempts to rid itself of its socialist image all proved highly debilitating to the Farmer-Laborites. By 1940, observes Montgomery, the MFLP's membership had disastrously declined to 4,000: the end arrived in 1944 in the merger movement with the Democrats. On a national level, the seemingly massive opportunities for independent labour politics presented between 1937 and 1939 were shattered by divisions within labour's ranks. The Communist Party had already effectively pledged its support to Roosevelt in line with its turn to a Popular Front strategy. The Socialist Party, torn by internal faction fights, increasingly cooled in the post-1936 period towards the notion of independent labour or farmer-labour politics. And most crucially, at least according to Mike Davis, the AFL's war against the CIO during the late 1930s, including opposition to any political candidate favourable towards the CIO, effectively split the labour vote and 'undermined the base of state third-party movements, city-wide labor tickets, and the left wing of the New Deal'. In sum, and despite the 'quixotic' politics of the AFL, by the early 1940s organised labour had consummated its marriage with the Democratic Party. And the latter, given its representation of capitalists, southern planters and workers, epitomised the continuing American tradition of widely based coalition politics to a much greater extent than its more working-class-based British counterpart, the Labour Party.[39]

Table 5.4 Trade-union Membership and Density in Britain, 1931–9

	Union membership (000s)	Density (%)
1931	4,624	24.0
1932	4,444	23.0
1933	4,392	22.6
1934	4,590	23.5
1935	4,867	24.9
1936	5,295	26.9
1937	5,842	29.6
1938	6,053	30.5
1939	6,298	31.6

Source: G. S. Bain and R. Price, op. cit., p. 37

POPULAR MOVEMENTS IN BRITAIN

Trade Unionism and Industrial Protest

Industrial and trade-union developments in 1930s Britain were far less dramatic than in New Deal America. As seen in Table 5.4, trade-union membership followed a similar trajectory to that of its American counterpart. The worst years of the Slump, 1930–3, saw an accelerated decline of British trade unionism, but, as in America, the years from 1934 to 1939 saw a considerable strengthening of the movement. Indeed, and in the absence of the massive 'new' unionist upsurge associated with the CIO, British unionism increased by 42.7 per cent between 1933 and 1939.[40] Coalmining unions recovered from their nadir of 1933 to increase their membership by almost 30 per cent. But it was in bricks and building, chemicals and allied trades, electrical goods, and in metals and engineering – areas of economic recovery or the sites of 'new' industries – that rapid gains in both numbers and union density (often from relatively small bases) were recorded. There were also important conflicts in transport (especially among busmen) and motor cars. But cars remained largely unorganised up to 1939 and beyond.

In somewhat different circumstances to the American case, the revival of British trade unionism took place during a period of relatively strong economic recovery (thus demonstrating both the importance and insufficiency of economic developments to trends in trade unionism). In both countries trade unionism throughout the 1930s remained above the 1913 level. In America the highpoint of 1920 was consistently surpassed between 1937 and 1939, whereas the 6,298,000 recorded union members in Britain in 1939 (the record for the 1930s) fell short of both the

6,533,000 for 1918 and the 8,348,000 for 1920. But British trade unionism retained much of its comparative strength and resiliency. Thus, apart from the numerical superiority of American unions in 1939, British trade unionism continued to enjoy both absolutely higher numbers and much higher density than its American counterpart during the 1930s. As in the United States, the Second World War would provide a further boost to the fortunes of trade unionism in Britain.

To proceed to a more detailed breakdown, the history of trade unionism and industrial protest in 1930s Britain can usefully be divided into the pre- and post-1934 years. In both periods we witness an ongoing, if variable, dialectical process between official trade-union moderation and attempts to stimulate rank-and-file militancy.

In the midst of the Slump unions busied themselves in attempting to fend off or lessen the cuts in wages demanded by employers. And, as noted by Chris Wrigley, 'while trade union leaders such as Bevin negotiated lesser cuts ... in many sectors rank-and-file movements sprang up in 1932 and 1933 to oppose cuts or demand the restoration of the rates cut'. The year 1932 saw the inaugural conference of the Railwaymen's Vigilance Movement, and mass support for the demands of the London Busmen's Rank and File Committee that the redundancies and wage cuts declared by the company be withdrawn. In the event the company agreed to their withdrawal upon condition of the introduction of improved and faster schedules. Attempts to reorganise methods of work, by means of the Bedaux system, sparked off numerous disputes in this period: in cars and hosiery in 1932; in parts of woodworking in 1933; and in metalworking in Manchester between 1933 and 1935. There was protracted and widespread conflict in cotton concerning wage cuts and proposed increases in the number of looms operated by each weaver. The year 1929 had seen almost 400,000 cotton operatives locked out. At its height, in 1932, the 'More Looms' dispute led to 'the greatest clash Lancashire had seen since the Plug Riots of 1842'. Having been defeated on both the wages and more looms issues, the cotton workers were, observes Hinton, subjected to 'a vicious circle of speed-up, competitive wage-cutting and factory closures'. Government intervention was eventually required in order to restore collective bargaining in weaving.[41]

The early 1930s also saw 'hunger marches', mainly organised by the Communist-dominated National Unemployed Workers' Movement, and protests against the 'means test'. The latter was introduced in 1931 in order to officially scrutinise the 'transitional' relief claims made by those who had exhausted their entitlement to twenty-six weeks unemployment benefit. As Stevenson remarks, the means test became 'one of the most despised aspects of the inter-war years', signifying a fall from respect for those workers subjected to the prying and frequently condescending attitudes and attentions of members of the local Public Assistance Committee.[42] Opposition to the introduction of the means test was often led by local Labour parties. But, in addition to its organisation of the hunger marches, the NUWM also played a key anti-means test role. Indeed, despite official opposition from the national Labour Party (which instructed local parties and trades councils not to help the NUWM), the NUWM claimed a membership of between 50,000 and 100,000 in 1931–2. Wal Hannington and his comrades organised national hunger marches to London in 1930, 1932, 1934 and 1936. None of these marches received the Labour Party's official support, although in 1934 and 1936 Party members did ignore the leadership's bans. (The famous Jarrow March of 1935 was organised by Ellen Wilkinson, the Labour MP, but the TUC and the Labour Party's National Executive still did not offer co-operation.) The considerable national and local impact of the NUWM in the early 1930s has been noted by Cronin:

> When the national Government came to power in August 1931 on a programme of reducing benefits, the NUWM was able to lead substantial resistance among the unemployed. A hunger march was organized from Wales to the TUC meeting in Bristol in September, and a bitter clash with police resulted. In the next month, demonstrations took place in Cardiff, Nottingham, Manchester. Derby and numerous other industrial towns ... from November 1931 through February 1932 demonstrations spread to Yorkshire, the Northeast, Merseyside and the potteries. Some 40,000 signed petitions in Birmingham, while 100,000 marched on Tyneside ... In the autumn there were riots in Birkenhead and a national hunger march to London, met by a crowd of nearly 100,000.[43]

Such important instances of protest must, however, be set against the largely defensive and disillusioned mood of workers and organised labour during the first half of the decade. Labour had suffered a major electoral defeat in 1931; its record on unemployment was in tatters, and it had been deserted by two of its key leaders. The trade-union leadership was advocating caution and moderation at all costs. Troublesome 'agitators' were to be purged from the movement. The 1932 strike in cotton would prove to be the last national strike in Britain before the outbreak of the Second World War. And, despite the undoubted successes of the NUWM, large numbers of the unemployed did not organise, and most unions did little to relate to those out of work. Influential in the NUWM, the Communist Party was widely distrusted in the labour movement, and its success in cultivating rank-and-file movements was not particularly marked in the years before 1935–6. In truth the industrial wing of the labour movement was dominated by cautious and hard-headed pragmatists, intent upon patiently achieving the long haul to renewed strength and respectability in the wake of the disasters of 1926 and 1931, and in the midst of depression. Much like the beleaguered Samuel Gompers of the late 1890s, they were dismissive of 'extreme' flights of fancy. Finally, Britain did not experience protests comparable in breadth and depth to those shaking American capitalism in 1933 and 1934.[44]

Economic recovery from 1934 onwards improved the fortunes of trade unionism. Thus Wrigley:

> By the mid-1930s the unions were no longer in retreat. Advances in wages were being pressed for, often with vigour. In 1934 the aggregate number of working days lost through strikes and lock-outs had fallen below 1 million for the first time since the figures had been compiled ... During 1935–39 the average number of days lost was just under 2 million per year. Of these, half the days lost took place in the coal mining industry.[45]

In 1935 the Miners' Federation launched a campaign which resulted in considerable wage increases and a return to national bargaining. Economic recovery and rearmament stimulated trade unionism in engineering and metals, union membership in these sectors increasing by 80 per cent, from 551,300 to 993,700, between 1933 and 1939. The Amalgamated Engineering Union, in particular, grew rapidly and organised increasing numbers of semi-skilled workers. Vastly increased expenditure upon aircraft, guaranteed orders, and extremely high profits and greatly quickened demand for labour meant that the aircraft industry became a very strong centre of trade unionism and shop stewards' organisation in the late 1930s, 'By 1939', records Wrigley, 'strike action was at its greatest for the decade with strikes in the aircraft industry accounting for about an eighth of all days lost in the metal, engineering and shipbuilding sector'. Unionism in electrical engineering likewise grew apace.[46]

As Richard Hyman has noted, 'in the more favourable conditions of the later 1930s, it is clear that independence and assertiveness recovered'.[47] This was particularly the case at shopfloor level. 'Taylorite' innovations, the rapid growth of piecework bargaining, the quickened demand for labour, the frequent inability of the dominant industry-wide bargaining system to respond quickly or flexibly enough to workplace grievances, and the general hostility of the union leadership towards shopfloor organisation, all provided the opportunity for a renewal of unofficial shopfloor initiatives. As in the early 1930s, members of the Communist Party played a key role in resurgent rank-and-file militancy in transport, car production, engineering and elsewhere. Having abandoned, in 1932, the 'entryist' tactics of the National Minority Movement, Communist Party members had turned instead to creating genuinely indigenous rank-and-file movements within specific industries. But they continued to face formidable opposition from Ernest Bevin of the TGWU and other moderate trade-union leaders. Bevin and Deakin thus 'crushed the Busmen's Rank and File Movement after the Coronation Strike of May 1937, which involved nearly 25,000 London busmen'.[48] Communist or exceptionally ardent rank-and-file spirits were expelled from the TGWU. Similarly, communists were outlawed from positions of elected office in the GMWU. And, as Stevenson declares, the 'T.U.C. remained firmly in the control of right-wing unionists who exerted considerable influence over the Labour Party in the years after 1931'.[49]

Still, by the end of the 1930s British trade unionism was in a reasonably strengthened state. In comparison with the early–mid 1930s workers were generally better paid, organised and able to enjoy improved conditions of work and holidays with pay. And radical workplace organisation had not been uniformly defeated. Thus Richard Price's favourable judgement:

> By the outbreak of war, the groundwork had been laid for the transformation of industrial relations. Workplace organisation had re-established itself, had begun to encroach upon managerial prerogatives, and had secured considerable gains in the core war industries.[50]

The Political Arena

No such revival was evident in the case of the Labour Party. By 1939 the National Government had been in power ever since the catastrophic events of 1931. In the latter year Labour's support at the polls had in fact been higher than in either 1923 or 1924. But, as Stevenson has argued, the 1931 election saw a 'massive reduction' in three-cornered contests and Labour fighting unsuccessfully against united opposition. A glaring indictment of the 'first past the post' electoral system, the 6.5 million votes cast for the Labour Party returned a mere 52 MPs (including ILPers). The fact that the Liberal decline continued (the Party's combined total of roughly 2.25 million votes representing a fall of 3 million from the Liberal vote of 1929), and that Labour now stood as the major opposition party, did little to quell the feelings of overwhelming failure and disappointment.[51]

Reactions to Labour's defeat varied. On the Left of the Party there still prevailed the belief that capitalism had displayed its innate contradictions and, above all, its descent into crisis. Political and economic logic demanded, therefore, that socialists abandon all attempts to apply capitalist solutions to the ills of the system (as exemplified by the actions of Snowden), to place paramount importance upon Labour's 'fitness to govern' (as epitomised by MacDonald), to seek to extract gradually better conditions for workers from capitalism, and to assume office with minority support and thus lack an effective mandate to implement a full-blown socialist programme. As Stafford Cripps declared in 1931:

> It is my profound belief that if Labour again forms a minority government it will be the finish of the Labour Party. Socialism cannot be brought about by a minority government and if the Labour Party does not intend to bring in an active programme of immediate socialism when it next comes to office, I shall have no further use for it.

Rejecting the 'gradualism' of MacDonald, Cripps and others on the Labour Left did not, however, reject parliamentarianism. As Roger Spalding has demonstrated, Cripps and many others (including Gaitskell and Attlee) did nevertheless seek both a profound and immediate parliamentary transition to socialism and the enactment of Emergency Powers by a future Labour government 'to protect itself against capitalist sabotage'.[52]

Institutionalised in the Socialist League (created in 1932 out of the link between the National ILP Affiliation Committee and the Society for Socialist Inquiry and Propaganda) left-Labour ideas and policies won some notable victories at the Labour Party's annual conferences between 1932 and 1934. Formal Party commitments to socialist measures during the period of office of the next Labour government, to nationalisation of the joint-stock banks in addition to the Bank of England, to the creation of a national investment board, to guaranteed workers' representation on the boards of nationalised industries, and to opposition to war and war preparations were indicative of these victories.[53]

By the time of the Party's conference of 1934 matters had, however, changed considerably. Above all, largely through the mechanism of the National Joint Council, the Labour Party was increasingly dominated by the cautious, narrow, economistic and gradualist 'vision' of the trade-union leaders. At the 1934 conference the Socialist League was trounced. And the Party's adoption of a new programme, 'For Socialism and Peace', to be achieved gradually and consensually, signalled the triumph of incremental 'labourism' or, at best, moderate reformism.[54] Henceforth, the dominant Labour emphases were to be upon 'pragmatism', 'commonsense' and opposition to 'extremism'.

The Socialist League's defeat in 1934 was symptomatic of the increasingly wider failings of the Left to make significant headway in British society. The Communist Party, as noted earlier, continued to perform important work among the unemployed. The Party was also active in campaigns to gain wider access to the countryside (the Kinder Scout 'mass trespass' of 1932 being the most famous of these campaigns) and better recreational facilities for the mass of people. But in terms of both membership and electoral performance, the CP failed to become a strong force. Membership fluctuated from 3–4,000 during the late 1920s to 2,500 at the end of 1930 to 6,000 in 1932. The Party's 'class-against-class' policy, under which the ILP, the Labour Party and the TUC were denounced as enemies of the revolution and the working class, undoubtedly did little to attract mass support in Britain. The Party was very active in parts of the Scottish and South Wales coalfields, where many of Macintyre's 'Little Moscows' were to be found. And in Rhondda East and West Fife the Communists won more than 20 per cent of the vote in the 1931 general election. However, most of the Party's candidates in 1931 lost their deposits.[55]

If the early 1930s Communist Party failed to successfully challenge the militant moderation of Labour's leaders, so also did the ILP and the more 'right-wing' sections of the Labour Party influenced by Keynes. The ILP disaffiliated from the Labour Party in 1932 and, at least in policy terms, exerted little influence upon the direction of the labour movement thereafter. Mistrusted by both the trade unions and the Labour Left (as variously being anti-socialist, too Liberal and too 'intellectual'), Keynesianism, notes Ben Pimlott, 'entered Labour policy by way of the Right'. It was the group centred upon Gaitskell, Durbin, Jay and Clark which increasingly preached the virtues of demand-led economic management and ameliorative social reform. But only in the post-1945 period would Keynesian 'revisionism' become Labour's dominant guiding light.[56]

At the local level it appears that Labour's moderate reformism had, at least within the general framework of left-wing politics, become hegemonic by the mid 1930s. Despite the sketchy nature of the overall picture and the urgent need for more comparative studies of local politics, certain broad patterns are discernible. First, in 1932 and 1933 there was a great deal of rank-and-file Labour hostility to the introduction of the means test, and in some towns, such as Bolton, Labour refused to administer the test. Significantly, Labour performed well at the polls in Bolton in 1933. More generally, however, local Labour parties usually did not withdraw their representatives from the Public Assistance Committees. The dominant aims were 'to ensure that the PACs paid generous terms' and to campaign against 'the strict application of the Means Test' (Reynolds and Laybourn). Labour was thus committed to mitigating rather than fundamentally challenging the operation of the system of unemployment relief.[57]

In Nelson, Bolton, West Yorkshire, the west of Scotland and South Wales local Labour parties did continue the crusading social-welfarist spirit of the 1920s. Demands for better housing and slum clearance, free secondary education, the creation of direct labour departments, improved welfare facilities and heightened senses of civic responsibility, idealism and pride figured centrally in the politics of these towns and regions during the early 1930s.[58]

Two key issues do, however, remain barely investigated: the general typicality of the progressive Labour policies pursued in the West Riding of Yorkshire and elsewhere; and the extent to which the impetus underlying Labour's crusading and largely oppositional local zeal slackened from 1933–4 onwards. In Bolton, for example, there is no doubt that the politics of confrontation (revolving largely around the issues of 'responsibility to the ratepayers' and the principles and operation of the means test) gave way, between 1933 and the late 1930s, to the politics of compromise, indeed bland consensus, between Labour and the Tories. Paul Harris informs us that Labour in Bolton reconciled itself to the principle of 'economy' in local government. Bolton's Tories reciprocated by accepting the need for direct labour, better schools, more playing fields and more scholarships. Both parties agreed upon the overriding importance of 'trusteeship', of the responsible and efficient management of local affairs in the interests of the 'whole community'. Herein lay extremely powerful influences upon the development of mild reformism. In a similar way the politics of civic pride and advancement in Coventry were concerned far more with the advancement of the interests of the 'community' than with a battle to militantly further the claims of a specific class.[59] Yet Labour's notion of its own constituency or community may well have become more gender specific than in the 1920s. Certainly, as noted earlier, women and their specific social-welfarist concerns were increasingly afforded a subordinate role in local Labour parties in Preston and Liverpool during the 1930s. The same may well have been true elsewhere.

Finally, Labour's local 'rise' was uneven during the first half of the 1930s. There were important and widespread municipal gains during 1933 and 1934, as seen most spectacularly in the capture of the London County Council. But many of the new 'boom' towns of the south and Midlands resisted Labour's preferred embrace. And in various contexts throughout the country the fear induced by insecurity and the threat of unemployment, or the powerlessness resulting from dependence upon the employer for work, induced working-class quiescence and apolitical behaviour.[60]

Future research must provide comprehensive answers to the issues and lacuna noted above. Preliminary investigation would nevertheless suggest that, locally as well as nationally, mid-1930s Labour was going hard for the 'middle ground' of British politics, paramount importance being attached to compromise, consensus and militant moderation. In the face of adversity (as noted in so many other historical contexts in the course of this book) transformative goals were surrendered to the more 'realistic' aims of step-by-step advancement.

It was thus as a 'realistic' and 'responsible' (yet 'socialist') party that Labour entered the 1935 general election.[61] Hopes within the mainstream of the Party were relatively high. Above all, Labour seemed to have recovered much of its pre-1931 strength and purpose. Thus Cronin:

> By 1935 ... the Labour party had fended off challenges from the ILP and the Socialist League and had prevented any serious erosion of support to the right or left. Instead, Labour had moved resolutely to the centre and fallen back, in its time of distress, upon its critical allies in the trade union movement ... it managed to emerge in 1935 as more resolute, practical and united.[62]

The Party had increased its membership from around 215,000 in 1928 to the 400,000 mark, and the local election results augured well for the general election. Many of the Party believed that, at best, outright victory or, at worst, between 200 and 250 seats were within Labour's grasp.

The result was a disappointment. Labour did achieve a measure of recovery, increasing its number of seats from 59 to 154; and the share of the vote received, 37.8 per cent, was even higher than in 1929. But Labour's attacks on the National Government's economic record failed to sway sufficient voters. The government, in turn, asked voters to consider economic recovery and the housing boom, and 'promised more efforts to assist the distressed areas, extension of old age pensions, and the raising of the school-leaving age to fifteen'. Baldwin reaffirmed the government's commitment to the 'peace through security' strategy of the League of Nations, and 'declared that rearmament was necessary to fill in gaps in national defence' (Cook and Stevenson). Labour maintained its solid support in the coalfields, but generally failed to capture the ex-Liberal vote, that of the (especially southern) middle class, and many of the votes cast by workers in the new service and distributive industries. Within the more traditional working-class areas Labour's performance was very uneven: good in parts of London, Scotland and South Wales; extremely poor in Birmingham; and a grave disappointment in the Lancashire textile towns (where only 4 of the seats lost in 1931 were recaptured). John Stevenson has provided a good summary of Labour's mixed fortunes:

> the single most remarkable feature of working-class politics in the slump was the continued loyalty of millions of working-class voters to the Labour Party. But there were important qualifications to this apparent strength. Regional variations cut across class lines. Lancashire retained a deviant pattern among the older industrial

areas where the Labour Party only took 28 seats in 1935 as against 40 in 1929. There were no Labour seats in Birmingham, while the north-east retained distinctive features ... outside Greater London it had only two seats in the whole of southern England. While many poorer voters still voted Conservative ... many of the voters in the new industrial and suburban areas had also failed to come over to Labour.[63]

Thus defeated in 1935, Labour steadfastly pursued its middle-of-the-road position down to the outbreak of the Second World War. Criticised for failing to give unequivocal support to the Republican cause in Spain, for refusing to oppose the National Government's rearmament programme, for being insufficiently tough in its attitude to fascists at home, and too enamoured of the 'appeasers' of the League of Nations, the Labour Party was nevertheless consistently militant in its treatment of domestic left-wingers. The Socialist League, for example, adopting a United-Front strategy between 1935 and 1937, was banned by Labour for collaborating with Communists. (The League disbanded in 1937.) From 1937 onwards many left-wingers buried their differences to work together in the anti-fascist Popular Front. However, prizing its political independence and denouncing the 'dictatorships in Berlin and Moscow', the Labour Party opposed the Popular Front. Indeed, Bevan, Cripps and others were expelled from the Party on account of their Popular Front activities.[64]

Militant moderation did not, however, suggest that any major change had taken place in Labour's popularity, at both local and national levels, between the election of 1935 and the outbreak of war in 1939. Cook and Stevenson's conclusion is apposite:

> Between ... 1935 and ... 1939, the pattern of by-election results was very similar to the results of the 1931–5 period. Labour did well, with many big swings in its favour; but none of the swings was large enough to suggest an overall Labour majority.[65]

It was probably of great comfort to the Labour Party leadership that the Left's failures were of an even greater magnitude. The Communist Party, notwithstanding its valuable anti-fascist activities at home and abroad and its influential role in many rank-and-file industrial struggles, remained of minor political importance. And ex-Socialist League members were increasingly moving from 'revolutionary socialism to radical patriotism' (Spalding). In truth, much like the 1980s, the 1930s was a decade of capitalist crisis *and* Conservative political hegemony.

Before proceeding to an evaluation of the class-based characteristics of 1930s British and American protest movements, we must briefly consider two key questions in relation to the British experience. Why did the Labour Party fail to achieve greater political successes during the 1930s? And why did the country as whole not move to the Left? Both questions have been posed before. The intention is to make a contribution to ongoing debates.[66]

As Ross McKibbin has argued, Labour had the misfortune to be in office when Britain was hit by capitalist crisis. Few, if any governments could realistically have introduced policies sufficient to negate the effects of the Slump, at least over the short term. But I would argue that this was not the whole story. We have seen that MacDonald's government failed to take a determined and united radical stand on both economic theory and economic policy. Despite lofty-sounding appeals to the higher good of socialism, labour socialism was basically empty of practical content, and in 1930 and 1931 the government capitulated to 'orthodoxy'. There were alternatives available, but the leading figures in the government were more interested in demonstrating their 'responsibility' and 'respectability' than a bold and radical vision. In fact, as so often since 1931, many of Labour's policies were to the detriment of workers; and were perceived to contradict the hopes and promises of 1929. Workers could and did respond to appeals to the 'national interest', but Labour's notion of the national good often did not appear to adequately recognise the full contribution of the working class to the social whole. Alan Fowler's observations in relation to the Lancashire cotton workers are most relevant:

> The Labour Party's record in office, 1929–31, did not build on or enhance its appeal to cotton operatives. Wage cuts, unemployment, changes in unemployment pay, the failure of the Clynes' Report and the Indian boycott all discredited Labour with the cotton workforce long before Ramsey MacDonald's 'betrayal'. Labour did not recover in Lancashire until 1945.

Fowler proceeds to inform us that, given Lancashire's established tradition of mill work for married women, the Anomalies Act was bitterly resented. Thus the high hopes of 1929, which had seen Labour dramatically improve its showing in Lancashire (capturing an unprecedented 41 of the country's 66 parliamentary seats), were dashed. In 1931, 'not a single textile constituency returned a Labour MP and all the cotton trade union MPs were defeated'.[67] Labour's fall from grace, among the 'traditional' working class, the unemployed, and the mass electorate, was thus far from beyond its control.

From 1931 onwards Labour was in an extremely difficult position. The National Government effectively stabilised the ship of state, was seen to possess confidence and assurance in its 'natural' right to govern, and was increasingly aided by economic recovery, the flowering of the 'new' industries, improved living standards, and the more extensive growth of a secure, consumer-oriented and predominantly Conservative middle class. The rise of a more privatised and individualistic working class in services and distribution also seemed to restrict Labour's 'natural' constituency. Notwithstanding this largely unfavourable context, Labour did continue to attract millions of predominantly working-class voters. The question is: could Labour have done more? Given its counterfactual nature, the question necessarily invites speculation. But this has not generally been a deterrent to historians of Labour. Ben Pimlott, for example, maintains that the largely negative and unhelpful influences of the Labour Left (setting an impossible socialist agenda for the Party, advocating alliances with 'despotic' Communists and others beyond the Party, erecting barriers against Keynesian influence, and constantly sniping at the elected leadership), 'so far from encouraging brave initiatives, inhibited the Party leadership and restricted its room for manoeuvre'. Contrary to the views of many of the Labour Left and Marxist historians, 'the Labour Party', argues Pimlott, 'has never been a mass movement, still less a revolutionary vanguard. It was founded as, and remains, an electoral machine.' Furthermore, 'the purpose of the Labour Party has not been to create a socialist (or liberal) Britain, still less to create a "mighty force of Socialist faith" ... Thus', concludes Pimlott,

> the Labour Party might have played an important part in the events which preceded the Second World War. That this role was minor was not because of its excessive moderation, or its Parliamentarianism, or because it did not try to politicise the working class. Rather, it was due to an inability to try new approaches, and to show flexibility at a critical time, *because of the political strait-jacket which its own internal conflicts had imposed*. Labour might have been in the vanguard of the Keynesian revolution ... Later, Labour had a chance to lead a broad united opposition against the inadequacies of Chamberlain's foreign policy. Instead it chose to maintain a debilitating exclusiveness, resisting ... new economic ideas, and permitting the divisions among critics of Government foreign and defence policy to continue almost until it was too late.[68]

If the Labour Left constitutes Pimlott's central villain of the piece, then Chris Cook and John Stevenson identify Labour's continued adherence to 'socialism' as an important electoral liability. Thus, while most certainly averse to the view that all Labour's problems in the 1930s were reducible to its 'socialism', Cook and Stevenson do observe that, 'even Cole' (G.D.H. Cole, a prominent socialist), 'accepted that it had been a grave mistake to campaign with too much emphasis on Socialism' during the 1935 election.[69]

My response to Cook and Stevenson is to suggest that there was precious little 'socialism' on offer, at least in relation to the statements and policies of Labour's national leadership, during the 1930s. We have earlier seen that the Socialist League did make a considerable imprint upon Conference policies during 1932 and 1933. But the reversals of the 1934 Labour Party conference effectively marked the end of socialist domination. Thereafter, the unions held sway.

Pimlott's arguments are flawed in several ways. Not only does he presuppose the nature and aims of the Labour Party to be fixed and unchanging, but he is insufficiently 'alive to nuance and complexity. It is thus far too simplistic to mainly attribute the deficiencies of the 1930s Labour Party to the presence of the Left and internal divisions. Largely endorsing the view of Miliband, I have hopefully demonstrated that there was a powerful logic to mainstream Labour's 'rush to the centre', irrespective of the activities of a socialist Left. On balance, Labour's lack of boldness in addressing the problems of the unemployed and the rise of Fascism would have prevailed in the absence of the Socialist League. Labour could indeed have done more, but chose to act only in accordance with its principles of moderation and gradualism.

Pimlott further argues that Labour's primary role as an electoral machine was incompatible with socialism. But this remains more of an assertion than a proven fact. I certainly do not perceive any *necessary* incompatibility between electoralism and socialism. As we have seen, during the 1920s many men and women at the grassroots saw Labour as an electoral force with the power to *transform* the quality of their lives. By the mid 1930s such hopes had been scaled down to take into account the more depressing realities of life. But the point to note is that raised expectations, indeed hopes of transformation, were not confined to members of revolutionary vanguardist organisations.

Questions relating to expectations, hopes and needs take us into the areas of working-class culture and the relationship which prevailed during the 1930s between working-class culture and Labour politics.

A number of historians, such as Pimlott, Cronin, and Cook and Stevenson have identified a close link between the nature of Labour's development and the character of working-class life.[70] The suggestion made is that Labour's moderation and modest goals, indeed its failure to achieve political hegemony, were partly rooted in the increasingly defensive, intensely 'close', and limited practices and goals of working-class culture. I would argue that there is measure of truth in this thesis. During the 1930s the experiences of defeat, depression and insecurity did move many workers to lower their expectations, and to 'dig in' for survival. For many loyalty to Labour was an increasingly natural extension of loyalty to family, neighbourhood and 'those of our kind'. In sum, part of Labour politics could be seen as a mirror-image to large parts of working-class life. Once again, this was not, however, the complete picture. Culture did not 'give' politics in any simple, unme-

diated way. Politics possessed their own life, capable, as agent, of moulding culture. And it would be more correct to say that mainstream
Labour appealed to the more limited and modest aspects of working-
class life than working-class culture as a whole. Indeed, there were
workers in the 'new' industries and services whose expectations and
'needs' dramatically expanded. We must accordingly be more attentive
to the cultures and politics of these workers as well as those out of
work and/or employed in the more traditional sectors.

Finally, as noted in previous chapters, we must be both sensitive to
the complex and changing meanings of culture and more probing in our
investigations. For example, a bald portrayal of the majority of the
Lancashire working class of the 1930s as, 'stolidly politically apathetic
and conservative in all senses of the word',[71] does scant justice to the
complexities of working-class lives. It also fails, as does much work on
inter-war popular culture, to relate adequately to working-class people
within their own terms of reference, within their own value-systems,
ideas and expectations. As the more sensitive treatments of Stephen
Jones and Ross McKibbin have shown, unemployed workers and others
were far from being the dull, apathetic mass too often portrayed in the
historical literature.[72]

A further and major, if grossly neglected and under-researched, factor
in dashing Labour's hopes was the continued vitality of popular Conservatism. During the 1930s Conservatism not only consolidated its
base among the salaried middle class, but, as noted earlier, also exerted
considerable appeal among 'new' workers in the south and some sections
of the older working class. Birmingham, the West Midlands and parts of
industrial Lancashire were particularly important areas of working-class
Toryism. A variety of factors – associations with 'economy' and 'living
with one's means' rather than 'socialist profligacy'; economic 'safety
first', recovery, and improved living standards for some; with a range
of cultural attributes such as 'niceness', 'respectability' and 'family virtues'; and with political moderation, patriotism stability and steadfast-
ness – may well have been at the root of the Conservatives' continued
mass appeal.[73] But our knowledge and understanding is slight. The need
for further research is urgent.

In answer to our second question – why did the country as a whole
not move to the Left during the 1930s? – one is tempted to answer,
why should it have so moved? Revolutionary images – of the Left Book
Club, of the battle of Cable St, of the hunger marches, of the International Brigade and of Left intellectuals – were, while extremely
important, hardly representative of the dominant themes and developments of the decade. Mass unemployment was, as we have seen, one
aspect of a much more varied economic picture. In itself, unemployment

is rarely, if ever, sufficient spur to revolutionary activity; and in the 1930s living standards rose for those in work. Sections of the unemployed did march, and did concern themselves with 'the politics of the dole', seeking to ensure adequate levels of maintenance. And the NUWM did lead a successful campaign in 1935 against the new nationally based unemployment benefit rates introduced by the Unemployment Assistance Board. But the NUWM was in decline during the second half of the decade.[74] The membership of the Communist Party increased to 18,000 during the late 1930s, and would be further strengthened during the war. But, as we have seen, the forces of the Left, embracing the Labour Party and groups on its left flank, were too divided and commanded insufficient support to effect a major leftwards shift. The majority of the middle and lower-middle classes were staunchly patriotic. Conservatism was dominant. And the ruling class was reasonably united. In these circumstances Britain successfully maintained its reputation for stability, order and peaceful, gradual change.

CLASS AND POPULAR MOVEMENTS

In conclusion, we must return to a key leitmotif of this book: the extent to which popular movements were informed by class. There is no doubt that class was present in both countries. We have seen that its influence considerably varied during the inter-war period, being, for example, far more prominent in 1930s rather than 1920s America, and in many respects at its strongest in Britain during the 1920s (especially up to and including 1926 in the industrial sphere, and up to 1929 politically). Still, by the late 1930s both countries possessed strong independent labour organisations, particularly in relation to the trade-union movement. Politically, there was greater continuity in America: the Democratic Party had successfully accommodated the popular upsurges of the 1930s. In Britain the Labour Party had broken the mould of two-party politics, and had become the major party of opposition.

In terms of our second criterion of class, constituency, there is little doubt that the American labour movement, and especially the CIO, had made massive advances. A new and greatly enlarged constituency, rooted above all in the sons of the 'new' immigrants, and to a lesser extent in blacks and women, now dominated the unions in the mass-production industries. In contrast to the 1880s and the decade between 1912 and 1922, the mass protests of the 1930s had resulted in more durable trade-union gains, crucially protected by the state. The more established unions of the AFL had also survived the Great Depression to demonstrate recovered strength in 1939. In Britain inter-war trade unionism had consolidated, indeed expanded, its base among a wide range of largely non-skilled workers. In contrast to the late nineteenth century, the 'new' general unions now held sway within the trade-union world. Ironically, these unions had become more bureaucratised and centralised than the 'old' craft unions, and had increasingly adopted many of the moderate and conciliatory policies traditionally associated with the nineteenth-century 'aristocratic' unions. Limited gains had also been registered in 'new' sectors of the economy.

The social characteristics of our respective labour movements must also be set against the wider features of the working class. In the United States many of the ethnic and other sources of fragmentation, so evident during the 1920s, were increasingly overshadowed during the 1930s by an enhanced sense of class unity. This increased sense of class solidarity did not mean that all divisions suddenly dissolved; but it did signify greater levels of cultural toleration and co-operation among all manner of workers.[75] The massive fact of economic crisis, complete with mass unemployment and widespread loss of faith in established employer and other institutions, provided the key stimulus to heightened class action. In Britain, despite the continued profundity of class-based cultural ties and loyalties, there was increasing evidence during the 1930s of differential experiences and sharper divisions within the working class. Massive slum-clearance programmes disrupted 'traditional' communities. Above all the 'affluent' and more privatised workers in the growth sectors of the south and the Midlands knew little of the hardships of the 'hard core' unemployed in the north, Scotland and Wales. Migration from depressed to booming regions did ensure that some contacts were retained with family and kin; and employer speed-up, anti-unionism and 'Taylorism' were marked features of the growth industries. But the regional concentration of the unemployed meant that their voices and protests meant little in the streets of Luton and parts of Oxford and London.[76]

Conflict – our final yardstick of class – was manifestly present in both countries. In 1930s America millions of workers expressed ideas and undertook actions which met with acute hostility from employers. Conflict, albeit on a lesser scale than in the years between 1916 and 1922, was widespread. This 1930s pattern once again stood in marked contrast to the 1920s. In Britain most employers had long since accommodated themselves to the existence of trade unionism. But the period up to 1926 and the second half of the 1930s witnessed serious industrial conflicts revolving around questions of authority and power, wage levels, conditions of work, and the attempted reorganisation of production methods.

In both countries the expression of views and patterns of behaviour which conflicted with the perceived interests of capital, did not signify the dominance of revolutionary class consciousness among workers. Throughout the inter-war years, and especially during the 1930s, communists and revolutionary socialists played very important roles, particularly as shopfloor militants and industrial leaders, in labour movements in both countries. But the class consciousness expressed by the vast majority of workers was both more modest and 'limited' than that articulated by revolutionaries. Despite the formal socialistic rhetoric of parts of the British labour movement, the dominant aims of British and American workers were to 'civilise', 'moralise', 'tame', and indeed to transform, in more human as opposed to cash-based ways, the capitalism of unregulated markets, unfettered individualism and unbridled profit maximisation. And integral to the process of change was the advancement of collective working-class power and influence within a more regulated and 'moral' economy and society.[77] In truth, workers in both countries were intent upon achieving, in very changed circumstances, the 'due balance, protection and reward' for labour sought by the Chartists and the Workingmen in the 1830s.

Notwithstanding the continued absence of mass-based independent labour politics in the United States, the very revival and strength of class among 1930s American workers once again invalidates the notion of American exceptionalism. In addition, the failure of the Left in Britain and the mild reformism of the Labour Party compel us to reconsider the characteristics of class and politics in 1930s Britain.

By the early 1940s the achievement of 'due balance, protection and reward' for organised workers no longer seemingly necessitated either acute or prolonged class conflict. In both Britain and the United States the demands of organised labour, or at least the trade-union movement, had been officially accommodated to degrees largely unmatched in the past. Wartime experiences would further advance the processes of accommodation and assimilation. Simultaneously, however, 'the end of history' was not at hand. Class conflict as well as class collaboration informed the war years. Furthermore, by 1945 workers' needs and expectations had greatly expanded, and heightened demands were made of the capitalist system. The dialectic between conflict and consensus, stability and change, would continue into the post-war period.

Conclusion

This book and its companion volume have been centrally concerned with the issues of class making and breaking, and class and exceptionalism. At this point it is appropriate to offer the reader a summary of the various conclusions reached.

We have consistently argued that an absolute notion of American 'exceptionalism' is wide of the mark. There is no 'normal' or 'essential' law of working-class development and consciousness. Class, as defined in these volumes, exerted a powerful influence among both British and American workers from the late eighteenth century to the outbreak of the Second World War. This influence rose and fell in relation to time and place, but of its significant presence there can surely be little doubt. In the field of workplace relations both industrial and class conflicts were, especially in the face of chronic and aggressive employer antiunionism, frequently more acute in the United States than in Britain. As seen in their capacities to build and re-create independent organizations with large constituencies, in their daily opposition to the increasing powers and unbridled profit maximisation of employers, and in their values and practices of mutualism and personal and collective independence, workers offered important alternatives to the acquisitive individualism of their respective capitalisms.

British and American workers sought to create more civilised, harmonious and morally informed social orders in which workers and all 'true citizens' would receive their 'due protection and reward', and in which greater equity would prevail. For the most part this 'civilising mission' did not embrace the transformation of capitalism by means of revolutionary socialism. Workers' legacies of democratic practice, the primacy of rational thought and human agency, and collective duties and responsibilities combined with individual freedom and independence merit special note in late twentieth-century capitalist contexts of unrestrained greed and individualism, appalling inequality, the seeming rule of commodities and markets over people, widespread cynicism, and growing social isolation and apparent powerlessness. Organised labour would do well to look beyond the 'bloc vote,' narrow instrumentalism and incremental gradualism in order to rediscover its 'true' roots and inspirations.

We have also argued that class-based ways of seeing and acting were more durable in Britain. Time and time again American workers built impressive class-based organisations and ideologies only to see them quickly destroyed. Racism, ethnic conflicts and other sources of internal working-class fragmentation were frequently instrumental in undermining, for a time at least, class in American. But, in addition to the more heterogeneous character of the American working class, we have enumerated the greater flexibility of the American political system, the more widespread nature of property ownership and the promise of mobility, and state and employer repression as factors which variously thwarted and smashed the appeal of class. In Britain class was forced to contend with a range of competing loyalties, ranging from 'producerism' to ethnically based definitions of 'the People'. But, generally speaking, more proletarianised Britain witnessed the stronger development of an increasingly reformist kind of class.

On a more abstract level, it is hoped this study has shown, in opposition to the claims of many post-structuralists, that the adoption of a class-based, historical-materialist form of analysis is perfectly compatible with due attention to language and the construction of identity, complexity, change, contradiction and individual distinctiveness. It is all too easy, and fundamentally flawed, to fashionably set up unitary and undifferentiated models of class, and then correctly demolish such models in the name of complexity, difference and deconstruction. But, as we have been at pains to demonstrate, classes are never simple, unified wholes. Change and contradiction lie at the very heart of a historical-materialist approach to class. They key factor is to investigate and evaluate the overall interactions between sources of unity and division, solidarity and fragmentation among workers. Complexity and individual choice and perception are, despite many claims to the contrary, hardly the inventions of present-day scholars. And, at a very basic level, one does not have to travel far beyond most university libraries, whether in New Haven or Manchester, to encounter the persistence, indeed intensification, of class-based inequalities.

Current, and in all probability future, trends in labour and social history are/will move beyond the class-based problematic of this book. This is to be welcomed. Greater attention to gender, race, ideas and language, and indeed institutions is to be applauded. But we must not get carried away in our applause, to adopt an essentially uncritical stance towards the filling of gaps in our knowledge. Such gaps must, of course, be filled. But neither ideas and language, nor institutions and the study of race and gender constitute, *in themselves*, sufficient means of the historical investigation of workers, their movements, and relations with the wider society. It is, above all, the study of the *interactions* of the various levels and practices over time – of the 'making and breaking' of concepts against evidence, of the relations between human agency and conditioning; words, actions and their unintended consequences; women and men; institutions, individuals and social processes; and of language, politics, economics and social structure – which constitute 'good history'. And, as demonstrated by a long line of distinguished historians from Marx to Montgomery, the study of the material aspects of life and of changing patterns of consciousness and 'experience' constitute essential parts of adequate historical investigation. The future will hopefully see the further theoretical and empirical development of the insights provided by historical materialism.

Notes

CHAPTER ONE

1. A. D. Chandler, Jr., *The Visible Hand: The Managerial Revolution in American Business* (1978), Chs. 9–11.
2. S. Wood (ed.), *The Degradation of Work? Skill, Deskilling and the Labour Process* (1982), Introduction and Ch. 7 by C. R. Littler; C. R. Littler, 'A Comparative Analysis of Managerial Structures and Strategies', in H. F. Gospel and C. R. Littler (eds.), *Managerial Strategies and Industrial Relations: An Historical and Comparative Study* (1983).
3. R. J. Oestreicher, 'Urban Working Class Political Behavior and Theories of American Electoral Politics, 1870–1940', *Journal of American History*, 74, 4 (March 1988), pp. 1259–60; D. Montgomery, 'Labor and the Republic in Industrial America, 1860–1920', *Le Mouvement Social*, no. 111 (April–June 1980), pp. 205–6.
4. P. S. Bagwell and G. E. Mingay, *Britain and America: A Study of Economic Change, 1850–1939* (1970), p. 1.
5. E. H. Hunt, *British Labour History 1815–1914* (1988), p. 144.
6. E. J. Hobsbawm, *World of Labour: Further Studies in the History of Labour* (1984), pp. 180, 196–7.
7. J. Hinton, *Labour and Socialism: A History of the British Labour Movement 1867–1974* (1983), pp. 26–7; E. H. Hunt, op. cit., pp. 28–31.
8. R. McKibbin, *The Ideologies of Class: Social Relations in Britain 1880–1950*, (1990), p. 2.
9. E. J. Hobsbawm, op. cit., p. 196.
10. Ibid., pp. 200–7.
11. M. A. Jones, *The Limits of Liberty: American History 1607–1980* (1983) p. 320.
12. B. Laurie, *Artisans into Workers: Labor in Nineteenth-century America* (1989), p. 115.
13. P. S. Bagwell and G. E. Mingay, op. cit., p. 5; E. H. Hunt, op. cit., p. 26; P. Passell and S. P. Lee, *A New Economic View of American History* (1979), p. 272.
14. M. A. Jones, op. cit., p. 295; D. Montgomery, *The Fall of the House of Labor: The Workplace, the State and American Labor Activism, 1865–1925* (1982), p. 51; P. Passell and S. P. Lee, op. cit., pp. 266–9.
15. P. S. Bagwell and G. E. Mingay, op. cit., pp. 1–2, Ch. 3.
16. E. H. Hunt, op. cit., pp. 176–7, K. Lunn, 'Immigrants and Strikes: Some British Case Studies, 1870–1914', in K. Lunn (ed.), *Race and Labour in Twentieth-Century Britain* (1985).
17. S. B. Saul, *The Myth of the Great Depression 1873–1896* (1969). See also S. Pollard, *Britain's Prime and Britain's Decline: The British Economy 1870–1914* (1989), Ch. 1.

18. E. P. Thompson, 'The Peculiarities of the English', *Socialist Register* (1965); D. Nicholls, 'A Subordinate Bourgeoisie? The Question of Hegemony in Modern British Capitalist Society', in C. Barker and D. Nicholls (eds.), *The Development of British Capitalist Society: A Marxist Debate* (1988); L. G. Sandberg, 'The Entrepreneur and Technological Change', in R. C. Floud and D. McCloskey (eds.), *The Economic History of Britain Since 1700, Vol. 2, 1860 to the 1970s* (1981), p. 1; S. Pollard, op. cit., pp. xi, 27, 40, 44, 257, 261, 265, 268.

19. E. J. Hobsbawm, *Industry and Empire* (1971), pp. 187–8.

20. R. C. Floud, 'Britain 1860–1914: A Survey', in R. C. Floud and D. McCloskey (eds.), op. cit., p. 1.

21. See, for example, the illuminating comments in the *Mosley Industrial Commission to the United States of America, Oct.–Dec. 1902. Report of the Delegates* (Manchester 1903).

22. See, for example, M. A. Jones, op. cit., Ch. 16; R. M. Robertson and G. M. Walton, *History of the American Economy* (1983), Ch. 20.

23. D. Montgomery, 'Labor and the Republic', op. cit., p. 202.

24. R. C. Floud, op. cit., pp. 9–11.

25. S. B. Saul, op. cit., pp. 13–15, 54–5.

26. J. Livingston, 'The Social Analysis of Economic History and Theory: Conjectures on Late Nineteenth-century American Development', *American Historical Review*, 92, 1 (Feb. 1987), especially pp. 72–9, 93–5; D. M. Gordon, R. Edwards and M. Reich, *Segmented Work Divided Workers: The Historical Transformation of Labor in the United States* (1984), pp. 94–9. See also the important 'Symposium on *The Fall of the House of Labor*', *Labor History*, 30 (1989), especially pp. 106–8 (Jacoby) and 126–7 (Montgomery).

27. J. Livingston, op. cit., p. 78; D. Montgomery, *The Fall of the House of Labor*, (1989), pp. 51–2, 171.

28. K. Burgess, *The Origins of British Industrial Relations: The Nineteenth Century Experience* (1975), Ch. IV; J. L. White, 'Lancashire Cotton Textiles', in C. J. Wrigley (ed.), *A History of British Industrial Relations 1875–1914* (1982); W. Lazonick, 'The Cotton Industry', in B. Elbaum and W. Lazonick (eds.), *The Decline of the British Economy* (1986).

29. K. Burgess, op. cit., pp. 269–85; J. L. White, op. cit., pp. 219–22.

30. K. Burgess, op. cit., pp. 254–5, 265–73.

31. A. J. McIvor, 'Cotton Employers' Organisations and Labour Relations, 1890–1939', in J. A. Jowitt and A. J. McIvor (eds.), *Employers and Labour in the English Textile Industries 1850–1939* (1988), pp. 9–10; H. A. Turner, *Trade Union Growth Structure and Policy* (1962), pp. 123–4.

32. Per Bolin-Hort, *Work Family and the State: Child Labour and the Organization of Production in the British Cotton Industry, 1780–1920* (1989), p. 256.

33. J. Melling, 'Scottish Industrialists and the Changing Character of Class Relations in the Clyde Region', in T. Dickson (ed.), *Capital and Class in Scotland* (1982), pp. 71–2, 77–8.

34. Ibid., pp. 72–4; J. Benson, 'Coalmining', in C. J. Wrigley (ed.), op. cit., pp. 188–200.

35. J. Melling, op. cit., pp. 80, 96–101. See also the astute observations by John Foster in *Labour History Review*, 55, 1 (1990), pp. 64–8.

36. T. C. Smout, *A Century of the Scottish People 1830–1950* (1986), pp. 3–4, 248, 260–1.

37. J. Zeitlin, 'The Labour Strategies of British Engineering Employers 1890–1922' in H. F. Gospel and C. R. Littler (eds.), op. cit., pp. 26–7; id., 'Engineers and Compositors: A Comparison', in R. Harrison and J. Zeitlin (eds.), *Divisions of Labour: Skilled Workers and Technological Change in Nineteenth Century Britain* (1985), pp. 185–250. See also, J. Melling, op. cit., pp. 76–8; K. Burgess, 'The Political Economy of British Engineering Workers During the First World War', in L. Haimson and C. Tilly (eds.), *Strikes, Wars and Revolutions in an International Perspective* (1989).

38. J. Zeitlin, in R. Harrison and J. Zeitlin, op. cit., p. 228.

39. Ibid., pp. 229–36; S. Tolliday, 'The Failure of Mass Production Unionism in the Motor Industry, 1914–39', in C. J. Wrigley (ed.), *A History of British industrial Relations. Vol. II: 1914–1939* (1987).

40. R. McKibbin, op. cit., pp. 15–16.

41. B. Lancaster, *Radicalism Cooperation and Socialism: Leicester Working-Class Politics 1860–1906* (1987), Chs. 2, 3, 6 and 9.

42. D. Brody, *Steelworkers in America: The Nonunion Era* (1969), Ch. 1; D. Montgomery, *The Fall* op. cit., pp. 27–9; R. M. Robertson and G. A. Walton, op. cit., pp. 427–8.

43. D. Brody, op. cit., p. 2.

44. Ibid., pp. 7–17, 31–2. Ch. IV.

45. A. Dawson, 'The Parameters of Craft Consciousness: The Social Outlook of the Skilled Worker, 1890–1920', in D. Hoerder (ed.), *American Labor and Immigration History, 1877–1920s: Recent European Research* (1983), pp. 138–9; id., 'The Paradox of Dynamic Technological Change and the Labor Aristocracy in the United States, 1880–1914', *Labor History*, 20 (1979), pp. 325–51.

46. D. Brody, op. cit., p. 31.

47. D. Montgomery, *The Fall*, pp. 12, 42.

48. D. Brody, op. cit., Ch. II.

49. D. Brody, op. cit., Ch. III; D. Montgomery, op. cit., pp. 22–4; J. Holt, 'Trade Unionism in the British and US Steel Industries, 1880–1914: A Comparative Study', in C. Emsley (ed.), *Essays in Comparative History: Economy, Society and Politics in Britain and America 1850–1920* (1984), pp. 125–46.

50. J. Holt, op. cit., pp. 128, 131; D. Brody, op. cit., p. 75.

51. D. Brody, op. cit., pp. 119–26.

52. D. Brody, *Labor in Crisis: The Steel Strike of 1919* (1965), pp. 39–43, 74–5, 151–8.

53. D. Montgomery, *The Fall*, op. cit., p. 123.

54. Per Bolin-Hort, op. cit., p. 271.

55. Ibid., p. 273.

56. D. Montgomery, *The Fall*, op. cit., pp. 156–7; P. T. Silvia, Jr., 'The Position of Workers in a Textile Community: Fall River in the Early 1880s', *Labor History*, 16, 2 (Spring 1975), especially pp. 232, 237–41; I. Cohen, 'Workers' Control in the Cotton Industry: A Comparative Study of British and American Mule Spinning', *Labor History*, 26, 1 (Winter 1985), pp. 81–3; R. Howard, 'Progress in the Textile Trades', in G. E. McNeill (ed.), *The Labor Movement: The Problem of Today* (1887, 1971 reprint).

57. Per Bolin-Hort, op. cit., pp. 186–7.

58. I. Cohen, 'American Management and British Labor: Lancashire Immigrant Spinners in Industrial New England', *Comparative Studies in Society and History*, 27 (1985), pp. 633–4; T. K. Hareven, 'The Laborers of Manchester, New Hampshire 1912–1922: The Role of Family and Ethnicity in Adjustment to Industrial Life', *Labor History*, 16, 2 (Spring 1975), pp. 250–1, 262.

59. D. Montgomery, *The Fall*, op. cit., pp. 55–6, 212–13.

60. D. Montgomery, *Workers' Control in America: Studies in the History of Work Technology and Labor Struggles* (1984), p. 118.

61. D. Montgomery, *The Fall*, op. cit., p. 45.

62. D. Montgomery, *Workers' Control*, pp. 48–57.

63. Ibid., p. 60.

64. Ibid., pp. 63, 81, 83, 99, 122; id., *The Fall*, pp. 457–64.

65. On scientific management see, F. W. Taylor, *The Principles of Scientific Management* (1911); D. Nelson, *Frederick W. Taylor and the Rise of Scientific Management* (1980); H. Braverman, *Labor and Monopoly Capital: The Degradation of Work in the Twentieth Century* (1974), Ch. 4; C. R. Littler, *The Development of the Labour Process in Capitalist Societies: A Comparative Study of Work Organisation in Britain, Japan and the U.S.A.* (1982), Chs. 5, 10 and 11; D. Montgomery, *The Fall*, op. cit., pp. 189–91, 216–33; id., *Workers' Control*, op. cit., pp. 32–3, 48, 101, 113–14.

66. H. Braverman, op. cit., pp. 86, 90.

67. D. Montgomery, *Workers' Control*, op. cit., pp. 101, 113, 117–19. For the introduction and impact of Taylorism see id., *The Fall*, op. cit., p. 229; 'Symposium', op. cit., pp. 108, 127–8; C. R. Littler, op. cit., pp. 180–1.

68. D. Montgomery, *Workers' Control*, op. cit., pp. 118–19.

69. Ibid., pp. 63–83.

70. J. Melling, 'Scottish Industrialists', op. cit., pp. 73–4.

71. D. Montgomery, *The Fall*, op. cit., p. 57.

72. A. Chandler, Jr., op. cit., especially Chs. 9–11.

73. R. M. Robertson and G. M. Walton, op. cit., pp. 422–33.

74. J. Cronin, 'Strikes 1870–1914', in C. J. Wrigley (ed.), Vol. 1, op. cit., p. 83; E. H. Hunt, op. cit., p. 30.

75. J. Benson, *British Coalminers in the Nineteenth Century: A Social History* (1989), p. 19.

76. K. McClelland and A. Reid, 'Wood, Iron and Steel: Technology, Labour and Trade Union Organisation in the Shipbuilding Industry, 1840–1914', in R. Harrison and J. Zeitlin (eds.), op. cit., p. 154.

77. B. Elbaum and W. Lazonick (eds.), op. cit., p. 3.

78. I. Cohen, 'American Management and British Labor', op. cit., pp. 633–4.

79. J. Holt, op. cit., p. 141.

80. K. McClelland and A. Reid, op. cit., p. 154; J. Benson, *British Coalminers*, op. cit., pp. 12–13; J. Zeitlin, 'Engineers and Compositors', op. cit., pp. 230–1.

81. B. Elbaum and W. Lazonick (eds.), op. cit., pp. 3–5, 10.

82. E. J. Hobsbawm, *Industry and Empire*, op. cit., pp. 186–92; M. Dintenfass, *The Decline of Industrial Britain 1870–1980* (1992).

83. A. Dawley, 'Paths to Power After the Civil War', in P. Buhle and A. Dawley (eds.), *Working for Democracy: American Workers from the Revolution to the Present* (1985), p. 41.

84. J. Holt, op. cit., p. 145.
85. J. Foster, 'A Century of Scottish Labour', *Labour History Review*, 55, 1 (1990), pp. 66–8; J. Melling, 'Scottish Industrialists', op. cit.; W. R. Garside and H. F. Gospel, 'Employers and Managers: Their Organisational Structure and Changing Industrial Strategies', in C. J. Wrigley (ed.), Vol. 1, op. cit., pp. 105–12; J. Holt, op. cit., p. 142.
86. B. Elbaum and W. Lazonick, 'An Institutional Perspective on British Decline', in B. Elbaum and W. Lazonick (eds.), op. cit., pp. 2–3.
87. See the review of Wiener's book by J. Baxendale in *History Workshop Journal*, 21 (Spring 1986).
88. I. Cohen, 'Workers' Control in the Cotton Industry', op. cit., especially pp. 84–5; W. Lazonick, 'The Cotton Industry', in B. Elbaum and W. Lazonick (eds.), op. cit., pp. 24–30; L. G. Sandberg, *Lancashire in Decline* (1974), p. 80; Per Bolin Hort, op. cit., pp. 175–7, 185, 194–9; A. Fowler, 'Trade Unions and Technological Change: The Automatic Loom Strike, 1908', *Bulletin of the North-West Labour History Society*, 6 (1979–80).
89. K. McClelland and A. Reid., op. cit., pp. 155–7, 165; J. Melling, 'Scottish Industrialists', op. cit., pp. 77–8; C. R. Littler, 'A Comparative Analysis of Managerial Structures and Strategies', op. cit.; K. Burgess, 'The Political Economy of British Engineering Workers', op. cit., p. 291; J. Zeitlin, 'The Labour Strategies of British Engineering Employers', op. cit., pp. 48–9; B. Elbaum and W. Lazonick (eds.), op. cit., p. 6.
90. P. Temin, *Causal Factors in American Economic Growth in the Nineteenth Century* (1975); K. Burgess, *The Origins of British Industrial Relations*, op. cit., p. 234.
91. E. J. Hobsbawm, *Industry and Empire*, op. cit., p. 192; S. Pollard, op. cit., pp. 108–14.
92. K. Burgess, *The Origins of British Industrial Relations* op. cit., pp. 248–9, 291–3.
93. B. Jessop, 'Recent Theories of the Capitalist State', *Cambridge Journal of Economics*, 1 (1977), pp. 353–73; P. K. Edwards, 'The Political Economy of Industrial Conflict: Britain and the United States', *Economic and Industrial Democracy*, 4 (1983), especially pp. 478–81; P. K. Edwards kindly supplied me with a copy of this article.
94. J. Saville *1848: The British State and the Chartist Movement*, (1987); N. Kirk, *The Growth of Working Class Reformism* (1985) pp. 25–6, 152–4; R. J. Looker and D. Coates, 'The State and the Working Class in Nineteenth-Century Europe', in J. Anderson (ed.), *The Rise of the Modern State* (1986).
95. R. McKibbin, op. cit., pp. 18, 24–5, 28–9, 38; C. J. Wrigley, 'The Government and Industrial Relations', in C. J. Wrigley (ed.), Vol. 1, op. cit.
96. For debates concerning the role of the state towards organised labour and the working class during the First World War see, C. J. Wrigley, 'The First World War and State Intervention in Industrial Relations 1914–18', in C. J. Wrigley (ed.), Vol. 2, op. cit., especially pp. 31, 52–7; A. Reid, 'Dilution, Trade Unionism and the State in Britain During the First World War', in S. Tolliday and J. Zeitlin (eds.), *Shop Floor Bargaining and the State: Historical and Comparative Perspectives* (1985), especially pp. 47–8; J. Hinton, *Labour and Socialism*, op. cit., Ch. 6; K. Burgess, 'The Political Economy of British Engineering Workers', op. cit., pp. 299–316; J. Melling, 'Scottish Industrialists, op. cit., pp. 104–34; J. Melling, 'Whatever

Happened to Red Clydeside? Industrial Conflict and the Politics of Skill in the First World War', *International Review of Social History*, Vol. XXXV (1990), pp. 3–32; J. Foster, 'Strike Action and Working-Class Politics on Clydeside 1914–1919', ibid., Vol. XXXV (1990).

97. H. Harris, 'The Snares of Liberalism? Politicians, Bureaucrats and the Shaping of Federal Labour Relations Policy in the United States, ca. 1915–47', in S. Tolliday and J. Zeitlin (eds.), op. cit., p. 152.

98. Ibid., pp. 152–3. For state hostility towards organised labour see also, J. Brecher, *Strike!* (1972); D. Montgomery, 'Labor and the Republic', op. cit., p. 209; J. H. M. Laslett, 'State Policy Towards Labour and Labour Organizations, 1830–1939: Anglo-American Union Movements', in P. Mathias and S. Pollard (eds.), *The Cambridge Economic History of Europe*, Vol. 8 (1989), especially pp. 516–20.

99. H. Harris, op. cit., pp. 153–5; C. L. Tomlins, *The State and the Unions: Labor Relations, Law and the Organized Labor Movement in America 1880–1960* (1985), pp. 74–7; P. K. Edwards, 'Strikes and Politics in the United States, 1900–1919', in L. Haimson and C. Tilly (eds.), op. cit., pp. 253–4.

100. J. Greene, 'The Strike at The Ballot Box: The American Federation of Labor's Entrance into Election Politics, 1906–1909', *Labor History*, 32, 2 (Spring 1991).

101. D. Montgomery, *The Fall*, op. cit., pp. 302–3; id., *Workers' Control*, op. cit., p. 75.

102. D. Montgomery, *The Fall*, op. cit., pp. 356–7; S. Skowronek, *Building a New American State: The Expansion of National Administrative Capacities* (1982).

103. D. Montgomery, 'Immigrants, Industrial Unions, and Social Reconstruction in the United States, 1916–1923', *Labour/Le Travail*, 13 (Spring 1984), pp. 103–4.

104. S. Wood (ed.), op. cit., especially Introduction.

105. A. Dawson, 'The Paradox of Dynamic Technological Change', op. cit., p. 332.

106. C. More, 'Skill and the Survival of Apprenticeship', in S. Wood (ed.), op. cit.; R. Penn, 'Skilled Manual Workers in the Labour Process', in ibid.; J. Belchem, *Industrialization and the Working Class (1990)*, Ch. 18.

107. For alienation and commodity fetishism see, T. B. Bottomore and M. Rubel, *Karl Marx: Selected Writings in Sociology and Social Philosophy* (1976), pp. 177–8; K. Marx, *The Economic and Philosophical Manuscripts of 1844* (1967), pp. 106–19.

108. D. Montgomery, *The Fall*, op. cit., p. 215.

109. Ibid., pp. 327–8; D. M. Gordon, R. Edwards and M. Reich, op. cit., Ch. 4; E. H. Hunt, op. cit., pp. 73–4, 99–100, 276–7, 296–8; E. J. Hobsbawm, *Worlds of Labour*, op. cit., Chs. 9 and 11.

110. D. Montgomery, *The Fall*, op. cit., p. 42.

111. P. Joyce, *Work Society and Politics* (1980), pp. 339–40.

112. R. M. Robertson and G. M. Walton, op. cit., pp. 437–8; B. Laurie, *Artisans into Workers*, op. cit., p. 127; J. Hinton, op. cit., p. 26 (although Hunt gives a higher percentage. E. H. Hunt, op. cit., p. 73).

113. P. R. Shergold, ' "Reefs of Roast Beef": The American Worker's Standard of Living in Comparative Perspective', in D. Hoerder (ed.), op. cit., pp. 81–5.

114. D. M. Gordon, R. Edwards and M. Reich, op. cit., pp. 119–20; D. Montgomery, *The Fall*, op. cit., pp. 70, 172. But see Dawson ('The Paradox', op. cit., p. 332) for the view that 'occupational differentials showed some tendency to widen' between 1860 and 1890.

115. E. H. Hunt, op. cit., p. 100.

116. E. J. Hobsbawm, *Worlds of Labour*, op. cit., Chs. 10 and 11.

117. Ibid., p. 207.

118. S. J. Kleinberg, *The Shadow of the Mills: Working Class Families in Pittsburgh 1870–1907* (1989), pp. 49–51.

119. D. Montgomery, 'Labor in the Industrial Era', in R. B. Morris (ed.), *A History of the American Worker* (1983), pp. 97, 101–2.

120. Ibid., pp. 94–6, 139–48.

121. J. Bodnar, 'Immigration, Kinship and the Rise of Working Class Realism', *Journal of Social History*, 14 (1980), pp. 45–65; R. J. Oestreicher, 'Urban Working Class Political Behavior', op. cit. p. 1274; D. Montgomery, 'To Study the People: The American Working Class', *Labor History*, 21, 4 (Fall 1980), pp. 499, 502.

122. R. J. Oestreicher, *Solidarity and Fragmentation: Working People and Class Consciousness in Detroit 1875–1900* (1986), pp. 13, 27 (footnote 26); S. Thernstrom, *The Other Bostonians* (1973); S. J. Kleinberg, op. cit., pp. 12–13, 53–64; H. Gutman and I. Berlin, *Power and Culture* (1987), p. 394.

123. G. S. Jones, *Languages of Class: Studies in English Working-class History 1832–1982* (1983), Ch. 4; N. Kirk, ' "Traditional" Working Class Culture and the "Rise of Labour": Some preliminary Questions and Observations', *Social History*, (May 1991).

124. J. Bodnar, op. cit.; D. Emmons, *The Butte Irish: Class and Ethnicity in an American Mining Town 1875–1925* (1989), pp. 38, 182–212. See also the review of Emmons' book by J. R. Barrett in *International Labor and Working Class History*, 37 (Spring 1990), pp. 41–51.

125. E. J. Hobsbawm, *Worlds of Labour*, op. cit., pp. 190–3, 209–13; D. Montgomery, 'Symposium', *Labor History* (1989), pp. 132–4; id., *The Fall*, op. cit., pp. 138–40, 171, 327–8.

126. S. Thernstrom, 'Working Class Social Mobility in Industrial America', in P. N. Stearns and D. J. Walkowitz (eds.), *Workers in the Industrial Revolution: Recent Studies of Labor in the United States and Europe* (1974); P. Johnson, *Saving and Spending: The Working Class Economy in Britain 1870–1939* (1985), especially Conclusion.

127. E. J. Hobsbawm, *Worlds of Labour*, op. cit., p. 207.

128. N. Kirk, 'The Myth of Class? Workers and the Industrial Revolution in Stockport', *Bulletin of the Society for the Study of Labour History*, 51, 1 (April 1986), pp. 41–2.

129. D. Montgomery, *The Fall*, op. cit., pp. 327–8.

130. S. J. Kleinberg, op. cit., pp. 79–80. See also D. Montgomery, 'Labor in the Industrial Era', op. cit., pp. 90–7.

131. D. Montgomery, 'Immigrants, Industrial Unions, and Social Reconstruction', op. cit., p. 108; M. A. Jones, *American Immigration* (1969), p. 208.

132. R. Asher, 'Union Nativism and the Immigrant Response', *Labor History*, 23, 3 (Summer 1982), especially pp. 327–31; A. T. Lane, *Solidarity or Survival? American Labor and European Immigrants 1830–1924* (1987);

C. Collomp, 'Unions, Civics and National Identity: Organized Labor's Reaction to Immigration, 1881–1897', *Labor History*, 29, 4 (Fall 1988).

133. S. J. Kleinberg, op. cit., pp. 46–52; S. B. Warner, Jr., *Streetcar Suburbs: The Process of Growth in Boston 1870–1900* (1971).

134. R. J. Oestreicher, *Solidarity and Fragmentation*, op. cit., pp. 39–43, 60–7, Chs. 3 and 6; D. Brody, *Steelworkers in America*, op. cit., pp. 119–21; T. K. Hareven, 'The Laborers of Manchester', op. cit., pp. 260–1.

135. S. J. Kleinberg, op. cit., pp. 12–19; R. J. Oestreicher, *Solidarity and Fragmentation*, op. cit., Ch. 2; J. Bodnar, *The Transplanted: A History of Immigrants in Urban America* (1985).

136. 'Symposium', *Labor History* (1989), pp. 119, 131.

137. G. Grob, *Workers and Utopia: A Study of Ideological Conflict in the American Labor Movement 1865–1900* (1976), especially Introduction, Ch. VIII, and Conclusion; S. Perlman, *A Theory of the Labor Movement* (1928).

138. G. S. Bain and R. Price, *Profiles of Union Growth: A Comparative Statistical Portrait of Eight Countries* (1980), pp. 37, 88.

139. E. J. Hobsbawm, *Worlds of Labour*, op. cit., p. 211; J. Hinton, op. cit., Ch. 8; R. McKibbin, *The Evolution of the Labour Party 1910–1924* (1974). But see also E. Olssen, 'The Case of the Socialist Party that Failed', *Labor History*, 29, 4 (Fall 1988), pp. 448–9.

140. D. Montgomery, 'Labor and the Republic', op. cit., p. 215.

141. R. J. Oestreicher, 'Urban Working Class Political Behavior', op. cit., pp. 1270–4.

142. P. Joyce, 'A People and a Class: How Industrial Workers saw the Social Order in Nineteenth-century England', unpublished paper presented to the Labour Studies seminar, Manchester University (November 1990); M. Kazin, 'A People Not a Class: Rethinking the Political Language of the Modern US Labor Movement', in M. Davis and M. Sprinker (eds.), *Reshaping the US Left: Popular Struggles in the 1980s* (1988).

143. P. F. Clarke, *Lancashire and the New Liberalism* (1971), pp. 25–82; N. Kirk, *The Growth of Working Class Reformism*, op. cit., pp. 335–47; J. Vincent, *The Formation of the British Liberal Party 1857–68* (1972), pp. 112–18, 131–53, 273.

144. K. Laybourn and J. Reynolds, *Liberalism and the Rise of Labour 1890–1918* (1984), pp. 2–7, 18.

145. R. J. Oestreicher, 'Urban Working Class Political Behavior', op. cit., p. 1272.

CHAPTER TWO

1. J. Hinton, *Labour and Socialism*, op. cit., p. 24.

2. In 1901 the Taff Vale Railway Company was awarded £23,000 in receipt of damages incurred during a strike on the Taff Vale railway. The award was made against the Amalgamated Society of Railway Servants, and negated the widespread belief that the acts of 1871 and 1875 had rendered trade unions (as collective organisations) exempt from claims for damages. The Osborne judgment 'in effect prohibited union expenditure upon anything other than strictly trade objectives' (E. H. Hunt, p. 324). The Liberal railwayman, W. V. Osborne, had successfully contested his contribution to the Labour Party via his trade-union subscription. The judg-

ment constituted a severe, if in the event, shortlived setback to unions' financial contributions to the Labour Party.

3. E. H. Hunt, *British Labour History*, op. cit., p. 250.

4. G. S. Bain and R. Price, op. cit., p. 37.

5. P. S. Foner, *History of the Labor Movement in the United States*, (1972) Vol. 1, Ch. 17.

6. D. Montgomery, *Beyond Equality: Labor and the Radical Republicans 1862–1872* (1967), op. cit., pp. 140–1.

7. P. S. Foner, *The Great Labor Uprising of 1877* (1977), p. 8.

8. B. Laurie, *Artisans into Workers*, op. cit., pp. 142, 149, 156.

9. D. Montgomery, 'Labor in the Industrial Era', in R. B. Morris (ed.), op. cit., pp. 108–9.

10. D. Montgomery, *Workers Control in America*, op. cit., p. 93.

11. J. G. Rayback, *A History of American Labor* (1966), Chs. XI–XV; G. Grob, *Workers and Utopia* op. cit., Chs. 8, 9 and Conclusion; P. S. Bagwell and G. E. Mingay, op. cit., pp. 201–8.

12. G. Grob, *Workers and Utopia* op. cit., Ch. 3 and Conclusion; L. Fink, *Workingmens Democracy: The Knights of Labor and American Politics* (1983), p. xii.

13. D. Montgomery, 'On Goodwyn's Populists', *Marxist Perspectives*, 1, 1 (1978).

14. For the 'new' labour history see, L. Fink, 'The New Labor History and the Power of Historical Pessimism: Consensus, Hegemony and the Case of the Knights of Labor', *Journal of American History*, 75, 1 (June 1988); D. Montgomery, *The Fall*, op. cit., Introduction; A. J. Reid, 'The Division of Labour and Politics in Britain, 1880–1920', in W. J. Mommsen and H-G. Husung (eds.), *The Development of Trade Unionism in Great Britain and Germany, 1880–1914* (1985), especially pp. 150–1, 158–63; E. F. Biagini and A. J. Reid (eds.) *Currents of Radicalism: Popular Radicalism Organised Labour and Party Politics in Britain 1850–1914* (1991), 1.

15. The following section on British trade unionism relies heavily upon E. H. Hunt, op. cit., Ch. 8; J. Hinton, op. cit., Chs. 1 and 2; J. Lovell, *British Trade Unions 1875–1933* (1977), Ch. 1.

16. N. Kirk, op. cit., Ch. 6.

17. A Howe, *The Cotton Masters, 1830–1860* (1984), pp. 44–6; P. Joyce, *Work Society and Politics*, op. cit., Ch. 1.

18. A. Bullen, *The Lancashire Weavers Union: A Commemorative History* (1984); A. Bullen and A. Fowler, *The Cardroom Workers Union: A Centenary History of the Amalgamated Association of Card and Blowing Room Operatives* (1986), pp. 39–47.

19. H. A. Turner, op. cit., pp. 126–38, III, 2.

20. J. Mason, 'Spinners and Minders', and A. Bullen, 'The Founding of The Amalgamation', in A. Fowler and T. Wyke (eds.), *The Barefoot Aristocrats: A History of the Amalgamated Association of Operative Cotton Spinners* (1987).

21. The following pages on mining depend heavily upon J. Benson, *British Coalminers in the Nineteenth Century* (1989), pp. 189–213; E. H. Hunt, op. cit., pp. 252–4; J. Hinton, op. cit., pp. 20–1. See also F. Reid, 'Alexander MacDonald and the Crisis of the Independent Collier, 1872–1874', in R. Harrison (ed.), *The Independent Collier*, (1978).

22. T. Matsumura, *The Labour Aristocracy Revisited: The Victorian Flint-Glass Makers 1850–1880* (1983).

23. J. P. D. Dunbabin, ' "The Revolt of the Field": The Agricultural Labourers' Movement in the 1870s', *Past and Present*, 26 (1963); J. Hinton, op. cit., pp. 18–20.

24. J. Hinton, op. cit., p. 17.

25. For the period 1875–1888 see J. Lovell, op. cit., pp. 10–11, 15–17; E. L. Taplin, *The Dockers Union: A Study of the National Union of Dock Labourers 1889–1922* (1986), pp. 25–7; J. Liddington and J. Norris, *One Hand Tied Behind Us: The Rise of the Women's Suffrage Movement* (1984), II and V. For the notion of 'co-exploitation' see E. J. Hobsbawm, *Labouring Men*, op. cit., pp. 297–300. The employment of helpers was widespread among American craft and skilled workers. See D. Montgomery, *The Fall*, op. cit., pp. 11–22.

26. E. H. Hunt, op. cit., pp. 263–4; N. Kirk, op. cit., pp. 288–9.

27. E. H. Hunt, op. cit., p. 268, E. Frow and M. Katanka (eds.), *1868: Year of the Unions: A Documentary Survey* (1968).

28. A. Reid, 'The Division of Labour and Politics in Britain, 1880–1920', op. cit., pp. 155–8.

29. E. H. Hunt, op. cit., p. 281.

30. D. Montgomery, *Beyond Equality*, op. cit., Ch. IV; id., 'Strikes in Nineteenth-Century America', *Social Science History*, 4, 1 (Feb. 1980); S. J. Ross, *Workers on the Edge: Work, Leisure and Politics in Industrializing Cincinnati 1788–1890* (1985), op. cit., Ch. 8; P. S. Foner, *History of the Labor Movement in the United States*, Vol. 1, Chs. 17 and 18; S. Wilentz, 'The Rise of the American Working Class, 1776–1877', in J. C. Moody and A. K. Harris (eds.), *Perspectives on American Labor History: The Problems of Synthesis* (1990), op. cit., especially pp. 117–34; G. E. McNeill, 'Progress of the Movement from 1861 to 1886', in G. E. McNeill (ed.), op. cit.

31. It is extremely difficult to provide accurate membership figures for American unions during these post-bellum years. As seen in the case of the Crispins, many officially enrolled members failed to maintain consistent payment of their union dues (but continued to be counted as members). The Crispins were a powerful force, but did not merit the *American Workman*'s description as being, 'the foremost trade organisation of the world'. See N. Kirk, 'Technology and Boot and Shoe Workers 1860–1905', unplublished M.A. dissertation (University of Warwick, 1969); F. K. Foster, 'Shoemakers in the Movement', in G. E. McNeill (ed.), op. cit.

32. D. Montgomery, *Beyond Equality*, op. cit., pp. 151 ff.

33. Ibid., p. 178, Ch. 6, p. 334.

34. For the National Labor Union see ibid., pp. 176–96.

35. E. Foner, *Reconstruction: America's Unfinished Revolution 1863–1877* (1988), p. 477.

36. For an excellent study of the ways in which such impositions were partly responsible for the New York City Draft Riots of 1863 see I. Bernstein, *The New York City Draft Riots: Their Significance for American Society and Politics in the Age of the Civil War* (1990), especially Ch. 3.

37. S. J. Ross, op. cit., pp. 193–4.

38. D. Montgomery, *Beyond Equality*, op. cit., pp. 188–9, 327–32.

39. E. Foner, *Reconstruction*, op. cit., pp. 515–16; L. Goodwyn, *The Populist*

Moment: A Short History of the Agrarian Revolt in America (1978), Introduction.

40. For material on women see D. Montgomery, 'Labor in the Industrial Era', op. cit., pp. 94–6; P. S. Foner, *History of the Labor Movement*, op. cit., pp. 341–4, 382–8; A. K. Harris, *Out to Work* (1982); M. J. Buhle, 'Gender and Labor History', in J. C. Moody and A. K. Harris (eds.), op. cit.; M. H. Blewett, *Men, Women and Work* (1988) pp. 167–90.

41. Within the WWA there were continuous conflicts between those middle-class women, especially Anthony, who wished to make the struggle for female suffrage a top priority, and those wage-earning women who emphasised the economic and social causes of their poverty and oppression. Anthony's suggestion in 1869 that employers in New York City recruit women to break a male printers' strike led to the withdrawal of working-class women from the WWA. See A. K. Harris, op. cit., pp. 95–7.

42. P. S. Foner, *Organized Labor and the Black Worker 1619–1981*, Chs. 2 and 3; I. Bernstein, op. cit., pp. 27–31, 35–6, 119–20; B. Laurie, *Artisans into Workers*, op. cit., pp. 158–9.

43. E. Foner, *Reconstruction*, op. cit., pp. 479–80.

44. L. Fink, *Workingmens Democracy*, op. cit., Ch. 6.

45. E. Foner, *Reconstruction*, op. cit., especially Ch. 4; id., 'Languages of Change: Sources of Black Ideology during the Civil War and Reconstruction', in L. V. Mannucci (ed.), *The Languages of Revolution* (1989); G. D. Jaynes, *Branches Without Roots: Genesis of the Black Working Class in the American South 1862–1882* (1986), Chs. 7 and 8; P. J. Rachleff, *Black Labor in the South: Richmond Virginia 1865–1900* (1984), especially Chs. 2 and 3; R. L. Ransom and R. Sutch, *One Kind of Freedom: The Economic Consequence of Emancipation* (1977); H. G. Gutman, *The Black Family in Slavery and Freedom 1750–1925* (1976).

46. E. Foner, *Reconstruction*, op. cit., p. 136.

47. G. Wright, *Old South New South: Revolutions in the Southern Economy Since the Civil War* (1986), p. 85.

48. Ibid., pp. 89. 93–4; G. D. Jaynes, op. cit., Ch. 9.

49. N. I. Painter, *Exodusters: Black Migration to Kansas after Reconstruction* (1976), Pt. I, Ch. 5.

50. P. S. Foner, *Organized Labor and the Black Worker*, op. cit., Ch. 2; W. C. Hine, 'Black Organized Labor in Reconstruction Charleston', *Labor History*, 25, 4 (Fall 1984).

51. P. S. Foner, op. cit., p. 26; G. D. Jaynes, op. cit., pp. 114, 120; L. Fink, *Workingmens Democracy*, op. cit., pp. 169–70; H. G. Gutman, 'Labor in the Land of Lincoln: Coal Miners on the Prairie', in H. G. Gutman and I. Berlin, *Power and Culture*, op. cit., especially pp. 175, 203.

52. G. D. Jaynes, op. cit., pp. 256, 264.

53. D. Montgomery, *Beyond Equality*, op. cit., Ch. 5; M. Davis 'Why the U.S. Working Class is Different', *New Left Review*, 23 (Sept.-Oct. 1980), especially pp. 9–25.

54. D. Montgomery, op. cit., pp. 249–60, Ch. 9.

55. Ibid., pp. 177–8.

56. Ibid., Ch. 11, especially pp. 444–7; E. Foner, *Reconstruction*, op. cit., p. 478.

57. S. J. Ross, op. cit., pp. 199–201. Michael Kazin's emphasis upon the pri-

macy of the producerist, populist and racist (as opposed to revolutionary socialist) discourses of modern American labour has led to an underestimation of the influence of non-socialist class-based actions and ideas among American workers and the interplays between class, race, populism and producerism. Much in the manner of Stedman Jones and Joyce, Kazin employs an absolute, ideal standard of class. This standard camouflages the depth and extent of class in America. See M. Kazin, 'A People Not a Class', op. cit.

58. E. Foner, op. cit., p. 514. The following section on social protest during the depression is indebted to id., pp. 514–16; B. Laurie, *Artisans into Workers*, op. cit., pp. 134–5, 142–3; H. G. Gutman, 'Trouble on the Railroads in 1873–1874: Prelude to the 1877 Crisis?', in H. G. Gutman, *Work Culture and Society*, (1977); id., 'Two Lockouts in Pennsylvania, 1873–1874', in ibid.

59. D. Montgomery, 'Labour in the Industrial Era', in R. B. Morris (ed.), op. cit., pp. 106–7.

60. Foner has produced the most exhaustive account of the strikes of 1877. See P. S. Foner *The Great Labor Uprising of 1877*, op. cit., especially Preface, Chs. X and XI.

61. Ibid., Ch. IX.

62. H. G. Gutman, 'The Workers Search for Power: Labor in the Gilded Age', in H. W. Morgan (ed.), *The Gilded Age: A Reappraisal* (1963).

63. E. Foner, op. cit., p. 517; M. Kazin, 'A People Not a Class', op. cit., p. 264.

64. B. Laurie, op. cit., p. 136.

65. H. Perkin, *The Origins of Modern English Society 1780–1880* (1972), pp. 389–407.

66. For the 'new unionist' upsurge see, H. A. Clegg, A. Fox and A. F. Thompson, *A History of British Trade Unions since 1889*, Vol. 1 (1964); D. Howell, *British Workers and the Independent Labour Party 1888–1906* (1984), Ch. 6; H. Pelling, *A History of British Trade Unionism* (1963); J. Hinton, op. cit., pp. 45–51; E. H. Hunt, op. cit., pp. 295–311; J. Lovell, op. cit., Ch. 2; and the essays by E. J. Hobsbawm ('The "New Unionism" Reconsidered'), S. Pollard ('The New Unionism in Britain: Its Economic Background'), and R. Hyman ('Mass Organisation and Militancy in Britain: Contrasts and Continuities') in W. J. Mommsen and H-G. Husung (eds.), *The Development of Trade Unionism in Great Britain and Germany*, op. cit.

67. E. H. Hunt, op. cit., pp. 299–300; J. Hinton, op. cit., p. 31; J. Liddington and J. Norris, op. cit., Chs. II and V; L. Middleton (ed.), *Women in the Labour Movement* (1977); A. V. John, 'A Miner Struggle? Women's Protests in Welsh Mining History', *Llafur*, 4, 1 (1984); E. Gordon, *Women and the Labour Movement in Scotland*, (1991), Ch. 6.

68. R. Hyman, *Mass Organisation and Militancy*, op. cit. p. 251.

69. J. Lovell, 'The Significance of the Great Dock Strike of 1889 in British Labour History', in W. J. Mommsen and H-G Husung (eds.), op. cit., pp. 105–13.

70. J. Lovell, *British Trade Unions*, op. cit., Ch. 2; A. J. Reid, 'Old Unionism Reconsidered: The Radicalism of Robert Knight, 1870–1900', in E. F. Biagini and A. J. Reid (eds.), *Currents of Radicalism*, op. cit.

71. D. Howell, op. cit., Ch. 6; J. L. White, *Tom Mann* (1991).

72. D. Howell, op. cit., p. 113.

73. R. Hyman, 'Mass Organisation and Militancy', op. cit., pp. 251–3; D. Howell, op. cit., Ch. 4; P. S. Bagwell, 'The New Unionism in Britain: The Railway Industry', in W. J. Mommsen and H.-G. Husung (eds.), op. cit.

74. R. M. Jones, *The North Wales Quarrymen 1874–1922* (1981), especially Chs. 7 and 8; R. M. Jones and J. Lovecy, 'Slate Workers in Wales, France and the United States: A Comparative Study, 1870–1920', *Llafur*, 4, 4 (1986).

75. K. Burgess, *The Origins of British Industrial Relations*, op. cit., p. 288.

76. J. Hinton, op. cit., p. 65.

77. J. Benson, *British Coalminers*, op. cit., pp. 198–9.

78. J. Lovell, *British Trade Unions*, op. cit., p. 43.

79. J. Hinton, op. cit., Ch. 5; E. H. Hunt, op. cit., pp. 318–34; B. Holton, *British Syndicalism 1900–1914* (1976).

80. P. S. Bagwell, op. cit.; R. Hyman, op. cit., pp. 259–60; E. L. Taplin, op. cit., pp. 84–107.

81. J. Hinton, op. cit., p. 86.

82. J. L. White, 'Lancashire Cotton Textiles', in C. J. Wrigley (ed.), Vol. 1, op. cit., p. 224.

83. J. Hinton, op. cit., p. 89.

84. R. Hyman, op. cit., pp. 258–61; J. Lovell, op. cit., p. 46; J. Hinton, op. cit., p. 98.

85. J. L. White, '1910–14 Reconsidered', in J. E. Cronin and J. Schneer (eds.), *Social Conflict and the Political Order in Modern Britain* (1982).

86. In the United States persistent and widespread state and employer hostility towards trade unionism did give rise to acute periods of conflict and radicalism. All too often, however, the very successes of employer offensives against trade unionism not only debilitated the movement but also induced accommodation and bitter despair among workers.

87. R. Geary, 'Tonypandy and Llanelli Revisited', *Llafur*, 4, 4 (1986); R. Hyman, op. cit. p. 262.

88. J. Schneer, 'The War, the State and the Workplace: British Dockers During 1914–1918', in J. E. Cronin and J. Schneer (eds.), op. cit.; J. Stevenson, *British Society 1914–45* (1984), pp. 55–70, 85–9; J. M. Winter, *Socialism and the Challenge of War: Ideas and Politics in Britain 1912–18* (1974); B. Waites, *A Class Society at War: England 1914–18* (1987); J. Hinton, op. cit., Ch. 6; J. Lovell, op. cit., Ch. 5.

89. For debates concerning 'Red Clydeside' see the articles (op. cit.) by J. Melling and J. Foster, *International Review Social History*, XXXV (1990); A. J. Reid, 'Dilution, Trade Unionism and the State in Britain during the First World War', in S. Tolliday and J. Zeitlin (eds.), op. cit.; J. Hinton, *The First Shop Stewards Movement* (1973); I. McLean, *The Legend of Red Clydesdie* (1983).

90. J. Stevenson, op. cit., p. 87.

91. J. E. Cronin, 'Coping with Labour, 1918–1926', in J. E. Cronin and J. Schneer (eds.), op. cit., p. 114.

92. J. Stevenson, op. cit., p. 101.

93. A. Reid, 'Glasgow Socialism', *Social History*, XI, 1 (Jan. 1986).

94. J. Hinton, *The First Shop Stewards Movement*, op. cit., Ch. 1; R. Davidson, 'The Myth of the Servile State', *Bulletin of the Society for the Study*

of Labour History, 29 (Autumn 1974); A. J. Reid, 'Dilution, Trade Unionism and the State', op. cit.

95. J. Hinton, *Labour and Socialism*, op. cit., pp. 98–102.
96. J. Melling 'Industrial Conflict and the Politics of Skill', *International
     Review of Social History*, XXXV (1990), pp. 30–2.
97. For a review of the literature dealing with relations between 'rank-and-
     file' workers and union officials see, E. Arnesen, 'Crusades Against Crisis:
     A View from the United States on the "Rank and File" Critique and
     Other Catalogues of Labour History's Alleged Ills', *International Review
     of Social History*, XXXV (1990).
98. For accounts of the 'Great Upheaval' I have consulted B. Laurie, *Artisans
     into Workers*, op. cit., pp. 156–75; S. J. Ross, op. cit., Ch. 11; S. Levine,
     *Labor's True Women: Carpet Weavers, Industrialization and Labor
     Reform in the Gilded Age* (1984), Introduction and Ch. 4; R. J. Oestrei-
     cher, *Solidarity and Fragmentation*, op. cit., Ch. 5.
99. D. Montgomery, 'Strikes in Nineteenth-Century America', op. cit., p. 98;
     M. Shefter, 'Trade Unions and Political Machines: The Organization and
     Disorganization of the American Working Class in the Late Nineteenth
     Century', in I. Katznelson and A. R. Zolberg (eds.), *Working Class Forma-
     tion* (1986), p. 236.
100. L. Fink, *Workingmens Democracy*, op. cit., pp. xii–xiii.
101. Ibid., pp. 121–2; S. Stromquist, *A Generation of Boomers: The Pattern of
     Railroad Labor Conflict in Nineteenth-Century America* (1987), pp. 32,
     49, 56, 60, 69.
102. B. Laurie, op. cit., p. 169.
103. S. J. Ross, op. cit., pp. 270–1, 275–7, 280, 283–4, 291–2. See R. J. Oest-
     reicher (op. cit., Ch. 5) for May Day in Detroit.
104. R. J. Oestreicher, op. cit., especially pp. 89–96, 112–19, 162–8; S. Levine,
     op. cit., Chs. 5 and 6; L. Fink, op. cit., especially Preface and Ch. 1; B.
     Laurie, op. cit., Ch. 5. See also G. E. McNeill, 'History of the Knights
     of Labor', in G. E. McNeill (ed.), op. cit.
105. B. Laurie, op. cit., p. 142. It is, however, important to note that alliances
     with the American Railway Union and Populism revived the fortunes of
     the Knights in the early 1890s.
106. L. Fink, op. cit., p. 9.
107. S. Levine, op. cit., p. 121: M. H. Blewett, op. cit., Ch. 8.
108. S. Levine, op. cit., pp. 109–10, 118–27, 133.
109. B. Laurie, op. cit., pp. 160–3; N. I. Painter, 'Black Workers From Recon-
     struction to the Great Depression', in P. Buhle and A. Dawley (eds.), op.
     cit., especially pp. 65–6; P. J. Rachleff, op. cit. Chs. 7 and 8; L. Fink,
     op. cit., Chs. 6 and 8.
110. H. G. Gutman, 'The Negro and the United Mine Workers of America:
     The Career and Letters of Richard L. Davis and Something of Their
     Meaning, 1890–1900', in H. G. Gutman, *Work, Culture and Society*, op.
     cit.
111. L. Fink, op. cit., p. 4; B. Laurie, op. cit., p. 150.
112. For an incisive examination of the Knights' and many other nineteenth-
     century radicals' attitude towards the state see L. Fink, op. cit., Ch. 2.
113. B. D. Palmer, *Descent into Discourse: The Reification of Language and
     the Writing of Social History* (1990), pp. 108–18.
114. R. J. Oestreicher, op. cit., pp. 90–6, 103.

115. Many national unions were increasingly critical of the Knights' refusal to respect their autonomy and their jurisdictional 'rights'. As illustrated above all in cigarmaking, the Knights' leaders were accused of supporting dual unionism and even strikebreaking (especially against Gompers' and Strasser's Cigar Makers' International Union). Matters came to a head in 1886 when the Knights ordered all cigar makers who were members of both the Order and the CMIU to withdraw from the latter or leave the Order. Many trade unionists, largely irrespective of their political leanings, were critical of Powderly's actions and joined the AFL. See R. J. Oestreicher (op. cit., Ch. 6) for an informed discussion of the points of disagreement between national unionists and the Knights' leadership. See also B. Laurie, op. cit., pp. 170–5; P. J. Rachleff, op. cit., Chs. 10 and 11; L. Fink, op. cit., p. 133; B. C. Nelson, *Beyond the Martyrs: A Social History of Chicago's Anarchists 1870–1900* (1988).

116. L. Fink, op. cit., p. 226.

117. This section on agrarian radicalism is particularly indebted to L. Goodwyn, *The Populist Moment*, (1978); C. V. Woodward's superbly evocative *Tom Watson: Agrarian Radical* (1972); D. Montgomery, 'On Goodwyn's Populists', op. cit.; and the essays by S. Hahn and R. C. McMath (op. cit.) in S. Hahn and J. Prude (eds.), *The Countryside in the Age of Capitalist Transformation*, (1985).

118. Argument centres around price levels (for agricultural produce in relation to general price trends), incomes and outgoings (rates of interest, railroad rates and so on). See D. C. North, T. L. Anderson and P. J. Hill, *Growth and Welfare in the American Past* (1983), Ch. XI; G. M. Walton and R. M. Robertson, *History of the American Economy*, op. cit., pp. 362–9.

119. For Populism as a backward-looking conspiracy see R. Hofstadter, *The Age of Reform: From Bryan to F. D. R.* (1955). For counter-blasts see L. Goodwyn, op. cit., pp. 334–42; W. T. K. Nugent, *The Tolerant Populists* (1963); O. E. Clanton, *Kansas Populism: Ideas and Men* (1969); N. Pollack, *The Populist Response to Industrial America: Midwestern Populist Thought* (1962). John Hicks' *The Populist Revolt* (1931) constitutes the pioneering work on the subject.

120. L. Goodwyn, op. cit., p. 20.

121. C. V. Woodward, op. cit., p. 136.

122. Ibid., pp. 178, 217–19.

123. L. Goodwyn, op. cit., pp. 117–23.

124. D. Montgomery, 'On Goodwyn's Populists', op. cit.; L. Goodwyn, op. cit., Ch. 5, and pp. 231–63.

125. G. Wright, op. cit., p. 115.

126. L. Goodwyn, op. cit., pp. 108–12.

127. For the later years of Populism see ibid., Ch. 8; C. V. Woodward, op. cit., Chs. xx–xxiv; D. Montgomery, op. cit.

128. C. V. Woodward, op. cit., p. 219.

129. G. Wright, op. cit., pp. 122–3; C. V. Woodward, *Origins of the New South 1877–1913* (1951), pp. 321–95.

130. G. Wright, op. cit., pp. 117, 119, 133.

131. C. V. Woodward, *Tom Watson*, op. cit., p. 178.

132. S. B. Kaufman, *Samuel Gompers and the Origins of the American Federation of Labor 1848–1896* (1973), pp. 186–9.

133. C. V. Woodward, *Tom Watson*, op. cit., pp. 217–18.

134. D. Montgomery, 'Labor in the Industrial Era', op. cit., p. 111; B. Laurie, op. cit., p. 193.

135. The most dramatic account of the Homestead lockout was provided in 1893 by Pittsburgh journalist, Arthur G. Burgoyne. See his *The Homestead Strike of 1892* (1979).

136. D. Montgomery, *The Fall*, op. cit., pp. 38–9. The quotes by Snowden and Paxson are taken from Montgomery's book.

137. For the Pullman boycott and its aftermath see B. Laurie, op. cit., pp. 204–10; S. Stromquist, *A Generation of Boomers*, op. cit., pp. 89–99, 257–8.

138. S. Stromquist, 'Looking Both Ways: Ideological Crisis and Working Class Recomposition in the 1890s', unpublished paper (1984), especially pp. 15–24, 32. I am grateful to the author for permission to quote from his paper.

139. Ibid., especially pp. 55–71; D. Brody, *Steelworkers in America*, op. cit., Ch. V; M. Davis, 'Why the U.S. Working Class is Different', op. cit., pp. 33–5; B. Laurie, op. cit., pp. 195–7; A. Saxton, *The Indispensable Enemy: Labor and the Anti-Chinese Movement in California* (1975), especially Ch. 12; A. H. Spear, *Black Chicago: The Making of a Negro Ghetto 1890–1920* (1967), Ch. 2; G. Mink, *Old Labor and New Immigrants in American Political Development: Union Party and State 1875–1920* (1986), Ch. 1.

140. For the AFL see B. Laurie, op. cit., Ch. 6; M. Shefter, op. cit., pp. 259–66; S. B. Kaufman, op. cit.; W. M. Dick, *Labor and Socialism in America: The Gompers Era* (1972); J. H. M. Laslett, 'Samuel Gompers and the Rise of American Business Unionism', in M. Dubofsky and W. Van Tine (eds.), *Labor Leaders in America* (1987); S. Gompers, *Seventy Years of Life and Labor*, 2 Vols. (1925); C. L. Tomlins, *The State and the Unions*, op. cit., Ch. 3; L. Fink, 'American Labor History', in E. Foner (ed.), *The New American History* (1990); W. Forbath, *Law and the Shaping of the American Labor Movement* (1991).

141. D. Montgomery, *The Fall*, op. cit., pp. 5–6.

142. B. Laurie, op. cit., pp. 192–8; A. K. Harris, *Out to Work*, op. cit., pp. 153–9; M. Tax, *The Rising of the Women: Feminist Solidarity and Class Conflict 1880–1917 (1980)*; N. S. Dye, *As Equals and as Sisters: Feminism Unionism and the Women's Trade Union League of New York* (1980).

143. D. Brody, *Workers in Industrial America: Essays on the Twentieth Century Struggle* (1981), pp. 83–6.

144. J. Greene, 'The Strike at the Ballot Box" ', op. cit., pp. 166–7.

145. J. R. Commons, 'The American Federation of Labor', in C. M. Rehmus, D. B. McLaughlin and F. H. Nesbitt (eds.), *Labor and American Politics: A Book of Readings* (1978), pp. 87–94; S. Gompers, 'Should a Labor Party be Formed?', in ibid., pp. 103–7.

146. J. Greene, op. cit., pp. 169ff.

147. M. Rogin, 'Voluntarism: The Political Functions of an Anti-Political Doctrine', *Industrial and Labor Relations Review*, 15 (July 1962); W. Forbath, op. cit.

148. D. Montgomery, *The Fall*, op. cit., pp. 357, 364–5, 373–7.

149. S. Gompers, 'Should a Labor Party be Formed?', op. cit., p. 107.

150. See, for example, G. Grob, *Workers and Utopia*, op. cit., Chs. 6 and 7.

151. S. B. Kaufman, op. cit., pp. 165, 173–4; C. L. Tomlins, op. cit., pp. 61, 63, 76.

152. A. K. Harris, op. cit., pp. 155–6, 165–6; L. W. Tentler, *Wage Earning Women: Industrialization Work and Family Life in the United States 1900–1930* (1979); R. M. Jacoby, 'The Women's Trade Union League and American Feminism', in M. Cantor and B. Laurie (eds.), *Class, Sex and the Woman Worker* (1977); N. S. Dye, 'Creating a Feminist Alliance: Sisterhood and Class Conflict in the New York Women's Trade Union League, 1903–1914', in ibid.

153. For socialist activity within the AFL see D. Montgomery, *The Fall*, op. cit., pp. 281–310; J. H. M. Laslett and S. M. Lipset (eds.), *Failure of a Dream?: Essays in the History of American Socialism* (1974); J. Weinstein, *The Decline of Socialism in America 1912–1925* (1967); J. H. M. Laslett, *Labour and the Left: A Study of Socialist and Radical Influences in the American Labor Movement 1881–1924* (1970); M. Kazin, *Barons of Labor: The San Francisco Building Trades and Union Power in the Progressive Era* (1987), pp. 148–50, 160–2.

154. M. Kazin, op. cit., pp. 114–20, Ch. 6 and Conclusion.

155. G. M. Fink, *Labor's Search for Political Order: The Political Behavior of the Missouri Labor Movement 1890–1940* (1973); id., 'The Rejection of Voluntarism', in C. M. Rehmus, D. B. McLaughlin and F. H. Nesbitt (eds.), op. cit., pp. 108–29; I. Yellowitz, *Labor and the Progressive Movement in New York State 1897–1916* (1965); M. Kazin, op. cit., p. 283.

156. S. Stromquist, 'Looking Both Ways', op. cit., p. 62.

157. P. Taft, 'Workers of a New Century,', in R. B. Morris, op. cit., pp. 122–5; E. Jameson, 'Imperfect Unions: Class and Gender in Cripple Creek, 1894–1904', in M. Cantor and B. Laurie (eds.), op. cit., pp. 166–8, 189–93.

158. D. Emmons, op. cit., pp. 183–5, 221–36, 244–8, Chs. 8, 10 and Epilogue.

159. M. Kazin, op. cit., Ch. 9.

160. D. Montgomery, *The Fall*, op. cit., pp. 288–9.

161. D. Montgomery, *Workers Control in America*, op. cit., pp. 93–8.

162. P. Taft, op. cit., pp. 125–6.

163. D. Montgomery, *Workers Control in America*, op. cit., pp. 107–8.

164. Ibid., pp. 103–4; 127–34; J. Haydu, *Between Craft and Class: Skilled Factory Workers and Factory Politics in the United States and Britain 1890–1922* (1988) for a comparison between the 'factory politics' of skilled metal workers in Coventry and Bridgeport. For the involvement of 'new' immigrants in strikes and trade unionism in Britain see K. Lunn, 'Immigrants and Strikes', op. cit.; B. Williams, 'The beginnings of Jewish Trade Unionism in Manchester, 1889–1891', in K. Lunn (ed.), *Hosts Immigrants and Minorities: Historical Responses to Newcomers in British Society 1870–1914* (1980); K. Lunn, 'Reactions to Lithuanian and Polish Immigrants in the Lanarkshire Coalfield, 1880–1914', in ibid; J. Buckman, *Immigrants and Class Struggle: The Jewish Immigrant in Leeds 1880–1914* (1983).

165. D. Montgomery, 'Immigrants, Industrial Unions and Social Reconstruction', *Labour/Le Travail*, 13 (Spring 1984), p. 104; id., 'Nationalism, American Patriotism, and Class Consciousness Among Immigrant Workers in the United States in the Epoch of World War I', in D. Hoerder (ed.), *Struggle a Hard Battle: Essays on Working-Class Immigrants* (1986), p. 329.

166. D. Montgomery, *The Fall*, op. cit., p. 332.

167. D. Montgomery, 'Nationalism, American Patriotism', op. cit., pp. 330–3.

168. D. Montgomery, *Workers Control in America*, op. cit., pp. 103, 124, 127–34.

169. D. Montgomery, 'Immigrants, Industrial Unions and Social Reconstruction', op. cit., pp. 105–6; id., *The Fall* p. 427.

170. D. Montgomery, *The Fall*, op. cit., pp. 373–376, 377, 393–5; S. Meyer, 'Adapting the Immigrant to the Line: Americanization in the Ford Factory, 1914–1921', *Journal of Social History*, 14, 1 (Fall 1980).

171. D. Montgomery, *The Fall*, op. cit., p. 370.

172. D. Montgomery, 'Nationalism, American Patriotism', op. cit., pp. 334–5.

173. D. Montgomery, *Workers Control in America*, op. cit., p. 100. Montgomery's work has conclusively shown that fierce industrial conflicts at Homestead, Turtle Creek and Bridgeport, in the coalfields and on the railways and elsewhere generated strong *class* (as opposed to purely industrial and sectional) attachments and conflicts.

174. D. Montgomery, *Workers Control in America*, op. cit., p. 99.

175. D. Brody, *Labor in Crisis*, op. cit., especially Chs. 4 and 5.

176. D. Montgomery, *Workers Control in America*, op. cit., p. 100; J. R. Barrett, *Work and Community in the Jungle: Chicago's Packinghouse Workers 1894–1922* (1987), pp. 191–202, 255–63; R. Halpern, 'Race, Ethnicity and Union in the Chicago Stockyards, 1917–1922', *International Review of Social History*, XXXVII (1992).

177. For the post-war scene in Britain see J. E. Cronin, 'Coping with Labour, 1918–1926', in J. E. Cronin and J. Schneer (eds.), op. cit.; J. Stevenson, *British Society*, op. cit., pp. 97–102.

178. J. Foster, 'Strike Action and Working Class Politics', op. cit., pp. 38, 54–9.

179. A. Marwick, *The Deluge: British Society and the First World War* (1975), pp. 20–6, 203–10, 300–5.

180. D. Montgomery, *Workers Control in America*, op. cit., p. 99.

181. D. Brody, *Labor in Crisis*, op. cit., pp. 39–44, 132–3, 162–3; P. S. Foner, *Organized Labor and the Black Worker*, op. cit., Chs. 10 and 11; D. Montgomery, *The Fall*, op. cit., pp. 378–83.

182. D. Brody, *Labor in Crisis*, op. cit., p. 134.

183. D. Montgomery, *The Fall*, op. cit., p. 408.

184. J. J. Bukowczyk, 'The Transformation of Working-Class Ethnicity: Corporate Control, Americanization, and the Polish Immigrant Middle Class in Bayonne, New Jersey, 1915–1925', *Labor History*, 25, 1 (Winter 1984).

185. D. Brody, 'The Rise and Decline of Welfare Capitalism', in his *Workers in Industrial America*, op. cit., J. D. Hall, R. Korstad and J. Leloudis, 'Cotton Mill People: Work, Community and Protest in the Textile South, 1880–1940', *American Historical Review*, 91 (1986); D. Montgomery, *The Fall* op. cit., pp. 415–16, 453–7, 459–64.

186. D. Montgomery, *The Fall*, pp. 393–4, 406–10.

187. J. E. Cronin, 'Coping With Labour', op. cit., p. 128.

188. P. Fryer, *Staying Power: The History of Black People in Britain* (1985), pp. 298–316; J. Jenkinson, 'The Glasgow Race Disturbances of 1919', in K. Lunn (ed.), *Race and Labour*, op. cit.; N. Evans, 'Regulating the Reserve Army: Arabs, Blacks and the Local State in Cardiff, 1919–45', in ibid.

189. E. J. Hobsbawm, *Labouring Men*, op. cit., Ch. 10; G. Marks, *Unions in*

Politics: Britain Germany and the United States in the Nineteenth and Twentieth Centuries (1989), pp. 199, 204–17. It is, however, interesting to note that in 1905 William English Walling, the American socialist, argued that non-skilled unionism was more advanced (by means of industrial organisation) in the United States than in Britain. See W. E. Walling, 'British and American Trade Unionism', *Annals of the American Academy of Political and Social Science*, Vol. XXVLI (1905). I am grateful to Steve Sapolsky for this reference.

190. D. Montgomery, 'Strikes in Nineteenth-Century America', op. cit., pp. 88–9.

191. N. Kirk, *The Growth of Working Class Reformism*, op. cit., pp. 270–2.

192. D. Montgomery, 'Strikes in Nineteenth-Century America', op. cit., p. 93;

193. E. J. Hobsbawm, 'Economic Fluctuations and Some Social Movements since 1800', *Labouring Men*, op. cit., Ch. 8; J. Lovell, *British Trade Unions*, op. cit., Ch. 2.

194. D. Montgomery, 'Strikes in Nineteenth-Century America', op. cit., p. 84; M. Shefter, 'Trade Unions and Political Machines', op. cit., p. 236; E. J. Hobsbawm, *Labouring Men*, op. cit., p. 127.

195. J. Zeitlin, 'From Labour History to the History of Industrial Relations', *Economic History Review*, second series XL (1987); R. Price, ' "What's in a Name?" Workplace History and "Rank and Filism" ', *International Review of Social History*, XXXIV (1989).

196. R. Price, 'The Future of British Labour History', *International Review of Social History*, XXXVI (1991–2), p. 257.

197. S. Pollard 'The New Unionism in Britain', in W. J. Mommsen and H-G. Husung (eds.), op. cit., pp. 39–41; J. E. Cronin, 'Strikes 1870–1914', in C. J. Wrigley (ed.), *A History of British Industrial Relations 1875–1914*, op. cit. But for continued inequality and poverty see H. Perkin, *The Rise of Professional Society; England Since 1880* (1989), especially pp. 101–15; S. Meacham, *A Life Apart*: The English Working Class 1890–1914 (1977).

198. See the essays (op. cit.) by K. Burgess, P. S. Bagwell and A. Reid in W. J. Mommsen and H-G Husung (eds.) op. cit: K. McClelland and A. Reid, 'Wood, Iron and Steel' (op. cit., pp. 168, 170, 174) for exclusive policies on the part of the Boilermakers' Society towards platers' helpers (who constituted a direct threat to the jobs of the skilled) and more inclusive policies towards the caulkers (who did not constitute a threat to other trades); G. Mink, op. cit.; D. Brody, *Steelworkers in America*, op. cit., Ch. XII; M. Kazin, op. cit., p. 105. For the hostile and indifferent attitudes of male cigar makers in the CMIU towards the organisation of women in cigarmaking see P. A. Cooper, *Once a Cigar Maker: Men, Women and Work Culture in American Cigar Factories 1900–1919* (1987), Ch. 8.

199. J. Lovell, 'The Significance of the Great Dock Strike of 1889 in British Labor History', in W. J. Mommsen and H-G Husung (eds.), op. cit., pp. 106–7.

200. B. Laurie, op. cit., pp. 190–1; J. H. M. Laslett, *Labor and the Left*, op. cit., Ch. 3.

201. D. Emmons, op. cit., p. 184. It should, however, be noted that a rift soon developed between the WFM and the IWW. In 1911 the WFM re-entered the AFL. See J. H. M. Laslett, op. cit., Ch. 7 for the WFM.

202. For nineteenth-century railway developments see S. Stromquist, *A Gener-*

ation of Boomers, op. cit., Ch. 2, pp. 263–5. For twentieth-century railroad unionism see D. Montgomery, *The Fall*, op. cit., pp. 365–9.

203. J. Holt, 'Trade Unionism in the British and U.S. Steel Industries', in C. Emsley (ed.), op. cit., pp. 126–8.

204. P. Duffy, 'Conflict and Continuity in the Manchester Building Trades, 1833–1870', unpublished M.A. dissertation, Manchester Polytechnic (1990), especially pp. 45, 54–5, 72, 87; R. Price, *Masters Unions and Men: Work Control in Building and the Rise of Labour 1830–1914* (1980), pp. 50–1, 78–9.

205. See, for example, B. Lancaster, *Radicalism Cooperation and Socialism*, op. cit., pp. 100–9. For the complex relations between skilled and non-skilled see A. Reid, 'The Division of Labour and Politics in Britain', op. cit., especially pp. 154–8.

206. J. Haydu, op. cit., pp. 211–21.

207. M. Kazin, op. cit., Chs. 9 and 10; D. Emmons, op. cit., Ch. 8.

208. S. Stromquist, 'Looking Both Ways', op. cit., p. 7.

209. C. J. Wrigley, 'Labour and the Trade Unions', in K. D. Brown (ed.), *The First Labour Party 1906–1914* (1985), p. 149.

210. This is particularly the case with Reid, Zeitlin and Tanner. See, for example, A. Reid, 'The Division of Labour and Politics', op. cit.; D. Tanner, *Political Change and the Labour Party 1900–1918* (1990), especially Introduction and Conclusion. For a critique see N. Kirk (ed.) *Class and History* (forthcoming, Scolar 1994).

211. J. R. Barrett, *Work and Community in the Jungle*, op. cit., pp. 273–4; D. Brody, *Labor in Crisis*, op. cit.; id., *The Butcher Workmen: A Study of Unionization* (1964); E. Foner, 'Class, Ethnicity and Radicalism in the Gilded Age: The Land League and Irish America', in his *Politics and Ideology in the Age of the Civil War* (1980), for an astute examination of the interactions between class and ethnicity. In contrast to Foner, Gwendolyn Mink underestimates the degrees of fluidity and complexity between class, ethnicity and race. Mink draws an exaggerated picture of necessary structural conflict (rooted in labour market competition) between 'new' immigrants and mainstream labour. This partial account underestimates varied responses and relationships, the degree of diversity within the AFL, and the importance of class in allegedly 'exceptionalist' America. See, G. Mink, *Old Labor and New Immigrants*, op. cit., especially 17–19, 35–41, Ch. 2. See J. Greene's useful review of Mink's book in *International Labor and Working Class History*, 34 (Fall 1988), especially pp. 122–3.

212. D. Emmons, op. cit., p. 235.

213. M. Kazin, op. cit., Chs. 1 and 2.

214. It should be noted that the behaviour of neither Emmons' conservative miners nor of Stedman Jones' resigned proletarians amounted to class, at least as defined by this author. In both cases anti-capitalist ideas and conflicts were largely absent; and independent working-class cultural and organisational forms coexisted with, and at times were overshadowed by, cross-class and (in the case of Butte) strong inter-class ethnic institutions and practices. In Butte the Irish miners also jealously guarded their domination of job opportunities.

215. For criticisms of Stedman Jones see N. Kirk, ' "Traditional Working-Class Culture" ', *Social History*, op. cit.; J. M. Winter, 'Trade Unions and the

Labour Party in Britain', in W. J. Mommsen and H.-G. Husung (eds.)
op. cit., especially pp. 364–7.

216. E. J. Hobsbawm, 'The Making of the Working Class 1870–1914', in his
Worlds of Labour, op. cit., pp. 194–6.

217. J. R. Barrett, op. cit., pp. 202–24; M. Kazin, op. cit., pp. 162–71.

218. M. Kazin, op. cit., pp. 24–8; J. T. Cumbler, *Working Class Community
in Industrial America* (1979). See the interesting comparative work on
coalminers by Roger Fagge, 'A Comparison of the Miners of South Wales
and West Virginia, 1900–1922: Patterns of Militancy', paper presented to
the International Mining History Congress, Bochum, Sept. 1989.

CHAPTER THREE

1. E Foner, 'Why is There No Socialism in the United States', *History
Workshop Journal*, 17 (Spring 1984), p. 59.

2. P. Kleppner, *The Cross of Culture: A Social Analysis of Midwestern Politics
1850–1900* (1971).

3. R. J. Oestreicher, 'Urban Working Class Political Behavior', op. cit.,
especially pp. 1261–2, 1267–9.

4. A. Dawley, *Class and Community* (1982), p. 70.

5. G. Marks, *Unions in Politics*, op. cit., p. 217.

6. R. J. Oestreicher, op. cit., p. 1270.

7. J. Belchem, *Class Party and the Political System in Britain 1867–1914*
(1990), p. 8. Belchem provides a very useful review of the key political
issues of the period.

8. E. and E. Marx-Aveling, *The Working Class Movement in America* (1887);
H. Pelling, *America and the British Left From Bright to Bevan* (1956),
pp. 62–5; K. Marx and F. Engels, *Letters to Americans 1848–1895* (1953),
pp. 157–8, 161–9, 184–5.

9. E. F. Biagini and A. J. Reid (eds.), op. cit., pp. 5–6, 12–19; K. D. Brown
(ed.) *The First Labour Party 1906–1914* (1985), Introduction.

10. D. Howell, *British Workers and the Independent Labour Party*, op. cit.,
pp. 123–8, 277–82.

11. J. K. Walton, *Lancashire: A Social History*, op. cit., p. 264.

12. The following pages on popular Liberalism owe much to E. F. Biagini
and A. J. Reid (eds.), op. cit., especially Chs. 1 and 5; N. Kirk, *The
Growth of Working Class Reformism*, op. cit., pp. 161–6; P. F. Taylor,
'Popular Politics and Labour-Capital Relations in Bolton 1825–1850' (D.
Phil., Lancaster University, 1991), Ch. 3 and pp. 295–303; J. Foster, *Class
Struggle and the Industrial Revolution* (1974), op. cit., Ch. 7; T. C. Smout,
A Century of the Scottish People, op. cit., pp. 239–51; J. Vincent, *The
Formation of the British Liberal Party* (1972), op. cit., Ch. 2; P. Joyce,
Visions of the People: Industrial England and the Question of Class (1991),
Ch. 2; P. F. Clarke, *Lancashire and the New Liberalism* (1971), Chs. 2
and 3.

13. P. F. Clarke, op. cit., p. 32.

14. In the 1841 parliamentary election Hindley stood at Ashton on the
remarkable platform of support for the entire Charter, repeal of the New
Poor Law, opposition to the new police, and the release of the Welsh
Chartist, John Frost. Sykes notes that 'A substantial body of opinion in
the N (ational) C (harter) A (ssociation) . . . favoured supporting him,

but the Chartists eventually decided to remain neutral.' R. A. Sykes, 'Popular Politics and Trade Unionism in South East Lancashire, 1829–1842' D. Phil. Thesis, University of Manchester, 1982), p. 498.

15. N. Kirk, *The Growth*, op. cit., p. 164.

16. For this 'change of heart', see ibid., pp. 291–301; P. Joyce, *Work Society and Politics* (1980), op. cit., Ch. 4.

17. N. Kirk, op. cit., pp. 294–5.

18. See R. Q. Gray, *The Labour Aristocracy in Victorian Edinburgh* (1976); G. Crossick, *An Artisan Élite in Victorian Society: Kentish London 1840–1880* (1978). There appears to be growing support for the view that the 'turn' to popular Liberalism in some Lancashire mill towns both took place earlier and constituted less of a mid-century 'break' than I have suggested. See P. F. Taylor, op. cit., Ch. 3; E. F. Biagini and A. J. Reid (eds.), op. cit., Ch. 1; and M. J. Winstanley's work on Oldham (*Historical Journal*, 36, 3 (1993).

19. N. Kirk, op. cit., p. 297.

20. Ibid., pp. 180–1, 182–9, 207–21.

21. P. Joyce, *Visions of the People*, op. cit., Ch. 2 (especially p. 47).

22. B. Harrison and P. Hollis, 'Chartism, Liberalism and the Life of Robert Lowery', *English Historical Review*, LXXXII (1967); T. R. Tholfsen, *Working Class Radicalism in Mid Victorian England* (1976).

23. N. Kirk, op. cit., p. 184.

24. T. C. Smout, op. cit., pp. 245–6.

25. P. Joyce, op. cit., p. 61.

26. N. Kirk, op. cit., pp. 179–80.

27. P. Joyce, 'The Factory Politics of Lancashire in the Later Nineteenth Century', *Historical Journal*, 18, 3 (1975).

28. J. Vernon, 'Popular Politics, the Language of Independence and the Question of Party, 1808–1868', unpublished paper (1991), p. 19. I am grateful to the author for permission to quote from his paper.

29. N. Kirk, op. cit., Ch. 5.

30. J. K. Walton, *Lancashire: A Social History*, op. cit., pp. 248–9.

31. T. Koditschek, *Class Formation and Urban-Industrial Society: Bradford 1750–1850* (1990), Ch. 18.

32. For the conventional viewpoint see J. Vincent, op. cit., p. 145; J. Cole, *Rochdale Revisited: A Town and its People*, Vol. 2 (1990), pp. 38–9; id., 'Chartism in Rochdale', unpublished m.s. (1986). I am grateful to John Cole for permission to read his manuscript.

33. J. Cole, 'Chartism in Rochdale' (Manchester Polytechnic 1986) unpublished m.s., op. cit., p. 54.

34. Jones is quoted in K. Tiller, 'Late Chartism: Halifax 1847–58', in J. A. Epstein and D. Thompson (eds.), *The Chartist Experience* (1982), p. 325.

35. J. Cole, *Rochdale Revisited*, op. cit., pp. 37, 41–4; id., 'Chartism in Rochdale', unpublished m.s., (1986) op. cit.

36. K. Tiller, op. cit., pp. 337–41.

37. See P. F. Taylor, op. cit., Introduction and Ch. 3.

38. See, for example, *Bolton Chronicle*, 12 June, 10 July, 31 July 1852. I am extremely grateful to Peter Taylor for providing me with Bolton newspaper references for both the 1852 and 1859 elections.

39. For the 1859 election see *Bolton Chronicle*, 12 Feb., 16, 23, 30 April, 27 August, 24 December of that year.

40. For popular Toryism see P. F. Clarke, op. cit., Chs. 2 and 3; P. Joyce, *Work Society and Politics* (1980), op. cit., Chs. 6 and 7; N. Kirk, op. cit., Ch. 7.

41. J. K. Walton, op. cit., pp. 253–7, 259, 262–3.

42. P. Joyce, op. cit., pp. 38, 324.

43. Ibid., p. 323.

44. Ibid., p. 323; N. Kirk, op. cit., p. 336.

45. For Stephens see N. Kirk, op. cit., pp. 255–6; P. Joyce, op. cit., pp. 151, 253–5, 295–7.

46. P. Joyce, op. cit., p. 325.

47. N. Kirk, op. cit., pp. 316–7, 337–9.

48. P. Joyce, op. cit., p. 250.

49. N. Kirk, op. cit., p. 338; P. Joyce, op. cit., p. 254.

50. N. Kirk, op. cit., p. 339.

51. P. J. Waller, *Democracy and Sectarianism* (1981), pp. 12–19, 155, Ch. 11; J. K. Walton, op. cit., pp. 262–3.

52. E. J. Evans, *The Forging of the Modern State*, (1985), pp. 348, 350; J. K. Walton, *Disraeli* (1990), pp. 2–8, Ch. 5.

53. J. Belchem, op. cit., pp. 26–7; M. Taylor, 'John Bull and the Iconography of Public Opinion in England, c1712–1929', *Past and Present*, 134 (1992).

54. P. Joyce, op. cit., pp. 187, 189–91.

55. P. Joyce, op. cit., pp. 187–91, 215–17; D. Walsh, 'Operative Conservatism in Lancashire, 1833–1846: Some Comments on a Changing Political Culture' (Dept of Politics and Contemporary History, University of Salford, Occasional Paper no. 11, 1987), pp. 35, 39ff., 56. For a fine discussion of political cultures see, G. Trodd, 'Political Change and the Working Class in Blackburn and Burnley, 1880–1914', (D. Phil., University of Lancaster, 1978).

56. A. J. Lee, 'Conservatism, Traditionalism and the British Working Class, 1880–1918', in D. E. Martin and D. Rubinstein (eds.), *Ideology and the Labour Movement: Essays Presented to John Saville* (1979), especially pp. 85–9.

57. G. Trodd, op. cit., p. 163.

58. Ibid., p. 171.

59. See, for example, J. Lawrence, 'Class and Gender in the Making of Urban Toryism, 1860–1914', unpublished paper (1991). I am grateful to the author for permission to cite. For a critique of the views which regard working-class Toryism as 'deviant' see, A. J. Lee, op. cit., especially p. 85.

60. A. D. Taylor, 'Chartism and Popular Politics in London and Manchester, 1848–1852', M.A. Seminar (Manchester Polytechnic, Dec. 1991). I gratefully acknowledge the author's permission to cite.

61. J. K. Walton, *Lancashire: A Social History*, op. cit., p. 258; C. Buckley, 'The Unionist Party in North-West England, 1906–1914, with special reference to the Manchester area' (D.Phil., University of Manchester, 1985), Vol. 1, pp. 1–3. I am grateful to the author for the loan of his thesis.

62. B. Coleman, *Conservatism and the Conservative Party in Nineteenth-Century Britain* (1988); M. Pugh, *The Tories and the People 1880–1935* (1985); F. O'Gorman, *British Conservatism: Conservative Thought From Burke to Thatcher* (1986).

63. P. Joyce, op. cit., pp. 283–4.

64. Ibid., pp. 269–70.

65. Ibid., p. 270; J. A. Garrard, 'Parties, Members and Voters After 1867', in T. R. Gourvish and A. O'Day (eds.), *Later Victorian Britain 1867–1900* (1988), especially pp. 131–4.

66. L. Walker, 'Party Political Women: A Comparative Study of Liberal Women and the Primrose League, 1890–1914', in J. Rendall (ed.), *Equal or Different: Women's Politics 1800–1914* (1987).

67. Thus Martin Pugh informs us (in *The Tories and the People*, op. cit., p. 43) that, 'In Mid-Victorian England the natural role for a politically ambitious woman was that of political hostess'. Women could also (see, for example, L. Walker, op. cit., p. 165) be drawn into politics on the basis of family and community traditions and connections.

68. M. Pugh, op. cit., pp. 12–18, Ch. 3.

69. Ibid., pp. 50–2; L. Walker, op. cit., p. 178.

70. L. Cooper, 'The Organisation of Women by Political Parties, 1880–1914', unpublished m.s. (1991). The author has kindly permitted me to cite her m.s. See also, M. Pugh, op. cit., p. 2.

71. L. Walker, op. cit., pp. 169, 188.

72. Ibid., pp. 169, 172, 180–2, 190–1.

73. Ibid., pp. 172, 184.

74. J. Vernon, op. cit., p. 22; L. Cooper, op. cit., especially pp. 15–17, 25–6.

75. For the various emphases see, M. J. Buhle, *Women and American Socialism 1870–1920* (1981), pp. 117–18; C. Rowan, ' "Mothers Vote Labour!" The State, the Labour Movement and Working-Class Mothers, 1900–1918', in R. Brunt and C. Rowan (eds.), *Feminism Culture and Politics* (1982), p. 74; J. Hannam, ' "In the Comradeship of the Sexes Lies the Hope of Progress and Social Regeneration": Women in the West Riding ILP, c. 1890–1914', in J. Rendall (ed.), op. cit. p. 222; P. Hollis, 'Women in Council: Separate Spheres, Public Space' in ibid.

76. J. Lawrence, op. cit., pp. 35–6; J. Belchem, op. cit., Ch. 3.

77. J. Belchem, op. cit., Ch. 4.

78. P. Joyce, op. cit., pp. 268–9.

79. J. A. Garrard, op. cit., pp. 129, 134–44.

80. J. Belchem, op. cit., pp. 53–4; J. Charlton, 'A Study of Labour in Britain to 1940', (D. Phil., University of Leeds, 1991), pp. 170–4, 237.

81. J. Belchem, op. cit., p. 19; J. K. Walton, *Disraeli*, op. cit., Ch. 5; J. Spain, 'Trade Unionists, Gladstonian Liberals, and the labour law reforms of 1875', in E. F. Biagini and A. J. Reid (eds.), op. cit.

82. E. H. H. Green, 'Conservatism and the Mass Electorate: Perception and Response c 1884–1914', unpublished paper (1991). I am grateful to the author for permission to quote.

83. P. Joyce, op. cit., p. 324; E. H. Green, op. cit.

84. J. Belchem, op. cit., pp. 53–4.

85. M. Shefter, 'Trade Unions and Political Machines', in I. Katznelson and A. R. Zolberg (eds.), *Working Class Formation*, op. cit., p. 247.

86. A. Dawley, *Class and Community*, op. cit., pp. 238–9.

87. L. Goodwyn, *The Populist Moment* op. cit., p. 5.

88. I. Bernstein, *The New York City Draft Riots* op. cit., pp. 188–9.

89. D. Montgomery, *Beyond Equality*, op. cit., pp. 72–89.

90. E. Foner, *Reconstruction*, op. cit., pp. 221–5, 228–39.

91. Ibid., p. 484; D. Montgomery, op. cit., pp. 230, 260, Ch. 9, pp. 446–7.

92. R. Harrison, *Before the Socialists* (1965), Ch. 2; H. Pelling, *America and the British Left*, op. cit., Ch. 2. See M. Ellison (*Support for Secession: Lancashire and the American Civil War* (1972)) for the view that high levels of unemployment and suffering during the Cotton Famine and charges of northern 'hypocrisy', resulted in significant levels of support for the South in the cotton towns of Lancashire and Cheshire. See also, P. Joyce, op. cit., p. 150. For a convincing critique of Ellison see T. Barley, *Myths of the Slave Power: Confederate Slavery Lancashire Workers and the Alabama* (1992).

93. E. Foner, op. cit., p. 484.

94. D. Montgomery, op. cit., pp. 334, 340–56, Ch. 11.

95. M. Shefter, op. cit., p. 251.

96. D. Montgomery, op. cit., pp. 48–59; R. J. Oestreicher, 'Urban Working Class Political Behavior', op. cit., p. 1262; I. Bernstein, op. cit., pp. 8ff.

97. L. Goodwyn, *The Populist Moment*, op. cit., p. 4.

98. For Democratic politics in New York City during the 1850s and 1860s see, respectively, A. Bridges, *A City in the Republic* (1987), Ch. 8 and I. Bernstein, op. cit. Ch. 6.

99. I. Bernstein, op. cit., pp. 9–10, 112–13, 117, 146.

100. Ibid., pp. 113, 195–8.

101. L. Goodwyn, op. cit., pp. 5–6.

102. M. Shefter, op. cit., pp. 248–9.

103. E. Foner, op. cit., pp. 484–5, 523ff; M. Shefter, op. cit., p. 248.

104. E. Foner, op. cit., p. 518; M. Shefter, op. cit., pp. 247–8.

105. M. Shefter, op. cit., pp. 210–12; J. H. M. Laslett, 'State Policy Towards Labour', op. cit.

106. D. Montgomery, 'Labor in the Industrial Era', in R. B. Morris (ed.), op. cit., p. 104.

107. D. Montgomery, 'To Study the People', *Labor History*, 21, 4 (1980), p. 507.

108. S. J. Ross, op. cit., pp. 201–5.

109. For developments in Massachusetts see A. Dawley, op. cit., pp. 196–9; E. Foner, op. cit., pp. 482–4; D. Montgomery, *Beyond Equality*, op. cit., pp. 265–95.

110. I. Bernstein, (op. cit., pp. 209–41) for developments in New York City.

111. H. G. Gutman, *Work Culture and Society* (1976), op. cit., pp. 278–9; id., *Power and Culture*, op. cit., pp. 163ff., 194–6, 209ff. As Gutman observed, the character and extent of worker and labour movement involvement in local Gilded Age politics merit further investigation.

112. Quoted in P. S. Foner, *The Great Labor Uprising*, op. cit., p. 222. The following section on labour politics in 1877 is largely indebted to Foner's study, especially pp. 220–7.

113. P. S. Foner, *The Workingmen's Party of the United States: A History of the First Marxist Party in the Americas* (1984); A. Dawley, 'Paths to Power After the Civil War', in P. Buhle and A. Dawley (eds.), op. cit.; M. Shefter, op. cit., pp. 222, 243; A. Dawley, *Class and Community*, op. cit., pp. 199–207.

114. L. Goodwyn, op. cit., pp. 12–14.

115. My study of politics during the 'Great Upheaval' owes much to L. Fink, *Workingmen's Democracy*, op. cit., pp. xiii, 25–35.

116. Ibid., Ch. 6; N. I. Painter, *Exodusters*, op. cit., pp. 35, 39, 43. We must,

however, heed Painter's general conclusion that bi-racial bipartisanship was (p. 39) 'comparatively rare in the post-Reconstruction South . . . interracial politics remained the exception, the color line the rule'.

117. A. Dawley, 'Paths to Power', op. cit., p. 48.
118. S. J. Ross, op. cit., Ch. 12.
119. L. Fink, op. cit., pp. 225–7.
120. Ibid., p. 60.
121. Ibid., pp. 32–3.
122. Although, as demonstrated by several historians, British workers' opposition to the state as intrusive inspector, regulator and 'improver' of their lives remained very strong. Male trade unionists much preferred to achieve good wages, job security and decent conditions by their own collective efforts rather than by means of an interventionist state. Some also feared that extended state benefits and welfare would undermine their independence, the notion of the 'family wage', and their patriarchal role in the household. There was, nevertheless, a heightened awareness of the pro-labour benefits to be won from a more democratic and accountable state (housing, better sanitation, the repeal of anti-trade-union legislation and so on) at both national and (especially) local levels. See, H. Pelling, 'The Working Class and the Welfare State', in his *Popular Politics and Society in Late Victorian Britain* (1979); J. Belchem, op. cit., p. 70; P. Thane, 'The Working Class and State "Welfare" in Britain, 1880–1914', *Historical Journal*, 27, 4 (1984); id., 'The Labour Party and State "Welfare" ', in K. D. Brown (ed.), *The First Labour Party*, op. cit., p. 185.
123. See, for example, the introduction to Bruce Laurie's *Artisans into Workers*, op. cit.
124. K. Marx and F. Engels, *On Britain* (1953), pp. 509–10 (Marx to W. Liebknecht Feb. 11, 1878, Engels to E. Bernstein June 17, 1879, Engels to G. V. Plekhanov May 21, 1894).
125. V. I. Lenin, *Left Wing Communism: An Infantile Disorder* (1973 edition), pp. 60, 62.
126. K. Marx and F. Engels, op. cit., pp. 534–6 (Engels to F. A. Sorge May 12, 1894, Engels to H. Schluter Jan. 1 1895).
127. For the various debates see G. Marks, *Unions in Politics*, op. cit., Ch. 6; J. H. M. Laslett, 'State Policy Towards Labour', op. cit., pp. 523–4.
128. E. Foner, 'Why is There No Socialism', op. cit., p. 60.
129. Although Weinstein probably exaggerates the strength of the Socialist Party in the post-1912 period. See J. Weinstein, *The Decline of Socialism*, op. cit., pp. 93–118; J. H. M. Laslett (*Labor and the Left*, op. cit., pp. 301–2) for a convincing critique of continued strength; H. Pelling, *American Labor* (1968), Ch. V; N. Salvatore, *Eugene V. Debs: Citizen and Socialist* (1982), especially pp. 266–72, 289–302, Ch. 10.
130. P. Buhle, 'Socialists and Wobblies', in P. Buhle and A. Dawley (eds.), op. cit., p. 53.
131. D. Montgomery, *Workers Control*, op. cit., pp. 70–1.
132. G. Marks, op. cit., pp. 203–4.
133. J. Weinstein, op. cit. pp. ix, 16–25, 27–9; J. H. M. Laslett, 'State Policy Towards Labour', op. cit., p. 523; P. Buhle, op. cit., pp. 52–3.
134. M. J. Buhle, op. cit., pp. 117–18.
135. Ibid., pp. 106–40, Chs. 4 and 8; C. Leinenweber, 'The Class and Ethnic

Bases of New York City Socialism, 1904–1915', *Labor History*, 22 (Winter 1981).

136. See Ch. 2 above; D. Montgomery, *The Fall*, op. cit., pp. 314–27.

137. J. H. M. Laslett, 'State Policy Towards Labour', op. cit., p. 523; id., *Labor and the Left*, op. cit., Conclusion; J. Karabel, 'The Failure of American Socialism Reconsidered', *Socialist Register* (1979).

138. G. Marks, op. cit., pp. 200–2.

139. For the failures of independent labour politics see ibid., pp. 202–4; M. Kazin, *Barons of Labor*, op. cit., p. 150, Chs. 7–9; D. Montgomery, 'The Farmer-Labor Party', in P. Buhle and A. Dawley (eds.), op. cit.

140. For Progressivism see M. A. Jones, *The Limits of Liberty*, op. cit., Ch. 19; J. A. Thompson, *Progressivism* (1979); M. Kazin, op. cit., pp. 146–52, 283–7; H. Pelling, *American Labor*, op. cit., pp. 123–6; G. M. Fink, 'The Rejection of Voluntarism', *Industrial and Labor Relations Review*, 26 (Jan. 1973).

141. D. Montgomery, 'The Farmer-Labor Party', op. cit.; J. L. Sundquist, *Dynamics of the Party System: Alignment and Realignment of Political Parties in the United States* (1983), Ch. 9; J. Weinstein, op. cit., Ch. 8; R. M. Valelly, *Radicalism in the States: The Minnesota Farmer-Labor Party and the American Political Economy* (1989).

142. D. Montgomery, *The Fall*, op. cit., pp. 406–7, 434–7.

143. For the contemptuous attitudes of some socialists towards popular culture see C. Waters, *British Socialists and the Politics of Popular Culture 1884–1914* (1990), especially Ch. 6.

144. D. Howell, *British Workers and the Independent Labour Party*, op. cit., pp. 327–35.

145. J. Hannam, op. cit.; J. Liddington and J. Norris, op. cit., Ch. VIII; C. Rowan, op. cit., especially pp. 67–73; C. Waters, op. cit., pp. 165–70; D. Howell, op. cit., p. 335; E. Gordon, op. cit., Ch. 7.

146. M. Pugh, 'Labour and Women's Suffrage', in K. D. Brown (ed.), *The First Labour Party*, op. cit.; P. Pugh, *Educate Agitate Organize: 100 Years of Fabian Socialism* (1984), Ch. 10.

147. K. Hunt, 'Women and the Social Democratic Federation: Some Notes on Lancashire', in *Women and the Labour Movement*, North-West Labour History Society Bulletin, 7 (1980–1), especially pp. 51ff.

148. R. Roberts, *The Classic Slum* (1971) p. 16; E. J. Hobsbawm, 'Hyndman and the S.D.F.', in his *Labouring Men* (1964), op. cit., p. 232.

149. D. Howell, op. cit., p. 1.

150. E. J. Hobsbawm, 'The Fabians Reconsidered', in *Labouring Men*, op. cit.

151. See Kirk's review of Patricia Pugh's book in *Labor History* 27, 3 (Summer 1986), pp. 463–4.

152. D. Howell, op. cit., pp. 144–56; W. H. Fraser, 'The Labour Party in Scotland', in K. D. Brown (ed.), op. cit.

153. D. Tanner, op. cit., pp. 2–10, 419–20; J. Belchem, op. cit., pp. 4–5, 44–51, Ch. 5.

154. See, for example, E. F. Biagini and A. J. Reid (eds.), op. cit.; K. D. Brown, 'The Edwardian Labour Party', in K. D. Brown (ed.), op. cit., p. 11.

155. K. D. Brown (ed.), op. cit., pp. 1, 2; E. H. Hunt, op. cit., p. 324; J. Belchem, op. cit., p. 63.

156. D. Tanner, op. cit., p. 426.

157. L. Fink, *Workingmen's Democracy*, op. cit., p. 229.

158. William Forbath's argument that the very strength and hostility of the courts (especially their ability to render legislative gains unconstitutional) greatly strengthened the voluntarist/non-partisan case as opposed to the transformative goals of the socialists and advocates of independent labour politics, is important if not totally convincing. Despite the courts' powers of judicial review, workers (and especially miners) continued to lobby for favourable legislation. Gains were achieved by legislative means at local and state levels. And radicals and socialists both within and outside the AFL believed that root-and-branch action was necessary to fundamentally change the state. In Britain both Taff Vale and, unintentionally, the Osborne case worked to the benefit of independent Labour politics. In the United States the sheer power, levels of success, and persistence of anti-labour courts did, however, often lead to worker defeats, radical disillusionment, resignation to the strength of the 'system' and fortify the defensive, 'digging in', approach of the mainstream AFL. Forbath, Tomlins and others are to be congratulated upon their attempt to 'bring the state back in' to historical explanation. But the nature and role of the judiciary constitutes, in itself, insufficient explanation of the failure of socialist and independent labour strategies. A complete explanatory picture would go beyond the state to include the social composition of the working class, the structure of politics, developments at the workplace and so forth (i.e. the state as relatively rather than fully autonomous). See W. Forbath, op. cit.

159. See E. Foner, ('Why is There No Socialism', op. cit.) for an incisive and lucid review of the literature on American socialism. For the British situation see J. Belchem, op. cit., Chs. 5 and 6.

160. J. H. M. Laslett, 'State Policy Towards Labour', op. cit., p. 529; R. Fagge, op. cit., pp. 8–10, 14–20.

161. E. and K. F-Wolf, 'Trade Union Evangelism: Religion and the AFL in the Labor Forward Movement, 1912–16', in M. H. Frisch and D. J. Walkowitz (eds.), Working Class America (1983).

162. D. Montgomery, The Fall, op. cit., pp. 302–10; J. H. M. Laslett, op. cit., p. 526.

163. A Shallice, 'Liverpool Labourism and Irish Nationalism in the 1920s and 1930s', North-West Labour History Society Bulletin, 8 (1982–3); J. Smith, 'Labour Tradition in Glasgow and Liverpool', History Workshop Journal, XVII (Spring 1984); D. Howell, op. cit., pp. 142–3; S. Fielding, 'A Separate Culture? Irish Catholics in Working-Class Manchester and Salford, c1890–1939', in A. Davies and S. Fielding (eds.), Workers Worlds: Cultures and Communities in Manchester and Salford 1880–1939 (1992).

164. The following section is indebted to J. L. Sundquist, op. cit., especially pp. 154–70.

165. J. Greene, 'Dinner-Pail Politics: Employers, Workers and Political Organization in the Progressive Era', unpublished m.s., History Dept., University of Missouri-Kansas City (1992), especially pp. 43–8. I am grateful to Julie Greene for permission to quote her m.s.

166. J. H. M. Laslett, Labor and the Left, op. cit., p. 302.

167. M. Kazin, op. cit., Conclusion; M. A. Jones, op. cit., Ch. 19; J. H. M. Laslett, 'State Policy Towards Labour', op. cit., p. 519; S. Stromquist, 'United States of America', in M. van der Linden and J. Rojahn (eds.),

The Formation of Labour Movements 1870–1914: An International Perspective, Vol. 2 (1990).

168. L. Fink, op. cit., p. 228; S. P. Hays, 'The Changing Structure of the City in Industrial America', *Journal of Urban History*, 1, (Nov. 1974).

169. M. Kazin, op. cit., p. 285.

170. For debates concerning the nature and underpinnings of late nineteenth- and early twentieth-century popular Conservatism see H. Pelling's review of Nordlinger and McKenzie and Silver entitled 'Working Class Conservatives', *Historical Journal*, 13, 2 (1970); J. Belchem, op. cit., pp. 26–32; A. J. Lee, op. cit., especially p. 93; C. Buckley, thesis, op. cit., Ch. 1 (Vol. 1); G. Trodd, thesis, op. cit., p. 223; R. McKibbin, *The Ideologies of Class: Social Relations in Britain 1880–1950* (1991), Ch. 9.

171. See the splendid Ch. 6 in G. Trodd, thesis, op. cit.

172. N. Kirk, ' "Traditional" Working Class Culture', op. cit.

173. Prominent among the more recent studies have been, R. McKibbin, *The Evolution of the Labour Party*, op. cit.; D. Tanner, op. cit.; B. Lancaster, *Radicalism, Cooperation and Socialism*, op. cit.; K. Laybourn and J. Reynolds, *Liberalism and the Rise of Labour*, op. cit.; P. Thane, 'Labour and Local Politics: Radicalism, Democracy and Social Reform, 1880–1914', in E. F. Biagini and A. J. Reid (eds.), op. cit. I am grateful to Pat Thane for sending me a copy of her article in advance of publication.

174. C. J. Wrigley, 'Liberals and the Desire for Working Class Representatives in Battersea, 1886–1922', in K. D. Brown (ed.), *Essays in Anti-Labour History* (1974); J. Davis, 'Radical Clubs and London Politics, 1870–1900', in D. Feldman and G. S. Jones (eds.), *Metropolis: London Histories and Representations Since 1800* (1989); S. Pennybacker, ' "The Millenium by Return of Post": Reconsidering London Progressivism, 1889–1907', in ibid.; P. Thane, op. cit.

175. See the first chapter in E. F. Biagini and A. J. Reid (eds.), op. cit.; D. Tanner, op. cit., Introduction and Conclusion.

176. Duncan Tanner has rightly drawn our attention to the *complexities* of the relationship between Labour and Liberalism, and the strengths and weaknesses of the cases argued by P. F. Clarke and R. McKibbin. Tanner's ultimate insistence that (p. 441) 'The rise of Labour between 1885 and 1931 cannot be explained by an expanding class consciousness' is, however, too bald and unsubstantiated an assertion to carry much weight. Much like Alastair Reid, Tanner constructs a flawed model of class (of workers more or less *totally unified* by economic and cultural factors and largely frozen in time), attributes this model to advocates of class, and then proceeds to the process of demolition. In such ways are the Marxist, Hobsbawm (Reid's special target) and the non-Marxist, McKibbin, attacked. Reminiscent of many of the methodological and substantive attacks upon E. P. Thompson's notion of 'The Making of the English Working Class', Tanner's and Reid's arguments fail to ultimately convince. They do not do justice to the complexities and acute senses of change over time, and intricate interplays between elements of unity and disunity in working-class life to be found in the work of Hobsbawm and McKibbin. Complexity, contradiction *and* class are, as emphasised by a long line of historical materialists, often close companions. See D. Tanner (op. cit., pp. 2–4, 6, 7, 8, 319, 419–20, 431) for further amplification of his views upon class. Also, N. Kirk (ed.), *Class and History* (forthcoming, 1994)

for essays in favour of historical materialism and the importance of class. A. J. Reid, *Social Classes and Social Relations in Britain 1850–1914* (1992), Chs. 3 and 5.

177. J. Belchem, op. cit., pp. 44–5.

178. S. Pennybacker, op. cit., pp. 150–2.

179. J. Belchem, op. cit., pp. 63–7.

180. See, in addition to the references in notes 173 and 174, D. Howell, op. cit., pp. 123–8, 277–82; J. Hill, 'Manchester and Salford Politics and the Early Development of the Independent Labour Party', *International Review of Social History*, 26 (1981), especially p. 192; G. Trodd, thesis, op. cit., Ch. 6; N. Kirk, ' "Traditional" Working Class Culture', op. cit., especially p. 211 and note. 33; D. Gilbert, *Class Community and Collective Action: Social Change in Two British Coalfields 1850–1926* (1992), especially pp. 107–9, 170–85; H. Francis and D. Smith, *The Fed: A History of the South Wales Miners in the Twentieth Century* (1980).

181. For such debates see R. McKibbin, *The Ideologies of Class*, op. cit., Ch. 3; D. Tanner, op. cit., pp. 99–123.

182. For models of working-class culture see, N. Kirk, op. cit., especially pp. 203–7; J. T. Cumbler, *Working Class Community*, op. cit.; R. J. Oestreicher, *Solidarity and Fragmentation*, op. cit.; J. R. Barrett, op. cit.; D. J. Walkowitz, *Worker City Company Town: Iron and Cotton-Worker Protest in Troy and Cohoes New York 1855–1884* (1978).

183. N. Kirk, op. cit.; F. G. Couvares, 'The Triumph of Commerce: Class Culture and Mass Culture in Pittsburgh', in M. H. Frisch and D. J. Walkowitz (eds.), op. cit. For an interesting and enjoyable account of the leisure patterns of (especially young) women, see K. Peiss, *Cheap Amusements: Working Women and Leisure in Turn-of-the-Century New York* (1986).

184. R. Rosenzweig, *Eight Hours For What We Will: Workers and Leisure in an Industrial City 1870–1920* (1983), p. 223.

185. O. Zuntz, *The Changing Face of Inequality: Urbanization, Industrial Development and Immigrants in Detroit 1880–1920* (1982), pp. 3–6. Zuntz shows that increased social and economic inequality in Detroit went hand-in-hand with strong ethnic allegiance.

186. The quote is from F. G. Couvares, op. cit., p. 146; R. Rosenzweig, op. cit., p. 4.

187. R. Rosenzweig, op. cit., pp. 223, 225; O. Zuntz, op. cit., Chs. 13 and 14.

188. N. Kirk, op. cit., p. 203; E. J. Hobsbawm, *Worlds of Labour*, op. cit., Chs. 10 and 11.

189. M. Savage, *The Dynamics of Working Class Politics: The Labour Movement in Preston 1880–1940* (1987), pp. 53–4, 200–3; R. S. W. Davies, 'Class, Religion and Gender: Liverpool Labour Party and Women, 1918–1939', in J. Belchem (ed.), *Popular Politics Riot and Labour: Essays in Liverpool History 1790–1940* (1992); P. Thane, 'The Women of the British Labour Party and Feminism, 1906–1945', in H. L. Smith (ed.), *British Feminism in the Twentieth Century* (1990); J. M. Lawson, M. Savage and A. Warde, 'Gender and Local Politics: Struggles Over Welfare Policies, 1918–1939', in L. Murgatroyd et al., *Localities Class and Gender* (1985).

190. As emphasised by Gerstle, the meanings of 'Americanism' were, however, by no means solely synonymous with integrated conservatism. In some cases distinctly radical interpretations were made by workers. See, G.

Gerstle, *Working Class Americanism: The Politics of Labor in a Textile City, 1914–1960* (1989).

CHAPTER FOUR

1. J. Potter, *The American Economy Between the World Wars* (1985), p. 55.
2. See ibid., pp. 15, 55–89; P. Fearon, *War Prosperity and Depression: The U.S. Economy 1917–45* (1987), Ch. 3.
3. T. Kemp, *The Climax of Capitalism: The U.S. Economy in the Twentieth Century* (1990), p. 24.
4. Ibid., pp. 25–6.
5. G. Gerstle, *Working Class Americanism*, op. cit., Introduction; L. Cohen, *Making a New Deal: Industrial Workers in Chicago 1919–1939* (1990), Ch. 3. See also Michael Denning, 'The End of Mass Culture', *International Labor and Working-Class History*, 37 (Spring 1990).
6. P. Fearon, op. cit., Ch. 2.
7. D. Montgomery, 'Thinking About American Workers in the 1920s', *International Labor and Working Class History*, 32 (Fall 1987), pp. 10–11.
8. P. Fearon, op. cit., pp. 101–4.
9. D. Montgomery, op. cit., pp. 9–12; J.D. Hall, R. Korstad and J. Leloudis, op. cit.
10. T. Kemp, op. cit., p. 25.
11. F. Stricker, 'Affluence for Whom? Another Look at Prosperity and the Working Classes in the 1920s', *Labor History*, 24, 1 (Winter 1983).
12. The following picture of the 1920s is indebted to J. Stevenson, *British Society*, op. cit., Ch. 4; and the essays by N. Von Tunzelmann ('Britain 1900–45: a survey'), I. Drummond ('Britain and the World Economy, 1900–45'), S. Howson ('Slump and Unemployment'), and B.W.E. Alford ('New Industries for Old? British Industry between the Wars'), in R. Floud and D. McCloskey (eds.), op. cit.
13. E.J. Hobsbawm, *Industry and Empire*, op. cit., p. 223.
14. J. Stevenson, op. cit., pp. 186–7.
15. The famous Hawthorne experiments of 1927, held at Western Electric's telephone-assembly plant near Chicago, 'focused on the work group as the key to productivity'. See J.R. Green, *The World of the Worker: Labor in Twentieth-Century America* (1980), pp. 106–7.
16. J.D. Hall, R. Korstad and J. Leloudis, op. cit., especially pp. 267–70.
17. S. Fraser, 'Dress Rehearsal for the New Deal: Shop-Floor Insurgents, Political Elites and Industrial Democracy in the Amalgamated Clothing Workers', in M. Frisch and D.J. Walkowitz (eds.), op. cit.
18. D. Brody, 'The Rise and Decline of Welfare Capitalism', in his *Workers in Industrial America*, op. cit.; R. Schatz, *The Electrical Workers: A History of Labor at General Electric and Westinghouse 1923–60* (1983), Ch. 1.
19. H.M. Gitelman, 'Welfare Capitalism Reconsidered', *Labor History*, 33, 1 (Winter 1992); S. Jacoby, *Employing Bureaucracy* (1985), Ch. 6.
20. D. Brody, op. cit., p. 61.
21. D. Montgomery, op. cit., p. 5.
22. D. Brody, op. cit., p. 134.
23. J.E. Cronin, *Labour and Society in Britain 1918–1979* (1984), p. 52; E.J. Hobsbawm, op. cit., p. 214.

24. E.J. Hobsbawm, op. cit., p. 215; L. Hannah, *The Rise of the Corporate Economy: The British Experience* (1976), Chs. 3, 4, 6 and 9.

25. See, for example, S.G. Jones, 'Work, Leisure and the Political Economy of the Cotton Districts Between the Wars', *Textile History*, 18, 1 (1987), especially pp. 47–8.

26. J. Stevenson, op. cit., p. 112.

27. R. Price, *Labour in British Society*, op. cit., p. 179; C.J. Wrigley (ed.), *A History of British Industrial Relations*, Vol. 2, op. cit., p. 110.

28. H.F. Gospel, 'Employers and Managers: Organisation and Strategy, 1914–39', in C.J. Wrigley (ed.), op. cit., pp. 174–6; J.E. Cronin, op. cit., pp. 94–5.

29. S.G. Jones, op. cit., pp. 47–9.

30. For the development of welfarism see H.F. Gospel, op. cit., pp. 179–80; R.C. Whiting, *The View from Cowley: The Impact of Industrialization Upon Oxford 1918–1939* (1983); J. McG. Davies, 'A Twentieth Century Paternalist: Alfred Herbert and the Skilled Coventry Workman', in B. Lancaster and T. Mason (eds.), *Life and Labour in a Twentieth Century City: The Experience of Coventry* (1986).

31. S. Tolliday, 'High Tide and After: Coventry's Engineering Workers and Shopfloor Bargaining, 1945–80', in B. Lancaster and T. Mason (eds.), op. cit.; id., 'The Failure of Mass Production Unionism', in C.J. Wrigley (ed.), op. cit.

32. J. Castle, 'Factory Work for Women: Courtaulds and GEC between the Wars', in B. Lancaster and T. Mason (eds.), op. cit., pp. 162–3; J. Stevenson, op. cit., p. 200; A. Fowler and T. Wyke (eds.), *The Barefoot Aristocrats*, op. cit., Ch. 9; A. Fowler, 'Lancashire Cotton Trade Unionism in the Inter-War Years', in J.A. Jowitt and A.J. McIvor (eds.), op. cit.

33. J.E. Cronin, op. cit., p. 52.

34. H.F. Gospel, op. cit., p. 179.

35. J. Melling, 'Employers and the Rise of Supervisory Unionism', in C.J. Wrigley (ed.), op. cit., especially pp. 270–5.

36. R. Price, op. cit., p. 181.

37. W. Lazonick, 'The Cotton Industry', in B. Elbaum and W. Lazonick (eds.), op. cit.; J.D. Hall, R. Korstad and J. Leloudis, op. cit., especially pp. 269–78; J.D. Hall et al., *Like a Family: The Making of a Southern Cotton Mill World* (1987); A. Fowler, 'Spinners in the Inter-War Years', in A. Fowler and T. Wyke (eds.), op. cit.

38. J. Melling, op. cit., p. 272; J. Hinton, *Labour and Socialism*, op. cit., Chs. 7 and 8.

39. D. Montgomery, op. cit., pp. 4–5; T. Skocpol, 'Political Responses to Capitalist Crisis: Neo-Marxist Theories of the State and the Case of the New Deal', *Politics and Society*, 10, 2 (1980).

40. The following paragraphs on occupational changes are indebted to J.E. Cronin, op. cit., pp. 56–7; J. Stevenson, op. cit., pp. 185–6; R.H. Zieger, *American Workers American Unions 1920–1985* (1986), p. 4; J. Potter, op. cit., pp. 39–40.

41. A. Dawley, 'Workers, Capital and the State in the Twentieth Century', in J.C. Moody and A.K. Harris (eds.), op. cit., p. 155.

42. J. Hinton, op. cit., pp. 121–2.

43. D. Montgomery, op. cit., pp. 10, 12, 18; J. Higham, *Strangers in the Land:*

Patterns of American Nativism 1860–1925 (1963), Chs. 10 and 11; M.A. Jones, op. cit., pp. 438–9.

44. A.K. Harris, *Out to Work*, op. cit., p. 224; M.W. Greenwald, *Women War and Work: The Impact of World War 1 on Women Workers in the United States* (1980), pp. 15–45, Conclusion.

45. A.K. Harris, op. cit., pp. 257–60; J.R. Green, op. cit., pp. 105, 113.

46. A.K. Harris, op. cit., Ch. 8; S.P. Benson, ' "The Customers Ain't God": The Work Culture of Department-Store Saleswomen, 1890–1940', in M.H. Frisch and D.J. Walkowitz (eds.), op. cit.; id., 'The 1920s Through the Looking Glass of Gender: A Response to David Montgomery', *International Labor and Working Clas History*, 32 (Fall 1987), especially pp. 33–7.

47. For women's employment in Britain see J.E. Cronin, op. cit., pp. 55–7; G. Braybon, *Women Workers in the First World War: The British Experience* (1981); J. Lewis, 'In Search of a Real Equality: Women Between the Wars', in F. Gloversmith (ed.), *Class Culture and Social Change: A New View of the 1930s* (1980); J. Stevenson, op. cit., pp. 169–71; E. Roberts. *Women's Work 1840–1940* (1990), Ch. 1.

48. M. Savage, 'Trade Unionism, Sex Segregation and the State: Women's Employment in "New Industries" in inter-war Britain', *Social History*, 13, 2 (May 1988), p. 214.

49. J. Castle, 'Factory Work for Women', op. cit.

50. For the above-mentioned debates see S. Walby, *Patriarchy at Work: Patriarchal and Capitalist Relations in Employment* (1986); L. Grant, 'Women in a Car Town: Coventry, 1920–45', in P. Hudson and W.R. Lee (eds.), *Women's Work*, op. cit.; M. Savage, op. cit., especially pp. 217–18.

51. J. Lewis, op. cit., pp. 210–14; N. Whiteside, 'Social Welfare and Industrial Relations 1914–39', in C.J. Wrigley (ed.), op. cit., pp. 227–8.

52. J. Lewis, op. cit., pp. 230–2; A.K. Harris, 'Problems of Coalition-Building: Women and Trade Unions in the 1920s', in R. Milkman (ed.), *Women Work and Protest: A Century of U.S. Women's Labor History* (1985), especially pp. 119, 133; J. Stevenson, op. cit., pp. 161, 167, 180–1; H.L. Smith (ed.), op. cit.

53. For improved living standards see J. Stevenson, op. cit., pp. 116–29; S. Pollard, *The Development of the British Economy 1914–1980* (1989), pp.186–91; B.W.E. Alford, *Depression and Recovery? British Economic Growth 1918–1939* (1972); D.H. Aldcroft, *The Inter War Economy: Britain 1919–1939* (1970), Ch. 10; S. Glynn and J. Oxborrow, *Interwar Britain: A Social and Economic History* (1976), Ch. 1; J.E. Cronin, op. cit., pp. 86–8; S.G. Jones, *Workers at Play: A Social and Economic History of Leisure 1918–1939* (1986), Ch. 1.

54. R.H. Zieger, op. cit., p. 5; P. Fearon, op. cit., pp. 65–7; D. Brody, op. cit., p. 62.

55. D. Brody, op. cit., pp. 63–4.

56. P. Johnson, 'Working Class Consumption and Working-Class Collectivism in Inter-War Britain', unpublished paper presented to Anglo-German Working-class Culture conference, Lancaster University, March 1988, pp. 4–5. I am grateful to the author for permission to cite.

57. J.K. Walton, *Lancashire: A Social History*, op. cit., pp. 338–9; P. Johnson, op. cit., p. 5.

58. T. Kemp, op. cit., p. 31; P. Fearon, op. cit., pp. 62–4; I. Bernstein, *The Lean*

Years: A History of the American Worker 1920–1933 (1960), pp. 47–74; J. Potter, op. cit., pp. 69–70.

59. J. Stevenson, op. cit., p. 120; J.K. Walton, op. cit., pp. 338–41; A. Davies, *Leisure, Gender and Poverty: Working Class Culture in Salford and Manchester 1900–1939* (1992), p. 40.

60. The following section on poverty relies heavily upon A. Davies, op. cit., Ch. 1 and p. 54; J.K. Walton, op. cit., pp. 343–8.

61. C.J. Wrigley (ed.), op. cit., p. 7; A. Exell, 'Morris Motors in the 1930s', *History Workshop Journal*, 6 (1978).

62. C. Webster, 'Healthy or Hungry Thirties?', *History Workshop Journal*, 13 (1982), especially pp. 124–5.

63. See, for example, M. Davis, *Prisoners of the American Dream: Politics and Economy in the History of the U.S. Working Class* (1986), pp. 55–6.

64. F. Stricker, op. cit., pp. 23, 32–3.

65. A. Davies, op. cit., Ch. 3; M. Tebbutt, *Making Ends Meet: Pawnbroking and Working Class Credit* (1984); M.S. Rice, *Working Class Wives: Their Health and Conditions* (1938 and 1981); C. Chinn, *They Worked All Their Lives: Women of the Urban Poor in England 1880–1939* (1988); E. Roberts, *A Woman's Place: An Oral History of Working-Class Women 1890–1940* (1984).

66. P. Ayres and J. Lambertz, 'Marriage Relations, Money and Domestic Violence in Working-Class Liverpool, 1919–39', in J. Lewis (ed.), *Labour and Love: Women's Experience of Home and Family 1850–1940* (1986).

67. See, especially, S.G. Jones, *Workers at Play*, op. cit., Ch. 2; J. Richards, *The Age of the Dream Palace: Cinema and Society in Britain 1930–39* (1984).

68. A. Davies, op. cit., Ch. 4.

69. M. Tebbutt, ' "You Couldn't Help but Know": Public and Private Spaces in the Lives of Working-Class Women, 1918–39', *Manchester Region History Review*, VI (1992), p. 79. For women and consumerism in America see M.P. Ryan, *Womanhood in America* (1975). For the importance of the notions of domesticity and privacy (as affording controlled space) to working-class women and their families on the new housing estates see A. Hughes and K. Hunt, 'A Culture Transformed? Women's Lives in Wythenshawe in the 1930s', in A. Davies and S. Fielding (eds.), op. cit.

70. M. Denning, op. cit.

71. R. and H. Lynd, *Middletown* (1929); D. Brody, op. cit., pp. 64–5.

72. J.R. Green, op. cit., pp. 114–15.

73. J. H. Goldthorpe, et al., *The Affluent Worker in the Class Structure* (1969); F. Devine, 'Social Identities, Class Identity and Political Perspectives', *Sociological Review* (1992). I am grateful to the author for a copy of this article.

74. J. Bukowczyk, 'The Transforming Power of the Machine', *International Labor and Working-Class History*, 34 (Fall 1988), p. 34.

75. L. Cohen, op. cit., pp. 156–7.

76. Ibid., p. 156.

77. D. Montgomery, op. cit., p. 19; J. Bukowczyk, 'The Transformation of Working-Class Ethnicity', op. cit., pp. 545–77.

78. J. Higham, op. cit., Chs. 10 and 11; J.R. Green, op. cit., pp. 115–19.

79. P. Johnson, *Saving and Spending*, op. cit., conclusion; R. Roberts, *The*

Classic Slum, op. cit., Ch. 1; N. Kirk, ' "Traditional" Working-Class Culture', op. cit.; P.J. Harris, 'Social Leadership and Social Attitudes in Bolton, 1919–1939' (D.Phil., Lancaster University, 1973).

80. J. Hinton, op. cit., p. 128; R. McKibbin, 'Class and Conventional Wisdom: The Conservative Party and the "Public" in Inter-war Britain', in his *The Ideologies of Class*, op. cit., for a very stimulating discussion of the cultural and ideological roots of Tory hegemony.

81. J.E. Cronin, op. cit., p. 86.

82. N. Evans, ' "The War after the War": Racial Violence and the Post-War Crisis in Britain, 1919–1925', paper presented to the Milan Group in Early American History (Milan, June 1992). I am grateful to the author for permission to quote from his paper.

83. N. Kirk, ' "Traditional" Working-Class Culture', op. cit., p. 216.

84. R. Roberts, op. cit., pp. 219–21; D. Gilbert, op. cit., Ch. 3.

85. D. Montgomery, op. cit., p. 14.

86. I. Bernstein, op. cit., pp. 130–1.

87. J.D. Hall, R. Korstad and J. Leloudis, op. cit., especially pp. 271–7; I. Bernstein, op. cit., prologue.

88. S. Fraser, op. cit., especially pp. 216–17; I. Bernstein, op. cit., p. 85.

89. I. Bernstein, op. cit., pp. 84, 136–41; J.R. Green, op. cit., pp. 127–32.

90. I. Bernstein, op. cit., pp. 84–5, 109–17; R.A. Christie, *Empire in Wood: A History of the Carpenters Union* (1956).

91. H.J. Harris, 'The Snares of Liberalism', op. cit., p. 160.

92. M. Greenwald, op. cit., Ch. 1; S. Porter-Benson, 'Through the Looking Glass of Gender', op. cit., especially p. 36; J.R. Green, op. cit., pp. 125–6; S.D. Spero and A.L. Harris, *The Black Worker* (1931); P.S. Foner, *Organized Labor and the Black Worker*, op. cit.; R.T. Penn, 'Survival Strategies among African-American Women Workers: A Continuing Process', in R. Milkman (ed.), op. cit.; M. Frederickson, ' "I Know which Side I'm on": Southern Women in the Labor Movement in the Twentieth Century', in ibid.

93. A.K. Harris, op. cit., pp. 120–4; S.P. Benson, op. cit., p. 36; J.R. Green, op. cit., p. 126.

94. I. Bernstein, op. cit., Ch. 4.

95. For the difficulties facing British labour during the 1920s see C.J. Wrigley, 'The Trade Unions between the Wars' in C.J. Wrigley (ed.), op. cit.; J.E. Cronin, 'Coping with Labour', op. cit.; id., *Labour and Society in Britain*, op. cit., Ch. 3; J. Hinton, op. cit., Chs. 7 and 8; J. Stevenson, 'The United Kingdom', in S. Salter and J. Stevenson (eds.), *The Working Class and Politics in Europe and America 1929–1945* (1990).

96. A. Fowler, 'Spinners in the Inter-War Years', op. cit.; id., 'Lancashire Cotton Trade Unionism in the Inter-War Years', op. cit.; C.J. Wrigley (ed.), op. cit., pp. 94–7, 171.

97. R. Hyman, 'Rank-and-File Movements and Workplace Organisation, 1914–39', in C.J. Wrigley (ed.), op. cit., pp. 139–43; C.J. Wrigley, 'The Trade Unions between the Wars', op. cit., pp. 98–9; J. Hinton, op. cit., pp. 137–8.

98. The following section on the general strike and its aftermath is indebted to C.L. Mowat, *Britain between the Wars 1918–1940* (1968), Ch. 6; M. Morris, *The British General Strike* (1976); J. Skelley (ed.), *The General*

Strike 1926 (1976); J. Hinton, op. cit., Ch. 8; R. Lowe, 'The Government and Industrial Relations', in C.J. Wrigley (ed.), op. cit., pp. 194–5.

99. C.J. Wrigley, op. cit., p. 99.

100. J. Hinton, op. cit., pp. 120–5; C.J. Wrigley, op. cit., pp. 108–9; J. Stevenson, *British Society*, op. cit., pp. 175–6.

101. J.E. Cronin, 'Coping with Labour', op. cit., p. 130; D. Montgomery, op. cit., p. 14; J. Hinton, op. cit., p. 140; C.J. Wrigley, op. cit., pp. 120–1; R. Lowe, op. cit., pp. 198–9.

102. C.J. Wrigley, op. cit., p. 120.

103. D. Howell, unpublished papers presented to the Labour Studies Seminar (Manchester University), Nov. 1991, and the Northern Marxist Historians Group, April 1992. I am grateful to the author for permission to cite.

104. J.L. Sundquist, op. cit., Ch. 9.

105. Ibid., pp. 186–7; D. Montgomery, *The Fall*, op. cit., pp. 434–7; id., 'The Farmer-Labor Party', op. cit., pp. 77–8; J.R. Green, op. cit., pp. 127–30.

106. D. Montgomery, 'The Farmer-Labor Party', op. cit.; R.M. Valelly, *Radicalism in the States*, op. cit., and the review of Valelley's book by M. Goldfield in *International Labor and Working-Class History*, 40 (Fall 1991), pp. 132–5.

107. For post-1924 political developments among workers see J.L. Sundquist, op. cit., pp. 189–97; I. Bernstein, op. cit., pp. 75–80; P. Renshaw, 'The United States of America', in S. Salter and J. Stevenson (eds.), op. cit., pp. 244–5.

108. J. Stevenson, 'The United Kingdom', op. cit., p. 132. See also J. Saville, 'May Day 1937', in A. Briggs and J. Saville (eds.), *Essays in Labour History 1918–1939* (1977), p. 235; J.E. Cronin, *Labour and Society in Britain*, op. cit., p. 47. See the special issue, entitled the Labour Party 1900–1990 of the *Journal of Regional and Local Studies*, 10, 1 (1990).

109. A. Fowler, 'Lancashire Cotton Trade Unionism and the Decline of the Lancashire Cotton Industry 1914–1939', unpublished paper presented to the Politics, Economy and Society research group, Manchester Polytechnic, May 1992. I am grateful to the author for permission to cite.

110. R. McKibbin, 'Class and Conventional Wisdom', op. cit.

111. R. MacDonald, *Socialism: Critical and Constructive* (n.d.), especially pp. 279–80.

112. M. Savage, op. cit., pp. 173–80, Ch. 8; R.S.W. Davies, 'Class, Religion and Gender', op. cit.; P. Thane, 'The Women of the British Labour Party' op. cit. Linda Walker, a member of the Manchester Women's History Group, is also currently working on women in the Labour Party.

113. In addition to the references listed in note 112, see N. Kirk, ' "Traditional" Working-Class Culture', op. cit., especially pp. 211–15; J.A. Gillespie, 'Economic and Political Chnage in the East End of London during the 1920s' (D.Phil., University of Cambridge, 1984), pp. 38–50, 75–7, Ch. 8; 'Conference Report', *Society for the Study of Labour History Bulletin*, 39 (Autumn 1979).

114. R. McKibbin, 'The Economic Policy of the Second Labour Government, 1929–1931', in his *The Ideologies of Class*, op. cit., especially pp. 215–18; J.E. Cronin, *Labour and Society*, op. cit., pp. 97–100.

115. A. Thorpe, *The British General Election of 1931* (1991), p. 4.

116. For the above-mentioned changes see, for example, M. Savage, op. cit., pp. 197–8; R.S.W. Davies, op. cit., p. 15.

CHAPTER FIVE

1. T. Kemp, op. cit., p. 72; J. Potter, op. cit., Ch. 4; P. Fearon, op. cit., Part II.
2. E.J. Hobsbawm, *Industry and Empire*, op. cit., pp. 208–9; A. Davies, op. cit., p. 25; N. Whiteside, op. cit., pp. 228–30.
3. For debates concerning recovery see B.W.E. Alford, *Depression and Recovery*, op. cit.; id., 'New Industries for Old?', op. cit., especially pp. 315–31.
4. J. Stevenson, *British Society*, op. cit., p. 118.
5. The following paragraphs on unemployed protests are indebted to J.R. Green, op. cit., pp. 137–9; R.H. Zieger, op. cit., pp. 14–19; D. Milton, *The Politics of U.S. Labor: From the Great Depression to the New Deal* (1982), Ch. 1; I. Bernstein, *The Turbulent Years: A History of the American Worker 1933–1941* (1969), Chs. 3 and 4.
6. D. Milton, op. cit., p. 30.
7. Ibid., pp. 31–2.
8. J.D. Hall, R. Korstad and J. Leloudis, op. cit., p. 277.
9. D. Montgomery and R. Schatz, 'Facing Layoffs', in D. Montgomery, *Workers' Control in America*, op. cit., pp. 140–9.
10. J.D. Hall, R. Korstad and J. Leloudis, op. cit., pp. 280–4; D. Milton, op. cit., Ch. 2.
11. D. Brody, 'Labor and the Great Depression: The Interpretive Prospects', in *Workers in Industrial America*, op. cit., p. 134.
12. M. Davis, 'The Barren Marriage of American Labor and the Democratic Party', in *Prisoners of the American Dream*, op. cit., pp. 56–7.
13. R. Schatz, 'Union Pioneers: The Founders of Local Unions at General Electric and Westinghouse, 1923–1937', *Journal of American History*, 66, 3 (Dec. 1979), especially pp. 594–601.
14. D. Brody, 'The New Deal and the Labor Movement', in *Workers in Industrial America*, op. cit., p. 139; M. Davis, op. cit., pp. 55–6.
15. For developments from 1935 to the war see P. Renshaw, op. cit.; I. Bernstein, op. cit., Chs. 7–12. See also the specific studies by S. Jefferys, *Management and Managed: Fifty Years of Crisis at Chrysler* (1986), Chs. 3 and 4; P. Friedlander, *The Emergence of a UAW Local: A Study in Class and Culture* (1975); D. Nelson, *American Rubber Workers and Organized Labor 1900–1941* (1988); S. Fine, *Sit-Down: The General Motors Strike of 1936–1937* (1969); and for the war years N. Lichtenstein, *Labor's War at Home: The CIO in World War II* (1982).
16. D. Brody, 'The Emergence of Mass-Production Unionism', in *Workers in Industrial America*, op. cit., pp. 100–2.
17. D. Montgomery and R. Schatz, op. cit., pp. 145–6.
18. L. Cohen, op. cit., pp. 333–41.
19. For women and the CIO see ibid., pp. 346–8; A.K. Harris, *Out to Work*, op. cit., pp. 268–9; M. Frederickson, op. cit.; M.P. Lasky, ' "Where I was a Person": The Ladies Auxiliary in the 1934 Minneapolis Teamsters' Strikes', in R. Milkman (ed.), op. cit.; S.H. Strom, ' "We're no Kitty Foyles": Organizing Office Workers for the Congress of Industrial Organizations, 1937–50', in ibid.
20. D. Brody, op. cit., pp. 103–13; M. Davis, op. cit., p. 60; A. Preis, *Labor's Giant Step: Twenty Years of the CIO* (1972), Chs. 8 and 9.
21. D. Montgomery, 'To Study the People', op. cit., p. 511.

22. D.M. Gordon, R. Edwards and M. Reich, op. cit., pp. 178–81.
23. A. Dawley, 'Workers, Capital and the State', op. cit., pp. 169–70; M. Dubofsky and W. Van Tine, 'John L. Lewis and the Triumph of Mass Production Unionism', and S. Fraser, 'Sidney Hillman: Labor's Machiavelli', in M. Dubofsky and W.V. Tine (eds.), op. cit.
24. G. Wright, *Old South New South*, op. cit., Ch. 7.
25. See, for example, M. Dubofsky, 'Not so "Turbulent Years": Another Look at the American 1930s', *Amerika Studien/American Studies*, 24 (1979).
26. M. Davis, op. cit., p. 53; R. Schatz, *The Electrical Workers*, op. cit., pp. 63–7; A. Dawley, op. cit., p. 168; P. Friedlander, op. cit., Chs. 1 and 2.
27. D. Montgomery, 'The Study the People', op. cit., p. 510.
28. D. Brody, 'Labor and the Great Depression: The Interpretive Prospects', in *Workers in Industrial America*, op. cit., pp. 128–9.
29. R. Schatz, op. cit., p. xii.
30. For continued employer claims to autonomy and 'moral authority' within the workplace see H.J. Harris, *The Right to Manage: Industrial Relations Policies of American Business in the 1940s* (1982).
31. For the attitudes and policies of Roosevelt, the state and the NIRA see H.J. Harris, 'The Snares of Liberalism', op. cit., especially pp. 164ff.; P.K. Edwards, 'The Political Economy of Industrial Conflict', op. cit., especially pp. 478–89; D. Brody, 'The New Deal and the Labor Movement', in *Workers in Industrial America*, op. cit., pp. 138–46; C.L. Tomlins, *The State and the Unions*, op. cit., Pt. II.
32. B. Jessop, 'Recent Theories of the Capitalist State', op. cit.
33. J.R. Green, op. cit., pp. 147–50; M. Davis, op. cit., p. 67.
34. J.R. Green, 'Labor and the New Deal', in P. Buhle and A. Dawley (eds.), op. cit., p. 89; H.J. Harris, 'The Snares of Liberalism', op. cit., p. 171; D. Brody, op. cit., pp. 139–40.
35. R.H. Zieger, op. cit., pp. 19–20.
36. D. Montgomery, 'The Farmer-Labor Party', op. cit., p. 79.
37. D. Brody, 'Labor and the Great Depression', op. cit., p. 127; M. Davis, op. cit., p. 66.
38. M. Davis, op. cit., pp. 67–9.
39. For the failure of independent labour politics during the second half of the 1930s see ibid., pp. 69–73; D. Montgomery, op. cit.; J.R. Green, op. cit., pp. 87–91; E. Olssen, 'The Case of the Socialist Party that Failed', op. cit., especially pp. 420, 449.
40. C.J. Wrigley, 'The Trade Unions between the Wars', op. cit., p. 116. Much of the following material on trade unionism is heavily indebted to Chris Wrigley's lucid and informative overview.
41. J. Hinton, op. cit., p. 141.
42. J. Stevenson, *British Society*, op. cit., pp. 276–7.
43. J. Saville, 'May Day 1937', op. cit., p. 240; J.E. Cronin, *Labour and Society*, p. 96.
44. J.E. Cronin, op. cit., p. 97; C.J. Wrigley, op. cit., p. 108; J. Stevenson, 'The United Kingdom', op. cit., pp. 138–9.
45. C.J. Wrigley, op. cit., p. 113.
46. Ibid., pp. 116–19.
47. R. Hyman, 'Rank-and-File Movements', op. cit., pp. 138ff.
48. C.J. Wrigley, op. cit., pp. 112–13.

49. C. Cook and J. Stevenson, *The Slump: Society and Politics during the Depression* (1977), p. 280.
50. R. Price, *Labour in British Society*, op. cit., p. 190.
51. J. Stevenson, 'The United Kingdom', op. cit., pp. 133–4.
52. The quote from Cripps is to be found in R. Spalding, 'Revolutionary Socialism to Radical Patriotism: The British Labour Left, 1931–1945' (M.Phil. thesis, University of East Anglia, 1991). I am grateful to the author for a copy of his thesis. Much of what follows on the Socialist League is indebted to Spalding.
53. J.E. Cronin, op. cit., pp. 100–1; P. Seyd, 'Factionalism within the Labour Party: The Socialist League, 1932–37', in A. Briggs and J. Saville (eds.), op. cit.; R. Spalding, op. cit., pp. 21–33.
54. R. Miliband, *Parliamentary Socialism: A Study in the Politics of Labour* (1975), Chs. VII and VIII.
55. For the activities of the C.P. during these years see N. Branson, *History of the Communist Party of Great Britain 1927–1941* (1985), Chs. 6–8; J. Stevenson, 'The United Kingdom', op. cit., pp. 135–7; A. Howkins, 'Class against Class: The Political Culture of the Communist Party of Great Britain, 1930–35', and J. Lowerson, 'Battles for the Countryside', in F. Gloversmith (ed.), op. cit.; S.G. Jones, *Workers at Play*, op. cit., pp. 189–94; S. Macintyre, *Little Moscows: Communism and Working-Class Militancy in Inter-War Britain* (1980).
56. B. Pimlott, *Labour and the Left in the 1930s* (1986), pp. 200–1; E. Durbin, *New Jerusalems: The Labour Party and the Economics of Democratic Socialism* (1985).
57. P.J. Harris, 'Social Leadership and Social Attitudes' op. cit., p. 412; J.K. Walton, op. cit., p. 347; J. Reynolds and K. Laybourn, *Labour Heartland: A History of the Labour Party in West Yorkshire during the Interwar Years 1918–1939* (1987), pp. 112–15.
58. See, for example, J. Reynolds and K. Laybourn, op. cit., Ch. 5.
59. P.J. Harris, op. cit., pp. 405, 408, 412–13; F. Carr, 'Municipal Socialism: Labour's Rise to Power', and B. Lancaster and T. Mason, 'Society and Politics in Twentieth-Century Coventry', in B. Lancaster and T. Mason (eds.), op. cit.
60. The relationship between powerlessness and working-class quiescence is explored by A. Warde, 'Conditions of Dependence: Working-Class Quiescence in Lancaster in the Twentieth Century', *International Review of Social History*, XXXV (1990).
61. For the 1935 election see J. Reynolds and K. Laybourn, op. cit., pp. 122–9; J. Stevenson, 'The United Kingdom', op. cit., pp. 144–5; C. Cook and J. Stevenson, op. cit., Ch. XIII.
62. J.E. Cronin, op. cit., p. 102.
63. J. Stevenson, 'The United Kingdom', op. cit., p. 145.
64. R. Spalding, op. cit., Ch. 3.
65. C. Cook and J. Stevenson, op. cit., pp. 260–3.
66. See, for example, C. Cook and J. Stevenson, op. cit., Chs. XIII and XIV. For a critique of Cook and Stevenson see A. Howkins and J. Saville, 'The Nineteen Thirties: A Revisionist History', *Socialist Register* (1979).
67. A. Fowler, 'Lancashire Cotton Trade Unionism and the Decline of the Lancashire Cotton Industry', op. cit.; J.K. Walton, *Lancashire: A Social History*, op. cit., p. 349.

68. B. Pimlott, op. cit., pp. 194, 196–7, 200–3.
69. C. Cook and J. Stevenson, op. cit., p. 259.
70. See, for example, J.E. Cronin, op. cit., Ch. 5.
71. Brenda Crosby, 'The Lancashire Campaign of the British Union of Fascists, 1934–5' (M.A., University of Lancaster, 1977), quoted in J.K. Walton, op. cit., p. 351.
72. S.G. Jones, *Workers at Play*, op. cit., pp. 117–18; R. McKibbin, 'The "Social Psychology" of Unemployment in Inter-war Britain', in *The Ideologies of Class*, op. cit.
73. R. McKibbin, 'Class and Conventional Wisdom', op. cit.; J. Richards, 'Cinemagoing in Worktown', unpublished paper presented to the Anglo-German Working-Class Culture conference, Lancaster University, March 1988. I am grateful to the author for permission to cite a very stimulating paper which draws attention to the links between politics and cultural characteristics.
74. J. Stevenson, *British Society*, op. cit., pp. 290–1.
75. B. Nelson, 'The Uneven Development of Class and Consciousness', *Labor History*, 32, 4 (1991), pp. 585–91; and the comments by W. Licht and L. Cohen in ibid.
76. P. Johnson, 'Working-Class Consumption and Working-Class Collectivism', op. cit., pp. 11–15.
77. L. Cohen, *Making a New Deal*, op. cit., pp. 355–6.

Index

Compiled by Terry Wyke

Cooper, Lynn 203, 204
corporate capitalism 3, 5, 31–41,
  57–61, 130, 262–3, 268
  in Britain 31–5, 283–4; in USA 32–5;
  compared 31–41
corporate retardation in Britain 37–41
cotton industry
  disputes 68, 71, 102, 103
  employer strategies 15, 24–7, 33–4,
    68, 70
  entrepreneurial failure 286–7
  trade unionism 8, 12, 68–74, 98–9,
    100, 101, 104, 105, 315–16
  in Scotland 16–17
  in USA 24–7, 33–4, 276–7, 281
  women in industry 70–1
  workers' living standards 298
Cotton Famine (1861–5) 68–9
Cook, Christopher 358, 361, 362
Courtaulds 284
Courtauld, Samuel 285
Couvares, Francis G. 262
Coventry, Warwickshire 7, 165, 285,
  357
craft unionism 132, 155
craft workers, presence and status 19,
  46–9
Criminal Law Amendment Act (1871)
  207
Cripple Creek, Colorado 143
Cripps, Sir Stafford 355, 359
Crofters' Land War 76
Cronin, James 33, 112, 154, 282, 285,
  289, 292, 295, 315, 321, 329, 335,
  352, 358, 362
Crook, Joseph 188
crop lien system 89, 125, 127
Crossick, Geoffrey 198

Dagenham, Essex 285
Daily News 309
Dallas, Texas 127
Daley, Marcus 144, 171
Dangerfield, George 109
Dan River Mill, Virginia 310
Darwen, Lancashire 297
Daughters of St. Crispin 81, 86
Davidson, Roger 114
Davies, Andrew 299
Davies, Sam 327
Davis, John 256

Davis, Mike 339, 342, 343–4, 348
Dawley, Alan 174, 209–10, 248, 288,
  343, 344
Dawson, Andrew 22, 46, 47, 48
Deakin, Arthur 354
Debs, Eugene 133, 134, 164, 232
deindustrialization 288
De Leon, Daniel 136, 231, 234, 242,
  246
Democratic Party 5–6, 61, 86, 87, 173,
  174, 208, 224, 249, 250, 270, 323
  and blacks 215–16
  character and ideology 214–17, 218,
    236
  and immigrants 214–15, 303
  and working class 45, 127, 219, 221
  and AFL 43, 44, 138–9, 166, 235
  and CIO 348–9
Denver, Colorado 134
deskilling 19, 31, 46–7, 132
Detroit, Michigan 10, 56, 336
Die Arbeiter Union 222
Disraeli, Benjamin 200, 206, 207
Distillers' and Cattle Feeders' Trust 32
dockers 76, 77, 111
Dockers' Union 163
Dock Strike, London (1889) 98
Dock, Wharf, Riverside and General
  Labourers' Union 99, 100
Douai, Adolph 222
'driving' in cotton industry 15
'dual unionism' 242, 246
Dubofsky, Melvyn 343
Duffy, Pat 165
Dukinfield, Cheshire 69
Durbin, Elizabeth 356

East Lancashire Amalgamated
  Powerloom Weavers' Friendly
  Association 70, 71, 73
Economic Advisory Council 322
economic growth in Britain and USA
  11, 38–9, 273–9
Edinburgh, Scotland 181
Edwards, Paul 346, 347
Edwards, Richard 48, 49, 50
eight-hour campaign 83, 91, 94, 157,
  161, 162, 215, 220, 221, 223–4
Eight Hour Bill (1916) 146
Eight Hour Leagues 117
Elbaum, Bernard 33, 38